# Traditions & ENCOUNTERS

### SECOND EDITION

## A BRIEF GLOBAL HISTORY

### TO 1500
### VOLUME I

**JERRY H. BENTLEY**
*University of Hawai`i*

**HERBERT F. ZIEGLER**
*University of Hawai`i*

**HEATHER E. STREETS-SALTER**
*Washington State University*

With Additional Material from

Taking Sides
Clashing Views in World History, Volume 1
The Ancient World to the Pre-Modern Era

Fourth Edition

Joseph R. Mitchell
*Howard Community College*

Helen Buss Mitchell
*Howard Community College*

## Instructor: Clif Stratton

Boston   Burr Ridge, IL   Dubuque, IA   New York   San Francisco   St. Louis
Bangkok   Bogotá   Caracas   Lisbon   London   Madrid
Mexico City   Milan   New Delhi   Seoul   Singapore   Sydney   Taipei   Toronto

The McGraw·Hill Companies

Traditions & Encounters: A Brief Global History, Second Edition
Volume I: To 1500
With Additional Material from Taking Sides
Instructor: Clif Stratton

This book is a McGraw-Hill Learning Solutions textbook and contains select material from the following sources:
*Traditions and Encounters: A Brief Global History, Volume I: To 1500*, Second Edition by Jerry H. Bentley, Herbert F. Ziegler and Heather E. Streets-Salter. Copyright © 2010, 2008 by The McGraw-Hill Companies, Inc.
*Taking Sides: Clashing Views in World History, Volume 1: The Ancient World to the Pre-Modern Era*, Fourth Edition by Joseph R. Mitchell and Helen Buss Mitchell. Copyright © 2012, 2011, 2008, 2002 by The McGraw-Hill Companies, Inc.
Both are reprinted with permission of the publisher. Many custom published texts are modified versions or adaptations of our best-selling textbooks. Some adaptations are printed in black and white to keep prices at a minimum, while others are in color.

1 2 3 4 5 6 7 8 9 0  DIG DIG  13 12 11

ISBN-13: 978-0-07-753412-7
ISBN-10: 0-07-753412-3

*Learning Solutions Representative: Mary Park*
*Production Editor: Constance Kuhl*
*Printer/Binder: Digital Impressions*

# Brief Table of Contents

# Table of Contents

## PART II

## THE FORMATION OF CLASSICAL SOCIETIES, 500 B.C.E. TO 500 C.E. 84

---

## PART III

## THE POSTCLASSICAL ERA, 500 TO 1000 C.E.   184

---

## PART IV

# AN AGE OF CROSS-CULTURAL INTERACTION, 1000 TO 1500 C.E. 262

Taking Sides/Clashing Views Volume 1: The Ancient World to the Pre-Moderen Er
Fourth Editon, 0078050073

# PRIMARY SOURCES FROM THE

# A BRIEF NOTE ON USAGE

This book qualifies dates as B.C.E. ("Before the Common Era") or C.E. ("Common Era"). In practice, B.C.E. refers to the same epoch as B.C. ("Before Christ"), and C.E. refers to the same epoch as A.D. (*Anno Domini,* a Latin term meaning "in the year of the Lord"). As historical study becomes a global, multicultural enterprise, however, scholars increasingly prefer terminology that does not apply the standards of one society to all the others. Thus reference in this book to B.C.E. and C.E. reflects emerging scholarly convention concerning the qualification of historical dates.

Measurements of length and distance appear here according to the metric system, followed by their English-system equivalents in parentheses.

The book transliterates Chinese names and terms into English according to the *pinyin* system, which has largely displaced the more cumbersome Wade-Giles system. Transliteration of names and terms from other languages follows contemporary scholarly conventions.

WORLD HISTORY IS ABOUT PEOPLE. But it is easy to lose people in the telling of history. *Traditions and Encounters: A Brief Global History* is not merely a recounting of the facts of history. Rather, we wanted to tell the story of people in history, the traditions they embraced and the encounters with other cultures that brought about inevitable change.

It is the interaction of these traditions and encounters that provides the key to making sense of our past. Human communities furthered themselves not by remaining isolated, but by interacting with others and exploring the benefits and risks of reaching out. The vitality of history—and its interpretation—lies in understanding the nature of individual traditions and the scope of encounters that punctuated every significant event in human history.

*Traditions & Encounters: A Brief Global History* provides a global vision of history that grows increasingly meaningful in a shrinking world. The theme of ***traditions*** draws attention to the formation, maintenance, and sometimes collapse of individual societies. Because the world's peoples have also interacted regularly with one another since the earliest days of human history, the theme of ***encounters*** directs attention to communications, interactions, networks, and exchanges that have linked individual societies to their neighbors and others in the larger world.

TELLING THE STORY OF PEOPLE

The themes of traditions and encounters are at the heart of every chapter in the text. They provide a lens through which to interpret the affairs of humankind and the pressures that continue to shape history. All aspects of the text support these themes—from the organization of chapters, engaging stories of the world's peoples, to the robust map program and critical-thinking features.

## ORGANIZATION: SEVEN ERAS OF GLOBAL HISTORY

We discuss the world's development through time by organizing it into seven eras of global history. These eras, treated successively in the seven parts of this book, represent coherent epochs that form the larger architecture of world history as we see it. Every region of the world is discussed in each of the seven eras. The eras owe their coherence in large part to the networks of transportation, communication, and exchange that have linked peoples of different societies at different times in the past. This structure allows us to make cross-cultural comparisons that help frame world history for students to put events in a perspective that renders them more understandable.

# FEATURES THAT ENRICH
# THE HISTORY EXPERIENCE

This text contains a carefully selected range of tools to enhance student comprehension and interest. These tools are crafted to underscore the vital theme of "traditions and encounters," encourage critical thinking, and reinforce the global view of the course. Among these tools are several new and remodeled features that strengthen these objectives further.

- **Revised Part Openers.** Seven newly designed part openers begin with an introduction that outlines the themes running through all the chapters in that part. This information creates a strong framework for understanding the details of individual chapters. New part-opening maps preview the cultures and regions discussed in a given era.

- **Chapter-opening Vignettes** draw the reader into the larger story and allow students to remember that world history is really about people.

- **New Part Closers.** The last chapter of each era now concludes with an interpretive summary called "Bringing It All Together." This feature encourages the student to assimilate material from all chapters in the era and to apply the broader theme of traditions and encounters.

- **Sources from the Past.** Found in every chapter, "Sources from the Past" boxes bring the past to life by spotlighting significant primary source documents relevant to the chapter, such as poems, journal accounts, religious writings, and letters. We place the documents in context and explain their significance, and thought-provoking questions prompt readers to contextualize and think critically about key issues raised in the document. For this edition, we carefully reviewed our existing selections and replaced ten of them with compelling new choices.

- **New Map Program.** The entire map program has been revised for clarity, greater detail, and more topographical information. Maps now include newly written captions and critical-thinking questions that draw attention to the geographical dimensions of historical developments.

- **New Study Terms.** A list of important terms (with page references) has been added to the end of each chapter.

MAP 7.1 | The Mauryan and Gupta empires, 321 B.C.E.–550 C.E. The Mauryan and Gupta dynasties both originated in the kingdom of Magadha. **Why was this region so important in ancient India? What advantages did it offer for purposes of trade and communication with other regions?**

Both the Mauryan and Gupta empires made their capital in Pataliputra, near the Ganges River.

- **New "Thinking About" Questions.** Each chapter presents two new critical thinking questions—one on "traditions" and one on "encounters"—to further reinforce the underlying themes of the text.

- **Chronology.** Found in each chapter, the chronology box lists the most important dates and events discussed in the chapter. These revised timelines have been relocated to the third page of each chapter for easier access.

- **New Photos and Illustrations.** The second edition has nearly 100 new illustrations and photographs. Many photo and illustration captions now include critical-thinking questions to link the text's illustrations to the chapter discussion.

- **Expanded Pronunciation Guide.** This expanded guide appears along the bottom of pages and helps readers with unfamiliar names and terms. The pronunciations can also be found in the text's glossary.

- **Links for Primary Source Investigator (PSI).** Links to our customized online archive of primary source documents and images can be found throughout the book in the chapter margins.

- **Summary.** Clearly written chapter-ending summaries remind students of the highlights in each chapter.

- **New Study Terms.** A list of important study terms recaps important concepts and people from each chapter.

- **For Further Reading.** Fully updated in the second edition, these annotated lists of references that end each chapter provide readers with a starting point for research assignments or their own study.

THINKING ABOUT
*Traditions*

**TRADITIONS IN STATES AND SOCIETIES IN SUB-SAHARAN AFRICA.** Geographical barriers posed many difficulties for cross-cultural interaction between sub-Saharan African societies and other societies in north Africa and Eurasia. In what ways did the relative isolation imposed by these barriers contribute to the persistence of distinctly sub-Saharan traditions regarding religion, culture, and community organization in this period?

# CHANGES FOR THE SECOND EDITION

In preparing this second edition of *Traditions & Encounters: A Brief Global History,* we have revised, updated, and reorganized the text to stay current with recent world historical scholarship and to remain true to the goals of a brief textbook.

Significant modifications to the second edition include:

- **New Chapter 16, "Christian Western Europe during the Middle Ages."** By combining elements of former chapters 14 and 17, we strengthen the book's story about Christianity and place Europe in a world perspective. This change provides coverage that is broader, deeper, and more focused.

- **New Chapter 33, "The Cold War and the End of Empires."** By combining elements of former chapters 34 and 35, we strategically join the discussion of two contemporaneous issues that affected one another: the relationship between the cold war and its effect on the empires.

- **Expanded Chapter 34, "A World without Borders."** This concluding chapter provides a more timely discussion of the contemporary world with added coverage of the Middle East and a broader discussion of globalization in the context of world history.

- **A Briefer Text.** Many instructors told us that brevity was one of the most important aspects of this text. Following their lead, and implementing the changes described above, we have succeeded in making the second edition even shorter by one chapter with 34 instead of 35 chapters.

- **New Sources from the Past.** Primary source documents highlight individual voices from the human past. We carefully reviewed our existing Sources from the Past selections, which appear in each chapter, and updated ten of them with compelling new selections.

# WHAT'S NEW IN EACH CHAPTER?

Other notable chapter changes and revisions include the following:

**In Every Chapter...** New and expanded critical thinking features including: Thinking about Traditions and Thinking about Encounters questions; photo and figure captions with probing questions; new map program with visual pointers and questions; new photos; study terms.

**Chapter 1** Revised discussion of the Hebrew patriarch Abraham, and an expanded section on early Jewish communities. New Sources from the Past selection: the Sumerian flood story in *The Epic of Gilgamesh*.

**Chapter 2** Revised discussion of early economic specialization and trade in Nile societies.

**Chapter 4** Revised discussion of Olmec society and trade.

**Chapter 7** New Sources from the Past: "The Teachings of Buddha."

**Chapter 9** New chapter ending summary.

**Chapter 12** Revised discussion of early Japan.

**Chapter 15** Expanded discussion of Bantu migrations. New Sources from the Past selection: "Ibn Battuta on Muslim Society at Mogadishu."

**Chapter 16** New discussions of the establishment of regional states in early Europe; the Franks and the temporary revival of empire; serfs and the growth of an agricultural economy; and the conversion of western Europe to Christianity. Expanded discussion of the Crusades. New chapter ending summary.

**Chapter 18** New chapter ending summary.

**Chapter 20** New Sources from the Past selection: Galileo Galilei, "Letter to the Grand Duchess Christina."

**Chapter 21** Revised description and question for the primary source from the past: "First Impressions of Spanish Forces." Expanded discussion of tobacco farming in North America.

**Chapter 22** New discussion of African-American music.

**Chapter 24** New Sources from the Past selection: Sultan Selim I, "Letter to Shah Ismail of Persia."

**Chapter 26** New Sources from the Past selection: "Testimony for the Factory Act of 1833: Working Conditions in England."

**Chapter 27** Expanded discussion of the annexation of New Mexico.

**Chapter 29** Expanded discussion on the Armenian massacre and the influenza pandemic of 1918.

**Chapter 30** New Sources from the Past selection: *Mein Kampf*.

**Chapter 31** New Sources from the Past selection: Mohandas Gandhi.

**Chapter 33** New discussion on apartheid in South Africa. Expanded discussion on decolonization and global cold war. New Sources from the Past selection: "National Security Council Paper Number 68."

**Chapter 34** Expanded chapter on globalization. New discussions on Consumption and Cultural Interaction and The Age of Access.

# SUPPLEMENTS

## *Primary Source Investigator Online*

McGraw-Hill's Primary Source Investigator (PSI), available online at www.mhhe.com/psi, is designed to support and enrich the text discussion in *Traditions & Encounters: A Brief Global History*. PSI gives instructors and students access to more than 700 primary and secondary sources including documents, images, maps, and videos. Students can use these resources to formulate and defend their arguments as well as further their understanding of the topics discussed in each chapter. All assets are indexed alphabetically as well as by type, subject, place, and time period, allowing students and instructors to locate resources quickly and easily.

**Primary Source Documents:** Newly updated for this edition of *Traditions & Encounters*, this database includes items from a wide range of contemporary accounts. Each document is accompanied by a detailed description and a series of critical thinking questions that draw students into the content and engage them in thoughtful analysis. Sources include private papers, government documents, and publications.

**Images:** This extensive collection includes photographs of artifacts and buildings as well as contemporary paintings, engravings, and drawings. Each image is also accompanied by a description and critical thinking question.

**Interactive Maps:** Each map's legend is interactive, allowing students to see historical change over time and compare various factors in the order of their choice.

**Research and Writing Center:** The PSI Research and Writing Center provides a wide range of resources to assist you in writing papers, conducting research, and organizing your efforts to achieve success in college. Divided into four sections, the Writing Center provides tips regarding achieving success in college, tools for conducting research and formatting your materials, avoiding plagiarism, and writing an effective paper.

INSTRUCTOR RESOURCES IN PSI

**Faculty Guide:** The Faculty Guide provides easy reference to all learning assets, both in the text and on PSI, available to teachers and students. Each chapter is accompanied by a rich list of resources, including **PowerPoint slides, image bank, outline maps, book maps,** and **test bank questions,** all keyed to the chapter. In addition to assets, the Faculty Guide also includes a chapter overview, a list of themes, lecture strategies, discussion suggestions, suggestions for further reading, and chapter-specific film recommendations.

# ADDITIONAL RESOURCES FOR STUDENTS

- **The Online Learning Center (OLC) for Students** at www.mhhe.com/bentleybrief2e provides students with a wide range of tools that will help them test their understanding of the book. It includes chapter overviews, interactive maps, multiple choice and essay quizzes, matching and identification games, as well as primary source indexes for further research.

- Two **After the Fact Interactive** units are available for use with *Traditions & Encounters:* "After the Fact Interactive: Tracing the Silk Roads" for volume 1 (ISBN 0-07-281843-3) and "After the Fact Interactive: Envisioning the Atlantic World" for volume 2 (ISBN 0-07-281844-1). These rich, visually appealing modules on CD-ROM allow students to be apprentice historians, examining a variety of multimedia primary source material and constructing arguments based on their research.

# ADDITIONAL RESOURCES FOR INSTRUCTORS

- The **Online Learning Center (OLC) for Instructors** at www.mhhe.com/bentley brief2e contains several instructor tools, including a link to the Teacher's Edition of Primary Source Investigator (www.mhhe.com/psi) and PowerPoint presentations for each chapter. The instructor side of the OLC is password protected to prevent tampering. Please contact your local McGraw-Hill sales representative for details.

- A **Computerized Test Bank,** McGraw-Hill's EZ Test, allows you to quickly create a customized test using the publisher's supplied test banks or your own questions. You decide the number, type, and order of test questions with a few simple clicks. EZ Test runs on your computer without a connection to the Internet.

- **Videos** on topics in world history are available through the Films for Humanities and Sciences collection. Contact your local McGraw-Hill sales representative for further information.
- **Classroom Performance System (CPS).** The Classroom Performance System brings ultimate interactivity to *Traditions & Encounters: A Brief Global History*. CPS is a wireless polling system that gives you immediate feedback from every student in the class. Use CPS to ask questions during your lecture that have been prepared by McGraw-Hill or enter your own questions. A complete CPS Tutorial is available at www.einstruction.com.

This text is available as an eTextbook at *www.CourseSmart.com*. At CourseSmart your students can take advantage of significant savings off the cost of a print textbook, reduce their impact on the environment, and gain access to powerful Web tools for learning. CourseSmart eTextbooks can be viewed online. The eTextbooks allow students to do full text searches, add highlighting and notes, and share notes with classmates. CourseSmart has the largest selection of eTextbooks available anywhere. Visit *www.CourseSmart.com* to learn more and to try a sample chapter.

## *McGraw-Hill Higher Education. Connect. Learn. Succeed.*

McGraw-Hill Higher Education's mission is to help prepare students for the world that awaits them. With textbooks, e-books, and other digital instructional content, as well as experiential learning and assignment/assessment platforms, McGraw-Hill enables instructors to connect with their students more closely. In turn, students can learn to their full potential and, thus, succeed academically now and in the real world. Learn more at www.mhhe.com.

# ACKNOWLEDGMENTS

Many individuals have contributed to this book, and the authors take pleasure in recording deep thanks for all the comments, criticism, advice, and suggestions that helped to improve the work. Special thanks to the editorial and production teams at McGraw-Hill: Chris Freitag, Matthew Busbridge, Thom Holmes, Lisa Pinto, Brett Coker, Cassandra Chu, Kim Adams, and Sheryl Rose, who provided crucial support by helping the authors work through difficult issues and solving the innumerable problems of content, style, organization, and design that arise in any project to produce a history of the world.

## *Academic Reviewers*

This edition continues to reflect many discerning suggestions made by instructors of the world history course. We would like to acknowledge the contributions of the following reviewers who suggested many of the changes implemented here in the second edition:

Wayne Ackerson
*Salisbury University*

Patrick Albano
*Fairmont State University*

Gene Barnett
*Calhoun Community College*

Kathryn Braund
*Auburn University*

David Brosius
*Air Force Academy/USAFA*

Samuel Brunk
*University of Texas, El Paso*

Robert Carriedo,
*US Air Force Academy/USAFA*

Patricia Colman
*Moorpark College*

Kevin Dougherty
*University of Southern Mississippi*

Tim Dowling
*Virginia Military Institute*

Christopher Drennan
*Clinton Community College*

Shawn Dry
*Oakland Community College*

Sarah Franklin
*University of Southern Mississippi*

Ernie Grieshaber
*Minnesota State University-Mankato*

Theodore Kallman
*San Joaquin Delta Community College*

David Katz
*Mohawk Valley Community College*

Richard Kennedy
*Mount Olive College*

Janine Lanza
*Wayne State University*

David Massey
*Bunker Hill Community College*

Anne Osborne
*Rider University, Lawrenceville, NJ*

Charles Parker
*Saint Louis University*

Brian Plummer
*Asuza Pacific University*

William Rodner
*Tidewater Community College*

Pamela Sayre
*Henry Ford Community College*

David Schmidt
*Bethel College*

Jerry Sheppard
*Mount Olive College*

Kyle Smith
*Grand Valley State University*

Michael Snodgrass
*Indiana University Purdue University Indianapolis*

Paul Steeves
*Stetson University*

Elisaveta Todorova
*University of Cincinnati*

Judith Walden
*College of the Ozarks*

Kathleen Warnes
*Grand Valley State University*

Kurt Werthmuller
*Azusa Pacific University*

Sherri West
*Brookdale Community College*

Kenneth Wilburn
*East Carolina University*

Jeffrey Wilson
*University of New Orleans*

William Zogby
*Mohawk Valley Community College*

We are also grateful to the valued reviewers who contributed to the creation of the first edition of the text. Their ideas and comments continue to inform the planning of subsequent editions:

Heather J. Abdelnur
*Blackburn College*

Wayne Ackerson
*Salisbury University*

William H. Alexander
*Norfolk State University*

Michael Balyo
*Chemeketa Community College*

Diane Barefoot
*Caldwell Community College, Watauga Campus*

Gene Barnett
*Calhoun Community College*

John Boswell
*San Antonio College*

W. H. Bragg
*Georgia College and State University*

Robert Brown
*UNC Pembroke*

Gayle Brunelle
*California State University, Fullerton*

Marybeth Carlson
*University of Dayton*

Kay J. Carr
*Southern Illinois University*

Jon Davidann
*Hawaii Pacific University*

Mitch Driebe
*Andrew College*

Shawn Dry
*Oakland Community College*

Shannon Duffy
*Loyola University of New Orleans*

Robert J. Flynn
*Portland Community College*

Deanna D. Forsman
*North Hennepin Community College*

Kristine Frederickson
*Brigham Young University*

James Fuller
*University of Indianapolis*

Jessie Ruth Gaston
*California State University, Sacramento*

George W. Gawrych
*Baylor University*

Deborah Gerish
*Emporia State University*

Gary G. Gibbs
*Roanoke College*

Candace Gregory
*California State University, Sacramento*

Jillian Hartley
*Arkansas Northeastern College*

Gregory Havrilcsak
*The University of Michigan, Flint*

John K. Hayden
*Southwest Oklahoma State University*

# About the Authors

**JERRY H. BENTLEY** is professor of history at the University of Hawai`i and editor of the *Journal of World History*. He has written extensively on the cultural history of early modern Europe and on cross-cultural interactions in world history. His research on the religious, moral, and political writings of the Renaissance led to the publication of *Humanists and Holy Writ: New Testament Scholarship in the Renaissance* (1983) and *Politics and Culture in Renaissance Naples* (1987). His more recent research has concentrated on global history and particularly on processes of cross-cultural interaction. His book *Old World Encounters: Cross-Cultural Contacts and Exchanges in Pre-Modern Times* (1993) studies processes of cultural exchange and religious conversion before modern times, and his pamphlet *Shapes of World History in Twentieth-Century Scholarship* (1996) discusses the historiography of world history. His current interests include processes of cross-cultural interaction and cultural exchange in modern times.

**HERBERT F. ZIEGLER** is an associate professor of history at the University of Hawai`i. He has taught world history since 1980 and currently serves as director of the world history program at the University of Hawai`i. He also serves as book review editor of the *Journal of World History*. His interest in twentieth-century European social and political history led to the publication of *Nazi Germany's New Aristocracy* (1990). He is at present working on a study that explores from a global point of view the demographic trends of the past ten thousand years, along with their concomitant technological, economic, and social developments. His other current research project focuses on the application of complexity theory to a comparative study of societies and their internal dynamics.

**HEATHER E. STREETS-SALTER** is an associate professor of history at Washington State University, where she teaches world history at the graduate and undergraduate levels. She has been teaching at WSU since 1998 and is the director of the WSU history department's world history Ph.D. program. Streets-Salter was also co-editor of *World History Connected: the ejournal of Learning and Teaching* from 2003 to 2008. Recent publications include *Martial Races: The Military, Race, and Masculinity in British Imperial Culture, 1857–1914* (2004). She is currently researching nineteenth- and twentieth-century imperialism as a global phenomenon rather than as a strictly national issue. Her next book will explore the connections between French Indochina, the Dutch East Indies, and British Malaya as a way of demonstrating that the various national empires learned from, imitated, and stayed in contact with one another.

# TRADITIONS & ENCOUNTERS

# I

# The Early Complex Societies, 3500 to 500 B.C.E.

EARLY ANDEAN STATES (CH. 4)

EARLY MESOAMERICA (CH. 4)

INDO-EUROPEAN HOMELAND (CH. 1)

KINGDOM OF ISRAEL (CH. 1)

KINGDOM OF EGYPT (CH. 2)

PHOENICIA (CH. 1)

MESOPOTAMIAN EMPIRES (CH. 1)

EARLY ARYAN INDIA (CH. 3)

EARLY CHINA (CH. 3)

EARLY SOCIETIES OF OCEANIA (CH. 4)

BANTU HOMELAND (CH. 2)

KINGDOM OF NUBIA (CH. 2)

About 12,000 years ago, humans crossed an important threshold when they began to experiment with agriculture. It quickly became clear that cultivation of crops provided a larger and more reliable food supply than foraging. Groups that turned to agriculture experienced rapid population growth, and they settled into permanent communities. Some of these developed into cities and became the world's first complex societies.

The term *complex society* refers to a form of large-scale social organization in which productive agricultural economies produced surplus food. That surplus allowed some people to devote their time to specialized tasks, other than food production, and to congregate in urban settlements. During the centuries from 3500 to 500 B.C.E., complex societies arose independently in several regions of the world, including Mesopotamia, Egypt, northern India, China, Mesoamerica, and the central Andean region of South America. Each established political authorities, built states with formal governmental institutions, collected surplus agricultural production in the form of taxes or tribute, and redistributed wealth. Complex societies also traded with other peoples, and they often sought to extend their authority to surrounding territories.

Complex societies were able to generate and preserve much more wealth than smaller societies. When bequeathed to heirs and held within particular families, this accumulated wealth became the foundation for social distinctions. These societies developed different kinds of social distinctions, but all recognized several classes of people, including ruling elites, common people, and slaves.

All early complex societies also created sophisticated cultural traditions. Most of them either invented or borrowed a system of writing, which quickly came to be used to construct traditions of literature, learning, and reflection. All the complex societies organized systems of formal education that introduced intellectual elites to skills such as writing and astronomical observation deemed necessary for their societies' survival. In addition, all of these societies explored the nature of humanity, the world, and the gods.

Although all the early complex societies shared some common features, each nevertheless developed distinct cultural, political, social, and economic traditions of its own. These distinctions were based, at least initially, on geographical differences and the differing availability of resources. For instance, the absence or presence of large supplies of freshwater, of river or ocean transport, of mountains or desert, or of large draft animals or domesticable plants helped structure the shape of early economic activities, cultural beliefs, and state structures. As a result, early complex societies in different parts of the world grew into a variety of rich and unique cultures.

At the same time, none of the early complex societies developed their distinct cultures in complete isolation. Indeed, each interacted with neighboring peoples, with whom they traded valuable items, fought, married, and borrowed ideas about government, philosophy, or religion. In many ways, these encounters were crucial to the development of early complex societies. Because of this, it seems clear that, even in the earliest complex societies, connections between peoples were an important part of the human story.

# The Foundations of Complex Societies

By far, the most familiar individual of ancient Mesopotamian society was a man named Gilgamesh. According to historical sources, Gilgamesh was the fifth king of the city of Uruk. He ruled about 2750 B.C.E., and he led his community in its conflicts with Kish, a nearby city that was the principal rival of Uruk.

Gilgamesh was a figure of Mesopotamian mythology and folklore as well as history. He was the subject of numerous poems and legends, and Mesopotamian bards made him the central figure in a cycle of stories known collectively as the *Epic of Gilgamesh*. As a figure of legend, Gilgamesh became the greatest hero figure of ancient Mesopotamia. According to the stories, the gods granted Gilgamesh a perfect body and endowed him with superhuman strength and courage. The legends declare that he constructed the massive city walls of Uruk as well as several of the city's magnificent temples to Mesopotamian deities.

The stories that make up the *Epic of Gilgamesh* recount the adventures of this hero and his cherished friend Enkidu as they sought fame. They killed an evil monster, rescued Uruk from a ravaging bull, and matched wits with the gods. In spite of their heroic deeds, Enkidu offended the gods and fell under a sentence of death. His loss profoundly affected Gilgamesh, who sought for some means to cheat death and gain eternal life. He eventually found a magical plant that had

 **The Epic of Gilgamesh**
www.mhhe.com/
bentleybrief2e

the power to confer immortality, but a serpent stole the plant and carried it away, forcing Gilgamesh to recognize that death is the ultimate fate of all human beings. Thus, while focusing on the activities of Gilgamesh and Enkidu, the stories explored themes of friendship, loyalty, ambition, fear of death, and longing for immortality. In doing so they reflected the interests and concerns of the complex, urban-based society that had recently emerged in Mesopotamia.

Yet such interests and concerns had their foundation deep in the human past. By the time Mesopotamian society emerged, our own species of human, *Homo sapiens*, had existed for about two hundred thousand years. These humans, who themselves descended from earlier hominids, were already accomplished problem solvers and thinkers long before urban societies developed. In fact, early human communities were responsible for laying the social, economic, and cultural foundations on which their descendants built increasingly complex societies—especially through the domestication of plants and animals and by establishing agricultural economies.

Indeed, productive agricultural economies supported the development of the first known complex societies during the

❮ *A wall relief from an Assyrian palace of the eighth century B.C.E. depicts Gilgamesh as a heroic figure holding a lion.*

**Uruk** (OO-rook)

**hominid** (HAW-mih-nihd)

# CHRONOLOGY

| | |
|---|---|
| 4 million–1 million years ago | Era of first hominids, *Australopithecus* |
| 2.5 million–200,000 years ago | Era of *Homo erectus* |
| 200,000 years ago | Early evolution of *Homo sapiens* |
| 40,000 years ago | First appearance of *Homo sapiens sapiens* |
| 10,000–8000 B.C.E. | Early experimentation with agriculture |
| 4000–3500 B.C.E. | Appearance of cities in southwest Asia |
| 3200–2350 B.C.E. | Era of Sumerian dominance in Mesopotamia |
| 3000 B.C.E.–1000 C.E. | Era of Indo-European migrations |
| 2350–1600 B.C.E. | Era of Babylonian dominance in Mesopotamia |
| 2334–2315 B.C.E. | Reign of Sargon of Akkad |
| 1792–1750 B.C.E. | Reign of Hammurabi |
| 1450–1200 B.C.E. | Era of Hittite dominance in Anatolia |
| 1000–612 B.C.E. | Era of Assyrian dominance in Mesopotamia |
| 1000–970 B.C.E. | Reign of Israelite king David |
| 970–930 B.C.E. | Reign of Israelite king Solomon |
| 722 B.C.E. | Assyrian conquest of the kingdom of Israel |
| 605–562 B.C.E. | Reign of Nebuchadnezzar |
| 600–550 B.C.E. | New Babylonian empire |
| 586 B.C.E. | New Babylonian conquest of the kingdom of Judah |

fourth millennium B.C.E. Such societies, in which sizable numbers of people lived in cities and extended their political, social, economic, and cultural influence over large regions, emerged first in southwest Asia, particularly in Mesopotamia. As these complex societies developed and grew, people found that they needed to resolve disputes that inevitably arose as individual and group interests conflicted. In Mesopotamia, settled agricultural peoples in search of order recognized political authorities and built states. The establishment of states in turn encouraged the creation of empires, as some states sought to extend their power by imposing their rule on neighboring lands.

Apart from stimulating the establishment of states, urban society in Mesopotamia also promoted the emergence of social classes, thus giving rise to increasingly complex social and economic structures. Cities fostered specialized labor, and the efficient production of high-quality goods in turn stimulated trade. Furthermore, early Mesopotamia developed distinctive cultural traditions as Mesopotamians invented a system of writing and supported organized religions.

Mesopotamian and other peoples regularly interacted with one another, which helped further the geographic reach of Mesopotamian society. Some Indo-European peoples also had direct dealings with their Mesopotamian contemporaries, with effects crucial for both Indo-European and Mesopotamian societies. Other Indo-European peoples never heard of Mesopotamia, but they employed Mesopotamian inventions such as wheels and metallurgy when undertaking extensive migrations that profoundly influenced historical development throughout much of Eurasia from western Europe to India and beyond. Even in the earliest days of city life, the world was the site of frequent and intense interaction between peoples of different societies.

# THE TRANSITION TO AGRICULTURE

Between twelve and six thousand years ago, humans crossed a critical threshold of immense significance for the species, and the earth more generally, when they began to domesticate plants and animals. That transition to agriculture led to a population explosion, which enabled human communities to establish themselves in far greater numbers around the world than ever before. Agriculture also led to new forms of social organization, which ultimately resulted in the birth of the world's first urban centers.

# The Paleolithic Era

HOMO SAPIENS    *Homo sapiens* ("consciously thinking human")—the direct ancestor of our own subspecies, *Homo sapiens sapiens*—evolved about two hundred thousand years ago from a hominid ancestry that originated in east Africa about four to five million years ago. *Homo sapiens* possessed larger brains and greater intelligence than earlier hominids—a feature that enabled them to adapt to widely varying environmental conditions and to displace earlier hominid species. More than one hundred thousand years ago, communities of *Homo sapiens* began to spread throughout the temperate lands of the eastern hemisphere. Using their intelligence to make warm clothes and shelters, *Homo sapiens* soon established communities in progressively colder regions. Then, between sixty and fifteen thousand years ago, *Homo sapiens* took advantage of land bridges exposed by lowered sea levels and spread to Indonesia, New Guinea, Australia, and, finally, the Americas. Thus by about fifteen thousand years ago, communities of *Homo sapiens* had appeared in almost every habitable region of the world.

For most of human existence—indeed, from the evolution of the first hominids until about twelve thousand years ago—our ancestors foraged for their food. In other words, they hunted wild animals or gathered edible products of naturally growing plants. That reliance on foraging characterized what historians and archaeologists call the *paleolithic era,* or the "old stone age."

The conditions of foraging economies decisively influenced all dimensions of the human experience during the paleolithic era. For instance, because of constant mobility in the search for food, a foraging economy virtually prohibits individuals from accumulating private property and basing social distinctions on wealth. In the absence of accumulated wealth, hunters and gatherers of paleolithic times probably lived a relatively egalitarian existence. Some scholars believe that this relative social equality also extended to relations between the sexes, because all members of a paleolithic group made important contributions to the survival of the community. Although meat from the hunt (provided by men) was the most highly prized item in the paleolithic diet, plant foods (provided by women) were essential to survival and sustained communities when the hunt did not succeed. Because of the thorough interdependence of the sexes from the viewpoint of food production, paleolithic society probably did not encourage the domination of one sex by the other.

Spread of the earliest humans
www.mhhe.com/bentleybrief2e

# The Neolithic Era

Between twelve and six thousand years ago, human communities in a variety of locations underwent profound economic, social, and political changes when they began to experiment with the domestication of plants and animals. Scientists refer to this period as the *neolithic era,* or "new stone age," because of the polished stone tools associated with peoples who relied on cultivation for subsistence.

Neolithic peoples sought to ensure themselves of more regular food supplies by encouraging the growth of edible crops and bringing wild animals into dependence on human keepers. Many scholars believe that women most likely began the systematic care of plants. As the principal gatherers in foraging communities, women in neolithic societies probably began to nurture plants instead of simply collecting available foods in the wild. Meanwhile, instead of just stalking game with the intention of killing it for meat, neolithic men began to capture animals and domesticate them by providing for their needs and supervising their breeding. Over a period of decades and centuries, these practices gradually led to the formation of agricultural economies.

*Homo sapiens*  (HOH-moh SAY-pyans)
*Homo sapiens sapiens*  (HOH-moh SAY-pyans SAY-pyans)
**paleolithic** (pey-lee-oh-LITH-ik)
**neolithic** (nee-uh-LITH-ik)

THE EARLY SPREAD OF AGRICULTURE    The transition to agriculture—including both the cultivation of crops and the domestication of animals—emerged independently in several parts of the world. The earliest evidence of agricultural activity discovered so far dates to the era after 9000 B.C.E. in southwest Asia (modern-day Iraq, Syria, and Turkey). Between 9000 and 7000 B.C.E., agriculture also emerged among African peoples inhabiting the southeastern margin of the Sahara desert (modern-day Sudan), and then among the peoples of sub-Saharan west Africa (in the vicinity of modern Nigeria) between 8000 and 6000 B.C.E. In east Asia, residents of the Yangzi River valley began to cultivate crops as early as 6500 B.C.E., and their neighbors to the north in the Yellow River valley did the same after 5500 B.C.E. In southeast Asia the cultivation of crops dates from an indeterminate but very early time, probably 3000 B.C.E. or earlier. In the western hemisphere, inhabitants of Mesoamerica (central Mexico) cultivated plants as early as 4000 B.C.E., and residents of the central Andean region of South America (modern Peru) followed suit after 3000 B.C.E. It is also possible that the Amazon River valley was yet another site of independently invented agriculture.

Once established, agriculture spread rapidly. As a result, foods originally cultivated in only one region also spread widely, as merchants, migrants, or other travelers carried knowledge of these foods to agricultural lands that previously had relied on different crops. However, agriculture did not spread rapidly because it was easier than foraging. On the contrary, agriculture involved long hours of hard physical labor—clearing land, preparing fields, planting seeds, pulling weeds, and harvesting crops—and thus probably required more work than paleolithic foraging. Yet agriculture had its own appeal in that it made possible the production of abundant food supplies, which in turn allowed human populations to grow to unprecedented levels. For example, historians estimate that before agriculture, about 10,000 B.C.E., the earth's human population was about four million. By 500 B.C.E., after agriculture had spread to most world regions, the human population had risen to about one hundred million.

THE DEVELOPMENT OF SOCIAL DISTINCTIONS    Such rapidly increasing populations encouraged neolithic peoples to adopt new forms of social organization. Because they devoted their time to cultivation rather than to foraging, neolithic peoples did not continue the migratory life of their paleolithic predecessors but, rather, settled near their fields in permanent villages. Most people in neolithic villages cultivated crops or kept animals, and many even continued to hunt and forage for wild plants. But a surplus of food enabled some individuals to concentrate their time and talents on enterprises that had nothing to do with the production of food, especially pottery making, metallurgy, and textile production. Moreover, the concentration of people into permanent settlements and the increasing specialization of labor provided the first opportunity for individuals to accumulate considerable wealth. The institutionalization of privately owned landed property—which occurred at an uncertain date after the introduction of agriculture—enhanced the significance of accumulated wealth. Because land was (and remains) the ultimate source of wealth in any agricultural society, ownership of land carried enormous economic power. When especially successful individuals managed to consolidate wealth in their families' hands and kept it there for several generations, clearly defined social classes emerged.

ÇATAL HÜYÜK    Within four thousand years of its introduction, agriculture had dramatically transformed the face of the earth. Human beings multiplied prodigiously, congregated in densely populated quarters, placed the surrounding lands under cultivation, and domesticated several species of animals. Besides altering the physical appearance of the earth, agriculture transformed the lives of human beings. Even a modest neolithic village dwarfed a paleolithic band of a few dozen hunters and gatherers. In larger villages and towns, with their populations of several thousand people, their specialized labor, and

**Çatal Hüyük**  (chat-l-hoo-yook)

their craft industries, social relationships became more complex than would have been conceivable during paleolithic times.

Excavations carried out at Çatal Hüyük, one of the best-known neolithic settlements, have helped confirm that view. Located in south-central Anatolia (modern Turkey), Çatal Hüyük grew from a small village to a bustling town of five thousand inhabitants between its settlement in 7250 B.C.E. and its abandonment in 5400 B.C.E. Archaeological evidence indicates that because the site was close to large obsidian deposits, Çatal Hüyük became a center for production and trade in obsidian tools. The wealth generated from such trade in turn allowed increasing specialization of labor, so that residents eventually manufactured and traded pots, textiles, leather, beads, and jewelry at the site. Gradually, dense populations, specialized labor, and complex social relations such as those that developed at Çatal Hüyük gave rise to an altogether new form of social organization—the city.

# THE QUEST FOR ORDER

The earliest known cities grew out of agricultural villages and towns in the valleys of the Tigris and Euphrates rivers in Mesopotamia (modern-day Iraq). During the fourth millennium B.C.E., human population increased rapidly in the area, which in turn presented inhabitants with the challenge of keeping order in a large-scale society. Over time, by experimentation and adaptation, they created states and governmental machinery that brought political and social order to their territories. Moreover, effective political and military organization enabled them to build regional empires and extend their authority to neighboring peoples.

## Mesopotamia: "The Land between the Rivers"

The place-name *Mesopotamia* comes from two Greek words meaning "the land between the rivers." Mesopotamia receives little rainfall, but the Tigris and the Euphrates brought large volumes of freshwater to the region. Early cultivators realized that by tapping these

Irrigable land between the Tigris and Euphrates rivers.

**MAP 1.1** | Early Mesopotamia, 3000–2000 B.C.E. Note the locations of Mesopotamian cities in relation to the Tigris and Euphrates rivers. *In what ways were the rivers important for Mesopotamian society?*

rivers, building reservoirs, and digging canals, they could irrigate fields of barley, wheat, and peas. Small-scale irrigation began in Mesopotamia soon after 6000 B.C.E.

SUMER   Artificial irrigation led to increased food supplies, which in turn supported a rapidly increasing human population and attracted migrants from other regions. Human numbers grew especially fast in the land of Sumer in the southern half of Mesopotamia. By about 5000 B.C.E. the Sumerians were constructing elaborate irrigation networks that helped them realize abundant agricultural harvests. By 3000 B.C.E. the population of Sumer approached one hundred thousand—an unprecedented concentration of people in ancient times—and the Sumerians were the dominant people of Mesopotamia.

SEMITIC MIGRANTS   While supporting a growing population, the wealth of Sumer also attracted migrants from other regions. Most of the new arrivals were Semitic peoples—so called because they spoke tongues in the Semitic family of languages, including Akkadian, Aramaic, Hebrew, and Phoenician. Semitic peoples were nomadic herders who went to Mesopotamia from the Arabian and Syrian deserts to the south and west. They often intermarried with the Sumerians, and they largely adapted to Sumerian ways.

The remains of Ur
www.mhhe.com/
bentleybrief2e

SUMERIAN CITY-STATES   Beginning about 4000 B.C.E., as human numbers increased in southern Mesopotamia, the Sumerians built the world's first cities. These cities differed markedly from the neolithic villages that preceded them. Unlike the earlier settlements, the Sumerian cities were centers of political and military authority, and their jurisdiction extended into the surrounding regions. Moreover, bustling marketplaces that drew buyers and sellers from near and far turned the cities into economic centers as well. Finally, the cities also served as cultural centers where priests maintained organized religions and scribes developed traditions of writing and formal education. For almost a millenium, from 3200 to 2350 B.C.E., a dozen Sumerian cities—Eridu, Ur, Uruk, Lagash, Nippur, Kish, and others—dominated public affairs in Mesopotamia.

These cities all experienced internal and external pressures that prompted them to establish states—formal governmental institutions that wielded authority throughout their territories. Internally, the cities needed recognized authorities to maintain order and ensure that inhabitants cooperated on community projects. With their expanding populations, the cities also needed to prevent conflicts between urban residents from escalating into serious civic disorder. In addition, because agriculture was crucial to the welfare of urban residents, the cities all became city-states: they not only controlled public life within the city walls but also oversaw affairs in surrounding agricultural regions.

While preserving the peace, recognized authorities were also needed to organize work on projects of value to the entire community. Palaces, temples, and defensive walls dominated all the Sumerian cities. Particularly impressive were the ziggurats—distinctive stepped pyramids that housed temples and altars to the principal local deity. More important, however, were the irrigation systems that supported productive agriculture and urban society. As their population grew, the Sumerians expanded their networks of reservoirs and canals, whose construction and maintenance required untold thousands of laborers and provided precious water for Sumerian crops.

SUMERIAN KINGS   As the wealth of Sumerian cities grew, they began to face increasing external problems from raiders outside the cities. The cities responded to that threat by building defensive walls and organizing military forces. Thus the need to recruit, train, equip, maintain, and deploy military forces created another demand for recognized authority. To answer that demand, the earliest Sumerian governments were probably made up of assemblies of prominent men who made decisions on behalf of the whole

Sumerians (soo-MEHR-ee-uhns)

Semitic (suh-MIHT-ihk)

ziggurats (ZIG-uh-rahts)

**SUMERIAN ZIGGURAT.** | The massive temple of the moon god Nanna-Suen (sometimes known as Sin) dominated the Sumerian city of Ur. Constructing temples of this size required a huge investment of resources and thousands of laborers. *How might commoners have viewed such massive structures?*

community. By about 3000 B.C.E., however, most Sumerian cities were ruled by individual kings who claimed absolute authority within their realms. By 2500 B.C.E. city-states ruled by kings dominated public life in Sumer.

## The Course of Empire

Conflicts between city-states often led to war between ambitious or aggrieved kings. However, after 2350 B.C.E. a series of conquerors sought to put an end to these constant conflicts by building empires that supervised the affairs of numerous subject cities and peoples.

SARGON OF AKKAD    The first of these conquerors was Sargon of Akkad. A talented administrator and brilliant warrior, Sargon (2370–2315 B.C.E.) began his career as a minister to the king of Kish. About 2334 B.C.E. he organized a coup against the king, recruited an army, and went on the offensive against the Sumerian city-states. He conquered the cities one by one, destroyed their defensive walls, and placed them under his own governors and administrators. Sargon financed his empire by seizing control of trade routes and taxing the goods that traveled along them, which allowed him to transform his capital at Akkad into the wealthiest and most powerful city in the world. At the high point of his reign, his empire embraced all of Mesopotamia, and his armies had ventured as far afield as the Mediterranean and the Black Sea.

By about 2150 B.C.E. Sargon's empire had collapsed in the midst of rebellion from within and invasion from outsiders. Yet the memory of his deeds, recorded in legends and histories as well as in his own works of propaganda, inspired later conquerors to follow his example. Most prominent of these later conquerors was the Babylonian Hammurabi

**Hammurabi** (hahm-uh-RAH-bee)

**HAMMURABI'S LAWS.** | This handsome basalt stele shows Hammurabi receiving his royal authority from the sun god, Shamash. Some four thousand lines of Hammurabi's laws are inscribed below. *Why would it have been important to emphasize Hammurabi's connection to divinity?*

Drawing of Khorsabad, an Assyrian city
www.mhhe.com/bentleybrief2e

(reigned 1792–1750 B.C.E.), who styled himself "king of the four quarters of the world." Hammurabi improved on Sargon's administrative techniques by relying on centralized bureaucratic rule and regular taxation rather than on suppression and plunder.

HAMMURABI'S LAWS    By these means Hammurabi developed a more efficient and predictable government than his predecessors and also spread its costs more evenly over the population. Hammurabi also sought to maintain his empire by providing it with a code of law, which became the most extensive and complete Mesopotamian law code up to that point. In the prologue to his laws, Hammurabi proclaimed that the gods had chosen him "to promote the welfare of the people, . . . to cause justice to prevail in the land, to destroy the wicked and evil, [so] that the strong might not oppress the weak, to rise like the sun over the people, and to light up the land." Hammurabi's laws established high standards of behavior and stern punishments for violators. They prescribed death penalties for murder, theft, fraud, false accusations, sheltering of runaway slaves, failure to obey royal orders, adultery, and incest. Civil laws regulated prices, wages, commercial dealings, marital relationships, and the conditions of slavery.

The code relied heavily on the principle that offenders should suffer punishments resembling their violations. However, the code did not treat all social classes equally and demanded lesser punishments for those of higher classes who committed crimes against those of lower classes. In addition, local judges did not always follow the prescriptions of Hammurabi's code: indeed, they frequently relied on their own judgment when deciding cases that came before them. Nevertheless, Hammurabi's laws established a set of common standards that lent some degree of cultural unity to the far-flung Babylonian empire.

Eventually, the wealth of the Babylonian empire attracted invaders. Foremost among them were the Hittites, who had built a powerful empire in Anatolia (modern-day Turkey). By about 1595 B.C.E. the Babylonian empire had crumbled before Hittite assaults. For several centuries after the fall of Babylon, southwest Asia was a land of considerable turmoil, as regional states competed for power and position while migrants and invaders struggled to establish footholds for themselves in Mesopotamia and neighboring regions.

THE ASSYRIAN EMPIRE    Imperial rule returned to Mesopotamia with the Assyrians, a people from northern Mesopotamia who had built a compact state in the Tigris River valley during the nineteenth century B.C.E. Taking advantage of their location on trade routes running both north-south and east-west, the Assyrians built flourishing cities at Assur and Nineveh. They built a powerful and intimidating army by organizing their forces into standardized units and placing them under the command of professional officers chosen on the basis of merit and skill. They supplemented infantry with cavalry forces and light, swift, horse-drawn chariots, which they borrowed from the Hittites. These chariots were devastating instruments of war that allowed archers to attack their enemies from rapidly moving platforms.

Many states jockeyed for power following the collapse of the Babylonian empire, but after about 1300 B.C.E. the Assyrians gradually extended their authority to much of south-

**Assyrians** (uh-SEER-ee-uhns)

**MAP 1.2** | Mesopotamian empires, 1800–600 B.C.E. Mesopotamian empires facilitated interactions between peoples from different societies. Consider the various land, river, and sea routes by which peoples of Mesopotamia, Anatolia, and Egypt were able to communicate with one another in the second and first millennia B.C.E.

The distinctive shape of the Assyrian empire closely correlates to areas that could be irrigated by large rivers.

west Asia. At its high point, during the eighth and seventh centuries B.C.E., the Assyrian empire embraced not only Mesopotamia but also Syria, Palestine, much of Anatolia, and most of Egypt.

Like most other Mesopotamian peoples, the Assyrians relied on the administrative techniques pioneered by their Babylonian predecessors, and they followed laws much like those enshrined in the code of Hammurabi. They also preserved a great deal of Mesopotamian literature in huge libraries maintained at their large and lavish courts. Yet Assyrian domination was extremely unpopular and proved impossible to maintain. In 612 B.C.E. a combination of internal unrest and external assault brought the empire down.

PSI map | Mesopotamian empires
www.mhhe.com/bentleybrief2e

**THE NEW BABYLONIAN EMPIRE** For half a century, from 600 to 550 B.C.E., Babylon once again dominated Mesopotamia during the New Babylonian empire, sometimes called the Chaldean empire. King Nebuchadnezzar (reigned 605–562 B.C.E.) lavished wealth and resources on his capital city. Babylon occupied some 850 hectares (more than 2,100 acres), and the city's defensive walls were reportedly so thick that a four-horse chariot could turn around on top of them. Within the walls there were enormous palaces and 1,179 temples, some of them faced with gold and decorated with thousands of statues. When one of the king's wives longed for flowering shrubs from her mountain

**Nebuchadnezzar** (neb-uh-kud-NEZ-er)

homeland, Nebuchadnezzar had them planted in terraces above the city walls, and the hanging gardens of Babylon have symbolized the city's luxuriousness ever since.

By this time, however, peoples beyond Mesopotamia had acquired advanced weapons and were experimenting with techniques of administering large territories. As a result, in the mid–sixth century B.C.E. Mesopotamians largely lost control of their affairs, and foreign conquerors absorbed them into their own empires.

# THE FORMATION OF A COMPLEX SOCIETY AND SOPHISTICATED CULTURAL TRADITIONS

With the emergence of cities and the congregation of dense populations in urban spaces, specialized labor proliferated. The Mesopotamian economy became increasingly diverse, and trade linked the region with distant peoples. Clearly defined social classes emerged, as small groups of people concentrated wealth and power in their own hands, and Mesopotamia developed into a patriarchal society that vested authority largely in adult males. Mesopotamians also allocated some of their resources to individuals who worked to develop sophisticated cultural traditions, including the invention of writing, which enabled them to record information for future retrieval. Indeed, writing soon became a foundation for education, science, literature, and religious reflection.

## *Economic Specialization and Trade*

When large numbers of people began to congregate in cities and work at tasks other than agriculture, they vastly expanded the stock of human skills. Craftsmen refined techniques inherited from earlier generations and experimented with new ways of doing things. Pottery making, textile manufacture, woodworking, leather production, brick making, stonecutting, and masonry all became distinct occupations in the world's earliest cities.

BRONZE METALLURGY  Metallurgical innovations ranked among the most important developments that came about because of specialized labor. About 3500 B.C.E. experimentation with copper metallurgy led to the invention of bronze when Mesopotamian metalworkers learned to alloy copper with tin. Unlike pure copper, bronze is both hard and strong, and it quickly became the preferred metal for military weaponry as craftsmen turned out swords, spears, axes, shields, and armor made of the recently invented metal. And although bronze was expensive, over a long period Mesopotamian farmers also began to use bronze knives and bronze-tipped plows instead of tools made of bone, wood, stone, or obsidian.

IRON METALLURGY  After about 1000 B.C.E. Mesopotamian craftsmen began to manufacture effective tools and weapons with iron as well as bronze. Whereas early experimentation with iron metallurgy resulted in products that were too brittle for heavy-duty uses, by about 1300 B.C.E. craftsmen from Hittite society in Anatolia (discussed later in this chapter) developed techniques of forging exceptionally strong iron tools and weapons. As knowledge of those techniques spread, Assyrian conquerors made particularly effective use of them by forging iron weapons to build their empire. Iron also had the advantage of being less expensive than bronze, which quickly made it the metal of choice for weapons and tools.

THE WHEEL  Other craftsmen focused on devising efficient means of transportation based on wheeled vehicles and sailing ships, both of which facilitated long-distance trade. Sumerians first invented the wheel in about 3500 B.C.E., and they were building wheeled carts by 3000 B.C.E. Wheeled carts and wagons enabled people to haul heavy

loads of bulk goods over much longer distances than human porters or draft animals could
manage. The wheel rapidly diffused from Sumer to neighboring lands, and within a few
centuries it had become a standard means of overland transportation.

**SHIPBUILDING** Sumerians also experimented with technologies of maritime
transportation. By 3500 B.C.E. they had built watercraft that allowed them to venture into
the Persian Gulf and beyond. By 2300 B.C.E. they were trading regularly with merchants
of Harappan society in the Indus River valley of northern India (discussed in chapter 3),
which they reached by sailing through the Persian Gulf and the Arabian Sea. During the
time of the Babylonian empire, Mesopotamians traded extensively with peoples in all
directions: they imported silver from Anatolia, cedarwood from Lebanon, copper from
Arabia, gold from Egypt, tin from Persia, lapis lazuli from Afghanistan, and semiprecious
stones from northern India.

## The Emergence of a Stratified Patriarchal Society

With their increasingly specialized labor and long-distance trade, cities provided many more
opportunities for the accumulation of wealth than ever before. As a result, social distinctions in Mesopotamia became much more sharply defined than those in neolithic villages.

**SOCIAL CLASSES** In early Mesopotamia the ruling classes originally consisted
of kings and nobles who were elected to their positions because of their valor and success
as warriors. However, royal status soon became hereditary, as kings arranged for their sons
to succeed them. Nobles were mostly members of royal families and other close supporters of the kings and thus controlled significant wealth and power. Members of the ruling
class displayed their high status through large-scale construction projects and by lavishly
decorating their capital cities.

**TEMPLE COMMUNITIES** Closely allied with the ruling elites were priests and
priestesses, many of whom were younger relatives of the rulers. The principal role of the
priestly elites was to intervene with the gods to ensure good fortune for their communities.
In exchange for those services, priests and priestesses lived in temple communities and received offerings of food, drink, and clothing from city inhabitants. Temples also generated
income from the vast tracts of land that they owned and large workshops that they maintained. Because of their wealth, temples provided comfortable livings for their inhabitants,
and they also served the needs of the larger community. For instance, temples functioned as
banks where individuals could store wealth, and they helped underwrite trading ventures to

**COMMONERS IN MESOPO-TAMIA.** | Gypsum carving of an elderly couple from the city of Nippur about 2500 B.C.E. *How does this figure give us insight into daily life among the Sumerians?*

distant lands. They also helped those in need by taking in orphans, supplying grain in times of famine, and providing ransoms for community members captured in battle.

Apart from the ruling and priestly elites, Mesopotamian society included less privileged classes of free commoners, dependent clients, and slaves. Free commoners mostly worked as peasant cultivators in the countryside on land owned by their families, although some also worked in the cities as builders, craftsmen, or professionals. Dependent clients possessed no property and usually worked as agricultural laborers on estates owned by others. Free commoners and dependent clients all paid taxes—usually in the form of surplus agricultural production—that supported the ruling classes, military forces, and temple communities. In addition, free commoners and dependent clients were subject to conscription by ruling authorities to provide labor services for large-scale construction projects such as roads, city walls, irrigation systems, temples, and public buildings.

SLAVES    Slaves came from three main sources: prisoners of war, convicted criminals, and heavily indebted individuals who sold themselves into slavery to satisfy their obligations. Some slaves worked as agricultural laborers on the estates of nobles or temple communities, but most were domestic servants in wealthy households. Many masters granted slaves their freedom, often with a financial bequest, after several years of good service.

In addition to recognizing differences of rank, wealth, and social status, Mesopotamians built a patriarchal society that vested authority over public and private affairs in adult men. Men made most of the important decisions within households and dominated public life as well. In effect, men ruled as kings, and decisions about policies and public affairs rested almost entirely in their hands.

GENDER ROLES    Hammurabi's laws throw considerable light on sex and gender relations in ancient Mesopotamia. The laws recognized men as heads of their households and entrusted all major family decisions to their judgment. Men even had the power to sell their wives and children into slavery to satisfy their debts. In the interests of protecting the reputations of husbands and the legitimacy of offspring, the laws prescribed death by drowning as the punishment for adulterous wives, as well as for their partners, while permitting men to engage in consensual sexual relations with concubines, slaves, or prostitutes without penalty.

In spite of their subordinate legal status, women made their influence felt in Mesopotamian society. At ruling courts women sometimes advised kings and their governments. A few women wielded great power as high priestesses who managed the enormous estates belonging to their temples. Others obtained a formal education and worked as scribes—literate individuals who prepared administrative and legal documents for governments and private parties. Women also pursued careers as midwives, shopkeepers, brewers, bakers, tavern keepers, and textile manufacturers.

During the second millennium B.C.E., however, Mesopotamian men progressively tightened their control over the social and sexual behavior of women. To protect family fortunes and guarantee the legitimacy of heirs, Mesopotamians insisted on the virginity of brides at marriage, and they forbade casual socializing between married women and men outside their family. By 1500 B.C.E. and probably even earlier, married women in Mesopotamian cities had begun to wear veils when they ventured beyond their own households in order to discourage the attention of men from other families. This concern to control women's social and sexual behavior spread throughout much of southwest Asia and the Mediterranean basin, where it reinforced patriarchal social structures.

## *The Development of Written Cultural Traditions*

The world's earliest known writing came from Mesopotamia. Sumerians invented a system of writing about the middle of the fourth millennium B.C.E. to keep track of commercial transactions and tax collections. They first experimented with pictographs representing animals, agricultural products, and trade items that figured prominently in tax and

*The* Epic of Gilgamesh *is the oldest surviving epic poem in history, dating from about 2500 B.C.E. As part of his adventures, Gilgamesh seeks the secret of immortality from a wise man named Ut-napishtim. During the visit, Ut-napishtim tells him how the god Ea alerted him to a plot by the gods to destroy humankind by a massive flood. Here, Ut-napishtim recounts the story to Gilgamesh.*

The *Epic of Gilgamesh*
www.mhhe.com/
bentleybrief2e

This is the message:
"Man of Shuruppak, son of Ubara-Tutu,*
Dismantle your house, build a boat.
Leave possessions, search out living things.
Reject chattels⁺ and save lives!
Put aboard the seed of all living things, into the boat.
The boat that you are to build
Shall have her dimensions in proportion,
Her width and length should be in harmony,
Roof her like the Apsu."**
I realized and spoke to my master Ea,
"I have paid attention to the words that you spoke
    in this way,
My master, and I shall act upon them. . . .
I loaded her with everything there was,
Loaded her with all the silver,
Loaded her with all the gold
Loaded her with all the seed of living things, all of them.
I put on board the boat all my kith and kin.
Put on board cattle from open country, wild beasts from
    open country, all kinds of craftsmen. . . .
That hour arrived; . . .
I saw the shape of the storm,
The storm was terrifying to see.
I went aboard the boat and closed the door. . . .
For six days and seven nights
The wind blew, flood and tempest overwhelmed the land;
When the seventh day arrived the tempest, flood and
    onslaught

Which had struggled like a woman in labor, blew them-
    selves out.
The sea became calm, the wind grew quiet, the flood
    held back.
[S]ilence reigned, for all mankind had returned to clay. . . .
The boat came to rest on Mount Nimush.⁺⁺ . . .
When the seventh day arrived,
I put out and released a dove.
The dove went; it came back,
For no perching place was visible to it; and it turned
    round.
I put out and released a swallow.
The swallow went; it came back,
For no perching place was visible to it, and it turned
    round.
I put out and released a raven.
The raven went, and saw the waters receding.
And it ate, preened, lifted its tail and did not turn round.

*This refers to Ut-napishtim
+ Property
** The realm of freshwater under the earth
++ A mountain in modern Iraq

■ **Discuss the similarities between the flood story above and the story of Noah's Ark from the Old Testament. Why are these stories so similar?**

SOURCE: Thomas Sanders et al. *Encounters in World History: Sources and Themes from the Global Past*, Vol. I. Boston: McGraw-Hill, 2006, pp. 40–41.

commercial transactions. By 3100 B.C.E. conventional signs representing specific words had spread throughout Mesopotamia.

A writing system that depends on pictures is useful for purposes such as keeping records, but it is a cumbersome way to communicate abstract ideas. Beginning about 2900 B.C.E. the Sumerians developed a more flexible system of writing that used graphic symbols to represent sounds, syllables, and ideas as well as physical objects. By combining pictographs and other symbols, the Sumerians created a powerful writing system.

CUNEIFORM WRITING   When writing, a Sumerian scribe used a stylus fashioned from a reed to impress symbols on wet clay. Because the stylus left lines and wedge-shaped marks, Sumerian writing is known as *cuneiform*, a term that comes from two Latin words meaning "wedge-shaped." When dried in the sun or baked in an oven, the clay hardened and preserved a permanent record of the scribe's message. Babylonians, Assyrians, and other peoples later adapted the Sumerians' script to their own languages, and the tradition of cuneiform writing continued for more than three thousand years.

Though originally invented for purposes of keeping records, writing clearly had potential that went far beyond the purely practical matter of storing information. Mesopotamians relied on writing to communicate complex ideas about the world, the gods, human beings, and their relationships with one another. Indeed, writing made possible the emergence of a distinctive cultural tradition that shaped Mesopotamian values for almost three millennia.

ASTRONOMY AND MATHEMATICS   Literacy led to a rapid expansion of knowledge. Mesopotamian scholars devoted themselves to the study of astronomy and mathematics—both important sciences for agricultural societies. Knowledge of astronomy helped them prepare accurate calendars, which in turn enabled them to chart the rhythms of the seasons and determine the appropriate times for planting and harvesting crops. They used their mathematical skills to survey agricultural lands and allocate them to the proper owners or tenants. Some Mesopotamian conventions persist to the present day: Mesopotamian scientists divided the year into twelve months, for example, and they divided the hour into sixty minutes, each composed of sixty seconds.

THE EPIC OF GILGAMESH   Mesopotamians also used writing to communicate abstract ideas, investigate intellectual problems, and reflect on human beings and their place in the world. Best known of the reflective literature from Mesopotamia is the *Epic of Gilgamesh,* completed after 2000 B.C.E. In recounting the experiences of Gilgamesh and Enkidu, the epic explored themes of friendship, relations between humans and the gods, and especially the meaning of life and death. The stories of Gilgamesh and Enkidu resonated so widely that for some two thousand years—from the time of the Sumerian city-states to the fall of the Assyrian empire—they were the principal vehicles for Mesopotamian reflections on moral issues.

# THE BROADER INFLUENCE OF MESOPOTAMIAN SOCIETY

While building cities and regional states, Mesopotamians deeply influenced the development and experiences of peoples living far beyond their own lands. Often their wealth and power attracted the attention of neighboring peoples. Sometimes Mesopotamians projected their power to foreign lands and imposed their ways by force. Occasionally migrants left Mesopotamia and carried their inherited traditions to new lands. Mesopotamian influence did not completely transform other peoples and turn them into carbon copies of Mesopotamians. On the contrary, other peoples adopted Mesopotamian ways selectively and adapted them to their own needs and interests. Yet the broader impact of Mesopotamian society shows that, even in early times, complex agricultural societies organized around cities had strong potential to influence the development of distant human communities.

## *Hebrews, Israelites, and Jews*

The best-known cases of early Mesopotamian influence involved Hebrews, Israelites, and Jews, who preserved memories of their historical experiences in an extensive collection of sacred writings. Hebrews were speakers of the ancient Hebrew language. Israelites formed a branch of Hebrews who settled in Palestine (modern-day Israel) after 1300 B.C.E. Jews descended from southern Israelites who inhabited the kingdom of Judah. For more than two thousand years, Hebrews, Israelites, and Jews interacted constantly with Mesopotamians and other peoples as well, with profound consequences for the development of their own societies.

**THE EARLY HEBREWS**   The earliest Hebrews were pastoral nomads who inhabited lands between Mesopotamia and Egypt during the second millennium B.C.E. As Mesopotamia prospered, some of the Hebrews settled in the region's cities. According to the Hebrew scriptures (the Old Testament of the Christian Bible), the Hebrew patriarch Abraham came from the Sumerian city of Ur, but he migrated to northern Mesopotamia about 1850 B.C.E. Abraham's descendants continued to recognize many of the deities, values, and customs common to Mesopotamian peoples. Hebrew law, for example, borrowed heavily from Hammurabi's code. The Hebrews also told the story of a devastating flood that had destroyed all early human society, which was a variation on similar flood stories related from the earliest days of Sumerian society. One early version of the story made its way into the *Epic of Gilgamesh.* The Hebrews altered the story and adapted it to their own interests and purposes, but their familiarity with the flood story shows that they participated fully in the larger society of Mesopotamia.

**MIGRATIONS AND SETTLEMENT IN PALESTINE**   According to their scriptures, some Hebrews migrated from Palestine to Egypt during the eighteenth century B.C.E. About 1300 B.C.E., however, this branch of the Hebrews departed under the leadership of Moses and returned to Palestine. Organized into a loose federation of twelve tribes, those Hebrews, known as the Israelites, fought bitterly with other inhabitants of Palestine and carved out a territory for themselves. Eventually the Israelites abandoned their inherited tribal structure in favor of a Mesopotamian-style monarchy that brought all their twelve tribes under unified rule. During the reigns of King David (1000–970 B.C.E.) and King Solomon (970–930 B.C.E.), Israelites dominated the territory between Syria and the Sinai peninsula. They built an elaborate and cosmopolitan capital city at Jerusalem and entered into diplomatic and commercial relations with Mesopotamians, Egyptians, and Arabian peoples. Like other peoples of southwest Asia, the Israelites made use of iron technology to strengthen their military forces and produce tough agricultural implements.

**MOSES AND MONOTHEISM**   After the time of Moses, however, the religious beliefs of the Israelites developed along increasingly distinctive lines. Whereas the early Hebrews had recognized many of the same gods as their Mesopotamian neighbors, Moses embraced monotheism: he taught that there was only one god, known as Yahweh, who was a supremely powerful deity, the creator and sustainer of the world. Yahweh expected his followers to worship him alone, and he demanded that they observe high moral and ethical standards. In the Ten Commandments, a set of religious and ethical principles that Moses announced to the Israelites, Yahweh warned his followers against destructive and antisocial behavior such as lying, theft, adultery, and murder. Between about 1000 and 400 B.C.E., the Israelites' religious leaders compiled their teachings in a set of holy scriptures known as the Torah (Hebrew for "doctrine" or "teaching"), which laid down Yahweh's laws and outlined his role in creating the world and guiding human affairs. The Torah taught that Yahweh would reward those who obeyed his will and punish those who did not.

**ASSYRIAN AND BABYLONIAN CONQUESTS**   The Israelites placed increasing emphasis on devotion to Yahweh as they experienced a series of political and military setbacks. Following King Solomon's reign, tribal tensions led to the division of the community into a large kingdom of Israel in the north and a smaller kingdom of Judah in the land known as Judea to the south. In 722 B.C.E. Assyrian forces conquered the northern kingdom and deported many of its inhabitants to other regions, causing many of the deported to lose their identity as Israelites. In 586 B.C.E., the New Babylonian empire toppled the kingdom of Judah and destroyed Jerusalem, forcing many residents into exile. Unlike their cousins to the north, however, most of these Israelites maintained

**monotheism**  (mah-noh-THEE-iz'm)

**Yahweh**  (YAH-way)

their religious identity, and many of the deportees eventually returned to Judea, where they became known as Jews.

Ironically, perhaps, the Israelites' devotion to Yahweh intensified during this era of turmoil. Between the ninth and sixth centuries B.C.E., a series of prophets urged the Israelites to rededicate themselves to their faith and obey Yahweh's commandments. Failure to do so, they warned, would be punished by Yahweh in the form of conquest by foreigners. Many Israelites took the Assyrian and Babylonian conquests as proof that the prophets accurately represented Yahweh's mind and will.

The exiles who returned to Judea after the Babylonian conquest did not abandon hope for a state of their own, and even organized several small Jewish states as tributaries to the larger empires that dominated the area. But the returnees also built a distinctive religious community based on their conviction that they had a special relationship with Yahweh. This conviction enabled the Jews to maintain a strong sense of identity as a people distinct from others, even as they participated fully in the development of a larger complex society in southwest Asia. Over the longer term, Jewish monotheism, scriptures, and moral concerns also profoundly influenced the development of Christianity and Islam.

# The Phoenicians

Phoenician artifacts
www.mhhe.com/
bentleybrief2e

**PHOENICIAN TRADE NETWORKS** North of the Israelites' kingdom in Palestine, the Phoenicians occupied a narrow coastal plain between the Mediterranean Sea and the Lebanon Mountains. They spoke a Semitic language, referring to themselves as Canaanites and their land as Canaan. (The term *Phoenician* comes from early Greek references.) Sometime after 3000 B.C.E., the Phoenicians established a series of city-states ruled by local kings, the most important of which were Tyre, Sidon, Beirut, and Byblos. Though not a numerous or militarily powerful people, the Phoenicians influenced societies throughout the Mediterranean basin because of their trade and communication networks. Their meager lands did not permit development of a large agricultural society, so after about 2500 B.C.E. the Phoenicians turned increasingly to industry and trade. Although the Phoenicians traded overland, they were also excellent sailors, and they built the best ships of their times. Between 1200 and 800 B.C.E., they dominated Mediterranean trade. They established commercial colonies in Rhodes, Cyprus, Sicily, Sardinia, Spain, and north Africa. They sailed far and wide in search of raw materials, which took them well beyond the Mediterranean: Phoenician merchant ships visited the Canary Islands, coastal ports in Portugal and France, and even the distant British Isles, and adventurous Phoenician mariners made exploratory voyages to the Azores Islands and down the west coast of Africa as far as the Gulf of Guinea.

**ALPHABETIC WRITING** Like the Hebrews, the Phoenicians largely adapted Mesopotamian cultural traditions to their own needs. Their gods, for example, were mostly adapted from Mesopotamian gods. The Phoenicians also creatively adapted the Mesopotamian practice of writing by experimenting with simpler alternatives to cuneiform. By 1500 B.C.E. Phoenician scribes had devised an early alphabetic script consisting of twenty-two symbols representing consonants (the Phoenician alphabet had no symbols for vowels). Learning twenty-two letters and building words with them was much easier than memorizing the hundreds of symbols employed in cuneiform. Because alphabetic writing required much less investment in education than did cuneiform writing, more people were able to become literate than ever before.

Alphabetic writing spread widely as the Phoenicians traveled and traded throughout the Mediterranean basin. About the ninth century

# THINKING ABOUT *Traditions*

**TRADITIONS IN EARLY COMPLEX SOCIETIES.** In the period between 3500 and 500 B.C.E., peoples such as the Sumerians, Assyrians, Hittites, and Phoenicians independently developed distinctive characteristics in terms of architecture, economic pursuits, and technology. What were some of the defining characteristics that marked these societies as different from one another, and why might these differences have arisen? Think carefully here about geographical location, the presence or absence of plants and animals, and the availability of resources.

Phoenicians (fi-NEE-shins)

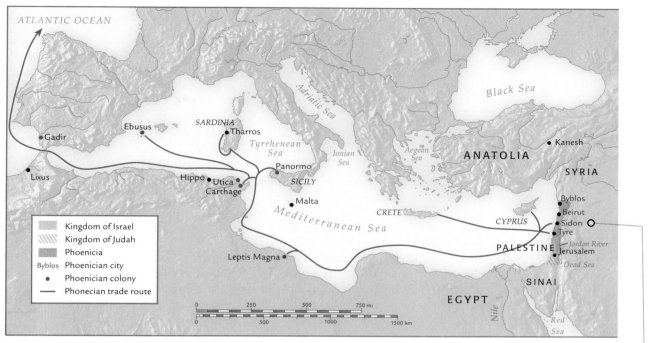

**MAP 1.3** | Israel and Phoenicia, 1500–600 B.C.E. Note the location of Israel and Phoenicia with respect to Mesopotamia, Egypt, and the Mediterranean Sea. *How might geographic location have influenced communications and exchanges between Israel, Phoenicia, and other lands of the region?*

**The coastal position of Phoenician cities was conducive to trade by sea.**

B.C.E., for example, Greeks modified the Phoenician alphabet and added symbols representing vowels. Romans later adapted the Greek alphabet to their own language and passed it along to their cultural heirs in Europe. In later centuries alphabetic writing spread to central Asia, south Asia, and southeast Asia, and ultimately throughout most of the world.

# THE INDO-EUROPEAN MIGRATIONS

After 3000 B.C.E. Mesopotamia was a prosperous, productive region where peoples from many different communities mixed and mingled. But Mesopotamia was only one region in a much larger world of interaction and exchange. Mesopotamians and their neighbors all dealt frequently with peoples from regions far beyond southwest Asia. Among the most influential of these peoples in the third and second millennia B.C.E. were those who spoke various Indo-European languages. Their migrations throughout much of Eurasia profoundly influenced historical development in both southwest Asia and the larger world.

## *Indo-European Origins*

**INDO-EUROPEAN LANGUAGES**   During the eighteenth and nineteenth centuries, linguists noticed that many languages of Europe, southwest Asia, and India featured remarkable similarities in vocabulary and grammatical structure. Ancient languages displaying these similarities included Sanskrit (the sacred language of ancient India), Old Persian, Greek, and Latin. Because of the geographic regions where these tongues are found, scholars refer to them as Indo-European languages. Major subgroups of the Indo-European family of languages include Indo-Iranian, Greek, Balto-Slavic, Germanic,

| NORTH SEMITIC | | | GREEK | | ETRUSCAN | LATIN | |
| --- | --- | --- | --- | --- | --- | --- | --- |
| EARLY PHOENICIAN | EARLY HEBREW | PHOENICIAN | EARLY | CLASSICAL | EARLY | EARLY | CLASSICAL |
| K | K | ⋊ | ◁ | A | A | A | A |
| 9 | 9 | 9 | 9 | B | B | B | B |
| 1 | ⅂ | 1 | 1 | Γ | ⌐ | | C |
| △ | ◁ | ◁ | △ | △ | ⌒ | ◠ | D |

Italic, and Celtic. English belongs to the Germanic subgroup of the Indo-European family of languages.

After noticing linguistic similarities, scholars sought a way to explain the close relationship between the Indo-European languages. The only persuasive explanation for the high degree of linguistic coincidence was that speakers of Indo-European languages were all descendants of ancestors who spoke a common tongue and migrated from their original homeland. As migrants established separate communities and lost touch with one another, their languages evolved along different lines, adding new words, pronunciations, and spellings but retaining the basic grammatical structure of their original speech.

THE INDO-EUROPEAN HOMELAND   The original homeland of Indo-European speakers was probably the steppe region of modern-day Ukraine and southern Russia, where the earliest of them built a society between about 4500 and 2500 B.C.E. A central feature of Indo-European society was the domestication of wild horses from the Eurasian steppe about 4000 B.C.E. Horses were initially used for food and soon thereafter for riding as well. When Sumerian knowledge of bronze metallurgy spread to the Indo-European homeland about 3000 B.C.E., Indo-European speakers devised ways to hitch horses to carts, wagons, and chariots. The possession of domesticated horses vastly magnified the power of the Indo-Europeans. Horses enabled them to develop transportation technologies that were much faster and more efficient than other alternatives. Furthermore, because of their strength and speed, horses provided Indo-European speakers with a tremendous military advantage over peoples they encountered. It is perhaps significant that many groups of Indo-European speakers considered themselves superior to other peoples: the terms *Aryan, Iran,* and *Eire* (the official name of the modern Republic of Ireland) all derive from the Indo-European word *aryo,* meaning "nobleman" or "lord."

## Indo-European Expansion and Its Effects

THE NATURE OF INDO-EUROPEAN MIGRATION   Horses also provided Indo-European speakers with a means of expanding far beyond their original homeland. As they flourished in southern Russia, Indo-European speakers experienced a population explosion, which prompted some of them to move into the sparsely inhabited eastern steppe or even beyond the grasslands altogether. The earliest Indo-European migrations began about 3000 B.C.E. and continued until about 1000 B.C.E. Like early movements of other peoples, these were not mass migrations so much as gradual and incremental processes that resulted in the spread of Indo-European languages and ethnic communities, as small groups of people established settlements in new lands, which then became foundations for further expansion.

THE HITTITES   The most influential Indo-European migrants in ancient times were the Hittites. About 1900 B.C.E. the Hittites migrated to the central plain of Anatolia, where they imposed their language and rule on the region's inhabitants. During the

## TABLE 1.1 — Similarities in Vocabulary Indicating Close Relationships between Select Indo-European Languages

| English | German | Spanish | Greek | Latin | Sanskrit |
|---------|--------|---------|--------|-------|----------|
| father | vater | padre | pater | pater | pitar |
| one | ein | uno | hen | unus | ekam |
| fire | feuer | fuego | pyr | ignis | agnis |
| field | feld | campo | agros | ager | ajras |
| sun | sone | sol | helios | sol | surya |
| king | könig | rey | basileus | rex | raja |
| god | gott | dios | theos | deus | devas |

seventeenth and sixteenth centuries B.C.E., they built a powerful kingdom and established close relations with Mesopotamian peoples. They traded with Babylonians and Assyrians, adapted cuneiform writing to their Indo-European language, and accepted many Mesopotamian deities into their own pantheon. In 1595 B.C.E. the Hittites toppled the mighty Babylonian empire of Mesopotamia, and for several centuries thereafter they were the dominant power in southwest Asia. Between 1450 and 1200 B.C.E. their authority extended to eastern Anatolia, northern Mesopotamia, and Syria down to Phoenicia. After 1200 B.C.E. the unified Hittite state dissolved, but a Hittite identity survived, along with the Hittite language, throughout the era of the Assyrian empire and beyond.

WAR CHARIOTS    The Hittites were responsible for two technological innovations—the construction of light, horse-drawn war chariots and the refinement of iron metallurgy—that greatly strengthened their own society and influenced other peoples throughout much of the ancient world. The Hittites' speedy chariots were crucial in their campaign to establish a state in Anatolia. Following the Hittites' example, Mesopotamians soon added chariot teams to their own armies, and Assyrians made especially effective use of chariots in building their empire. Indeed, chariot warfare was so effective—and its techniques spread so widely—that charioteers became the elite strike forces in armies throughout much of the ancient world from Rome to China.

IRON METALLURGY    After about 1300 B.C.E. the Hittites also refined the technology of iron metallurgy, which enabled them to produce effective weapons cheaply and in large quantities. Hittite methods of iron production diffused rapidly and eventually spread throughout all of Eurasia. (Peoples of sub-Saharan Africa independently invented iron metallurgy.) Hittites were not the original inventors either of horse-drawn chariots or of iron metallurgy: in both cases they built on Mesopotamian precedents. But in both cases they clearly improved on existing technologies and introduced innovations that other peoples readily adopted.

INDO-EUROPEAN MIGRATIONS TO THE WEST AND EAST    While the Hittites were building a state in Anatolia, other Indo-European speakers migrated from the steppe to different regions. Some went east into central Asia, venturing as far as the Tarim Basin (now western China) by 2000 B.C.E. Meanwhile, other Indo-European migrants moved west. One wave of migration took Indo-European speakers into Greece after 2200 B.C.E., with their descendants

## THINKING ABOUT *Encounters*

ENCOUNTERS IN EARLY COMPLEX SOCIETIES. Despite important differences between the early complex societies, it is nevertheless clear that significant interaction occurred among them. What were the mechanisms by which such interaction occurred (i.e., trade, transport), and what evidence do scholars have that these early societies influenced one another?

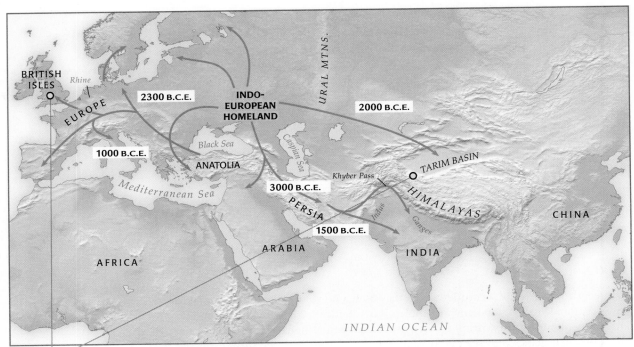

**The distance between the British Isles and the Tarim Basin is about 4000 miles.**

**MAP 1.4** | Indo-European migrations, 3000–1000 B.C.E. Consider the vast distances over which Indo-European migrants established communities. *Would it have been possible for speakers of Indo-European languages to spread so widely without the aid of domesticated horses?*

moving into central Italy by 1000 B.C.E. Another migratory wave established an Indo-European presence farther to the west. By 2300 B.C.E. some Indo-European speakers had made their way from southern Russia into central Europe (modern Germany and Austria), by 1200 B.C.E. to western Europe (modern France), and shortly thereafter to the British Isles, the Baltic region, and the Iberian peninsula. Yet another, later, wave of migrations established an Indo-European presence in Iran and India. About 1500 B.C.E. the Medes and the Persians migrated into the Iranian plateau, while the Aryans began filtering into northern India. As in earlier migrations, Indo-European migrants borrowed from, influenced, and mixed with the settled peoples they discovered and in so doing shaped future historical developments in each area.

**Aryans** (AYR-ee-uhns)

## SUMMARY

Building on neolithic foundations, Mesopotamian peoples constructed societies much more complex, powerful, and influential than those of their predecessors. Through their city-states, kingdoms, and regional empires, Mesopotamians created formal institutions of government that extended the authority of ruling elites to all corners of their states, and they occasionally mobilized forces that projected their power to distant lands. They generated several distinct social classes. Specialized labor fueled productive economies and encouraged the establishment of long-distance trade networks. They devised systems of writing, which enabled them to develop sophisticated cultural traditions. They deeply influenced other peoples, such as the Hebrews and the Phoenicians, throughout southwest Asia and the eastern Mediterranean basin. They had frequent dealings also with Indo-European peoples. Although Indo-European society emerged far to the north of Mesopotamia, speakers of Indo-European languages migrated widely and established societies throughout much of Eurasia. Sometimes they drew inspiration from Mesopotamian practices, and sometimes they developed their own practices that influenced Mesopotamians and others as well. Thus, already in remote antiquity, the various peoples of the world profoundly influenced one another through cross-cultural interaction and exchange.

# STUDY TERMS

Aryans (24)
Assyrians (12)
bronze (14)
chariot (23)
cuneiform (17)
Gilgamesh (17)
Hammurabi (11)
Hebrews (18)

Hittites (22)
*Homo sapiens* (7)
Indo-European migrations (21)
Israelites (18)
Mesopotamia (9)
monotheism (19)
neolithic era (7)

New Babylonian empire (13)
paleolithic era (7)
Phoenician (20)
Sargon of Akkad (11)
Sumerians (10)
wheel (14)
Yahweh (19)

# FOR FURTHER READING

Elizabeth Wayland Barber. *Women's Work: The First 20,000 Years.* New York, 1994. Fascinating study of ancient textiles, which the author argues was a craft industry dominated by women from the earliest times.

David Christian. *Maps of Time: An Introduction to Big History.* Berkeley, 2004. A brilliant study that considers human history in the context of natural history since the big bang.

Jared Diamond. *The Third Chimpanzee: Evolution and the Future of the Human Animal.* New York, 1992. An insightful guide to human evolution and its significance for human behavior.

Andrew George, trans. *The Epic of Gilgamesh.* London, 1999. A careful study and fresh translation of the best-known Mesopotamian literary work prepared on the basis of recently discovered texts.

J. P. Mallory. *In Search of the Indo-Europeans: Language, Archaeology, and Myth.* London, 1989. Carefully reviews modern theories about early Indo-European speakers in light of both the linguistic and the archaeological evidence.

Marc van de Mieroop. *A History of the Ancient Near East, ca 3000–323 B.C.* Oxford, 2004. A concise and readable history of ancient Mesopotamia and neighboring societies.

Hans J. Nissen. *The Early History of the Ancient Near East, 9000–2000 B.C.* Trans. by E. Lutzeier. Chicago, 1988. A brilliant synthesis of scholarship on the development of cities and complex society in Mesopotamia and neighboring regions.

James B. Pritchard, ed. *Ancient Near Eastern Texts Relating to the Old Testament.* 2 vols. 3rd ed. Princeton, 1975. Important collection of primary sources in translation, emphasizing parallels between the ancient Hebrews and other peoples.

Michael Roaf. *Cultural Atlas of Mesopotamia and the Ancient Near East.* New York, 1990. Richly illustrated volume with well-informed essays on all dimensions of Mesopotamian history.

Bruce D. Smith. *The Emergence of Agriculture.* New York, 1995. Concentrates on the initial domestication of plant and animal species in world regions where agriculture developed.

# Early African Societies and the Bantu Migrations

## 2

For almost three thousand years, Egyptian embalmers preserved the bodies of deceased individuals through a process of mummification. Egyptian records rarely mention the techniques of mummification, but the Greek historian Herodotus traveled in Egypt about 450 B.C.E. and briefly explained the craft. The embalmer first used a metal hook to draw the brain of the deceased out through a nostril, then removed the internal organs through an incision made alongside the abdomen, washed them in palm wine, and sealed them with preservatives in stone vessels. Next, the embalmer washed the body, filled it with spices and aromatics, and covered it for about two months with natron, a naturally occurring salt substance. When the natron had extracted all moisture from the body, the embalmer cleansed it again and wrapped it with strips of fine linen covered with resin. Adorned with jewelry, the preserved body then went into a coffin bearing a painting or a sculpted likeness of the deceased.

**Canopic Coffinette of Tutankhamon**
www.mhhe.com/
bentleybrief2e

Careful preservation of the body was only a part of the funerary ritual for prominent Egyptians. Ruling elites, wealthy individuals, and sometimes common people as well laid their deceased to rest in expensive tombs equipped with furniture, tools, weapons, and ornaments that the departed would need in their next lives. Relatives periodically brought food and wine to nourish the deceased in their new dimension of existence.

Egyptian funerary customs were reflections of a prosperous agricultural society. Food offerings consisted mostly of local agricultural products, and scenes painted on tomb walls often depicted workers preparing fields or cultivating crops. Moreover, bountiful harvests explained the accumulation of wealth that supported elaborate funerary practices, and they also enabled some individuals to devote their efforts to specialized tasks such as embalming. Agriculture even influenced religious beliefs. Many Egyptians believed fervently in a life beyond the grave, and they likened the human experience of life and death to the agricultural cycle in which crops grow, die, and come to life again in another season.

❮ *Excavations surrounding the pyramids, as seen from the air.*

As Mesopotamians built a productive agricultural society in southwest Asia and as Indo-European peoples introduced domesticated horses to much of Eurasia, cultivation and herding also transformed African societies. African agriculture first took root in the Sudan, then moved into the Nile River valley and also to most parts of sub-Saharan Africa. Agriculture flourished

**Nubia** (NOO-bee-uh)

# CHRONOLOGY

| | |
|---|---|
| 9000 B.C.E. | Origins of Sudanic herding |
| 7500 B.C.E. | Origins of Sudanic cultivation |
| 3100 B.C.E. | Unification of Egypt |
| 3100–2660 B.C.E. | Archaic Period of Egyptian history |
| 2660–2160 B.C.E. | Egyptian Old Kingdom |
| 2600–2500 B.C.E. | Era of pyramid building in Egypt |
| 2500–1450 B.C.E. | Early kingdom of Kush with capital at Kerma |
| 2040–1640 B.C.E. | Egyptian Middle Kingdom |
| 2000 B.C.E. | Beginnings of Bantu migrations |
| 1550–1070 B.C.E. | Egyptian New Kingdom |
| 1479–1425 B.C.E. | Reign of Pharaoh Tuthmosis III |
| 1473–1458 B.C.E. | Reign of Queen Hatshepsut (coruler with Tuthmosis III) |
| 1353–1335 B.C.E. | Reign of Pharaoh Amenhotep IV (Akhenaten) |
| 900 B.C.E. | Invention of iron metallurgy in sub-Saharan Africa |
| 760 B.C.E. | Conquest of Egypt by King Kashta of Kush |

particularly in the fertile Nile valley, and abundant harvests soon supported fast-growing populations. That agricultural bounty underwrote the development of Egypt, the most prosperous and powerful of the early agricultural societies in Africa, and also of Nubia, Egypt's neighbor to the south.

Distinctive Egyptian and Nubian societies began to take shape in the valley of the Nile River during the late fourth millennium B.C.E., shortly after the emergence of complex society in Mesopotamia. Like their Mesopotamian counterparts, Egyptians and Nubians drew on agricultural surpluses to organize formal states, support specialized laborers, and develop distinctive cultural traditions. Also like Mesopotamians, Egyptian and Nubian residents of the Nile valley had regular dealings with peoples from other societies. They drew inspiration for political and social organization both from Mesopotamia and from their African neighbors to the south. In addition, they both traded with and competed against Mesopotamians, Phoenicians, Africans, and others, which resulted in increasing connections with other societies as well as intermittent military conflict.

Indeed, like their counterparts in Mesopotamia, Egyptian and Nubian societies developed from their earliest days in a larger world of interaction and exchange. Just as the peoples of southwest Asia influenced one another, so inhabitants of the Nile valley mixed and mingled with peoples from the eastern Mediterranean, southwest Asia, and sub-Saharan Africa. Just as Indo-European peoples migrated to new lands and established communities that transformed much of Eurasia, so Bantu peoples migrated from their original homeland in west Africa and established settlements that brought profound change to much of sub-Saharan Africa. By no means were Egypt and Nubia isolated centers of social development. Instead, they were only a small part of a much larger world of interacting societies.

# EARLY AGRICULTURAL SOCIETY IN AFRICA

Egypt was the most prominent of early African societies, but it was by no means the only agricultural society, or even the only complex, city-based society of ancient Africa. On the contrary, Egypt emerged alongside Nubia and other agricultural societies in sub-Saharan Africa. Indeed, agricultural crops and domesticated animals reached Egypt from sub-Saharan Africa by way of Nubia as well as from southwest Asia. Favorable geographic conditions enabled Egyptians to build an especially productive agricultural economy that supported a powerful state, while Nubia became home to a somewhat less prosperous but nonetheless sophisticated society. After taking shape as distinctive societies, Egypt had regular dealings with both eastern Mediterranean and southwest Asian peoples, and Nubia linked Egypt and the eastern Mediterranean basin with the peoples and societies of sub-Saharan Africa.

**Bantu** (BAHN-too)

# Climatic Change and the Development of Agriculture in Africa

African agriculture emerged in the context of gradual but momentous changes in climatic conditions. About 10,000 B.C.E., after the end of the last ice age, the area now occupied by the Sahara desert was mostly a grassy steppe with numerous lakes, rivers, and streams. Indeed, climatic and geographic conditions were similar to those of the Sudan—a region of savanna and grassland that stretches across the African continent between the Sahara to the north and the tropical rain forest to the south.

EARLY SUDANIC AGRICULTURE  After about 9000 B.C.E., peoples of the eastern Sudan domesticated cattle and became nomadic herders but also continued to collect wild grains. After 7500 B.C.E. they established permanent settlements and began to cultivate sorghum. Meanwhile, after about 8000 B.C.E., inhabitants of the western Sudan began to cultivate yams in the region between the Niger and Congo rivers. Sudanic agriculture became increasingly diverse over the following centuries: sheep and goats arrived from southwest Asia after 7000 B.C.E., and Sudanic peoples began to cultivate gourds, watermelons, and cotton after 6500 B.C.E.

Agricultural productivity—and the need for order—led Sudanic peoples to organize small-scale states. By about 5000 B.C.E. many Sudanic peoples had formed small monarchies ruled by kings who were viewed as divine or semidivine beings. Sudanic peoples also developed religious beliefs that reflected their agricultural society. They recognized a single divine force as the source of good and evil, and they associated it with rain—a matter of concern for any agricultural society.

CLIMATIC CHANGE  After 5000 B.C.E. the northern half of Africa became much hotter and drier than before. The Sahara desert in particular became increasingly arid and uninhabitable. This process of desiccation drove both humans and animals to regions that offered reliable sources of water such as lakes and rivers. One of those regions was the valley of the Nile River, the principal source of water flowing through north Africa.

THE NILE RIVER VALLEY  Fed by rain and snow in the mountains of east Africa, the Nile, which is the world's longest river, courses some 6,695 kilometers (4,160 miles) from its source at Lake Victoria to its outlet through the delta to the Mediterranean Sea. Each spring, rain and melting snow swell the river, which surges north through the Sudan and Egypt. Until the completion of the high dam at Aswan in 1968, every year the Nile flooded the plains downstream. When the waters receded, they left behind a layer of rich, fertile muck, and those alluvial deposits supported a remarkably productive agricultural economy throughout the Nile River valley.

# Egypt and Nubia: "Gifts of the Nile"

Agriculture transformed the entire Nile River valley, with effects that were most dramatic in Egypt. In ancient times, Egypt referred not to the territory embraced by the modern state of Egypt but, rather, to the ribbon of land bordering the lower third of the Nile between the Mediterranean and the river's first cataract (an unnavigable stretch of rapids and waterfalls) near Aswan. Egypt enjoyed a much larger floodplain than most of the land to the south known as Nubia, the middle stretches of the Nile valley between the river's first and sixth cataracts. As the Sahara became increasingly arid, cultivators flocked to the Nile valley and established societies that depended on intensive agriculture. Because of their broad floodplains, Egyptians were able to take better advantage of the Nile's annual floods than their neighbors to the south, and they turned Egypt into an especially productive agricultural region that was capable of supporting a much larger population than were Nubian lands. Because of its prosperity, the Greek historian Herodotus proclaimed Egypt the "gift of the Nile."

Herodotus & Egypt
www.mhhe.com/
bentleybrief2e

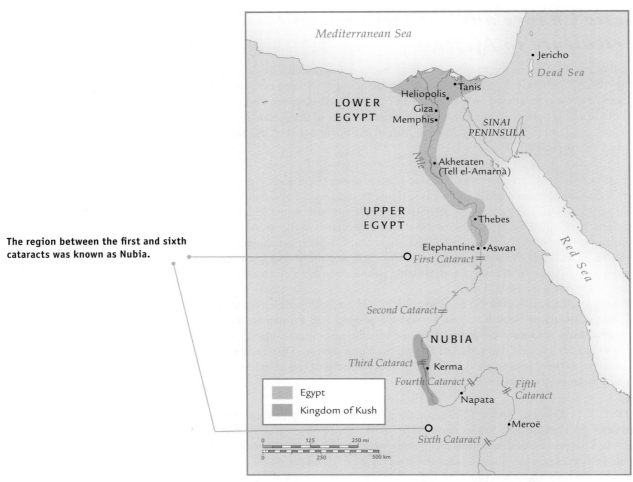

The region between the first and sixth cataracts was known as Nubia.

**MAP 2.1** | The Nile valley, 3000–2000 B.C.E. Note the difference in size between the kingdom of Egypt and the kingdom of Kush. *What geographical conditions favored the establishment of large states north of the first cataract of the Nile River?*

Counting livestock, a model from a tomb
www.mhhe.com/ bentleybrief2e

**EARLY AGRICULTURE IN THE NILE VALLEY**  Geography ensured that Egypt and Nubia would come under the influence of both sub-Saharan Africa and the eastern Mediterranean basin, since the Nile River links the two regions. About 10,000 B.C.E. migrants from the Red Sea hills in northern Ethiopia traveled down the Nile valley and introduced to Egypt and Nubia the practice of collecting wild grains as well as their language, which became the language of ancient Egypt. After 5000 B.C.E., as the African climate grew hotter and drier, Sudanic peoples moved down the Nile, introducing Egypt and Nubia to crops such as gourds and watermelons and domesticated animals such as cattle and donkeys. About the same time, wheat and barley reached Egypt and Nubia from Mesopotamia by traveling up the Nile from the Mediterranean.

Both Egyptians and Nubians relied heavily on agriculture at least by 5000 B.C.E. Egyptian cultivators went into the floodplains in the late summer, after the recession of the Nile's annual flood, sowed their seeds without extensive preparation of the soil, allowed their crops to mature during the cool months of the year, and harvested them during the winter and early spring. With less-extensive floodplains, Nubians relied more on prepared fields and irrigation by waters diverted from the Nile. As in Mesopotamia, high agricultural productivity led to a rapid increase in population throughout the Nile valley. Demographic pressures soon forced Egyptians in particular to develop more intense and sophisticated methods of agriculture as cultivators found it necessary to move beyond the Nile's immediate floodplains to areas that required careful preparation and irrigation. By

4000 B.C.E. agricultural villages dotted the Nile's shores from the Mediterranean in the north to the river's fourth cataract in the south. As in Mesopotamia, dense human population in Egypt and Nubia brought a need for formal organization of public affairs. Although geographical barriers in the form of seas and desert meant that neither area faced external dangers to the extent that Mesopotamia did, the two areas still needed to maintain order and organize community projects. As a result, both Egyptians and Nubians created states and recognized official authorities.

The earliest Egyptian and Nubian states were small kingdoms much like those instituted in the Sudan after 5000 B.C.E. Indeed, it is likely that the notion of divine or semidivine rulers reached Egypt and Nubia from the eastern and central Sudan. In any case, small kingdoms appeared first in southern Egypt and Nubia after 4000 B.C.E., and by 3300 B.C.E. small local kingdoms organized public life throughout Egypt as well as Nubia.

## *The Unification of Egypt*

**MENES** By 3500 B.C.E. political and economic competition fueled numerous skirmishes and small-scale wars between the Nile kingdoms. Some kingdoms overcame their neighbors and gradually expanded until they controlled sizable territories. About 3100 B.C.E. Egyptian rulers drew on the considerable agricultural and demographic advantages of Egypt's large population and broad floodplains to forge all the territory between the Nile delta and the river's first cataract into a powerful and unified kingdom. Tradition holds that unified rule came to Egypt in the person of a conqueror named Menes (sometimes identified with an early Egyptian ruler called Narmer). Menes was an ambitious minor official from southern Egypt (known as Upper Egypt, since the Nile flows north) who rose to power and extended his authority north and into the delta (known as Lower Egypt). According to tradition, Menes founded the city of Memphis, near modern Cairo, which stood at the junction of Upper and Lower Egypt. Memphis served as Menes' capital and eventually became the cultural as well as the political center of ancient Egypt.

Menes and his successors built a centralized state ruled by the pharaoh, the Egyptian king. The early pharaohs claimed to be gods living on the earth in human form, the owners and absolute rulers of all the land. In that respect, they continued the tradition of divine kingship inherited from the early agricultural societies of the Sudan. Over time, Egyptians viewed rulers as offspring of Amon, a sun god. They considered the ruling pharaoh a human sun overseeing affairs on the earth, just as Amon was the sun supervising the larger cosmos, and they believed that after his death the pharaoh actually merged with Amon.

**THE ARCHAIC PERIOD AND THE OLD KINGDOM** The power of the pharaohs was greatest during the first millennium of Egyptian history—the eras known as the Archaic Period (3100–2660 B.C.E.) and the Old Kingdom (2660–2160 B.C.E.). The most enduring symbols of their authority and divine status are the massive pyramids constructed during the Old Kingdom as royal tombs, most of them during the century from 2600 to 2500 B.C.E. These enormous monuments stand today at Giza, near Cairo, as testimony to the pharaohs' ability to marshal Egyptian resources. The largest is the pyramid of Khufu (also known as Cheops), which involved the precise cutting and fitting of 2.3 million limestone blocks weighing up to 15 tons, with an average weight of 2.5 tons. Scholars estimate that construction of Khufu's pyramid required the services of some eighty-four thousand laborers working eighty days per year for twenty years.

**RELATIONS BETWEEN EGYPT AND NUBIA** Even after the emergence of the strong pharaonic state, the fortunes of Egypt and Nubia remained closely intertwined. Egyptians had strong interests in Nubia for both political and commercial

**Menes** (mee-neez)

**EARLY AGRICULTURE IN EGYPT.** | A painting from the tomb of a priest who lived about the fifteenth century B.C.E. depicts agricultural workers plowing and sowing crops in southern Egypt.

Diagram of the pyramids
www.mhhe.com/
bentleybrief2e

reasons: they were wary of Nubian kingdoms that might threaten Upper Egypt, and they desired products such as gold, ivory, ebony, and precious stones that were available only from southern lands. Meanwhile, Nubians had equally strong interests in Egypt: they wanted to protect their independence from their large and powerful neighbor to the north, and they sought to profit by controlling trade down the Nile.

**THE EARLY KINGDOM OF KUSH**  Tensions led to frequent violence between Egypt and Nubia throughout the Archaic Period and the Old Kingdom. Indeed, Egypt dominated Lower Nubia (the land between the first and second cataracts of the Nile) for more than half a millennium, from about 3000 to 2400 B.C.E. This Egyptian presence in the north forced Nubian leaders to concentrate their efforts at political organization farther to the south in Upper Nubia. By about 2500 B.C.E. they had established a powerful kingdom, called Kush, with a capital at Kerma, about 700 kilometers (435 miles) south of Aswan. Though not as powerful as united Egypt, the kingdom of Kush became a formidable and wealthy state in its own right.

In spite of constant tension and frequent hostilities, Egypt and Nubia remained connected in many ways. About 2300 B.C.E., for example, the Egyptian explorer Harkhuf made four expeditions to Nubia. He returned from one of his trips with a caravan of some three hundred donkeys bearing exotic products from tropical Africa, as well as a dancing dwarf, and his cargo stimulated Egyptian desire for trade with southern lands. Meanwhile, by the end of the Old Kingdom, Nubian mercenaries had become quite prominent in Egyptian armies. In fact, they often married Egyptian women and assimilated into Egyptian society.

## Turmoil and Empire

**THE MIDDLE KINGDOM**  Toward the end of the Old Kingdom, high agricultural productivity made several regions of Egypt so prosperous and powerful that they were able to ignore the pharaohs and pursue their own interests. As a result, the central state declined and eventually disappeared altogether during a long period of upheaval and unrest (2160–2040 B.C.E.). Pharaonic authority returned with the establishment of the Middle Kingdom (2040–1640 B.C.E.). Pharaohs of the Middle Kingdom were not as powerful as their predecessors of the Old Kingdom, but they effectively stabilized Egypt and supervised relations with neighboring lands.

**THE HYKSOS**  Gradually, however, Egypt came under the pressure of foreign peoples from southwest Asia, particularly a Semitic people whom Egyptians called the Hyksos ("foreign rulers"). Little information survives about the Hyksos, but it is clear that they were horse-riding nomads. Indeed, their horse-drawn chariots, which they learned about from Hittites and Mesopotamians, provided them with a significant military advantage over Egyptian forces. They enjoyed an advantage also in their weaponry: the Hyksos used bronze weapons and bronze-tipped arrows, whereas Egyptians relied mostly on wooden weapons and arrows with stone heads. About 1674 B.C.E. the Hyksos captured Memphis and levied tribute throughout Egypt.

Hyksos rule provoked a strong reaction especially in Upper Egypt, where disgruntled nobles organized revolts against the foreigners. They adopted horses and chariots for their own military forces. They also equipped their troops with bronze weapons. Working from Thebes and later from Memphis, Egyptian leaders gradually pushed the Hyksos out of the Nile delta and founded a powerful state known as the New Kingdom (1550–1070 B.C.E.).

Pharaohs of the New Kingdom presided over a prosperous and productive society. Agricultural surpluses supported a population of perhaps four million people as well as an army and an elaborate bureaucracy that divided responsibilities among different offices.

**Kush** (kuhsh)
**Hyksos** (HICK-sohs)

*Many Egyptians wrote brief autobiographies that they or their descendants had carved into their tombs. One of the most famous autobiographies from the Old Kingdom is that of Harkhuf, a royal official who became governor of Upper Egypt before 2300 B.C.E. The inscriptions in his tomb mention his four expeditions to Nubia to seek valuable items and report on political conditions there. The inscriptions also include the text of a letter from the boy-pharaoh Neferkare expressing his appreciation for Harkhuf's fourth expedition and his desire to see the dancing dwarf that Harkhuf had brought back from Nubia.*

The majesty of [Pharaoh] Mernere, my lord, sent me together with my father . . . to [the Upper Nubian kingdom of] Yam to open the way to that country. I did it in seven months; I brought from it all kinds of beautiful and rare gifts, and was praised for it greatly.

His majesty sent me a second time alone. . . . I came down [the Nile] bringing gifts from that country in great quantity, the likes of which had never before been brought back to this land [Egypt]. . . .

Then his majesty sent me a third time to Yam. . . . I came down with three hundred donkeys laden with incense, ebony, . . . panther skins, elephant's tusks, throw sticks, and all sorts of good products.

[The letter of Pharaoh Neferkare to Harkhuf:] Notice has been taken of this dispatch of yours which you made for the King of the Palace, to let one know that you have come down in safety from Yam with the army that was with you. You have said in this dispatch of yours that you have brought all kinds of great and beautiful gifts. . . . You have said in this dispatch of yours that you have brought a pygmy of the god's dances from the land of the horizon-dwellers [the region of Nubia southeast of Egypt], like the pygmy whom the [royal official] Bawerded brought from Punt [Ethiopia and Somalia] in the time of King Isesi. You have said to my majesty that his like has never been brought by anyone who [visited] Yam previously.

Truly you know how to do what your lord loves and praises. Truly you spend day and night planning to do what your lord loves, praises, and commands. His majesty will provide you many worthy honors for the benefit of your son's son for all time, so that all people will say, when they hear what my majesty did for you: "Does anything equal what was done for the sole companion Harkhuf when he came down from Yam, on account of the vigilance he showed in doing what his lord loved, praised, and commanded?"

Come north to the residence at once! Hurry and bring with you this pygmy whom you brought from the land of the horizon-dwellers live, hale, and healthy, for the dances of the god, to gladden the heart, to delight the heart of King Neferkare who lives forever! When he goes down with you into the ship, get worthy men to be around him on deck, lest he fall into the water! When he lies down at night, get worthy men to lie around him in his tent. Inspect ten times at night! My majesty desires to see this pygmy more than the gifts of the mineland [the Sinai peninsula] and of Punt!

When you arrive at the residence and this pygmy is with you live, hale, and healthy, my majesty will do great things for you, more than was done for the [royal official] Bawerded in the time of King Isesi, in accordance with my majesty's wish to see this pygmy. Orders have been brought to the chief of the new towns and the companion, overseer of priests to command that supplies be furnished from what is under the charge of each from every storage depot and every temple that has not been exempted.

■ How does Harkhuf's autobiography illuminate early Egyptian interest in Nubia and the processes by which Egyptians of the Old Kingdom developed knowledge about Nubia?

SOURCE: Miriam Lichtheim, ed. *Ancient Egyptian Literature*. 3 vols. Berkeley: University of California Press, 1973, 1:25–27.

EGYPTIAN IMPERIALISM    Pharaohs of the New Kingdom also worked to extend Egyptian authority well beyond the Nile valley and the delta. After expelling the Hyksos, they sought to prevent new invasions by seizing control of regions that might pose threats in the future. Most vigorous of the New Kingdom pharaohs was Tuthmosis III

**Tuthmosis** (tuh-MOE-sis)

**MAP 2.2** | Imperial Egypt, 1400 B.C.E. Compare the territory ruled by the New Kingdom with the earlier kingdom of Egypt as represented in Map 2.1. *Why was the New Kingdom able to expand so dramatically to the north and south? Why did it not expand to the east and west also?*

Areas of Egyptian expansion during the New Kingdom

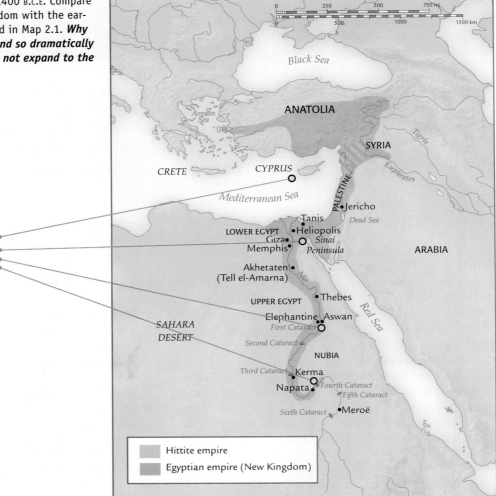

(reigned 1479–1425 B.C.E.). After seventeen campaigns that he personally led to Palestine and Syria, Tuthmosis dominated the coastal regions of the eastern Mediterranean as well as north Africa. Rulers of the New Kingdom also turned their attention to the south and restored Egyptian dominance in Nubia. Thus for half a millennium Egypt was an imperial power throughout much of the eastern Mediterranean basin and southwest Asia as well as most of the Nile River valley.

After the New Kingdom, Egypt entered a long period of political and military decline. Just as Hyksos rule provoked a reaction in Egypt, so Egyptian rule provoked reactions in the regions subdued by pharaonic armies. Local resistance drove Egyptian forces out of Nubia and southwest Asia; then Kushite and Assyrian armies invaded Egypt itself.

**THE REVIVED KINGDOM OF KUSH** By 1100 B.C.E. Egyptian forces were in full retreat from Nubia, and in the tenth century B.C.E. Nubian leaders organized a new kingdom of Kush with a capital at Napata, located just below the Nile's fourth cataract. By the eighth century B.C.E., rulers of this revived kingdom of Kush were powerful enough to invade Egypt. King Kashta conquered Thebes about 760 B.C.E. and founded a Kushite dynasty that ruled Egypt for almost a century. Kashta's successors consolidated Kushite authority in Upper Egypt, claimed the title of pharaoh, and eventually extended their rule to the Nile delta and beyond.

Meanwhile, as Kushites pushed into Egypt from the south, Assyrian armies equipped with iron weapons bore down from the north. During the mid–seventh century B.C.E.,

**NUBIAN TRIBUTE TO EGYPT.** | A wall painting from the tomb of an Egyptian imperial official in Nubia depicts a delegation of Nubians bringing tribute in the forms of exotic beasts, animal skins, and rings of gold. *What kinds of products are the delegates bringing, and why?*

while building their vast empire, the Assyrians invaded Egypt, campaigned as far south as Thebes, drove out the Kushites, and subjected Egypt to Assyrian rule. After the mid–sixth century B.C.E., like Mesopotamia, Egypt fell to a series of foreign conquerors who built vast empires throughout southwest Asia and the eastern Mediterranean region.

# THE FORMATION OF COMPLEX SOCIETIES AND SOPHISTICATED CULTURAL TRADITIONS

As in Mesopotamia, cities and the congregation of dense populations encouraged the emergence of specialized labor in the early agricultural societies of Africa. Clearly defined social classes emerged throughout the Nile valley, and both Egypt and Nubian lands built patriarchal societies that placed authority largely in the hands of adult males. The Egyptian economy was especially productive, and because of both its prosperity and its geographic location, Egypt figured as a center of trade, linking lands in southwest Asia, the eastern Mediterranean, and sub-Saharan Africa. Meanwhile, like southwest Asia, the Nile valley was a site of sophisticated cultural development. Writing systems appeared in both Egypt and Nubia, and writing soon became a principal medium of literary expression and religious reflection as well as a means for preserving governmental records and commercial information.

## *The Emergence of Cities and Stratified Societies*

**CITIES OF THE NILE VALLEY**    Cities were not as prominent in early societies of the Nile River valley as they were in ancient Mesopotamia. Nevertheless, several major cities emerged and guided affairs in both Egypt and Nubia. In Egypt, Memphis, Thebes, Heliopolis, and Tanis all became important political, administrative, or cultural

**SOCIAL STRATIFICATION IN EGYPTIAN SOCIETY.** | Building pyramids and other large structures involved heavy work, especially by the less privileged classes. Here an Egyptian manuscript painting produced about 1000 B.C.E. depicts a supervisor overseeing a group of laborers as they drag a sled loaded with building blocks.

centers. In Nubia, Kerma, Napata, and Meroë all took their turn as political capitals between about 2500 B.C.E. and 100 C.E.

Limestone relief of Akhenaten & Nefertiti
www.mhhe.com/ bentleybrief2e

**SOCIAL CLASSES** In Egypt and Nubia alike, ancient cities were centers of considerable accumulated wealth, which encouraged the development of social distinctions and hierarchies. Like the Mesopotamians, ancient Egyptians recognized a series of well-defined social classes. Egyptian peasants and slaves played roles in society similar to those of their Mesopotamian counterparts: they supplied the hard labor that made complex agricultural society possible. The organization of the ruling classes, however, differed considerably between Mesopotamia and Egypt. Instead of a series of urban kings, as in Mesopotamia, Egyptians recognized the pharaoh as a supreme central ruler. In addition, rather than depending on nobles who owed their positions to their birth, Egypt relied on professional military forces and an elaborate bureaucracy of administrators and tax collectors who served the central government. Thus, in Egypt much more than in Mesopotamia, individuals of common birth could attain high positions in society through government service.

Surviving information illuminates Egyptian society much better than Nubian, but it is clear that Nubia also was the site of a complex, hierarchical society in ancient times. Indeed, cemeteries associated with Nubian cities clearly reveal social and economic distinctions. Tombs of wealthy and powerful individuals were often elaborate structures—comfortable dwelling places tastefully decorated with paintings and filled with expensive goods such as gold jewelry, gems, fine furniture, and abundant supplies of food. In contrast, graves of commoners were much simpler, although they usually contained jewelry, pottery, personal ornaments, and other goods to accompany the departed.

**PATRIARCHAL SOCIETY** Like their Mesopotamian counterparts, both Egyptian and Nubian peoples built patriarchal societies that vested authority over public and private affairs in their men. With rare exceptions men were the rulers in both Egyptian and Nubian private as well as public life, and decisions about government policies rested mostly in men's hands.

Yet women made their influence felt in ancient Egyptian and Nubian societies much more than in contemporary Mesopotamia. In Egypt, women of the royal family sometimes served as regents for young rulers. In one notable case, a woman took power as pharaoh herself: Queen Hatshepsut (reigned 1473–1458 B.C.E.) served as coruler with her stepson Tuthmosis III. However, the notion of a female ruler may have been unsettling to many Egyptians. In what seems to have been an effort to present her in unthreatening guise, a monumental statue of Queen Hatshepsut depicts her wearing the stylized beard traditionally associated with the pharaohs. In Nubia, in contrast, there is abundant evidence of many women rulers in the kingdom of Kush. Some ruled in their own right, others reigned jointly with male kings, and many governed also in the capacity of regents. Meanwhile, other women wielded considerable power as priestesses in the numerous religious cults observed in Egypt and Nubia. A few women also obtained a formal education and worked as scribes.

## *Economic Specialization and Trade*

With the formation of complex, city-based societies, peoples of the Nile valley were able to draw on a rapidly expanding stock of human skills. Bronze metallurgy made its way from Mesopotamia to both Egypt and Nubia, and by 1000 B.C.E. Sudanic peoples independently developed a technology of iron production that eventually spread to most parts of sub-Saharan Africa. Pottery, textile manufacture, woodworking, leather production, stonecutting, and masonry all became distinct occupations in cities throughout the Nile valley. Specialized labor and the invention of efficient transportation technologies encouraged the development of trade networks that linked the Nile valley to a much larger world.

BRONZE METALLURGY   Nile societies were much slower than their Mesopotamian counterparts to adopt metal tools and weapons. Whereas the production of bronze flourished in Mesopotamia by 3000 B.C.E., use of bronze implements became widespread in Egypt only after the seventeenth century B.C.E., when the Hyksos relied on bronze weapons to impose their authority on the Nile delta. Although Egyptians equipped their own forces with bronze weapons after expelling the Hyksos, the high cost of copper and tin kept bronze out of the hands of most people. Indeed, bronze was considered so valuable that officers weighed the bronze tools issued to workers at royal tombs to ensure that craftsmen did not shave slivers off them for personal uses.

IRON METALLURGY   Bronze was even less prominent in Nubian societies than in Egypt. During the centuries after 1000 B.C.E., however, the southern Nile societies made up for their lack of bronze with the emergence of large-scale iron production. Furnaces churned out iron implements both in Nubia and in west Africa at least by 500 B.C.E. Meroë in particular became a site of large-scale iron production. Indeed, archaeologists who excavated Meroë in the early twentieth century C.E. found enormous mounds of slag still remaining from ancient times.

TRANSPORTATION   Nile craftsmen also worked from the early days of agricultural society to devise efficient means of transportation. Before 3500 B.C.E. Egyptians already traveled up and down the Nile with ease. Because the Nile flows north, boats could ride the currents from Upper to Lower Egypt. Meanwhile, prevailing winds blow almost year-round from the north, so that by raising a sail, boats could easily make their way upriver from Lower to Upper Egypt. Soon after 3000 B.C.E. Egyptians sailed beyond the Nile into the Mediterranean, and by about 2000 B.C.E. they had also thoroughly explored the waters of the Red Sea, the Gulf of Aden, and the western portion of the Arabian Sea. Egyptians also made use of Mesopotamian-style wheeled vehicles for local transport as well as donkey caravans for overland transport.

In Nubia, navigation on the Nile was less convenient than in Egypt because unnavigable cataracts made it necessary to transport goods overland before continuing on the

THINKING ABOUT *Traditions*

**TRADITIONS IN EARLY AFRICAN SOCIETIES.** Egyptian kingdoms flourished along the Nile River as a result of the fertile alluvial soils that made agriculture so productive. What were some of the distinctive styles of ruling, monument building, and religious worship in this prosperous agricultural society, and why might they have developed differently than in Nubia?

**Hatshepsut** (hat-SHEP-soot)

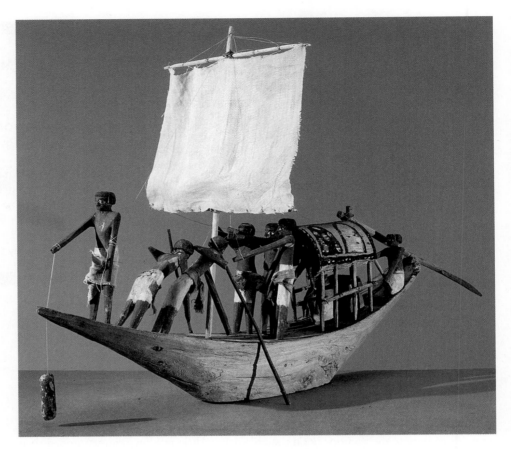

**EGYPTIAN RIVER TRANS-PORT.** | A wooden model found in a tomb shows how Egyptians traveled up and down the Nile River. Produced about 2000 B.C.E., this sculpture depicts a relatively small boat with a mast, sail, rudder, and poles to push the vessel through shallow waters. Many wall and tomb paintings confirm the accuracy of this model. *Why is the figure in front trying to gauge the water's depth?*

river. Moreover, sailing ships heading upriver could not negotiate a long stretch of the Nile around the fourth cataract because winds blow the same direction that currents flow. As a result, Nubian societies had to rely more than Egyptians on overland transport by wheeled vehicles and donkey caravan.

**TRADE NETWORKS** In both Egypt and Nubia, specialized labor and efficient means of transportation encouraged the development of long-distance trade. By the time of the Old Kingdom, trade flowed regularly between Egypt and Nubia. Exotic African goods such as ivory, ebony, leopard skins, ostrich feathers, gemstones, gold, and slaves went down the Nile in exchange for pottery, wine, honey, and finished products from Egypt. Among the most prized Egyptian exports were fine linen textiles woven from the flax that flourished in the Nile valley as well as high-quality decorative and ornamental objects such as boxes, furniture, and jewelry produced by skilled artisans.

Egyptian merchants looked north as well as south. They traded with Mesopotamians as early as 3500 B.C.E., and after 3000 B.C.E. they were active throughout the eastern Mediterranean basin. Since Egypt has very few trees, Egyptian ships regularly imported huge loads from Lebanon. Pharaohs especially prized aromatic cedar for their tombs, and one record from about 2600 B.C.E. mentions an expedition of forty ships hauling cedar logs. In exchange for cedar, Egyptians offered gold, silver, linen textiles, leather goods, and dried foods such as lentils.

After the establishment of the New Kingdom, Egyptians also traded through the Red Sea and the Gulf of Aden with an east African land they called Punt—probably modern-day Somalia and Ethiopia. From Punt they imported gold, ebony, ivory, cattle, aromatics, and slaves. Thus, as in southwest Asia, specialization of labor and efficient technologies of transportation not only quickened the economies of complex societies in Egypt and Nubia but also encouraged their interaction with peoples of distant lands.

# Early Writing in the Nile Valley

**HIEROGLYPHIC WRITING**   Writing appeared in Egypt at least by 3200 B.C.E., possibly as a result of Mesopotamian influence. As in Mesopotamia, the earliest Egyptian writing was pictographic, but Egyptians soon supplemented their pictographs with symbols representing sounds and ideas. Early Greek visitors to Egypt marveled at the large and handsome pictographs that adorned Egyptian monuments and buildings. Since the symbols were particularly prominent on temples, the visitors called them hieroglyphs, from two Greek words meaning "holy inscriptions." Hieroglyphic writing also survives on sheets of papyrus, a paper-like material fashioned from the insides of papyrus reeds, which flourish along the Nile River. The hot, dry climate of Egypt has preserved large numbers of papyrus texts bearing administrative and commercial records as well as literary and religious texts.

Although striking and dramatic, hieroglyphs were also somewhat cumbersome. Egyptians went to the trouble of using hieroglyphs for formal writing and monumental inscriptions, but for everyday affairs they commonly relied on the hieratic ("priestly") script, a simplified, cursive form of hieroglyphs. Hieratic appeared in the early centuries of the third millennium B.C.E., and Egyptians made extensive use of the script for more than three thousand years, from about 2600 B.C.E. to 600 C.E. Hieratic largely disappeared after the middle of the first millennium C.E., when Egyptians adapted the Greek alphabet to their own language and developed alphabetic scripts known as the demotic ("popular") and Coptic ("Egyptian") scripts.

**MEROITIC WRITING**   Nubian peoples spoke their own languages, but all early writing in Nubia was Egyptian hieroglyphic writing. Indeed, over the centuries, Egypt wielded great cultural influence in Nubia, especially during times when Egyptian political and military influence was strong in southern lands. After about the fifth century B.C.E., however, Egyptian cultural influence declined noticeably in Nubia. After the transfer of the Kushite capital from Napata to Meroë, Nubian scribes even devised an alphabetic script for the Meroitic language. They borrowed Egyptian hieroglyphs but used them to represent sounds rather than ideas and so created a flexible writing system. Many Meroitic inscriptions survive, both on monuments and on papyrus. However, although scholars have ascertained the sound values of the alphabet, the Meroitic language itself is so different from other known languages that no one has been able to decipher Meroitic texts.

# The Development of Organized Religious Traditions

**AMON AND RE**   Like their counterparts in other world regions, Egyptians and Nubians believed that deities played prominent roles in the world and that proper cultivation of the gods was an important community responsibility. The principal gods revered in ancient Egypt were Amon and Re. Amon was originally a local Theban deity associated with the sun, creation, fertility, and reproductive forces, and Re was a sun god worshiped at Heliopolis. During the Old Kingdom and the Middle Kingdom, priests increasingly associated the two gods with each other and honored them in the combined cult of Amon-Re. At Heliopolis a massive temple complex supported priests who tended to the cult of Amon-Re and studied the heavens for astronomical purposes. When Egypt became an imperial power during the New Kingdom, some devotees suggested that Amon-Re might even be a universal god who presided over all the earth.

---

**hieroglyphics** (heye-ruh-GLIPH-iks)

**hieratic** (hahy-uh-RAT-tik)

**Amon-Re** (AH-mohn RAY)

**THE CULT OF OSIRIS.** Osiris (seated at right) receives a recently deceased individual, while attendants weigh the heart of another individual against a feather. This illustration comes from a papyrus copy of the *Book of the Dead* that was buried with a royal mummy.

*Egyptian Book of the Dead* www.mhhe.com/ bentleybrief2e

**ATEN AND MONOTHEISM**    For a brief period the cult of Amon-Re faced a monotheistic challenge from the god Aten, another deity associated with the sun. Aten's champion was Pharaoh Amenhotep IV (reigned 1353–1335 B.C.E.), who changed his name to Akhenaten in honor of his preferred deity. Akhenaten considered Aten the world's "sole god, like whom there is no other." This faith represented one of the world's earliest expressions of monotheism—the belief that a single god rules over all creation. As long as Akhenaten lived, the cult of Aten flourished. But when the pharaoh died, traditional priests mounted a fierce counterattack, restored the cult of Amon-Re to privileged status, and nearly annihilated the worship and even the memory of Aten.

**MUMMIFICATION**    Whereas Mesopotamians believed with Gilgamesh that death brought an end to an individual's existence, many Egyptians believed that death was not an end so much as a transition to a new dimension of existence. The yearning for immortality helps to explain the Egyptian practice of mummifying the dead. During the Old Kingdom, Egyptians believed that only the ruling elites would survive the grave, so they mummified only pharaohs and their close relatives. During the Middle and New Kingdoms, however, Egyptians came to think of eternal life as a condition available to normal mortals as well as members of the ruling classes. Mummification never became general practice in Egypt, but with or without preservation of the body, a variety of religious cults promised to lead individuals of all classes to immortality.

**CULT OF OSIRIS**    The cult of Osiris attracted particularly strong popular interest. According to the myths surrounding the cult, Osiris's evil brother Seth murdered him and scattered his dismembered parts throughout the land, but the victim's loyal wife, Isis, retrieved his parts and gave her husband a proper burial. Impressed by her devotion, the gods restored Osiris to life as god of the underworld, the dwelling place of the departed.

Egyptians also associated Osiris with immortality and honored him through a religious cult that demanded observance of high moral standards. Following their deaths, individual souls faced the judgment of Osiris, who had their hearts weighed against a feather symbolizing justice. Those with heavy hearts carrying a burden of evil and guilt did not merit immortality, whereas those of pure heart and honorable deeds gained the gift of eternal life. Thus Osiris's cult held out hope of eternal reward for those who behaved according to high moral standards.

**NUBIAN RELIGIOUS BELIEFS**    Nubian peoples observed their own religious traditions, but very little written information survives to throw light on their religious beliefs. The most prominent of the Nubian deities was the lion-god Apedemak,

**Akhenaton** (ahk-eh-NAH-ton)

often depicted with a bow and arrows, who served as war god for the kingdom of Kush. Another deity, Sebiumeker, was a creator god and divine guardian of his human devotees. Alongside native traditions, Egyptian religious cults were quite prominent in Nubia, especially after the aggressive pharaohs of the New Kingdom imposed Egyptian rule on the southern lands. Nubian peoples did not mummify the remains of their deceased, but they built pyramids similar to those of Egypt, although smaller, and they embraced several Egyptian gods. Amon was the preeminent Egyptian deity in Nubia as in Egypt itself. Osiris was also popular in Nubia, where he sometimes appeared in association with the native deity Sebiumeker. However, Egyptian gods did not displace native gods so much as they joined them in the Nubian pantheon. Indeed, Nubians often identified Egyptian gods with their own deities or endowed the foreign gods with traits important in Nubian society.

## THINKING ABOUT *Encounters*

**ENCOUNTERS IN EARLY AFRICAN SOCIETIES.** Egyptian and Nubian kingdoms were positioned in such a way that they provided crucial links between the Mediterranean basin on the one hand and sub-Saharan Africa on the other. In what ways did trade and contact with distant regions shape Egyptian and Nubian ideas about religion, written expression, technology, and agriculture?

# BANTU MIGRATIONS AND EARLY AGRICULTURAL SOCIETIES OF SUB-SAHARAN AFRICA

Like their counterparts in southwest Asia, Egyptian and Nubian societies participated in a much larger world of interaction and exchange. Mesopotamian societies developed under the strong influences of long-distance trade, diffusions of technological innovations, the spread of cultural traditions, and the far-flung migrations of Semitic and Indo-European peoples. Similarly, quite apart from their dealings with southwest Asian and Mediterranean peoples, Egyptian and Nubian societies developed in the context of widespread interaction and exchange in sub-Saharan Africa. The most prominent processes unfolding in sub-Saharan Africa during ancient times were the migrations of Bantu-speaking peoples and the establishment of agricultural societies in regions where Bantu speakers settled. Just as Sudanic agriculture spread to the Nile valley and provided an economic foundation for the development of Egyptian and Nubian societies, it also spread to most other regions of Africa south of the Sahara and supported the emergence of distinctive agricultural societies.

## *The Dynamics of Bantu Expansion*

THE BANTU    Among the most influential peoples of sub-Saharan Africa in ancient times were those who spoke Bantu languages. The original Bantu language was one of many related tongues in the larger Niger-Congo family of languages widely spoken in west Africa after 4000 B.C.E. The earliest Bantu speakers inhabited a region embracing the eastern part of modern Nigeria and the southern part of modern Cameroon. Members of this community referred to themselves as *bantu* (meaning "persons" or "people"). The earliest Bantu speakers settled mostly along the banks of rivers, which they navigated in canoes, and in open areas of the region's forests. They cultivated yams and oil palms, and in later centuries they added millet and sorghum. They also kept goats and raised guinea fowl. They lived in clan-based villages headed by chiefs who conducted religious rituals and represented their communities in dealings with neighboring villages. They traded regularly with hunting and gathering peoples who inhabited the tropical forests. Bantu cultivators provided these forest peoples with pottery and stone axes in exchange for meat, honey, and other forest products.

---

**Sebiumeker** (sehb-ih-meh-kur)

Agriculture spread to sub-Saharan
Africa with the Bantu migrations.

BANTU MIGRATIONS    Unlike most of their neighbors, the Bantu displayed
an early readiness to migrate to new territories. By 3000 B.C.E. they were slowly spreading south into the west African forest, and after 2000 B.C.E. they expanded rapidly to the
south toward the Congo River basin and east toward the Great Lakes, absorbing local
populations of hunting, gathering, and fishing peoples into their own agricultural societies. Over the centuries, as some groups of Bantu speakers settled and others moved on
to new territories, their languages differentiated into more than five hundred distinct but
related tongues. (Today more than ninety million people speak Bantu languages, which
collectively constitute the most prominent family of languages in sub-Saharan Africa.)
Like the Indo-European migrations discussed in chapter 1, the Bantu migrations were not
mass movements of peoples. Instead, they were intermittent and incremental processes
that resulted in the gradual spread of Bantu languages and ethnic communities, as small
groups moved to new territories and established settlements, which then became foundations for further expansion. By 1000 C.E. Bantu-speaking peoples occupied most of Africa
south of the equator.

The precise motives of the early Bantu migrants are unknown, but it seems likely that
population pressures drove the migrations. When settlements grew uncomfortably large
and placed strains on available resources, small groups left their parent communities and
moved to new territories. As they moved, Bantu migrants placed pressures on the forest
dwellers, sometimes clashing with them over land resources but often intermarrying and
absorbing them into Bantu agricultural society.

**IRON AND MIGRATION**   After about 1000 B.C.E., the pace of Bantu migrations quickened, as Bantu peoples began to produce iron tools and weapons. Iron tools enabled Bantu cultivators to clear land and expand the zone of agriculture more effectively than before, while iron weapons strengthened the hand of Bantu groups against adversaries and competitors for land or other resources. Thus iron metallurgy supported rapid population growth among the Bantu while also lending increased momentum to their continuing migrations.

## Early Agricultural Societies of Sub-Saharan Africa

Several smaller migrations took place alongside the spread of Bantu peoples in sub-Saharan Africa. Between 3500 and 1000 B.C.E., southern Kushite herders pushed into parts of east Africa (modern-day Kenya and Tanzania), while Sudanese cultivators and herders moved into the upper reaches of the Nile River (now southern Sudan and northern Uganda). Meanwhile, Mande-speaking peoples who cultivated African rice established communities along the Atlantic estuaries of west Africa, and other peoples speaking Niger-Congo languages spread the cultivation of okra from forest regions throughout much of west Africa.

**SPREAD OF AGRICULTURE**   Among the most important effects of Bantu and other migrations was the establishment of agricultural societies throughout most of sub-Saharan Africa. Between 1000 and 500 B.C.E., cultivators extended the cultivation of yams and grains deep into east and south Africa (modern-day Kenya, Malawi, Mozambique, Zimbabwe, and South Africa), while herders introduced sheep and cattle to the region. About the same time, Bantu and other peoples speaking Niger-Congo languages spread the intensive cultivation of yams, oil palms, millet, and sorghum throughout west and central Africa while also introducing sheep, pigs, and cattle to the region. By the late centuries B.C.E., agriculture had reached almost all of sub-Saharan Africa except for densely forested regions and deserts.

As cultivation and herding spread throughout sub-Saharan Africa, agricultural peoples built distinctive societies and cultural traditions. Most Bantu and other peoples lived in communities of a few hundred individuals led by chiefs. Many peoples recognized groups known as age sets, or age grades, consisting of individuals born within a few years of one another. Members of each age set jointly assumed responsibility for tasks appropriate to their levels of strength, energy, maturity, and experience. During their early years, for example, members of an age set might perform light public chores. At maturity, members jointly underwent elaborate initiation rites that introduced them to adult society. Older men cultivated fields and provided military service, and women tended to domestic chores and sometimes traded at markets. In later years, members of age sets served as community leaders and military officers.

**AFRICAN CULTIVATORS**   African cultivators and herders also developed distinctive cultural and religious traditions. Both Sudanic and Niger-Congo peoples (including Bantu speakers), for example, held monotheistic religious beliefs by 5000 B.C.E. Sudanic peoples recognized a single, impersonal divine force that they regarded as the source of both good and evil. They believed that this divine force could take the form of individual spirits, and they often addressed the divine force through prayers to intermediary spirits. The divine force itself, however, was ultimately responsible for rewards and punishments meted out to human beings. For their part, Niger-Congo peoples recognized a single god originally called Nyamba who created the world and established the principles that would govern its development, then stepped back and allowed the world to proceed on its own. Individuals did not generally address this distant creator god directly but, rather, offered their prayers to ancestor spirits and local territorial spirits believed to inhabit the world and influence the fortunes of living humans. Proper attention to these spirits would ensure them good fortune, they believed, whereas their neglect would bring punishment or adversity from disgruntled spirits.

Individual communities frequently borrowed religious elements from other communities and adapted their beliefs to changing circumstances or fresh understandings of the world. Migrations of Bantu and other peoples in particular resulted in a great deal of cultural mixing and mingling, and religious beliefs often spread to new communities in the wake of population movements. After 1000 B.C.E., for example, as they encountered Sudanic peoples and their reverence of a single divine force that was the source of good and evil, many Bantu peoples associated the god Nyamba with goodness. As a result, this formerly distant creator god took on a new moral dimension that brought him closer to the lives of individuals. Thus changing religious beliefs sometimes reflected widespread interactions among African societies.

## SUMMARY

Like other world regions, Africa was a land in which peoples of different societies regularly traded, communicated, and interacted with one another from ancient times. African agriculture and herding first emerged in the Sudan, then spread both to the Nile River valley and to arable lands throughout sub-Saharan Africa. Agricultural crops and domesticated animals from southwest Asia soon made their way into the Nile valley. With its broad floodplains, Egypt became an especially productive land, while Nubia supported a smaller but flourishing society. Throughout the Nile valley, abundant agricultural surpluses supported dense populations and the construction of prosperous societies with sophisticated cultural traditions. Elsewhere in sub-Saharan Africa, populations were less dense, but the migrations of Bantu and other peoples facilitated the spread of agriculture, and later iron metallurgy as well, throughout most of the region. Meanwhile, the Nile River served as a route of trade and communication linking Egypt and the Mediterranean basin to the north with the Sudan and sub-Saharan Africa to the south. Only in the context of migration, trade, communication, and interaction is it possible to understand the early development of African societies.

## STUDY TERMS

Akhenaton (40)
Amon-Re (39)
Archaic Period (31)
Aten (40)
Bantu (28)
Bantu migrations (42)
cult of Osiris (40)
Egypt (29)
Hatshepsut (37)

hieratic script (39)
hieroglyphics (39)
Hyksos (32)
Kush (32)
Menes (31)
Meroitic writing (39)
Middle Kingdom (32)
mummification (27)

New Kingdom (32)
Nile River (29)
Nubia (27)
Old Kingdom (31)
pharaoh (31)
pyramids (31)
Sebiumeker (41)
Tuthmosis III (33)

Cyril Aldred. *The Egyptians.* Rev. ed. New York, 1984. A popular, well-illustrated, and reliable survey of ancient Egyptian history.

Christopher Ehret. *An African Classical Age: Eastern and Southern Africa in World History, 1000 B.C. to A.D. 400.* Charlottesville, Va., 1998. A pathbreaking volume focusing on eastern and southern Africa and drawing on both linguistic and archaeological evidence.

————. *The Civilizations of Africa: A History to 1800.* Charlottesville, Va., 2001. An important contribution that views Africa in the context of world history.

Zahi Hawass. *Silent Images: Women in Pharaonic Egypt.* New York, 2000. A prominent archaeologist draws on both textual and artifactual evidence in throwing light on women's experiences in ancient Egypt.

Miriam Lichtheim, ed. *Ancient Egyptian Literature.* 3 vols. Berkeley, 1973–80. An important collection of primary sources in translation that reflects the results of recent scholarship.

Roderick James McIntosh. *The Peoples of the Middle Niger: The Island of Gold.* Oxford, 1998. Fascinating volume emphasizing the environmental context of west African history.

Jan Vansina. *Paths in the Rainforests: Toward a History of Political Tradition in Equatorial Africa.* Madison, 1990. A brilliant synthesis concentrating on central Africa by one of the world's foremost historians of Africa.

Derek A. Welsby. *The Kingdom of Kush: The Napatan and Meroitic Empires.* London, 1996. Draws on both written and archaeological sources in tracing the development of ancient Nubia and charting its relationship with Egypt.

# Early Societies in South and East Asia

## 3

For a god, Indra was a very rambunctious fellow. According to the stories told about him by the Aryans, Indra had few if any peers in fighting, feasting, or drinking. The Aryans were a herding people who spoke an Indo-European language and who migrated to south Asia in large numbers after 1500 B.C.E. In the early days of their migrations they took Indra as their chief deity. The Aryans told dozens of stories about Indra and sang hundreds of hymns in his honor. One favorite story described how Indra brought rain to the earth by killing a dragon who lived in the sky and hoarded water in the clouds. When the dragon fell to earth, its weight caused such turmoil in the atmosphere that it rained enough to fill seven rivers in northern India. Those rivers, in turn, brought life-giving waters to inhabitants of the region.

A warrior such as Indra was a useful god for the Aryans, because as they migrated into south Asia they came into frequent conflict with Dravidian peoples already living there. For a thousand years and more, Aryans looked on the rowdy, raucous war god as a ready source of inspiration as they sought to build a society in an already occupied land.

In ancient China, heroic figures were quite different. Legends tell stories of heroes who invented agriculture, domesticated animals, taught people to marry and live in families, created music, introduced the calendar, and instructed people in the arts and crafts. Most dashing of those heroes was a sage-king named Yu, who helped lay the foundations of Chinese society by rescuing China from the devastating floodwaters of the Yellow River. Rather than dam the river as his predecessors had done, Yu dredged it and dug canals parallel to the river to allow the floodwaters to flow harmlessly out to sea.

The legends say that Yu worked on the river for thirteen years without ever returning home. Once, he passed by the gate to his home and heard his wife and children crying out of loneliness, but he continued on his way rather than interrupt his flood-control work. Because he tamed the Yellow River, Yu became a popular hero, and poets praised the man who protected fields and villages from deadly and destructive floods. By exalting Yu as an exemplar of virtue, Chinese moralists promoted the values of social harmony and selfless, dedicated work that the sage-king represented.

Archaeological excavations show that China was a site of paleolithic communities as early as four hundred thousand years ago. In south Asia, humans appeared at least two hundred thousand years ago, long before the Aryans introduced Indra to south Asia. Yet, as in Mesopotamia and Egypt, population

《 *Sandstone bust of a distinguished man, perhaps a priest-king, from Mohenjo-daro.*

**Yu** (yoo)

# CHRONOLOGY

## SOUTH ASIA

| | |
|---|---|
| 8000–7000 B.C.E. | Beginnings of agriculture in south Asia |
| 2500–2000 B.C.E. | High point of Harappan society |
| 1900 B.C.E. | Beginning of Harappan decline |
| 1500 B.C.E. | Beginning of Aryan migration to India |
| 1500–500 B.C.E. | Vedic age |
| 1400–900 B.C.E. | Composition of the *Rig Veda* |
| 1000 B.C.E. | Early Aryan migrations into the Ganges River valley |
| 1000 B.C.E. | Emergence of *varna* distinctions |
| 1000–500 B.C.E. | Formation of regional kingdoms in northern India |
| 800–400 B.C.E. | Composition of the principal Upanishads |
| 750 B.C.E. | Establishment of first Aryan cities in the Ganges valley |
| 500 B.C.E. | Aryan migrations to the Deccan Plateau |

## EAST ASIA

| | |
|---|---|
| 2200–1766 B.C.E. | Xia dynasty |
| 1766–1122 B.C.E. | Shang dynasty |
| 1122–256 B.C.E. | Zhou dynasty |
| 403–221 B.C.E. | Period of the Warring States |

pressures in both east and south Asia induced human groups to begin experimenting with agriculture. By 7000 B.C.E. agriculture had taken root in India's Indus River valley, and by 3000 B.C.E. it had spread throughout much of the Indian subcontinent. In roughly the same period, between 7000 and 5000 B.C.E., people in China's Yangzi River valley domesticated and became dependent on rice, while people farther north in the Yellow River valley learned to cultivate and depend on millet.

In both south and east Asia, agricultural surpluses encouraged the growth of complex societies. Indeed, people in both locations developed bustling cities. By 3000 B.C.E. people in India's Indus River valley built south Asia's first cities in what has come to be known as *Harappan* society. Harappan society collapsed about 1500 B.C.E., just as Aryans moved into India in large numbers, which created a period of turmoil and conflict. Eventually, however, Aryan peoples interacted and intermarried with the indigenous Dravidians, and that combination led to the development of a distinctive society and a rich cultural tradition. In China, three dynastic states based in the Yellow River valley brought much of China under their authority during the second millennium B.C.E. In the process they forged many local communities into a larger Chinese society. At the same time, all three dynasties had frequent dealings with neighboring peoples to the west, who linked China to other societies and brought knowledge and technologies from afar. As in early Mesopotamia and Egypt, then, complex society in both south and east Asia promoted the development of distinctive social and cultural traditions in the context of cross-cultural interaction and exchange.

# HARAPPAN SOCIETY

Like societies in Mesopotamia and Egypt, the earliest urban society in south Asia was built by Dravidian peoples in the valley of a river, the Indus, whose waters were available for irrigation of crops. This society—called Harappan society after one of its two chief cities—thrived between about 3000 B.C.E. and 1900 B.C.E. As it fell into decline over the next four hundred years, Indo-European migrants from the northwest began to settle in south Asia. Although Indo-Europeans initially clashed with the indigenous Dravidians, over time the two groups mixed and became indistinguishable from each other. In the process, they created a unique social and religious order that helped shape south Asian society until modern times.

Although scholars know that cities were evolving in the Indus region by 3000 B.C.E., it is impossible to follow the development of Harappan society in detail. One reason is that many of the earliest Harappan physical remains lie below the existing water table and thus are inaccessible to archaeologists. Another reason is the lack of deciphered written records, because scholars have so far been unable to understand

**Dravidian** (drah-VIHD-een)

**Harappan** (huh-RUHP-puhn)

the complex pictographic Harappan script. As a result, our understanding of Harappan society depends entirely on the study of accessible material remains.

THE INDUS RIVER    If the Greek historian Herodotus had known of Harappan society, he might have called it "the gift of the Indus." Like the Nile, the Indus draws its waters from rain and melting snow in towering mountains—in this case, the Hindu Kush and the Himalayas. As the waters reach the lowlands, the Indus deposits huge quantities of silt on its banks. Although the Indus periodically caused extensive destruction from flooding, it did make agricultural society possible in northern India. Early cultivators sowed their crops along its banks in September, after the flood receded, and harvested their crops the following spring.

As in Mesopotamia and Egypt, agricultural surpluses in India vastly increased the food supply, stimulated population growth, and supported the establishment of cities and specialized labor. Between 3000 and 2500 B.C.E., the agricultural surplus of the Indus valley fed two large cities, Harappa and Mohenjo-daro, as well as subordinate cities and a vast agricultural hinterland. Harappan society embraced much of modern-day Pakistan and a large part of northern India as well—a territory of about 1.3 million square kilometers (502,000 square miles)—and thus was considerably larger than either Mesopotamian or Egyptian society.

HARAPPA AND MOHENJO-DARO    No evidence survives concerning the Harappan political system, although archaeological excavations do not suggest a royal or imperial authority. However, both Harappa and Mohenjo-daro had city walls, a fortified citadel, and a large granary, suggesting that they served as centers of political authority and sites for the collection and redistribution of taxes paid in the form of grain. The two cities represented a considerable investment of human labor and other resources: both featured marketplaces, temples, public buildings, extensive residential districts, and broad streets laid out on a carefully planned grid.

Mohenjo-daro statue of a bearded man
www.mhhe.com/bentleybrief2e

The two cities clearly established the patterns that shaped the larger society: weights, measures, architectural styles, and even brick sizes were consistent throughout the land. This standardization no doubt reflects the prominence of Harappa and Mohenjo-daro as powerful and wealthy cities whose influence touched all parts of Harappan society, as well as the degree to which the Indus River facilitated trade, travel, and communication among the far-flung regions of Harappan society.

SPECIALIZED LABOR AND TRADE    Like other complex societies in ancient times, Harappa engaged in trade, both domestic and foreign. Pottery, tools, and decorative items produced in Harappa and Mohenjo-daro found their way to all corners of the Indus valley, while the cities imported precious metals and stones from neighboring peoples in Persia and the Hindu Kush mountains. During the period about 2300 to 1750 B.C.E., they also traded with Mesopotamians, mostly via ships that followed the coastline of the Arabian Sea between the mouth of the Indus River and the Persian Gulf.

## Harappan Society and Culture

SOCIAL DISTINCTIONS    Like societies in Mesopotamia and Egypt, Harappan society generated considerable wealth. Excavations at Mohenjo-daro show that at its high point, from about 2500 to 2000 B.C.E., the city was a thriving economic center with a population of about forty thousand. The wealth of Harappan society, like that in Mesopotamia and Egypt, encouraged the formation of social distinctions. It is clear from Harappan dwellings that rich and poor lived in very different styles. In Mohenjo-daro, for example, many people lived in one-room tenements in barracks-like structures, but there were also individual houses of two and three stories with a dozen rooms and an interior

Plan for a Mohenjo-daro house
www.mhhe.com/bentleybrief2e

Indus (IN-duhs)

Harappans traded with distant societies by land and sea.

**MAP 3.1** | Harappan society and its neighbors, ca. 2000 B.C.E. Compare Harappan society with its Mesopotamian and Egyptian contemporaries with respect to size. *What conditions would have been necessary to enable trade to flow between the Indus River valley and Mesopotamia?*

courtyard, as well as a few even larger houses. Almost all houses had private bathrooms with showers and toilets that drained into city sewage systems, which themselves were among the most sophisticated of the ancient world.

In the absence of deciphered writing, Harappan beliefs and values are very difficult to interpret. Even without written texts, however, material remains shed some tantalizing light on Harappan society. Like other early agricultural societies, Harappans venerated gods and goddesses they associated with creation and procreation. They recognized a mother goddess and a horned fertility god, and they held trees and animals sacred because of their associations with vital forces. In fact, many scholars believe that some Harappan deities survived the collapse of the larger society and later found places in the Hindu pantheon, because they have noticed striking similarities between Harappan and Hindu deities—especially those associated with fertility and procreation.

HARAPPAN DECLINE    Sometime after 1900 B.C.E. Harappan society entered a period of decline. A primary cause was ecological degradation: in clearing the land for cultivation and firewood, Harappans deforested the Indus valley. In the process, they facilitated soil erosion and desertification. Over a period of half a millennium or more, most of the Indus valley became a desert: agriculture is possible there today only with the aid of artificial irrigation. These climatic and ecological changes reduced agricultural yields, and Harappan society faced a subsistence crisis during the centuries after 1900 B.C.E. By about 1700 B.C.E. the populations of Harappa and Mohenjo-daro had abandoned the cities, and by 1500 B.C.E. even the smaller Harappan cities had almost entirely collapsed.

**MOHENJO-DARO.** | This aerial view of the excavations at Mohenjo-daro illustrates the careful planning and precise layout of the city. *What does the layout of this city reveal about the lifestyle of the people who lived there?*

# THE INDO-EUROPEAN MIGRATIONS AND EARLY ARYAN INDIA

During the second millennium B.C.E., just as Harappan society declined, bands of foreigners filtered into the Indian subcontinent via the Hindu Kush mountains and settled throughout the Indus valley and beyond. Most prominent were nomadic and pastoral peoples speaking Indo-European languages who called themselves Aryans ("noble people"). By about 1500 B.C.E. they had begun to establish small herding and agricultural communities throughout northern India.

Their migrations took place over several centuries and thus did not constitute an invasion or a military campaign. Even so, it is clear that Indo-European migrants clashed with Dravidians and other peoples already settled in India. However, in the centuries after 1500 B.C.E., Dravidian and Indo-European peoples increasingly intermingled, in the process laying the social and cultural foundations that would influence Indian society to the present day.

## *The Aryans and India*

**THE EARLY ARYANS** When they entered India, the Aryans depended heavily on a pastoral economy. They especially prized their horses and herds of cattle. Horses were quite valuable because of their expense and rarity: horses do not breed well in India,

**Aryan** (AIR-ee-uhn)

so it was necessary for Aryans to replenish their stock by importing animals from central Asia. Like their Indo-European cousins to the north, the Aryans harnessed horses to carts, and they also hitched them to chariots for use in warfare. Meanwhile, cattle became the principal measure of wealth in early Aryan society. The Aryans consumed both dairy products and beef, and they often calculated prices in terms of cattle.

THE VEDAS    The early Aryans did not use writing but instead preserved extensive collections of religious and literary works by transmitting them orally from one generation to another in their sacred language, Sanskrit. The earliest of these orally transmitted works were the *Vedas,* which were collections of hymns, songs, prayers, and rituals honoring the various gods of the Aryans. There are four *Vedas,* the earliest and most important of which is the *Rig Veda,* a collection of 1,028 hymns addressed to Aryan gods. Although it was compiled between about 1400 and 900 B.C.E., Aryan priests committed the *Rig Veda* to writing only in about 600 B.C.E.

While the *Vedas* represent a priestly perspective on affairs because of their function in transmitting religious knowledge, they also shed considerable light on early Aryan society in India. Indeed, in view of their importance as historical sources, scholars refer to Indian history during the millennium between 1500 and 500 B.C.E. as the Vedic age.

THE VEDIC AGE    The *Vedas* reflect a boisterous society in which the Aryans clashed repeatedly with the Dravidians and other peoples—referred to in the texts as *dasas,* meaning "enemies" or "subject peoples"—already living in India. The *Vedas* identify Indra, the Aryan war god and military hero, as one who ravaged citadels, smashed dams, and destroyed forts the way age consumes cloth garments. These characterizations suggest that competition over land and resources fueled intermittent conflict between Aryan and Dravidian peoples. The Aryans also fought ferociously among themselves. They did not have a state or common government but, rather, formed hundreds of chiefdoms organized around herding communities and agricultural villages. Because of their close proximity, this practice encouraged competition for resources and created enormous potential for conflict.

ARYAN MIGRATIONS IN INDIA    During the early centuries of the Vedic age, Aryan groups settled in the Punjab, the upper Indus River valley that straddles the modern-day border between northern India and Pakistan. After 1000 B.C.E. they began to settle in the area between the Himalayan foothills and the Ganges River, where they learned to make iron tools and to practice agriculture. Agricultural surpluses encouraged larger populations and more complex social organization, and by about 750 B.C.E., Aryans had established the first small cities in the Ganges River valley. Population growth also encouraged further migration. Thus, by 500 B.C.E. Aryan groups had migrated as far south as the northern Deccan, a plateau region in the southern cone of the Indian subcontinent about 1,500 kilometers (950 miles) south of the Punjab.

As they settled into permanent communities and began to rely more on agriculture than on herding, the Aryans gradually lost the tribal political organization they had brought into India and instead evolved more formal political institutions. Indeed, between 1000 and 500 B.C.E., tribal chiefdoms increasingly developed into regional kingdoms, and for centuries these became the most common form of political organization on the subcontinent.

## Origins of the Caste System

Although the Aryans did not build large imperial states, they did construct a well-defined social order. In fact, in some ways their social hierarchy served to maintain the order and stability that states and political structures guaranteed in other societies. The Aryan social structure, known today as the caste system, rested on sharp hereditary distinctions between individuals and groups, according to their occupations and roles in society.

*Vedas* (VAY-duhs)

**CASTE AND VARNA** Caste identities developed gradually as the Aryans established settlements throughout India. Initially, increased interaction with Dravidian peoples probably prompted Aryans to base social distinctions on either Aryan or Dravidian ancestry. In part, those distinctions may have arisen from differences in complexion between the Aryans, who referred to themselves as "wheat-colored," and the darker-skinned Dravidians. Indeed, the Aryan term *varna,* which refers to the major social classes, comes from the Sanskrit word meaning "color." However, over time Aryans and Dravidians mixed, mingled, interacted, and intermarried to the point that distinguishing between them was impossible.

Brahmins
www.mhhe.com/
bentleybrief2e

After about 1000 B.C.E. the Aryans increasingly recognized four main *varnas: brahmins* (priests), *kshatriyas* (warriors and aristocrats), *vaishyas* (cultivators, artisans, and merchants), and *shudras* (landless peasants and serfs). Some centuries later, probably about the end of the Vedic age, they added the category of the *untouchables*—people who performed dirty or unpleasant tasks, such as butchering animals or handling dead bodies, and who theoretically became so polluted from their work that their very touch could defile individuals of higher status.

**SUBCASTES AND JATI** Until about the sixth century B.C.E., the four *varnas* described Vedic society reasonably well. Because they did not live in cities and did not yet pursue many specialized occupations, the Aryans had little need for a more complicated social order. Over the longer term, however, a much more elaborate scheme of social classification emerged. As Vedic society became more complex and generated increasingly specialized occupations, the caste system served as the umbrella for a complicated hierarchy of subcastes known as *jati,* which were hereditary categories largely determined by occupation. By the eighteenth and nineteenth centuries C.E., in its most fully articulated form, the system featured several thousand *jati,* which prescribed individuals' roles in society in minute detail.

Castes and subcastes deeply influenced the lives of individual Indians through much of history. Members of a *jati* ate with one another and intermarried, and they cared for those who became ill or fell on hard times. Elaborate rules dictated forms of address and specific behavior appropriate for communication between members of different castes and subcastes. Violation of *jati* rules could result in expulsion from the larger group. That penalty was serious, since an outcast individual could not function well and sometimes could not even survive when shunned by members of the larger society.

**CASTE AND SOCIAL MOBILITY** The caste system never functioned in an absolutely rigid or inflexible manner but, rather, operated so as to accommodate social change. Individuals sometimes prospered on the basis of their own initiative, or else they could fall on hard times and move down in the social hierarchy. More often, however, social mobility came about as members of *jati* improved their condition collectively. Achieving upward mobility was not an easy matter—it often entailed moving to a new area, or at least taking on a new line of work—but the possibility of improving individual or group status helped to dissipate social tensions. In addition, the caste system enabled foreign peoples to find a place in Indian society by allowing newcomers to organize into well-defined groups that eventually came to adopt caste identities.

By the end of the Vedic age, caste distinctions had become central institutions in Aryan India. Whereas in other lands states and empires maintained public order, in India the caste system served as a principal foundation of social stability. Individuals have often identified more closely with their *jati* than with their cities or states, and castes have played a large role in maintaining social discipline in India.

**ARYAN SWORD.** | This bronze sword manufactured by Aryan craftsmen was a much stronger and more effective weapon than those available to Harappan defenders.

*varna* (VUHR-nuh)

**brahmins** (BRAH-minz)

**kshatriyas** (SHUHT-ree-uhs)

**vaishyas** (VEYESH-yuhs)

**shudras** (SHOO-druhs)

**THE LAWBOOK OF MANU** While building an elaborate social hierarchy on the foundations of caste and *varna* distinctions, the Aryans also constructed a strongly patriarchal social order on the basis of gender distinctions. At the time of their migrations into India, men already dominated Aryan society. All priests, warriors, and tribal chiefs were men, and the Aryans recognized descent through the male line. Women influenced affairs within their own families but enjoyed no public authority. As the Aryans settled in agricultural communities throughout India, they maintained this thoroughly patriarchal society. Only males could inherit property, unless a family had no male heirs, and only men could preside over family rituals that honored departed ancestors.

A text from about the first century B.C.E., called the *Lawbook of Manu,* illustrates the patriarchal ideologies that helped structure Indian society. Although composed after the Vedic age, the *Lawbook of Manu* reflected the society constructed earlier under Aryan influence. The author advised men to treat women with honor and respect, but he insisted that women remain subject to the guidance of the principal men in their lives. The *Lawbook* also specified that the most important duties of women were to bear children and maintain wholesome homes for their families.

# RELIGION IN THE VEDIC AGE

As the caste system emerged and helped to organize Indian society, distinctive cultural and religious traditions also took shape. The Aryans entered India with traditions and beliefs that met the needs of a mobile and often violent society. As they spread throughout India and mixed with the Dravidians, however, the Aryans encountered new religious ideas they considered intriguing and persuasive. The resulting fusion of Aryan traditions with Dravidian beliefs and values laid the foundation for Hinduism, a faith immensely popular in India and parts of southeast Asia for more than two millennia.

## Aryan Religion

As in Mesopotamia, Egypt, and other lands, religious values in India reflected the larger society. For example, during the early centuries following the Aryan migrations, the focus on Indra the war god testified to the instability and turbulence of early Vedic society. Also important to those early beliefs was the proper performance of ritual sacrifices. Through sacrifices, Aryans hoped to win the favor of the gods to ensure military success, large families, long life, and abundant herds of cattle. But those rewards required constant attention to religious ritual: proper honor for the gods called for households to have brahmins perform no fewer than five sacrifices per day—a time-consuming and expensive obligation.

**SPIRITUALITY** As the centuries passed, many Aryans became dissatisfied with the sacrificial cults of the Vedas, which increasingly seemed like sterile rituals rather than a genuine means of communicating with the gods. Beginning about 800 B.C.E. many thoughtful individuals left their villages and retreated to the forests of the Ganges valley, where they lived as hermits and reflected on the relationships between human beings, the world, and the gods. These mystics drew considerable inspiration from the religious beliefs of Dravidian peoples, who often worshiped nature spirits that they associated with fertility and the generation of new life. Dravidians also believed that human souls took on new physical forms after the deaths of their bodily hosts. The notion that souls could experience transmigration and reincarnation—that an individual soul could depart one body at death and become associated with another body through a new birth—intrigued thoughtful people and encouraged them to try to understand the principles that governed the fate of souls. As a result, a remarkable tradition of religious speculation emerged.

## The Blending of Aryan and Dravidian Values

This tradition achieved its fullest development in a body of works known as the *Upanishads,* which began to appear late in the Vedic age, about 800 to 400 B.C.E. The word *upanishad* literally means "a sitting in front of," and it refers to the practice of disciples

**ARYAN WOMAN AND CHILD.** | This greenish blue schist carving illustrates the devotion of a mother to her child.

gathering before a sage for discussion of religious issues. The Upanishads often took the form of dialogues that explored the *Vedas* and the religious issues that they raised.

BRAHMAN, THE UNIVERSAL SOUL   The Upanishads taught that each person participates in a larger cosmic order and forms a small part of a universal soul, known as *Brahman*. Whereas the physical world is a theater of change, instability, and illusion, Brahman is an eternal, unchanging, permanent foundation for all things that exist—hence the only genuine reality. The authors of the Upanishads believed that individual souls were born into the physical world, not once, but many times: they believed that souls appeared most often as humans, but sometimes as animals, and possibly even occasionally as plants or other vegetable matter.

TEACHINGS OF THE UPANISHADS   The Upanishads developed several specific doctrines that helped to explain this line of thought. One was the doctrine of *samsara*, which held that upon death, individual souls go temporarily to the World of the Fathers and then return to earth in a new incarnation. Another was the doctrine of *karma*, which accounted for the specific incarnations that souls experienced. According to this doctrine, individuals who lived virtuous lives and fulfilled all their duties could expect rebirth into a purer and more honorable existence—for example, into a higher and more distinguished caste. Those who accumulated a heavy burden of karma, however, would suffer in a future incarnation by being reborn into a difficult existence, or perhaps even into the body of an animal or an insect.

The Upanishads also encouraged the cultivation of personal integrity—a self-knowledge that would incline individuals naturally toward both ethical behavior and union with Brahman. In addition, they taught respect for all living things, animal as well as human. Animal bodies, after all, might well hold incarnations of unfortunate souls suffering the effects of a heavy debt of karma. A vegetarian diet thus became a common feature of the ascetic regime.

Yet even under the best of circumstances, the cycle of rebirth involved a certain amount of pain and suffering. The authors of the Upanishads sought to escape the cycle altogether and attain the state of *moksha*, which they characterized as a deep, dreamless sleep that came with permanent liberation from physical incarnation. This goal was difficult to reach, since it entailed severing all ties to the physical world and identifying with the ultimate reality of Brahman, the universal soul. The two principal means to the goal were asceticism and meditation, which could help individuals purge themselves of desire for the comforts of the physical world.

RELIGION AND VEDIC SOCIETY   Just as the Aryan focus on Indra reflected early Aryan society, so the religious views of the Upanishads dovetailed with the social order of the late Vedic age. Indeed, the doctrines of samsara and karma certainly reinforced the Vedic social order: they explained why individuals were born into their castes, and they encouraged individuals to observe their caste duties in hopes of enjoying a more comfortable and honorable incarnation in the future. However, these doctrines were not simply cynical means of controlling Vedic society. Indeed, the sages who gave voice to these doctrines were conscientiously attempting to deal with meaningful spiritual and intellectual problems. Like Greek philosophers, Christian theologians, and many others, the authors of the Upanishads sought ultimate truth and certain knowledge in an ideal world that transcends our own.

**Upanishads** (oo-pah-NIH-shuhds)

**samsara** (suhm-SAH-ruh)

**karma** (KAHR-mah)

*moksha* (MOHK-shuh)

# POLITICAL ORGANIZATION IN EARLY CHINA

As in the Indus River valley of India, fertile river valleys in China allowed villages and towns to flourish along their banks. The most important of these valleys were those of the Yellow and Yangzi rivers, which supported settlements of agriculturalists after about 7000 B.C.E. By the late years of the third millennium B.C.E., these small settlements began to give way to much larger regional states. Among the most notable were those of the Xia, Shang, and Zhou dynasties, which progressively brought much of China under their authority and laid a political foundation for the development of a distinctive Chinese society.

**THE YELLOW RIVER**   Like the Indus, the Yellow River is boisterous and unpredictable. It rises in the mountains bordering the high plateau of Tibet, and it courses almost 4,700 kilometers (2,920 miles) before emptying into the Yellow Sea. It takes its name, Huang He, meaning "Yellow River," from the vast quantities of light-colored soil that it picks up along its route. So much soil becomes suspended in the Yellow River that the water turns yellow. The soil gradually builds up, raising the river bed and forcing the water out of its established path, periodically unleashing tremendous floods. The Yellow River has caused so much destruction that it has earned the nickname "China's Sorrow." Despite the periodic damage caused by the Yellow River, however, the soil it deposits is extremely fertile and easy to work, so even before the introduction of metal tools, cultivators using wooden implements could bring in generous harvests. As in India, agricultural surpluses resulted in increased population, which eventually gave rise to complex societies.

Chinese legends speak of three ancient dynasties—the Xia, the Shang, and the Zhou— that arose before the Qin and Han dynasties brought China under unified rule in the third century B.C.E. These dynasties were hereditary states that extended their control over progressively larger regions, although none of them embraced all the territory claimed by later Chinese dynasties.

## The Xia and Shang Dynasties

**THE XIA DYNASTY**   The Xia dynasty emerged about 2200 B.C.E. and was one of the earliest to organize public life in China on a large scale. Ancient legends credit the dynasty's founder, the sage-king Yu, with the organization of effective flood-control projects on the Yellow River: thus here, as in Mesopotamia and Egypt, the need to organize large-scale public works projects helped to establish recognized authorities and formal political institutions. Although no information survives about the political institutions of the Xia, the dynasty's rulers probably exercised power throughout the middle Yellow River valley by controlling the leaders of individual villages. By extending formal control over this region, the Xia dynasty established a precedent for hereditary monarchical rule in China.

**THE SHANG DYNASTY**   According to the legends, the last Xia king was an oppressive despot who lost his realm to the founder of the Shang dynasty. In fact, the Xia state probably gave way gradually before the Shang, which arose in a region to the south and east of the Xia realm. Tradition assigns the Shang dynasty to the period 1766 to 1122 B.C.E., and archaeological discoveries have largely confirmed those dates. Because the Shang dynasty left written records as well as mate-

---

### THINKING ABOUT *Traditions*

**TRADITIONS IN EARLY SOCIETIES IN SOUTH AND EAST ASIA.** In the period between 3000 and 500 B.C.E., sophisticated, stratified, and wealthy states developed in both China and India. Although each society shared concerns with morality and ethics, their approaches to religion and social organization were quite distinct. Think carefully about these differences in approach, and try to explain how such differences might have arisen.

---

**Yangzi** (YAHNG-zuh)

**Xia** (shyah)

**MAP 3.2** | The Xia, Shang, and Zhou dynasties, 2200–256 B.C.E. Note that the three dynasties extended their territorial reach through time. *How might technological considerations explain the increasing size of early Chinese states?*

Note the many cities that served as capitals

rial remains, the basic features of early Chinese society come into much clearer focus than they did during the Xia.

**BRONZE METALLURGY AND CHARIOTS**
Technology helps to explain the rise and success of the Shang dynasty. Bronze metallurgy transformed Chinese society during Shang times and indeed may well have enabled Shang rulers to displace the Xia dynasty. Bronze metallurgy—together with horses, horse-drawn chariots, and other wheeled vehicles—came to China with Indo-European migrants from southwest Asia. Although the Xia dynasty already made limited use of bronze tools and weapons, Shang ruling elites managed to monopolize the production of bronze in the Yellow River valley. Thus, control over bronze production strengthened Shang forces against those of the Xia, and they had little difficulty imposing their rule on agricultural villages and extending their influence throughout much of the Yellow River valley.

Shang kings extended their rule to a large portion of northeastern China centered on the modern-day province of Henan. Like state builders in other parts of the world, the kings claimed a generous portion of the surplus agricultural production from the regions they controlled and then used that surplus to support military forces, political allies, and others who could help them maintain their rule.

**SHANG POLITICAL ORGANIZATION**  The Shang state rested on a vast network of walled towns whose local rulers recognized the authority of the Shang kings. During the course of the dynasty, Shang kings may have controlled one thousand or more towns. According to tradition, the Shang capital moved six times during the course of the dynasty. Though originally chosen for political and military reasons, in each case the capital also became an important social, economic, and cultural center—the site not only of administration and military command but also of bronze foundries, arts, crafts, trade, and religious observances.

King Tang, first ruler of the Shang
www.mhhe.com/bentleybrief2e

**THE SHANG CAPITAL AT YIN**  Excavations have revealed much about the workings of the Shang dynasty. One remarkable site is Yin, near modern Anyang, which was the Shang capital during the last two or three centuries of the dynasty. Archaeologists working at Yin have identified a complex of royal palaces, archives with written documents, several residential neighborhoods, two large bronze foundries, several workshops used by craftsmen, and scattered burial grounds. Eleven large and lavish tombs constructed for Shang kings have received particular attention. The graves included thousands of objects—chariots, weapons, bronze goods, pottery, carvings, and sacrificial victims, including dogs, horses, and scores of human beings intended to serve the deceased royals in another existence. One tomb alone contained skeletons of more than three hundred sacrificial victims who joined the Shang king in death.

A ritual wine vessel from the Shang Dynasty
www.mhhe.com/bentleybrief2e

The Xia and Shang dynasties were not the only states that developed in ancient China, although legendary and historical accounts paid special attention to them because of their location in the Yellow River valley, where the first Chinese imperial states rose in later times. Indeed, archaeological excavations are making it clear that similar states dominated other regions at the same time the Xia and the Shang ruled the Yellow River valley. Recent excavations, for example, have unearthed evidence of a very large city at Sanxingdui in modern-day Sichuan province (southwestern China). Occupied about 1700 to 1000 B.C.E., the city was roughly contemporaneous with the Shang dynasty, and it probably served as the capital of a regional kingdom.

# The Zhou Dynasty

**THE RISE OF THE ZHOU**  Although little information survives to illustrate the principles of law, justice, and administration by which Shang rulers maintained order, the picture becomes more clear in the practices of the Zhou dynasty, which succeeded the Shang as the preeminent political authority in northern China. Dwelling in the Wei River valley of northwestern China (modern Shaanxi province), the Zhou were a tough people who battled Shang forces and eventually won recognition as kings of the western regions. But the ambitions of the two dynasties collided in the late twelfth century B.C.E. According to Zhou accounts, the last Shang king was a criminal fool who gave himself over to wine, women, tyranny, and greed. As a result, many of the towns and political districts subject to the Shang transferred their loyalties to the Zhou, who toppled the Shang king's government in 1122 B.C.E. and replaced it with their own state. The new dynasty ruled most of northern and central China, at least nominally, until 256 B.C.E.

**THE MANDATE OF HEAVEN**  In justifying the deposition of the Shang, spokesmen for the Zhou dynasty articulated a set of principles that influenced Chinese thinking about government and political legitimacy until the twentieth century. The Zhou theory of politics rested on the assumption that heavenly powers granted the right to govern—"the mandate of heaven"—to an especially deserving individual known as the son of heaven. The ruler had the duty to govern conscientiously, to observe high standards of honor and justice, and to maintain order and harmony within his realm. As long as he did so, the heavenly powers would approve of his work, the cosmos would enjoy stability, and the ruling dynasty would retain its mandate to govern. If a ruler failed in his duties, however, chaos and suffering would afflict his realm, the cosmos would fall out of balance, and the displeased heavenly powers would withdraw the mandate to rule and transfer it to a more deserving candidate. On the basis of that reasoning, spokesmen for the new dynasty explained the fall of the Shang and the transfer of the mandate of heaven to the Zhou.

**POLITICAL ORGANIZATION**  The Zhou state was much larger than the Shang. In fact, it was so extensive that a single central court could not rule the entire land effectively. As a result, Zhou rulers relied on a decentralized administration: they entrusted power, authority, and responsibility to subordinates who in return owed allegiance, tribute, and military support to the central government. During the early days of the dynasty, that system worked reasonably well. Gradually, however, subordinates established their own bases of power, which allowed them to become more independent of the Zhou dynasty. In addition, iron production spread rapidly across China in the first millennium B.C.E., and Zhou subordinates took advantage of the technology to outfit their own forces with weapons to resist the central government.

**DECLINE OF THE ZHOU**  After the early eighth century B.C.E., Zhou rule deteriorated as nomadic invaders forced the royal court from their capital at Hao. Although the dynasty survived, it never regained its authority, and competing states fought ferociously with one another in hopes of establishing themselves as leaders of a new political order. So violent were the last centuries of the Zhou dynasty that they are known as the Period of the Warring States (403–221 B.C.E.). The Zhou dynasty officially ended in 256 B.C.E. when the last king abdicated his position under pressure from his ambitious subordinate, the king of Qin. Only with the establishment of the Qin dynasty in 221 B.C.E. did effective central government return to China.

**Zhou** (JOH)

**Qin** (Chin)

# SOCIETY AND FAMILY IN ANCIENT CHINA

In China, as in India, the introduction of agriculture enabled individuals to accumulate wealth and preserve it within their families. Social distinctions began to appear during neolithic times, and after the establishment of the Xia, Shang, and Zhou dynasties the distinctions became even sharper. Throughout China the patriarchal family emerged as the institution that most directly influenced individuals' lives and their roles in the larger society.

## The Social Order

RULING ELITES    Already during the Xia dynasty, but especially under the Shang and the early Zhou, the royal family and allied noble families occupied the most honored positions in Chinese society. They resided in large, palatial compounds made of pounded earth, and they lived on the agricultural surplus and taxes delivered by their subjects. One of the hallmarks of these elites was their conspicuous consumption of bronze, which was far too expensive for most people to afford. Indeed, ruling elites controlled much of the bronze weaponry that existed in northern China and also supplied their households with elaborately decorated cast-bronze utensils and vessels. Ruling elites consumed bronze in such staggering quantities that the tomb of Yi of Zeng, a provincial governor of the late Zhou dynasty, contained a collection of bronze weapons and decorative objects that weighed almost eleven tons.

A privileged class of hereditary aristocrats rose from the military allies of Shang and Zhou rulers. These aristocrats possessed extensive landholdings, and their standard of living was much more refined than that of the commoners and slaves who worked their fields and served their needs. They were served by a small class of free artisans and craftsmen, including bronzesmiths, jewelers, jade workers, and silk manufacturers, who enjoyed a reasonably comfortable existence because of aristocratic patronage.

PEASANTS    Far less comfortable was a large class of semiservile peasants who populated the Chinese countryside. They owned no land but provided agricultural, military, and labor services for their lords in exchange for plots to cultivate, security, and a portion of the harvest. They lived like their neolithic predecessors in small, partially subterranean houses excavated to a depth of about one meter (three feet) and protected from the elements by thatched walls and roofs. Women's duties included mostly indoor activities such as wine making, weaving, and cultivation of silkworms, whereas men spent most of their time outside working in the fields, hunting, and fishing.

SLAVES    Finally, there was a sizable class of slaves, most of whom were enemy warriors captured during battles between the many competing states of ancient China. Slaves performed hard labor, such as the clearing of new fields or the building of city walls, that required a large workforce.

BRONZE VESSEL.   |   The delicate design of this bronze wine vessel displays the high level of craftsmanship during the late Shang dynasty. *Why did the elite classes prefer objects made of bronze?*

## Family and Patriarchy

Throughout human history the family has served as the principal institution for the socialization of children and the preservation of cultural traditions. In China the extended family emerged as a particularly influential institution during neolithic times, and it continued to play a prominent role in shaping both private and public affairs after the appearance of the Xia, Shang, and Zhou states. Indeed, the early dynasties ruled their territories largely through family and kinship groups.

*Peasants in ancient China mostly did not own land. Instead, they worked as tenants on plots allotted to them by royal or aristocratic owners, who took sizable portions of the harvest for their own uses. In the following poem from the* Book of Songs, *a collection of verses dating from Zhou times, peasants liken their lords to rodents, protest the bite lords take from the peasants' agricultural production, and threaten to abandon the lords' lands for a neighboring state where conditions are better.*

Large rats! Large rats!
Do not eat our millet.
Three years have we had to do with you.
And you have not been willing to show any regard for us.
We will leave you,
And go to that happy land.
Happy land! Happy land!
There shall we find our place.
Large rats! Large rats!
Do not eat our wheat.
Three years have we had to do with you.
And you have not been willing to show any kindness to us.
We will leave you,
And go to that happy state.
Happy state! Happy state!
There shall we find ourselves aright.

Large rats! Large rats!
Do not eat our springing grain!
Three years have we had to do with you,
And you have not been willing to think of our toil.
We will leave you,
And go to those happy borders.
Happy borders! Happy borders!
Who will there make us always to groan?

■ How might you go about judging the extent to which these verses throw reliable light on class relations in ancient China?

SOURCE: James Legge, trans. *The Chinese Classics,* 5 vols. London: Henry Frowde, 1893, 4:171–72.

**VENERATION OF ANCESTORS**   One reason for the pronounced influence of the Chinese family was the veneration of ancestors, a practice with roots in neolithic times. This practice was based on the belief that dead ancestors had the power to support and protect their surviving families, but only if their descendants displayed proper respect and ministered to the spirits' needs. A family could expect to prosper only if all its members—dead as well as living—worked cooperatively toward common interests. Thus, the family became an institution linking departed generations to the living and helped build a strong ethic of family solidarity.

**PATRIARCHAL SOCIETY**   In the absence of organized religion or official priesthood in ancient China, the patriarchal head of the family presided at ceremonies honoring ancestors' spirits. As mediator between the family's dead and living members, the family patriarch possessed tremendous authority. Indeed, Chinese society vested authority principally in elderly males who headed their households. And, like its counterparts in other regions, Chinese patriarchy intensified with the emergence of large states. During neolithic times Chinese men wielded public authority, but they won their rights to it by virtue of the female line of their descent. Gradually, however, Chinese society lost its matrilineal character. By the later Shang and Zhou dynasties, women lived increasingly in the shadow of men, and even queens and empresses were honored only as a result of being associated with their illustrious husbands.

**patriarch** (PAY-tree-ahrk)

# EARLY CHINESE WRITING AND CULTURAL DEVELOPMENT

Early Chinese myths and legends explained the origins of the world, the human race, agriculture, and the various arts and crafts. But Chinese thinkers saw no need to organize those ideas into systematic religious traditions. Although they often spoke of an impersonal heavenly power, they did not recognize a personal supreme deity who intervened in human affairs or took special interest in human behavior. Nor did ancient China support a large class of priests like those of Mesopotamia, Egypt, and India. As a result, it was family patriarchs who represented the interests of living generations to the spirits of departed ancestors.

In that environment, writing served as the foundation for a distinctive secular cultural tradition in ancient China. Surviving evidence suggests that writing came into extensive use during the Shang dynasty. As in other lands, writing in east Asia quickly became an indispensable tool of government as well as a means of expressing ideas and offering reflections on human beings and their world.

## THINKING ABOUT *Encounters*

**ENCOUNTERS IN EARLY SOCIETIES IN SOUTH AND EAST ASIA.** Both Chinese and Indian (Aryan) societies developed in the context of interactions with peoples outside their own territories or social groupings: in China with nomads to the north and west, and in India with indigenous Dravidian peoples. How did these interactions influence the development of Chinese and Indian trade, social structure, or culture?

## Oracle Bones and Early Chinese Writing

In Mesopotamia and India, merchants pioneered the use of writing. In China, however, the earliest known writing served the interests of rulers rather than traders. Writing in China goes back at least to the early part of the second millennium B.C.E. Surviving records indicate that scribes at the Shang royal court kept written accounts of important events on strips of bamboo or pieces of silk. Unfortunately, almost all those materials have perished, along with their messages. Yet one medium employed by ancient Chinese scribes has survived the ravages of time. Recognized just over a century ago, inscriptions on oracle bones have thrown tremendous light both on the Shang dynasty and on the early stages of Chinese writing.

Shang oracle bone
www.mhhe.com/
bentleybrief2e

**ORACLE BONES** Oracle bones were the principal instruments used by fortune-tellers in ancient China. Diviners inscribed a question on a specially prepared broad bone—such as the shoulder blade of a sheep—and then subjected it to heat. When heated, the bone developed networks of splits and cracks. The fortune-teller then studied the patterns and determined the answer to the question inscribed on the bone. Often the diviner recorded the answer on the bone, and later scribes occasionally added further information about the events that actually came to pass.

Most of the oracle bones have come from royal archives, and the questions posed on them clearly reveal the day-to-day concerns of the Shang royal court. Will the season's harvest be abundant or poor? Will the queen bear a son or a daughter? Taken together, bits of information preserved on the oracle bones have allowed historians to piece together an understanding of the political and social order of Shang times.

Even more important, the oracle bones offer the earliest glimpse into the tradition of Chinese

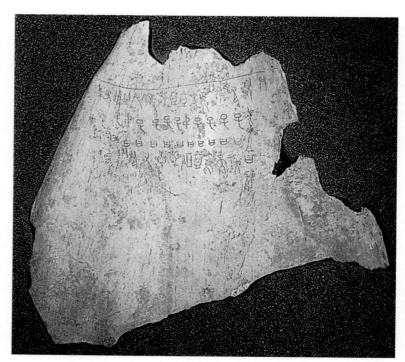

**CHINESE ORACLE BONE.** | Oracle bone from Shang times with an inscribed question and cracks caused by exposure of the bone to heat.

| | Turtle | Horse |
|---|---|---|
| Oracle bone script of the Shang dynasty (16th century–11th century B.C.E.) | | |
| Zhou dynasty script (11th century–3rd century B.C.E.) | | |
| Qin dynasty script (221–207 B.C.E.) | | |
| Han dynasty script (207 B.C.E.–220 C.E.) | | |
| Modern script (3rd century C.E.–present) | | |
| Contemporary script, People's Republic of China (1950–the present) | | |

**CHINESE WRITING.** | The evolution of Chinese characters from the Shang dynasty to the present. *In what ways did the characters above change over time?*

writing. The earliest form of Chinese writing, like Sumerian and Egyptian writing, was the pictograph—a conventional or stylized representation of an object. The characters used in contemporary Chinese writing are direct descendants of those used in Shang times. Scholars have identified more than two thousand characters inscribed on oracle bones, most of which have a modern counterpart. Over the centuries, written Chinese characters have undergone considerable modification: generally speaking, they have become more stylized, conventional, and abstract. Yet the affinities between Shang and later Chinese written characters are apparent at a glance.

The political interests of the Shang kings may have accounted for the origin of Chinese writing, but once established, the technology was available for other uses. Because Shang writing survives only on oracle bones and a small number of bronze inscriptions, however, evidence for the expanded uses of writing comes only from the Zhou dynasty and later times.

**ZHOU LITERATURE** Indeed, the Zhou dynasty produced books of poetry and history, manuals of divination and ritual, and essays dealing with moral, religious, philosophical, and political themes. Best known of these works are the reflections of Confucius and other late Zhou thinkers (discussed in chapter 6), which served as the intellectual foundation of classical Chinese society. But many works won recognition in Zhou society, including the popular *Book of Changes* (a manual instructing diviners in the art of foretelling the future), the *Book of History* (a collection of documents that justified the Zhou state), the *Book of Etiquette* (a manual in the arts of polite behavior), and—most notable of all—the *Book of Songs* (a collection of verses).

Unfortunately, most other Zhou writings have perished. One important reason for this is that when the imperial house of Qin ended the chaos of the Period of the Warring States and brought all of China under tightly centralized rule in 221 B.C.E., the victorious emperor ordered the destruction of all writings that did not have some immediate utilitarian value. Only a few items escaped, hidden away for a decade or more until scholars and writers could once again work without fear of persecution. These few survivors represent the earliest development of Chinese literature and moral thought.

# ANCIENT CHINA AND THE LARGER WORLD

High mountain ranges, forbidding deserts, and turbulent seas stood between China and other early societies of the eastern hemisphere. These geographic features did not entirely prevent communication between China and other lands, but they hindered the establishment of direct long-distance trade relations such as those linking Mesopotamia with Harappan India or those between the Phoenicians and other peoples of the Mediterranean basin. Nevertheless, like other early societies, ancient China developed in the context of a larger world of interaction and exchange. Trade, migration, and the expansion of Chinese agricultural society all ensured that peoples of the various east Asian and central Asian societies would have regular dealings with one another. Chinese cultivators had particularly intense relations—sometimes friendly and sometimes hostile—with their neighbors to the north, the west, and the south.

## Relations with Nomadic Peoples of Central Asia

**STEPPE NOMADS**   From the valley of the Yellow River, Chinese agriculture spread to the north and west. As this expansion occurred, Chinese cultivators encountered nomadic peoples who had built pastoral societies in the grassy steppes of central Asia. These lands were too arid to sustain large agricultural societies, but their grasses supported large herds of livestock. By 2200 B.C.E. these nomads were already experienced horseback riders, had learned the technology of bronze metallurgy, and had introduced large numbers of heavy wagons into the steppes. After about 1000 B.C.E. several clusters of nomadic peoples organized powerful herding societies on the Eurasian steppes.

**NOMADIC SOCIETY**   Nomadic peoples did little farming but instead concentrated on herding their animals, driving them to regions where they could find food and water. Because nomadic peoples ranged widely over the grassy steppes of central Asia, they served as links between agricultural societies to the east and west. They were prominent intermediaries in trade networks spanning central Asia. They also brought knowledge of bronze metallurgy and horse-drawn chariots from southwest Asia. Nomadic peoples depended on agricultural societies for grains and finished products, such as textiles and metal goods, which they could not readily produce for themselves. In exchange for those products, they offered horses, which flourished on the steppes, and their services as links to other societies. Yet the Chinese and nomadic peoples always had tense relations. Indeed, they often engaged in bitter wars, and nomadic raids posed a constant threat to the northern and western regions of China.

## The Southern Expansion of Chinese Society

**THE YANGZI VALLEY**   Chinese influence spread to the south as well as to the north and west. There was no immediate barrier to cultivation in the south: indeed, the valley of the Yangzi River supports even more intensive agriculture than is possible in the Yellow River basin. In fact, the moist, subtropical climate of southern China lent itself readily to the cultivation of rice: ancient cultivators sometimes raised two crops of rice per year.

But intensive cultivation of rice depended on the construction and maintenance of an elaborate irrigation system that allowed cultivators to flood their paddies and release the waters at the appropriate time. The Shang and Zhou states provided sources of authority that could supervise a complex irrigation system, and harvests in southern China—along with the population—increased dramatically during the second and first millennia B.C.E.

**THE STATE OF CHU**   Agricultural surpluses and growing populations led to the emergence of cities, states, and complex societies in the Yangzi as well as the Yellow River valley. During the late Zhou dynasty, the powerful state of Chu, situated in the central region of the Yangzi, governed its affairs autonomously and challenged the Zhou for supremacy. By the end of the Zhou dynasty, Chu and other states in southern China were in regular communication with their counterparts in the Yellow River valley.

**CHINESE AGRICULTURE.**   |   Terraced rice paddies in the river valleys of southern China have long produced abundant harvests. *What is the advantage of terraces in agriculture?*

They adopted Chinese political and social traditions as well as Chinese writing, and they built societies closely resembling those of the Yellow River valley. As a result, although only the northern portions of the Yangzi River valley fell under the authority of the Shang and Zhou states, by the end of the Zhou dynasty all of southern China formed part of an emerging larger Chinese society.

# SUMMARY

Agricultural peoples in south and east Asia built complex societies that in broad outline were much like those to the west. Particularly in the valleys of the Yellow River, the Yangzi River, and the Indus River, early Chinese and Indian cultivators organized states, developed social distinctions, and established sophisticated cultural traditions. Their languages, writing, beliefs, and values differed considerably from one another and from those of their contemporaries in other societies, and these cultural elements lent distinctiveness to both Chinese and Indian society. Moreover, inhabitants of both ancient China and India managed to trade and communicate with peoples of other societies. As a result, wheat cultivation, bronze and iron metallurgy, horse-drawn chariots, and wheeled vehicles all made their way from southwest Asia in ancient times. Thus, in south and east Asia, as in other parts of the eastern hemisphere, agriculture demonstrated its potential to provide a foundation for large-scale social organization and to support interaction and exchange between peoples of different societies.

# STUDY TERMS

Aryans (51)
Brahman (55)
brahmins (53)
caste (52)
Dravidian (48)
Harappan (48)
Indus River (49)
*jati* (53)
karma (55)
kshatriyas (53)

mandate of heaven (58)
*moksha* (55)
oracle bones (61)
Qin (58)
samsara (55)
Shang dynasty (56)
shudras (53)
untouchables (53)
Upanishads (54)

vaishyas (53)
*varna* (53)
*Vedas* (52)
Vedic age (52)
Xia dynasty (56)
Yangzi (56)
Yellow River (56)
Yu (47)
Zhou dynasty (58)

# FOR FURTHER READING

F. R. Allchin. *The Archaeology of Early Historic South Asia: The Emergence of Cities and States.* Cambridge, 1995. A collection of scholarly essays on the roles of cities and states in ancient India.

Cyril Birch, ed. *Anthology of Chinese Literature.* 2 vols. New York, 1965. Collection of primary sources in translation.

Nicola di Cosmo. *Ancient China and Its Enemies: The Rise of Nomadic Power in East Asian History.* Cambridge, 2002. An insightful study analyzing the emergence of pastoral nomadism and relations between Chinese cultivators and nomadic peoples in ancient times.

David N. Keightley, ed. *The Origins of Chinese Civilization.* Berkeley, 1983. An important collection of scholarly articles dealing with all aspects of early Chinese society.

Jonathan Mark Kenoyer. *Ancient Cities of the Indus Valley Civilization.* Oxford, 1998. A well-illustrated volume that synthesizes recent archaeological and linguistic scholarship on Harappan society.

J. P. Mallory. *In Search of the Indo-Europeans: Language, Archaeology, and Myth.* London, 1989. Carefully reviews modern theories about early Indo-European speakers in light of both the linguistic and the archaeological evidence.

Juan Mascaró, trans. *The Upanishads.* London, 1965. A superb English version of selected Upanishads by a gifted translator.

Shereen Ratnagar. *Encounters: The Westerly Trade of the Harappan Civilization.* Delhi, 1981. Relies on archaeological discoveries in examining commercial relations between Harappan society and Mesopotamia.

Jessica Rawson. *Ancient China: Art and Archaeology.* New York, 1980. An outstanding and well-illustrated volume with especially strong treatment of archaeological discoveries.

Robert L. Thorp. *China in the Early Bronze Age: Shang Civilization.* Philadelphia, 2006. Authoritative synthesis of archaeological studies that places the Shang dynasty in its historical context.

# Early Societies in the Americas and Oceania

n early September of the year 683 C.E., a Maya man named Chan Bahlum grasped a sharp obsidian knife and cut three deep slits into the skin of his penis. He inserted into each slit a strip of paper made from beaten tree bark so as to encourage a continuing flow of blood. His younger brother Kan Xul performed a similar rite, and other members of his family also drew blood from their own bodies.

The bloodletting observances of September 683 C.E. were political and religious rituals, acts of deep piety performed as Chan Bahlum presided over funeral services for his recently deceased father, Pacal, king of the Maya city of Palenque in the Yucatan peninsula. The Maya believed that the shedding of royal blood was essential to the world's survival. Thus, as Chan Bahlum prepared to succeed his father as king of Palenque, he let his blood flow copiously.

Throughout Mesoamerica, Maya and other peoples performed similar rituals for a millennium and more. Maya rulers and their family members regularly spilled their own blood. Men commonly drew blood from the penis, like Chan Bahlum, and women often drew from the tongue. Both sexes occasionally drew blood also from the earlobes, lips, or cheeks, and they sometimes increased the flow by pulling long, thick cords through their wounds.

According to Maya priests, the gods had shed their own blood to water the earth and nourish crops of maize, and they expected human beings to honor them by imitating their sacrifice. By spilling human blood the Maya hoped to please the gods and ensure that life-giving waters would bring bountiful harvests to their fields. By inflicting painful wounds not just on their enemies but on their own bodies as well, the Maya demonstrated their conviction that bloodletting rituals were essential to the coming of rain and the survival of their agricultural society.

This agricultural society was the product of a distinctive tradition. Human groups migrated to the Americas and Oceania long after they had established communities throughout most of the eastern hemisphere, but long before any people began to experiment with agriculture. Their migrations took place during ice ages, when glaciers locked up much of the earth's water, causing sea levels all over the world to decline precipitously—sometimes by as much as 300 meters (984 feet). For thousands of years, temporary land bridges joined regions that both before and after the ice ages were separated by the seas. One land bridge linked Siberia with Alaska. Another

❮ *In this Mayan mural from Bonampak in modern Mexico, war captives prepare to be sacrificed by their captors.*

**Maya** (MY-uh)

**Yucatan** (yoo-kah-TAN)

# CHRONOLOGY

## AMERICAS

| | |
|---|---|
| 13,000 B.C.E. | Human migration to North America from Siberia |
| 8000–7000 B.C.E. | Origins of agriculture in Mesoamerica |
| 4000 B.C.E. | Origins of maize cultivation in Mesoamerica |
| 3000 B.C.E. | Origins of agriculture in South America |
| 1200–100 B.C.E. | Olmec society |
| 1000–300 B.C.E. | Chavín cult |
| 200 B.C.E.–750 C.E. | Teotihuacan society |
| 300–1100 C.E. | Maya society |
| 300–700 C.E. | Mochica society |

## OCEANIA

| | |
|---|---|
| 60,000 B.C.E. | Human migration to Australia and New Guinea |
| 3000 B.C.E. | Origins of agriculture in New Guinea |
| 3000 B.C.E. | Austronesian migrations to New Guinea |
| 1500–500 B.C.E. | Lapita society |
| 1500 B.C.E.–700 C.E. | Austronesian migrations to Pacific islands |

joined the continent of Australia to the island of New Guinea. Human groups took advantage of those bridges by migrating to new lands.

When the earth's temperature rose and the glaciers melted, beginning about eighteen thousand years ago, the waters returned and flooded low-lying lands around the world. Eventually, the seas once again divided Asia from America by the body of water known as the Bering Strait, and they also separated Australia and New Guinea. By that time, however, human communities had become well established in each of those areas.

The return of high waters did not put an end to human migrations. Human groups fanned out from Alaska and ventured to all corners of North, Central, and South America. Beginning about 3000 B.C.E. coastal peoples of southeast Asia built large sailing canoes and established human settlements in the previously uninhabited islands of the Pacific Ocean. By about 700 C.E. human beings had established communities in almost every habitable part of the world.

Although they were separated by large bodies of water, by no means did human migrants to the Americas and Oceania lead completely isolated lives. On the contrary, there were frequent and sometimes regular interactions between peoples of different societies within the Americas and within Oceania. It is likely that at least fleeting encounters took place as well between peoples of the eastern and western hemispheres, although very little evidence survives to throw light on the nature of those encounters in early times. Yet even as they dealt with peoples of other societies, the first inhabitants of the Americas and Oceania also established distinctive societies of their own.

Despite their different origins and their distinctive political, social, and cultural traditions, peoples of the Americas and Oceania built societies that in some ways resembled those of the eastern hemisphere. Human communities independently discovered agriculture in several regions of North America and South America, and migrants introduced cultivation to the inhabited Pacific islands as well. With agriculture came increasing populations, settlement in towns, specialized labor, formal political authorities, hierarchical social orders, long-distance trade, and organized religious traditions. The Americas also generated large, densely populated societies featuring cities, monumental public works, imperial states, and sometimes traditions of writing as well. Thus, like their counterparts in the eastern hemisphere, the earliest societies of the Americas and Oceania reflected a common human tendency toward the development of increasingly complex social forms.

# EARLY SOCIETIES OF MESOAMERICA

Much is unclear about the early population of the Americas by human communities. Several archaeological excavations suggest that at least a few human groups had made their way to the Americas by 15,000 B.C.E. or earlier, although it is not clear whether they arrived by land or by water. However, it is clear that large-scale migration to the Americas began after 13,000 B.C.E., as humans made their way in large numbers across the Bering land bridge. Once in the Americas, humans quickly populated all habitable regions of the western hemisphere. By 9500 B.C.E. they had reached the southernmost part of South America, more than 17,000 kilometers (10,566 miles) from the Bering land bridge.

The earliest human inhabitants of the Americas lived exclusively by hunting and gathering. Beginning about 8000 B.C.E., however, large game animals became scarce, partly because they did not adapt well to the rapidly warming climate and partly because of overhunting by expanding human communities. By 7500 B.C.E. many species of large animals in the Americas were well on the road to extinction. To survive, some human communities supplemented the foods they gathered with fish and small game. Others turned to agriculture, and they gave rise to the first complex societies in the Americas.

# The Olmecs

EARLY AGRICULTURE IN MESOAMERICA    By 8000 to 7000 B.C.E. the peoples of Mesoamerica—the region from the central portion of modern Mexico to Honduras and El Salvador—had begun to experiment with the cultivation of beans, chili peppers, avocados, squashes, and gourds. By 4000 B.C.E. they had discovered the agricultural potential of maize, which soon became the staple food of the region. Later they added tomatoes to the crops they cultivated. Agricultural villages appeared soon after 3000 B.C.E., and by 2000 B.C.E. agriculture had spread throughout Mesoamerica.

Early Mesoamerican peoples had a diet rich in cultivated foods, but most large animals of the western hemisphere were not susceptible to domestication. For that reason, Mesoamericans were unable to harness animal energy as did the peoples of the eastern hemisphere. As a result, human laborers prepared fields for cultivation, and human porters carried trade goods on their backs. Mesoamericans had no need for wheeled vehicles, which would have been useful only if draft animals had been available to pull them.

CEREMONIAL CENTERS    Toward the end of the second millennium B.C.E., the tempo of Mesoamerican life quickened as elaborate ceremonial centers with monumental pyramids, temples, and palaces arose alongside the agricultural villages. These were not cities like those that existed in the eastern hemisphere, because only members of the ruling elite, priests, and those who tended to their needs were permanent residents. Instead, most people lived in surrounding villages and gathered in the ceremonial centers only on special occasions or on market days.

OLMECS: THE "RUBBER PEOPLE"    The earliest known ceremonial centers of the ancient Americas appeared on the coast of the Gulf of Mexico, near the modern Mexican city of Veracruz, and they served as the nerve center of the Olmecs, the first complex society of the Americas. Historians and archaeologists have systematically studied Olmec society only since the 1940s, and many questions about them remain unanswered. Even their proper name is unknown: the term *Olmec* (meaning "rubber people") did not come from the ancient people themselves but derives instead from the rubber trees that flourish in the region they inhabited. Nevertheless, some of the basic features of Olmec society have become reasonably clear, and it is certain that Olmec cultural traditions influenced all complex societies of Mesoamerica until the arrival of European peoples in the sixteenth century C.E.

The first Olmec ceremonial center arose about 1200 B.C.E. on the site of the modern town of San Lorenzo, and it served as their capital for some four hundred years. When the influence of San Lorenzo waned, leadership passed to new ceremonial centers at La Venta (800–400 B.C.E.) and Tres Zapotes (400–100 B.C.E.). These sites defined the heartland of Olmec society, where agriculture produced rich harvests. The entire region receives

**Mesoamerica** (mez-oh-uh-MER-i-kuh)

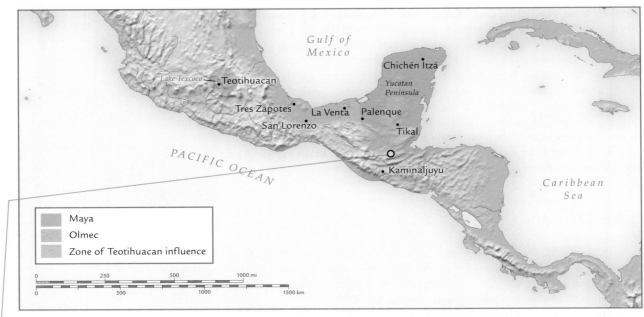

**Note how much larger Maya society was than Teotihuacan or the earlier Olmec society.**

**MAP 4.1** | Early Mesoamerican societies, 1200 B.C.E.–1100 C.E. Describe the different geographical settings of the early Mesoamerican societies represented here. Consider the extent to which geographical and environmental conditions influenced the historical development and daily life of these societies.

abundant rainfall; so, like the Harappans, the Olmecs constructed elaborate drainage systems to divert waters that otherwise might have flooded their fields or destroyed their settlements.

Olmec altar from La Venta
www.mhhe.com/
bentleybrief2e

**OLMEC SOCIETY** Olmec society was probably authoritarian in nature. Common subjects delivered a portion of their harvests for the maintenance of the elite classes living in the ceremonial centers and provided labor for large-scale construction projects. Indeed, untold thousands of laborers were required to build the temples, pyramids, altars, sculptures, and tombs that characterized each Olmec ceremonial center.

Common subjects also provided appropriate artistic adornment for the elites in Olmec capitals. The most distinctive artistic creations of the Olmecs were colossal human heads—possibly likenesses of rulers—sculpted from basalt rock. The largest of these sculptures stands 3 meters (almost 10 feet) tall and weighs some twenty tons. In the absence of draft animals and wheels, human laborers had to move rocks to the ceremonial centers. The largest sculptures required the services of about one thousand laborers.

**TRADE IN JADE AND OBSIDIAN** Olmec influence extended to much of the central and southern regions of modern Mexico and beyond to modern Guatemala and El Salvador. The Olmecs spread their influence partly by military force, but trade was a prominent link between the Olmec heartland and the other regions of Mesoamerica. Indeed, the Olmecs obtained both jade and obsidian—used for decorative objects and for cutting tools, respectively—from distant regions in the interior of Mesoamerica.

Among the many mysteries surrounding the Olmecs, one of the most perplexing concerns the decline and fall of their society. The Olmecs systematically destroyed their ceremonial centers at both San Lorenzo and La Venta and then deserted the sites. Archaeologists study-

**La Venta** (lah BEHN-tah)

**Tres Zapotes** (TRACE-zah-POE-tace)

ing those sites found statues broken and buried, monuments defaced, and the capitals themselves burned. Although intruders may have ravaged the ceremonial centers, many scholars believe that the Olmecs deliberately destroyed their capitals, perhaps because of civil conflicts or doubts about the effectiveness and legitimacy of the ruling classes. In any case, Olmec society collapsed and disappeared by about 100 B.C.E.

# Heirs of the Olmecs: The Maya

During the thousand years following the Olmecs' disappearance about 100 B.C.E., complex societies arose in several Mesoamerican regions and carried on many of the legacies of the Olmecs. Human population grew dramatically, and ceremonial centers cropped up at sites far removed from the Olmec heartland. Some of them evolved into genuine cities that attracted large populations of permanent residents and encouraged increasing specialization of labor. Networks of long-distance trade linked the new urban centers and extended their influence to all parts of Mesoamerica. Within the cities themselves, priests devised written languages and compiled a body of astronomical knowledge. In short, Mesoamerican societies developed in a manner roughly parallel to that of their counterparts in the eastern hemisphere.

OLMEC COLOSSAL HEAD. | This particular head was carved from basalt rock between 1000 and 600 B.C.E. and discovered at La Venta. Olmecs carved similar heads for their ceremonial centers at San Lorenzo and Tres Zapotes. *In the absence of wheeled vehicles, how could human laborers have moved these enormous sculptures?*

THE MAYA    The earliest heirs of the Olmecs were the Maya, who created a remarkable society in the region now occupied by southern Mexico, Guatemala, Belize, Honduras, and El Salvador. Although Maya society originally appeared in the fertile Guatemalan highlands beginning in the third century B.C.E., after the fourth century C.E. it flourished mostly in the poorly drained Mesoamerican lowlands, where thin, tropical soils quickly lost their fertility. To enhance the agricultural potential of their region, the Maya built terraces designed to trap silt carried by the numerous rivers passing through the lowlands. By artificially retaining rich earth, they dramatically increased the agricultural productivity of their lands. They harvested maize in abundance, and they also cultivated cotton, from which they wove fine textiles highly prized both in their own society and by trading partners in other parts of Mesoamerica. Maya cultivators also raised cacao, the large bean that is the source of chocolate. Cacao was a precious commodity consumed mostly by nobles in Maya society. They whisked powdered cacao into water to create a stimulating beverage, and they sometimes even ate the bitter cacao beans as snacks. The product was so valuable that the Maya used cacao beans as money.

Drawing of a Maya fortress city
www.mhhe.com/
bentleybrief2e

TIKAL    The Maya organized themselves politically into scores of small city-kingdoms. From about 300 to 900 C.E., the Maya built more than eighty large ceremonial centers in the lowlands—all with pyramids, palaces, and temples—as well as numerous smaller settlements. Some of the larger centers attracted dense populations and evolved into genuine cities. Foremost among them was Tikal, the most important Maya political center between the fourth and ninth centuries C.E. At its height, roughly 600 to 800 C.E., Tikal was a wealthy and bustling city with a population approaching forty thousand. It boasted enormous paved plazas and scores of temples, pyramids, palaces, and public buildings. The Temple of the Giant Jaguar, a stepped pyramid rising sharply to a height of 47 meters (154 feet), dominated the skyline and represented Tikal's control over the surrounding region, which had a population of about five hundred thousand.

MAYA WARFARE    The Maya kingdoms fought constantly with one another. Victors generally destroyed the peoples they defeated and took over their ceremonial centers, but the purpose of Maya warfare was not so much to kill enemies as to capture them in hand-to-hand combat on the battlefield. Warriors won enormous prestige when they brought back important captives from neighboring kingdoms. Ultimately, most captives ended their lives either as slaves or as sacrificial victims to Maya gods. High-ranking captives

Tikal (tee-KAHL)

in particular often underwent ritual torture and sacrifice in public ceremonies on important occasions.

**CHICHÉN ITZÁ** Bitter conflicts between small kingdoms were a source of constant tension in Maya society. Only about the ninth century C.E. did the state of Chichén Itzá in the northern Yucatan peninsula seek to construct a larger society by integrating captives into their own society instead of killing them. Some captives refused the opportunity and went to their deaths as proud warriors, but many agreed to recognize the authority of Chichén Itzá. Between the ninth and eleventh centuries C.E., Chichén Itzá organized a loose empire that brought a measure of political stability to the northern Yucatan.

**MAYA DECLINE** By about 800 B.C.E., however, most Maya populations had begun to desert their cities. Within a century Maya society was in full decline everywhere except the northern Yucatan, where Chichén Itzá continued to flourish. Historians have suggested many possible causes of the decline, including invasion, internal dissension and civil war, failure of the system of water control, ecological problems caused by destruction of the forests, the spread of epidemic diseases, and natural catastrophes such as earthquakes. Possibly several problems combined to destroy Maya society. It is likely that debilitating civil conflict and excessive siltation of agricultural terraces caused particularly difficult problems for the Maya. In any case, the population declined, the people abandoned their cities, and long-distance trade came to a halt. Meanwhile, the tropical jungles of the lowlands encroached on human settlements and gradually smothered the cities, temples, pyramids, and monuments of a once-vibrant society.

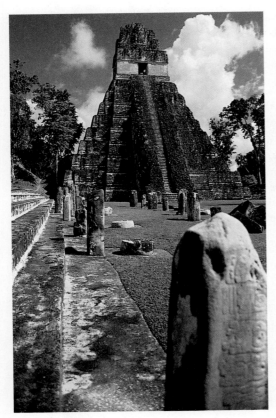

**MAYA TEMPLE OF THE GIANT JAGUAR.** | This temple, built in the city of Tikal, served as the funerary pyramid for Lord Cacao, a prominent Maya ruler of the late sixth and early seventh centuries C.E. *What kind of message might a monument of this size have been trying to convey?*

## *Maya Society and Religion*

In addition to kings and ruling families, Maya society included a large class of priests who maintained an elaborate calendar and transmitted knowledge of writing, astronomy, and mathematics. A hereditary nobility owned most land and cooperated with the kings and the priests by organizing military forces and participating in religious rituals. Maya merchants also came from the ruling and noble classes, because they served not only as traders but also as ambassadors to neighboring lands and allied peoples. Maya society also generated several other distinct social classes. Professional architects and sculptors oversaw construction of large monuments and public buildings. Artisans specialized in the production of pottery, tools, and cotton textiles. Finally, large classes of peasants and slaves fed the entire society and provided physical labor for the construction of cities and monuments.

Building on the achievements of their Olmec predecessors, Maya priests studied astronomy and mathematics, and they devised both a sophisticated calendar and an elaborate system of writing. They understood the movements of heavenly bodies well enough to plot planetary cycles and to predict eclipses of the sun and the moon. They invented the concept of zero and used a symbol to represent zero mathematically, which facilitated their manipulation of large numbers. By combining their astronomical and mathematical observations, Maya priests calculated the length of the solar year at 365.242 days—about seventeen seconds shorter than the figure reached by modern astronomers.

**THE MAYA CALENDAR** Maya priests constructed the most elaborate calendar of the ancient Americas, which reflected a powerful urge to identify meaningful cycles of time. The Maya calendar interwove two kinds of year: a solar year of 365 days governed the agricultural cycle, and a ritual year of 260 days governed daily affairs by organizing time into twenty "months" of 13 days apiece. The Maya believed that each day derived certain specific characteristics from its position in both the solar and the ritual calendar and that the combined attributes of each day would determine the fortune of activities undertaken on that day. It took fifty-two years for the two calendars to work through all possible combinations of days and return simultaneously to their respective starting points. Maya priests carefully studied the various opportunities and dangers that would come together on a given day in hopes that they could determine which activities were safe to initiate. The Maya attributed especially great significance to the fifty-two-year periods in which the two calendars ran. They believed that the end of a cycle would bring monumental changes and that ultimately the world would end after one such cycle.

MAYA WRITING    The Maya also expanded on the Olmec tradition of written inscriptions. In doing so they created the most flexible and sophisticated of all the early American systems of writing. The Maya script contained both ideographic elements (like Chinese characters) and symbols for syllables. Scholars have begun to decipher this script only since the 1960s, and it has become clear that writing was just as important to the Maya as it was to early complex societies in the eastern hemisphere. Most Maya writing survives today in the form of inscriptions on temples and monuments, because sixteenth-century Spanish conquerors and missionaries destroyed untold numbers of books in hopes of undermining native religious beliefs. Today only four books of the ancient Maya survive, all dealing with astronomical and calendrical matters.

MAYA RELIGIOUS THOUGHT    Surviving inscriptions and other writings shed considerable light on Maya religious and cultural traditions. The *Popol Vuh,* a Maya creation myth, taught that the gods had created human beings out of maize and water, the ingredients that became human flesh and blood. Thus Maya religious thought reflected the fundamental role of agriculture in their society, much like religious thought in early complex societies of the eastern hemisphere. Maya priests also taught that the gods kept the world going and maintained the agricultural cycle in exchange for honors and sacrifices performed for them by human beings.

BLOODLETTING RITUALS    The most important of those sacrifices involved the shedding of human blood, which the Maya believed would prompt the gods to send rain to water their crops of maize. Some bloodletting rituals centered on war captives. Before sacrificing the victims by decapitation, their captors cut off the ends of their fingers or lacerated their bodies so as to cause a copious flow of blood in honor of the gods. Yet the Maya also frequently and voluntarily shed their own blood as a means of displaying reverence to their gods.

THE MAYA BALL GAME    Apart from the calendar and sacrificial rituals, the Maya also inherited a distinctive ball game from the Olmecs. The game usually involved teams of two to four members apiece. Its object was for players to score points by propelling a rubber ball through a ring or onto a marker without using their hands. The Maya used a solid rubber ball about 20 centimeters (8 inches) in diameter, which was both heavy and hard. Players needed great dexterity and skill to maneuver it accurately using only their feet, legs, hips, torso, shoulders, or elbows. The game was extremely popular: almost all Maya ceremonial centers, towns, and cities had stone-paved courts on which players performed publicly.

The Maya played the ball game for several reasons. Sometimes individuals competed for sporting purposes, and sometimes the game was used as a ritual that honored the conclusion of treaties. High-ranking captives often engaged in forced public competition in which the stakes were their very lives: losers became sacrificial victims and faced torture and execution immediately following the match. Alongside some ball courts were skull racks that bore the decapitated heads of losing players. Thus Maya concerns to please the gods by shedding human blood extended even to the realm of sport.

*Popol Vuh* (paw-pawl vuh)

**MAYA STONE RELIEF SCULPTURE.** In this relief, a Maya king from Yaxchilán (between Tikal and Palenque in the southern Yucatan peninsula) holds a torch over a woman from the royal family as she draws a thorn-studded rope through a hole in her tongue, so as to shed her blood in honor of the Maya gods.

Mayan ball court
www.mhhe.com/
bentleybrief2e

## The *Popol Vuh* on the Creation of Human Beings

*The* Popol Vuh *outlines traditional Maya views on the creation of the world and human beings. The version of the work that survives today dates from the mid–sixteenth century, but it reflects beliefs of a much earlier era. According to the* Popol Vuh, *the gods wanted to create intelligent beings that would recognize and praise them. Three times they tried to fashion such beings out of animals, mud, and wood, but without success. Then they decided to use maize and water as their ingredients.*

And here is the beginning of the conception of humans, and of the search for the ingredients of the human body. So they spoke, the [gods] Bearer, Begetter, the Makers, Modelers named Sovereign Plumed Serpent:

"The dawn has approached, preparations have been made, and morning has come for the provider, nurturer, born in the light, begotten in the light. Morning has come for humankind, for the people of the face of the earth," they said. It all came together as they went on thinking in the darkness, in the night, as they searched and they sifted, they thought and they wondered.

And here their thoughts came out in clear light. They sought and discovered what was needed for human flesh. . . . Broken Place, Bitter Water Place is the name: the yellow corn, white corn came from there. . . .

And these were the ingredients for the flesh of the human work, the human design, and the water was for the blood. It became human blood, and corn was also used by the Bearer, Begetter. . . .

And then the yellow corn and white corn were ground, and Xmucane did the grinding nine times. Corn was used, along with the water she rinsed her hands with, for the creation of grease; it became human fat when it was worked by the Bearer, Begetter, Sovereign Plumed Serpent, as they are called. . . .

It was staples alone that made up their flesh.

These are the names of the first people who were made and modeled.

This is the first person: Jaguar Quitze.

And now the second: Jaguar Night.

And now the third: Mahucutah.

And the fourth: True Jaguar.

And these are the names of our first mother-fathers. They were simply made and modeled, it is said; they had no mother and no father. We have named the men by themselves. No woman gave birth to them, nor were they begotten by the builder, sculptor, Bearer, Begetter. By sacrifice alone, by genius alone they were made, they were modeled by the Maker, Modeler, Bearer, Begetter, Sovereign Plumed Serpent. And when they came to fruition, they came out human:

They talked and they made words.

They looked and they listened.

They walked, they worked. . . .

And then their wives and women came into being. Again, the same gods thought of it. It was as if they were asleep when they received them, truly beautiful women were there with Jaguar Quitze, Jaguar Night, Mahucutah, and True Jaguar. With their women there they became wider awake. Right away they were happy at heart again, because of their wives.

Celebrated Seahouse is the name of the wife of Jaguar Quitze.

Prawn House is the name of the wife of Jaguar Night.

Hummingbird House is the name of the wife of Mahucutah.

Macaw House is the name of the wife of True Jaguar.

So these are the names of their wives, who became ladies of rank, giving birth to the people of the tribes, small and great.

■ Discuss the extent to which this account of human creation reflects the influences on Maya society of both agriculture and the untamed natural world.

SOURCE: Dennis Tedlock, trans. *Popol Vuh: The Definitive Edition of the Mayan Book of the Dawn of Life and the Glories of Gods and Kings.* New York: Simon and Schuster, 1985, pp. 163–65, 167.

## *Heirs of the Olmecs: Teotihuacan*

While the Maya flourished in the Mesoamerican lowlands, a different society arose to the north in the highlands of Mexico. For most of human history, the valley of central Mexico, situated some two kilometers (more than a mile) above sea level, was the site of several large lakes fed by the waters coming off the surrounding mountains. Although environmental changes have caused most of the lakes to disappear, in earlier times their abundant supplies of freshwater, fish, and waterfowl attracted human settlers.

The earliest settlers in the valley of Mexico channeled some of the waters from the mountain streams into their fields and established a productive agricultural society. The earliest center of this society was the large and bustling city of Teotihuacan, located about 50 kilometers (31 miles) northeast of modern Mexico City.

**THE CITY OF TEOTIHUACAN**   Teotihuacan was probably a large agricultural village by 500 B.C.E., but by the end of the millennium its population approached fifty thousand. By the year 100 C.E., the city's two most prominent monuments, the colossal pyramids of the sun and the moon, dominated the skyline. The Pyramid of the Sun is the largest single structure in Mesoamerica. It occupies nearly as much space as the pyramid of Khufu in Egypt, though it stands only half as tall. At its high point, about 400 to 600 C.E., Teotihuacan was home to almost two hundred thousand inhabitants, a thriving metropolis with scores of temples, several palatial residences, neighborhoods with small apartments for the masses, busy markets, and hundreds of workshops for artisans and craftsmen.

Detail from Teotihuacan
www.mhhe.com/
bentleybrief2e

The organization of a large urban population, along with the hinterland that supported it, required a recognized source of authority. Unfortunately, scholars have little information about the character of that authority, since books and written records from the city did not survive. Yet paintings and murals suggest that Teotihuacan was a theocracy of sorts. Priests figure prominently in the works of art, and scholars interpret many figures as representations of deities.

**THE SOCIETY OF TEOTIHUACAN**   Apart from rulers and priests, Teotihuacan's population included cultivators, artisans, and merchants. Artisans of Teotihuacan were especially famous for their obsidian tools and fine orange pottery. Professional merchants traded the products of Teotihuacan throughout Mesoamerica, from the region of modern Guatemala City in the south to Durango and beyond in the north.

Until about 500 C.E. there was little sign of military organization in Teotihuacan. The city did not have defensive walls, and works of art rarely depicted warriors. Yet the influence of Teotihuacan extended to much of modern Mexico and beyond. Apparently, the city's influence derived less from military might than from its ability to produce fine manufactured goods that appealed to consumers in distant markets.

Teotihuacan (tay-oh-tee-wa-KAHN)

**CULTURAL TRADITIONS** Like the Maya, the residents of Teotihuacan built on cultural foundations established by the Olmecs. They played the ball game, adapted the Olmec calendar to their own uses, and expanded the Olmecs' graphic symbols into a complete system of writing. Unfortunately, because their books have all perished, it is impossible to know exactly how they viewed the world and their place in it. Works of art suggest that they recognized an earth god and a rain god, and it is certain that they carried out human sacrifices during their religious rituals.

**DECLINE OF TEOTIHUACAN** Teotihuacan began to experience increasing military pressure from other peoples about 500 C.E. About the middle of the eighth century, invaders sacked and burned the city, destroying its books and monuments. After that catastrophe most residents deserted Teotihuacan, and the city slowly fell into ruin.

# EARLY SOCIETIES OF SOUTH AMERICA

By about 12,000 B.C.E. hunting and gathering peoples had made their way across the narrow isthmus of Central America and into South America. Those who migrated into the region of the northern and central Andes mountains hunted deer, llama, alpaca, and other large animals. Both the mountainous highlands and the coastal regions below benefited from a cool and moist climate that provided natural harvests of squashes, gourds, and wild potatoes. Beginning about 8000 B.C.E., however, the climate of this whole region became increasingly warm and dry, and the changes placed pressure on natural food supplies. To maintain their numbers, the human communities of the region began to experiment with agriculture. Here, as elsewhere, agriculture encouraged population growth, the establishment of villages and cities, the building of states, and the elaboration of organized cultural traditions. During the centuries after 1000 B.C.E., the central Andean region generated complex societies parallel to those of Mesoamerica.

## *Early Andean Society and the Chavín Cult*

Although they were exact contemporaries, early Mesoamerican and Andean societies developed largely independently. Geography discouraged the establishment of communications between the Andean region and Mesoamerica because neither society possessed abundant pack animals or a technology to facilitate long-distance transportation. Although some agricultural products and technologies diffused slowly from one area to the other, neither the Andes mountains nor the lowlands of modern Panama and Nicaragua offered an attractive highway linking the two regions.

Geography made even communications within the central Andean region difficult. Deep valleys crease the western flank of the Andes mountains as rivers drain waters from the highlands to the Pacific Ocean, so transportation and communication between the valleys have always been very difficult. Nevertheless, powerful Andean states sometimes overcame the difficulties and influenced human affairs over a broad geographical range.

Most of the early Andean heartland came under cultivation between 2500 and 2000 B.C.E. The coastal regions probably developed complex societies first, since cultivators there experienced abundant harvests as a result of crops such as beans, peanuts, and sweet potatoes, and supplemented them with the rich marine life of the Pacific Ocean. Settlements likely appeared somewhat later in the Andean highlands, but it is clear that potatoes were being cultivated in the region after about 2000 B.C.E. By 1800 B.C.E. peoples in all the Andean regions had begun to fashion distinctive styles of pottery and to build temples and pyramids in large ceremonial centers.

A ceramic effigy of a shaman
www.mhhe.com/ bentleybrief2e

**MAP 4.2** | Early societies of Andean South America, 1000 B.C.E.–700 C.E. The early societies of Andean South America occupied long, narrow territories between the Andes Mountains and the Pacific Ocean. *Why did these societies not occupy territories to the east?*

Caribbean Sea

Orinoco River

Equator

Napo R.

Amazon River

PACIFIC OCEAN

Chavín de Huántar

ANDES MOUNTAINS

Lake Titicaca

Moche and Chimu

Huari

Tiahuanaco

0      050      1000 mi

0      1000      2000 km

**Early Andean societies had to cope with extremely mountainous territories.**

**THE CHAVÍN CULT**    Shortly after the year 1000 B.C.E., a new religion appeared in the central Andes. The Chavín cult, which enjoyed enormous popularity during the period 900 to 800 B.C.E., spread through most of the territory occupied by modern Peru and then vanished about 300 B.C.E. Although scholars do not understand the precise significance of the cult, it is clear that Andean society became increasingly complex during this period. Weavers devised techniques of producing elaborate, intricately patterned cotton textiles. Artisans manufactured large, light, and strong fishnets from cotton string. Craftsmen experimented with minerals and discovered techniques of gold, silver, and copper metallurgy and used them to make jewelry as well as small tools.

**EARLY CITIES**    There is no evidence to suggest that Chavín cultural and religious beliefs led to the establishment of a state or any organized political order. Indeed, they probably inspired the building of ceremonial centers rather than the making of true cities. As the population increased and society became more complex, however, cities began to appear shortly after the disappearance of the Chavín cult. Beginning about 200 B.C.E. large cities emerged at the modern-day sites of Huari, Pucara, and Tiahuanaco. Each of these early Andean cities had a population exceeding ten thousand, and each also featured large public buildings, ceremonial plazas, and extensive residential districts.

## Early Andean States: Mochica

Along with cities there appeared regional states. The earliest Andean states arose in the many valleys on the western side of the mountains. These states emerged when conquerors unified the valleys and organized them into integrated societies. They coordinated the building of irrigation systems so that the lower valleys could support intensive agriculture, and they established trade and exchange networks that tied the highlands, the central valleys, and the coastal regions together. Each region contributed its own products to the larger economy of the valley: from the highlands came potatoes, llama meat, and alpaca wool; the central valleys supplied maize, beans, and squashes; and the coasts provided sweet potatoes, fish, and cotton.

**THE MOCHICA STATE**    Because early Andean societies did not make use of writing, their beliefs, values, and ways of life remain largely hidden. Surviving fortifications as well as art suggest that early Andean states relied heavily on arms to introduce order and maintain stability within their realms. In addition, art from the early Andean state of Mochica—which dominated the coasts and valleys of northern Peru from about 300 to 700 C.E.—offers a detailed and expressive depiction of early Andean society in all its variety. Most Mochica art survives in the form of pottery vessels, many of which depict individuals' heads or represent the major gods and various subordinate deities and demons. Most interesting, perhaps, are those that illustrate scenes in the everyday life of the Mochica people: warriors leading captives bound by ropes, women working in a textile factory under the careful eye of a supervisor, and beggars looking for handouts on a busy street. Even in the absence of writing, Mochica artists left abundant evidence of a complex society with considerable specialization of labor.

 **Moche corn goddess** www.mhhe.com/ bentleybrief2e

**MOCHICA ARTWORK.**
Many Mochica pots portray human figures and often depict distinctive characteristics of individuals or typical scenes from daily life. This pot represents two women helping a man who consumed a little too much maize beer.

Mochica was only one of several large states that dominated the central Andean region during the first millennium C.E. Although they integrated the regional economies of the various Andean valleys, none of these early states was able to impose order on the entire region or even to dominate a portion of it for very long. The exceedingly difficult geographical barriers posed by the Andes mountains presented challenges that ancient technology and social organization simply could not meet. As a result, at the end of the first millennium C.E., Andean society exhibited regional differences much sharper than those of Mesoamerica and early complex societies in the eastern hemisphere.

# EARLY SOCIETIES OF OCEANIA

Human migrants entered Australia and New Guinea at least 60,000 years ago, and possibly earlier than that. They arrived in watercraft—probably canoes fitted with sails—but because of the low sea levels of that era, the migrants did not have to cross large stretches of open ocean. These earliest inhabitants of Oceania also migrated—perhaps over land when sea levels were still low—to the Bismarcks, the Solomons, and other small island groups near New Guinea. Beginning about 5,000 years ago, seafaring peoples from southeast Asia settled the northern coast of New Guinea and then ventured farther and established communities in the island groups of the western Pacific Ocean. By the middle centuries of the first millennium C.E., their descendants had established communities in all the habitable islands of the Pacific Ocean.

## Early Societies in Australia and New Guinea

Human migrants reached Australia and New Guinea long before any people had begun to cultivate crops or keep herds of domesticated animals. As a result, the earliest inhabitants of Australia and New Guinea lived by hunting and gathering. Once rising seas covered the land bridge connecting Australia and New Guinea about 10,000 years ago, however, human societies in each area followed radically different paths. While the aboriginal peoples of Australia continued as hunting and gathering societies, in New Guinea communities turned to agriculture: beginning about 3000 B.C.E. the cultivation of root crops such as yams and taro and the keeping of pigs and chickens spread rapidly throughout the island.

### EARLY HUNTING AND GATHERING SOCIETIES IN AUSTRALIA
Like hunting and gathering peoples elsewhere, the aboriginal Australians lived in small, mobile communities that undertook seasonal migrations in search of food. Over the centuries, they learned to exploit the resources of the various ecological regions of Australia. Plant foods, including fruits, berries, roots, nuts, seeds, shoots, and green leaves, constituted the bulk of their diet. To supplement their plant-based diet, they used axes, spears, clubs, nets, lassos, snares, and boomerangs to bring down animals ranging in size from rats to giant kangaroos, which grew to a height of 3 meters (almost 10 feet), and to catch fish, waterfowl, and small birds.

### AUSTRONESIAN PEOPLES  In New Guinea, seafaring peoples from southeast Asia introduced agriculture to the island about 5,000 years ago when they began to establish trading and settlement communities on the northern coast. These sail-

**Mochica** (moh-CHEE-kah)

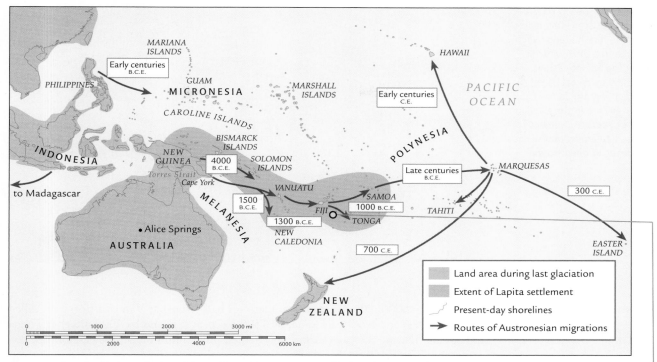

**MAP 4.3** | Early societies of Oceania, 1500 B.C.E.–700 C.E. Notice the routes that Austronesian migrants followed. *What technologies enabled Austronesian peoples to travel so widely and to maintain an extensive communication and exchange network in the western and central regions of the Pacific Ocean?*

**Note how many centuries it took for humans to populate most of the islands in the Pacific Ocean.**

ors spoke Austronesian languages (whose modern relatives include Malayan, Indonesian, and Polynesian) and were highly skilled in seafaring technologies. They sailed the open ocean in large canoes equipped with outriggers, which stabilized their craft and reduced the risks of long voyages. By paying close attention to winds, currents, stars, cloud formations, and other natural indicators, they learned how to find distant lands reliably and return home safely.

**EARLY AGRICULTURE IN NEW GUINEA**  Austronesian seafarers came from societies that depended on the cultivation of root crops and the herding of animals. When they settled in New Guinea, they introduced yams, taro, pigs, and chickens to the island, and the indigenous peoples themselves soon followed suit. Within a few centuries agriculture and herding had spread to all parts of New Guinea. There, as in other lands, agriculture brought population growth and specialization of labor: after the change to agriculture, permanent settlements, pottery, and carefully crafted tools appeared throughout the island.

## The Peopling of the Pacific Islands

**AUSTRONESIAN MIGRATIONS TO POLYNESIA**  Austronesian-speaking peoples possessed a sophisticated maritime technology as well as agricultural expertise, and they established human settlements in the islands of the Pacific Ocean. Their outrigger canoes enabled them to sail safely over long distances of open ocean, and their food crops and domesticated animals enabled them to establish agricultural societies in the islands. Once they had established coastal settlements in New Guinea, Austronesian seafarers sailed easily to the Bismarck and Solomon islands east of New Guinea. From there they undertook exploratory voyages that led them to previously unpopulated islands.

Stone heads, Easter Island
www.mhhe.com/
bentleybrief2e

By about 1500 B.C.E. Austronesian mariners had arrived at Vanuatu (formerly called New Hebrides) and New Caledonia, by 1300 B.C.E. at Fiji, and by 1000 B.C.E. at Tonga and Samoa. During the late centuries of the first millennium B.C.E., they established settlements in Tahiti and the Marquesas. From there they launched ventures that took them to the most remote outposts of Polynesia, which required them to sail over thousands of nautical miles of blue water. They reached the islands of Hawai`i in the early centuries C.E., Easter Island by 300 C.E., and the large islands of New Zealand by 700 C.E.

### AUSTRONESIAN MIGRATIONS TO MICRONESIA AND MADAGASCAR

While one branch of the Austronesian-speaking peoples populated the islands of Polynesia, other branches sailed in different directions. From the Philippines some ventured to the region of Micronesia, which includes small islands and atolls such as the Mariana, Caroline, and Marshall islands of the western Pacific. Others looked west from their homelands in Indonesia, sailed throughout the Indian Ocean, and became the first human settlers of the large island of Madagascar off the east African coast.

### THE LAPITA PEOPLES

The earliest Austronesian migrants to sail out into the blue water of the Pacific Ocean and establish human settlements in Pacific islands are known as the Lapita peoples. No one knows what they called themselves: the name Lapita comes from a beach in New Caledonia where some of the earliest recognizable Lapita artifacts came to the attention of archaeologists. It is clear, however, that between about 1500 and 500 B.C.E., Lapita peoples maintained communication and exchange networks throughout a large region extending about 4,500 kilometers (2,800 miles) from New Guinea and the Bismarck Archipelago to Samoa and Tonga.

Wherever they settled, Lapita peoples established agricultural villages where they raised pigs and chickens and introduced the suite of crops they inherited from their Austronesian ancestors. They supplemented their crops and domesticated animals with fish and seaweed from nearby waters, and they soon killed off most of the large land animals and birds that were suitable for human consumption. They left abundant evidence of their presence in the form of their distinctive pottery decorated with stamped geometric designs.

For about 1,000 years, Lapita peoples maintained extensive networks of trade and communication across vast stretches of open ocean. Their agricultural settlements were largely self-sufficient, but they placed high value on some objects from distant islands. Their pottery was a principal item of long-distance exchange, as was high-quality obsidian, which

**Lapita** (lah-PEE-tah)

they sometimes transported over thousands of kilometers, since it was available at only a few sites of Lapita settlement. Other trade items brought to light by archaeologists include shell jewelry and stone tools. Indeed, it is clear that, like their counterparts in other regions of the world, the earliest inhabitants of the Pacific islands maintained regular contacts with peoples well beyond their own societies.

CHIEFLY POLITICAL ORGANIZATION  After about 500 B.C.E. Lapita trade networks fell into disuse, probably because the various Lapita settlements had grown large enough that they could supply their own needs. By the middle part of the first millennium B.C.E., Lapita and other Austronesian peoples had established hierarchical chiefdoms in the Pacific islands. Contests for power and influence between ambitious subordinates frequently caused tension and turmoil, but the possibility of migration offered an alternative to conflict. Indeed, the spread of Austronesian peoples throughout the Pacific islands came about partly because of population pressures and conflicts that encouraged small parties to seek fresh opportunities in more hospitable lands.

Over the longer term, descendants of Lapita peoples built strong, chiefly societies, particularly on large islands with relatively dense populations, such as those of the Tongan, Samoan, and Hawaiian groups. In Hawai`i, for example, militarily skilled chiefs cooperated closely with priests, administrators, soldiers, and servants in ruling their districts. Chiefs and their retinues claimed a portion of the agricultural surplus produced by their subjects, and they sometimes required subjects to deliver additional products, such as fish, birds, or timber. Chiefs and their administrators also vied with the ruling classes of neighboring districts, led public ritual observances, and oversaw irrigation systems that watered the taro plants that were crucial to the survival of Hawaiian society. Eventually, the chiefly and aristocratic classes became so entrenched and powerful that they regarded themselves as divine or semidivine, and the law of the land prohibited common subjects from even gazing directly at them.

THINKING ABOUT *Encounters*

**ENCOUNTERS IN EARLY SOCIETIES IN THE AMERICAS AND OCEANIA.** Although all of the early complex societies in the Americas and Oceania engaged in long-distance trade with neighboring societies, it seems clear that such interactions were more difficult to sustain over the long term than they were in the complex societies of Africa and Eurasia. What factors contributed to these difficulties? What might the existence of such interactions—despite such difficulties—tell us about early complex societies more generally?

## SUMMARY

Very little writing survives to illuminate the historical development of early societies in the Americas and Oceania. Thus it is impossible to offer the sort of richly detailed account of their political organization, social structures, and cultural traditions that historians commonly provide for societies of the eastern hemisphere. Nevertheless, it is clear that migrations to the Americas and Oceania represented continuations of population movements that began with *Homo erectus* and early *Homo sapiens,* resulting eventually in the establishment of human communities in almost all habitable parts of the earth. Moreover, it is clear that the earliest inhabitants of the Americas and Oceania built productive and vibrant societies whose development roughly paralleled that of their counterparts in the eastern hemisphere. Many communities depended on an agricultural economy, and with their surplus production they supported dense populations, engaged in specialized labor, established formal political authorities, constructed hierarchical social orders, carried on long-distance trade, and formed distinctive cultural traditions. The early historical development of the Americas and Oceania demonstrates once again the tendency of agriculture to encourage human communities to construct ever more elaborate and complex forms of social organization.

# STUDY TERMS

Austronesian peoples (78)
bloodletting rituals (73)
cacao (71)
Chavín cult (76)
Chichén Itzá (72)
colossal heads (71)
Lapita peoples (80)
La Venta (70)

maize (71)
Maya (71)
Maya ball game (73)
Mesoamerica (69)
Mochica (77)
Oceania (78)
Olmecs (69)

*Popul Vuh* (73)
San Lorenzo (70)
Temple of the Giant Jaguar (71)
Teotihuacan (74)
Tikal (71)
Tres Zapotes (70)
Yucatan (67)

# FOR FURTHER READING

Robert McC. Adams. *The Evolution of Urban Society.* Chicago, 1966. Provocative analysis comparing the development of Mesopotamian and Mesoamerican societies by a leading archaeologist.

Ignacio Bernal. *Mexico before Cortez: Art, History, and Legend.* Trans. by W. Barnstone. Garden City, 1963. Judicious survey by a leading student of ancient Mesoamerica.

Geoffrey Blainey. *Triumph of the Nomads: A History of Aboriginal Australia.* Melbourne, 1975. A sympathetic account of Australia before European arrival, well informed by archaeological discoveries.

Michael D. Coe. *The Maya.* 4th ed. London, 1987. Well-illustrated popular account by one of the world's leading scholars of the Maya.

David Freidel, Linda Schele, and Joy Parker. *Maya Cosmos: Three Thousand Years on the Shaman's Path.* New York, 1993. Fascinating investigation of Maya conceptions of the world and their continuing influence in the present day.

K. R. Howe. *The Quest for Origins: Who First Discovered and Settled the Pacific Islands?* Honolulu, 2003. Reviews the numerous theories advanced to explain the arrival of human populations and the establishment of human societies in the remote islands of the Pacific Ocean.

Jesse D. Jennings, ed. *The Prehistory of Polynesia.* Cambridge, Mass., 1979. Brings together essays by prominent scholars on Polynesia before the arrival of Europeans in the Pacific Ocean.

Friedrich Katz. *The Ancient American Civilizations.* Trans. by K. M. L. Simpson. New York, 1972. Detailed survey that compares the experiences of Mesoamerica and Andean South America.

Charles C. Mann. *1491: New Revelations of the Americas before Columbus.* New York, 2006. Summarizes a great deal of archaeological research on the pre-Columbian Americas.

Michael E. Mosley. *The Incas and Their Ancestors: The Archaeology of Peru.* Rev. ed. London, 2001. A comprehensive survey of Andean history through the era of the Incas.

Linda Schele and Mary Ellen Miller. *The Blood of Kings: Dynasty and Ritual in Maya Art.* New York, 1986. A richly illustrated volume that explores Maya society through works of art and architecture as well as writing.

Dennis Tedlock, trans. *Popol Vuh: The Definitive Edition of the Mayan Book of the Dawn of Life and the Glories of Gods and Kings.* New York, 1985. The best translation of the *Popol Vuh,* with an excellent introduction.

# Bringing It All Together

## Part I | The Early Complex Societies, 3500 to 500 B.C.E.

As we have seen in chapters 1–4, early complex societies—whether in Mesopotamia, Egypt, India, China, or the Americas—shared certain common features. This is because all of these societies were responding to similar pressures: in the areas where prosperous agricultural communities grew large enough to develop into cities, each sought to secure protection from outsiders, to establish and maintain internal order, and to ensure the maintenance of property and wealth among the groups who prospered most from settled urban life. The responses to these common pressures resulted, in each case, to the development of political authorities, warrior groups, class and social distinctions, religious and philosophical beliefs, and systems of education.

Furthermore, early complex societies interacted with neighboring peoples for purposes of trade, war, conquest, or intermarriage. Although these encounters with outsiders were more extensive and ranged over longer dis-

tances in early Mesopotamia, Egypt, India, and China than in either Mesoamerica, the Andes, or Oceania, they nevertheless made important contributions to all of the early complex societies. In some cases, as in early India, these interactions contributed to changes in the religious worldview of the Aryans; in others, as in early Egypt and Mesoamerica, they facilitated the exchange of luxury trade items over long distances. Indeed, material items, technologies, and ideas regularly flowed both into and out of the early complex societies. Thus, connections and encounters between peoples were important to the development of early complex societies from their beginnings.

While all of the early complex societies developed common features and responded to similar pressures, they obviously did not turn out exactly alike. Rather, each developed political structures, cultural beliefs, social customs, and economic systems that reflected unique local and regional conditions. For example, although each of the societies discussed in chapters 1–4 sought ways to maintain internal order and to conceptualize the meaning of life and death, the ways they did so were quite different: Indian society developed the caste system, Chinese society emphasized the importance of family and ancestor worship, and Mesoamerican societies sought to re-create the cycle of life through ritual sacrifice. Thus, despite important similarities between early complex societies, it is equally important to explore the rich variety of traditions that developed in response to the needs and pressures of urban agricultural life in distant parts of the world.

# II

# The Formation of Classical Societies, 500 B.C.E. to 500 C.E.

UNIFICATION OF CHINA (CH. 6)

SILK ROAD CULTURAL EXCHANGE (CH. 9)

CLASSICAL INDIA (CH. 7)

PERSIAN EMPIRES (CH. 5)

GREEK AND ROMAN SOCIETY (CH. 8)

In the millennium between about 500 B.C.E. and 500 C.E., several early complex societies achieved particularly high degrees of internal organization, extended their authority over extremely large regions, and elaborated especially influential cultural traditions. Because their legacies have endured so long and have influenced the ways that literally billions of people have led their lives, historians often refer to them as classical societies.

Although the classical societies of Persia, China, India, and the Mediterranean differed from one another in many ways, they all shared several common challenges. One such challenge was that of administering vast territories without advanced technologies of transportation and communication. To meet that challenge, classical rulers standardized systems of governance, law, and taxation; built roads and transportation networks; and encouraged trade and communication between the sometimes far-flung regions under their authority. In some cases, rulers also encouraged the people under their influence to adopt particular religious, social, or cultural beliefs and practices as a way of promoting unity within their realms.

Most of the classical societies were also aggressively expansionist. As a result, their leaders were prepared to use powerful armies to conquer new areas, to fend off the advances of competing states, and to quell rebellion within their own territories. Indeed, one of the central problems most classical societies faced was how to balance the need to create loyalty and unity among their diverse subjects with the realities of authoritarian, foreign, and often unwanted rule. Heavy taxation and stiff labor requirements were particularly distasteful to many subjects of the classical societies, and these sometimes contributed to rebellions and civil wars that threatened the very survival of the societies themselves.

Another shared feature of all the classical societies was that each sponsored and maintained a vast system of roads and ports, which resulted in a dramatic increase in long-distance trade. This trade encouraged economic integration within and between societies, and various regions came to depend on one another for agricultural products and manufactured items. In fact, long-distance trade was such an important feature of the classical societies that a well-established network of land and sea routes, known collectively as the silk roads, linked lands as distant as China and Europe.

Finally, all the classical societies generated sophisticated cultural and religious traditions that offered guidance on moral, religious, political, and social issues. Because of the extensive trade networks that linked distant regions, many of these traditions spread along the trade routes and shaped peoples and cultures in societies far from their origin. Thus, even though each of the classical societies adopted outside traditions selectively, for most of the classical period cultural borrowing was more widespread than it had been in the period of the early complex societies.

Accelerated interaction also carried the seeds of disintegration because disease pathogens travelled the trade routes alongside people, goods, and ideas. In the second and third centuries C.E., epidemic diseases afflicted most societies along the silk roads, disrupting long-distance trade and creating severe social unrest. As a result, many societies turned inward and sacrificed long-distance connections for local and regional concerns.

Over the centuries since the height of their influence, many of the specific political, social, economic, and cultural features of the classical societies have disappeared. Yet their legacies deeply influenced future societies and in many ways continue to influence the lives of the world's peoples. Appreciation of the legacies of classical societies is thus crucial to understanding the world's historical development.

# The Empires of Persia

## 5

The Greek historian Herodotus relished a good story, and he related many a tale about the Persian empire and its conflicts with other peoples, including Greeks. One story had to do with a struggle between Cyrus, leader of the expanding Persian realm, and Croesus, ruler of the powerful and wealthy kingdom of Lydia in southwestern Anatolia (modern Turkey). Croesus noted the growth of Persian influence with concern and asked the Greek oracle at Delphi whether to go to war against Cyrus. The oracle responded that an attack on Cyrus would destroy a great kingdom.

Overjoyed, Croesus lined up his allies and prepared for war. In 546 B.C.E. he provoked Cyrus to engage the formidable Lydian cavalry. The resulting battle was hard fought but inconclusive. Because winter was approaching, Croesus disbanded his troops and returned to his capital at Sardis, expecting Cyrus to retreat as well. But Cyrus was a vigorous and unpredictable warrior, and he pursued Croesus to Sardis. When he learned of the pursuit, Croesus hastily assembled an army to confront the invaders. Cyrus threw it into disarray, however, by advancing a group of warriors mounted on camels, which spooked the Lydian horses and sent them into headlong flight. Cyrus's army then surrounded Sardis and took the city after a siege of only two weeks. Croesus was taken captive and afterward became an advisor to Cyrus. Herodotus could not resist pointing out that events proved the Delphic oracle right: Croesus's attack on Cyrus did indeed lead to the destruction of a great kingdom—his own.

The victory over Lydia was a major turning point in the development of the Persian empire. Lydia had a reputation as a kingdom of fabulous wealth, partly because it conducted maritime trade with Greece, Egypt, and Phoenicia as well as overland trade with Mesopotamia and Persia. Lydian wealth and resources gave Cyrus tremendous momentum as he extended Persian authority to new lands and built the earliest of the vast imperial states of classical times.

Classical Persian society began to take shape during the sixth century B.C.E. when warriors conquered an enormous region from the Indus River to Egypt and southeastern Europe. Indeed, the very size of the Persian empire created political and administrative problems for its rulers. Once they solved those problems, however, a series of Persian-based empires governed much of the territory between India and the Mediterranean Sea for more than a millennium—from the mid–sixth century B.C.E. until the early seventh century C.E.—and brought centralized political organization to many distinct peoples living over vast geographic spaces.

❮ *Gold plaque depicting a figure who was perhaps a priest in Achaemenid times.*

**Cyrus** (SIGH-ruhs)
**Croesus** (CREE-suhs)

# CHRONOLOGY

| | |
|---|---|
| 7th–6th centuries B.C.E. (?) | Life of Zarathustra |
| 558–330 B.C.E. | Achaemenid dynasty |
| 558–530 B.C.E. | Reign of Cyrus the Achaemenid |
| 521–486 B.C.E. | Reign of Darius |
| 334–330 B.C.E. | Invasion and conquest of the Achaemenid empire by Alexander of Macedon |
| 323–83 B.C.E. | Seleucid dynasty |
| 247 B.C.E.–224 C.E. | Parthian dynasty |
| 224–651 C.E. | Sasanid dynasty |

In organizing their realm, Persian rulers relied heavily on Mesopotamian techniques of administration, but they also created institutions and administrative procedures of their own. In addition, they invested resources in the construction of roads and highways to improve communications and mobility across the empire. As a result of those efforts, central administrators were able to send instructions throughout the empire, dispatch armies in times of turmoil, and ensure that local officials would carry out imperial policies.

The organization of the vast territories embraced by the classical Persian empires had important social, economic, and cultural implications. Because high agricultural productivity allowed more people to work at tasks other than cultivation, classes of bureaucrats, administrators, priests, craftsmen, and merchants increased in number. Meanwhile, social extremes between the wealthy and the poor became more pronounced. In addition, good roads across the empire allowed Persian society to serve as a commercial and cultural bridge between Indian and Mediterranean societies. As a result, Persia became an important link in long-distance trade networks as well as a conduit for the exchange of philosophical and religious ideas. Indeed, Persian religious traditions inspired religious thinkers subject to Persian rule and deeply influenced Judaism, Christianity, and Islam.

# THE RISE AND FALL OF THE PERSIAN EMPIRES

The empires of Persia arose in the arid land of Iran. For centuries Iran had developed under the shadow of the wealthier and more productive Mesopotamia to the west while absorbing migrations and invasions of nomadic peoples coming out of central Asia. During the sixth century B.C.E., rulers of the province of Persia in southwestern Iran embarked on a series of conquests that resulted in the formation of an enormous empire. For more than a millennium, four ruling dynasties—the Achaemenids (558–330 B.C.E.), the Seleucids (323–83 B.C.E.), the Parthians (247 B.C.E.–224 C.E.), and the Sasanids (224–651 C.E.)—maintained a continuous tradition of imperial rule in much of southwest Asia.

## *The Achaemenid Empire*

Achaemenid and Seleucid empires
www.mhhe.com/bentleybrief2e

**THE MEDES AND THE PERSIANS**   The origins of classical Persian society trace back to the late stages of Mesopotamian society. During the centuries before 1000 B.C.E., two closely related Indo-European peoples known as the Medes and the Persians migrated from central Asia to Persia, where they lived in loose subjection to the Babylonian and Assyrian empires. The Medes and the Persians shared many cultural traits with their distant cousins the Aryans, who had migrated into India. Like the Aryans, they were mostly pastoralists, although they also practiced a limited amount of agriculture. They also possessed considerable military power: like other Indo-Europeans, they were skilled equestrians and expert archers. They also organized themselves by clans rather than by states, although they did recognize leaders who collected taxes and delivered tribute to their Mesopotamian overlords.

**CYRUS'S CONQUESTS**   When the Assyrian and Babylonian empires weakened in the sixth century B.C.E., the Medes and the Persians launched their first bid for empire in the person of Cyrus the

**Achaemenid** (ah-KEE-muh-nid)

**Medes** (meeds)

**MAP 5.1** | The Achaemenid and Seleucid empires, 558–83 B.C.E. Compare the size of the Achaemenid empire to the earlier Mesopotamian and Egyptian empires discussed in chapters 1 and 2. *What role did the Royal Road and other highways play in the maintenance of the Achaemenid empire?*

**Darius's empire stretched 3,000 km from East to West.**

Achaemenid (reigned 558–530 B.C.E.). Cyrus proved to be a tough, wily leader and an outstanding military strategist, whose conquests laid the foundation for the first Persian empire. In 558 B.C.E. Cyrus became king of the Persian tribes, which he ruled from his mountain fortress at Pasargadae. In 553 B.C.E. he initiated a rebellion against his Median overlord, whom he crushed within three years. By 548 B.C.E. he had brought all of Iran under his control, and he began to look for opportunities to expand. In 546 B.C.E., as we know, he conquered the powerful kingdom of Lydia in Anatolia. Between 545 B.C.E. and 539 B.C.E. he campaigned in central Asia and Bactria (modern Afghanistan). In a swift campaign of 539 B.C.E., he seized Babylonia, whose vassal states immediately recognized him as their lord. Within twenty years Cyrus went from minor regional king to ruler of an empire that stretched from India to the borders of Egypt. Had he lived long enough, Cyrus no doubt would have mounted a campaign against Egypt, the largest and wealthiest neighboring state outside his control. But in 530 B.C.E. he fell, mortally wounded, while protecting his northeastern frontier from nomadic raiders.

DARIUS  Cyrus's empire survived and expanded during the reigns of his successors. His son Cambyses (reigned 530–522 B.C.E.) conquered Egypt in 525 B.C.E. His younger kinsman Darius (reigned 521–486 B.C.E.) then extended the empire both east and west. Indeed, Darius's armies pushed into northwestern India as far as the Indus River, absorbing the northern Indian kingdom of Gandhara, while also capturing Thrace, Macedonia, and the western coast of the Black Sea in southeastern Europe. By the late sixth century B.C.E., Darius presided over an empire stretching some 3,000 kilometers (1,865 miles) from the Indus River in the east to the Aegean Sea in the west and 1,500 kilometers (933 miles) from Armenia in the north to the first cataract of the Nile River in the south. With

**Pasargadae** (pah-SAR-gah-dee)

**RUINS OF PERSEPOLIS.**
This image shows the imperial reception hall and palaces. Try to imagine the size and grandeur of the buildings these columns supported.

a population of some thirty-five million, Darius's realm was by far the largest empire the world had yet seen.

Yet Darius was more important as an administrator than as a conqueror. Governing a far-flung empire of so many ethnic groups, languages, and traditions was a much more difficult challenge than conquering it. To maintain their empire, the Achaemenids needed to establish lines of communication with all parts of their realm and design institutions that would enable them to administer their territories efficiently. Their solutions not only made it possible for the Achaemenid empire to survive but also pioneered administrative techniques that would outlast their own dynasty and influence political life in southwestern Asia for centuries to come.

The palace at Persepolis
www.mhhe.com/
bentleybrief2e

**PERSEPOLIS**   Soon after his rise to power, Darius began to centralize his administration. About 520 B.C.E. he started to build a new capital of astonishing magnificence at Persepolis. Darius intended Persepolis to serve not only as an administrative center but also as a monument to the Achaemenid dynasty. From the time of Darius to the end of the Achaemenid dynasty in 330 B.C.E., Persepolis served as the nerve center of the Persian empire—a resplendent capital bustling with advisors, ministers, diplomats, scribes, accountants, translators, and bureaucratic officers of all descriptions. Even today, massive columns and other ruins bespeak the grandeur of Darius's capital.

**ACHAEMENID ADMINISTRATION: THE SATRAPIES**   The government of the Achaemenid empire depended on a finely tuned balance between central initiative and local administration. Like their Mesopotamian predecessors, the Achaemenids appointed governors to serve as agents of the central administration and oversee affairs in the various regions. Darius divided his realm into twenty-three administrative and taxation districts he called satrapies, with each governed by an official satrap. Yet the Achaemenids did not try to push direct rule on their subjects: although most satraps were Persian, the Achaemenids recruited local officials to fill almost all other administrative posts.

**Cambyses** (kam-BIE-sees)
**Aegean** (ih-GEE-an)
**Persepolis** (per-SEP-uh-lis)

The Achaemenid rulers employed two strategies to discourage distant satraps from allying with local groups or trying to become independent of Achaemenid authority. First, each satrapy had a contingent of military officers and tax collectors who served as checks on the satraps' power and independence. Second, the rulers created a new category of officials—essentially imperial spies—known as "the eyes and ears of the king." These agents traveled throughout the empire with their own military forces, conducting surprise audits of accounts and procedures in the provinces and collecting intelligence reports. Taken together, these two strategies helped prevent the vast Achaemenid empire from splitting into a series of independent kingdoms.

**TAXATION AND LAW**   Darius also sought to improve administrative efficiency by regularizing tax levies and standardizing laws. Instead of exacting irregular tribute payments from subject lands as his predecessors had done, Darius instituted regular, formal tax levies. Each satrapy was now required to pay a set quantity of silver to the imperial court every year. To simplify the process, Darius issued standardized coins—a move that also fostered trade throughout his empire. Equally important, beginning in 520 B.C.E., Darius also sought to bring the many legal systems of his empire closer to a single standard. The point was not to abolish the existing laws of individual lands or peoples to impose a uniform law code on his entire empire. Rather, Darius wished to codify the laws of his subject peoples, modifying them when necessary to harmonize them with the legal principles observed in the empire as a whole.

**ROADS AND COMMUNICATIONS**   Alongside administrative and legal policies, the Achaemenid rulers took other measures to knit their far-flung realm into a coherent whole. They built good roads across their realm, notably the Persian Royal Road, which stretched some 2,575 kilometers (1,600 miles) from the Aegean port of Ephesus to Sardis in Anatolia, through Mesopotamia along the Tigris River, to Susa in Iran, with an extension to Pasargadae and Persepolis. Caravans took some ninety days to travel this road, lodging at inns along the well-policed route.

The imperial government also organized a courier service and built 111 postal stations at intervals of 40 to 50 kilometers (25 to 30 miles) along the Royal Road. Each station kept a supply of fresh horses, enabling couriers to speed from one end of the Royal Road to the other in a week's time. The Achaemenids also improved existing routes between Mesopotamia and Egypt, and they built a new road between Persia and the Indus River to link the imperial center with the satrapy of Gandhara in northwestern India. In addition to improving communications, these roads facilitated trade, which helped to integrate the empire's various regions into a larger economy.

## Decline and Fall of the Achaemenid Empire

**THE ACHAEMENID COMMONWEALTH**   The Achaemenids' roads and administrative machinery enabled them to govern a vast empire and extend Persian influences throughout their territories. Persian concepts of law and justice administered by trained imperial officials linked peoples from the Mediterranean Sea to the Indus River in a larger Persian society. Political stability made it possible to undertake enormous public works projects such as the construction of *qanat* (underground canals), which led to enhanced agricultural production and population growth. Iron metallurgy spread to all parts of the empire, and by the end of the Achaemenid dynasty, iron tools were common in Persian agricultural communities. Peoples in the various regions of the Achaemenid empire maintained their ethnic identities, but all participated in a larger Persian commonwealth.

Eventually, however, difficulties between rulers and subject peoples undermined the integrity of the empire. Cyrus and Darius both consciously pursued a policy of toleration

satraps (SAY-traps)

*qanat* (kah-NAHT)

**STONE CARVING FROM PERSEPOLIS.** | This carving shows an enthroned Darius (with his son Xerxes standing behind him) receiving a high court official, as incense burners perfume the air. *What purpose might the formality of this reception have served?*

Darius enthroned with Xerxes behind him
www.mhhe.com/
bentleybrief2e

in administering their vast multicultural empire: they took great care to respect the values and cultural traditions of the peoples they ruled. In Mesopotamia, for example, they portrayed themselves not as Persian conquerors but, rather, as legitimate Babylonian rulers and representatives of Marduk, the patron deity of Babylon. Cyrus also won high praise from Jews in the Achaemenid empire, since he allowed them to return to Jerusalem and rebuild the temple that Babylonian conquerors had destroyed in 586 B.C.E.

Darius's successor, Xerxes (reigned 486–465 B.C.E.), retreated from this policy of toleration, however, flaunted his Persian identity, and sought to impose his own values on conquered lands. That policy caused enormous ill will, especially in Mesopotamia and Egypt, where peoples with their own cultural traditions resented Xerxes' pretensions. Although Xerxes successfully repressed rebellions against his rule in Mesopotamia and Egypt, resentment of Persian conquerors continued to fester, and it caused serious problems for the later Achaemenids.

**THE PERSIAN WARS** In fact, efforts to control their ethnic Greek subjects helped to bring about the collapse of the Achaemenid empire. Ethnic Greeks inhabited many of the cities in Anatolia—particularly in the region of Ionia on the Aegean coast of western Anatolia—and they maintained close economic and commercial ties with their cousins in the peninsula of Greece. The Ionian Greeks fell under Persian domination during the reign of Cyrus. They became restive under Darius's Persian governors who oversaw their affairs, and in 500 B.C.E. the Ionian cities rebelled, expelled or executed their governors, and asserted their independence. Their rebellion launched a series of conflicts known as the Persian Wars (500–479 B.C.E.).

The conflict between the Ionian Greeks and the Persians expanded considerably when the cities of peninsular Greece sent fleets to aid their kinsmen in Ionia. Darius managed to put down the rebellion and reassert Achaemenid authority, but he and his successors became entangled in a difficult and ultimately destructive effort to extend their authority to the Greek peninsula. Indeed, after some initial successes against the Greeks, the Persians suffered a rout at the battle of Marathon (490 B.C.E.), and they returned home without achieving their goals. Ten years later, in 480 B.C.E., a renewed Persian attempt to conquer the Greek cities ended in costly defeats for the Persians. Thereafter, for almost 150 years the Persian empire continued to spar intermittently with the Greek cities without achieving victory.

**ALEXANDER OF MACEDON** The standoff ended with the rise of Alexander of Macedon, often called Alexander the Great (discussed more fully in chapter 8). In 334 B.C.E. Alexander invaded Persia with an army of some forty-eight thousand tough, battle-hardened Macedonians. Though far smaller than the Persian army in numbers, the well-disciplined Macedonians carried heavier arms and employed more sophisticated military tactics than their opponents. As a result, they sliced through the Persian empire and dealt their adversaries a series of devastating defeats. In 331 B.C.E. Alexander shattered Achaemenid forces at the battle of Gaugamela, and within a year the empire founded by Cyrus had dissolved.

Alexander led his forces into Persepolis and proclaimed himself heir to the Achaemenid rulers. After a brief season of celebration, Alexander and his forces ignited a blaze—perhaps intentionally—that destroyed Persepolis. The conflagration was so great that when archaeologists first began to explore the ruins of Persepolis in the eighteenth century, they found layers of ash and charcoal up to 1 meter (3 feet) deep.

The Achaemenid empire had crumbled, but its legacy was by no means exhausted. Alexander portrayed himself in Persia and Egypt as a legitimate successor of the Achaemenids who observed their precedents and deserved their honors. He retained the Achaemenid administrative structure, and he even confirmed the appointments of many satraps and other officials. As it happened, Alexander had little time to enjoy his conquests, because he died in 323 B.C.E. after a brief effort to extend his empire to India. But the states that succeeded him—the Seleucid, Parthian, and Sasanid empires—continued to employ a basically Achaemenid structure of imperial administration.

**ALEXANDER OF MACEDON.** Tetradrachm of Kingdom of Thrace with head of deified Alexander the Great, struck under Lysimachos. *Photograph © 2010 Museum of Fine Arts, Boston.*

# The Seleucid, Parthian, and Sasanid Empires

**THE SELEUCIDS** After Alexander died, his chief generals carved his empire into three large realms, which they divided among themselves. The choicest realm, which included most of the former Achaemenid empire, went to Seleucus (reigned 305–281 B.C.E.), who had commanded an elite corps of guards in Alexander's army. Like Alexander, Seleucus and his successors retained the Achaemenid systems of administration and taxation as well as the imperial roads and postal service. The Seleucids also founded new cities throughout the realm and attracted Greek colonists to occupy them. These new cities greatly stimulated trade and economic development both within the Seleucid empire and beyond.

As foreigners, the Seleucids faced opposition from native Persians. Satraps often revolted against Seleucid rule and tried to establish their independence. The Seleucids soon lost their holdings in northern India, and the seminomadic Parthians progressively took over Iran during the third century B.C.E. The Seleucids continued to rule a truncated empire until 83 B.C.E., when Roman conquerors put an end to their empire.

**THE PARTHIANS** Meanwhile, the Parthians established themselves as lords of a powerful empire based in Iran that they extended to Mesopotamia. The Parthians had occupied the region of eastern Iran around Khurasan since Achaemenid times. They retained many of the customs and traditions of nomadic peoples from the steppes of central Asia. They did not have a centralized government, for example, but organized themselves into a federation of clans. They were also skillful warriors, accustomed to defending themselves against constant threats from nomadic peoples farther east.

As they settled and turned increasingly to agriculture, the Parthians discovered that they could resist nomadic invasions better by feeding their horses on alfalfa during the winter. The alfalfa allowed the animals to grow much larger and stronger than the small horses and ponies of nomadic peoples who had to forage on the steppes in winter. The larger Parthian horses could then support heavily armed warriors outfitted with metal armor, which served as an effective shield against the arrows

**Macedon** (MAS-ih-don)

**Gaugamela** (GAW-guh-mee-luh)

**Seleucids** (sih-LOO-sihds)

**THINKING ABOUT** *Traditions*

**TRADITIONS IN THE EMPIRES OF PERSIA.** One of the problems of the Achaemenids, Seleucids, Parthians, and Sasanids was that some of the peoples each empire conquered strongly resented what they viewed as rule by foreigners. At times, such resentment contributed to the toppling of one empire for another. How did the Persian-based empires try to balance the imposition of their rule from above with the cultural and ethnic identities of the people they conquered, and why did this balance sometimes fail?

**PARTHIAN SCULPTURE.**
Gold sculpture of a nomadic horseman discharging an arrow. This figurine dates from the fifth or fourth century B.C.E. and might well represent a Parthian.

A coin with Mithradates I
www.mhhe.com/
bentleybrief2e

of the steppe nomads. Indeed, few existing forces could stand up to Parthian heavy cavalry.

As early as the third century B.C.E., the Parthians began to wrest their independence from the Seleucids. The Parthian satrap revolted against his Seleucid overlord in 238 B.C.E., and during the following decades his successors gradually enlarged their holdings. Mithradates I, the Parthians' greatest conqueror, came to the throne about 171 B.C.E. and transformed his state into a mighty empire. By about 155 B.C.E. he had consolidated his hold on Iran and had also extended Parthian rule to Mesopotamia.

PARTHIAN GOVERNMENT    The Parthians portrayed themselves as enemies of the foreign Seleucids and as restorers of rule in the Persian tradition. To some extent that characterization was accurate. The Parthians largely followed the example of the Achaemenids in structuring their empire: they governed through satraps, employed Achaemenid techniques of administration and taxation, and built a lavish capital city. But the Parthians also retained elements of their own steppe traditions. For example, they did not develop nearly as centralized a regime as the Achaemenids or the Seleucids but, rather, vested a great deal of authority and responsibility in their clan leaders. These men—who frequently served as satraps—could be troublesome, because they frequently rebelled against the imperial government from their regional bases.

For about three centuries the Parthians presided over a powerful empire between India and the Mediterranean. Beginning in the first century C.E., they faced pressure in the west from the expanding Roman empire. On three occasions in the second century C.E., Roman armies captured the Parthian capital at Ctesiphon. Combined with internal difficulties caused by rebellious satraps, Roman pressure contributed to the weakening of the Parthian state. During the early third century C.E., internal rebellion brought it down.

THE SASANIDS    Once again, though, the tradition of imperial rule continued, this time under the Sasanids, who came from Persia and claimed direct descent from the Achaemenids. The Sasanids toppled the Parthians in 224 C.E. and ruled until 651 C.E., re-creating much of the splendor of the Achaemenid empire. From their cosmopolitan capital at Ctesiphon, the Sasanid "king of kings" provided strong rule from Parthia to Mesopotamia. Sasanid merchants traded actively with peoples to both the east and the west, and they introduced into Iran the cultivation of crops such as rice, sugarcane, citrus fruits, eggplant, and cotton that came west over the trade routes from India and China.

During the reign of Shapur I (239–272 C.E.), the Sasanids stabilized their western frontier and created a series of buffer states between themselves and the Roman empire. After Shapur, the Sasanids did not expand militarily but entered into a standoff relationship with the Kushan empire in the east and the Roman and Byzantine empires in the west. None of those large empires was strong enough to overcome the others, but they contested border areas and buffer states, sometimes engaging in lengthy and bitter disputes that sapped the energies of all involved.

These continual conflicts seriously weakened the Sasanid empire in particular. The empire came to an end in 651 C.E. when Arab warriors killed the last Sasanid ruler, overran his realm, and incorporated it into their rapidly expanding Islamic empire. Yet even conquest by external invaders did not end the legacy of classical Persia, since Arab conquerors adopted Persian administrative techniques and cultural traditions for their own use in building a new Islamic society.

**Mithradates** (mihth-rah-DAY-teez)
**Ctesiphon** (TES-uh-phon)
**Sasanids** (suh-SAH-nids)

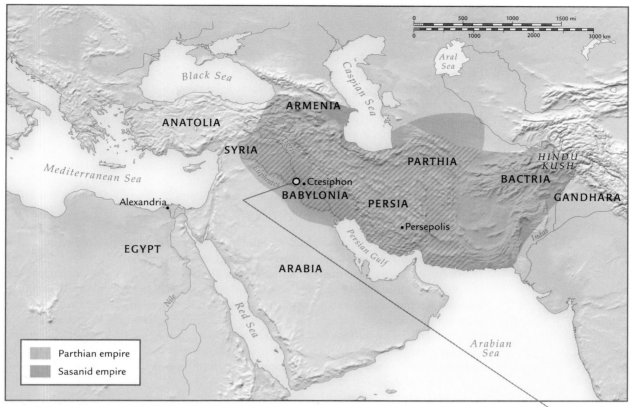

**MAP 5.2** | The Parthian and Sasanid empires, 247 B.C.E.–651 C.E. Note the location of the Parthian and Sasanid empires between the Mediterranean Sea and northern India. *What roles did these two empires play in facilitating or hindering communications between lands to their east and west?*

Ctesiphon was the capital of both the Parthian and Sasanid empires.

# IMPERIAL SOCIETY AND ECONOMY

Throughout the eastern hemisphere during the classical era, public life and social structure became much more complicated than they had been during the days of the early complex societies. Centralized imperial governments needed large numbers of administrative officials, which led to the emergence of educated classes of bureaucrats. Stable empires also enabled many individuals to engage in trade or other specialized labor. Some of these individuals accumulated vast wealth, which led to increased distance and tensions between rich and poor. Meanwhile, slavery became more common than in earlier times. The prominence of slavery had to do partly with the expansion of imperial states, which often enslaved conquered foes, but it also reflected the increasing gulf between rich and poor, which placed such great economic pressure on some individuals that they had to give up their freedom in order to survive. All these developments had implications for the social structures of classical societies in Persia as well as China, India, and the Mediterranean basin.

## Social Development in Classical Persia

During the early days of the Achaemenid empire, Persian society reflected its nomadic steppe origins. When the Medes and the Persians migrated to Iran, their social structure was very similar to that of the Aryans in India, consisting primarily of warriors, priests, and peasants. Family and clan relationships were extremely important in the organization of Persian political and social affairs. Male warriors headed the clans, which retained much of their influence long after the establishment of the Achaemenid empire.

IMPERIAL BUREAUCRATS    The development of a cosmopolitan empire and the requirements of imperial administration, however, called for a new class of educated bureaucrats, who to a large extent undermined the position of the old warrior elite. Although the bureaucrats did not directly challenge the patriarchal warriors, their crucial role in running the day-to-day affairs of the empire guaranteed them a prominent and comfortable place in Persian society. By the time of the later Achaemenids and the Seleucids, Persian cities were home to masses of administrators, tax collectors, and record keepers. The bureaucracy even included a substantial corps of translators, who facilitated communications among the empire's many linguistic groups. Imperial survival depended on these literate professionals, and high-ranking bureaucrats came to share power and influence with warriors and clan leaders.

FREE CLASSES    The bulk of Persian society consisted of free individuals such as artisans, craftspeople, farmers, merchants, and low-ranking civil servants. Priests and priestesses were also prominent urban residents, along with servants who maintained the temple communities in which they lived. In Persian society, as in earlier Mesopotamian societies, members of the free classes participated in religious observances conducted at local temples, and they had the right to share in the income that temples generated from their agricultural operations and from craft industries such as textile production that the temples organized. The weaving of textiles was mostly the work of women, who received rations of grain, wine, beer, and sometimes meat from the imperial and temple workshops that employed them.

In the countryside the free classes included peasants who owned land as well as landless cultivators who worked on properties owned by the state, temple communities, or other individuals. Free residents of rural areas had the right to marry and move as they wished, and they could seek better opportunities in the cities or in military service. The Persian empires embraced a great deal of parched land that received little rainfall, and free residents of the countryside contributed much of the labor that went into the building and maintenance of irrigation systems. Most remarkable of those systems were underground canals known as *qanat,* which allowed cultivators to distribute water to fields without losing large quantities to evaporation through exposure to the sun and open air. Numerous *qanat* crisscrossed the Iranian plateau in the heartland of the Persian empire, where extreme scarcity of water justified the enormous investment of human labor required to build the canals.

SLAVES    A large class of slaves also worked in both the cities and the countryside. Individuals passed into slavery by two main routes. Most were prisoners of war who became slaves as the price of survival. Other slaves came from the ranks of free subjects who accumulated debts that they could not satisfy. In the cities, for example, merchants, artisans, and craftsmen borrowed funds to purchase goods or open shops, while in the countryside small farmers facing competition from large-scale cultivators borrowed against their property and liberty to purchase tools, seed, or food. Failure to repay those debts in a timely fashion often forced the borrowers not only to forfeit their property but also to sell their children, their spouses, or themselves into slavery.

## Economic Foundations of Classical Persia

Agriculture was the economic foundation of classical Persian society. Like other classical societies, Persia needed large agricultural surpluses to support military forces and administrative specialists as well as residents of cities who were artisans, crafts workers, and merchants rather than cultivators. The Persian empires embraced several regions of exceptional fertility—notably Mesopotamia, Egypt, Anatolia, and northern India—and they prospered by mobilizing the agricultural surpluses of those lands.

**AGRICULTURAL PRODUCTION**     Barley and wheat were the grains cultivated most commonly in the Persian empires. Peas, lentils, mustard, garlic, onions, cucumbers, dates, apples, pomegranates, pears, and apricots supplemented the cereals in diets throughout Persian society, and beer and wine were the most common beverages. In most years agricultural production far exceeded the needs of cultivators, making sizable surpluses available for sale in the cities or for distribution to state servants through the imperial bureaucracy. Vast quantities of produce flowed into the imperial court from state-owned lands. Even though they are incomplete, surviving records show that in 500 B.C.E., during the middle period of Darius's reign, the imperial court received almost eight hundred thousand liters of grain, quite apart from vegetables, fruits, meat, poultry, fish, oil, beer, wine, and textiles. Officials distributed some of this produce to the imperial staff as wages in kind, but much of it also found its way into the enormous banquets that Darius organized for as many as ten thousand guests.

**TRADE**     Agriculture was the foundation of the Persian economy, but long-distance trade grew rapidly during the course of the Persian empires and linked lands from India to Egypt in a vast commercial zone. Each region of the Persian empire contributed particular products to the imperial economy, from the gold and ivory of India to the semiprecious stones of Iran, and from the metals of Anatolia to the textiles and grain of Egypt. Several conditions promoted the growth of trade: the relative political stability maintained by the Persian empires, the general prosperity of the realm, the use of standardized coins, and the availability of good trade routes, including long-established routes, newly constructed highways such as the Persian Royal Road, and sea routes through the Red Sea, the Persian Gulf, and the Arabian Sea. Markets operated regularly in all the larger cities of the Persian empires, and the largest cities, such as Babylon, also were home to banks and companies that invested in commercial ventures.

Long-distance trade of this sort became especially prominent during the reigns of Alexander of Macedon and his Seleucid successors. The cities they established and the colonists they attracted stimulated trade throughout the whole region from the Mediterranean to northern India. Indeed, Greek migrants facilitated cultural as well as commercial exchanges by encouraging the mixing and mingling of religious faiths, art styles, and philosophical speculation throughout the Persian realm.

# THINKING ABOUT
## *Encounters*

**ENCOUNTERS IN THE EMPIRES OF PERSIA.** Between the mid–sixth century B.C.E. and the early seventh century C.E., Persian-based empires ruled a variety of diverse peoples and territories between India and the Mediterranean Sea. What effects did these empires have on the movement of people and goods across their territories, and how did such movement alter or modify the ways people thought about themselves and others?

# RELIGIONS OF SALVATION IN CLASSICAL PERSIAN SOCIETY

Cross-cultural influences were especially noticeable in the development of Persian religion. Persians came from the family of peoples who spoke Indo-European languages, and their earliest religion closely resembled that of the Aryans of India. During the classical era, however, the new faith of Zoroastrianism emerged and became widely popular in Iran and to a lesser extent also in the larger Persian empires. Zoroastrianism reflected the cosmopolitan society of the empires, and it profoundly influenced the beliefs and values of Judaism, Christianity, and Islam.

## Zarathustra and His Faith

The earliest Persian religion recognized many of the same gods as the ancient Aryans, and their priests performed sacrifices similar to those conducted by the brahmins in India. Like the Aryans, the ancient Persians glorified strength and martial virtues, and the cults of both peoples sought principally to bring about a comfortable material existence for their practitioners.

ZARATHUSTRA    During the classical era Persian religion underwent considerable change, as moral and religious thinkers sought to adapt their messages to the circumstances of a complex, cosmopolitan society. One result was Zoroastrianism, which emerged from the teachings of Zarathustra. Though Zarathustra was undoubtedly a historical person, little certain information survives about his life and career. It is not even clear when he lived, though most scholars date his life to the late seventh and early sixth centuries B.C.E. He came from an aristocratic family, and he probably was a priest who became disenchanted with the traditional religion. In any case, when he was about twenty years old, Zarathustra left his family and home in search of wisdom. After about ten years of travel, he experienced a series of visions and became convinced that the supreme god, whom he called Ahura Mazda (the "wise lord"), had chosen him to serve as his prophet and spread his message.

THE GATHAS    Like his life, Zarathustra's doctrine remains largely unknown, since many of the earliest Zoroastrian teachings were not preserved in writing. Only during the Seleucid dynasty did Zoroastrian priests, known as *magi*, begin to preserve religious texts in writing, and only under the Sasanids did they compile their scriptures in a holy book known as the *Avesta*. Nevertheless, many of Zarathustra's own compositions survive because of the diligence by which magi preserved them through oral transmission. Known as the *Gathas*, Zarathustra's works were hymns that he composed in honor of the various deities that he recognized. Apart from the *Gathas*, ancient Zoroastrian literature included a wide variety of hymns, liturgical works, and treatises on moral and theological themes. Though some of these works survive, the arrival of Islam in the seventh century C.E. and the subsequent decline of Zoroastrianism resulted in the loss of most of the Avesta and later Zoroastrian works.

ZOROASTRIAN TEACHINGS    Zarathustra and his followers were not strict monotheists. They recognized Ahura Mazda as a supreme deity and the creator of all good things, but Zarathustra also praised six lesser deities in the *Gathas*. Furthermore, he believed that Ahura Mazda engaged in a cosmic conflict with an independent adversary, an evil and malign spirit known as Angra Mainyu (the "destructive spirit" or "hostile spirit"). Following a struggle of some twelve thousand years, Zarathustra believed, Ahura Mazda and the forces of good would ultimately prevail, and Angra Mainyu and the principle of evil would disappear forever. At that time individual human souls would undergo judgment and would experience the rewards or punishments they deserved.

**Zoroastrianism** (zohr-oh-ASS-tree-ahn-iz'm)

**Zarathustra** (zar-uh-THOO-struh)

*Gathas* (GATH-uhs)

Zarathustra did not call for ascetic renunciation of the world in favor of a future heavenly existence. On the contrary, he considered the material world a blessing that reflected the benevolent nature of Ahura Mazda. His moral teachings allowed human beings to enjoy the world and its fruits—including wealth, sexual pleasure, and social prestige—as long as they did so in moderation and behaved honestly toward others. Zoroastrians have often summarized their moral teachings in the simple formula "good words, good thoughts, good deeds."

**ZOROASTRIAN DIVINE IMAGE.** | A gold clasp or button of the fifth century B.C.E. with the symbol of Ahura Mazda as a winged god.

**POPULARITY OF ZOROASTRIANISM** Zarathustra's teachings began to attract large numbers of followers during the sixth century B.C.E., particularly among Persian aristocrats and ruling elites. Wealthy patrons donated land and established endowments for the support of Zoroastrian temples. The Achaemenid era saw the emergence of a sizable priesthood, whose members conducted religious rituals, maintained a calendar, taught Zoroastrian values, and preserved Zoroastrian doctrine through oral transmission.

Beginning with Darius, the Achaemenid emperors closely associated themselves with Ahura Mazda and claimed divine sanction for their rule. Darius ordered stone inscriptions celebrating his achievements, and in those monuments he clearly revealed his devotion to Ahura Mazda and his opposition to the principle of evil. In one of his inscriptions, Darius praised Ahura Mazda as the great god who created the earth, the sky, and humanity and who moreover elevated Darius himself to the imperial honor. With the aid of imperial sponsorship, Zoroastrian temples cropped up throughout the Achaemenid realm. The faith was most popular in Iran, but it attracted sizable followings also in Mesopotamia, Anatolia, Egypt, and other parts of the Achaemenid empire even though there was no organized effort to spread it beyond its original homeland.

 Shapur I with Ahura Mazda
www.mhhe.com/
bentleybrief2e

# Religions of Salvation in a Cosmopolitan Society

The arrival of Alexander of Macedon inaugurated a difficult era for the Zoroastrian community. During his Persian campaign, Alexander's forces burned many temples and killed numerous magi. Because at that time the magi still transmitted Zoroastrian doctrines orally, an untold number of hymns and holy verses disappeared. The Zoroastrian faith survived, however, and the Parthians cultivated it to rally support against the Seleucids.

**OFFICIALLY SPONSORED ZOROASTRIANISM** During the Sasanid dynasty, however, Zoroastrianism experienced a revival. As self-proclaimed heirs to the Achaemenids, the Sasanids identified closely with Zoroastrianism and supported it zealously. Indeed, the Sasanids often persecuted other faiths if they seemed likely to become popular enough to challenge the supremacy of Zoroastrianism.

With generous imperial backing, the Zoroastrian faith and the magi flourished as never before. Theologians prepared written versions of the holy texts and collected them in the Avesta. They also explored points of doctrine and addressed difficult questions of morality and theology. Ordinary people flocked to Zoroastrian temples, where they prayed to Ahura Mazda and participated in rituals. The Zoroastrian faith faced severe difficulties in the seventh century C.E. when Islamic conquerors toppled the Sasanid empire. The conquerors did not outlaw the religion altogether, but they placed political and financial pressure on the magi and Zoroastrian temples. Some Zoroastrians fled their homeland and found refuge in India, where their descendants, known as Parsis ("Persians"), continue even today to observe Zoroastrian traditions. But most Zoroastrians remained in Iran and eventually converted to Islam. Only a few thousand faithful maintain a Zoroastrian community in modern-day Iran.

**INFLUENCE OF ZOROASTRIANISM** Meanwhile, even though Zoroastrianism ultimately declined in its homeland, the cosmopolitan character of the Persian realm offered it opportunities to influence other religious faiths. In particular, Jews living in Persia during Achaemenid times adopted several specific teachings of Zoroastrianism,

**Parsis** (pahr-SEES)

*Like many other religious faiths of classical times, Zoroastrianism encouraged the faithful to observe high moral and ethical standards. In this hymn from the* **Gathas,** *Zarathustra relates how Ahura Mazda and Angra Mainyu—representatives of good and evil, respectively—made choices about how to behave based on their fundamental natures. Human beings did likewise, according to Zarathustra, and ultimately all would experience the rewards and punishments that their choices merited.*

In the beginning, there were two Primal Spirits, Twins
    spontaneously active;
These are the Good and the Evil, in thought, and in word,
    and in deed:
Between these two, let the wise choose aright;
Be good, not base.

And when these Twin Spirits came together at first,
They established Life and Non-Life,
And so shall it be as long as the world shall last;
The worst existence shall be the lot of the followers of evil,
And the Good Mind shall be the reward of the followers
    of good.

Of these Twin Spirits, the Evil One chose to do the worst;
While the bountiful Holy Spirit of Goodness,
Clothing itself with the mossy heavens for a garment,
    chose the Truth;
And so will those who [seek to] please Ahura Mazda with
    righteous deeds, performed with faith in Truth. . . .

And when there cometh Divine Retribution for the Evil One,
Then at Thy command shall the Good Mind establish the
    Kingdom of Heaven, O Mazda,
For those who will deliver Untruth into the hands of
    Righteousness and Truth.

Then truly cometh the blow of destruction on Untruth,
And all those of good fame are garnered up in the Fair
    Abode,
The Fair Abode of the Good Mind, the Wise Lord, and of
    Truth!

O ye mortals, mark these commandments—
The commandments which the Wise Lord has given, for
    Happiness and for Pain;
Long punishment for the evil-doer, and bliss for the fol-
    lower of Truth,
The joy of salvation for the Righteous ever afterwards!

■ What assumptions does Zarathustra make about human nature and the capacity of human beings to make morally good choices out of their own free will?

SOURCE: D. J. Irani. *The Divine Songs of Zarathustra.* London: George Allen & Unwin, 1924.

which later found their way into the faiths of Christianity and Islam as well. These teachings included the notion that an omnipotent and beneficent deity was responsible for all creation, the idea that a purely evil being worked against the creator god, the conviction that the forces of good will ultimately prevail over the forces of evil after a climactic struggle, the belief that human beings must strive to observe the highest moral standards, and the doctrine that individuals will undergo judgment, after which the morally upright will experience rewards in paradise while evildoers will suffer punishments in hell. These teachings, which have profoundly influenced Judaism, Christianity, and Islam, all derived ultimately from the faith of Zarathustra and his followers.

## SUMMARY

The Achaemenid empire inaugurated a new era of world history. The Achaemenids borrowed military and administrative techniques devised earlier by Babylonian and Assyrian rulers, but they applied those techniques on a much larger scale than did any of their Mesopotamian predecessors. In doing so they conquered a vast empire and then governed its diverse lands and peoples with tolerable success for more than two centuries. The Achaemenids demonstrated how it was possible to build and maintain a massive imperial state, and their example inspired later efforts to establish similar large-scale imperial states based in Persia and other Eurasian lands as well. The Achaemenid and later Persian empires integrated much of the territory from the Mediterranean Sea to the Indus River into a commonwealth in which peoples of different regions and ethnic groups participated in a larger economy and society. By sponsoring regular and systematic interactions between peoples of different communities, the Persian empires wielded tremendous cultural as well as political, social, and economic influence. Indeed, Persian religious beliefs helped to shape moral and religious thought throughout much of southwest Asia and the Mediterranean basin. Zoroastrian teachings were particularly influential: although Zoroastrianism declined after the Sasanid dynasty, its doctrines decisively influenced the fundamental teachings of Judaism, Christianity, and Islam.

# STUDY TERMS

Achaemenids (88)
Ahura Mazda (98)
Alexander of Macedon (92)
*Avesta* (98)
battle of Marathon (92)
Croesus (87)
Cyrus (87)
Darius (89)
*Gathas* (98)

magi (98)
Medes (88)
Mithradates I (94)
Parthians (93)
Pasargadae (89)
Persepolis (90)
Persian Royal Road (91)
Persian Wars (92)

Persians (95)
*qanat* (91)
Sasanids (94)
satraps (91)
Seleucids (93)
Shapur I (94)
Xerxes (92)
Zarathustra (98)

# FOR FURTHER READING

Mary Boyce, ed. *Textual Sources for the Study of Zoroastrianism.* Totowa, N.J., 1984. Sources in translation with numerous explanatory comments by the author.

Maria Brosius. *Women in Ancient Persia, 559–331 B.C.* Oxford, 1996. Carefully examines both Persian and Greek sources for information about women and their role in Achaemenid society.

John Curtis and Nigel Tallos, eds. *Forgotten Empire: The World of Ancient Persia.* Berkeley, 2005. A lavishly illustrated collection of essays on various aspects of the Achaemenid Empire.

Muhammad A. Dandamaev and Vladimir G. Lukonin. *The Culture and Social Institutions of Ancient Iran.* Ed. by P. L. Kohl. Cambridge, 1989. Scholarly account that brings the results of Russian research to bear on the Achaemenid empire.

Richard C. Foltz. *Spirituality in the Land of the Noble: How Iran Shaped the World's Religions.* Oxford, 2004. Includes an accessible discussion of the Zoroastrian faith.

Richard N. Frye. *The Heritage of Central Asia: From Antiquity to the Turkish Expansion.* Princeton, 1996. Briefly sketches the history of various Iranian-speaking peoples in the steppes of central Asia as well as on the Iranian plateau.

Susan Sherwin-White and Amélie Kuhrt. *From Samarkhand to Sardis: A New Approach to the Seleucid Empire.* Berkeley, 1993. Detailed scholarly analysis of the Seleucid empire concentrating on political and economic matters.

Mark van de Mieroop. *A History of the Ancient Near East, ca. 3000–323 B.C.* Oxford, 2004. A concise and readable history that concludes with the Achaemenid Empire.

Mortimer Wheeler. *Flames over Persepolis.* New York, 1968. Deals with Alexander's conquest of the Achaemenid empire and especially the spread of Greek art styles throughout the Persian empire.

Robert C. Zaehner. *The Dawn and Twilight of Zoroastrianism.* London, 1961. An important interpretation of Zoroastrianism that concentrates on the Achaemenid and Sasanid periods.

# The Unification of China

6

In the year 99 B.C.E., Chinese imperial officials sentenced the historian Sima Qian to punishment by castration. For just over a decade, Sima Qian had worked on a project that he had inherited from his father, a history of China from earliest times to his own day. That project brought Sima Qian high prominence at the imperial court. Thus, when he spoke in defense of a dishonored general, his views attracted widespread attention. The emperor reacted furiously when he learned that Sima Qian had publicly expressed opinions that contradicted the ruler's judgment and ordered the historian to undergo his humiliating punishment.

Human castration was by no means uncommon in premodern times. Thousands of boys and young men of undistinguished birth underwent voluntary castration in China and many other lands as well to pursue careers as eunuchs. Ruling elites often appointed eunuchs, rather than nobles, to sensitive posts because eunuchs did not sire families and so could not build power bases to challenge established authorities. As personal servants of ruling elites, eunuchs sometimes came to wield enormous power.

Castration was not an appealing alternative, however, to educated elites and other prominent individuals: indeed, Chinese men of honor normally avoided the penalty by taking their own lives. Yet Sima Qian chose to endure his punishment. In a letter to a friend he explained that suicide would mean that his work would forever unwritten. To transmit his understanding of the Chinese past, then, Sima Qian opted to live and work in disgrace until his death about 90 B.C.E.

During his last years Sima Qian completed a massive work consisting of 130 chapters, most of which survive. He composed historical accounts of the emperors' reigns and biographical sketches of notable figures, including ministers, statesmen, generals, empresses, aristocrats, scholars, officials, merchants, and rebels. He even described the societies of neighboring peoples with whom the Chinese sometimes conducted trade and sometimes made war. As a result, Sima Qian's efforts still provide the best information available about the development of early imperial China.

A rich body of political and social thought prepared the way for the unification of China under the Qin and Han dynasties. Confucians, Daoists, Legalists, and others formed schools of thought and worked to bring political and social stability to China during the chaotic years of the late Zhou dynasty and the Period of the Warring States. Legalist ideas contributed directly to unification by

❮ *The Han emperor discusses classical texts with Confucian scholars.*

**Qin** (chin)

# CHRONOLOGY

| | |
|---|---|
| sixth century B.C.E. (?) | Laozi |
| 551–479 B.C.E. | Confucius |
| 403–221 B.C.E. | Period of the Warring States |
| 390–338 B.C.E. | Shang Yang |
| 372–289 B.C.E. | Mencius |
| 298–238 B.C.E. | Xunzi |
| 280–233 B.C.E. | Han Feizi |
| 221–207 B.C.E. | Qin dynasty |
| 206 B.C.E.–9 C.E. | Former Han dynasty |
| 141–87 B.C.E. | Reign of Han Wudi |
| 9–23 C.E. | Reign of Wang Mang |
| 25–220 C.E. | Later Han dynasty |

outlining means by which rulers could strengthen their states. The works of the Confucians and the Daoists were not directly concerned with unification, but both schools of thought profoundly influenced Chinese political and cultural traditions over the long term.

Rulers of the Qin and Han dynasties adopted Legalist principles and imposed centralized imperial rule on all of China. Like the Achaemenids of Persia, the Qin and Han emperors ruled through an elaborate bureaucracy, and they built roads that linked the various regions of China. They went further than the Persian emperors in their efforts to foster cultural unity in their realm. They imposed a common written language throughout China and established an educational system based on Confucian thought and values. For almost 450 years the Qin and Han dynasties guided the fortunes of China and established a strong precedent for centralized imperial rule.

Especially during the Han dynasty, political stability brought economic prosperity. High agricultural productivity supported the development of iron and silk industries, and Chinese goods found markets in central Asia, India, the Persian Empire, and even the Mediterranean basin. In spite of economic prosperity, however, later Han society experienced deep divisions between rich landowners and poor peasants. Those divisions eventually led to civil disorder and the emergence of political factions, which ultimately brought the Han dynasty to an end.

# IN SEARCH OF POLITICAL AND SOCIAL ORDER

The late centuries of the Zhou dynasty led eventually to the chaos associated with the Period of the Warring States (403–221 B.C.E.). Yet the political turmoil of that period also resulted in a remarkable cultural flowering, because it forced thoughtful people to reflect on the proper roles of human beings in society. Some sought to identify principles that would restore political and social order. Others concerned themselves with a search for individual tranquility apart from society. Three schools of thought that emerged during those centuries of confusion and chaos—Confucianism, Daoism, and Legalism—exercised a particularly deep influence on Chinese political and cultural traditions.

## *Confucius and His School*

CONFUCIUS  The first Chinese thinker who addressed the problem of political and social order in a straightforward and self-conscious way was Kong Fuzi (551–479 B.C.E.)—"Master Philosopher Kong," as his disciples called him, or Confucius, as he is known in English. He came from an aristocratic family in the state of Lu in northern China, and for many years he sought an influential post at the Lu court. But Confucius was a strong-willed man who often did not get along well with others. He could be quite cantankerous: he was known to lodge bitter complaints, for

**Zhou** (joh)

**Confucianism** (kuhn-FEW-shuhn-iz'm)

example, if someone undercooked or overcooked his rice. Not surprisingly, then, he refused to compromise his beliefs in the interest of political expediency, and he insisted on observing principles that frequently clashed with state policy. As a result, Confucius was unable to obtain a high position at the Lu court. Confucius then sought employment with other courts in northern China but after a decade of travel found none willing to accept his services. In 484 B.C.E., bitterly disappointed, he returned to Lu, where he died five years later.

Although Confucius never realized his ambition, he left an enduring mark on Chinese society through his work as an educator and a political advisor. He attracted numerous disciples who aspired to political careers, and those disciples compiled the master's sayings and teachings in a book known as the *Analects*—a work that has profoundly influenced Chinese political and cultural traditions.

**CONFUCIAN IDEAS** Confucius's thought was fundamentally moral, ethical, and political in character. It was also thoroughly practical: Confucius did not address philosophical or religious questions but focused instead on the proper ordering of human relationships. In an age when bureaucratic institutions were not yet well developed, Confucius believed that the best way to promote good government was to fill official positions with individuals who were both well educated and extraordinarily conscientious. Thus Confucius concentrated on the formation of what he called *junzi*—"superior individuals"—who did not allow personal interests to influence their judgments.

In the absence of an established educational system and a formal curriculum, Confucius had his disciples study works of poetry and history that provided insight into human nature. He and his students carefully examined works produced during the Zhou dynasty, such as the *Book of Songs,* the *Book of History,* and the *Book of Rites,* concentrating especially on their practical value for prospective administrators. As a result of Confucius's influence, literary works of the Zhou dynasty became the core texts of the traditional Chinese education. For more than two thousand years, until the early twentieth century C.E., talented Chinese seeking government posts followed a program of study deriving from the one developed by Confucius in the fifth century B.C.E.

**CONFUCIUS.** | No contemporary portrait of Confucius survives, but artists have used their imaginations and depicted him in many ways over the years. This portrait of 1735 identifies Confucius as "the Sage and Teacher" and represents him in the distinctive dress of an eighteenth-century Confucian scholar-bureaucrat.

**CONFUCIAN VALUES** For Confucius, though, ideal government officials needed more than an advanced education: they also needed a strong sense of moral integrity and a capacity to deliver wise and fair judgments. Several qualities were particularly important to Confucius. One of them he called *ren,* by which he meant an attitude of kindness and benevolence or a sense of humanity. Confucius explained that individuals possessing *ren* were courteous, respectful, diligent, and loyal—characteristics desperately needed in government officials. Another quality of central importance was *li,* a sense of propriety, which called for individuals to behave appropriately: they should treat all other human beings with courtesy, while showing special respect and deference to elders or superiors. Yet another quality that Confucius emphasized was *xiao,* filial piety, which obliged children to respect their parents and other family elders, look after their welfare, support them in old age, and remember them along with other ancestors after their deaths.

*li* (LEE)

*xiao* (SHAYOH)

Confucius emphasized personal qualities such as *ren, li,* and *xiao* because he believed that individuals who possessed those traits would gain influence in the larger society and in the process would lead others by their example. Only through enlightened leadership by morally strong individuals, Confucius believed, was there any hope for the restoration of political and social order in China. Thus his goal was not simply the cultivation of personal morality for its own sake but also the creation of *junzi* who could bring order and stability to China.

Because Confucius expressed his thought in general terms, later disciples could adapt it to the particular problems of their times. Indeed, the flexibility of Confucian thought helps to account for its remarkable longevity and influence in China. Two later disciples of Confucius—Mencius and Xunzi—illustrate especially well the ways in which Confucian thought lent itself to adaptation.

MENCIUS    Mencius (372–289 B.C.E.) was the most learned man of his age and the principal spokesman for the Confucian school. During the Period of the Warring States, he traveled widely throughout China as a political advisor. Mencius firmly believed that human nature was basically good; thus he placed special emphasis on the Confucian virtue of *ren* and advocated government by benevolence and humanity. This principle implied that rulers would levy light taxes, avoid wars, support education, and encourage harmony and cooperation. In his lifetime, Mencius's advice had little practical effect, and critics charged that his views about human nature were naïve. Over the long term, however, his ideas deeply influenced the Confucian tradition. Since about the tenth century C.E., many Chinese scholars have considered Mencius the most authoritative of Confucius's early expositors.

XUNZI    Like Confucius and Mencius, Xunzi (298–238 B.C.E.) was a man of immense learning, but unlike his predecessors, he also served for many years as a government administrator. His practical experience encouraged him to develop a less optimistic view of human nature than Mencius's. Xunzi believed that human beings selfishly pursued their own interests and resisted making any voluntary contribution to the larger society. He considered strong social discipline the best means to bring order to society. Thus, whereas Mencius emphasized the Confucian quality of *ren,* Xunzi emphasized *li.* He advocated the establishment of clear, well-publicized standards of conduct that would set limits on the pursuit of individual interests and punish those who neglected their obligations to the larger society.

Like Confucius and Mencius, however, Xunzi also believed that it was possible to improve human beings and restore order to society. That fundamental optimism was a basic characteristic of Confucian thought. It explains the high value that Confucian thinkers placed on education and public behavior, and it accounts also for their activist approach to public affairs. Confucians involved themselves in society: they sought government positions and made conscientious efforts to solve political and social problems and to promote harmony in public life.

## Daoism

Some contemporaries, however, regarded Confucian activism as little more than misspent energy. Among the most prominent of these critics were the Daoists. Like Confucianism, Daoism developed in response to the turbulence of the late Zhou dynasty and the Period of the Warring States. But unlike the Confucians, the Daoists considered it pointless to waste time on social activism. Instead, the Daoists devoted their energies to reflection and

---

*junzi* (juhn-zee)
**Mencius** (MEN-shi-us)
**Xunzi** (SHOON-dzuh)
**Daoism** (DOW-iz'm)

*Confucius never composed formal writings, but his disciples collected his often pithy remarks into a work known as the* Analects *(Sayings). Referred to as "the Master" in the following excerpts from the* Analects, *Confucius consistently argued that only good men possessing moral authority could rule effectively.*

The Master said, "He who exercises government by means of his virtue may be compared to the north polar star, which keeps its place, while all the stars turn toward it. . . ."

The Master said, "If the people be led by laws, and uniformity be imposed on them by punishments, they will try to avoid the punishment, but will have no sense of shame."

"If they be led by virtue, and uniformity be provided for them by the rules of propriety, they will have the sense of shame, and moreover will become good. . . ."

The duke Ai asked, saying, "What should be done in order to secure the submission of the people?" Confucius replied, "Advance the upright and set aside the crooked, and then the people will submit. Advance the crooked and set aside the upright, and then the people will not submit."

Ji Kang asked how to cause the people to reverence their ruler, to be faithful to him, and to go on to seek virtue. The Master said, "Let him preside over them with gravity; then they will reverence him. Let him be filial and kind to all; then they will be faithful to him. Let him advance the good and teach the incompetent; then they will eagerly seek to be virtuous. . . ."

Zigong asked about government. The Master said, "The requisites of government are that there be sufficiency of food, sufficiency of military equipment, and the confidence of the people in their ruler." Zigong said, "If it cannot be helped, and one of these must be dispensed with, which of the three should be foregone first?" "The military equipment," said the Master.

Zigong again asked, "If it cannot be helped, and one of the remaining two must be dispensed with, which of them should be foregone?" The Master answered, "Part with the food. From olden times, death has been the lot of all men; but if the people have no faith in their rulers, there is no standing for the state. . . ."

Ji Kang asked Confucius about government, saying, "What do you say to killing the unprincipled for the good of the principled?" Confucius replied, "Sir, in carrying on your government, why should you use killing at all? Let your evinced desires be for what is good, and the people will be good. The relation between superiors and inferiors is like that between the wind and the grass. The grass must bend when the wind blows across it. . . ."

The Master said, "When a prince's personal conduct is correct, his government is effective without the issuing of orders. If his personal conduct is not correct, he may issue orders, but they will not be followed."

■ Compare Confucius's understanding of moral virtue with Zarathustra's notion of morality discussed in the previous chapter.

SOURCE: James Legge, trans. *The Chinese Classics,* 7 vols. Oxford: Clarendon Press, 1893, 1:145, 146, 152, 254, 258–59, 266. (Translations slightly modified.)

introspection, in hopes that they could understand how to live in harmony with the natural principles that governed the world. The Daoists believed that, over time, this approach would bring harmony to society as a whole, as people ceased to meddle in affairs that they could not understand or control.

LAOZI AND THE DAODEJING    According to Chinese tradition, the founder of Daoism was a sixth-century B.C.E. sage named Laozi. Although Laozi has been credited with composing the *Daodejing (Classic of the Way and of Virtue),* the basic exposition of Daoist beliefs, it is almost certain that the book acquired its definitive form over several centuries. After the *Daodejing,* the most important Daoist work was the *Zhuangzi,* named

*Daodejing* (DOW-DAY-JIHNG)

*Zhuangzi* (joo-wong-dz)

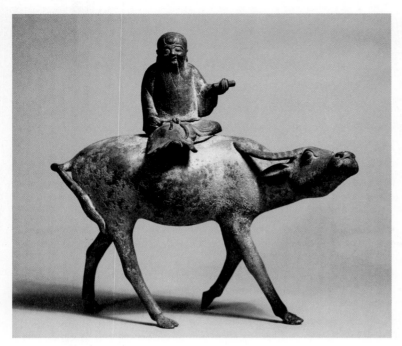

**LAOZI.** | A jade statue produced about the tenth century C.E. depicts the sage Laozi on an ox. Legends reported that Laozi rode a blue ox from China to central Asia when spreading his teachings. *Why is Laozi depicted wearing common, simple clothing?*

after its author, the philosopher Zhuangzi (369–286 B.C.E.), which provided a well-reasoned compendium of Daoist views.

**THE DAO** Daoism represented an effort to understand the fundamental character of the world and nature. The central concept of Daoism is the elusive concept of *dao*, meaning "the way," or more specifically "the way of nature" or "the way of the cosmos." In the *Daodejing, dao* figures as the original force of the cosmos, an eternal principle that governs all the workings of the world. Yet the *Daodejing* envisioned *dao* as a supremely passive force and spoke of it mostly in negative terms: *dao* does nothing, and yet it accomplishes everything. *Dao* resembles water, which is soft and yielding, yet is also so powerful that it eventually erodes even the hardest rock placed in its path. *Dao* also resembles the cavity of a pot: although it is nothing more than an empty space, it makes the pot a useful tool.

Daoists believed that human beings should live in harmony with the passive and yielding nature of *dao*. To the Daoists, that meant retreating from the world of politics and administration. Ambition and activism had only brought the world to a state of chaos. The proper response to that situation was to cease frantic striving and live in as simple a manner as possible.

**THE DOCTRINE OF WUWEI** Thus early Daoists recognized as the chief moral virtue the trait of *wuwei*—disengagement from active involvement in worldly affairs. *Wuwei* required that individuals refrain from advanced education and personal striving, and that they live simply, unpretentiously, and in harmony with nature.

*Wuwei* also had implications for state and society: the less government, the better. Instead of expansive kingdoms, the *Daodejing* envisioned a world of tiny, self-sufficient communities where people had no desire to conquer their neighbors or even to trade or visit with them.

Although Daoist thought opposed the activism of Confucianism, in fact the Daoist encouragement of self-knowledge appealed strongly to many Confucians. And, since neither Confucianism nor Daoism was an exclusive faith, it was possible for individuals to study the Confucian curriculum and take administrative posts in the government while devoting their private hours to reflection on human nature and the place of humans in the larger world—to live as Confucians by day, as it were, and Daoists by night.

## Legalism

Ultimately, neither Confucian activism nor Daoist retreat was able to solve the problems of the Period of the Warring States. Order returned to China only after the emergence of a third school of thought—that of the Legalists—which promoted a practical and ruthlessly efficient approach to statecraft. Unlike the Confucians, the Legalists did not concern themselves with ethics, morality, or propriety. Unlike the Daoists, the Legalists cared nothing about the place of human beings in nature. Instead, they devoted their attention exclusively to the state, which they sought to strengthen and expand at all costs.

**SHANG YANG AND HAN FEIZI** Legalist doctrine emerged from the insights of men who were active in Chinese political affairs during the late fourth century B.C.E. Most notable of them was Shang Yang (ca. 390–338 B.C.E.), who served as chief

*wuwei* (woo-WAY)

minister to the duke of the Qin state in western China. His policies survive in a work titled *The Book of Lord Shang*. Though a clever and efficient administrator, Shang Yang was despised because of his power and ruthlessness. Thus, when his patron died, Shang's enemies at court executed him, mutilated his body, and annihilated his family. Another Legalist theorist, Han Feizi (ca. 280–233 B.C.E.) also fell afoul of ambitious men at the Qin court. During his life, Han Feizi synthesized Legalist ideas in a collection of powerful and well-argued essays on statecraft. However, his enemies forced him to commit suicide by taking poison. Thus, the Legalist state itself consumed the two foremost exponents of Legalist doctrine.

**THINKING ABOUT** *Traditions*

**TRADITIONS IN THE UNIFICATION OF CHINA.** Although the Qin and Han dynasties built large empires that encompassed a variety of peoples and languages, they insisted on a cultural unity that emphasized the primacy of Chinese customs and traditions over other traditions. What measures did the two dynasties use to impose this cultural unity, and how successful were they?

**LEGALIST DOCTRINE**   Shang Yang, Han Feizi, and other Legalists reasoned that the foundations of a state's strength were agriculture and armed forces. Since both lines of work directly advanced the interests of the state, Legalists sought to channel as many individuals as possible into cultivation or military service. Meanwhile, they discouraged others from pursuing what they believed were less useful careers as merchants, entrepreneurs, scholars, educators, philosophers, poets, or artists.

The Legalists expected to harness subjects' energy by means of clear and strict laws—hence the name "Legalist." Their faith in laws distinguished the Legalists clearly from the Confucians, who relied on education and example to induce individuals to behave appropriately. The Legalists believed that this was not enough: to persuade individuals to serve the needs of the state, they imposed a strict legal regimen that clearly outlined expectations and provided severe punishment for violators. They believed that if people feared to commit small crimes, they would hesitate all the more before committing great crimes. Thus Legalists imposed harsh penalties for even minor infractions: individuals could suffer amputation of their hands or feet, for example, for disposing of trash in the street. The Legalists also established the principle of collective responsibility before the law, whereby all members of a family or a community were liable to be punished along with the actual violator.

The Legalists' principles of government did not win them much popularity. Yet Legalist doctrine lent itself readily to practical application, and Legalist principles of government quickly produced remarkable results for rulers who adopted them. In fact, Legalist methods put an end to the Period of the Warring States and brought about the unification of China.

# THE UNIFICATION OF CHINA

During the Period of the Warring States, rulers of several regional states adopted elements of the Legalist program. Legalist doctrines met the most enthusiastic response in the state of Qin, in western China, where Shang Yang and Han Feizi oversaw the implementation of Legalist policies. The Qin state soon dominated its neighbors and imposed centralized imperial rule throughout China. Qin rule survived for only a few years, but the succeeding Han dynasty followed the Qin example by governing China through a centralized imperial administration.

China under the Qin dynasty
www.mhhe.com/
bentleybrief2e

## *The Qin Dynasty*

**THE KINGDOM OF QIN**   During the fourth and third centuries B.C.E., the Qin state underwent a remarkable round of economic, political, and military development. Shang Yang encouraged peasant cultivators to migrate to the sparsely populated state by granting them private plots. That policy dramatically boosted agricultural production

**Han Feizi** (hahn-fay-zi)

while it simultaneously weakened the economic position of the hereditary aristocratic classes. As a result, Qin rulers found fewer obstacles to establishing centralized, bureaucratic rule throughout their state. Meanwhile, they devoted their newfound wealth to the organization of a powerful army equipped with the most effective iron weapons available. During the third century B.C.E., Qin rulers attacked one state after another, absorbing each new conquest into their centralized structure, until finally they had brought China for the first time under the sway of a single state.

THE FIRST EMPEROR  In 221 B.C.E., Qin Shihuangdi, the king of Qin (reigned 221–210 B.C.E.), proclaimed himself the First Emperor and decreed that his descendants would reign for thousands of generations. In fact, the dynasty lasted only fourteen years, dissolving in 207 B.C.E. because of civil insurrections. Yet the Qin dynasty had a significance out of proportion to its short life, because like the Achaemenid empire in Persia, the Qin dynasty established a tradition of centralized imperial rule that later rulers sought to emulate.

Like his ancestors in the kingdom of Qin, the First Emperor of China ignored the nobility and ruled his empire through a centralized bureaucracy. He governed from his capital at Xianyang, near the modern city of Xi'an. The remainder of China he divided into administrative provinces and districts, and he entrusted the implementation of his policies to officers of the central government who served at his pleasure. He disarmed regional military forces, and he built roads to facilitate communications and the movement of armies. He also drafted laborers by the hundreds of thousands to build a massive defensive barrier that was a precursor to the Great Wall of China.

RESISTANCE TO QIN POLICIES  It is likely that many Chinese welcomed the political stability introduced by the Qin dynasty, but it did not win universal acceptance. Confucians, Daoists, and others launched a vigorous campaign of criticism. In an effort to reassert his authority, Qin Shihuangdi ordered execution for those who criticized his regime. In the year following this decree, for example, he sentenced some 460 scholars residing in the capital to be buried alive for their criticism of his regime. Qin Shihuangdi also demanded that all books of philosophy, ethics, history, and literature be burned. Although he spared some works on medicine, fortune-telling, and agriculture on the grounds that they had some utilitarian value, many classical literary or philosophical works were lost.

QIN CENTRALIZATION  The First Emperor launched several initiatives that enhanced the unity of China. In keeping with his policy of centralization, he standardized the laws, currencies, weights, and measures of the various regions of China. Previously, regional states had organized their own legal and economic systems, which often hampered commerce and communications across state boundaries. Uniform coinage and legal standards encouraged the integration of China's various regions into a society more tightly knit than ever before. The roads and bridges that Qin Shihuangdi built throughout his realm, like those built in other classical societies, also encouraged economic integration because they facilitated interregional commerce.

STANDARDIZED SCRIPT  Perhaps even more important than his legal and economic policies was the First Emperor's standardization of Chinese script. Before the Qin dynasty, regional Chinese scripts had developed along different lines and had become mutually unrecognizable. In hopes of ensuring better understanding and uniform application of his policies, Qin Shihuangdi mandated the use of a common script throughout his empire. The regions of China continued to use different spoken languages, as they do

PSI img  The Great Wall
www.mhhe.com/
bentleybrief2e

Qin Shihuangdi (chin she-huang-dee)

Xianyang (SHYAHN-YAHNG)

Xi'an (shee-ahn)

**MAP 6.1** | China under the Qin dynasty, 221–207 B.C.E. Compare the size of Qin territories to those of earlier Chinese kingdoms depicted in Map 3.2. **How is it possible to account for the greater reach of the Qin dynasty?**

These defensive walls were precursors to China's Great Wall, which was built during the Ming dynasty (1368–1644 C.E.)

today, but they wrote those languages with a common script—just as if Europeans spoke English, French, German, and other languages but wrote them all down in Latin. In China, speakers of different languages use the same written symbols, which enables them to communicate in writing across linguistic boundaries.

In spite of his ruthlessness, Qin Shihuangdi ranks as one of the most important figures in Chinese history. The First Emperor established a precedent for centralized imperial rule, which remained the norm in China until the early twentieth century. He also pointed China in the direction of political and cultural unity, and with some periods of interruption, China has remained politically and culturally unified to the present day.

**TOMB OF THE FIRST EMPEROR** Qin Shihuangdi died in 210 B.C.E. His final resting place was a lavish tomb constructed by some seven hundred thousand drafted laborers as a permanent monument to the First Emperor. Rare and expensive grave goods accompanied the emperor in burial, along with sacrificed slaves, concubines, and many of the craftsmen who designed and built the tomb. Qin Shihuangdi was laid to rest in an elaborate underground palace lined with bronze and protected by traps and crossbows rigged to fire at intruders. Buried in the vicinity of the tomb itself was an entire army of magnificently detailed life-size pottery figures to guard the emperor in death.

The terra-cotta army of Qin Shihuangdi protected his tomb, but it could not save his successors or his empire. The First Emperor had conscripted millions of laborers from

Emperor Qin's tomb
www.mhhe.com/
bentleybrief2e

**THE TOMB OF QIN SHIHUANGDI.** | One detachment of the formidable, life-size, terra-cotta army buried in the vicinity of Qin Shihuangdi's tomb to protect the emperor after his death. *What does the construction of such an elaborate tomb tell us about Qin Shihuangdi's ability to command resources?*

all parts of China to work on massive public works projects. Although these projects increased productivity and promoted the integration of China's various regions, they also generated tremendous ill will among the drafted laborers. Revolts began in the year after Qin Shihuangdi's death, and in 207 B.C.E. waves of rebels overwhelmed the Qin court, slaughtering government officials and burning state buildings. The Qin dynasty quickly dissolved in chaos.

## The Early Han Dynasty

LIU BANG    The bloody end of the Qin dynasty might well have ended the experiment with centralized imperial rule in China. However, centralized rule returned almost immediately, largely because of a determined commander named Liu Bang. Judging from the historian Sima Qian's account, Liu Bang was not a colorful or charismatic figure, but he was a persistent man and a methodical planner. He surrounded himself with brilliant advisors and enjoyed the unwavering loyalty of his troops. By 206 B.C.E. he had restored order throughout China and established himself at the head of a new dynasty.

Liu Bang called the new dynasty the Han, in honor of his native land. The Han dynasty turned out to be one of the longest and most influential in all of Chinese history. It lasted for more than four hundred years, from 206 B.C.E. to 220 C.E., although for a brief period (9–23 C.E.) a usurper temporarily displaced Han rule. Thus historians conventionally divide the dynasty into the Former Han (206 B.C.E.–9 C.E.) and the Later Han (25–220 C.E.).

The Han dynasty consolidated the tradition of centralized imperial rule that the Qin dynasty had pioneered. During the Former Han, emperors ruled from Chang'an, a cosmopolitan city near modern Xi'an that became the cultural capital of China. During the Later Han, the emperors moved their capital east to Luoyang, also a cosmopolitan city and second in importance only to Chang'an throughout much of Chinese history.

**EARLY HAN POLICIES** During the early days of the Han dynasty, Liu Bang attempted to follow a middle path between the decentralized political alliances of the Zhou dynasty and the tightly centralized state of the Qin to reap the advantages and avoid the excesses of both. On the one hand, he allotted large landholdings to members of the imperial family, in the expectation that they would provide a reliable network of support for his rule. On the other hand, he divided the empire into administrative districts governed by officials who served at the emperor's pleasure.

Liu Bang learned quickly that reliance on his family did not guarantee support for the emperor. In 200 B.C.E. an army of nomadic Xiongnu warriors besieged Liu Bang and almost captured him. He managed to escape—but without receiving the support he had expected from his family members. From that point forward, Liu Bang and his successors followed a policy of centralization. They reclaimed lands from family members, absorbed those lands into the imperial domain, and entrusted political responsibilities to an administrative bureaucracy. Thus, despite a brief flirtation with a decentralized government, the Han dynasty left as its principal political legacy a tradition of centralized imperial rule.

**THE MARTIAL EMPEROR: HAN WUDI** Much of the reason for the Han dynasty's success was the long reign of the dynasty's greatest and most energetic emperor, Han Wudi, the "Martial Emperor," who occupied the throne for fifty-four years, from 141 to 87 B.C.E. Han Wudi ruled his empire with vision and vigor. He pursued two policies in particular: administrative centralization and imperial expansion.

**HAN CENTRALIZATION** Domestically, Han Wudi worked strenuously to increase the authority and prestige of the central government. He built an enormous bureaucracy to administer his empire, and he relied on Legalist principles of government. He also continued the Qin policy of building roads and canals to facilitate trade and communication between China's regions. To finance the vast machinery of his government, he levied taxes on agriculture, trade, and craft industries, and he established imperial monopolies on the production of essential goods such as iron and salt. In building such an enormous governmental structure, Han Wudi faced a serious problem of recruitment. He needed thousands of reliable, intelligent, educated individuals to run his bureaucracy, but there was no institutionalized educational system in China that could provide a continuous supply of such people.

**THE CONFUCIAN EDUCATIONAL SYSTEM** Han Wudi addressed that problem in 124 B.C.E. by establishing an imperial university that prepared young men for government service. Personally, the Martial Emperor cared little for learning. In that respect he resembled all the other early Han emperors: Liu Bang once emptied his bladder in the distinctive cap worn by Confucian scholars in order to demonstrate his contempt for academic pursuits. Yet Han Wudi recognized that the success of his efforts at bureaucratic centralization would depend on a corps of educated officeholders. The imperial university took Confucianism—the only Chinese cultural tradition developed enough to provide rigorous intellectual discipline—as the basis for its curriculum. Ironically, then, although he relied on Legalist principles of government, Han Wudi ensured the long-term survival of the Confucian tradition by establishing it as the official imperial ideology.

**Xiongnu** (SHE-OONG-noo)

**MAP 6.2** | East Asia and central Asia at the time of Han Wudi, ca. 87 B.C.E. Note the indication in this map that Han authority extended to Korea and central Asia during the first century B.C.E. *What strategic value did these regions hold for the Han dynasty?*

**HAN IMPERIAL EXPANSION**  While he moved aggressively to centralize power and authority at home, Han Wudi pursued an equally vigorous foreign policy of imperial expansion. He invaded northern Vietnam and Korea, subjected them to Han rule, and brought them into the orbit of Chinese society. He ruled both lands through a Chinese-style government, and Confucian values followed the Han armies into the new colonies. Over the course of the centuries, the educational systems of both northern Vietnam and Korea drew their inspiration almost entirely from Confucianism.

The Xiongnu abduct Lady Wenji
www.mhhe.com/
bentleybrief2e

Lady Wenji's scroll
www.mhhe.com/
bentleybrief2e

**THE XIONGNU**  The greatest foreign challenge that Han Wudi faced came from the Xiongnu, a nomadic people from the steppes of central Asia. Like most of the other nomadic peoples of central Asia, the Xiongnu were superb horsemen. Although their weaponry was not as sophisticated as that of the Chinese, their mobility offered the Xiongnu a distinct advantage. When they could not satisfy their needs through peaceful trade, they mounted sudden raids into villages or trading areas, where they commandeered supplies and then rapidly departed. Because they had no cities or settled places to defend, the Xiongnu could quickly disperse when confronted by a superior force.

During the reign of Maodun (210–174 B.C.E.), their most successful leader, the Xiongnu ruled a vast federation of nomadic peoples that stretched from the Aral Sea to the Yellow Sea. Maodun brought strict military discipline to the Xiongnu. According to Sima Qian, Maodun once instructed his forces to shoot their arrows at whatever target he himself selected. He aimed in succession at his favorite horse, one of his wives, and his father's best horse, and he summarily executed those who failed to discharge their arrows. When his forces reliably followed his orders, Maodun targeted his father, who immediately fell under a hail of arrows, leaving Maodun as the Xiongnu chief.

With its highly disciplined army, the Xiongnu empire was a source of concern to the Han emperors. During the early days of the dynasty, they attempted to pacify the Xiongnu by paying them tribute—providing them with food and finished goods in hopes that they would refrain from mounting raids in China—or by arranging marriages between the ruling houses of the two peoples in hopes of establishing peaceful diplomatic relations. Neither method succeeded for long.

HAN EXPANSION INTO CENTRAL ASIA   Ultimately, Han Wudi decided to go on the offensive against the Xiongnu. He invaded central Asia with vast armies and brought much of the Xiongnu empire under Chinese military control. He pacified a long central Asian corridor extending almost to Bactria, which served as the lifeline of a trade network that linked much of the Eurasian landmass. He even planted colonies of Chinese cultivators in the oasis communities of central Asia. As a result of those efforts, the Xiongnu empire soon fell into disarray. For the moment, the Han state enjoyed uncontested hegemony in both east Asia and central Asia. Before long, however, economic and social problems within China brought serious problems for the Han dynasty itself.

THINKING ABOUT
*Encounters*

ENCOUNTERS IN THE UNIFICATION OF CHINA. During the Han dynasty, the Han emperors successfully projected their influence across a wide swath of east and central Asia, including much of modern China as well as Korea, Vietnam, and the central Asian desert. In what ways did this influence encourage interaction between the various peoples of the realm?

# FROM ECONOMIC PROSPERITY TO SOCIAL DISORDER

Already during the Xia, Shang, and Zhou dynasties, a productive agricultural economy supported the emergence of complex society in China. High agricultural productivity continued during the Qin and Han dynasties, and it supported the development of craft industries such as the forging of iron tools and the weaving of silk textiles. During the Han dynasty, however, China experienced serious social and economic problems as land became concentrated in the hands of a small, wealthy elite class. Social tensions generated banditry, rebellion, and even the temporary deposition of the Han state itself. Although Han rulers regained the throne, they presided over a much-weakened realm. By the early third century C.E., social and political problems brought the Han dynasty to an end.

## *Productivity and Prosperity during the Former Han*

PATRIARCHAL SOCIAL ORDER   The structure of Chinese society during the Qin and Han dynasties was very similar to that of the Zhou era. Patriarchal households averaged five inhabitants, although several generations of aristocratic families sometimes lived together in large compounds. During the Han dynasty, moralists sought to enhance the authority of patriarchal family heads by emphasizing the importance of filial piety and women's subordination to their menfolk. A widely read treatise titled *Admonitions for Women,* for example, emphasized humility, obedience, subservience, and devotion to their husbands as the virtues most appropriate for women. To Confucian moralists and government authorities alike, orderly, patriarchal families were the foundations of a stable society.

The vast majority of the Chinese population worked in the countryside cultivating grains and vegetables, which they harvested in larger quantities than ever before. The increased agricultural surplus allowed many Chinese to produce fine manufactured goods and to engage in trade.

IRON METALLURGY   During the Han dynasty, the iron industry entered a period of rapid growth. Han artisans experimented with production techniques and learned to craft fine utensils for both domestic and military uses. Iron pots, stoves, knives, needles, axes, hammers, saws, and other tools became standard fixtures in households that could not have afforded more expensive bronze utensils. The ready availability of iron also had important military implications. Craftsmen designed suits of iron armor to protect soldiers against arrows and blows, which helps to explain the success of Chinese armies against the Xiongnu and other nomadic peoples.

**HAN-ERA ARISTOCRATIC HOUSE.** | Clay model of an aristocratic house of the sort inhabited by a powerful clan during the Han dynasty. This model came from a tomb near the city of Guangzhou in southern China. *The Nelson-Atkins Museum of Art, Kansas City, Missouri. Purchase: William Rockhill Nelson Trust, 33-521.*

**SILK TEXTILES** Textile production—particularly sericulture, the manufacture of silk—became an especially important industry. The origins of sericulture date to the fourth millennium B.C.E., but only in Han times did sericulture expand from its original home in the Yellow River valley to most parts of China. Although silkworms inhabited much of Eurasia, Chinese silk was especially fine because of advanced sericulture techniques. Chinese producers bred their silkworms, fed them on finely chopped mulberry leaves, and carefully unraveled their cocoons so as to obtain long fibers of raw silk that they wove into light, strong, lustrous fabrics. (In other lands, producers relied on wild silkworms that ate a variety of leaves and chewed through their cocoons, leaving only short fibers that yielded lower-quality fabrics.) Chinese silk became a prized commodity in India, Persia, Mesopotamia, and even the distant Roman empire. Commerce in silk and other products led to the establishment of an intricate network of trade routes known collectively as the silk roads (discussed in chapter 9).

**PAPER** While expanding the iron and silk industries, Han craftsmen also invented paper. In earlier times Chinese scribes had written mostly on bamboo strips and silk fabrics, but about 100 C.E. Chinese craftsmen began to fashion hemp, bark, and textile fibers into sheets of paper. Although wealthy elites continued to read books written on silk rolls, paper soon became the preferred medium for most writing.

**POPULATION GROWTH** High agricultural productivity supported rapid demographic growth and general prosperity during the early part of the Han dynasty. Historians estimate that about 220 B.C.E., just after the founding of the Qin dynasty, the Chinese population was twenty million. By the year 9 C.E., at the end of the Former Han dynasty, it had tripled to sixty million. Meanwhile, taxes claimed only a small portion of production, yet state granaries bulged so much that their contents sometimes spoiled before they could be consumed.

## Economic and Social Difficulties

In spite of general prosperity, China began to experience economic and social difficulties in the Former Han period. The military adventures and the central Asian policy of Han Wudi caused severe economic strain. To finance his ventures, Han Wudi raised taxes and confiscated land and personal property from wealthy individuals, sometimes on the pretext that they had violated imperial laws. Those measures discouraged investment in manufacturing and trading enterprises, which in turn had a dampening effect on the larger economy.

**SOCIAL TENSIONS** Distinctions between rich and poor hardened during the course of the Han dynasty. Wealthy individuals wore fine silk garments and ate rich foods, whereas the poor classes made do with rough hemp clothing and a diet of mostly grain. By the first century B.C.E., social and economic differences had generated serious tensions, and peasants in hard-pressed regions began to organize rebellions in hopes of gaining a larger share of Han society's resources.

**LAND DISTRIBUTION** A particularly difficult problem concerned the distribution of land. Economic problems forced many small landowners to sell their property under unfavorable conditions or even to forfeit it in exchange for cancellation of their

**BURIAL SUIT.** | In Han times the wealthiest classes enjoyed the privilege of being buried in suits of jade plaques sewn together with gold threads, like the burial dress of Liu Sheng, who died in 113 B.C.E. at Manzheng in Hebei Province. Legend held that jade prevented decomposition of the deceased's body. Scholars have estimated that a jade burial suit like this one required ten years' labor. *What can such a suit tell us about the lives of the Chinese elite?*

debts. In extreme cases, individuals had to sell themselves and their families into slavery to satisfy their creditors. Owners of large estates not only increased the size of their holdings by absorbing the property of their less fortunate neighbors but also increased the efficiency of their operations by employing cheap labor.

By the end of the first century B.C.E., land had accumulated in the hands of a relatively small number of individuals who owned vast estates, while ever-increasing numbers of peasant cultivators led difficult lives with few prospects for improvement. Landless peasants became restive, and Chinese society faced growing problems of banditry and sporadic rebellion.

**THE REIGN OF WANG MANG** Tensions came to a head during the early first century C.E. when a powerful and respected Han minister named Wang Mang undertook a thoroughgoing program of reform. In 6 C.E. a two-year-old boy inherited the Han imperial throne. Because the boy was unable to govern, Wang Mang served as his regent. Many officials regarded Wang as more capable than members of the Han family and urged him to claim the imperial honor for himself. In 9 C.E. he did just that: announcing that the mandate of heaven had passed from the Han to his family, he seized the throne. Wang Mang then introduced a series of wide-ranging reforms that have prompted historians to refer to him as the "socialist emperor."

The most important reforms concerned landed property: Wang Mang limited the amount of land that a family could hold and ordered officials to break up large estates, redistribute them, and provide landless individuals with property to cultivate. Despite his good intentions, the socialist emperor attempted to impose his policy without adequate preparation and communication. The result was confusion: landlords resisted a policy that threatened their holdings, and even peasants found its application inconsistent and unsatisfactory. After several years of chaos, in 23 C.E. a coalition of disgruntled landlords and desperate peasants ended both his dynasty and his life.

## The Later Han Dynasty

Within two years a recovered Han dynasty returned to power, but it ruled over a weakened realm. Nevertheless, during the early years of the Later Han, emperors ruled vigorously in the manner of Liu Bang and Han Wudi. They regained control of the centralized administration and reorganized the state bureaucracy. They also maintained the Chinese presence in central Asia, continued to keep the Xiongnu in submission, and exercised firm control over the silk roads.

However, the Later Han emperors did not seriously address the problem of land distribution that had helped to bring down the Former Han dynasty. The wealthy classes still lived in relative luxury while peasants worked under difficult conditions. The empire continued to suffer the effects of banditry and rebellions organized by desperate peasants with few opportunities to improve their lot.

COLLAPSE OF THE HAN DYNASTY   In addition, the Later Han emperors were unable to prevent the development of factions at court that paralyzed the central government. Factions of imperial family members, Confucian scholar-bureaucrats, and court eunuchs sought to increase their influence, protect their own interests, and destroy their rivals. On several occasions relations between the various factions became so strained that they made war against one another. In 189 C.E., for example, a faction led by an imperial relative descended on the Han palace and slaughtered more than two thousand eunuchs in an effort to destroy them as a political force. In that respect the attack succeeded. From the unmeasured violence of the operation, however, it is clear that the Later Han dynasty had reached a point of internal weakness from which it could not easily recover. Indeed, early in the next century, the central government disintegrated, and for almost four centuries China remained divided into several large regional kingdoms.

# SUMMARY

The Qin state lasted for a short fourteen years, but it opened a new era in Chinese history. Qin conquerors imposed unified rule on a series of politically independent kingdoms and launched an ambitious program to forge culturally distinct regions into a larger Chinese society. The Han dynasty endured for more than four centuries and largely completed the project of unifying China. Han rulers built a centralized bureaucracy that administered a unified empire, thus establishing a precedent for centralized imperial rule in China. They also entered into a close alliance with Confucian moralists who organized a system of advanced education that provided recruits for the imperial bureaucracy. Moreover, on the basis of a highly productive economy stimulated by technological innovations, Han rulers projected Chinese influence abroad to Korea, Vietnam, and central Asia. Thus, like classical societies in Persia, India, and the Mediterranean basin, Han China produced a set of distinctive political and cultural traditions that shaped Chinese and neighboring societies over the long term.

# STUDY TERMS

*Analects* (105)
Confucianism (104)
*Daodejing* (107)
Daoism (106)
Former Han (112)
Han dynasty (112)
Han Wudi (113)
*junzi* (105)
Laozi (107)

Later Han (112)
Legalism (108)
*li* (105)
Liu Bang (112)
Maodun (114)
Mencius (106)
Qin (103)
Qin Shihuangdi (110)

*ren* (105)
Sima Qian (103)
Wang Mang (117)
*wuwei* (108)
*xiao* (105)
Xiongnu (113)
Xunzi (106)
Zhuangzi (107)

# FOR FURTHER READING

Thomas J. Barfield. *The Perilous Frontier: Nomadic Empires and China.* Cambridge, Mass., 1989. A provocative analysis of the relations between Chinese and central Asian peoples.

Sebastian De Grazia, ed. *Masters of Chinese Political Thought from the Beginnings to the Han Dynasty.* New York, 1973. A valuable collection of primary sources in translation, all of them bearing on political themes.

Mark Elvin. *The Pattern of the Chinese Past.* Stanford, 1973. A remarkable analysis of Chinese history by an economic historian who brings a comparative perspective to his work.

Cho-yun Hsu. *Han Agriculture: The Formation of Early Chinese Agrarian Economy (206 B.C.–A.D. 220).* Seattle, 1980. Studies the development of intensive agriculture in Han China and provides English translations of more than two hundred documents illustrating the conditions of rural life.

Michael Loewe. *The Government of the Qin and Han Empires, 221 B.C.E.–220 C.E.* Indianapolis, Ind., 2006. A reliable survey by a leading scholar.

Victor H. Mair, trans. *Tao Te Ching: The Classic Book of Integrity and the Way.* New York, 1990. A fresh and lively translation of the Daoist classic *Daodejing,* based on recently discovered manuscripts.

Frederick W. Mote. *Intellectual Foundations of China.* 2nd ed. New York, 1989. A compact and concise introduction to the cultural history of classical China.

Michele Pirazzoli-t'Serstevens. *The Han Dynasty.* Trans. by J. Seligman. New York, 1982. An excellent and well-illustrated survey of Han China that draws on archaeological discoveries.

Benjamin I. Schwartz. *The World of Thought in Ancient China.* Cambridge, Mass., 1985. A synthesis of classical Chinese thought by a leading scholar.

Arthur Waley, trans. *The Analects of Confucius.* New York, 1938. An English version of Confucius's sayings by a gifted translator.

# State, Society, and the Quest for Salvation in India

## 7

The earliest description of India by a foreigner came from the pen of a Greek ambassador named Megasthenes. As the diplomatic representative of the Seleucid emperor, Megasthenes lived in India for many years during the late fourth and early third centuries B.C.E., and he traveled throughout much of northern India. Although Megasthenes' book, the *Indika*, has long been lost, many quotations from it survive in Greek and Latin literature. These fragments clearly show that Megasthenes had great respect for the Indian land, people, and society.

Like travel writers of all times, Megasthenes included a certain amount of spurious information in his account of India. He wrote, for example, of ants the size of foxes that mined gold from the earth and fiercely defended their hoards from any humans who tried to steal them. Only by distracting them with slabs of meat, Megasthenes said, could humans safely make away with their treasure. He also reported races of monstrous human beings: some with no mouth who survived by breathing in the odors of fruits, flowers, and roots, others with the heads of dogs who communicated by barking.

Beyond the tall tales, Megasthenes offered a great deal of reliable information. He portrayed India as a fertile land that supported two harvests of grain per year. He described the capital of Pataliputra as a rectangle-shaped city situated along the Ganges River and surrounded by a moat and a massive timber wall with 570 towers and sixty-four gates. He mentioned large armies that used elephants as war animals. He pointed out the strongly hierarchical character of Indian society. He noted that two main schools of "philosophers" (Hindus and Buddhists) enjoyed special prominence as well as exemption from taxes, and he described the ascetic lifestyles and vegetarian diets followed by particularly devout individuals. In short, Megasthenes portrayed India as a wealthy land that supported a distinctive society with well-established cultural traditions.

*❮ A painting produced in the sixth century C.E. in the Ajanta caves of central India depicts individuals of different castes,* jati, *and ethnic groups in a crowd scene.*

In India as in Persia and China, the centuries after 500 B.C.E. witnessed the development of a classical society whose influence has persisted over the centuries. Its most prominent features were a well-defined social structure, which left individuals with few doubts about their position and role in society, and several popular religious traditions that helped to shape Indian beliefs and values. Two religions, Buddhism and Hinduism, also appealed strongly to peoples beyond the subcontinent.

For the most part, classical India fell under the sway of regional kingdoms rather than centralized empires. Yet the empires

| | |
|---|---|
| 563–483 B.C.E. | Life of Siddhartha Gautama, the Buddha |
| 540–468 B.C.E. | Life of Vardhamana Mahavira |
| 520 B.C.E. | Invasion of India by Darius of Persia |
| 327 B.C.E. | Invasion of India by Alexander of Macedon |
| 321–185 B.C.E. | Mauryan dynasty |
| 321–297 B.C.E. | Reign of Chandragupta Maurya |
| 268–232 B.C.E. | Reign of Ashoka Maurya |
| 182 B.C.E.–1 C.E. | Bactrian rule in northern India |
| 1–300 C.E. | Kushan empire in northern India and central Asia |
| 78–103 C.E. | Reign of Kushan emperor Kanishka |
| 320–550 C.E. | Gupta dynasty |

that did arise were crucial for the consolidation of Indian cultural traditions, because they sponsored cultural leaders and promoted their ideals throughout the subcontinent and beyond. The spread of Buddhism is a case in point: imperial support helped the faith secure its position in India and attract converts in other lands. Thus, even in the absence of a continuous imperial tradition like that of Persia or China, the social and cultural traditions of classical India not only shaped the lives and experiences of the subcontinent's inhabitants but also influenced peoples in distant lands.

# THE FORTUNES OF EMPIRE IN CLASSICAL INDIA

Following their migrations to India after 1500 B.C.E., the Aryans established a series of small kingdoms throughout the subcontinent. By the sixth century B.C.E., wars of expansion between these small kingdoms had resulted in the consolidation of several large regional kingdoms that dominated much of the subcontinent. Despite strenuous efforts, none of these kingdoms was able to establish hegemony over the others until the classical era, when the Mauryan and the Gupta dynasties founded centralized, imperial states that embraced much of India. However, neither empire survived long enough to establish centralized rule as a lasting feature of Indian political life.

## The Mauryan Dynasty and the Temporary Unification of India

The unification of India came about partly as a result of intrusion from beyond the subcontinent. About 520 B.C.E. the Persian emperor Darius crossed the Hindu Kush Mountains, conquered parts of northwestern India, and made the kingdom of Gandhara in the northern Punjab (the northern part of modern-day Pakistan) a province of the Achaemenid empire. Almost two centuries later, in 327 B.C.E., after overrunning the Persian empire, Alexander of Macedon crossed the Indus River and crushed the states he found there. Alexander remained in India for only two years, and he did not make a deep impression on the Punjabi people. Yet his campaign had an important effect on Indian history, since he created a political vacuum in northwestern India by destroying the existing states and then withdrawing his forces.

KINGDOM OF MAGADHA    Poised to fill the vacuum was the dynamic kingdom of Magadha, located in the central portion of the Ganges plain. By about 500 B.C.E. Magadha had emerged as the most important state in northeastern India. During the next two centuries, the kings of Magadha conquered the neighboring states and gained control of Indian commerce passing through the Ganges valley as well as overseas trade between India and Burma passing across the Bay of Bengal. The withdrawal of Alexander from the Punjab presented Magadha with a rare opportunity to expand.

CHANDRAGUPTA MAURYA    During the late 320s B.C.E., an ambitious adventurer named Chandragupta Maurya exploited that opportunity and laid the foundation for the Mauryan empire, the first state to bring a centralized, unified government to most of the Indian subcontinent. Chandragupta

**Chandragupta Maurya** (chuhn-dra-GOOP-tah MORE-yuh)

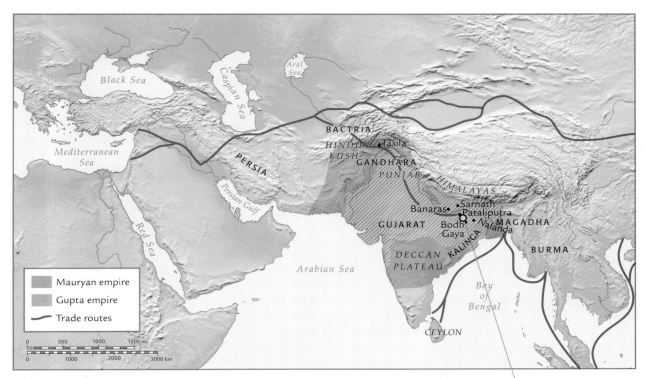

**MAP 7.1** | The Mauryan and Gupta empires, 321 B.C.E.–550 C.E. The Mauryan and Gupta dynasties both originated in the kingdom of Magadha. *Why was this region so important in ancient India? What advantages did it offer for purposes of trade and communication with other regions?*

Both the Mauryan and Gupta empires made their capital in Pataliputra, near the Ganges River.

began by seizing control of small, remote regions of Magadha and then worked his way gradually toward the center. By 321 B.C.E. he had overthrown the ruling dynasty and consolidated his hold on the kingdom. He then moved into the Punjab and brought northwestern India under his control. Next he ventured beyond the Indus River and conquered the Greek state in Bactria. By the end of the fourth century B.C.E., Chandragupta's empire embraced all of northern India from the Indus to the Ganges.

**CHANDRAGUPTA'S GOVERNMENT** A careful and systematic advisor named Kautalya devised procedures for the governance of Chandragupta's realm. Some of Kautalya's advice survives in the ancient Indian political handbook known as the *Arthashastra*. The *Arthashastra* outlined methods of administering the empire, overseeing trade and agriculture, collecting taxes, maintaining order, conducting foreign relations, and waging war. Kautalya also advised Chandragupta to make abundant use of spies, even including prostitutes in his stable of informants. Like the emperors of Persia and China, Chandragupta and Kautalya built a bureaucratic administrative system that enabled them to implement policies throughout the state.

**ASHOKA MAURYA** Tradition holds that Chandragupta abdicated his throne to become a monk and led such an ascetic life that he starved himself to death. Whether that report is true or not, it is certain that his son succeeded him in 297 B.C.E. and added most of

*Arthashastra* (UHRR-th-sha-strah)

**Kautalya** (KAHT-ahl-yah)

**Ashoka** (ah-SHOW-kuh)

**STONE COLUMN FROM THE REIGN OF ASHOKA.**
As a symbol of his rule, Ashoka had this sculpture of four lions mounted atop a column about 20 meters (66 feet) tall. The lion capital is the official symbol of the modern Republic of India. *Why might Ashoka have chosen the lion as a symbol of his rule?*

southern India to the growing empire. The high point of the Mauryan empire, however, came during the reign of Chandragupta's grandson Ashoka.

Ashoka began his reign (268–232 B.C.E.) as a conqueror. When he came to power, the only major region that remained independent of the Mauryan empire was the kingdom of Kalinga (modern Orissa) in the east-central part of the subcontinent. Kalinga was desirable territory for Ashoka because it controlled both land and sea trade routes between the Ganges plain and southern India. Thus Ashoka's first major undertaking as emperor was to conquer Kalinga and bring it under Mauryan control, which he did in a bloody campaign in 260 B.C.E. By Ashoka's estimate, 100,000 Kalingans died in the fighting, 150,000 were driven from their homes, and untold numbers of others perished in the ruined land.

In spite of that campaign, Ashoka is much better known as a governor than as a conqueror. With Kalinga subdued, Ashoka ruled almost the entire subcontinent—only the southernmost region escaped his control—and he turned his attention to the responsible government of his realm. As heir to the administrative structure that Chandragupta and Kautalya had instituted, Ashoka ruled through a tightly organized bureaucracy. He established his capital at the fortified and cosmopolitan city of Pataliputra (near modern Patna), where a central administration developed policies for the whole empire. A central treasury oversaw the efficient collection of taxes—a hallmark of Kautalya's influence—which supported legions of officials, accountants, clerks, soldiers, and other imperial employees. Ashoka communicated his policies throughout his realm by inscribing edicts in natural stone formations or on pillars that he ordered erected. In those promulgations, known as the rock and pillar edicts, Ashoka issued imperial decrees, encouraged his subjects to observe Buddhist values, and expressed his intention to serve as a fair, just, and humane ruler.

As a result of Ashoka's policies, the various regions of India became well integrated, and the subcontinent benefited from both an expanding economy and a stable government. Ashoka encouraged the expansion of agriculture by building irrigation systems. He encouraged trade by building roads, most notably a highway of more than 1,600 kilometers (1,000 miles) linking Pataliputra with Taxila, the chief political and commercial center of northern India, which offered access to Bactria, Persia, and other points west. Ashoka also provided comforts for administrators, merchants, and other travelers by planting banyan trees to offer shade, digging wells, and establishing inns along the roads.

**DECLINE OF THE MAURYAN EMPIRE**  Ashoka's policies did not long survive his rule, nor did his empire. Ashoka died in 232 B.C.E., and decline set in almost immediately. During its later years the Mauryan empire suffered from acute financial and economic difficulties. The empire depended on a strong army and a large corps of officials to administer imperial policy. Salaries for soldiers and bureaucrats were very expensive, and administrative costs soon outstripped the revenues that flowed into the central treasury. Because of their financial difficulties, the later Mauryan emperors were unable to hold the realm together. By about 185 B.C.E., almost fifty years after Ashoka's death, the Mauryan empire had disappeared.

## *The Emergence of Regional Kingdoms and the Revival of Empire*

**BACTRIAN RULE IN NORTHWESTERN INDIA**  Although the Mauryan empire came to an end, India did not crumble into anarchy. Instead, local rulers formed a series of kingdoms that brought order to large regions. Although regional

**Pataliputra** (pah-tal-ih-puh-trah)

kingdoms emerged throughout the subcontinent, historical records and archaeological excavations have thrown clearest light on developments in northern India. For almost two centuries after the collapse of the Mauryan empire, northwestern India fell under the rule of Greek-speaking conquerors from Bactria—Alexander of Macedon's imperial heirs who had mingled with local populations since establishing an independent Bactrian kingdom in the third century B.C.E. Bactria was a thriving commercial center linking lands from China in the east to the Mediterranean basin in the west, so Bactrian rule had the effect of promoting cross-cultural interaction and exchange in northern India. Large volumes of trade provided sources of revenue for the Bactrian rulers, and the city of Taxila flourished because of its strategic location on trade routes leading from northern India to Bactria.

**THE KUSHAN EMPIRE** Beginning in the late second century B.C.E., several groups of nomadic conquerors from central Asia attacked Bactria and eventually put an end to the Indo-Greek kingdom there. The most successful of those conquerors were the Kushans, who ruled a sizable empire embracing much of northern India and central Asia from about 1 to 300 C.E. Under Kanishka, the most prominent of the Kushan emperors (reigned 78–103 C.E.), the Kushan empire embraced modern-day Pakistan, Afghanistan, and northern India to Gujarat and the central part of the Ganges valley. Like the Indo-Greek Bactrians, the Kushans facilitated commerce between India and lands to the north. Indeed, the Kushan empire played a crucial role in the silk roads network (discussed in chapter 9) by pacifying much of the large region between Persia and China, thus making it possible for merchants to travel safely across long distances.

**THE GUPTA DYNASTY** In about 320 C.E., a new power—the Guptas—arose in the Ganges region and established a dynamic kingdom. Like the Mauryas, the Guptas based their state in Magadha, a crucial region because of its wealth, its dominance of the Ganges valley, and its role as intermediary between the various regions of the subcontinent. The empire was founded by Chandra Gupta (not related to Chandragupta Maurya), who forged alliances with powerful families in the Ganges region. His successors, Samudra Gupta (reigned 335–375 C.E.) and Chandra Gupta II (reigned 375–415 C.E.), took the former Mauryan capital of Pataliputra as their own, conquered many of the regional kingdoms of India, and established tributary alliances with others that elected not to fight. Only the Deccan Plateau and the southernmost part of the subcontinent remained outside the orbit of Gupta influence.

The Gupta empire was somewhat smaller in size than the Mauryan, and it also differed considerably in organization. Ashoka had insisted on knowing the details of regional affairs, which he closely monitored from his court at Pataliputra. The Guptas left local government and administration, and even the making of basic policy, in the hands of their allies in the various regions of their empire. Nevertheless, during the late fourth and early fifth centuries C.E., the Gupta dynasty brought stability and prosperity to much of the subcontinent.

**GUPTA DECLINE** The Guptas were eventually overcome, however, by the White Huns, a nomadic people from central Asia. For the first half of the fifth century, the Guptas repelled the Huns as they tried to invade across the Hindu Kush mountains from Bactria, but the defense cost them dearly in resources and eventually weakened their state. By the end of the fifth century, the Huns moved across the Hindu Kush almost at will and had established several kingdoms in northern and western India.

The Gupta dynasty continued in name only: regional governors progressively usurped imperial rights and powers, and contemporary documents do not even record the names of all the later Gupta emperors. Once again, imperial government survived only for a short term in India. Not until the establishment of the Mughal dynasty in the sixteenth

**TRADITIONS IN CLASSICAL INDIA.** Although classical Indian society did not develop long-lasting imperial traditions like classical Persia and China, people throughout the subcontinent nevertheless developed other traditions that promoted both social unity and social order. In what ways did the caste system function to promote this unity and order, and how might it have encouraged a shared sense of identity in India?

**Gupta** (GOOP-tah)

century C.E. did any state rule as much of India as the Mauryan and Gupta empires ruled. Memories of empire remained, to be sure, but for the most part large regional kingdoms dominated political life in India during the millennium between the Gupta and the Mughal dynasties.

# ECONOMIC DEVELOPMENT AND SOCIAL DISTINCTIONS

After spreading through the subcontinent, Aryan migrants turned increasingly from herding to agriculture. Once they learned the techniques of iron metallurgy after about 1000 B.C.E., they used iron axes and tools to advance into previously inaccessible regions, notably the jungle-covered valley of the Ganges River. Agricultural surpluses from these fertile lands supported large-scale states such as the regional kingdoms and the Mauryan and Gupta empires that organized Indian public life. Agricultural surpluses also encouraged the emergence of towns, the growth of trade, and further development of the caste system.

## Towns and Trade

After about 600 B.C.E. towns dotted the Indian countryside, especially in the northwestern corner of the subcontinent. These towns served the needs of a productive agricultural society by providing manufactured products for local consumption—pots, textiles, iron tools, and other metal utensils—as well as luxury goods such as jewelry destined for the wealthy and elite classes.

Flourishing towns maintained marketplaces and encouraged the development of trade. Within the subcontinent itself trade was most active along the Ganges River, although trade routes also passed through the Ganges delta east to Burma and down the east Indian coast to the Deccan and southern India. Roads built by Ashoka also facilitated overland commerce within the subcontinent.

LONG-DISTANCE TRADE   Meanwhile, the volume of long-distance trade also grew as large imperial states in China, southwest Asia, and the Mediterranean basin provided a political foundation enabling merchants to deal with their counterparts in distant lands. From India, long-distance trade passed overland in two directions: through the Hindu Kush mountains and the Gandharan capital of Taxila to Persia and the Mediterranean basin, and across the silk roads of central Asia to markets in China. Cotton, aromatics, black pepper, pearls, and gems were the principal Indian exports, in exchange for which Indian merchants imported horses and bullion from western lands and silk from China.

TRADE IN THE INDIAN OCEAN BASIN   During the Mauryan era merchants continued to use land routes, but they increasingly turned to the sea to transport their goods. Seaborne trade benefited especially from the rhythms of the monsoon winds that govern weather and the seasons in the Indian Ocean basin. During the spring and summer, the winds blow from the southwest, and during the fall and winter, they blow from the northeast. Once mariners recognized these rhythms, they could sail easily and safely before the wind to any part of the Indian Ocean basin.

As early as the fifth century B.C.E., Indian merchants had traveled to the islands of Indonesia and the southeast Asian mainland, where they exchanged pearls, cotton, black pepper, and Indian manufactured goods for spices and exotic local products. Many of those goods then traveled west through the Arabian Sea to the lands bordering the Persian Gulf and the Red Sea. Indian products also found markets in the Mediterranean basin. Indian pepper became so popular there that the Romans established direct commercial relations and built several trading settlements in southern India. Archaeologists in southern India have unearthed hoards of Roman coins that testify to the large volume of trade between classical India and Mediterranean lands.

Jewel-bedecked flying goddesses drop flowers on the earth from their perch in the heavens. Their gems and personal adornments reflect the tastes of upper-class women during the Gupta dynasty. This painting on a rock wall, produced about the sixth century C.E., survives in modern Sri Lanka.

## *Family Life and the Caste System*

GENDER RELATIONS   In the midst of urban growth and economic development, Indian moralists sought to promote stability by encouraging respect for strong patriarchal families and to promote the maintenance of a social order in which all members played well-defined roles. Although most people lived with members of their nuclear family, among the higher castes several generations of a family often lived in large compounds ruled by powerful patriarchs. Literary works suggest that women were largely subordinate to men. The two great Indian epics, the *Mahabharata* and the *Ramayana,* commonly portrayed women as weak-willed and emotional creatures and exalted wives who devoted themselves to their husbands.

During the early centuries C.E., patriarchal dominance became more pronounced in India. By the Gupta era child marriage was common: when girls were age eight or nine, their parents betrothed them to men in their twenties. Formal marriage took place just after the girls reached puberty. Wives often came to dominate domestic affairs in their households, but the practice of child marriage placed them under the control of older men and encouraged them to devote themselves to family matters rather than to public affairs in the larger society.

SOCIAL ORDER   After their arrival in India, the Aryans recognized four main castes, or classes of people: *brahmins* (priests), *kshatriyas* (warriors and aristocrats), *vaishyas*

*Mahabharata* (mah-hah-BAH-'rah-tah)
*Ramayana* (rah-MAY-yuh-nah)
*kshatriyas* (kuh-SHAT-tree-uhs)

**BUDDHIST TEMPLE SCULPTURE.** | Buddhist art often depicted individuals as models of proper social relationships. Here a sculpture from a Buddhist temple at Karli, produced about the first century C.E., represents an ideal Buddhist married couple. *What does the position of the images imply about the ideal relationship between husband and wife?*

(peasants and merchants), and *shudras* (serfs). Brahmins in particular endorsed this social order, which brought them honor, prestige, and sometimes considerable wealth as well.

CASTES AND GUILDS    However, as trade and industrial activity expanded, new groups of artisans, craftsmen, and merchants appeared, many of whom did not fit easily into the established structure. Individuals working in the same craft or trade usually joined together to form a guild, a corporate body that supervised prices and wages in a given industry and provided for the welfare of members and their families. Guild members lived in the same quarter of town, socialized with one another, intermarried, and cared for the group's widows, orphans, and needy.

In effect, the guilds functioned as subcastes based on occupation, known as *jati.* These *jati,* in turn, assumed much of the responsibility for maintaining social order in India. *Jati* regularly organized their own courts, through which they disciplined members, resolved differences, and regulated community affairs. Individuals who did not abide by group rules were liable to expulsion from the community. Thus Indian guilds and *jati* performed services that central governments provided in other lands. The tendency for individuals and their families to associate closely with others of the same occupation remained a prominent feature of Indian society well into modern times.

WEALTH AND THE SOCIAL ORDER    Beyond encouraging further development of the caste system, economic development in the subcontinent also generated tremendous wealth, which posed a serious challenge to the social order that arose in India following the Aryan migrations. Traditional social theory accorded special honor to the brahmins and the kshatriyas because of the worthy lives they had led during previous incarnations and the heavy responsibilities they assumed as priests, warriors, and rulers during their current incarnations. Members of the vaishya and shudra castes, on the other hand, had the obligation to work as directed by the higher castes. During the centuries after 600 B.C.E., however, trade and industry brought prosperity to many vaishyas and even shudras, who sometimes became wealthier and more influential in society than their brahmin and kshatriya contemporaries.

Economic development and social change in classical India had profound implications for the established cultural as well as the social order. The beliefs, values, and rituals that were meaningful in early Aryan society—especially the ritual sacrifices offered by brahmins—seemed increasingly irrelevant during the centuries after 600 B.C.E. Along with emerging towns, growing trade, increasing wealth, and a developing social structure, classical India saw the appearance of new religions that addressed the needs of the changing times.

# RELIGIONS OF SALVATION IN CLASSICAL INDIA

During the sixth and fifth centuries B.C.E., new religions and philosophies appealed to the interests of new social classes. Some of them tended toward atheistic materialism: members of the Charvaka sect, for example, believed that the gods were figments of the imagination, that brahmins were charlatans who enriched themselves by hoodwinking others, and that human beings came from dust and returned to dust like any other animal in the natural world. Others, such as the Jains, the Buddhists, and the Hindus, turned to intense spirituality as an alternative to the mechanical rituals of the brahmins.

*vaishyas* (VEYESH-yuhs)

*shudras* (SHOO-druhs)

**Charvaka** (CHAHR-vah-kuh)

# Jainism and the Challenge to the Established Cultural Order

**VARDHAMANA MAHAVIRA** Among the most influential of the new religions was Jainism. Although Jainist doctrines first appeared during the seventh century B.C.E., they became popular only when the great teacher Vardhamana Mahavira turned to Jainism in the late sixth century B.C.E. Mahavira (the "great hero") was born in northern India about 540 B.C.E. to a prominent kshatriya family. According to the semilegendary accounts of his life, he left home at age thirty to seek salvation by escaping from the cycle of incarnation. For twelve years he led an ascetic life wandering throughout the Ganges valley, after which he gained enlightenment. He abandoned all his worldly goods, even his clothes, and taught an ascetic doctrine of detachment from the world. For the next thirty years, until his death about 468 B.C.E., he expounded his thought to a group of disciples who formed a monastic order to perpetuate and spread his message. These disciples referred to Mahavira as *Jina* (the "conqueror"), and borrowing from this title his followers referred to themselves as *Jains*.

Much of the inspiration for Jainist doctrine came from the Upanishads. Jains believed that everything in the universe—humans, animals, plants, the air, bodies of water, and even inanimate physical objects—possessed a soul. As long as they remained trapped in terrestrial bodies, these souls experienced both physical and psychological suffering. Only by purification from selfish behavior could souls gain release from their imprisonment and attain a state of bliss.

**JAIN SCULPTURE.** | Mahavira with one of his disciples. Representations of the early Jains often depicted them in the nude because of their ascetic way of life.

**JAINIST ETHICS** Individuals underwent purification by observing the principle of *ahimsa,* or nonviolence to other souls. Devout Jainist monks went to extremes to avoid harming the millions of souls they encountered each day. They swept the ground before them as they walked to avoid causing harm to insects; they strained their drinking water through cloth filters to remove tiny animals they might unwittingly consume; they followed an abstemious and strictly vegetarian diet; they even wore masks and avoided making sudden movements so that they would not bruise or otherwise disturb the tiny souls inhabiting the surrounding air.

Jainist ethics were so demanding that few people other than devout monks could hope to observe them closely. For certain groups, however, Jainism represented an attractive alternative to the traditional cults. Indeed, since Jains believed all creatures had souls that should be protected equally, Jains did not recognize human social hierarchies based on caste or *jati.* It is not surprising, then, that their faith became popular especially among members of lower castes, including merchants, scholars, and literary figures. These people provided substantial lay support for the Jainist monks and helped to maintain the ideal of ahimsa as a prominent concern of Indian ethics. Indeed, the doctrine of ahimsa has been an especially influential teaching over the long term, both in India and beyond. Quite apart from some two million Indian individuals who maintain Jainist traditions in the present day, many Buddhists and Hindus recognize ahimsa as a fundamental element of their beliefs, and prominent reformers of the twentieth century C.E. such as Mohandas K. Gandhi and Martin Luther King Jr. relied on the doctrine of ahimsa when promoting social reform by nonviolent means.

In spite of the moral respect it has commanded and the influence it has wielded through the centuries, however, Jainism has always been the faith of a small minority. It has simply

**Jainism** (JEYEN-iz'm)

**Vardhamana** (vahr-duh-MAH-nuh)

**Upanishads** (oo-pan-NIH-shuhds)

*ahimsa* (uh-HIM-suh)

been too difficult for most people to observe. A more popular and practical alternative to the brahmins' cults came in the form of Buddhism.

## Early Buddhism

**SIDDHARTHA GUATAMA**   Like Mahavira, the founder of Buddhism, Siddhartha Gautama, came from a kshatriya family but gave up his position and inheritance to seek salvation. He was born about 563 B.C.E. in a small tribal state governed by his father in the foothills of the Himalayas. According to early accounts, Gautama lived a pampered and sheltered life in palaces and parks, because his father had determined that Gautama would never know misery. He married his cousin and excelled in the program of studies that would prepare him to succeed his father as governor.

Eventually, however, Gautama became dissatisfied with his comfortable life. One day, according to an early legend, while riding toward a park in his chariot, Gautama saw a man made miserable by age and infirmity. When he asked for an explanation of this unsettling sight, Gautama learned from his chariot driver that all human beings grow old and weak. On later outings Gautama learned that disease and death were also inevitable features of the human condition. When he then came into contact with a monk traveling by foot, Gautama learned that some individuals withdraw from the active life of the world to lead holy lives. Inspired, Gautama determined to take up a similar life for himself in the hope that it would help him to understand the phenomenon of suffering.

**GAUTAMA'S SEARCH FOR ENLIGHTENMENT**   About 534 B.C.E. Gautama left his wife and family and the comforts of home to lead the existence of a holy man. He wandered throughout the Ganges valley searching for spiritual enlightenment and an explanation for suffering. He sought enlightenment first by means of intense meditation and later through the rigors of extreme asceticism. None of those tactics satisfied him. Then, according to Buddhist legends, as he sat one day beneath a large bo tree in Bodh Gaya, southwest of Pataliputra, Gautama decided that he would remain exactly where he was until he understood the problem of suffering. For forty-nine days he sat in meditation as various demons tempted and threatened him to shake his resolution. On the forty-ninth day Gautama prevailed and received enlightenment: he understood both the problem of suffering and the means by which humans could eliminate it from the world. At that point, Gautama became the Buddha—the "enlightened one."

**THE BUDDHA AND HIS FOLLOWERS**   The Buddha publicly announced his doctrine for the first time about 528 B.C.E. at the Deer Park of Sarnath, near the Buddhist holy city of Banaras (modern Varanasi), in a sermon delivered to friends. Buddhists refer to this sermon as the "Turning of the Wheel of the Law" because it represented the beginning of the Buddha's quest to promulgate the law of righteousness. His teachings quickly attracted attention, and disciples came from all parts of the Ganges valley. He organized them into a community of monks who owned only their yellow robes and their begging bowls. For more than forty years, the Buddha led his disciples throughout much of northern India in hopes of bringing spiritual enlightenment to others.

**BUDDHIST DOCTRINE: THE DHARMA**   The core of the Buddha's doctrine, known as the Four Noble Truths, teaches that all life involves suffering; that desire is the cause of suffering; that elimination of desire brings an end to suffering; and that a disciplined life conducted in accordance with the Noble Eightfold Path brings the elimination of desire. The Noble Eightfold Path calls for individuals to lead balanced and moderate lives, rejecting both devotion to luxury and to regimes of extreme asceticism.

**Siddhartha Gautama** (sih-DHAR-tuh GAHW-tah-mah)
**Buddha** (BOO-duh)

Specifically, the Noble Eightfold Path demands right belief, right resolve, right speech, right behavior, right occupation, right effort, right contemplation, and right meditation. Taken together, the teachings of the Four Noble Truths and the Noble Eightfold Path constitute the Buddhist *dharma*—the basic doctrine shared by Buddhists of all sects.

Ultimately, Buddhists believed that a lifestyle based on the Buddhist dharma would lead to personal salvation, which meant an escape from the cycle of incarnation and attainment of *nirvana,* a state of perfect spiritual independence. Like the Jains, the Buddhists sought to escape the cycle of incarnation without depending on the services of the brahmins. Like the Jains, too, they did not recognize social distinctions based on caste or *jati*. As a result, their message appealed strongly to members of lower castes. Yet, because it did not demand the rigorous asceticism of Jainism, Buddhism became far more popular, especially with merchants.

APPEAL OF BUDDHISM   Apart from the social implications of the doctrine, there were several other reasons for the popularity of early Buddhism in India. One has to do with language. Following the example of the Buddha himself, early Buddhist monks and preachers avoided the use of Sanskrit, the literary language of the *Vedas* that the brahmins employed in their rituals, in favor of vernacular tongues that reached a much larger popular audience. Furthermore, early Buddhists recognized holy sites that served as focal points for devotion. Even in the early days of Buddhism, pilgrims flocked to Bodh Gaya, where Gautama received enlightenment, and the Deer Park of Sarnath, where as the Buddha he preached his first sermon. Also popular with the faithful were stupas—shrines housing

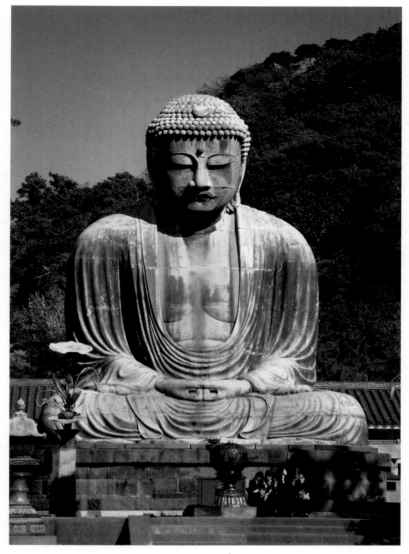

SCULPTURE OF THE BUDDHA.   | A confident and serene Buddha preaches his first sermon after his enlightenment at the Deer Park of Sarnath. *Why is the Buddha commonly depicted in this position?*

relics of the Buddha and his first disciples that pilgrims venerated while meditating on Buddhist values.

Yet another reason for the early popularity of Buddhism was the organization of the Buddhist movement. From the days of the Buddha himself, the most enthusiastic and highly motivated converts joined monastic communities where they dedicated their lives to the search for enlightenment and to preaching the Buddhist dharma to lay audiences. During the centuries following the Buddha's death, this monastic organization proved to be extremely efficient at spreading the Buddhist message and winning converts to the faith.

Buddha with devotees
www.mhhe.com/
bentleybrief2e

Buddhist statues at Sanchi
www.mhhe.com/
bentleybrief2e

**dharma** (DHUHR-muh)

**Buddhism** (BOO-diz'm)

**nirvana** (ner-VAHN-nah)

**stupas** (STOO-pahs)

**THE BUDDHIST STUPA AT SANCHI.** | This stupa was originally built by Ashoka and enlarged in later times.

ASHOKA'S SUPPORT   The early Buddhist movement also benefited from the official patronage and support of the Mauryan dynasty. The precise reason for Ashoka's conversion to Buddhism is unclear. Ashoka's own account, as preserved in one of his edicts, explains that the emperor adopted Buddhism about 260 B.C.E. after the war against Kalinga. Saddened by the violence of the war and the suffering of the Kalingans, Ashoka said that he decided to pursue his aims henceforth by means of virtue, benevolence, and humanity rather than arms. Quite apart from his sincere religious convictions, it is also likely that Ashoka found Buddhism appealing as a faith that could lend unity to his culturally diverse and far-flung realm. In any case, in honor of ahimsa, the doctrine of nonviolence, Ashoka banned animal sacrifices in Pataliputra, gave up his beloved hunting expeditions, and eliminated most meat dishes from the tables of his court. Ashoka rewarded Buddhists with grants of land, and he encouraged them to spread their faith throughout India. He built monasteries and stupas and made pilgrimages to the holy sites of Buddhism. Ashoka also sent missionaries to Bactria and Ceylon (modern Sri Lanka), thus inaugurating a process by which Buddhism attracted large followings in central Asia, east Asia, and southeast Asia.

## Mahayana Buddhism

From its earliest days Buddhism attracted merchants, artisans, and others of low rank in the traditional Indian social order. Its appeal was due both to its disregard for social classes and to its concern for ethical behavior instead of complicated ceremonies. Yet, even though it vastly simplified religious observances, early Buddhism made heavy demands on individuals seeking to escape from the cycle of incarnation. A truly righteous existence involved considerable sacrifice: giving up personal property, forsaking the search for social standing, and resolutely detaching oneself from the charms of family and the world. Although perhaps more attractive than the religion of the *brahmins,* Buddhism did not promise to make life easy for its adherents.

DEVELOPMENT OF BUDDHISM   Between the third century B.C.E. and the first century C.E., however, three new developments in Buddhist thought and practice reduced obligations of believers, opened new avenues to salvation, and brought explosive popularity to the faith. In the first place, whereas the Buddha had not considered himself divine, some of his later followers began to worship him as a god. Thus Buddhism acquired a devotional focus that helped converts channel their spiritual energies. In the second place, theologians articulated the notion of the *boddhisatva,* an enlightened being. Boddhisatvas were individuals who had reached spiritual perfection and merited the reward of nirvana, but who intentionally delayed their entry into nirvana to help others who were still struggling. Like Christian saints, boddhisatvas served as examples of spiritual excellence, and they provided a source of inspiration. Finally, Buddhist monasteries began to accept gifts from wealthy individuals and to regard the bequests as acts of generosity that merited salvation. Thus wealthy individuals could avoid the sacrifices demanded by early Buddhist teachings and still ensure their salvation.

**BODDHISATVA CARVING.** This carving dates from the second or third century C.E. It may represent Avalokitesvara, also known as the Lord of Compassion. Almost as perfect as the Buddha, Avalokitesvara had a reputation for protecting merchants and sailors, helping women conceive, and turning enemies into kindhearted friends.

**THE SPREAD OF MAHAYANA BUDDHISM**   Because these innovations opened the road to salvation for large numbers of people, their proponents called their faith the *Mahayana* (the "greater vehicle," which could carry more people to salvation), as opposed to the *Hinayana* (the "lesser vehicle"), a pejorative term for the earlier and stricter doctrine known also as Theravada Buddhism. During the early centuries C.E., Mahayana Buddhism spread rapidly throughout India and attracted many converts. In later centuries Mahayana Buddhism became established also in central Asia, China, Japan, and Korea. The stricter Theravada faith did not disappear, but since the first century C.E. most of the world's Buddhists have practiced Mahayana Buddhism.

**NALANDA**   Mahayana Buddhism flourished partly because of educational institutions that promoted the faith. During the Vedic era, Indian education was mostly an informal affair involving a sage and his students. When Jains and Buddhists organized monasteries, however, they began to establish educational institutions. Most monasteries provided basic education, and larger communities offered advanced instruction as well. Best known of all was the Buddhist monastery at Nalanda, founded during the Gupta dynasty in the Ganges River valley near Pataliputra. At Nalanda it was possible to study not only Buddhism but also the *Vedas,* Hindu philosophy, logic, mathematics, astronomy, and medicine. Nalanda soon became famous, and by the end of the Gupta dynasty, several thousand students may have been in residence there.

Buddhist priests in Sri Lanka and Cambodia
www.mhhe.com/bentleybrief2e

## *The Emergence of Popular Hinduism*

As Buddhism generated new ideas and attracted widespread popular interest, Hinduism underwent a similar evolution that transformed it into a popular religion of salvation. Although drawing inspiration from the *Vedas* and the Upanishads, popular Hinduism increasingly departed from the older traditions of the brahmins to meet the needs of ordinary people.

**THE BHAGAVAD GITA**   A short poetic work known as the *Bhagavad Gita* ("song of the lord") best illustrates both the expectations that Hinduism made of individuals and the promise of salvation that it held out to them. Scholars have dated the work at various points between 300 B.C.E. and 300 C.E., and it most likely underwent several rounds of revision before taking on its final form about 400 C.E. Yet it eloquently evokes the cultural climate of India between the Mauryan and the Gupta dynasties.

**THINKING ABOUT** *Encounters*

**ENCOUNTERS IN CLASSICAL INDIA.** Throughout the classical period, India was tied to vast overland trading networks linking it to central and east Asia, as well as ocean trading networks linking it to southeast and east Asia. How did the interactions promoted by these networks alter Indian society, and to what extent did these same networks allow for the diffusion of Indian cultural beliefs and practices?

**boddhisatvas** (BOH-dih-SAT-vuhs)

**Mahayana** (mah-huh-YAH-nah)

**Hinayana** (HEE-nah-yah-nuh)

**Theravada** (thehr-ah-VAH-dah)

*According to the sources written about the Buddha (born Siddhartha Gautama) after his death, his first sermon addressed the problem of human suffering. According to the Buddha, human suffering was the result of attachment to life's passions, to the body, to health, to things, or to people. In order to alleviate suffering, then, the Buddha advised a practice of non-attachment. Eventually, the goal was to reach a state of nirvana, or extinguishment, in which the soul is released from the cycle of rebirth and suffering.*

The world is full of suffering. Birth is suffering, old age is suffering, sickness and death are sufferings. To meet a man whom one hates is suffering. To be separated from a beloved one is suffering. To be vainly struggling to satisfy one's needs is suffering. In fact, life that is not free from desire and passion is always involved with distress. This is called the Truth of Suffering.

The cause of human suffering is undoubtedly found in the thirsts of the physical body and in the illusions of worldly passion. If these thirsts and illusions are traced to their source, they are found to be rooted in the intense desires of physical instincts. Thus, desire, having a strong will-to-live as its basis, seeks that which it feels desirable, even if it is sometimes death. This is called the Truth of the Cause of Suffering.

If desire, which lies at the root of all human passion, can be removed, then passion will die out and all human suffering will be ended. This is called the Truth of the Cessation of Suffering.

In order to enter into a state where there is no desire and no suffering, one must follow a certain Path. The stages of the Noble Eightfold Path are: Right Understanding, Right Purpose, Right Speech, Right Behavior, Right Livelihood, Right Effort, Right Mindfulness, and Right Concentration. This is called the Truth of the Noble Path to the Cessation of the Cause of Suffering.

People should keep these Truths clearly in mind, for the world is filled with suffering, and if anyone wishes to escape from suffering, he must sever the ties of worldly passion, which is the sole cause of suffering. The way of life which is free from all worldly passion and suffering can only be known through Enlightenment, and Enlightenment can only be attained through the discipline of the Noble Eightfold Path.

■ Consider the teachings of the Buddha in comparison to popular Hinduism as it was expressed in the *Bhagavad Gita*. How did the lessons of the Buddha differ from those of the *Bhagavad Gita*, especially regarding the advisability of involving oneself in the affairs of day-to-day life?

SOURCE: Thomas Sanders et al. *Encounters in World History: Sources and Themes from the Global Past*, Vol. I. Boston: McGraw-Hill, 2006, pp. 113–114.

Mahabharata map of important Hindu sites
www.mhhe.com/bentleybrief2e

Vishnu dreaming the universe
www.mhhe.com/bentleybrief2e

The work is a self-contained episode of the *Mahabharata,* one of the great epic poems of India. It presents a dialogue between Arjuna, a kshatriya about to enter battle, and his charioteer Krishna, who was in fact a human incarnation of the god Vishnu. The immediate problem addressed in the work was Arjuna's reluctance to fight: the enemy included many of his friends and relatives, and even though he recognized the justice of his cause, he shrank from the conflict. In an effort to persuade the warrior to fight, Krishna presented Arjuna with several lines of argument. In the first place, he said, Arjuna must not worry about harming his friends and relatives, because the soul does not die with the human body, and Arjuna's weapons did not have the power to touch the soul.

Krishna also held that Arjuna's caste imposed specific moral duties and social responsibilities on him. The duty of shudras was to serve, of vaishyas to work, of brahmins to learn the scriptures and seek wisdom. Similarly, Krishna argued, the duty of kshatriyas was to govern and fight. Indeed, Krishna went further and held that failure to fulfill caste duties was a grievous sin, whereas their observance brought spiritual benefits.

Finally, Krishna taught that Arjuna would attain everlasting peace if he devoted himself to the love, adoration, and service of Krishna himself. Arjuna should abandon his selfish and superficial personal concerns and surrender to the deeper wisdom of the god. As a reward, Arjuna would receive eternal salvation through unity with his god. Alongside understanding of the soul and caste duties, then, unquestioning faith and devotion would put Arjuna in the proper state of mind for the conflict by aligning his actions with divine wisdom and will. Krishna's teaching that faith would bring salvation helped inspire a tradition of ecstatic and unquestioning devotion in popular Hinduism.

**HINDU ETHICS**  Hindu ethics thus differed considerably from those of earlier Indian moralists. The Upanishads had taught that only through renunciation and detachment from the world could individuals escape the cycle of incarnation. As represented in the *Bhagavad Gita,* however, Hindu ethical teachings also held out the promise of salvation to those who participated actively in the world and met their caste responsibilities. To be sure, Krishna taught that individuals should meet their responsibilities in detached fashion and that they should not strive for material reward or recognition. Rather, they should perform their duties faithfully, with no thought as to their consequences.

Other works by early Hindu moralists acknowledged even more openly than did the *Bhagavad Gita* that individuals could lead honorable lives in the world. Indeed, Hindu ethics commonly recognized four principal aims of human life: *dharma,* obedience to religious and moral laws; *artha,* the pursuit of economic well-being and honest prosperity; *kama,* the enjoyment of social, physical, and sexual pleasure; and *moksha,* the salvation of the soul. According to Hindu moral precepts, a proper balance of *dharma, artha,* and *kama* would help an individual to attain *moksha.*

As devotional Hinduism evolved and became increasingly distinct from the teachings of the Upanishads and the older traditions of the brahmins, it also enhanced its appeal to all segments of Indian society. Hinduism offered salvation to masses of people who, as a matter of practical necessity, had to lead active lives in the world and thus could not hope to achieve the detachment envisioned in the Upanishads.

**POPULARITY OF HINDUISM**  Hinduism gradually displaced Buddhism as the most popular religion in India. Later Buddhist monks did not seek to communicate their message to the larger society in the zealous way of their predecessors but increasingly confined themselves to the comforts of monasteries richly endowed by wealthy patrons. Meanwhile, devotional Hinduism attracted political support and patronage, particularly from the Gupta emperors. The Guptas and their successors bestowed grants of land on Hindu *brahmins* and supported an educational system that promoted Hindu values. Just as Ashoka Maurya had advanced the cause of Buddhism, the Guptas and their successors later helped Hinduism become the dominant religious and cultural tradition in India. By about 1000 C.E., Buddhism had entered a noticeable decline in India, while Hinduism was growing in popularity. Within a few centuries devotional Hinduism and the more recently introduced faith of Islam almost completely eclipsed Buddhism in its homeland.

# SUMMARY

In India, as in classical Persia and China, a robust agricultural economy supported the creation of large-scale states and interregional trade. Although an imperial state did not become a permanent feature of Indian political life, the peoples of the subcontinent maintained an orderly society based on the caste system and regional states. Indian cultural and religious traditions reflected the conditions of the larger society in which they developed. Mahayana Buddhism and devotional Hinduism in particular addressed the needs of the increasingly prominent lay classes, and the two faiths profoundly influenced the religious life of Asian peoples over the long term of history.

# STUDY TERMS

ahimsa (129)
*artha* (135)
*Arthashastra* (123)
Ashoka (123)
*Bhagavad Gita* (133)
boddhisatva (133)
brahmin (127)
Buddhism (131)
Chandragupta Maurya (122)
dharma (131)

Four Noble Truths (130)
Gupta dynasty (125)
Hinayana Buddhism (133)
Jainism (129)
*kama* (135)
kshatriya (127)
Kushan empire (125)
Maghada (122)
*Mahabharata* (127)

Mahayana Buddhism (133)
Mauryan dynasty (122)
*moksha* (135)
nirvana (131)
Pataliputra (124)
shudra (128)
Siddhartha Gautama (130)
Theravada Buddhism (133)
*vaishya* (128)

# FOR FURTHER READING

Roy C. Amore and Larry D. Shinn. *Lustful Maidens and Ascetic Kings.* New York, 1981. Translations of stories and moral tales from Hindu and Buddhist writings.

Jeannine Auboyer. *Daily Life in Ancient India.* Trans. by S. W. Taylor. New York, 1965. An excellent and well-researched, though somewhat dated, introduction to Indian social history during the classical era.

Edward Conze. *Buddhism: Its Essence and Development.* New York, 1959. Systematic account of Buddhism from a theological point of view.

William Theodore De Bary, ed. *Sources of Indian Tradition.* 2 vols. 2nd ed. New York, 1988. Important collection of sources in translation.

Xinru Liu. *Ancient India and Ancient China: Trade and Religious Exchanges, A.D. 1–600.* Delhi, 1988. Important study exploring the early spread of Buddhism from India to central Asia and China.

Juan Mascaró, trans. *The Bhagavad Gita.* Harmondsworth, 1962. Brilliant and evocative English version by a gifted translator.

Jean W. Sedlar. *India and the Greek World: A Study in the Transmission of Culture.* Totowa, N.J., 1980. Important study of relations between India and Greece, based on solid research.

Romila Thapar. *Ashoka and the Decline of the Mauryas.* London, 1961. The best scholarly study of Ashoka and his reign.

———. *Early India: From the Origins to A.D. 1300.* Berkeley, 2003. A fresh view by one of the leading scholars of early Indian history.

Stanley Wolpert. *A New History of India,* 7th ed. New York, 2004. A concise and readable survey of Indian history.

# Mediterranean Society under the Greeks and the Romans

## 8

For a man who perhaps never existed, Homer has been a profoundly influential figure. According to tradition, Homer composed the two great epic poems of ancient Greece, the *Iliad* and the *Odyssey*. In fact, scholars now know that bards recited both poems for generations before Homer, and some believe that Homer was simply a convenient name for the otherwise anonymous scribes who committed the *Iliad* and the *Odyssey* to writing. Whether Homer ever really lived or not, the epics attributed to him deeply influenced the development of classical Greek thought and literature. The *Iliad* offered a Greek perspective on a campaign waged by a band of Greek warriors against the city of Troy in Anatolia during the twelfth century B.C.E. The *Odyssey* recounted the experiences of the Greek hero Odysseus as he sailed home after the Trojan War. The two works described scores of difficulties faced by Greek warriors, including battles, monsters, and conflicts among themselves. Between them, the two epics preserved a rich collection of stories that literary figures mined for more than a millennium.

The *Iliad* and the *Odyssey* also testify to the frequency and normality of travel, communication, and interaction in the Mediterranean basin during the second and first millennia B.C.E. Both works portray Greeks as expert and fearless seamen, almost as comfortable aboard their ships as on land, who did not hesitate to venture into the waters of what Homer called the "wine-dark sea." Homer lovingly described the sleek galleys in which Greek warriors raced across the waters, and he even had Odysseus construct a sailing ship single-handedly when he found himself shipwrecked on an island inhabited only by a goddess. The *Iliad* and the *Odyssey* make it clear that maritime links touched peoples throughout the Mediterranean basin in Homer's time and, further, that Greeks were among the most prominent seafarers of the age.

The maritime links established by the Greeks lived on long after the decline of classical Greek society. Indeed, the Romans took advantage of those links and used them to build a powerful society that dominated the whole Mediterranean basin by the first century C.E. By that time, Roman citizens found themselves living in a cosmopolitan world in which Roman administrators oversaw affairs from Anatolia and Palestine in the east to Spain and Morocco in the west.

Just as Homer's epics recall the world of the Greeks, the story of Paul of Tarsus reflects the cosmopolitan world of the

‹ *Pericles organized the construction of numerous marble buildings, partly with funds collected from poleis belonging to the Delian League. Most notable of his projects was the Parthenon, a temple dedicated to the goddess Athena, which symbolizes the prosperity and grandeur of classical Athens.*

**Ship fresco from Akroti**
www.mhhe.com/
bentleybrief2e

# CHRONOLOGY

| | |
|---|---|
| 2200–1100 B.C.E. | Minoan society |
| 1600–1100 B.C.E. | Mycenaean society |
| 800–338 B.C.E. | Era of the classical Greek polis |
| 509 B.C.E. | Establishment of the Roman republic |
| 500–479 B.C.E. | Persian Wars |
| 470–399 B.C.E. | Life of Socrates |
| 443–429 B.C.E. | Pericles' leadership in Athens |
| 431–404 B.C.E. | Peloponnesian War |
| 430–347 B.C.E. | Life of Plato |
| 384–322 B.C.E. | Life of Aristotle |
| 359–336 B.C.E. | Reign of Philip II of Macedon |
| 336–323 B.C.E. | Reign of Alexander of Macedon |
| 264–146 B.C.E. | Roman expansion in the Mediterranean basin |
| 106–43 B.C.E. | Life of Marcus Tullius Cicero |
| first century B.C.E. | Civil war in Rome |
| 46–44 B.C.E. | Rule of Gaius Julius Caesar as dictator |
| 31 B.C.E.–14 C.E. | Rule of Augustus |
| 4 B.C.E.–early 30s C.E. | Life of Jesus of Nazareth |
| first century C.E. | Life of Paul of Tarsus |
| 66–70 C.E. | Jewish War |

Romans. Born in the first century C.E., Paul was a devout Jew from Anatolia who accepted the Christian teachings of Jesus of Nazareth. Paul was a principal figure in the development of Christianity to an independent religious faith, largely because of his zealous missionary efforts to attract converts from outside as well as within the Jewish community. While promoting his adopted faith in Jerusalem about 55 C.E., however, Paul was attacked by a crowd of his enemies who believed his views were a threat to Judaism. The disturbance was so severe that Roman authorities intervened to restore order.

Under normal circumstances, Roman authorities would have delivered Paul to the leaders of his own ethnic community, where he would be dealt with according to custom. But knowing that Jewish leaders would probably execute him, Paul asserted his rights as a Roman citizen to appeal his case in Rome. Paul had never been to Rome, but this Anatolian traveling in Palestine called on the laws of the imperial center to determine his fate. Paul traveled across the Mediterranean to Rome, but his appeal did not succeed. Tradition holds that he was executed by imperial authorities out of concern that Christianity was a threat to the peace and stability of the empire.

Under both the Greeks and the Romans, the Mediterranean basin became much more tightly integrated than before as both societies organized commercial exchange and sponsored interaction throughout the region. In fact, under Greek and then Roman supervision, the Mediterranean served not as a barrier but, rather, as a highway. Moreover, this highway carried more than soldiers, citizens, and goods: it also carried ideas. Indeed, Greek philosophy—which generated a remarkable body of moral thought and philosophical reflection—shaped the cultural foundations of the Roman republic and empire, as educated Roman thinkers drew inspiration from their neighbors to the east. Later, this highway carried the Christian religion to all corners of the Roman empire.

Yet Greek and Roman societies also differed substantially, both in organization and in outlook. Early in the classical era, the Greeks lived in independent, autonomous city-states. Only after the late third century B.C.E. did they play prominent roles in the large, centralized empire established by their neighbors to the north in Macedon. Until then, the Greeks had integrated the societies and economies of distant lands mainly through energetic commercial activity over the Mediterranean sea-lanes. In contrast to the Greeks, the Romans built an extensive, centralized land empire. At its high point the Roman empire dominated the entire Mediterranean basin and parts of southwest Asia as well as north Africa and much of continental Europe and Britain. In addition, whereas Greek authorities did not sponsor an evangelical religion, Christianity eventually became the official religion of the Roman empire, which allowed the new religion to spread much more effectively than before.

# EARLY DEVELOPMENT OF GREEK SOCIETY

During the third millennium B.C.E., the peoples of the Balkan region and the Greek peninsula increasingly met and mingled with peoples from different societies who traveled and traded in the Mediterranean basin. As a result, early inhabitants of the Greek peninsula built their societies under the influence of Mesopotamians, Egyptians, Phoenicians, and others active in the region. Beginning in the ninth century B.C.E., the Greeks organized a series of city-states, which served as the political context for the development of classical Greek society.

## *Minoan and Mycenaean Societies*

KNOSSOS    During the late third millennium B.C.E., a sophisticated society arose on the island of Crete. Scholars refer to it as Minoan society, after Minos, a legendary king of ancient Crete. Between 2000 and 1700 B.C.E., the inhabitants of Crete built a series of lavish palaces throughout the island, most notably the enormous complex at Knossos decorated with vivid frescoes depicting Minoans at work and play. These palaces were the nerve centers of Minoan society: they were residences of rulers, and they also served as storehouses where officials collected taxes in kind from local cultivators.

Between 2200 and 1450 B.C.E., Crete was a principal center of Mediterranean commerce. By 2200 B.C.E. Cretans were traveling aboard advanced sailing craft of Phoenician design. Minoan ships sailed to Greece, Anatolia, Phoenicia, and Egypt, where they exchanged Cretan wine, olive oil, and wool for grains, textiles, and manufactured goods. After 1600 B.C.E. Cretans established colonies on Cyprus and many islands in the Aegean Sea.

DECLINE OF MINOAN SOCIETY    After 1700 B.C.E. Minoan society experienced a series of earthquakes, volcanic eruptions, and tidal waves. Between 1600 and 1450 B.C.E., Cretans embarked on a new round of palace building to replace structures destroyed by those natural catastrophes: they built luxurious complexes with indoor plumbing and drainage systems and even furnished some of them with flush toilets. After 1450 B.C.E., however, the wealth of Minoan society attracted a series of invaders, and by 1100 B.C.E. Crete had fallen under foreign domination. Yet Minoan traditions deeply influenced the inhabitants of nearby Greece.

MYCENAEAN SOCIETY    Beginning about 2200 B.C.E. migratory Indo-European peoples filtered into the Greek peninsula. By 1600 B.C.E. they had begun to trade with Minoan merchants and visit Crete, where they learned about writing and large-scale construction. After 1450 B.C.E. they also built massive stone fortresses and palaces throughout the southern part of the Greek peninsula, known as the Peloponnesus. Because the fortified sites offered protection, they soon attracted settlers, who built small agricultural communities. Their society is known as Mycenaean, after Mycenae, one of their most important settlements.

CHAOS IN THE EASTERN MEDITERRANEAN    From 1500 to 1100 B.C.E., the Mycenaeans expanded their influence beyond peninsular Greece. They largely overpowered Minoan society, and they took over the Cretan palaces. The Mycenaeans also established settlements in Anatolia, Sicily, and southern Italy. About 1200 B.C.E. the Mycenaeans engaged in a conflict with the city of Troy in Anatolia. This Trojan

**Minoan** (mih-NOH-uhn)

**Mycenaean** (meye-suh-NEE-uhn)

**Peloponnesus** (pell-uh-puh-NEE-suhs)

**Sparta and Athens were the two main rival poleis in classical Greece.**

**MAP 8.1** | Classical Greece, 800–350 B.C.E. Note the mountainous topography of the Greek peninsula and western Anatolia. *To what extent did geography encourage Greeks to venture into the Mediterranean Sea?*

War, which Homer recalled from a Greek perspective in his *Iliad,* coincided with invasions of foreign mariners in the Mycenaean homeland. Indeed, from 1100 to 800 B.C.E., chaos reigned throughout the eastern Mediterranean region. Invasions and civil disturbances made it impossible to maintain stable governments or even productive agricultural societies. Mycenaean palaces fell into ruin, the population sharply declined, and people abandoned most settlements.

# The World of the Polis

In the absence of a centralized state or empire, local institutions took the lead in restoring political order in Greece after the decline of Mycenaean society. The most important institution was the *polis,* or city-state. Over time, many of these *poleis* (the plural of *polis*) became lively commercial centers. They took on an increasingly urban character and extended their authority over surrounding regions. By about 800 B.C.E. many poleis had become bustling city-states that functioned as the principal centers of Greek society. The most important of the poleis were Sparta and Athens, whose contrasting constitutions help to illustrate the variety of political styles in classical Greece.

**polis** (POH-lihs)

**SPARTA** Sparta was situated in a fertile region of the Greek peninsula, whose lands the Spartans exploited by forcing neighboring peoples to perform agricultural labor. These *helots,* or servants of the Spartan state, were not slaves, but neither were they free to leave the land. Their role in society was to keep Sparta supplied with food. By the sixth century B.C.E., the helots probably outnumbered the Spartan citizens by more than ten to one, which meant that the Spartans constantly had to guard against rebellion. As a result, the Spartans devoted most of their resources to maintaining a powerful and disciplined military machine.

**SPARTAN SOCIETY** In theory, Spartan citizens were equal in status. To discourage the development of economic and social distinctions, Spartans observed an extraordinarily austere lifestyle. They did not wear jewelry or elaborate clothes, nor did they pamper themselves with luxuries or accumulate private wealth on a large scale. It is for good reason, then, that our adjective *spartan* refers to a lifestyle characterized by simplicity, frugality, and austerity.

Distinction among the ancient Spartans came by prowess, discipline, and military talent, which the Spartan educational system cultivated from an early age. All Spartans, men and women, underwent a rigorous regime of physical training. The sons of Spartan citizens left their homes at age seven and went to live in military barracks. At age twenty they began active military service, which they continued until retirement. Spartan women married when they reached age eighteen to twenty but did not live with their husbands. Only at about age thirty did men leave the barracks and set up a household with their wives and children. Although Spartan society had lost much of its ascetic rigor by the fourth century B.C.E., Spartan institutions nevertheless continued to reflect the larger society's commitment to military values.

**PAINTED SPARTAN VESSEL.** | This painted cup produced in Sparta about 550 B.C.E. depicts hunters attacking a boar. Spartans regarded hunting as an exercise that helped to sharpen fighting skills and aggressive instincts.

**ATHENS** Whereas Sparta sought to impose order by military means, Athenians relieved social tensions by establishing a government based on democratic principles. Indeed, Athenians opened government offices to all citizens and broadened the base of political participation in classical Greece. Citizenship was by no means open to all residents, however: only free adult males from Athens played a role in public affairs, leaving foreigners, slaves, and women with no direct voice in government.

**ATHENIAN SOCIETY** During the seventh century B.C.E., the gap between rich and poor around Athens widened considerably as increased trade brought prosperity to wealthy landowners. By the early sixth century B.C.E., a large class of underprivileged people were unhappy enough to wage war against their wealthy neighbors. To avert civil war, an Athenian aristocrat named Solon devised a solution to class conflict in Attica, the region around Athens.

**SOLON AND ATHENIAN DEMOCRACY** Solon forged a compromise between the classes. He allowed aristocrats to keep their lands, but he cancelled debts, forbade debt slavery, and liberated those already enslaved for debt. Solon also provided representation for the common classes in the Athenian government by opening the councils of the polis to any citizen wealthy enough to devote time to public affairs. During the late sixth and fifth centuries B.C.E., these reforms went even further as Athenian leaders paid salaries to officeholders so financial hardship would not exclude anyone from service.

**PERICLES** These reforms gradually transformed Athens into a democratic state. The high tide of Athenian democracy came under the leadership of the statesman Pericles, who became the most popular Athenian leader from 461 B.C.E. until his death in 429 B.C.E.

View of the Acropolis
www.mhhe.com/
bentleybrief2e

Pericles (PEH-rih-kleez)

Under the leadership of Pericles, Athens became the most sophisticated of the poleis, with a vibrant community of scientists, philosophers, poets, dramatists, artists, and architects.

# GREECE AND THE LARGER WORLD

Classical Greece
www.mhhe.com/
bentleybrief2e

As the poleis prospered, Greeks became increasingly prominent in the larger world of the Mediterranean basin. They established colonies along the shores of the Mediterranean Sea and the Black Sea, and they traded throughout the region. Eventually, their political and economic interests brought them into conflict with the expanding Persian empire. After a century of intermittent war, in the fourth century B.C.E. Alexander of Macedon toppled the Achaemenid empire and built an empire stretching from India to Egypt and Greece. His conquests created a vast zone of trade and communication that encouraged commercial and cultural exchange on an unprecedented scale.

## Greek Colonization

To relieve population pressures in the rocky Greek peninsula, Greeks began to establish colonies in other parts of the Mediterranean basin. Between the mid–eighth and the late sixth centuries B.C.E., they founded more than four hundred colonies along the shores of the Mediterranean Sea and the Black Sea.

**GREEK COLONIES** The Greeks established their first colonies in the central Mediterranean during the early eighth century B.C.E. The most popular sites were Sicily and southern Italy, particularly the region around modern Naples, which was itself originally a Greek colony called Neapolis ("new polis"). These colonies provided merchants not only with fertile fields that yielded large agricultural surpluses but also with convenient access to the copper, zinc, tin, and iron ores of central Italy.

Some of the Greek colonies were very distant from the Greek poleis.

**MAP 8.2** | Classical Greece and the Mediterranean basin, 800–500 B.C.E. All the Greek colonies were located on the coastlines of the Mediterranean Sea and the Black Sea. *In what ways did the colonies serve as links between Greece and the larger Mediterranean region?*

During the eighth and seventh centuries B.C.E., Greeks ventured into the Black Sea in large numbers and established colonies all along its shores. These settlements offered merchants access to rich supplies of grain, fish, furs, timber, honey, wax, gold, and amber as well as slaves captured in southern Russia and transported to markets in the Mediterranean.

Unlike their counterparts in classical Persia, China, and India, the Greeks did not build a centralized imperial state. Instead, colonies relied on their own resources and charted their own courses. Nevertheless, Greek colonization sponsored more communication, interaction, and exchange than ever before among Mediterranean lands and peoples. From the early eighth century B.C.E., colonies facilitated trade between their own regions and the Greek poleis. At the same time, colonization spread Greek language as well as cultural and political traditions throughout the Mediterranean basin. Thus Greek colonization had important political and social effects throughout the Mediterranean basin.

## Conflict with Persia

During the fifth century B.C.E., their links abroad brought the poleis of the Greek peninsula into direct conflict with the Persian empire in a long struggle known as the Persian Wars (500–479 B.C.E.). As the Persian emperors Cyrus and Darius tightened their grip on Anatolia, the Greek cities on the Ionian coast became increasingly restless. In 500 B.C.E. they revolted against Persian rule and expelled the Achaemenid administrators. In support of their fellow Greeks and commercial partners, the Athenians sent a fleet of ships to aid the Ionian effort.

THE PERSIAN WARS   Despite Athenian assistance, Darius repressed the Ionian rebellion in 493 B.C.E. Three years later, he mounted a campaign against peninsular Greece to punish them for their interference. Although greatly outnumbered, the Athenians routed the Persian army at the battle of Marathon and then marched back to Athens in time to fight off the Persian fleet. In spite of success in individual battles, however, neither side could secure a definitive victory over the other, and for more than a century Greeks and Persians continued to skirmish intermittently without decisive results.

THE DELIAN LEAGUE   Yet the Persian Wars did initiate serious conflict among the Greek poleis themselves. The cause was an alliance between the poleis known as the Delian League, which was formed to discourage further Persian actions in Greece. Because of its superior fleet, Athens became the leader of the alliance, benefiting greatly from the financial contributions of other poleis. However, once it was clear that the Persian threat no longer existed, the other poleis resented having to make contributions that seemed to benefit only the Athenians.

THE PELOPONNESIAN WAR   Ultimately, the tensions resulted in a bitter civil conflict known as the Peloponnesian War (431–404 B.C.E.). Poleis divided into two armed camps under the leadership of Athens and Sparta, the principal contenders for hegemony in the Greek world. By 404 B.C.E. the Spartans and their allies had forced the Athenians to unconditional surrender. However, Sparta's victory soon generated new jealousies, and new conflicts quickly broke out between the poleis. Meanwhile, as internal struggles weakened the poleis, a formidable power took shape in the north.

## The Macedonians and the Coming of Empire

THE KINGDOM OF MACEDON   Until the fourth century B.C.E., the kingdom of Macedon was a frontier state north of peninsular Greece. During the reign of King Philip II (359–336 B.C.E.), however, Macedon became a powerful, unified state with

Achaemenid (uh-KEE-muh-nid)

Peloponnesian (pell-uh-puh-NEE-suhn)

an impressive military machine. When Philip had consolidated his hold on Macedon, he turned his attention to two larger prizes: Greece and the Persian empire. Greece proved relatively easy to conquer: the Peloponnesian War had poisoned the poleis against one another, which hampered organized resistance. Thus in 338 B.C.E., after a campaign of twelve years, Philip had all of Greece under his control.

ALEXANDER OF MACEDON   Philip intended to use his conquest of Greece as a launching pad for an invasion of Persia but was prevented from doing so by an assassin who brought him down in 336 B.C.E. The invasion of Persia thus fell to his twenty-year-old son, Alexander of Macedon, often called Alexander the Great. Alexander soon assembled an army to invade the Persian empire. Alexander was a brilliant strategist and an inspired leader, and he inherited a well-equipped and highly spirited veteran force from his father. By 333 B.C.E. Alexander had subjected Ionia and Anatolia to his control; within another year he held Syria, Palestine, and Egypt; by 331 B.C.E. he controlled Mesopotamia and prepared to invade the Persian homeland. He took Pasargadae and burned the Achaemenid palace at Persepolis late in 331 B.C.E., and in 330 B.C.E. Alexander established himself as the new emperor of Persia.

ALEXANDER'S CONQUESTS   By 327 B.C.E. Alexander had larger ambitions: he took his army into India but was forced to return home when his troops refused to proceed any farther. By 324 B.C.E. Alexander and his army had returned to Susa in Mesopotamia. In June of 323 B.C.E., however, after an extended round of feasting and drinking, he suddenly fell ill and died at age thirty-three. Thus, although Alexander proved to be a brilliant conqueror, he did not live long enough to develop a system of administration for his vast realm.

## The Hellenistic Empires

Achaemenid & Seleucid Empires
www.mhhe.com/ bentleybrief2e

When Alexander died, his generals divided the empire into three large states. Antigonus took Greece and Macedon, which his Antigonid successors ruled until replaced by the Romans in the second century B.C.E. Ptolemy took Egypt, which the Ptolemaic dynasty ruled until the Roman conquest of Egypt in 31 B.C.E. Seleucus took the largest portion, the former Achaemenid empire stretching from Bactria to Anatolia, which his successors ruled until the Parthians displaced them during the second century B.C.E.

Arrian's The Life of Alexander
www.mhhe.com/ bentleybrief2e

THE HELLENISTIC ERA   Historians refer to the age of Alexander and his successors as the Hellenistic age—an era when Greek cultural traditions expanded their influence (*Hellas*) to a much larger world. Indeed, the Hellenistic empires governed cosmopolitan societies and sponsored interactions between peoples from Greece to India. Like imperial states in classical Persia, China, and India, the Hellenistic empires facilitated trade, and they made it possible for beliefs, values, and religions to spread over greater distances than ever before.

THE PTOLEMAIC EMPIRE   All the Hellenistic empires benefited handsomely from the new order through the supervision of extensive trade networks and efficient tax collection. Yet perhaps the wealthiest of the Hellenistic empires was Ptolemaic Egypt. Greek and Macedonian overlords did not interfere in Egyptian society, contenting themselves with the efficient organization of agriculture, industry, and tax collection. They maintained the irrigation networks and monitored the cultivation of crops and the payment of taxes. They also established royal monopolies over the most lucrative industries, such as textiles, salt making, and the brewing of beer.

**Antigonus** (an-TIG-uh-nuhs)

**Seleucid** (sih-LOO-sid)

**Ptolemaic** (TAWL-oh-may-ihk)

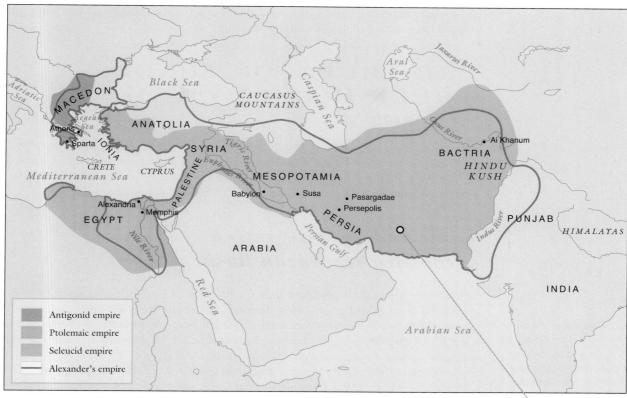

**MAP 8.3** | Boundaries of Alexander's former empire and of the Hellenistic empires that succeeded it about the year 275 B.C.E. Notice the difference in size between the three Hellenistic empires. *What would have been the economic and political advantages and disadvantages of each?*

The Seleucids were able to maintain control over such a large territory because of the many cities founded by Alexander of Macedon and his successors.

**ALEXANDRIA** Much of Egypt's wealth flowed to the Ptolemaic capital of Alexandria. Founded by Alexander at the mouth of the Nile, Alexandria served as the Ptolemies' administrative headquarters, but it became much more than a bureaucratic center. Alexandria's enormous harbor was able to accommodate 1,200 ships simultaneously, and the city soon became the most important port in the Mediterranean. Alongside Greeks, Macedonians, and Egyptians lived sizable communities of Phoenicians, Jews, Arabs, and Babylonians. The city was indeed an early megalopolis, where peoples of different ethnic, religious, and cultural traditions conducted their affairs. Under the Ptolemies, Alexandria also became the cultural capital of the Hellenistic world. It was the site of the famous Alexandrian Museum—a state-financed institute of higher learning where philosophical, literary, and scientific scholars carried on advanced research—and of the equally famous Alexandrian Library, which supported the scholarship sponsored by the museum and which, by the first century B.C.E., boasted a collection of more than seven hundred thousand works.

**THE SELEUCID EMPIRE** It was in the Seleucid realm, however, that Greek influence reached its greatest extent. The principal channels of that influence were the numerous cities that Alexander and his successors founded in the former Persian empire. Greek and Macedonian colonists flocked to these cities, where they created a Mediterranean-style urban society that left its mark on lands as distant as Bactria and India. Many Seleucids became familiar with Greek language, dress, literature, philosophy, art, and architecture. Emperor Ashoka of India himself had his edicts promulgated in Greek and Aramaic, the two most commonly used languages of the Hellenistic empires. Indeed, although the societies under Hellenistic domination did not lose their own customs, the Hellenistic empires, like classical states in Persia, China, and India, nevertheless brought distant lands into interaction by way of trade and cultural exchange.

# THE FRUITS OF TRADE: GREEK ECONOMY AND SOCIETY

The mountainous and rocky terrain of the Greek peninsula yielded only small harvests of grain, and the southern Balkan mountains hindered travel and communication. Indeed, until the construction of modern roads, much of Greece was more accessible by sea than by land. As a result, early Greek society depended heavily on maritime trade.

## Trade and the Integration of the Mediterranean Basin

TRADE   Although it produced little grain, much of Greece is ideally suited to the cultivation of olives and grapes. After the establishment of the poleis, the Greeks discovered that they could profitably concentrate their efforts on the production of olive oil and wine. Greek merchants traded these products around the Mediterranean, returning with abundant supplies of grain and other items as well.

By the early eighth century B.C.E., trade had generated considerable prosperity in the Greek world. Merchants and mariners linked Greek communities throughout the Mediterranean world—not only those in the Greek peninsula but also those in Anatolia, the Mediterranean islands, and the Black Sea region. These trade links contributed to a sense of a larger Greek community. Colonists recognized the same gods as their cousins in the Greek peninsula. They spoke Greek dialects, and they maintained commercial relationships with their native communities.

GREEK POTTERY VESSEL.   |   Harvesting olives. In this painting on a vase, two men knock fruit off the branches while a third climbs the tree to shake the limbs, and another gathers olives from the ground.

THE OLYMPIC GAMES   Greeks from all parts gathered periodically to participate in panhellenic festivals that reinforced their common bonds. Many of these festivals featured athletic, literary, or musical contests in which individuals sought to win glory for their polis. Best known of the panhellenic festivals were the Olympic Games. According to tradition, in 776 B.C.E. Greek communities from all parts of the Mediterranean sent their best athletes to the polis of Olympia to engage in contests of speed, strength, and skill. Events included footracing, long jump, boxing, wrestling, javelin tossing, and discus throwing. Winners of events received olive wreaths, and they became celebrated heroes in their home poleis. The ancient Olympic Games took place every four years for more than a millennium before quietly disappearing from Greek life. So, although they were not united politically, by the sixth century B.C.E. Greek communities had nevertheless established a sense of collective identity.

## Family and Society

PATRIARCHAL SOCIETY   With the establishment of poleis in the eighth century B.C.E., the nature of Greek family and society came into focus. Like urban societies in southwest Asia and Anatolia, the Greek poleis adopted strictly patriarchal family structures. Male family heads ruled their households, and fathers even had the right to decide whether to keep infants born to their wives. They could not legally kill infants, but they could abandon newborns in the mountains or the countryside, where they would soon die of exposure.

Greek women fell under the authority of their fathers, husbands, or sons. Upper-class Greek women spent most of their time in the family home and frequently wore veils when they ventured outside. In most of the poleis, women could not own landed property, but they sometimes operated small businesses such as shops and food stalls. The only public position open to Greek women was that of priestess of a religious cult. Sparta was something of a special case when it came to gender relations: there women participated in athletic contests, went about town by themselves, and sometimes even took up arms to defend the polis. Even in Sparta, however, men were family authorities, and men alone determined state policies.

Aristocratic families with extensive landholdings could afford to provide girls with a formal education, but in less privileged families all hands contributed to the welfare of the household. In rural families, men performed most of the outside work, while women took care of domestic chores and wove wool textiles. In artisan families living in the poleis, both men and women often participated in businesses and maintained stands or booths in the marketplace.

SLAVERY    Throughout the Greek world, as in other classical societies, slavery was a prominent means of mobilizing labor. Slaves came from several different backgrounds. Some entered slavery because they could not pay their debts. Many were soldiers captured in war. A large number came from the peoples with whom the Greeks traded: slave markets at Black Sea ports sold seminomadic Scythians captured in Russia, and Egyptians provided African slaves.

Greek law regarded all slaves as the private chattel property of their owners, and the conditions of slaves' lives depended on the needs and the temperament of their owners. In general, however, slaves who possessed special skills fared better than unskilled slaves. A slave named Pasion, for example, worked first as a porter and then as a clerk at a prominent Athenian bank during the late fifth and early fourth centuries B.C.E. Ultimately, Pasion gained his freedom, took over management of the bank, outfitted five warships from his own pocket, and won a grant of Athenian citizenship.

# THE CULTURAL LIFE OF CLASSICAL GREECE

During the eighth and seventh centuries B.C.E., as Greek merchants ventured throughout the Mediterranean basin, they became acquainted with the sophisticated cultural traditions of Mesopotamia and Egypt. They learned astronomy, science, mathematics, medicine, and magic from the Babylonians as well as geometry, medicine, and divination from the Egyptians. They also drew inspiration from the myths, religious beliefs, art motifs, and architectural styles of Mesopotamia and Egypt. About 800 B.C.E. they adapted the Phoenician alphabet to their own language. To the Phoenicians' consonants they added symbols for vowels and thus created an exceptionally flexible system for representing human speech in written form.

During the fifth and fourth centuries B.C.E., the Greeks combined those borrowed cultural elements with their own intellectual interests to elaborate a rich cultural tradition that exercised enormous influence in the Mediterranean basin and western Europe. The most distinctive feature of classical Greek culture was the effort to construct a consistent system of philosophy based purely on human reason.

**Pasion** (pahs-ee-on)

# Rational Thought and Philosophy

SOCRATES    The pivotal figure in the development of philosophy was Socrates (470–399 B.C.E.), a thoughtful Athenian driven by a powerful urge to understand human beings in all their complexity. Socrates did not commit his thought to writing, but his disciple Plato later composed dialogues that represented Socrates' views. He suggested that honor was far more important than wealth, fame, or other superficial attributes. He scorned those who preferred public accolades to personal integrity, and he insisted on the need to reflect on the purposes and goals of life. "The unexamined life is not worth living," he held, implying that human beings had an obligation to strive for personal integrity, behave honorably toward others, and work toward the construction of a just society.

In elaborating those views, Socrates often subjected traditional ethical teachings to critical scrutiny. That outraged some of his fellow citizens, who brought him to trial on charges that he corrupted the Athenian youths who joined him in the marketplace to discuss moral and ethical issues. A jury of Athenian citizens decided that Socrates had indeed passed the bounds of propriety and condemned him to death. In 399 B.C.E. Socrates drank a potion of hemlock sap and died in the company of his friends.

PLATO    Socrates' influence survived in the work of his most zealous disciple, Plato (430–347 B.C.E.), and in Plato's disciple Aristotle (384–322 B.C.E.). Inspired by his mentor's reflections, Plato elaborated a systematic philosophy of great subtlety. He presented his thought in a series of dialogues in which Socrates figured as the principal speaker. As time passed, Plato gradually formulated his thought into a systematic vision of the world and human society.

The cornerstone of Plato's thought was his theory of Forms, or Ideas. It disturbed Plato that he could not gain satisfactory intellectual control over the world. The quality of virtue, for example, meant different things in different situations, as did honesty, courage, truth, and beauty. How was it possible, then, to understand virtue as an abstract quality? In seeking an answer to that question, Plato developed his belief that the world in which we live is not the world of genuine reality, but only a pale and imperfect reflection of the world of Forms or Ideas. The secrets of this world, Plato argued, were available only to philosophers—those who applied their rational faculties to the pursuit of wisdom.

Though abstract, Plato's thought had important political and social implications. In his dialogue the *Republic,* for example, Plato argued that since philosophers were in the best position to understand ultimate reality, they would also be the best rulers. In effect, Plato advocated an intellectual aristocracy: the philosophical elite would rule, and less intelligent classes would work at functions for which their talents best suited them.

ARISTOTLE    During the generation after Plato, Aristotle elaborated a systematic philosophy that equaled Plato's work in its long-term influence. Unlike Plato, Aristotle believed that philosophers could rely on their senses to provide accurate information about the world and then depend on reason to sort out its mysteries. Aristotle explored the nature of reality in subtle metaphysical works, and he devised rigorous rules of logic in an effort to construct powerful and compelling arguments. His work provided such a coherent and comprehensive vision of the world that his later disciples called him "the master of those who know."

The Greek philosophers deeply influenced the development of European and Islamic cultural traditions. Until the seventeenth century C.E., most European philosophers regarded the Greeks as intellectual authorities. Christian and Islamic theologians alike went to great lengths to harmonize their religious convictions with the philosophical views of Plato and Aristotle. Thus, like philosophical and religious figures in other classical socie-

**SOCRATES.** | Tradition holds that Socrates was not a physically attractive man, but this statue emphasizes his sincerity and simplicity. *How does his clothing reinforce these aspects of his personality?*

**Socrates** (SAHK-rah-teez)

**Aristotle** (AHR-ih-stot-uhl)

*In one of his earliest dialogues, the* Apology, *Plato offered an account of Socrates' defense of himself during his trial before a jury of Athenian citizens. After the jury had convicted him and condemned him to death, Socrates reflected on the nature of death and reemphasized his commitment to virtue rather than to wealth or fame.*

And if we reflect in another way we shall see that we may well hope that death is a good thing. For the state of death is one of two things: either the dead man wholly ceases to be and loses all sensation; or, according to the common belief, it is a change and a migration of the soul unto another place. And if death is the absence of all sensation, like the sleep of one whose slumbers are unbroken by any dreams, it will be a wonderful gain. For if a man had to select that night in which he slept so soundly that he did not even see any dreams, and had to compare with it all the other nights and days of his life, and then had to say how many days and nights in his life he had slept better and more pleasantly than this night, I think that a private person, nay, even the great king of Persia himself, would find them easy to count, compared with the others. If that is the nature of death, I for one count it a gain. For then it appears that eternity is nothing more than a single night.

But if death is a journey to another place, and the common belief be true, that all who have died dwell there, what good could be greater than this, my judges? Would a journey not be worth taking if at the end of it, in the other world, we should be released from the self-styled judges of this world, and should find the true judges who are said to sit in judgment below? . . . It would be an infinite happiness to converse with them, and to live with them, and to examine them. Assuredly there they do not put men to death for doing that. For besides the other ways in which they are happier than we are, they are immortal, at least if the common belief be true.

And you too, judges, must face death with a good courage, and believe this as a truth, that no evil can happen to a good man, either in life, or after death. His fortunes are not neglected by the gods, and what has come to me today has not come by chance. I am persuaded that it is better for me to die now, and to be released from trouble. . . . And so I am hardly angry with my accusers, or with those who have condemned me to die. Yet it was not with this mind that they accused me and condemned me, but rather they meant to do me an injury. Only to that extent do I find fault with them.

Yet I have one request to make of them. When my sons grow up, visit them with punishment, my friends, and vex them in the same way that I have vexed you if they seem to you to care for riches or for anything other than virtue: and if they think that they are something when they are nothing at all, reproach them as I have reproached you for not caring for what they should and for thinking that they are great men when in fact they are worthless. And if you will do this, I myself and my sons will have received our deserts at your hands. But now the time has come, and we must go hence: I to die, and you to live. Whether life or death is better is known to God, and to God only.

■ How does Socrates' understanding of personal morality and its rewards compare and contrast with the Zoroastrian, Buddhist, and Hindu views discussed in earlier chapters?

SOURCE: F. J. Church, trans. *The Trial and Death of Socrates,* 2nd ed. London: Macmillan, 1886, pp. 76–78. (Translation slightly modified.)

---

ties, Plato and Aristotle provided a powerful intellectual framework that shaped thought about the world and human affairs for two millennia and more.

## *Popular Religion and Greek Drama*

DEITIES   Because most Greeks of the classical era did not have an advanced education, they turned to traditions of popular culture and popular religion rather than philosophy to seek guidance for human behavior. The Greeks did not recognize a single, exclusive, all-powerful god. Rather, they believed that in the beginning there was the formless void of chaos out of which emerged the earth, the mother and creator of all things. The earth then generated the sky, and together they produced night, day, sun, moon, and other natural phenomena. Struggles between the deities led to bitter heavenly battles, and ultimately Zeus, grandson of the earth and sky gods, emerged as paramount ruler of the divine realm. Zeus's heavenly court included scores of subordinate deities who had various responsibilities: the god Apollo promoted wisdom and justice, for example; the goddess Fortune brought unexpected opportunities and difficulties; and the Furies wreaked vengeance on those who violated divine law.

**RELIGIOUS CULTS** Like religious traditions in other lands, Greek myths sought to explain the world and the forces that shape it. They served also as foundations for religious cults based on individual poleis that contributed to a powerful sense of community in classical Greece. These religious cults varied widely: many conducted ritual observances in special places, for example, and some were open to only one sex. Before the fifth century B.C.E., many cults inspired emotional displays and spirited—sometimes frenzied—song and dance.

**TRAGIC DRAMA** During the fifth century B.C.E., however, as the poleis strengthened their grip on public and political life, the religious cults became progressively more tame. Instead of festivals, religious cults marked the year with the presentation of plays that examined relations between humans and the gods or reflected on ethics and morality. That transformation set the stage for the emergence of Greek dramatic literature, which sought to engage audiences in subtle reflection on complicated themes. The great tragedians—Aeschylus, Sophocles, and Euripides—whose lives spanned the fifth century B.C.E., explored the possibilities and limitations of human action. Comic dramatists such as Aristophanes also dealt with serious issues of human striving and responsible behavior by ridiculing the foibles of prominent public figures and calling attention to the absurd consequences of ill-considered action.

## Hellenistic Philosophy and Religion

As the Hellenistic empires seized the political initiative in the Mediterranean basin and eclipsed the poleis, residents ceased to regard their polis as the focus of individual and religious loyalties. Instead, they increasingly looked toward cultural and religious alternatives that ministered to the needs and interests of individuals living in a cosmopolitan society.

**THE HELLENISTIC PHILOSOPHERS** The most popular Hellenistic philosophers—the Epicureans, the Skeptics, and the Stoics—addressed individual needs by searching for personal tranquility and serenity. Epicureans, for example, identified pleasure as the greatest good. By *pleasure* they meant not unbridled hedonism but, rather, a state of quiet satisfaction that would shield them from the pressures of the Hellenistic world. Skeptics refused to take strong positions on political, moral, and social issues because they doubted the possibility of certain knowledge. The most respected and influential of the Hellenistic philosophers, however, were the Stoics. Unlike the Epicureans and the Skeptics, the Stoics did not seek to withdraw from the pressures of the world. Rather, they taught that individuals had the duty to aid others and lead virtuous lives in harmony with reason and nature.

**RELIGIONS OF SALVATION** Whereas the philosophers' doctrines appealed to educated elites, religions of salvation spread across the trade routes of the Hellenistic empires and enjoyed surging popularity in Hellenistic society. Mystery religions promised eternal bliss for initiates who observed their rites and lived in accordance with their doctrines. Some of these faiths spread across the trade routes and found followers far from

**Aeschylus** (ES-kuh-luhs)

**Epicureans** (ehp-ih-KYOOR-eeuhns)

**Stoics** (STOH-ihks)

their homelands. The Egyptian cult of Osiris, for example, became extraordinarily popular because it promised salvation for those who led honorable lives. Cults from Persia, Mesopotamia, Anatolia, and Greece also attracted disciples throughout the Hellenistic world.

Many of the mystery religions involved the worship of a savior whose death and resurrection would lead the way to eternal salvation for devoted followers. Some philosophers and religious thinkers speculated that a single, universal god might rule the entire universe, and that this god had a plan for the salvation of all humankind. Like the Hellenistic philosophies, then, religions of salvation addressed the interests of individuals searching for security in a complex world. Indeed, those interests continued to be of concern to peoples in the Mediterranean basin long after political dominance passed from the Greek to the Italian peninsula.

# ROME: FROM KINGDOM TO REPUBLIC

Founded in the eighth century B.C.E., the city of Rome was originally a small city-state ruled by a single king. In 509 B.C.E., however, the city's aristocrats deposed the king, ended the monarchy, and instituted a republic—a form of government in which delegates represent the interests of various constituencies. The Roman republic survived for more than five hundred years, and it was under the republican constitution that Rome came to establish itself as the dominant power in the Mediterranean basin.

## The Etruscans and Rome

**ROMULUS AND REMUS**    According to legend, the city of Rome was founded by Romulus, who—along with his twin brother, Remus—was abandoned as a baby by an evil uncle near the flooded Tiber River. Before the infants could drown, a kindly she-wolf found them and nursed them to health. The boys grew strong and courageous, and in 753 B.C.E. Romulus founded the city and established himself as its first king.

Capitoline wolf with Romulus & Remus
www.mhhe.com/ bentleybrief2e

Modern scholars do not tell so colorful a tale, but they do agree that bands of Indo-European migrants crossed the Alps and settled throughout the Italian peninsula beginning about 2000 B.C.E. Like their distant cousins in India, Greece, and northern Europe, these migrants blended with the neolithic inhabitants of the region, adopted agriculture, and established tribal federations. Sheepherders and small farmers occupied much of the Italian peninsula, including the future site of Rome. Bronze metallurgy appeared about 1800 B.C.E. and iron about 900 B.C.E.

**THE ETRUSCANS**    The Etruscans, a dynamic people, dominated much of Italy between the eighth and fifth centuries B.C.E. The Etruscans probably migrated to Italy from Anatolia. They settled first in Tuscany, the region around modern Florence, but they soon controlled much of Italy. They built thriving cities and established political and economic alliances between their settlements. They manufactured high-quality bronze and iron goods, and they worked gold and silver into jewelry. They built a fleet and traded actively in the western Mediterranean. During the late sixth century B.C.E., however, the Etruscans encountered a series of challenges from other peoples, and their society began to decline.

**THE KINGDOM OF ROME**    The Etruscans deeply influenced the early development of Rome. Like the Etruscan cities, Rome was a monarchy during the early days after its foundation, and several Roman kings were Etruscans. The kings ruled Rome through the seventh and sixth centuries B.C.E., and they provided the city with paved streets, public buildings, defensive walls, and large temples.

**Romulus** (ROM-yuh-luhs)

**Remus** (REE-muhs)

**Etruscans** (ih-TRUHS-kuhns)

Etruscan merchants drew a large volume of traffic to Rome, thanks partly to the city's geographical advantages. Rome enjoyed easy access to the Mediterranean by way of the Tiber River, but since it was not on the coast, it did not run the risk of invasion or attack from the sea. Already during the period of Etruscan dominance, trade routes from all parts of Italy converged on Rome. When Etruscan society declined, Rome was in a strong position to play a more prominent role both in Italy and in the larger Mediterranean world.

## The Roman Republic and Its Constitution

ESTABLISHMENT OF THE REPUBLIC   When the Roman nobility deposed the last Etruscan king and replaced him with a republic, they built the Roman forum at the heart of the city—a political and civic center filled with temples and public buildings where leading citizens tended to government business. They also instituted a republican constitution that entrusted executive responsibilities to two consuls who wielded civil and military power. Consuls were elected by an assembly dominated by the noble classes, known in Rome as the patricians, and they served one-year terms. The powerful Senate, whose members were mostly aristocrats with extensive political experience, advised the consuls and ratified all major decisions. When faced with crises, however, the Romans appointed an official, known as a dictator, who wielded absolute power for a term of six months. By providing for strong leadership during times of extraordinary difficulty, the republican constitution enabled Rome to maintain a reasonably stable society throughout most of the republic's history.

CONFLICTS BETWEEN PATRICIANS AND PLEBEIANS   Because the consuls and the Senate both represented the interests of the patricians, there was constant tension between the wealthy classes and the common people, known as the plebeians. Indeed, during the early fifth century B.C.E., relations between the classes became so strained that the plebeians threatened to secede from Rome. To maintain the integrity of the Roman state, the patricians granted plebeians the right to elect officials, known as tribunes, who represented their interests in the Roman government. Originally plebeians chose two tribunes, but the number eventually rose to ten. Tribunes had the power to intervene in all political matters, and they possessed the right to veto measures that they judged unfair.

Although tensions between the classes never disappeared, during the fourth century B.C.E. plebeians became eligible to hold almost all state offices and gained the right to have one of the consuls come from their ranks. By the early third century, plebeian-dominated assemblies won the power to make decisions binding on all of Rome. Thus, like fifth-century Athens, republican Rome gradually broadened the base of political participation.

## The Expansion of the Republic

Between the fourth and second centuries B.C.E., the people of Rome transformed their city from a small and vulnerable city-state to the center of an enormous empire. They began by consolidating their power in the Italian peninsula itself. Indeed, by the later fourth century they had emerged as the predominant power in the Italian peninsula. Roman success in the peninsula was partly a matter of military power and partly a matter of generous policies toward the peoples they conquered. Instead of ruling them as vanquished subjects, the Romans allowed conquered people to govern their internal affairs as long as they provided military support and did not enter into hostile alliances. In addition, conquered peoples were allowed to trade in Rome, to take Roman spouses, and even to gain Roman citizenship. These policies both provided Rome with essential support and eased the pain of conquest.

**plebeians** (plih-BEE-uhns)

**EXPANSION IN THE MEDITERRANEAN** With Italy under its control, Rome began to play a major role in the affairs of the larger Mediterranean basin and to experience conflicts with other Mediterranean powers. The principal power in the western Mediterranean during the fourth and third centuries B.C.E. was the city-state of Carthage, located near modern Tunis. Originally established as a Phoenician colony, Carthage enjoyed a strategic location that enabled it to trade actively throughout the Mediterranean. From the wealth generated by this commerce, Carthage became the dominant political power in north Africa (excluding Egypt), the southern part of the Iberian peninsula, and the western region of grain-rich Sicily as well. Meanwhile, the three Hellenistic empires that succeeded Alexander of Macedon continued to dominate the eastern Mediterranean.

**THE PUNIC WARS** Economic and political competition brought the Romans into conflict with Carthage first. Between 264 and 146 B.C.E., they fought three devastating conflicts known as the Punic Wars with the Carthaginians. The rivalry ended after Roman forces subjected Carthage to a long siege, conquered and burned the city, and forced some fifty thousand survivors into slavery. The Romans then annexed Carthaginian possessions in north Africa and Iberia—rich in grain, oil, wine, silver, and gold—and used those resources to finance continued imperial expansion.

Shortly after the beginning of the Carthaginian conflict, Rome became embroiled in conflicts with the Antigonids and the Seleucids in the eastern Mediterranean. Between 215 and 148 B.C.E., Rome fought five major wars, mostly in Macedon and Anatolia, against these opponents. As a result of these conflicts, Rome emerged as the preeminent power in the eastern as well as the western Mediterranean by the middle of the second century B.C.E.

# FROM REPUBLIC TO EMPIRE

Imperial expansion brought wealth and power to Rome, but these brought problems as well as benefits. Unequal distribution of wealth aggravated class tensions and gave rise to conflict over political and social policies. Meanwhile, the need to administer conquered lands efficiently strained the capacities of the republican constitution. During the first century B.C.E. and the first century C.E., Roman civil and military leaders gradually dismantled

**Carthage** (KAHR-thihj)

**MAP 8.4** | Expansion of the Roman republic to 146 B.C.E. By the mid-second century B.C.E., the Roman republic controlled extensive territories outside Italy. ***In what ways did Roman expansion encourage interactions and exchanges throughout the Mediterranean region?***

the republican constitution and imposed a centralized imperial form of government on the city of Rome and its empire.

## *Imperial Expansion and Domestic Problems*

In Rome, as in classical China and Greece, patterns of land distribution caused serious political and social tensions. Conquered lands fell largely into the hands of wealthy elites, who organized enormous plantations known as *latifundia*. Because they enjoyed economies of scale and often employed slave labor, owners of latifundia operated at lower costs than did owners of smaller holdings, who often had to sell out to their wealthier neighbors.

CIVIL WAR   During the second and first centuries B.C.E., relations between the classes became so strained that they led to violent social conflict and civil war. Roman politicians and generals jockeyed for power in support of either social reform or the privileged position of the wealthy elites, with bloody results on both sides. By the middle of the first century B.C.E., it had become increasingly clear that the Roman republic was not suitable for a large and growing empire. In this chaotic context Gaius Julius Caesar inaugurated the process by which Rome replaced its republican constitution with a centralized imperial form of government.

## *The Foundation of Empire*

Julius Caesar recognized the need for social reform and favored liberal policies that would ease the suffering of the poor. During the decade of the 60s B.C.E., he played an active role in Roman politics. He spent enormous sums of money sponsoring public spectacles—such as battles between gladiators and wild animals—which helped him build a reputation and win election to posts in the republican government. This activity kept him in the public eye and helped to publicize his interest in social reform. During the next decade Caesar led a Roman army to Gaul, which he conquered and brought into the still-growing Roman empire.

In 49 B.C.E. Caesar turned his army toward Rome itself after conservative leaders in the city sought to maneuver him out of power. By early 46 B.C.E. he had made himself master of the Roman state and named himself dictator—an office that he claimed for life rather

**latifundia** (lah-tee-FOON-dya)

than for the constitutional six-month term. Caesar then centralized military and political functions and brought them under his own control. He confiscated property from conservatives and distributed it to veterans of his armies and other supporters. He launched large-scale building projects in Rome as a way to provide employment for the urban poor. He also extended Roman citizenship to peoples in the imperial provinces.

**AUGUSTUS** Caesar never had the chance to consolidate his government, however, because in 44 B.C.E. members of the Roman elite stabbed him to death in the hopes of reestablishing the republic. Instead, they plunged Rome into thirteen more years of civil conflict. When the struggles ended, power belonged to Octavian, Caesar's nephew and adopted son. In a naval battle at Actium in Greece (31 B.C.E.), Octavian defeated his principal rival, Mark Antony, who had joined forces with Cleopatra, last of the Ptolemaic rulers of Egypt. Octavian then moved quickly to consolidate his rule. In 27 B.C.E. the Senate bestowed on him the title Augustus, a term with strong religious connotations suggesting the divine or semi-divine nature of its holder.

**AUGUSTUS'S ADMINISTRATION** Augustus's government was a monarchy disguised as a republic. He preserved traditional republican offices and forms of government and included members of the Roman elite in his government while at the same time fundamentally altering the nature of that government. He accumulated vast powers for himself and ultimately took responsibility for all important governmental functions. He reorganized the military system, creating a new standing army with commanders who owed allegiance directly to himself. He also was careful to place individuals loyal to him in all important positions. During his forty-five years of virtually unopposed rule, Augustus fashioned an imperial government that guided Roman affairs for the next three centuries.

## Continuing Expansion and Integration of the Empire

During the two centuries following Augustus's rule, Roman armies conquered distant lands and integrated them into a larger economy and society. At its high point, during the early second century C.E., the Roman empire embraced much of Britain and continental Europe as well as a continuous belt of possessions surrounding the Mediterranean and extending to rich agricultural regions inland, including Mesopotamia.

**ROMAN ROADS** Within the boundaries of the Roman empire itself, a long era of peace—known as the *pax romana,* or "Roman peace"—facilitated economic and political integration from the first to the middle of the third century C.E. Like their Persian, Chinese, Indian, and Hellenistic counterparts, the Romans integrated their empire by building networks of transportation and communication. Indeed, roads linked all parts of the Roman empire. One notable highway stretched more than 2,500 kilometers (1,554 miles) along the northeast imperial frontier from the Black Sea to the North Sea, parallel to the Danube and Rhine rivers. The roads permitted urgent travel and messages to proceed with remarkable speed: Tiberius, successor of Augustus as Roman emperor, once traveled 290 kilometers (180 miles) in a single day over Roman roads.

**ROMAN LAW** As armies spread Roman influence throughout the Mediterranean, jurists also worked to construct a rational body of law that would apply to all peoples under Roman rule. During the late republic and especially during the empire, the jurists articulated standards of justice and gradually applied them throughout Roman territory. They established the principle that defendants were innocent until proven guilty, and they ensured that defendants had a right to challenge their accusers before a judge in a court of law. Like transportation and communication networks, Roman law helped to integrate the diverse

**JULIUS CAESAR.** | This bust depicts a trim conqueror and a canny political leader.

Expansion of the Roman republic & empire
www.mhhe.com/bentleybrief2e

**THINKING ABOUT** *Encounters*

**ENCOUNTERS IN MEDITERRANEAN SOCIETY UNDER THE GREEKS AND ROMANS.** Both Greek and Roman society expanded well beyond their borders at the height of their respective influence in Mediterranean affairs. In what ways did Greek colonization and Roman empire-building facilitate and encourage the movement of goods, ideas, and people in the Mediterranean region?

**The Roman road system linked distant parts of the empire.**

**MAP 8.5** | The Roman empire, ca. 117 C.E. Compare this map of the Roman empire at its height with Map 8.4 showing territories controlled by the Roman republic almost two centuries earlier. *How important was the Romans' extensive road network for the maintenance of their enormous empire?*

lands that made up the empire, and the principles of Roman law continued to shape Mediterranean and European society long after the empire had disappeared.

# ECONOMY AND SOCIETY IN THE ROMAN MEDITERRANEAN

The rapid expansion of Roman influence and the imposition of Roman imperial rule brought economic and social changes to peoples throughout the Mediterranean basin. Good roads and the pax romana encouraged trade between regions. Existing cities benefited handsomely from the wealth generated by trade, and in the lands they conquered, the Romans founded new cities to serve as links between local regions and the larger Mediterranean economy. Meanwhile, like most other peoples of classical times, the Romans built a strictly patriarchal society and made extensive use of slave labor.

## *Trade and Urbanization*

COMMERCIAL AGRICULTURE   As the Roman empire became more integrated, agricultural production grew increasingly commercialized as well as specialized. Because it was possible to import grain at favorable prices from lands that routinely produced large surpluses, other regions could concentrate on the cultivation of fruits and vegetables or on the production of manufactured items. Greece, for example, concentrated on olives and vines, and Italy became a center for the production of pottery, glassware, and bronze goods.

**MEDITERRANEAN TRADE**   Specialized production of ⟨...⟩
modities and manufactured goods set the stage for vigorous trade. Sea-lan⟨...⟩
from Syria and Palestine to Spain and north Africa. Roman military and nava⟨...⟩
the seas largely free of pirates so that sizable cargoes could move safely over long ⟨...⟩
Indeed, the Mediterranean became essentially a Roman lake, which the Roman⟨...⟩
*mare nostrum* ("our sea").

**THE CITY OF ROME**   Much of the profit from Mediterranean trade flowed to
Rome, where it fueled remarkable urban development. In the first century C.E., some ten
thousand statues and seven hundred pools decorated the city. The Roman state financed
the construction of temples, bathhouses, public buildings, stadiums, and, perhaps most
important of all, aqueducts—built with concrete invented by Roman engineers—that
brought freshwater into the city from the neighboring mountains.

Pont du Gard
nhhe.com/
brief2e

**ROMAN CITIES AND THEIR ATTRACTIONS**   In addition to the
spectacular growth of Rome, urban growth and development took place in cities all over
the empire. And, as wealth concentrated in the cities, urban residents came to expect a
variety of comforts not available in rural areas. Roman cities enjoyed abundant supplies of
freshwater and elaborate sewage and plumbing systems. All sizable cities and even many
smaller towns had public baths and often swimming pools and gymnasia as well. Enormous circuses, stadiums, and amphitheaters provided sites for the entertainment of the
urban masses. Entertainment in stadiums often took forms now considered coarse and
cruel—battles to the death between gladiators or between humans and wild animals—but
urban populations flocked to such events, which they looked on as exciting diversions
from daily routine. The Roman Colosseum, a magnificent marble stadium and sports
arena opened in 80 C.E., provided seating for about fifty thousand spectators.

## Family and Society in Roman Times

**THE PATERFAMILIAS**   Roman law vested immense authority in male heads of
families, known as the *paterfamilias*—"father of the family." Roman law gave the paterfamilias the authority to arrange marriages for his children, determine the work or duties
they would perform, and punish them for offenses. He had rights also to sell them into
slavery and even to execute them.

Although the paterfamilias was legally endowed with extraordinary powers, women
usually supervised domestic affairs in Roman households, and by the time they reached
middle age they generally wielded considerable influence within their families. Also, although Roman law placed strict limits on the ability of women to receive inheritances,
clever individuals found ways to evade the law. During the third and second centuries
B.C.E., women came to possess a great deal of property, and by the first century B.C.E.,
many women supervised the financial affairs of family businesses and wealthy estates.

**SLAVERY**   Roman society made extensive use of slave labor: by the second century
C.E., slaves may have represented as much as one-third of the population of the Roman
empire. In the countryside they worked mostly on latifundia under extremely harsh conditions, often chained together in teams. In fact, discontent among rural slaves led to
several large-scale revolts, especially during the second and first centuries B.C.E. During
the most serious uprising, in 73 B.C.E., the escaped slave Spartacus assembled an army of
seventy thousand rebellious slaves. The Roman army dispatched eight legions, comprising
more than forty thousand well-equipped, veteran troops, to quell the revolt.

In the cities, conditions were much less difficult. Female slaves commonly worked
as domestic servants while males toiled as servants, laborers, craftsmen, shopkeepers, or

**nostrum** (NAHS-truhm)

**paterfamilias** (PAH-tehr fah-MEE-lyas)

**Spartacus** (SPAHR-tah-cus)

ners. As in Greece, slaves who had an education or possessed
... potential to lead comfortable lives. In urban areas it was also
... andatory, for masters to free slaves about the time they reached
... however, slaves remained under the strict authority of their masters,
busin...to sell them, arrange their family affairs, punish them, and even execute
som... offenses.
co...

# ... E COSMOPOLITAN
# ... EDITERRANEAN

The integration of the Mediterranean basin had important effects not only for the trade
and economy of the Roman empire but also for its cultural and religious traditions. Roads
and communication networks favored the spread of new popular religions. Most important of these over the long run was Christianity, which became the official religion of the
Roman empire and the predominant faith of the Mediterranean basin.

## *Greek Philosophy and Religions of Salvation*

**ROMAN DEITIES**    During the early days of their history, the Romans recognized
many gods and goddesses, who they believed intervened directly in human affairs. Jupiter
was the principal god, lord of the heavens, and Mars was the god of war, Ceres the goddess of grain, Janus the god who watched the threshold of individual houses, and Vesta
the goddess of the hearth. In addition to those major deities, most Roman households
honored tutelary deities, gods who looked after the welfare of individual families.

As the Romans expanded their political influence and built an empire, they encountered the religious and cultural traditions of other peoples. Often they adopted the deities
of other peoples and used them for their own purposes. From the Etruscans, for example,
they learned of Juno, the moon goddess, and Minerva, the goddess of wisdom, as well
as certain religious practices, such as divination of the future through examination of the
internal organs of ritually sacrificed animals.

**GREEK INFLUENCE**    The Romans also drew deep inspiration from the Greek
tradition of rational thought and philosophy, especially Stoicism. The Stoics' desire to
identify a set of universal moral standards based on nature and reason appealed strongly
to Roman intellectuals. Indeed, thinkers such as Marcus Tullius Cicero (106–43 B.C.E.)
readily adopted Stoic values. His letters and treatises emphasized the individual's duty to
live in accordance with nature and reason. He argued that the pursuit of justice was the
individual's highest public duty, and he scorned those who sought to accumulate wealth
or to become powerful through immoral, illegal, or unjust means. Through his speeches
and especially his writings, Cicero helped to establish Stoicism as the most prominent
school of moral philosophy in Rome.

**RELIGIONS OF SALVATION**    Whereas educated thinkers drew inspiration
from the Greeks, the masses found comfort in religions of salvation that established their
presence throughout the Mediterranean basin and beyond. These religions became prominent features in Rome during the late republic as well as under the empire. Many originated
in the far-flung realms of the empire, including the popular Anatolian cult of Mithras, the
Anatolian cult of the mother goddess Cybele, and the Egyptian cult of the goddess Isis.

**MITHRAISM**    The Mithraic religion provided divine sanction for human life and
especially for purposeful moral behavior. It brought together a community that welcomed
and nurtured like-minded individuals. Finally, it offered hope for individuals who conscientiously observed the cult's teachings by promising them ecstatic and mysterious union with

**Cicero** (SIHS-er-oh)

Mithras—who was strongly associated with military virtues such as strength, courage, and discipline—himself. During the late republic, Mithraic altars and temples appeared in military garrisons throughout the empire. During the early centuries C.E., administrators and merchants also became enchanted with Mithras, and his cult attracted followers among the male populations of all sizable communities and commercial centers in the Roman empire.

**CULT OF ISIS**   The cult of Mithras did not admit women, but cults dedicated to the Anatolian mother goddess Cybele, the Egyptian goddess Isis, and other deities made a place for both men and women. Indeed, the cult of Isis may have been the most popular of all the Mediterranean religions of salvation before the rise of Christianity. Devotees built temples to Isis throughout the Roman empire, and they adored the Egyptian goddess as a benevolent and protective deity who nurtured her worshipers and helped them cope with the stresses of life in cosmopolitan society. Like the Mithraic religion, the cult of Isis and other religions of salvation attracted followers in Rome and other cities throughout the Mediterranean basin. The immense popularity of these religions of salvation provides a context that helps to explain the remarkable success of Christianity in the Roman empire.

## Judaism and Early Christianity

**THE JEWS AND THE EMPIRE**   After the dissolution of the Jewish kingdom of David and Solomon in the early tenth century B.C.E., the Jewish people maintained their faith and their communities under various imperial regimes. At times, Jewish communities clashed with their imperial overlords, especially because monotheistic Jews refused to revere emperors as gods. As the Romans extended their empire in the eastern Mediterranean and brought the Jews in Palestine under their control, relations between the two became especially tense. Between 66 and 70 C.E., relations deteriorated to such a point that Palestinian Jews rose in rebellion against the Romans in what became known as the Jewish War.

**JESUS OF NAZARETH**   The Jews were decisively defeated in the war, which prompted some Jews to found new sects that looked for saviors to deliver them from Roman rule so they could practice their faith without interference. The early Christians were one such sect. The Christians formed their community around Jesus of Nazareth, a charismatic Jewish teacher whom they recognized as their savior. Born about the year 4 B.C.E., Jesus grew up at a time of high tension between Roman overlords and their Jewish subjects. He was a peaceful man who taught devotion to God and love for fellow human beings. He attracted large crowds because of a reputation for wisdom and miraculous powers, especially the ability to heal the sick.

Yet Jesus alarmed the Romans because he also taught that "the kingdom of God is at hand." To Jesus, the kingdom of God was a spiritual realm in which God would gather those faithful to him. To Roman administrators, however, his message sounded like a threat to Roman rule in Palestine, especially since crowds routinely accompanied Jesus. In an effort to forestall a new round of rebellion, Roman administrators executed Jesus by fixing him to a cross in the early 30s C.E.

**JESUS' EARLY FOLLOWERS**   Jesus' crucifixion did not put an end to his movement. Even after his execution Jesus' close followers strongly felt his presence and proclaimed that he had triumphed over death by rising from his grave. They called him "Christ," meaning "the anointed one," the savior who would bring individuals into the kingdom of God. They taught that he was the son of God and that his sacrifice served to offset the sins of those who had faith in him. They taught further that, like Jesus, the faithful would survive death and would experience eternal life in the spiritual kingdom of God. Following Jesus' teachings, the early Christians observed a demanding moral code and devoted themselves uncompromisingly to God. They also compiled a body of writings—accounts of Jesus' life, reports of his followers' works, and letters outlining Christian teachings—that gained recognition as the New Testament. Together with the Jews' Hebrew scriptures, which Christians referred to as the Old Testament, the New Testament became the holy book of Christianity.

**ROMAN PANTHEON.**
Built between 118 and 125 C.E., the Pantheon in Rome was a temple honoring all gods, and it survives as one of the outstanding examples of Roman architecture. With a diameter of 43 meters (141 feet), the building's dome was the largest constructed until the twentieth century. *What feelings might such a structure have evoked in worshipers?*

**PAUL OF TARSUS**    Jesus and his earliest followers were all Jews. Beginning about the middle of the first century C.E., however, some Christians avidly sought converts from non-Jewish communities in the Hellenistic world and the Roman empire. The principal figure in the expansion of Christianity beyond Judaism was Paul of Tarsus, a Jew from Anatolia who zealously preached his faith, especially in the Greek-speaking eastern region of the Roman empire. Paul taught a Christianity that attracted the urban masses in the same way as other religions of salvation that spread widely in the Roman empire. His doctrine called for individuals to observe high moral standards and to place their faith ahead of personal and family interests. His teaching also explained the world and human history as the results of God's purposeful activity so that it provided a framework of meaning for individuals' lives. Furthermore, Paul's doctrine promised a glorious future existence for those who conscientiously observed the faith.

**EARLY CHRISTIAN COMMUNITIES**    Yet for two centuries after the crucifixion of Jesus, there was no central authority for the fledgling church. Rather, individual communities selected their own supervisors, known as *bishops,* who oversaw priests and governed their jurisdictions according to their own best understanding of Christian doctrine. As a result, until the emergence of Rome as the principal seat of church authority in the third century C.E., Christians held doctrinal views and followed practices that varied considerably from one community to the next. Some religious leaders taught that Jesus had literally risen from the dead and come back to life, for example, and others held that his resurrection was a spiritual rather than physical matter. Only gradually did believers agree to recognize certain texts as authoritative scripture—the New Testament—and adopt them as fundamental guides for Christian doctrine and practice.

**THE GROWTH OF EARLY CHRISTIANITY**    Like the Jews from whose ranks they had sprung, the early Christians refused to honor the Roman state cults or revere the emperor as a god. As a result, Roman imperial authorities launched sporadic campaigns of persecution designed to eliminate Christianity as a threat to the empire. In spite of this repression, Christian numbers grew rapidly. During the first three centuries of the faith's existence, Christianity found its way to almost all parts of the Roman empire, and Christians established thriving communities throughout the Mediterranean basin and farther east in Mesopotamia and Iran. The remarkable growth of Christianity reflected the new faith's appeal particularly to the lower classes, urban populations, and women. Christianity accorded honor and dignity to individuals who did not enjoy high standing in Roman society, and it endowed them with a sense of spiritual freedom more meaningful than wealth, power, or social prominence. It taught the spiritual equality of the sexes and welcomed the contributions of both men and women. And it provided a promise of future glory for those who placed their faith in Jesus. Thus, although Christianity originated as a minor sect of Judaism, urban populations in the Roman empire embraced the new faith with such enthusiasm that by the third century C.E. it had become the most dynamic and influential religious faith in the Mediterranean basin.

# SUMMARY

Under Greek and Roman influence, Mediterranean lands became a tightly integrated society. Although the Greeks did not build a centralized empire, they dotted the Mediterranean and Black Sea shorelines with their colonies, and their merchant fleets stimulated both commercial and cultural interactions between peoples of distant lands. Greek merchants, soldiers, and administrators also played prominent roles in the extensive empires of Alexander and the Hellenistic rulers, and they left a remarkably rich and enduring cultural legacy. Building in part on both the cultural and the economic legacies of the Greeks, the Romans proceeded to construct a republic, and then an empire, that eventually administered lands as distant as Mesopotamia and Britain. Highly organized trade networks enabled peoples throughout the empire to concentrate on specialized agricultural or industrial production. Popular religions spread widely and attracted enthusiastic converts. Like Confucianism and Buddhism in classical China and India, rational philosophy and Christianity became prominent sources of intellectual and religious authority in the classical Mediterranean and continued to influence cultural development in the Mediterranean, Europe, and southwest Asia over the long term.

# STUDY TERMS

Alexander of Macedon (146)
Aristotle (150)
Athens (143)
Augustus (157)
Christians (161)
Cicero (160)
cult of Isis (161)
Delian League (145)
Epicureans (152)
Etruscans (153)
Jesus of Nazareth (161)
Jewish War (161)

Julius Caesar (156)
latifundia (156)
mare nostrum (159)
Minoan society (141)
Mithraism (160)
Mycenean society (141)
Olympic Games (148)
paterfamilias (159)
pax romana (157)
Peloponnesian War (145)
Persian Wars (145)

Plato (150)
plebians (154)
polis (142)
Ptolemaics (146)
Punic Wars (155)
Seleucids (147)
Senate (154)
Skeptics (152)
Socrates (150)
Sparta (143)
Stoics (152)

# FOR FURTHER READING

Martin Bernal. *Black Athena: The Afroasiatic Roots of Classical Civilization.* 2 vols. to date. New Brunswick, 1987–. Provocative and controversial study arguing for Egyptian and Semitic influences on early Greek society.

Henry C. Boren. *Roman Society.* 2nd ed. Lexington, 1992. An authoritative synthesis that places social and economic history in its political context.

Keith R. Bradley. *Discovering the Roman Family: Studies in Roman Social History.* New York, 1991. A provocative analysis of Roman family life with illustrations from individual experiences.

Peter Brown. *The Rise of Western Christendom: Triumph and Diversity, A.D. 200–1000.* 2nd ed. Oxford, 2003. A landmark analysis of early Christian history that incorporates the findings of recent scholarship.

F. M. Cornford. *Before and after Socrates.* Cambridge, 1965. A short but brilliant synthesis of classical Greek philosophy.

M. I. Finley. *Ancient Slavery and Modern Ideology.* Expanded ed. Princeton, 1998. Presents a thoughtful analysis of Greek and Roman slavery in light of modern slavery and contemporary debates.

Frederick C. Grant, ed. *Hellenistic Religions: The Age of Syncretism.* Indianapolis, 1953. Fascinating collection of translated documents and texts that throw light on religious and philosophical beliefs of the Hellenistic era.

Michael Grant. *Cities of Vesuvius: Pompeii and Herculaneum.* London, 1971. Fascinating glimpse of Roman society as reconstructed by archaeologists working at sites destroyed by the eruption of Vesuvius in 79 C.E.

Naphtali Lewis and Meyer Reinhold, eds. *Roman Civilization: Selected Readings.* 2 vols. 3rd ed. New York, 1990. A rich collection of translated texts and documents that illuminate Roman history and society.

Sarah B. Pomeroy. *Goddesses, Whores, Wives, and Slaves: Women in Classical Antiquity.* New York, 1995. Outstanding study analyzing the status and role of women in classical Greece and Rome.

# Cross-Cultural Exchanges on the Silk Roads

In the year 139 B.C.E., the Chinese emperor Han Wudi sent an envoy named Zhang Qian on a mission to lands west of China. The emperor's purpose was to find allies who could help combat the nomadic Xiongnu, who menaced the northern and western borders of the Han empire. From captives he had learned that other nomadic peoples in far western lands bore grudges against the Xiongnu, and he reasoned that they might ally with Han forces to pressure their common enemy.

The problem for Zhang Qian was that to communicate with potential allies against the Xiongnu, he had to pass directly through lands they controlled. Soon after Zhang Qian left Han territory, Xiongnu forces captured him. For ten years the Xiongnu held him in comfortable captivity: they allowed him to keep his personal servant, and they provided him with a Xiongnu wife, with whom he had a son. When suspicions about him subsided, however, Zhang Qian escaped with his family and servant. He even had the presence of mind to keep with him the yak tail that Han Wudi had given him as a sign of his ambassadorial status. He fled to the west and traveled as far as Bactria, but he did not succeed in lining up allies against the Xiongnu. While returning to China, Zhang Qian again fell into Xiongnu hands but managed to escape after one year's detention when the death of the Xiongnu leader led to a period of turmoil. In 126 B.C.E. Zhang Qian and his party returned to China and a warm welcome from Han Wudi.

Although his diplomatic efforts did not succeed, Zhang Qian's mission had far-reaching consequences. Apart from political and military intelligence about western lands and their peoples, Zhang Qian also brought back information of immense commercial value. While in Bactria about 128 B.C.E., he noticed Chinese goods—textiles and bamboo articles—offered for sale in local markets. Upon inquiry he learned that they had come from southwest China by way of Bengal. From that information he deduced the possibility of establishing trade relations between China and Bactria through India.

Han Wudi responded enthusiastically to this idea and dreamed of trading with peoples inhabiting lands west of China. From 102 to 98 B.C.E., he mounted an ambitious campaign that broke the power of the Xiongnu and pacified central Asia. His conquests simplified trade relations, since it became unnecessary to route commerce through India. The intelligence that Zhang Qian gathered during his travels thus contributed to the opening of the silk roads—the network of trade routes that linked lands as distant as China and the

*⟨ Tomb figure of a camel and a foreign rider. The majority of the silk road trade was handled by the nomadic peoples of central and western Asia.*

**Zhang Qian** (jung-chen)

# CHRONOLOGY

| | |
|---|---|
| third century B.C.E. | Spread of Buddhism and Hinduism to southeast Asia |
| second century B.C.E. | Introduction of Buddhism to central Asia |
| 139–126 B.C.E. | Travels of Zhang Qian in central Asia |
| first century B.C.E. | Introduction of Buddhism to China |
| second century C.E. | Spread of Christianity in the Mediterranean basin and southwest Asia |
| 184 C.E. | Yellow Turban rebellion |
| 216–272 C.E. | Life of Mani |
| 220 C.E. | Collapse of the Han dynasty |
| 284–305 C.E. | Reign of Diocletian |
| 313–337 C.E. | Reign of Constantine |
| 313 C.E. | Edict of Milan and the legalization of Christianity in the Roman empire |
| 325 C.E. | Council of Nicaea |
| 451 C.E. | Council of Chalcedon |
| 476 C.E. | Collapse of the western Roman empire |

Roman empire—and more generally to the establishment of relations between China and lands to the west.

China and other classical societies imposed political and military control over vast territories. They promoted trade and communication within their own empires, bringing regions that had previously been self-sufficient into a larger economy and society. They also fostered the spread of cultural, religious, and political traditions to distant regions, and they encouraged the construction of institutional frameworks that promoted the long-term survival of those traditions.

The classical societies established a broad zone of communication and exchange throughout much of the earth's eastern hemisphere. Trade networks crossed the deserts of central Asia and the depths of the Indian Ocean. Long-distance trade passed through much of Eurasia and north Africa, from China to the Mediterranean basin, and to parts of sub-Saharan Africa as well. That long-distance trade profoundly influenced the experiences of peoples and the development of societies throughout the eastern hemisphere. It brought wealth and access to foreign products, and it facilitated the spread of religious traditions beyond their original homelands. It also facilitated the transmission of disease. Indeed, the transmission of disease over the silk roads helped bring an end to the classical societies, since infectious and contagious diseases sparked devastating epidemics that caused political, social, and economic havoc. Long-distance trade thus had deep political, social, and cultural as well as economic and commercial implications for classical societies.

# LONG-DISTANCE TRADE AND THE SILK ROADS NETWORK

Ever since the earliest days of history, human communities have traded with one another, sometimes over long distances. Before classical times, however, long-distance trade was a risky venture. Ancient societies often policed their own realms effectively, but extensive regions were difficult to control. Trade passing between societies was therefore liable to interception by bandits or pirates. That risk increased the costs of long-distance transactions in ancient times.

During the classical era, two developments reduced the risks associated with travel and stimulated long-distance trade. First, rulers invested heavily in the construction of roads and bridges. They undertook these expensive projects primarily for military and administrative reasons, but roads also had the effect of encouraging trade within individual societies and facilitating exchanges between different societies. Second, classical societies pacified large stretches of Eurasia and north Africa. As a result, merchants did not face such great risk as in previous eras, the costs of long-distance trade dropped, and its volume rose dramatically.

**Han Wudi** (hahn-woo-dee)

# Trade Networks of the Hellenistic Era

The tempo of long-distance trade increased noticeably during the Hellenistic era, partly because of the many colonies established by Alexander of Macedon and the Seleucid rulers in Persia and Bactria. Though originally populated by military forces and administrators, these settlements soon attracted Greek merchants and bankers who linked the recently conquered lands to the Mediterranean basin. The Seleucid rulers controlled land routes linking Bactria, which offered access to Indian markets, to Mediterranean ports in Syria and Palestine.

Like the Seleucids, the Ptolemies maintained land routes—in their case, routes going south from Egypt to the kingdom of Nubia and Meroë in east Africa—but they also paid close attention to sea-lanes and maritime trade. They ousted pirates from sea-lanes linking the Red Sea to the Arabian Sea and the Indian Ocean. They also built several new ports, the most important being Berenice on the Red Sea, while Alexandria served as their principal window on the Mediterranean.

**THE MONSOON SYSTEM** Even more important, perhaps, mariners from Ptolemaic Egypt learned from Arab and Indian seamen about the monsoon winds that governed sailing and shipping in the Indian Ocean. During the summer the winds blow regularly from the southwest, whereas in the winter they come from the northeast. Knowledge of these winds enabled mariners to sail safely and reliably to all parts of the Indian Ocean basin.

**TRADE IN THE HELLENISTIC WORLD** Establishment and maintenance of these trade routes was an expensive affair calling for substantial investment in military forces, construction, and bureaucracies to administer the commerce that passed over the routes. But the investment paid handsome dividends. Long-distance trade stimulated economic development within the Hellenistic realms themselves, bringing benefits to local economies throughout the empires. Moreover, Hellenistic rulers closely supervised foreign trade and levied taxes on it, thereby deriving income even from foreign products. Thus with official encouragement, a substantial trade developed throughout the Hellenistic world, from Bactria and India in the east to the Mediterranean basin in the west.

Indeed, maritime trade networks through the Indian Ocean linked not only the large classical societies of Eurasia and north Africa but also smaller societies in east Africa. During the late centuries B.C.E., the port of Rhapta (located near Dar es Salaam in Tanzania) emerged as the principal commercial center on the east African coast. With increasing trade, groups of professional merchants and entrepreneurs emerged at Rhapta, and coins came into general use on the east African coast. Merchants of Rhapta imported iron goods such as spears, axes, and knives from southern Arabia and the eastern Mediterranean region in exchange for ivory, rhinoceros horn, tortoise shell, and slaves obtained from interior regions.

# The Silk Roads

The establishment of classical empires greatly expanded the scope of long-distance trade, as much of Eurasia and north Africa fell under the sway of one classical society or another. The Han empire maintained order in China and pacified much of central Asia, including a sizable corridor offering access to Bactria and western markets. The Parthian empire displaced the Seleucids in Persia and extended its authority to Mesopotamia. The Roman empire brought order to the Mediterranean basin. With the decline of the Mauryan dynasty, India lacked a strong imperial state, but the Kushan empire and other regional states provided stability and security, particularly in northern India, which favored long-distance trade.

The silk roads
www.mhhe.com/
bentleybrief2e

Ptolemaic (TAWL-oh-may-ihk)

**OVERLAND TRADE ROUTES** As the classical empires expanded, merchants and travelers created an extensive network of trade routes that linked much of Eurasia and north Africa. Historians refer to these routes collectively as the silk roads, since high-quality silk from China was one of the principal commodities exchanged over the roads. The overland silk roads took caravan trade from China to the Roman empire, thus linking the extreme ends of the Eurasian landmass. From the Han capital of Chang'an, the main silk road went west until it arrived at the Taklamakan desert, also known as the Tarim Basin. The silk road then split into two main branches that skirted the desert proper and passed through oasis towns that ringed it to the north and south. The branches came together at Kashgar (now known as Kashi, located in the westernmost corner of modern China). From there the reunited road went west to Bactria, where a branch forked off to offer access to Taxila and northern India, while the principal route continued across northern Iran. There it joined with roads to ports on the Caspian Sea and the Persian Gulf and proceeded to Palmyra (in modern Syria), where it met roads coming from Arabia and ports on the Red Sea. Continuing west, it terminated at the Mediterranean ports of Antioch (in modern Turkey) and Tyre (in modern Lebanon).

**SEA-LANES AND MARITIME TRADE** The silk roads also included a network of sea-lanes that sustained maritime commerce throughout much of the eastern hemisphere. From Guangzhou in southern China, sea-lanes through the South China Sea

**The silk roads connected cities as distant as Byzantium and Luoyang.**

**Chang'an** (chahng-ahn)

**Tyre** (tah-yer)

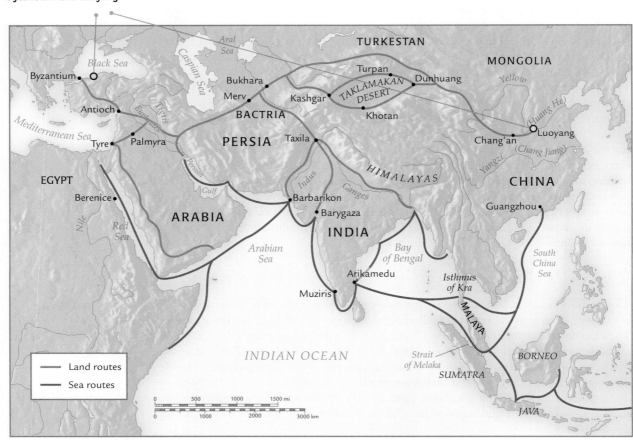

**MAP 9.1** | The silk roads, 200 B.C.E.–300 C.E. Note the extent of the land and sea routes known collectively as the silk roads. *Consider the political and economic conditions that would be necessary for regular travel and trade across the silk roads.*

**ROMAN GLASS BOWL.** | During the first century B.C.E. Romans developed advanced glass-blowing techniques that enabled them to produce wares like this. *What social group were bowls like these made for?*

**ROMAN COIN.** | This Roman coin, dated 189 C.E., depicts a merchant ship near the lighthouse at Alexandria. Ships like this regularly picked up pepper and cinnamon from India along with other cargoes.

linked the east Asian seaboard to the mainland and the islands of southeast Asia. Routes linking southeast Asia with Ceylon (modern Sri Lanka) and India were especially busy during classical times. From India, sea-lanes passed through the Arabian Sea to Persia and Arabia, and through the Persian Gulf and the Red Sea they offered access to land routes and the Mediterranean basin, which already possessed a well-developed network of trade routes.

TRADE GOODS    A wide variety of manufactured products and agricultural commodities traveled over the silk roads. Silk and spices traveled west from producers in southeast Asia, China, and India to consumers in central Asia, Iran, Arabia, and the Roman empire. Silk came mostly from China, and the fine spices—cloves, nutmeg, mace, and cardamom—all came from southeast Asia. Ginger came from China, cinnamon from China and southeast Asia, pepper from India, and sesame oil from India, Arabia, and southwest Asia. Spices were extremely important commodities in classical times because they had many more uses than they do in the modern world. They served not only as condiments and flavoring agents but also as drugs, anesthetics, aphrodisiacs, perfumes, aromatics, and magical potions. For the silk and spices they imported, western lands exchanged a variety of manufactured goods and other commodities, including horses and jade from central Asia and glassware, jewelry, textiles, and pottery from the Roman empire.

 "Battuta in China" www.mhhe.com/ bentleybrief2e

Zhang Qian was only one of many individuals who made very long journeys during classical times. Indeed, records indicate that merchants and diplomats from central Asia, China, India, southeast Asia, and the Roman empire traveled long distances in pursuit of trade and diplomacy. On a few occasions individuals even traveled across much or all of the eastern hemisphere between China and the Roman empire. A Chinese ambassador named Gang Ying embarked on a mission to distant western lands in 97 C.E. and proceeded as far as Mesopotamia before reports of the long and dangerous journey ahead persuaded him to return home. And Chinese sources reported the arrival in 166 C.E. of a delegation claiming to represent the Roman emperor Marcus Aurelius.

THE ORGANIZATION OF LONG-DISTANCE TRADE    Individual merchants did not usually travel from one end of Eurasia to the other, either by land or by sea. Instead, they handled long-distance trade in stages. On the caravan routes between China and Bactria, for example, Chinese and central Asian nomadic peoples dominated trade. Farther west, however, the Parthians took advantage of their power and geographic position to control overland trade within their boundaries. Once merchandise reached Palmyra, it passed mostly into the hands of Roman subjects such as Greeks, Jews, and Armenians, who were especially active in the commercial life of the Mediterranean basin.

"The Geography of Strabo: The Roman Empire"
www.mhhe.com/ bentleybrief2e

On the seas, the situation was similar: Malay and Indian mariners dominated trade in southeast Asian and south Chinese water, Persians and subjects of the Roman empire dominated the Arabian Sea, Parthians controlled the Persian Gulf, and the Roman empire dominated the Red Sea. Indeed, after Roman emperors absorbed Egypt in the first century C.E., their subjects carried on an especially brisk trade between India and the Mediterranean. The Greek geographer Strabo reported in the early first century C.E. that as many as 120 ships departed annually from the Red Sea for India. Meanwhile, since the mid-first century C.E., the Romans also had dominated both the eastern and the western regions of mare nostrum, the Mediterranean.

It is impossible to determine the quantity or the value of trade that passed over the silk roads in classical times, but it clearly made a deep impression on contemporaries. By the first century C.E., pepper, cinnamon, and other spices graced the tables of the wealthy classes in the Roman empire, where silk garments had become items of high fashion. Some Romans fretted that see-through silk attire would lead to moral decay, and others worried that hefty expenditures for luxury items would ruin the imperial economy. In both cases their anxieties testified to the powerful attraction of imported silks and spices for Roman consumers.

As it happened, long-distance trade more likely stimulated rather than threatened local economies. Yet long-distance trade did not occur in a vacuum. Commercial exchanges encouraged cultural and biological exchanges, some of which had large implications for classical societies.

# CULTURAL AND BIOLOGICAL EXCHANGES ALONG THE SILK ROADS

The silk roads served as magnificent highways for merchants and their commodities, but others also took advantage of the opportunities they offered to travel in relative safety over long distances. Merchants, missionaries, and other travelers carried their beliefs, values, and religious convictions to distant lands: Buddhism, Hinduism, and Christianity all traveled the silk roads and attracted converts far from their original homelands. Meanwhile, invisible travelers such as disease pathogens also crossed the silk roads and touched off devastating epidemics when they found fresh populations to infect. Toward the end of the classical era, epidemic disease that was spread over the silk roads caused dramatic demographic decline, especially in China and the Mediterranean basin and to a lesser extent in other parts of Eurasia as well.

## *The Spread of Buddhism and Hinduism*

By the third century B.C.E., Buddhism had become well established in northern India, and with the sponsorship of the emperor Ashoka the faith spread to Bactria and Ceylon. Buddhism was particularly successful in attracting merchants as converts. When they traveled, Buddhist merchants observed their faith among themselves and explained it to others. Gradually, Buddhism made its way along the silk roads to Iran, central Asia, China, and southeast Asia.

The Diamond Sutra
www.mhhe.com/ bentleybrief2e

BUDDHISM IN CENTRAL ASIA    Buddhism first established a presence in the oasis towns along the silk roads where merchants and their caravans found food, rest, lodging, and markets. The oases depended heavily on trade for their prosperity, and they allowed merchants to build monasteries and invite monks and scribes into their communities. Because they hosted travelers who came from different lands, spoke different

**Buddhism** (BOO-diz'm)

languages, and observed different religious practices, the oasis towns became cosmopolitan centers. As early as the second century B.C.E., many residents of the oases themselves adopted Buddhism, which was the most prominent faith of silk roads merchants for almost a millennium, from about 200 B.C.E. to 700 C.E.

BUDDHISM IN CHINA   From the oasis communities Buddhism spread to the steppe lands of central Asia and to China via the nomadic peoples who visited the oases to trade. In the early centuries C.E., they increasingly responded to the appeal of Buddhism, and by the fourth century C.E., they had sponsored the spread of Buddhism throughout much of central Asia. Foreign merchants also brought their faith to China in about the first century B.C.E. Although the religion remained unpopular among native Chinese for several centuries, the presence of Buddhist monasteries and missionaries in China's major cities did attract some converts. Then, in about the fifth century C.E., the Chinese began to respond enthusiastically to Buddhism. Indeed, during the postclassical era Buddhism became the most popular religious faith throughout all of east Asia, including Japan and Korea as well as China.

BUDDHISM AND HINDUISM IN SOUTHEAST ASIA
As Buddhism spread north from India into central Asia and China, both Buddhism and Hinduism also began to attract a following in southeast Asia. Once again, merchants traveling the silk roads—in this case the sea-lanes through the Indian Ocean—played prominent roles in spreading these faiths. By the first century C.E., clear signs of Indian cultural influence had appeared in many parts of southeast Asia. Many rulers converted to Buddhism, and others promoted the Hindu cults of Shiva and Vishnu. They built walled cities around lavish temples constructed in the Indian style, they adopted Sanskrit as a means of written communication, and they appointed Buddhist or Hindu advisors.

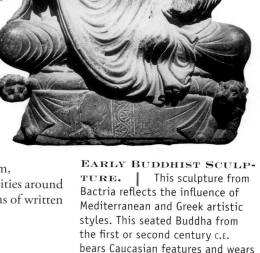

EARLY BUDDHIST SCULPTURE. | This sculpture from Bactria reflects the influence of Mediterranean and Greek artistic styles. This seated Buddha from the first or second century C.E. bears Caucasian features and wears Mediterranean-style dress.

# The Spread of Christianity

Early Christians faced intermittent persecution from Roman officials. During the early centuries C.E., Roman authorities launched a series of campaigns to stamp out Christianity, because most Christians refused to observe the state cults that honored emperors as divine beings. Imperial officials also considered Christianity a menace to society because zealous missionaries attacked other religions and generated sometimes violent conflict. Nevertheless, Christian missionaries took full advantage of the Romans' magnificent network of roads and sea-lanes, which enabled them to carry their message throughout the Roman empire and the Mediterranean basin.

CHRISTIANITY IN THE MEDITERRANEAN BASIN   During the second and third centuries C.E., countless missionaries worked zealously to attract converts. One of the more famous was Gregory the Wonderworker, a tireless missionary with a reputation for performing miracles, who popularized Christianity in central Anatolia during the mid-third century C.E. Contemporaries reported that Gregory not only preached Christian doctrine but also had access to impressive supernatural powers. Gregory and his fellow missionaries helped to make Christianity an enormously popular religion of salvation in the Roman empire. By the late third century C.E., in spite of continuing imperial opposition, devout Christian communities flourished throughout the Mediterranean basin in Anatolia, Syria, Palestine, Egypt, and north Africa as well as in Greece, Italy, Spain, and Gaul.

CHRISTIANITY IN SOUTHWEST ASIA   The young faith also traveled the trade routes and found followers beyond the Mediterranean basin. By the second century C.E., sizable Christian communities flourished throughout Mesopotamia and Iran, and a few Christian churches had appeared as far away as India. Christians also attracted

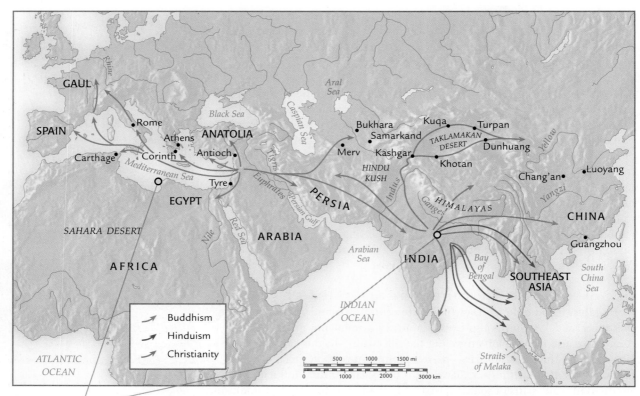

**Christianity spread predominantly to the west, while Buddhism and Hinduism spread to the south and the east.**

**MAP 9.2** | The spread of Buddhism, Hinduism, and Christianity, 200 B.C.E.–400 C.E. Compare the routes taken by Buddhism, Hinduism, and Christianity with the routes followed by merchants on silk roads depicted on Map 9.1. *How might you account for the similarities?*

large numbers of converts in southwest Asia and came to constitute—along with Jews and Zoroastrians—one of the major religious communities in the region.

Christian communities in Mesopotamia and Iran deeply influenced Christian practices in the Roman empire. To demonstrate utter loyalty to their faith, Christians in southwest Asia often followed strict ascetic regimes and sometimes even withdrew from family life and society. By the third century C.E., some Mediterranean Christians were so impressed by these practices that they began to live as hermits in isolated locations or to live exclusively among like-minded individuals who devoted their efforts to prayer and praise of God. Thus ascetic practices of Christians living in lands east of the Roman empire helped to inspire the formation of Christian monastic communities in the Mediterranean basin.

After the fifth century C.E., Christian communities in southwest Asia and the Mediterranean basin increasingly went separate ways. Most of the faithful in southwest Asia became Nestorians—followers of the Greek theologian Nestorius, who lived during the early fifth century and emphasized the human as opposed to the divine nature of Jesus. Mediterranean church authorities rejected Nestorius's views, and many of his disciples departed for Mesopotamia and Iran. Although they had limited dealings with Mediterranean Christians, the Nestorians spread their faith east across the silk roads, and by the early seventh century they had established communities in central Asia, India, and China.

**Zoroastrian** (zohr-oh-ASS-tree-ahn)

**Nestorian** (neh-STOHR-eeuhn)

# The Spread of Manichaeism

**MANI AND MANICHAEISM**  The explosive spread of Manichaeism dramatically illustrated how missionary religions made effective use of the silk roads trading network. Manichaeism was the faith derived from the prophet Mani (216–272 C.E.), a devout Zoroastrian from Babylon in Mesopotamia who also drew deep inspiration from Christianity and Buddhism. Because of the intense interaction between peoples of different societies, Mani promoted a syncretic blend of Zoroastrian, Christian, and Buddhist elements as a religious faith that would serve the needs of a cosmopolitan world.

**MANICHAEAN ETHICS**  Mani was a dualist: he viewed the world as the site of a cosmic struggle between the forces of light and darkness, good and evil. He urged his followers to reject worldly pleasures and to observe high ethical standards. Devout Manichaeans, known as "the elect," abstained from marriage, sexual relations, and personal comforts, dedicating themselves instead to prayer, fasting, and ritual observances. Less zealous Manichaeans, known as "hearers," led more conventional lives, but they followed a strict moral code and provided food and gifts to sustain the elect. Mani's doctrine had strong appeal because it offered a rational explanation for the presence of good and evil in the world while also providing a means for individuals to achieve personal salvation.

Mani was a fervent missionary and traveled widely to promote his faith. He also created a Manichaean church with its own services, rituals, hymns, and liturgies. His doctrine attracted converts first in Mesopotamia, and before Mani's death it had spread throughout the Sasanid empire and into the eastern Mediterranean region. In spite of its asceticism, Manichaeism appealed especially strongly to merchants, who adopted the faith as hearers and supported the Manichaean church. By the end of the third century C.E., Manichaean communities had appeared in all the large cities and trading centers of the Roman empire.

**MANICHAEAN PAINTING.** |  A cave painting from about the seventh century C.E. depicts a group of devout Manichaean faithful, whose austere regimen called for them to dress in plain white garments and keep their hair uncut and untrimmed.

**DECLINE OF MANICHAEISM**  Manichaeism soon came under tremendous pressure in both the Zoroastrian Sasanid state and the Roman empire. Mani himself died in chains as a prisoner of the Sasanid emperor, who saw Manichaeism as a threat to the public order. Authorities in the Roman empire also persecuted Manichaeans and largely exterminated the faith in the Mediterranean basin over the course of the fifth and sixth centuries. Yet Manichaeism survived in central Asia, where it attracted converts among nomadic Turkish peoples who traded with merchants from China, India, and southwest Asia. Like Buddhism, Hinduism, and Christianity, then, Manichaeism relied on the trade routes of classical times to extend its influence to new lands and peoples.

# The Spread of Epidemic Disease

Like religious faiths, infectious and contagious diseases also spread along the trade routes of the classical world. Aided by long-distance travelers, pathogens had opportunities to spread beyond their original environments and attack populations with no inherited or acquired immunities to the diseases they caused. The resulting epidemics took a ferocious toll in human lives.

**Manichaeism** (man-ih-KEE-iz'm)

**Sasanid** (suh-SAH-nid)

**EPIDEMIC DISEASES**   During the second and third centuries C.E., the Han and Roman empires suffered large-scale outbreaks of epidemic disease. The most destructive of these diseases were probably smallpox and measles, and epidemics of bubonic plague may also have erupted. All three diseases are devastating when they break out in populations without resistance, immunities, or medicines to combat them. As disease ravaged the two empires, Chinese and Roman populations declined sharply.

During the reign of Augustus, the population of the Roman empire stood at about sixty million people. During the second century C.E., epidemics reduced Roman population to forty-five million. Most devastating was an outbreak of smallpox that spread throughout the Mediterranean basin during the years 165 to 180 C.E. In combination with war and invasions, by 400 C.E. continuing outbreaks caused the population to decline even further, to about forty million. Whereas population in the eastern Mediterranean probably stabilized by the sixth century C.E., western Mediterranean lands experienced demographic stagnation until the tenth century.

Epidemics appeared slightly later in China than in the Mediterranean region. From fifty million people at the beginning of the millennium, Chinese population rose to sixty million in 200 C.E. As diseases found their way east, however, Chinese numbers fell back to fifty million by 400 C.E. and to forty-five million by 600 C.E. Thus by 600 C.E. both Mediterranean and Chinese populations had fallen by a quarter to a third from their high points during classical times.

**EFFECTS OF EPIDEMIC DISEASES**   Demographic decline in turn brought economic and social change. Trade within the empires declined, and both the Chinese and the Roman economies contracted. Both economies also moved toward regional self-sufficiency: whereas previously the Chinese and Roman states had integrated the various regions of their empires into a larger network of trade and exchange, after about 200 C.E. they increasingly embraced several smaller regional economies that concentrated on their own needs instead of the larger imperial market. Indeed, epidemic disease contributed to serious instability in China after the collapse of the Han dynasty, and in weakening Mediterranean society, it helped bring about the decline and fall of the western Roman empire.

# CHINA AFTER THE HAN DYNASTY

By the time epidemic diseases struck China, internal political problems had already begun to weaken the Han dynasty. By the late second century C.E., Han authorities had largely lost their ability to maintain order. Early in the third century C.E., the central government dissolved, and a series of autonomous regional kingdoms took the place of the Han state. With the disappearance of the Han dynasty, China experienced significant cultural change, most notably an increasing interest in Buddhism.

## *Internal Decay of the Han State*

The Han dynasty collapsed largely because of internal problems that its rulers could not solve. One problem involved the development of factions within the ranks of the ruling elites. The desire of some elites to advance their own prospects in the imperial government at the cost of others led to constant infighting and backstabbing among the ruling elites, which reduced the effectiveness of the central government. An even more difficult problem had to do with the perennial issue of land and its equitable distribution. In the last two centuries of the Han dynasty, large landowners gained new influence in the government. They

**THINKING ABOUT** *Encounters*

**ENCOUNTERS IN CROSS-CULTURAL EXCHANGES ON THE SILK ROADS.** During the classical era, large empires and regional states maintained order across large portions of Eurasia and north Africa, which allowed long-distance trade to expand dramatically. In addition to material goods, what other kinds of exchanges did the maintenance of these trading routes encourage?

*St. Cyprian, bishop of Carthage, was an outspoken proponent of Christianity during the early and middle decades of the third century C.E. When epidemic disease struck the Roman empire in 251 C.E., imperial authorities blamed the outbreak on Christians who refused to honor pagan gods. Cyprian refuted this charge in his treatise* **On Mortality,** *which described the symptoms of epidemic disease and reflected on its significance for the Christian community.*

It serves as validation of the [Christian] faith when the bowels loosen and drain the body's strength, when fever generated in bone marrow causes sores to break out in the throat, when continuous vomiting roils the intestines, when blood-shot eyes burn, when the feet or other bodily parts are amputated because of infection by putrefying disease, when through weakness caused by injuries to the body either mobility is impeded, or hearing is impaired, or sight is obscured. It requires enormous greatness of heart to struggle with resolute mind against so many onslaughts of destruction and death. It requires great loftiness to stand firm amidst the ruins of the human race, not to concede defeat with those who have no hope in God, but rather to rejoice and embrace the gift of the times. With Christ as our judge, we should receive this gift as the reward of his faith, as we vigorously affirm our faith and, having suffered, advance toward Christ by Christ's narrow path. . . .

Many of us [Christians] are dying in this epidemic—that is, many of us are being liberated from the world. The epidemic is a pestilence for the Jews and the pagans and the enemies of Christ, but for the servants of God it is a welcome event. True, without any discrimination, the just are dying alongside the unjust, but you should not imagine that the evil and the good face a common destruction. The just are called to refreshment, while the unjust are herded off to punishment: the faithful re-

ceive protection, while the faithless receive retribution. We are unseeing and ungrateful for divine favors, beloved brethren, and we do not recognize what is granted to us. . . .

How suitable and essential it is that this plague and pestilence, which seems so terrible and ferocious, probes the justice of every individual and examines the minds of the human race to determine whether the healthy care for the ill, whether relatives diligently love their kin, whether masters show mercy to their languishing slaves, whether physicians do not abandon those seeking their aid, whether the ferocious diminish their violence, whether the greedy in the fear of death extinguish the raging flames of their insatiable avarice, whether the proud bend their necks, whether the shameless mitigate their audacity, whether the rich will loosen their purse strings and give something to others as their loved ones perish all around them and as they are about to die without heirs.

■ To what extent do you think St. Cyprian was effective in his efforts to bring inherited Christian teachings to bear on the unprecedented conditions he and his followers faced?

SOURCE: Wilhelm von Hartel, ed. *S. Thasci Caecili Cypriani opera omnia* in *Corpus scriptorum ecclesiasticorum latinorum.* Vienna, 1868, vol. 3, pp. 305–6. (Translation by Jerry H. Bentley.)

reduced their share of taxes and shifted the burden onto peasants. They even formed private armies to advance the interests of their class.

**PEASANT REBELLION**   These developments provoked widespread unrest among peasants, who found themselves under increasing economic pressure with no means to influence the government. Pressures became particularly acute during the late second and third centuries when epidemics began to take their toll. In 184 C.E. peasant discontent fueled a large-scale uprising known as the Yellow Turban rebellion, so called because the rebels wore yellow headbands that represented the color of the Chinese earth and symbolized their peasant origins. Although quickly suppressed, the rebellion proved to be only the first in a series of insurrections that plagued the late Han dynasty.

**COLLAPSE OF THE HAN DYNASTY**   Meanwhile, Han generals increasingly usurped political authority. By 190 C.E. the Han emperor had become a mere puppet, and the generals effectively ruled the regions controlled by their armies. They allied with wealthy landowners of their regions and established themselves as warlords who

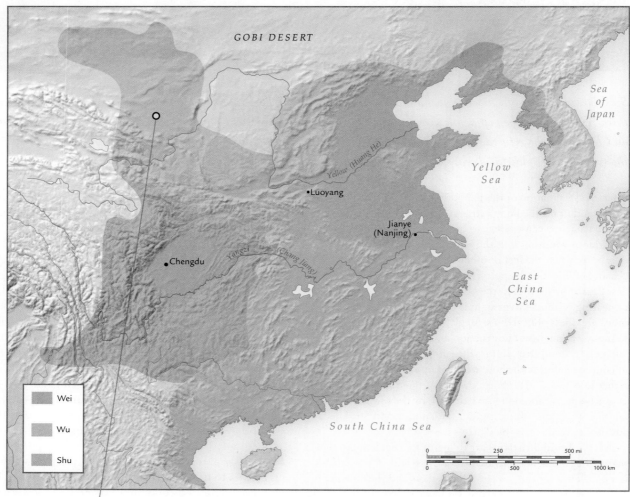

GOBI DESERT

Sea of Japan

Yellow Sea

Yellow (Huang He)

•Luoyang

Jianye (Nanjing) •

Chengdu •

Yangzi (Chang Jiang)

East China Sea

South China Sea

Wei

Wu

Shu

0     250     500 mi
0   500   1000 km

The Wei empire encompassed considerably less territory inhabited by northwestern nomadic groups than the Han empire had.

**MAP 9.3** | China after the Han dynasty, 200 C.E. Compare this map with Map 6.2 showing the Han empire at its height. *What geographical considerations might help explain why the Han empire broke up into the three kingdoms shown here?*

maintained a kind of rough order based on force of arms. In 220 C.E. they abolished the Han dynasty altogether and divided the empire into three large kingdoms.

Once the dynasty had disappeared, large numbers of nomadic peoples migrated into China, especially the northern regions, and they helped to keep China disunited for more than 350 years. Between the fourth and sixth centuries C.E., nomadic peoples established large kingdoms that dominated much of northern China as well as the steppe lands.

## Cultural Change in Post-Han China

In some ways the centuries following the fall of the Han dynasty present a spectacle of chaos and disorder. One kingdom toppled another, only to fall in its turn to a temporary successor. War and nomadic invasions led to population decline in much of northern China. By the mid-fifth century, contemporaries reported, the Former Han capital of Chang'an had no more than one hundred households and the Later Han capital of Luoyang resembled a trash heap more than a city.

CULTURAL ADAPTATION OF NOMADIC PEOPLES Beneath the disorderly surface of political events, however, several important social and cultural changes were taking place. First, nomadic peoples increasingly adapted to the Chinese environment and culture, and as the generations passed, distinctions between peoples of nomadic and Chinese ancestry became less and less obvious. Partly because of that development, a new imperial dynasty was eventually able to reconstitute a centralized imperial state in north China.

Second, with the disintegration of political order, the Confucian tradition lost much of its credibility. The original goal of Confucius and his early followers was to find some means to move from chaos to stability during the Period of the Warring States. When the Han dynasty collapsed, Confucianism seemed both ineffective and irrelevant.

Individuals who in earlier centuries might have committed themselves to Confucian values turned instead to Daoism and Buddhism. Daoism, from its origins in the Period of the Warring States, had originally appealed mostly to an educated elite. After the fall of the Han, however, Daoist sages widened its appeal by promising salvation to those who observed their doctrines and rituals and by offering the use of elixirs made of spices, herbs, and drugs that supposedly conferred health and immortality. Daoism attracted widespread interest among a population afflicted by war and disease and became much more popular than before, especially because it faced less competition from the Confucian tradition.

POPULARITY OF BUDDHISM    Even more important than Daoism for Chinese cultural history was Buddhism. After the fall of the Han empire, Buddhism received strong support from nomadic peoples who migrated into northern China and who in many cases had long been familiar with Buddhism in central Asia. Meanwhile, as a result of missionary efforts, the Indian faith began to attract a following among native Chinese as well. Indeed, between the fourth and sixth centuries C.E., Buddhism became well established in China. When a centralized imperial state took shape in the late sixth century C.E., Buddhism provided an important cultural foundation for the restoration of a unified political order.

# THE FALL OF THE ROMAN EMPIRE

A combination of internal problems and external pressures weakened the Roman empire and brought an end to its authority in the western portion of the empire, whereas in the eastern Mediterranean imperial rule continued until the fifteenth century C.E. In the Mediterranean basin as in China, imperial weakness and collapse coincided with significant cultural change, notably the increasing popularity of Christianity.

## *Internal Decay in the Roman Empire*

THE BARRACKS EMPERORS    As in the case of the Han dynasty, internal political problems go a long way toward explaining the fall of the Roman empire. Like their Han counterparts, the Roman emperors faced internal opposition. During the half century from 235 to 284 C.E., there were no fewer than twenty-six claimants to the imperial throne. Known as the "barracks emperors," most of them were generals who seized power, held it briefly, and then suddenly lost it when they were displaced by rivals or their own mutinous troops. Not surprisingly, most of the barracks emperors died violently. Only one is known for sure to have succumbed to natural causes.

**Confucianism** (kuhn-FEW-shun-iz'm)

**Daoism** (dow-ism)

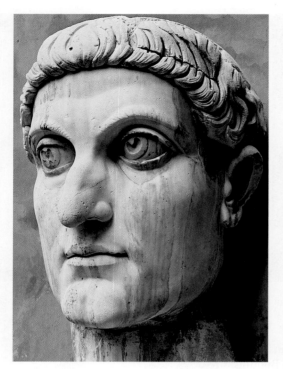

**CONSTANTINE.** | Only the colossal head of Constantine survives from a statue that originally stood about 14 meters (46 feet) tall.

The Roman empire also faced problems because of its sheer size. Even during the best of times, when the emperors could count on abundant revenues and disciplined armed forces, the sprawling empire posed a challenge for central governors. After the third century, as epidemics spread throughout the empire and its various regions moved toward local, self-sufficient economies, the empire as a whole became increasingly unmanageable.

**THE EMPEROR DIOCLETIAN** The emperor Diocletian (reigned 284–305 C.E.) attempted to deal with this problem by dividing the empire into two administrative districts: one in the east and one in the west. A coemperor ruled each district with the aid of a powerful lieutenant, and the four officials, known as the tetrarchs, were able to administer the vast empire more effectively than an individual emperor could. Diocletian was a skillful administrator. He managed to bring Rome's many armies, including unpredictable maverick forces, under firm imperial control. He also tried to deal with a crumbling economy by strengthening the imperial currency, forcing the government to adjust its expenditures to its income, and imposing price caps to dampen inflation. His economic measures were less successful than his administrative reforms, but they helped stabilize an economy ravaged by half a century of civil unrest.

Yet Diocletian's reforms encouraged ambition among the tetrarchs and their generals, and his retirement from the imperial office in 305 C.E. set off a round of internal struggles and bitter civil war. Already in 306 C.E. Constantine, son of Diocletian's coruler Constantius, moved to stake his claim as sole emperor. Once he had consolidated his grip on power in 324 C.E., Constantine ordered the construction of a new capital city, Constantinople, at a strategic site overlooking the Bosporus, the strait linking the Black Sea to the Sea of Marmara and beyond to the wealthy eastern Mediterranean. After 340 C.E. Constantinople became the capital of a united Roman empire.

**CONSTANTINE** Constantine himself was an able emperor. With the reunion of the eastern and western districts of the empire, however, he and his successors faced the same sort of administrative difficulties that Diocletian had attempted to solve by dividing the empire. As population declined and the economy contracted, emperors found it increasingly difficult to marshall the resources needed to govern and protect the vast Roman empire.

## Germanic Invasions and the Fall of the Western Roman Empire

Apart from internal problems, the Roman empire faced a formidable military threat from migratory Germanic peoples. Indeed, during the fifth century C.E., Germanic invasions brought an end to Roman authority in the western half of the empire, although imperial rule survived for an additional millennium in the eastern Mediterranean.

**GERMANIC MIGRATIONS** Germanic peoples had migrated from their homelands in northern Europe and lived on the eastern and northern borders of the Roman empire since the second century C.E. Most notable were the Visigoths, who came originally from Scandinavia and Russia. Like the nomadic peoples who moved into northern China after the fall of the Han dynasty, the Visigoths settled, adopted agriculture, and drew deep inspiration from Roman society. In the interests of social order, however, the

**Diocletian** (dah-yuh-KLEE-shuhn)

**Constantine** (KAHN-stuhn-teen)

Romans discouraged settlement of the Visigoths and other Germanic peoples within the empire, preferring that they constitute buffer societies outside imperial borders.

**THE HUNS**  During the late fourth century, the relationship between Visigoths and Romans changed dramatically when the nomadic Huns began an aggressive westward migration from their homeland in central Asia. The Huns were probably cousins of the nomadic Xiongnu who inhabited the central Asian steppe lands west of China. During the mid-fifth century C.E., the warrior-king Attila organized the Huns into a virtually unstoppable military juggernaut. Under Attila, the Huns invaded Hungary, probed Roman frontiers in the Balkan region, menaced Gaul and northern Italy, and attacked Germanic peoples living on the borders of the Roman empire.

**COLLAPSE OF THE WESTERN ROMAN EMPIRE**  Attila did not create a set of political institutions or a state structure, and the Huns disappeared as a political and military force soon after his death in 453 C.E. By that time, however, the Huns had placed such pressure on Visigoths and other Germanic peoples that they streamed en masse into the Roman empire in search of refuge. Once inside imperial boundaries, they encountered little effective resistance and moved around almost at will. They established

Fall of the Roman empire
www.mhhe.com/
bentleybrief2e

**MAP 9.4**  |  Germanic invasions and the fall of the western Roman empire between 450 and 476 C.E. Notice the many different groups that moved into western Roman territory in this period. *What might have motivated such movement, and why couldn't the western Roman empire prevent it?*

settlements throughout the western half of the empire—Italy, Gaul, Spain, Britain, and north Africa—where populations were less dense than in the eastern Mediterranean. Under the command of Alaric, the Visigoths even stormed and sacked Rome in 410 C.E. By the middle of the fifth century, the western part of the Roman empire was in a shambles. In 476 C.E. imperial authority came to an ignominious end when the Germanic general Odovacer deposed Romulus Augustulus, the last of the Roman emperors in the western half of the empire.

Unlike the Han dynasty, the Roman empire did not entirely disintegrate: imperial authority survived for another millennium in the eastern half of the empire, known after the fifth century C.E. as the Byzantine empire. In the western half, however, Roman authority dissolved, and nomadic peoples built successor states in regions formerly subject to Rome. Vandals and then Visigoths governed Spain, Franks ruled Gaul, Angles and Saxons invaded Britain, and Italy fell under the sway of a variety of peoples, including Visigoths, Vandals, and Lombards.

## Cultural Change in the Late Roman Empire

In the Roman empire, as in China, the collapse of the imperial state coincided with important social and cultural changes. The Germanic peoples who toppled the empire looked to their own traditions for purposes of organizing society and government. When they settled in the regions of the former empire, however, they absorbed a good deal of Roman influence. Over time, the mingling of Roman and Germanic traditions led to the emergence of an altogether new society—medieval Europe.

PROMINENCE OF CHRISTIANITY  Christianity was perhaps the most prominent survivor of the western Roman empire. During the fourth century C.E., several developments enhanced its influence throughout the Mediterranean basin. In the first place, Christianity won recognition as a legitimate religion in the Roman empire. In 312 C.E., while seeking to establish himself as sole Roman emperor, Constantine experienced a vision that impressed upon him the power of the Christian God. He believed that the Christian God helped him to prevail over his rivals, and he promulgated the Edict of Milan, which allowed Christians to practice their faith openly in the Roman empire. At some point during his reign, perhaps after his edict, Constantine himself converted to Christianity, and in 380 C.E. the emperor Theodosius proclaimed Christianity the official religion of the Roman empire. By the mid-fourth century, Christians held important political and military positions, and imperial sponsorship helped their faith to attract more converts than ever before.

Christianity also began to attract thoughtful and talented converts who articulated a Christian message for the intellectual elites of the Roman empire. The earliest Christians had come largely from the ranks of ordinary working people, and for three centuries the new faith grew as a popular religion of salvation favored by the masses, rather than as a reasoned doctrine of intellectual substance. During the fourth century, however, intellectual elites began to articulate Christianity in terms that were familiar and persuasive to the educated classes.

ST. AUGUSTINE  The most important and influential of those figures was St. Augustine (354–430 C.E.), bishop of the north African city of Hippo (modern-day Annaba in Algeria). Augustine had a fine education, and he was conversant with the leading intellectual currents of the day. During his youth he drew great inspiration from Stoicism and Platonism, and for nine years he belonged to a community of Manichaeans. Eventually he became disillusioned with both the Hellenistic philosophical school and

Odovacer (AHD-oh-vah-cer)

Byzantine (BIHZ-uhn-teen)

Theodosius (thee-hu-DOH-see-uhs)

Manichaeism, and in 387 C.E., while studying in Italy, he converted to Christianity. For the remainder of his life, he worked to reconcile Christianity with Greek and Roman philosophical traditions. More than any others, Augustine's writings helped make Christianity an intellectually respectable alternative to Hellenistic philosophy and to popular religions of salvation.

THE INSTITUTIONAL CHURCH    Besides winning the right to practice their faith openly and attracting intellectual talent, Christian leaders constructed an institutional apparatus that transformed a popular religion of salvation into a powerful church. In the absence of recognized leadership, the earliest Christians generated a range of conflicting and sometimes contradictory doctrines. To standardize their faith, Christian leaders instituted a hierarchy of church officials. At the top were five religious authorities—the bishop of Rome and the patriarchs of Jerusalem, Antioch, Alexandria, and Constantinople—who resided in the most important spiritual and political centers of the Roman empire. Subordinate to the five principal authorities were bishops, who presided over religious affairs in their districts, known as dioceses, which included all the prominent cities of the Roman empire. When theological disputes arose, the patriarchs and the bishops assembled in church councils to determine which views would prevail as official doctrine. The councils at Nicaea (325 C.E.) and Chalcedon (451 C.E.), for example, took up the difficult and contentious issue of Jesus' nature. Delegates at these councils proclaimed that Jesus was both fully human and fully divine at the same time, in contrast to Nestorians, Arians, and other Christian groups who held that Jesus was either primarily human or primarily divine.

As Roman imperial authority crumbled, the bishop of Rome, known as the pope (from the Latin *papa*, meaning "father"), emerged as spiritual leader of Christian communities in the western regions of the empire. As the only sources of established and recognized authority, the popes and the bishops of other important cities organized local government and defensive measures for their communities. They also mounted missionary campaigns to convert Germanic peoples to Christianity. Although Roman imperial authority disappeared, Roman Christianity survived and served as a foundation for cultural unity in lands that had formerly made up the western half of the Roman empire.

Nicaea (nahy-SEE-uh)
Chalcedon (KAL-suh-dawn)

ST. AUGUSTINE.    | This portrait shows St. Augustine holding a copy of his most famous work, *The City of God,* which sought to explain the meaning of history and the world from a Christian point of view. *In what ways does this portrait seek to represent St. Augustine as a deeply pious man?*

# SUMMARY

Between the last centuries of the first millennium B.C.E. and the first few centuries of the new millennium, the classical societies established a broad zone of exchange throughout much of Eurasia and north Africa. Long-distance trade along what has come to be known as the silk roads profoundly shaped the societies involved. Products like silk, jewels, and spices found new markets in far-distant regions, while ideas and religious beliefs from Buddhism to Christianity found new adherents and converts. Long-distance trade also facilitated the spread of epidemic disease, and by the second and third centuries C.E. disease had wreaked havoc among most of the classical societies. Indeed, coupled with severe internal conflicts as well as external threats, the disorder caused by epidemic disease helped contribute to the collapse of the Chinese Han dynasty as well as the Western Roman empire.

# STUDY TERMS

Attila the Hun (179)
Buddhism (170)
Byzantine empire (180)
Christianity (171)
Confucianism (177)
Constantine (178)
Constantinople (178)
Council of Chalcedon (181)
Council of Nicaea (181)

Daoism (177)
Diocletian (178)
Edict of Milan (180)
epidemic disease (173)
Gregory the Wonderworker (171)
Han dynasty (165)
Mani (173)
Manichaeism (173)

Nestorians (172)
Odovacer (180)
pope (181)
silk roads (167)
St. Augustine (180)
tetrarchs (178)
Visigoths (178)
Yellow Turban rebellion (175)

# FOR FURTHER READING

Thomas J. Barfield. *The Perilous Frontier: Nomadic Empires and China*. Cambridge, Mass., 1989. Provocative study of the Xiongnu and other central Asian peoples.

Jerry H. Bentley. *Old World Encounters: Cross-Cultural Contacts and Exchanges in Pre-modern Times*. New York, 1993. Studies the spread of cultural and religious traditions before 1500 C.E.

Averil Cameron. *The Later Roman Empire, A.D. 284–430*. Cambridge, Mass., 1993. A lively synthesis.

———. *The Mediterranean World in Late Antiquity, A.D. 395–600*. London, 1993. Like its companion volume just cited, a well-informed synthesis.

Edward Gibbon. *The Decline and Fall of the Roman Empire*. Many editions available. A classic account, still well worth reading, by a masterful historical stylist of the eighteenth century.

C. D. Gordon, ed. *The Age of Attila: Fifth-Century Byzantium and the Barbarians*. Ann Arbor, 1972. Translations of primary sources on the society and history of nomadic and migratory peoples.

Samuel Hugh Moffett. *A History of Christianity in Asia,* vol. 1. San Francisco, 1992. An important volume that surveys the spread of early Christianity east of the Roman empire.

Joseph A. Tainter. *The Collapse of Complex Societies*. Cambridge, 1988. Scholarly review of theories and evidence bearing on the fall of empires and societies.

Susan Whitfield. *Life along the Silk Road*. Berkeley, 1999. Focuses on the experiences of ten individuals who lived or traveled along the silk roads.

Francis Wood. *The Silk Road: Two Thousand Years in the Heart of Asia*. Berkeley, 2002. A brilliantly illustrated volume discussing the history of the silk roads from antiquity to the twentieth century.

# Bringing It All Together

**Part II** | **The Formation of Classical Societies, 500 B.C.E. to 500 C.E.**

In Part II, we have seen that the classical societies that developed in Persia, China, India, and the Mediterranean built on many of the traditions established by the early complex societies discussed in Part I. By the last half-millennium B.C.E., however, the classical societies had surpassed their predecessors in complexity, organization, and sophistication. As a result, they were able to expand further, to control more people and resources, and to trade longer distances than any human societies in the past.

The increased reach of classical societies created an ever-stronger need for rulers to impose their will efficiently across long distances, especially when their territories included diverse and potentially rebellious conquered peoples. Some, like the Achaemenid dynasty of Persia, established carefully designed administrations that divided oversight of their wide realms into manageable portions headed by loyal administrators. Many, including the Achaemenids, the Romans, and the Han dynasty of China, standardized systems of law and taxation as a means of encouraging uniformity throughout their realms. Others, like the rulers of Han China, established a uniform educational system from which all imperial administrators would be drawn.

Classical rulers also sought to impose their will and to promote unity within their realms by sponsoring particular philosophies, cultural practices, or religious beliefs. Thus, Greeks encouraged a sense of commonality between the diverse poleis and colonies by sponsoring the Olympic Games. In India, the Mauryan dynasty advocated Buddhism as a unifying system of belief, the Persian Sasanids sponsored Zoroastrianism as a state religion, and the Romans actively promoted Christianity after 380 C.E. Finally, all the classical societies sought to increase the efficiency of their administrations by establishing long-distance transportation and communication networks. While these networks aided imperial administration, they also allowed for a dramatic increase in long-distance trade. In turn, long-distance trade encouraged both the spread of religions such as Buddhism, Hinduism, and Christianity as well as the diffusion of disease pathogens that ultimately contributed to the disintegration of the classical societies.

By 500 C.E. classical societies in Persia, China, India, and the Mediterranean basin had either collapsed or fallen into decline. Yet all the classical societies left rich legacies that shaped political institutions, social orders, and cultural traditions for centuries to come. Moreover, by sponsoring commercial and cultural relations between different peoples, the classical societies laid a foundation for intensive and systematic cross-cultural interaction in later times.

# III

# The Postclassical Era, 500 to 1000 C.E.

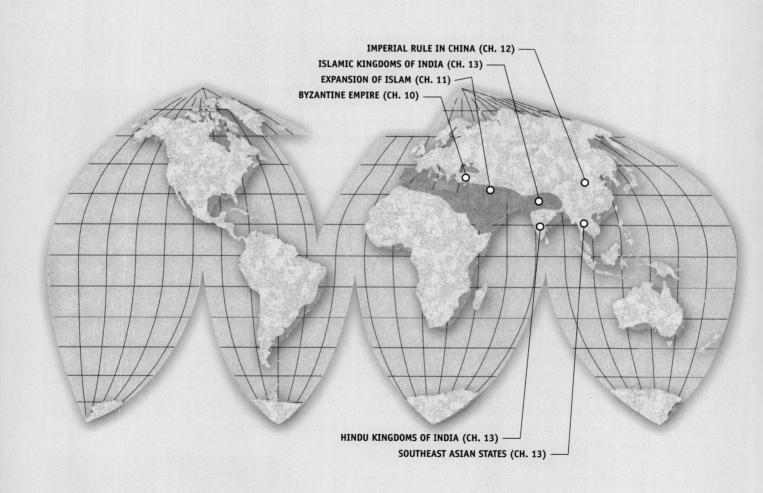

IMPERIAL RULE IN CHINA (CH. 12)

ISLAMIC KINGDOMS OF INDIA (CH. 13)

EXPANSION OF ISLAM (CH. 11)

BYZANTINE EMPIRE (CH. 10)

HINDU KINGDOMS OF INDIA (CH. 13)

SOUTHEAST ASIAN STATES (CH. 13)

The postclassical era was a period of major readjustment for societies throughout the eastern hemisphere. During the early centuries C.E., disease as well as both internal and external pressures brought serious instability to classical societies in China, India, southwest Asia, and the Mediterranean basin. Most of the classical empires collapsed under the strain. During the postclassical era the settled societies of the eastern hemisphere underwent political, social, economic, and cultural change that would shape their experiences over the long term.

The first task that settled societies faced in the postclassical era was the need to restore political and social order. In the eastern Mediterranean the eastern half of the Roman empire survived as the Byzantine empire but underwent political and social reorganization in order to deal with external pressures. In southwest Asia, Arab conquerors inspired by the recently founded Islamic faith asserted their authority over vast areas in southwest Asia and north Africa, and introduced their faith to India as well as Iberia. In China the Sui and Tang dynasties restored centralized imperial authority after almost four centuries of rule by competing regional kingdoms and nomadic conquerors. In India, in contrast, centralized imperial rule did not return: authority devolved instead to a series of regional kingdoms.

The reestablishment of political and social order enabled postclassical societies to revive networks of long-distance trade and participate more actively in processes of cross-cultural communication and exchange. As a result, the postclassical era was a time of rapid economic growth in most of the eastern hemisphere. Meanwhile, increased trade facilitated biological and technological as well as commercial exchanges: agricultural crops migrated far beyond the lands of their origin, and improved techniques of irrigation and cultivation spread through much of Eurasia. As agricultural production increased, so did human population, which allowed growing numbers of people to devote their efforts to trade and manufacturing rather than cultivation.

The postclassical era was also crucially important for the formation and development of cultural and religious traditions. Islam first appeared during the postclassical era, and it soon became the foundation of an expansive empire stretching from north Africa to northern India. Buddhism expanded beyond the Indian subcontinent and central Asia, attracting converts in east and southeast Asia. Christianity was the official faith of the Byzantine empire, where the Eastern Orthodox church emerged and gave shape to a distinctive form of Christianity that eventually spread to much of eastern Europe and Russia.

The empires and regional states of the postclassical era disappeared long ago, but the social, economic, and cultural legacies of the age are noticeable even today. Most notable, perhaps, religious and cultural traditions continue to flourish in lands where they first attracted converts in postclassical times. In some ways, then, the postclassical age survives even in the modern world.

# The Christian Commonwealth of Byzantium

## 10

According to the Byzantine historian Procopius, two Christian monks from Persia set out on a momentous journey about the middle of the sixth century C.E. The result of their travels was the introduction of high-quality silk production to the eastern Mediterranean. Although local crafts workers had long produced coarse fabrics from the cocoons of wild silkworms, fine silks had come to the Mediterranean only from China, where manufacturers closely guarded both their carefully bred strains of silkworms and the complex technology that yielded high-quality textiles. Mediterranean consumers obtained silk not directly from Chinese producers but, rather, through intermediaries subject to the Sasanid empire of Persia.

According to Procopius's account, the two Christian monks observed the techniques of silk production during the course of a mission to China. Upon departure they hollowed out their walking staffs and filled them with silkworm eggs, which they smuggled out of China, through their native land of Persia, and into the Byzantine empire.

The monks' motives are unknown. Whatever they may have been, though, it is certain that the monks by themselves could not have introduced a full-blown silk industry to Byzantium. The production of fine, Chinese-style silks required more than a few silkworm eggs. It also required understanding sophisticated technologies and elaborate procedures that must have reached the Byzantine empire by several different routes. Thus it seems that Procopius simplified a much more complex story.

In any case, Byzantine crafts workers did indeed learn how to produce high-quality silk fabrics. By the late sixth century, Byzantine silks matched Chinese silks in quality. Mediterranean consumers no longer relied on Chinese producers and Persian intermediaries, and local production of high-quality silk greatly strengthened the Byzantine economy. Thus Procopius's anonymous monks participated in a momentous transfer of technology between distant lands. Their efforts contributed to the vibrance of Byzantine society, and their story highlights the significance of cross-cultural interactions during the postclassical era.

During the centuries after 200 C.E., most of the classical societies faced a series of problems—epidemic disease, declining population, economic contraction, social and political turmoil, and military threats—that brought about their collapse. Only in the eastern Mediterranean did a classical empire survive. The eastern half of the Roman empire, known as the Byzantine empire, withstood the various problems that brought down other classical societies

❮ *A sixth-century icon depicting an enthroned Virgin Mary and infant Jesus attended by angels and saints.*

**Procopius** (proh-KOH-pee-uhs)

# CHRONOLOGY

| | |
|---|---|
| 313–337 | Reign of Constantine |
| 325 | Council of Nicaea |
| 329–379 | Life of St. Basil of Caesarea |
| 340 | Transfer of Roman government to Constantinople |
| 527–565 | Reign of Justinian |
| 717–741 | Reign of Leo III |
| 726–843 | Iconoclastic controversy |
| ninth century | Missions of St. Cyril and St. Methodius to the Slavs |
| 976–1025 | Reign of Basil II, "the Bulgar-Slayer" |
| 989 | Conversion of Prince Vladimir of Kiev to Orthodox Christianity |
| 1054 | Beginning of the schism between the eastern and western Christian churches |
| 1071 | Battle of Manzikert |
| 1202–1204 | Fourth crusade |
| 1453 | Fall of Constantinople |

and survived for almost a millennium after the collapse of the western Roman empire in the fifth century C.E.

The Byzantine empire did not reconstitute the larger Mediterranean society of classical times. The Roman empire had dominated an integrated Mediterranean basin; the Byzantine empire mostly faced a politically and culturally fragmented Mediterranean region. After the seventh century C.E., Islamic states controlled lands to the east and south of the Mediterranean, Slavic peoples dominated lands to the north, and western Europeans organized increasingly powerful states in lands to the west.

Nevertheless, the Byzantine empire was a political and economic powerhouse of the post-classical era. Until the twelfth century, Byzantine authority dominated the wealthy and productive eastern Mediterranean region. Manufactured goods from the Byzantine empire enjoyed a reputation for high quality in markets from the Mediterranean basin to India. The Byzantine empire also deeply influenced the historical development of the Slavic peoples of eastern Europe and Russia by introducing writing, Christianity, codified law, and sophisticated political organization into their lands. Because Byzantine political, economic, and cultural influence stretched so far, historians often refer to it as the "Byzantine commonwealth." Just as Greek and Roman initiative brought Mediterranean lands into a larger integrated society during classical times, Byzantine policies led to the formation of a large, multicultural zone of trade, communication, interaction, and exchange in eastern Europe and the eastern Mediterranean basin during the postclassical era.

# THE EARLY BYZANTINE EMPIRE

The Byzantine empire takes its name from Byzantion—latinized as Byzantium—a modest village that occupied a site of enormous strategic significance. Situated on a defensible peninsula and blessed with a magnificent natural harbor known as the Golden Horn, Byzantion had the potential to control the Bosporus, the strait of water leading from the Black Sea to the Sea of Marmara and beyond to the Dardanelles, the Aegean Sea, and the Mediterranean. Apart from its maritime significance, Byzantion also offered convenient access to the rich lands of Anatolia, southwestern Asia, and southeastern Europe.

Because of its strategic value, the Roman emperor Constantine designated Byzantion as the site of a new imperial capital, which he named Constantinople ("city of Constantine"). The imperial government moved to Constantinople in 340 C.E., and the new capital rapidly reached metropolitan dimensions. By the late fourth century, it was the most important political and military center of the eastern Roman empire, and it soon became the dominant economic and commercial center in the eastern Mediterranean basin. The city kept the name Constantinople until 1453 C.E., when it fell to the Ottoman Turks, who renamed it Istanbul. By convention, however, historians refer to the realm governed from Constantinople between the fifth and fifteenth centuries C.E. as the Byzantine empire, or simply as Byzantium, in honor of the original settlement.

**Byzantine** (BIHZ-uhn-teen)

**Aegean** (ih-JEE-uhn)

**MAP 10.1** | The Byzantine empire and its neighbors, 527–554 C.E. Compare this map with Map 11.2 showing the Roman empire at its height. **How did the territories of the Byzantine empire differ from those of the classical Roman empire?**

**Constantinople became the capital of the Byzantine empire.**

# The Later Roman Empire and Byzantium

The Byzantine empire originated as the eastern half of the classical Roman empire, which survived the collapse of the western Roman empire in the fifth century C.E. In its early days the Byzantine empire embraced Greece, the Balkan region, Anatolia, Syria, Palestine, Egypt, and northeast Africa. During the seventh and eighth centuries C.E., however, the southern regions of the empire fell into the hands of Arab Muslim conquerors. Nevertheless, Byzantium figured as a major power of the eastern Mediterranean basin until the thirteenth century C.E.

**THE LATER ROMAN EMPIRE**   As the western Roman empire crumbled, the eastern half of the empire remained intact, complete with roads, communications, lines of authority, and a set of functioning imperial institutions, all inherited from Roman predecessors. Yet the early Byzantine emperors faced challenges different from those of their predecessors, and they built a state significantly different from the classical Roman empire.

The principal challenges that confronted the late Roman and early Byzantine empires were the consolidation of the dynamic Sasanid dynasty (226–641 C.E.) in Persia and the invasions of migratory peoples from the north and east. The Sasanid emperors sought to rebuild the Achaemenid empire of classical Persia, a goal that brought them into conflict with Roman forces in Mesopotamia and Syria. Germanic invasions also menaced the late Roman empire. Because they did not have adequate resources to respond strongly to the threat on all fronts, Roman authorities concentrated on maintaining the integrity of the wealthy eastern portion of the empire.

**The Byzantine empire**
www.mhhe.com/
bentleybrief2e

**Sasanid** (suh-SAH-nid)

**Achaemenid** (uh-KEE-muh-nihd)

**THE EARLY BYZANTINE STATE**   The Byzantine emperors built a distinctive tradition of statecraft. Its most important feature was tightly centralized rule that concentrated power in the hands of a highly exalted emperor. This characteristic was noticeable already in the time of Constantine, who built his new capital to lavish standards. He filled it with libraries, museums, and artistic treasures, and he constructed magnificent marble structures—all in an effort to create a new Rome fit for the ruler of a mighty empire.

**CAESAROPAPISM**   Constantine also set a precedent by hedging his rule with an aura of divinity. Although he did not claim divine status as some of his imperial predecessors had, as the first Christian emperor he did claim divine favor and sanction for his rule. He intervened in theological disputes and used his political position to support views that he considered orthodox and condemn those he regarded as heretical. Constantine initiated a policy that historians call *caesaropapism,* whereby the emperor not only ruled as secular lord but also played an active and prominent role in ecclesiastical affairs.

Particularly after the sixth century, Byzantine emperors became absolute rulers. According to Roman law, emperors stood above the law: theoretically, they wielded absolute authority in political, military, judicial, financial, and religious matters. They also enjoyed the services of a large and complex bureaucracy. In combination, law and bureaucracy produced an exceptionally centralized state.

**THE BYZANTINE COURT**   Even dress and court etiquette drew attention to the lofty status of Byzantine rulers. The emperors wore heavily bejeweled crowns and dressed in magnificent silk robes dyed a dark, rich purple—a color reserved strictly for imperial use. High officials presented themselves to the emperor as slaves and before taking up matters of business prostrated themselves before him three times and kissed his hands and feet. By the tenth century, engineers had contrived a series of mechanical devices that worked dazzling effects and impressed foreign envoys at the Byzantine court: mechanical lions roared and swished their tails as ambassadors approached the emperor, and sometimes the imperial throne itself moved up and down to emphasize the awesome splendor of the emperor.

# *Justinian and His Legacy*

**JUSTINIAN AND THEODORA**   The most important of the early Byzantine emperors was Justinian (527–565 C.E.), an energetic and tireless worker known to his subjects as "the sleepless emperor," who profoundly influenced the development of the Byzantine empire with the aid of his ambitious wife Theodora. Both were intelligent, strong willed, and disciplined and used those qualities to build a strong empire and a grand imperial court.

Like Constantine, Justinian lavished resources on the imperial capital. During the early years of his rule, riots against high taxes had destroyed much of Constantinople. After Theodora persuaded him to deploy the imperial army and quash the disturbances, Justinian embarked on an ambitious construction program that thoroughly remade the city. The most notable building erected during that campaign was the church of Hagia Sophia, a magnificent domed structure that ranks as one of the world's most important examples of Christian architecture. Visitors marveled at the church's enormous dome, which they likened to the heavens encircling the earth, and they expressed awe at the gold, silver, and gems that decorated and illuminated Hagia Sophia. Over time, the church even acquired a reputation for working miraculous cures: its columns and doors reportedly healed the illnesses of people who stood beside them or touched them.

**JUSTINIAN'S CODE**   Justinian's most significant political contribution was his codification of Roman law. Almost immediately on taking the throne, Justinian ordered a thorough and systematic review of Roman law. On the basis of that work, he issued the

PSI img   Court of Theodora
www.mhhe.com/
bentleybrief2e

PSI img   Exterior of Hagia Sophia
www.mhhe.com/
bentleybrief2e

**Hagia Sophia** (HAH-yah soh-FEE-uh)

*Corpus iuris civilis (Body of the Civil Law),* which immediately won recognition as a definitive work. Later emperors updated Roman law by adding new provisions, but Justinian's code continued to serve as a source of legal inspiration and went on to influence civil law codes throughout much of western Europe.

**EMPEROR JUSTINIAN.** | Justinian wears imperial purple robes in this mosaic from the church of San Vitale in Ravenna. He is pictured in the company of ecclesiastical, military, and court officials. Notice the richness of Justinian's clothing in comparison to those around him.

BELISARIUS AND BYZANTINE CONQUESTS Justinian's most ambitious venture was his effort to reconquer the western Roman empire from Germanic peoples and reestablish Roman authority throughout the Mediterranean basin. Beginning in 533 he sent his brilliant general Belisarius on military campaigns that returned Italy, Sicily, northwestern Africa, and southern Spain to imperial hands. By the end of his reign in 565, Justinian had reconstituted a good portion of the classical Roman empire.

Justinian's accomplishment, however, did not long survive his own rule. Byzantium simply did not possess the resources to sustain Belisarius's conquests. Although Byzantium managed to hold on to a few areas in the Italian peninsula, Justinian's dream of restoring Roman authority throughout the Mediterranean basin soon faded. Indeed, Justinian's efforts clearly showed that the classical Roman empire was beyond recovery. While Justinian devoted his attention to the western Mediterranean, the Sasanids threatened Byzantium from the east and Slavic peoples approached from the north. Justinian's successors had no choice but to withdraw their resources from the western Mediterranean and redeploy them in the east. Even though Belisarius's reconquest of the western Roman empire was a spectacular military accomplishment, it was also something of an anachronism, since the lands of the eastern and western Mediterranean had already begun to follow different historical trajectories.

## Islamic Conquests and Byzantine Revival

After the seventh century C.E., the emergence of Islam and the development of a powerful and expansive Islamic state (topics discussed in chapter 11) posed a serious challenge to Byzantium. Inspired by their Islamic faith, Arab peoples conquered the Sasanid empire and overran Byzantine Syria, Palestine, Egypt, and north Africa. During the late seventh and early eighth centuries, Islamic forces even subjected Constantinople to prolonged siege (in 674–678 and again in 717–718). Byzantium resisted this northern thrust of Islam

*Corpus iuris civilis* (KOR-poos EW-rees sih-VEE-lees)
**Belisarius** (bel-uh-SAIR-ee-uhs)

**THE CHURCH OF HAGIA SOPHIA ("HOLY WIS-DOM").** | This church was built by Justinian and transformed into a mosque in the fifteenth century. The dome rises almost 60 meters (197 feet) above the floor, and its windows allow abundant light to enter the massive structure.

partly because of military technology. Byzantine forces used a weapon known as Greek fire—a devastating incendiary weapon compounded of sulphur, lime, and petroleum—which they launched at both the fleets and the ground forces of the invaders. Greek fire burned even when floating on water and thus created a serious hazard when deployed around wooden ships. On land it caused panic among enemy forces, since it was very difficult to extinguish and often burned troops to death. As a result of this defensive effort, the Byzantine empire retained its hold on Anatolia, Greece, and the Balkan region.

IMPERIAL ORGANIZATION    Though much reduced by the Islamic conquests, the Byzantine empire after the eighth century was also more compact and manageable. Also, Byzantine rulers initiated political and social adjustments that strengthened the empire that remained in their hands. The most important innovation was the reorganization of Byzantine society under the *theme* (imperial province) system. This system placed a *theme* under the jurisdiction of a general, who assumed responsibility for both its military defense and its civil administration. Generals received their appointments from the imperial government, which closely supervised their activities to prevent decentralization of power and authority. Generals recruited armies from the ranks of free peasants, who received allotments of land in exchange for military service. The armies proved to be effective military forces, and the system as a whole strengthened the class of free peasants, which in turn solidified Byzantium's agricultural economy. The *theme* system enabled Byzantine forces to mobilize quickly and resist further Islamic advances and also undergirded the political order and the social organization of the empire from the eighth through the twelfth century.

Indeed, Byzantium vastly expanded its influence between the late ninth and the late eleventh centuries. During the tenth century Byzantine forces shored up defenses in Anatolia and reconquered Syria from Arab Muslims. During the reign of Basil II (976–1025 C.E.), known as "Basil the Bulgar-Slayer," Byzantine armies turned west and crushed the neighboring Bulgars, who had built a large kingdom in the Balkans. After his victory at the battle of Kleidion in 1014 C.E., Basil reportedly commanded his forces to blind fourteen thousand Bulgarian survivors, though he spared one eye in a few, who then guided the others home. By the mid–eleventh century the Byzantine empire embraced lands from Syria and Armenia in the east to southern Italy in the west, from the Danube River in the north to Cyprus and Crete in the south. Byzantine expansion brought in so much wealth that Basil was able to waive the collection of taxes for two years. Once again, Byzantium dominated the eastern Mediterranean.

## *Byzantium and Western Europe*

TENSIONS BETWEEN BYZANTIUM AND WESTERN EUROPEAN STATES  While they went to war with their Arab Muslim and pagan Slavic neighbors, Byzantines also experienced tense relations with their Christian counterparts in the western Mediterranean. The Christian church of Constantinople conducted its affairs in Greek and was heavily influenced by the will of the caesaropapist emperors, whereas the Christian church of Rome conducted its affairs in Latin and rejected imperial interference in ecclesiastical matters. Church authorities in Byzantium regarded Roman Christians as poorly educated and uncouth. In return, church leaders in Rome considered their Byzantine counterparts insincere and insufficiently wary of heresy.

Political grievances also strained relations between Byzantium and western European lands. During the fifth and sixth centuries, imperial authorities could do little more than watch as Germanic peoples established successor states to the western Roman empire—lands that Byzantine emperors regarded as their rightful inheritance. Worse yet, some of the upstart powers claimed imperial authority for themselves. In 800, for example, the Frankish ruler Charlemagne received an imperial crown from the pope in Rome, thereby directly challenging Byzantine claims to imperial authority over western lands. Charlemagne's empire soon dissolved, but in 962 Otto of Saxony lodged his own claim to rule as emperor over the western lands of the former Roman empire. Adding injury to insult, Otto then attacked lands in southern Italy that had been in Byzantine possession since the days of Justinian.

# BYZANTINE ECONOMY AND SOCIETY

Byzantium dominated the political and military affairs of the eastern Mediterranean largely because of its strong economy. Ever since classical times, the territories embraced by the Byzantine empire had produced abundant agricultural surpluses, supported large numbers of crafts workers, and participated in trade with lands throughout the Mediterranean. Even after the collapse of the Roman empire, those territories continued to provide a solid material foundation for Byzantium, and they helped to make the Byzantine empire an economic powerhouse of the postclassical era.

**Charlemagne** (SHAHR-leh-mane)

# Rural Economy and Society

Until its conquest by Arab forces, Egypt was the major source of grain for Byzantium. Afterward, Anatolia and the lower Danube region served as the imperial breadbasket. All those lands produced reliable and abundant harvests of wheat, which supported large populations in Byzantium's major cities. Indeed, between the fifth and the early thirteenth centuries, Constantinople's population alone approached or exceeded one million people.

THE PEASANTRY  Byzantine economy and society were strongest when the empire supported a large class of free peasants who owned small plots of land. Besides serving as the backbone of the Byzantine military system, free peasants cultivated their land intensively in hopes of improving their families' fortunes. As in other societies, however, wealthy families sought to accumulate land and to control the labor of peasants for their own interests. Especially in the early centuries of the Byzantine empire, wealthy cultivators worked to bind peasants to their estates or to force them into sharecropping arrangements from which it was difficult to break free.

However, the invasions of the sixth and seventh centuries broke up many large estates and afforded peasants an opportunity to rebuild small holdings. The *theme* system strengthened the free peasantry by making land available to those who performed military service. The imperial government also made periodic efforts to prevent wealthy landowners from gaining control over peasant lands. Over the long term, however, wealthy landowners built ever-larger estates. From the eleventh century onward, they transformed the peasants into an increasingly dependent class, and by the thirteenth century free peasants accounted for only a small portion of the rural population.

DECLINE OF THE FREE PEASANTRY  The accumulation of landholdings in the hands of the wealthy had important implications for financial and military affairs. For one thing, large estates often received tax exemptions and so did not contribute their fair share to imperial coffers. Moreover, the decline of the free peasantry diminished the pool of recruits available for service in military forces organized under the *theme* system. Thus, the concentration of land and rural resources worked against the financial interests of the central government, and it caused political, military, and economic difficulties for the Byzantine state during the last three centuries of its existence.

# Industry and Trade

In spite of social and economic problems, Byzantium remained a wealthy land. Byzantine prosperity derived both from the empire's productive capacity and from the importance of Constantinople as a center of trade.

MANUFACTURING ENTERPRISES  Indeed, Constantinople was home to many artisans and crafts workers who enjoyed a reputation especially for their glassware, linen and woolen textiles, gems, jewelry, and fine work in gold and silver. In addition, after the arrival of silkworms, crafts workers added high-quality silk textiles to the list of products manufactured in the Byzantine empire. Silk was a most important addition to the economy, and Byzantium became the principal supplier of this fashionable fabric to lands in the Mediterranean basin. The silk industry was so important to the Byzantine economy that the government closely supervised every step in its production and sale. Regulations allowed individuals to participate in only one activity—such as weaving, dyeing, or sales—to prevent the creation of a monopoly in the industry by a few wealthy or powerful entrepreneurs.

TRADE  Situated astride routes going east and west as well as north and south, Constantinople also served as the main clearinghouse for trade in the western part of Eurasia. The merchants of Constantinople maintained direct commercial links with manufacturers and merchants in central Asia, Russia, Scandinavia, northern Europe, and the lands of the Black Sea and the Mediterranean basin. Byzantium dominated trade to such an extent that trading peoples recognized the Byzantine gold coin, the *bezant,* as the standard currency of the Mediterranean basin for more than half a millennium, from the sixth through the twelfth century.

Byzantium drew enormous wealth simply from the control of trade and the levying of customs duties on merchandise that passed through its lands. More important, Byzantium served as the western anchor of a Eurasian trading network that revived the silk roads of classical times. Silk and porcelain came to Constantinople from China, spices from India and southeast Asia. Carpets arrived from Persia, woolen textiles from western Europe, and timber, furs, honey, amber, and slaves from Russia and Scandinavia.

**THE ORGANIZATION OF TRADE** Banks helped to fuel Byzantine trade by advancing loans to individuals seeking to launch business ventures, and Byzantine merchants often formed partnerships that allowed them to pool their resources and limit their risks. Although neither banking nor partnership was an altogether new technique, Byzantine businessmen made much more extensive use of them than their predecessors had. In doing so, they both supported and stimulated a dynamic commercial economy.

## Urban Life

Constantinople had no rival among Byzantine cities. Subjects of the Byzantine empire referred to it simply as "the City." The heart of the City was the imperial palace, which employed twenty thousand workers as palace staff. Peacocks strutted through gardens filled with sculptures and fountains. Most famous was a gold fountain in the shape of a pineapple that spouted wine for imperial guests.

**HOUSING IN CONSTANTINOPLE** Aristocrats maintained enormous palaces that included courtyards, reception halls, libraries, and chapels. Women lived in separate apartments and did not receive male visitors from outside the household. Indeed, women often did not participate in banquets and parties, especially when wine flowed freely or when the affairs were likely to become so festive that they could compromise a woman's honor.

The less privileged classes of Constantinople occupied less splendid dwellings. Artisans and crafts workers usually lived in rooms above their shops, and clerks and government officials lived in multistory apartment buildings. Workers and the poor occupied dangerous and rickety tenements, sharing kitchens and sanitary facilities with their neighbors.

**ATTRACTIONS OF CONSTANTINOPLE** Even for the poor, though, the City had its attractions. As the heir to Rome, Constantinople was a city of baths, which were sites of relaxation and exercise as well as hygienic bathing. Taverns and restaurants offered settings for social gatherings—checkers, chess, and dice games were especially popular activities at taverns—and theaters provided entertainment in the form of song, dance, and striptease. Mass entertainment took place in the Hippodrome, a large stadium adjacent to the imperial palace. There Byzantine subjects watched chariot races, athletic matches, contests between wild animals, and circuses featuring clowns, jugglers, acrobats, and dwarfs.

# CLASSICAL HERITAGE AND ORTHODOX CHRISTIANITY

The first Christian emperor of the Roman empire gave both his name and his faith to Constantinople. Like the Byzantine state, however, Byzantine Christianity developed along distinctive lines, and it became a faith different from the early Christianity of the Roman empire. For one thing, the philosophy and literature of classical Greece had a much deeper influence in Byzantium than in western Europe. Byzantine church leaders also disagreed with their western counterparts on matters of doctrine, ritual, and church authority. By the mid–eleventh century, differences between the eastern and western churches had become so great that their leaders formally divided Mediterranean Christianity into the Eastern Orthodox and Roman Catholic churches.

## The Legacy of Classical Greece

Although local inhabitants spoke Greek, the official language of early Constantinople was Latin, the language of Rome. After the sixth century, however, Greek replaced Latin as the language of government in the Byzantine empire. Byzantine scholars often did not learn to read Latin, and they drew intellectual inspiration from the New Testament (originally composed in Greek) and the philosophy and literature of classical Greece rather than classical Rome.

BYZANTINE EDUCATION    The legacy of classical Greece was especially noticeable in Byzantine education. The Byzantine state considered education vitally important, since its bureaucracy called for large numbers of literate individuals to administer the empire. As a result, the state organized a school system that offered a primary education in reading, writing, and grammar, followed by studies of classical Greek literature, philosophy, and science. Because of this, basic literacy was widespread in Byzantine society.

BYZANTINE SCHOLARSHIP    Like the educational system, Byzantine scholarship reflected the cultural legacy of classical Greece. Byzantine scholars concentrated on the humanities—literature, history, and philosophy—rather than on the natural sciences or medicine. Byzantines with a literary education considered themselves the direct heirs of classical Greece, and they went to great lengths to preserve and transmit the classical legacy. Indeed, almost all literary and philosophical works of classical Greece that survive have come down to the present in copies made between the tenth and twelfth centuries in the Byzantine empire.

## The Byzantine Church

CHURCH AND STATE    The most distinctive feature of Byzantine Christianity was its close relationship with the imperial government. From the time of Constantine on, caesaropapist emperors participated actively in religious and theological matters. In 325 C.E., for example, Constantine organized the Council of Nicaea, which brought together bishops, spokesmen, and leaders from all the important Christian churches to consider the views of the Arians, who believed that Jesus had been a mortal human rather than a divine being coeternal with God. Although Constantine originally favored Arian views, he came to accept the view that Jesus was both human and divine and personally attended sessions of the Council of Nicaea to support it. His presence encouraged the council to endorse his preferred view as orthodox and to condemn Arianism as heresy.

The Byzantine emperors, in fact, treated the church as a department of state. They appointed individuals to serve as patriarch of Constantinople—the highest ecclesiastical official in the Byzantine church, counterpart of the pope in Rome—and they instructed patriarchs, bishops, and priests to deliver sermons that supported imperial policy. This caesaropapism was a source of constant conflict between imperial and ecclesiastical authorities, and sometimes even between emperors and their subjects. For example, Emperor Leo III (reigned 717–741 C.E.) sparked riots throughout the empire when he embarked on a policy of iconoclasm (literally, "the breaking of icons") in an attempt to prohibit the use of religious images and icons in churches. Although the policy was ultimately unsuccessful, it generated tremendous bitterness among ordinary people who were deeply attached to the religious imagery in their churches.

GREEK PHILOSOPHY AND BYZANTINE THEOLOGY    In its theology, Byzantine Christianity reflected the continuing influence of classical Greek philosophy. Theologians invested a great deal of time and intellectual energy in the examination of religious questions from a philosophical point of view. They looked to classical philosophy, for example, when seeking to understand the nature of Jesus and the extent to which he possessed both human and divine characteristics. Although these debates often became extremely technical, they illustrated an effort to understand Christian doctrine in light of the terms and concepts that classical philosophers had employed in their analysis of the world. A school maintained by the patriarch of Constantinople provided instruction for clergy and church officials in advanced theology of this sort. Thus, although it differed in many ways from Mediterranean society of classical times, Byzantium built its own cultural and religious traditions on a solid classical foundation.

## Monasticism and Popular Piety

Caesaropapist emperors, powerful patriarchs, and other high church officials concerned themselves with theological and ritual matters and rarely dealt directly with the lay population of the Byzantine church. Nor did the Byzantine laity have much interest in fine points of theology, and they positively resented policies such as iconoclasm that infringed on cherished patterns of worship. For religious inspiration, then, the laity looked not to the church hierarchy but to the local monasteries.

ASCETICISM    Byzantine monasticism grew out of the efforts of devout individuals to lead especially holy lives. Drawing inspiration from early Christian ascetics in Egypt, Mesopotamia, and Persia, these individuals observed regimes of extreme asceticism and self-denial. During the fifth century, for example, a few men and at least two women demonstrated their ascetic commitments by perching for years at a time atop tall pillars. Because of the extreme dedication of ascetics, disciples often gathered around them and established communities of men and women determined to follow their example. These communities became the earliest monasteries of the Byzantine church. They had few rules until St. Basil of Caesarea (329–379 C.E.), the patriarch of Constantinople during the mid–fourth century, urged them to give up their personal possessions and live communally, to observe the rule of elected superiors, and to devote themselves to work and prayer. After the fourth century, Basilian monasticism spread rapidly throughout the Byzantine empire.

**Nicaea** (nahy-SEE-uh)

**patriarch** (PAY-tree-ahrk)

**iconoclasts** (eye-KAHN-oh-klasts)

**asceticism** (uh-SET-uh-siz-uhm)

**BYZANTINE MONASTICISM**    Unlike their counterparts in western Europe and other lands, Byzantine monasteries for the most part did not become centers of education, study, learning, and scholarship. Yet monasteries under the rule of St. Basil had a reputation for piety and devotion that endeared them to the Byzantine laity. Basilian monks went to great lengths in search of mystical union with God through meditation and prayer. Some retired to remote destinations to lead lives of strict asceticism. The devotion of Basilian monks, in turn, inspired piety among the Byzantine laity because they represented a religious faith more immediate and meaningful than that of the theologians and ecclesiastical bureaucrats of Constantinople.

Monks and nuns also provided social services to their communities. They provided spiritual counsel to local laity, and they organized relief efforts by bringing food and medical attention to communities struck by disasters. They won the support of the Byzantine populace, too, when they vigorously opposed the policy of iconoclasm and fought to restore icons to churches and monasteries. Indeed, by setting examples of devotion and by tending to the needs and interests of the laity, monks helped to maintain support for their faith in the Byzantine empire.

## Tensions between Eastern and Western Christianity

Byzantine Christianity developed in tension particularly with the Christian faith of western Europe. During the centuries following Constantine's legalization of Christianity, church leaders in Jerusalem, Alexandria, Antioch, Constantinople, and Rome exercised great influence in the larger Christian community. Yet after Arab peoples conquered most of southwest Asia and introduced Islam there in the seventh century, the influence of the patriarchs in Jerusalem, Alexandria, and Antioch declined, leaving only Constantinople and Rome as the principal centers of Christian authority.

**CONSTANTINOPLE AND ROME**    The specific issues that divided the two Christian communities in Constantinople and Rome were religious and theological. Some ritual and doctrinal differences were relatively minor concerns over forms of worship and the precise wording of theological teachings. Byzantine theologians objected, for example, to the fact that western priests shaved their beards and used unleavened instead of leavened bread when saying Mass. Other differences concerned substantive theological matters, such as the precise relationship between God, Jesus, and the Holy Spirit.

**SCHISM**    Alongside these ritual and doctrinal differences, the Byzantine patriarchs and Roman popes disputed their respective rights and powers. Patriarchs argued for the autonomy of all major Christian jurisdictions, including that of Constantinople, whereas popes asserted the primacy of Rome as the sole seat of authority for all Christendom. Ultimately, relations became so strained that the eastern and western churches went separate ways. In 1054 C.E. the patriarch and the pope excommunicated each other, each refusing to recognize the other's church as properly Christian. Despite efforts at reconciliation, the resulting schism between eastern and western churches persists to the present day. In recognition of the split, historians refer to the eastern Christian church after 1054 as the Eastern Orthodox church and its western counterpart as the Roman Catholic church.

# THE INFLUENCE OF BYZANTIUM IN EASTERN EUROPE

By the second millennium C.E., a dynamic society founded on the Islamic faith had seized control of the lands on the Mediterranean's southern and eastern rims, and Byzantines and western Europeans contested the northern rim. Hemmed in and increasingly pressured by Islamic and western European societies, Byzantium entered a period of decline beginning about the late eleventh century.

As its Mediterranean influence waned, however, Byzantium turned its attention to eastern Europe and Russia. Through political, commercial, and cultural relations, Byzantium decisively influenced the history of Slavic peoples. The Byzantine state itself came to an end in the fifteenth century C.E. But because of the Byzantine commonwealth—the larger collection of societies in eastern Europe and the eastern Mediterranean basin that developed under Byzantine influence—the legacy of Byzantium survives and continues to shape the lives of millions of people in Russia and eastern Europe.

## Domestic Problems and Foreign Pressures

When Basil II, "the Bulgar-Slayer," died in 1025 C.E., the Byzantine empire was a political, military, and economic dynamo. Within fifty years, however, the empire was suffering from serious internal weaknesses and had endured a series of military reverses. Both domestic and foreign problems help to explain this decline.

SOCIAL PROBLEMS    Domestic problems arose, ironically, from the success of the *theme* system. Generals who governed the *themes* were natural allies of local aristocrats who held large tracts of land, and together they began to resist the policies of the imperial government. At times, they even mounted rebellions against central authorities. Moreover, by the mid–eleventh century aristocrats had accumulated vast estates that placed the free peasantry under increasing pressure. Since peasants provided the backbone of Byzantium's military system and agricultural economy, this caused both fiscal and military problems for the imperial government.

CHALLENGES FROM THE WEST    As domestic problems mounted, Byzantium also faced fresh foreign challenges. From the west came the Normans—a Scandinavian people who had seized and settled in Normandy (in northern France). During the early eleventh century, they established themselves as an independent power in southern Italy, and by midcentury they had taken control of southern Italy and expelled Byzantine authorities there.

During the twelfth and thirteenth centuries, the Normans and other western European peoples mounted a series of crusades—vast military campaigns intended to recapture Jerusalem and other sites holy to Christians from Muslims—and took the opportunity to carve out states in the heart of the Byzantine empire. They even conquered and sacked Constantinople in 1204. Although Byzantine forces recaptured the capital in 1261, the destruction of Constantinople dealt the Byzantine empire a blow from which it never completely recovered.

CHALLENGES FROM THE EAST    As Europeans expanded into Byzantine territory from the west, nomadic Turkish peoples invaded from the east. Most important among them were the Muslim Saljuqs, who beginning in the eleventh century sent waves of invaders into Anatolia. Given the military and financial problems of the Byzantine empire, the Saljuqs found Anatolia ripe for plunder. In 1071 they subjected the Byzantine army to a demoralizing defeat at the battle of Manzikert. Byzantine factions then turned on one another in civil war, allowing the Saljuqs almost free rein in Anatolia. By the late twelfth century, the Saljuqs had seized much of Anatolia, and crusaders from western Europe held most of the remainder.

The loss of Anatolia—the principal source of Byzantine grain, wealth, and military forces—sealed the fate of the Byzantine empire. A territorially truncated Byzantium survived until the mid–fifteenth century, but the late Byzantine empire enjoyed little autonomy and continually faced fresh challenges from Italian merchants, western European

Saljuqs (sahl-JYOOKS)

*Anna Comnena (1083–1148), daughter of the Byzantine emperor Alexius I (reigned 1081–1118), wrote the* Alexiad, *a laudatory history of her father's reign. In the following selection, she discusses his prosecution in 1110 of Bogomil heretics, who revived the dualist teachings of the Manichaeans. Her account makes it clear that the caesaropapist Byzantine emperors took seriously their commitment to the Orthodox church and their obligation to protect its interests.*

Later . . . there arose an extraordinary "cloud of heretics," a new hostile group, hitherto unknown to the Church. . . . Apparently it was in existence before my father's time, but was unperceived (for the Bogomils' sect is most adept at feigning virtue). No worldly hairstyles are to be seen among Bogomils: their wickedness is hidden beneath cloak and cowl. Your Bogomil wears a somber look; muffled up to the nose, he walks with a stoop, quietly muttering to himself—but inside he's a ravening wolf. This unpleasant race, like a serpent lurking in its hole, was brought to the light and lured out by my father with magical incantations. . . .

The fame of the Bogomils had by now spread to all parts, for the impious sect was controlled with great cunning by a certain monk called Basil. He had twelve followers whom he called "apostles" and also dragged along with him certain female disciples, women of bad character, utterly depraved. In all quarters he made his wicked influence felt and when the evil, like some consuming fire, devoured many souls, the emperor could no longer bear it. He instituted a thorough inquiry into the heresy. . . .

. . . Alexius condemned the heretics out of hand: chorus and chorus-leader alike were to suffer death by burning. When the Bogomils had been hunted down and brought together in one place, some clung to the heresy, but others denied the charges completely, protesting strongly against their accusers and rejecting the Bogomilian heresy with scorn. . . .

The emperor glared at them and said, "Two pyres will have to be lit today. By one a cross will be planted firmly in the ground. Then a choice will be offered to all: those who are prepared to die for their Christian faith will separate themselves from the rest and take up position by the pyre with the cross; the Bogomilian adherents will be thrown on the other. Surely it is better that even Christians should die than live to be hounded down as Bogomils and offend the conscience of the majority. Go away, then, all of you, to whichever pyre you choose." . . .

A huge crowd gathered and stood all about them. Fires were then lit, burning seven times more fiercely than usual. . . . The flames leapt to the heavens. By one pyre stood the cross. Each of the condemned was given his choice, for all were to be burnt. Now that escape was clearly impossible, the orthodox to a man moved over to the pyre with the cross, truly prepared to suffer martyrdom; the godless adherents of the abominable heresy went off to the other. Just as they were about to be thrown on the flames, all the bystanders broke into mourning for the Christians; they were filled with indignation against the emperor (they did not know of his plan). But an order came from him just in time to stop the executioners. Alexius had in this way obtained firm evidence of those who were really Bogomils. The Christians, who were victims of calumny, he released after giving them much advice; the rest [i.e., the Bogomils] were committed once again to prison, but the [Bogomil] "apostles" were kept apart. Later he sent for some of these men every day and personally taught them, with frequent exhortations to abandon their abominable cult. . . . And some did change for the better and were freed from prison, but others died in their heresy, still incarcerated, although they were supplied with plentiful food and clothing.

■ Why did Byzantine rulers go to such lengths to suppress heresy?

SOURCE: Anna Comnena. *The Alexiad of Anna Comnena*. Trans. by E. R. A. Sewter. Harmondsworth: Penguin, 1969, pp. 496–505. (Translation slightly modified.)

---

adventurers, and Turkish nomads. In 1453, after a long era of decline, the Byzantine empire came to an end when Ottoman Turks captured Constantinople and absorbed its territories into their own expanding realm.

## Early Relations between Byzantium and Slavic Peoples

By the time Constantinople fell, Byzantine traditions had deeply influenced the political and cultural development of Slavic peoples in eastern Europe and Russia. Close relations between Byzantium and Slavic peoples date from the sixth century. When Justinian de-

**MAP 10.2** | The Byzantine empire and its neighbors, ca. 1100 C.E. After the emergence of Islam, the Byzantine empire shrank dramatically in size. ***To what extent does the expansion of Islam help explain the fact that Byzantine influence was strongest in eastern Europe after the seventh century C.E.?***

Conversions to orthodox Christianity in Bulgaria contributed to the long-term influence of Byzantine culture in eastern Europe.

ployed Byzantium's military resources in the western Mediterranean, Slavic peoples from the north took advantage of the opportunity to move into Byzantine territory. Serbs and Croats moved into the Balkan peninsula, and Bulgars established a powerful kingdom in the lower Danube region.

Relations between Byzantium and Bulgaria were especially tense. By the eighth century, however, Byzantium had begun to influence Bulgarian politics and society. Byzantium and Bulgaria entered into political, commercial, and cultural relations. Members of Bulgarian ruling families often went to Constantinople for a formal education in Greek language and literature and followed Byzantine examples in organizing their court and capital.

**CYRIL AND METHODIUS** Byzantium also sent missionaries to Balkan lands, and Bulgars and other Slavic peoples began to convert to Orthodox Christianity. The most famous of the missionaries to the Slavs were Saints Cyril and Methodius, two brothers from Thessaloniki in Greece. During the mid–ninth century Cyril and Methodius conducted missions in Bulgaria and Moravia (which included much of the modern Czech, Slovakian, and Hungarian territories). While there, they devised an alphabet, known as the Cyrillic alphabet, for the previously illiterate Slavic peoples. Though adapted from written Greek, the Cyrillic alphabet represented the sounds of Slavic languages more precisely than did the Greek, and it remained in use in much of eastern Europe until supplanted by the Roman alphabet in the twentieth century. In Russia and most other parts of the former Soviet Union, the Cyrillic alphabet survives to the present day.

## THINKING ABOUT *Encounters*

**ENCOUNTERS IN THE CHRISTIAN COMMONWEALTH OF BYZANTIUM.** Although the Mediterranean world inhabited by the Byzantines was more politically fragmented than it had been under the Roman empire, the Byzantine empire nevertheless sustained both hostile and friendly encounters with Islamic peoples to the south and east, Slavic peoples to the north, and Europeans to the west. In what ways did these various encounters shape the Byzantine empire, and in what ways did Byzantine influence shape societies beyond imperial borders?

**MISSION TO THE SLAVS** The Cyrillic alphabet stimulated conversion to Orthodox Christianity. Missionaries translated the Christian scriptures and church rituals into Slavonic, and Cyrillic writing helped them explain Christian values and ideas in Slavic terms. Meanwhile, schools organized by missionaries ensured that Slavs would receive religious instruction alongside their introduction to basic literacy. As a result, Orthodox Christianity deeply influenced the cultural traditions of many Slavic peoples.

## Byzantium and Russia

North of Bulgaria another Slavic people began to organize large states: the Russians. About the mid–ninth century Russians created several principalities governed from thriving trading centers, notably Kiev. Strategically situated on the Dnieper River along the main trade route linking Scandinavia and Byzantium, Kiev became a wealthy and powerful center, and it dominated much of the territory between the Volga and the Dnieper from the tenth to the thirteenth century. Russian merchants visited Constantinople in large numbers and became well acquainted with Byzantine society. Russian princes sought alliances with Byzantine rulers and began to express an interest in Orthodox Christianity.

**THE CONVERSION OF PRINCE VLADIMIR** About 989 Prince Vladimir of Kiev converted to Orthodox Christianity and ordered his subjects to follow his example. After his conversion, Byzantine influences flowed rapidly into Russia. Cyrillic writing, literacy, and Orthodox missions all spread quickly throughout Russia. Byzantine teachers traveled north to establish schools, and Byzantine priests conducted services for Russian converts. For two centuries Kiev served as a conduit for the spread of Byzantine cultural and religious influence in Russia. Indeed, Byzantine art and architecture dominated Kiev and other Russian cities. The onion domes that are a distinctive feature of early Russian churches were the result of architects' efforts to imitate the domed structures of Constantinople using wood as their principal building material.

**THE GROWTH OF KIEV** The princes of Kiev established firm, caesaropapist control over the Russian Orthodox church—so called to distinguish it from the Eastern Orthodox church of the Byzantine empire. They also drew inspiration from Byzantine legal tradition and compiled a written law code for their lands. By controlling trade with Byzantium and other lands, they gained financial resources to build a flourishing society.

Eventually, Russians even claimed to inherit the imperial mantle of Byzantium. According to a popular theory of the sixteenth century, Moscow was the world's third Rome: the first Rome had fallen to Germanic invaders in the fifth century, whereas the second Rome, Constantinople, had fallen to the Turks a thousand years later. Moscow survived as the third Rome, the cultural and religious beacon that would guide the world to Orthodox Christian righteousness. Inspired by that theory, missionaries took their Russian Orthodox faith to distant lands. Thus, long after the collapse of the eastern Roman empire, the Byzantine legacy continued to work its influence through the outward reach of the Russian Orthodox church.

**BULGARIANS IN BYZANTIUM.** | This illustration from a twelfth-century manuscript depicts ninth-century incursions of Bulgarians into Byzantine territory, culminating in a lecture by the Bulgarian king to the Byzantine emperor, shown here with bound hands.

Church of the Resurrection
www.mhhe.com/
bentleybrief2e

## SUMMARY

The Byzantine empire originated as a survivor of the classical era. Byzantium inherited a hardy economy, a set of governing institutions, an imperial bureaucracy, an official religion, an established church, and a rich cultural tradition from classical Mediterranean society and the Roman empire. Byzantine leaders drew heavily on that legacy as they dealt with new challenges. Throughout Byzantine history, classical inspiration was especially noticeable in the imperial office, the bureaucracy, the church, and the educational system. Yet in many ways Byzantium changed profoundly over the course of its thousand-year history. After the seventh century the Byzantine empire shrank dramatically in size, and after the eleventh century it faced relentless foreign pressure from western Europeans and nomadic Turkish peoples. Changing times also brought transformations in Byzantine social and economic organization. Yet from the fifth to the twelfth century and beyond, Byzantium brought political stability and economic prosperity to the eastern Mediterranean basin, and Byzantine society served as a principal anchor supporting commercial and cultural exchanges in the postclassical world. Through its political, economic, and cultural influence, Byzantium also helped shape the development of the larger Byzantine commonwealth in eastern Europe and the eastern Mediterranean basin.

# STUDY TERMS

Arians (197)
asceticism (197)
Basil the Bulgar-Slayer (192)
Basilian monasticism (197)
battle of Manzikert (199)
Belisarius (191)
*bezant* (195)
Bosporus (188)
Byzantine (188)

caesaropapism (190)
Constantinople (188)
Council of Nicaea (196)
*Corpus iuris civilis* (191)
Cyrillic alphabet (201)
Eastern Orthodox church (196)
Hagia Sophia (192)
Hippodrome (196)

iconoclasm (197)
Justinian (190)
Normans (199)
patriarch (197)
Prince Vladimir of Kiev (202)
Saljuqs (199)
*theme* system (194)
Theodora (190)

# FOR FURTHER READING

Averil Cameron. *The Mediterranean World in Late Antiquity, A.D. 395–600.* London, 1993. A thoughtful synthesis that places Byzantium in the context of the late Roman empire.

Helen C. Evans, ed. *Byzantium: Faith and Power (1261–1557).* New York, 2004. A lavishly illustrated volume exploring religious life in the late Byzantine empire.

John V. A. Fine Jr. *The Early Medieval Balkans: A Critical Survey from the Sixth to the Late Twelfth Century.* Ann Arbor, 1983. An excellent introduction to Balkan history in the postclassical era.

Garth Fowden. *Empire to Commonwealth: Consequences of Monotheism in Late Antiquity.* Princeton, 1993. A provocative volume that interprets Byzantine political and cultural development as a monotheist Christian society.

Deno John Geanakoplos. *Byzantium: Church, Society, and Civilization Seen through Contemporary Eyes.* Chicago, 1984. Rich collection of translated documents that throw light on all aspects of Byzantine society.

J. M. Hussey. *The Byzantine World.* London, 1982. A brief and reliable survey.

Dimitri Obolensky. *The Byzantine Commonwealth: Eastern Europe, 500–1453.* New York, 1971. A well-informed overview of early Slavic history and relations between Byzantine and Slavic peoples.

Procopius. *History of the Wars, Secret History, and Buildings.* Trans. by A. Cameron. New York, 1967. Translations of writings by the most important historian in the time of Justinian.

Michael Psellus. *Fourteen Byzantine Rulers.* Trans. by E. R. A. Sewter. Harmondsworth, 1966. Memoirs of eleventh-century Byzantium by a highly placed advisor to several emperors.

Mark Whittow. *The Making of Byzantium, 600–1025.* Berkeley, 1996. Concentrates on Byzantine military and political relations with neighboring societies.

# The Expansive Realm of Islam

## 11

I n 632 C.E. the prophet Muhammad visited his native city of Mecca from his home in exile at Medina, and in doing so he set an example that devout Muslims have sought to emulate ever since. The *hajj*—the holy pilgrimage to Mecca—draws Muslims by the hundreds of thousands from all parts of the world to Saudi Arabia. Each year Muslims travel to Mecca by land, sea, and air to make the pilgrimage and visit the holy sites of Islam.

In centuries past the numbers of pilgrims were smaller, but their observance of the hajj was no less conscientious. By the ninth century, pilgrimage had become so popular that Muslim rulers went to some lengths to meet the needs of travelers passing through their lands. With the approach of the pilgrimage season, crowds gathered at major trading centers such as Baghdad, Damascus, and Cairo. There they lived in tent cities, surviving on food and water provided by government officials, until they could join caravans bound for Mecca. Muslim rulers invested considerable sums in the maintenance of roads, wells, cisterns, and lodgings that accommodated pilgrims—as well as police forces that protected travelers—on their journeys to Mecca and back.

The hajj was not only solemn observance but also an occasion for joy and celebration. Muslim rulers and wealthy pilgrims often made lavish gifts to caravan companions and others they met en route to Mecca. During her famous hajj of 976–977, for example, the Mesopotamian princess Jamila bint Nasir al-Dawla provided food and fresh green vegetables for her fellow pilgrims and furnished five hundred camels for handicapped travelers. She also purchased freedom for five hundred slaves and distributed fifty thousand fine robes among the common people of Mecca.

Most pilgrims did not have the resources to match Jamila's generosity, but for common travelers, too, the hajj became a special occasion. Merchants and craftsmen arranged business deals with pilgrims from other lands. Students and scholars exchanged ideas during their weeks of traveling together. For all pilgrims, participation in ritual activities lent new meaning and significance to their faith.

❮ *A fifteenth-century Persian manuscript depicts pilgrims praying at Mecca in the mosque surrounding the Ka'ba.*

The word *Islam* means "submission," signifying obedience to the rule and will of Allah, the only deity recognized in the strictly monotheistic Islamic religion. An individual who accepts the Islamic faith is a *Muslim,* meaning "one who has submitted." Though it began as one man's expression of unqualified faith in Allah, Islam quickly attracted followers. During the

hajj (HAHJ)

# CHRONOLOGY

| | |
|---|---|
| 570–632 | Life of Muhammad |
| 622 | The *hijra* |
| 632 | Muhammad's hajj |
| 650s | Compilation of the Quran |
| 661–750 | Umayyad dynasty |
| 750–1258 | Abbasid dynasty |
| 1050s | Establishment of Saljuq control over the Abbasid dynasty |
| 1126–1198 | Life of Ibn Rushd |

first century of the new faith's existence, Islam reached far beyond its Arabian homeland, bringing Sasanid Persia and parts of the Byzantine empire into its orbit. By the eighth century the realm of Islam stood alongside the Byzantine empire as a political and economic anchor of the postclassical world.

Islamic society originally reflected the nomadic and mercantile Arabian society from which Islam arose. Yet over time, Muslims drew deep inspiration from other societies as well. After toppling the Sasanid dynasty, Muslim conquerors adopted Persian techniques of government and finance to administer their lands. Persian literature, science, and religious values also found a place in Islamic society. During later centuries Muslims drew inspiration from Greek and Indian traditions as well.

While drawing influence from other societies, however, the Islamic faith thoroughly transformed the cultural traditions that it absorbed. The expansive realm of Islam eventually provided a political framework for trade and diplomacy over a vast portion of the eastern hemisphere, from west Africa to the islands of Southeast Asia. Many lands of varied cultural background thus became part of a larger society often called the *dar al-Islam*—an Arabic term that means the "house of Islam" and that refers to lands under Islamic rule.

# A PROPHET AND HIS WORLD

Islam arose in the Arabian peninsula, and the new religion faithfully reflected the social and cultural conditions of its homeland. Desert covers most of the peninsula, and agriculture is possible only in the well-watered area of Yemen in the south and in a few other places, such as the city of Medina, where oases provide water. Yet human communities have occupied Arabia for millennia. Nomadic peoples known as bedouin migrated through the deserts to find grass and water for their herds of sheep, goats, and camels. The bedouin organized themselves in family and clan groups. Individuals and their immediate families depended heavily on those kinship networks for support in times of need. In an environment as harsh and unforgiving as the Arabian desert, cooperation with kin often made the difference between life and death. As a result, bedouin peoples developed a strong sense of loyalty to their clans. Indeed, clan loyalties survived for centuries after the appearance of Islam.

Arabia also figured prominently in the long-distance trade networks of the postclassical era. Commodities arrived at ports on the Persian Gulf (near modern Bahrain), the Arabian Sea (near modern Aden), and the Red Sea (near Mecca), and then traveled overland by camel caravan to Palmyra or Damascus, which offered access to the Mediterranean basin. After the third century C.E., Arabia became an increasingly important link in long-distance trade networks. With the weakening of classical empires, trade routes across central Asia became increasingly insecure. In response, merchants abandoned the overland routes in favor of sea-lanes connecting with land routes in the Arabian peninsula. In the process, their trade allowed Arabian cities to thrive.

## Muhammad and His Message

MUHAMMAD'S EARLY LIFE    The prophet Muhammad came into this world of nomadic bedouin herders and merchants. Born about 570 C.E. into a reputable family of merchants in Mecca, Muhammad ibn Abdullah lost both of his parents as a young child. His grandfather and his uncle raised

bedouin (BEHD-oh-ihn)

Muhammad (muh-HAHM-mahd)

him and provided him with an education, but Muhammad's early life was difficult. As a young man, he worked for a woman named Khadija, a wealthy widow whom he married about the year 595. Through this marriage he gained wealth and a position of some prominence in Meccan society.

By age 30 Muhammad had established himself as a merchant. He made a comfortable life for himself in Arabian society, where peoples of different religious and cultural traditions regularly dealt with one another. Most Arabs recognized many gods, goddesses, demons, and nature spirits, whose favor they sought through prayers and sacrifices. Large communities of Jewish merchants also worked throughout Arabia, and many Arabs had converted to Christianity by Muhammad's time. Although he was not deeply knowledgeable about Judaism or Christianity, Muhammad had a basic understanding of both faiths.

**MUHAMMAD'S SPIRITUAL TRANSFORMATION** About 610 C.E., as he approached age 40, Muhammad underwent a profound spiritual experience that transformed his life and left a deep mark on world history. His experience left him with the convictions that in all the world there was only one true deity, Allah ("God"), that he ruled the universe, that idolatry and the recognition of other gods amounted to wickedness, and that Allah would soon bring his judgment on the world. Muhammad experienced visions, which he understood as messages or revelations from Allah, delivered through the archangel Gabriel (also recognized by Jews and Christians as a special messenger of God), instructing him to explain his faith to others. In accordance with instructions transmitted to him by Gabriel, Muhammad began to expound his faith to his family and close friends. Gradually, others showed interest in his message, and by about 620 C.E. a zealous and expanding minority of Mecca's citizenry had joined his circle.

**THE QURAN** Muhammad originally presented oral recitations of the revelations he received during his visions. As the Islamic community grew, his followers prepared written texts of his teachings. During the early 650s devout Muslims compiled these written versions of Muhammad's revelations and issued them as the Quran ("recitation"), the holy book of Islam. A work of magnificent poetry, the Quran communicates in powerful and moving terms Muhammad's understanding of Allah and his relation to the world, and it serves as the definitive authority for Islamic religious doctrine and social organization.

Apart from the Quran, several other sources have provided moral and religious guidance for the Islamic community. Most important after the Quran itself are traditions known as *hadith,* which include sayings attributed to Muhammad and accounts of his deeds. Regarded as less authoritative than the Quran and the *hadith,* but still important as inspirations for Islamic thought, were early works describing social and legal customs, biographies of Muhammad, and pious commentaries on the Quran.

## Muhammad's Migration to Medina

**CONFLICT AT MECCA** The growing popularity of Muhammad's preaching brought him into conflict with the ruling elites at Mecca. Muhammad's insistence that Allah was the only divine power in the universe struck many polytheistic Arabs as offensive and dangerous, since it disparaged long-recognized deities and spirits thought to wield influence over human affairs. The tensions also had a personal dimension. Mecca's ruling elites, who were also the city's wealthiest merchants, took it as a personal affront when Muhammad denounced greed as moral wickedness that Allah would punish.

Muhammad's attack on idolatry also represented an economic threat to those who owned and profited from the many shrines to deities that attracted merchants and pilgrims to Mecca. The best known of these shrines was a large black rock long considered to be the dwelling of a powerful deity. Housed in a cube-shaped building known as the Ka'ba, it drew worshipers from all over Arabia and brought considerable wealth to Mecca. As

Ka'ba at Mecca
www.mhhe.com/
bentleybrief2e

Quran (koorr-AHN)

Ka'ba (KAH-bah)

**THE QURAN.** | Current Islamic doctrine forbids artistic representations of Muhammad and Allah to prevent the worship of their images as idols. Although artists of previous centuries occasionally produced paintings of Muhammad, Islamic art has emphasized geometric design and calligraphy. This handsome page from a Quran written on vellum dates from the ninth or early tenth century.

Muhammad relentlessly condemned the idolatry officially promoted at the Ka'ba and other shrines, the ruling elites of Mecca began to persecute the prophet and his followers.

**THE HIJRA**  The pressure became so great that Muhammad and his followers were forced to migrate from Mecca in 622 C.E. They established themselves in Yathrib, a rival trading city north of Mecca, which they renamed Medina ("the city," meaning "the city of the prophet"). Known as the *hijra* ("migration"), Muhammad's move to Medina serves as the starting point of the official Islamic calendar.

**THE UMMA**  Once in Medina, Muhammad found himself at the head of a small but growing society in exile that needed guidance in practical as well as spiritual affairs. He organized his followers into a cohesive community called the *umma* ("community of the faithful") and provided it with a comprehensive legal and social code. He led this community both in daily prayers to Allah and in battle with enemies at Medina, Mecca, and other places. Remembering the difficult days of his own youth, he provided relief for widows, orphans, and the poor, and he made almsgiving a prime moral virtue.

**THE "SEAL OF THE PROPHETS"**  Muhammad's understanding of his religious mission expanded during his years at Medina. He began to refer to himself as a prophet, indeed as the "seal of the prophets"—the final prophet through whom Allah would reveal his message to humankind. Muhammad accepted the authority of earlier Jewish and Christian prophets, including Abraham, Moses, and Jesus, and he held the Hebrew scriptures and the Christian New Testament in high esteem. He also believed that Allah was one and the same as the Jews' Yahweh and the Christians' God. Muhammad taught, however, that the message entrusted to him was a more complete revelation of Allah and his will than Jewish and Christian faiths had made available. Thus, while at Medina, Muhammad came to see himself consciously as the messenger who communicated Allah's wishes and his plan for the world to all humankind.

*hijra* (HIHJ-ruh)

*umma* (UM-mah)

# The Establishment of Islam in Arabia

**MUHAMMAD'S RETURN TO MECCA**   Throughout their sojourn at Medina, Muhammad and his followers planned ultimately to return to their home in Mecca. In 629 C.E. they arranged with the authorities to participate in the annual pilgrimage to the Ka'ba, but they were not content with a short visit. In 630 they attacked Mecca and conquered the city. They forced the elites to adopt Muhammad's faith, and they imposed a government dedicated to Allah. They also destroyed the pagan shrines and replaced them with mosques, buildings that sought to instill a sense of sacredness and community where Muslims gathered for prayers. Only the Ka'ba escaped their efforts to cleanse Mecca of pagan monuments.

Muhammad and his followers denied that the Ka'ba was the home of a deity, but they preserved the black rock and its housing as a symbol of Mecca's greatness. In 632 Muhammad himself led the first Islamic pilgrimage to the Ka'ba, thus establishing the hajj as an example for all devout Muslims. Building on the conquest of Mecca, Muhammad and his followers launched campaigns against other towns and bedouin clans, and by the time of the prophet's death in 632, shortly after his hajj, they had brought most of Arabia under their control.

**THE FIVE PILLARS OF ISLAM**   Muhammad's faith and his personal leadership decisively shaped the values and the development of the Islamic community. The foundation of the Islamic faith as elaborated by Muhammad consists of obligations known as the Five Pillars of Islam: (1) Muslims must acknowledge Allah as the only god and Muhammad as his prophet. (2) They must pray to Allah daily while facing Mecca. (3) They must observe a fast during the daylight hours of the month of Ramadan. (4) They must contribute alms for the relief of the weak and the poor. (5) Finally, those who are physically and financially able must undertake the hajj and make at least one pilgrimage to Mecca. Although Islam has generated many schools and sects in the centuries since its appearance, the Five Pillars of Islam constitute a powerful framework that has bound the *umma* as a whole into a cohesive community of faith.

**JIHAD**   Some Muslims, though by no means all, have taken *jihad* as an additional obligation for the faithful. The term *jihad* literally means "struggle," and Muslims have understood its imperatives in various ways. In one sense, jihad imposes obligations on Muslims by requiring them to combat vice and evil. In another sense, jihad calls on Muslims to struggle against unbelief by spreading the word of Islam and seeking converts to the faith. In some circumstances, jihad also obliges Muslims to take up the sword and wage war against unbelievers who threaten Islam.

**ISLAMIC LAW: THE SHARIA**   Beyond the general obligations prescribed by the Five Pillars, Islamic holy law, known as the *sharia*, emerged during the centuries after Muhammad and offered detailed guidance on proper behavior in almost every aspect of life. Inspired by the Quran and elaborated by jurists and legal scholars, the sharia offered precise guidance on matters as diverse as marriage and family life, inheritance, slavery, business relationships, political authority, and crime. Through the sharia, Islam became more than a religious doctrine: it developed into a way of life.

# THE EXPANSION OF ISLAM

After Muhammad's death the Islamic community might well have unraveled and disappeared. Muhammad had made no provision for a successor, and there was serious division within the *umma* concerning the selection of a new leader. Many of the towns and bedouin clans that had recently accepted Islam took the opportunity of Muhammad's death

The growth of Islam
www.mhhe.com/
bentleybrief2e

---

**jihad** (jih-HAHD)

**sharia** (shah-REE-ah)

# SOURCES FROM THE PAST

## The Quran on Allah and His Expectations of Humankind

*The foundation of the Islamic faith is the understanding of Allah, his nature, and his plan for the world as outlined in the Quran. Through his visions Muhammad came to understand Allah as the one and only god, the creator and sustainer of the world in the manner of the Jews' Yahweh and the Christians' God. Those who rejected Allah and his message would suffer eternal punishment, whereas those who recognized and obeyed him would receive his mercy and secure his blessings.*

In the name of Allah, most benevolent, ever-merciful.
All praise be to Allah,
Lord of all the worlds,
Most beneficent, ever-merciful,
King of the Day of Judgement.
You alone we worship, and to You
alone turn for help.
Guide us (O Lord) to the path that is straight,
The path of those You have blessed,
Not of those who have earned Your anger,
nor those who have gone astray. . . .
Verily men and women who have come to submission,
men and women who are believers,
men and women who are devout,
truthful men and women,
men and women with endurance,
men and women who are modest,
men and women who give alms,
men and women who observe fasting,
men and women who guard their private parts,
and those men and women who remember God
   a great deal,
for them God has forgiveness and a great reward.
No believing men and women have any choice in a matter
after God and His Apostle [i.e., Muhammad] have
   decided it.
Whoever disobeys God and His Apostle
has clearly lost the way and gone astray. . . .
O you who believe, remember God a great deal,
And sing His praises morning and evening.
It is He who sends His blessings on you,
as (do) His angels, that He may lead you out of darkness
   into light,

for He is benevolent to the believers. . . .
I call to witness
the early hours of the morning,
And the night when dark and still,
Your Lord has neither left you,
nor despises you.
What is to come is better for you
than what has gone before;
For your Lord will certainly give you,
and you will be content.
Did He not find you an orphan
and take care of you?
Did He not find you poor
and enrich you?
So do not oppress the orphan,
And do not drive
the beggar away,
And keep recounting the favours of your Lord. . . .
Say: "He is God
the one the most unique,
God the immanently indispensable.
He has begotten no one,
and is begotten of none.
There is no one comparable to Him."

■ Compare the Quran's teachings on the relationship between Allah and human beings with the views of Zoroastrians, Jews, and Christians discussed in earlier chapters.

SOURCE: *Al-Qur'an: A Contemporary Translation.* Trans. by Ahmed Ali. Princeton: Princeton University Press, 1984, pp. 11, 358, 359, 540, 559.

to renounce the faith, reassert their independence, and break free from Mecca's control. Within a short time, however, the Islamic community had embarked on a stunningly successful round of military expansion that extended its political and cultural influence far beyond the boundaries of Arabia. Those conquests laid the foundation for the rapid growth of Islamic society.

## The Early Caliphs and the Umayyad Dynasty

**THE CALIPH** Because Muhammad was the "seal of the prophets," it was inconceivable that another prophet should succeed him. Shortly after Muhammad's death his advisors selected Abu Bakr, a genial man who was one of the prophet's closest friends and most devoted disciples, to serve as *caliph* ("deputy"). Thus Abu Bakr and later caliphs led the *umma* not as prophets but as substitutes for Muhammad. Abu Bakr became head of state for the Islamic community as well as chief judge, religious leader, and military commander. Under the new caliph's leadership, the *umma* went on the offensive against people who had renounced Islam after Muhammad's death, and within a year it had compelled them to recognize the faith of Islam and the rule of the caliph.

**THE EXPANSION OF ISLAM** Indeed, during the century after Muhammad's death, Islamic armies carried their religion and authority throughout Arabia into Byzantine and Sasanid territories and beyond. Although much less powerful than either the Byzantine empire or the Sasanid empire, Muslim armies fought with particular effectiveness because their leaders had unified tribal groups into a powerful state under the banner of Islam. Moreover, they attacked at a moment when the larger empires were preoccupied with internal difficulties. Between 633 and 637 C.E., Muslim forces seized Byzantine Syria

**Abu-Bakr** (a-BOO BAK-uhr)

**caliph** (KHA-leef)

### THINKING ABOUT *Traditions*

**TRADITIONS IN THE EXPANSIVE REALM OF ISLAM.** In the two hundred years after the death of Muhammad in 632, Islam expanded rapidly throughout Arabia and included large portions of west Asia and north Africa as well as part of western Europe. Given the large geographic scope of the Islamic realm, in what ways did the legal, social, and cultural traditions of Islam provide a measure of cultural unity among diverse peoples?

 **The Great Mosque at Córdoba** www.mhhe.com/ bentleybrief2e

**MAP 11.1** | The expansion of Islam, 632–733 C.E. During the seventh and eighth centuries, the new faith of Islam expanded rapidly and dramatically beyond its Arabian homeland. *How might you explain the spread of a new faith? What political and cultural effects followed from the expansion of Islam?*

Mecca is the holy city of Islam and the destination for pilgrims who make the hajj.

**ISLAMIC EXPANSION.**
The early expansion of Islam was a bloody affair. This illustration from an Arabic manuscript of the thirteenth century depicts a battle between Muhammad's cousin Ali and his adversaries.

PSI img · Shia pilgrims
www.mhhe.com/
bentleybrief2e

and Palestine and took most of Mesopotamia from the Sasanids. During the 640s they conquered Byzantine Egypt and north Africa. In 651 they toppled the Sasanid dynasty and incorporated Persia into their expanding empire. In 711 they conquered the Hindu kingdom of Sind in northwestern India. Between 711 and 718 they extended their authority to northwest Africa and crossed the Strait of Gibraltar, conquering most of the Iberian peninsula and threatening the Frankish kingdom in Gaul. By the mid–eighth century an immense Islamic empire ruled lands from India and the central Asian steppe lands in the east to northwest Africa and Iberia in the west.

During this rapid expansion the empire's rulers encountered problems of governance and administration. One problem had to do with the selection of caliphs. During the early decades after Muhammad's death, leaders of the most powerful Arab clans appointed the first four caliphs. Political ambitions, personal differences, and clan loyalties, however, soon led to the rise of factions and parties within the Islamic community.

**THE SHIA** Disagreements over succession led to the emergence of the Shia sect, the most important and enduring of all the alternatives to the faith observed by the majority of Muslims, known as Sunni Islam. The Shia sect originated as a party supporting the appointment of Ali—a cousin and son-in-law of Muhammad—and his descendants as caliphs. Ali did serve briefly as the fourth caliph (656–661 C.E.), but his enemies assassinated him, killed many of his relatives, and imposed their own candidate as caliph. Partisans of Ali then organized the Shia ("party") and furiously struggled to return the caliphate to the line of Ali. Although persecuted, the Shia survived and strengthened its identity by adopting doctrines and rituals distinct from those of the Sunnis ("traditionalists"), who accepted the legitimacy of the early caliphs. Shia partisans, for example, observed holy days in honor of their leaders and martyrs to their cause, and they taught that descendants of Ali were infallible, sinless, and divinely appointed to rule the Islamic community.

**THE UMAYYAD DYNASTY** After the assassination of Ali, the establishment of the Umayyad dynasty (661–750 C.E.) temporarily solved the problem of succession. The Umayyads ranked among the most prominent of the Meccan merchant clans, and their reputation and network of alliances helped them bring stability to the Islamic community. Despite their association with Mecca, the Umayyads established their capital at Damascus, a thriving commercial city in Syria, whose central location enabled them to maintain better communication with the vast and still-expanding Islamic empire.

**POLICY TOWARD CONQUERED PEOPLES** Although the Umayyads' dynasty solved the problem of succession, their tightly centralized rule and the favor they showed to their fellow Arabs generated an administrative problem. The Umayyads ruled the *dar al-Islam* as conquerors, and their policies favored the Arab military aristocracy by distributing both lands and positions of power among this privileged class. Such policies caused severe discontent among the scores of ethnic and religious groups embraced by the Umayyad empire. In addition, although the Arabs mostly allowed conquered peoples to observe their own religions, they levied a special head tax, called the *jizya,* on those who did not convert to Islam. Moreover, even those who converted did not enjoy access to wealth and positions of authority, which the Umayyads reserved almost exclusively for members of the Arab military aristocracy.

**Shia** (SHEE-'ah)

**Sunni** (SOON-nee)

**Umayyad** (oo-MEYE-ah)

*jizya* (JIHZ-yah)

**UMAYYAD DECLINE**   Beginning in the early eighth century, the Umayyad caliphs became alienated even from other Arabs as they devoted themselves increasingly to luxurious living rather than to moral leadership of the *umma*. By midcentury the Umayyad caliphs faced not only the continued resistance of the Shia faction but also the discontent of conquered peoples throughout their empire and even the disillusionment of Muslim Arab military leaders.

# The Abbasid Dynasty

**ABU AL-ABBAS**   Rebellion in Persia brought the Umayyad dynasty to an end. The chief leader of the rebellion was Abu al-Abbas, a descendant of Muhammad's uncle. Although he was a Sunni Arab, Abu al-Abbas allied readily with Shias and with non-Arab Muslims. During the 740s Abu al-Abbas's party seized control of Persia and Mesopotamia. In 750 his army shattered Umayyad forces in a great battle. Afterward Abu al-Abbas invited the remaining members of the Umayyad clan to a banquet under the pretext of reconciling their differences. Instead, during the festivities his troops slaughtered the Umayyads and annihilated the clan. Abu al-Abbas then founded the Abbasid dynasty, which was the principal source of authority in the *dar al-Islam* until the Mongols toppled it in 1258 C.E.

**THE ABBASID DYNASTY**   The Abbasid dynasty differed considerably from the Umayyad. For one thing, the Abbasid rulers did not show special favor to the Arab military aristocracy. Arabs continued to play a large role in government, but Persians, Egyptians, Mesopotamians, and others also rose to positions of wealth and power.

The Abbasid dynasty differed from the Umayyad also in that it was not a conquering dynasty. The Abbasids did clash intermittently with the Byzantine empire and nomadic peoples from central Asia, and in 751 they defeated a Chinese army at Talas River near Samarkand. The battle of Talas River was exceptionally important: it ended the expansion of China's Tang dynasty into central Asia (discussed in chapter 12), and it opened the door for the spread of Islam among Turkish peoples. Overall, however, the Abbasids did not expand their empire by conquest. The *dar al-Islam* as a whole continued to grow during the Abbasid era, but that was a result of largely autonomous Islamic forces rather than the policies of the caliphs.

**ABBASID ADMINISTRATION**   Instead of conquering new lands, the Abbasids largely contented themselves with administration—a considerable challenge given the empire's diversity of linguistic, ethnic, and cultural groups. In designing their administration, the Abbasids relied heavily on Persian techniques of statecraft. Central authority came from the court at the magnificent new city of Baghdad (capital of modern Iraq). From Baghdad, instructions flowed to the distant reaches of the Abbasid realm. In the provinces, governors represented the caliph and implemented his political and financial policies.

Learned officials known as *ulama* ("people with religious knowledge") and *qadis* ("judges") set moral standards in local communities and resolved disputes. *Ulama* and *qadis* were not priests—Islam does not recognize priests—but they had a formal education that emphasized study of the Quran and the sharia. *Ulama* were pious scholars who sought to develop public policy in accordance with the Quran and the sharia. *Qadis* heard cases at law and rendered decisions based on the Quran and the sharia. Because of their moral authority, *ulama* and *qadis* became extremely influential officials who helped to ensure widespread observance of Islamic values. The Abbasid caliphs also kept a standing army, maintained the network of roads they inherited from the Sasanids, and established bureaucratic ministries in charge of taxation, finance, coinage, and postal services.

**ABBASID DECLINE**   In the early ninth century, however, the Abbasid empire entered a period of decline, and disputes over succession seriously damaged its authority.

**Abbasid** (ah-BAH-sih)

Provincial governors took advantage of disorder in the ruling house by acting independently of the caliphs and building up local bases of power. Meanwhile, popular uprisings and peasant rebellions further weakened the empire.

As a result of these difficulties, the Abbasid caliphs became mere figureheads long before the Mongols extinguished the dynasty in 1258. In 945 members of a Persian noble family seized control of Baghdad and established their clan as the power behind the Abbasid throne. Later, imperial authorities in Baghdad fell under the control of the Saljuq Turks, a nomadic people from central Asia who also invaded the Byzantine empire. By the mid–eleventh century the Saljuqs took possession of Baghdad, and during the following decades they extended their authority to Syria, Palestine, and Anatolia. They retained Abbasid caliphs as nominal sovereigns, but for two centuries, until the arrival of the Mongols, the Saljuq *sultan* ("ruler") was the true source of power in the Abbasid empire.

# ECONOMY AND SOCIETY OF THE EARLY ISLAMIC WORLD

In the *dar al-Islam,* as in other agricultural societies, peasants tilled the land while manufacturers and merchants supported a thriving urban economy. Here, as in other lands, the creation of large empires had dramatic economic implications. The Umayyad and Abbasid empires created a zone of trade, exchange, and communication stretching from India to Iberia. Commerce throughout this zone served as a vigorous economic stimulus for both the countryside and the cities of the early Islamic world.

## *New Crops, Agricultural Experimentation, and Urban Growth*

**ISLAMIC MAP.** | A map produced in the eleventh century by the Arab geographer al-Idrisi shows the lands known and reported by Muslim merchants and travelers. Note that, in accordance with Muslim cartographic convention, this map places south at the top and north at the bottom.

**THE SPREAD OF FOOD AND INDUSTRIAL CROPS** As soldiers, administrators, diplomats, and merchants traveled throughout the *dar al-Islam,* they encountered plants, animals, and agricultural techniques peculiar to the empire's various regions. They often introduced particularly useful crops to new regions. The most important of the transplants traveled west from India and included staple crops such as sugarcane, rice, and new varieties of sorghum and wheat; vegetables such as spinach and artichokes; fruits such as oranges, bananas, coconuts, and mangoes; and industrial crops such as cotton, indigo, and henna.

**EFFECTS OF NEW CROPS** The introduction of these crops into the western regions of the Islamic world had wide-ranging effects. New food crops led to a richer and more varied diet. They also increased quantities of food available because they enabled cultivators to extend the growing season: since most of the transplanted crops grew well in high heat, cultivators in southwest Asia and other hot zones could plant an additional crop in the summer months instead of leaving their fields fallow. The result was a dramatic increase in food supplies.

**AGRICULTURAL EXPERIMENTATION** Travel and communication in the *dar al-Islam* also encouraged experimentation with agricultural methods. Cultivators paid close attention to methods of irrigation, fertilization, crop rotation, and the like, and they outlined their findings in hundreds of agricultural manuals. The combined effect of new crops and improved techniques was a far more productive agricultural economy, which in turn supported vigorous economic growth throughout the *dar al-Islam.*

**URBAN GROWTH** Increased agricultural production contributed to the rapid growth of cities in all parts of the Islamic world from India to Spain. All these cities—including, for example, Delhi, Merv, Isfahan, Damascus, Cairo, Córdoba, and Tangier—had flourishing markets supporting thousands of artisans, craftsmen, and merchants. Most of them were also important centers of industrial production, particularly of textiles, pottery, glassware, leather, iron, and steel.

One new industry appeared in Islamic cities during the Abbasid era: paper manufacture. When Arab forces defeated a Chinese army at the battle of Talas River in 751, they took prisoners skilled in paper production and learned the technique from them. Paper soon became popular throughout the Islamic world. Paper facilitated the keeping of administrative and commercial records, and it made possible the dissemination of books and treatises in larger quantities than ever before. By the tenth century, mills produced paper in Persia, Mesopotamia, Arabia, Egypt, and Spain, and the industry soon spread to western Europe.

## The Formation of a Hemispheric Trading Zone

From its earliest days Islamic society drew much of its prosperity from commerce. Muhammad himself was a merchant, and he held merchants in high esteem. By the time of the Abbasid caliphate, elaborate trade networks linked all the regions of the Islamic world and joined it to a larger, hemispheric economy.

**OVERLAND TRADE** When they overran the Sasanid empire, Muslim conquerors brought the prosperous trading cities of central Asia under control of the expanding *dar al-Islam*. Muslim merchants were then able to take advantage of the extensive road networks originally built during the classical era by imperial authorities in India, Persia, and the Mediterranean basin. To be sure, Umayyad and Abbasid rulers maintained the roads for military and administrative purposes, but those same roads also made excellent highways for merchants as well as missionaries and pilgrims.

**CAMELS AND CARAVANS** Overland trade traveled mostly by camel caravan. Although they are uncooperative beasts, camels endure the rigors of desert travel much better than horses or donkeys. Moreover, camels can carry heavy loads. During the early centuries C.E., camels became the favored beasts of burden in deserts and other dry regions. As camel transport became more common, the major cities of the Islamic world and central Asia built and maintained caravanserais—inns offering lodging for caravan merchants as well as food, water, and care for their animals.

**MARITIME TRADE** Meanwhile, innovations in nautical technology contributed to a steadily increasing volume of maritime trade in the Red Sea, Persian Gulf, Arabian Sea, and Indian Ocean. Arab and Persian mariners borrowed the compass from its Chinese inventors and used it to guide them on the high seas. From southeast Asian and Indian mariners they borrowed the lateen sail, a triangular sail that increased a ship's maneuverability. From the Hellenistic Mediterranean they borrowed the astrolabe, an instrument that enabled them to calculate latitude. Thus equipped, Arab and Persian mariners ventured throughout the Indian Ocean basin.

**BANKS** Banking also stimulated the commercial economy of the Islamic world. Banks had operated since classical antiquity, but Islamic banks of the Abbasid period conducted business on a much larger scale than their predecessors. They not only lent money

**SLAVERY IN THE ISLAMIC WORLD.** In this thirteenth-century manuscript illustration, merchants at a slave market in southern Arabia deal in black slaves captured in sub-Saharan Africa. Slaves traded in Islamic markets also came from Russia and eastern Europe.

A mosque lamp
www.mhhe.com/
bentleybrief2e

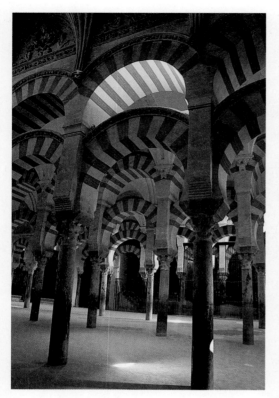

**THE MOSQUE AT CÓRDOBA.** | This mosque was originally built in the late eighth century and enlarged during the ninth and tenth centuries. One of the largest structures in the *dar al-Islam,* the mosque rests on 850 columns and features nineteen aisles. *Why are there no representations of Allah in the mosque?*

to entrepreneurs but also served as brokers for investments and exchanged different currencies. They established multiple branches that honored letters of credit known as *sakk* drawn on the parent bank. Thus merchants could settle accounts with distant business partners without having to deal in cash.

**THE ORGANIZATION OF TRADE**   Trade benefited also from refined techniques of business organization. Usually Islamic businessmen preferred not to embark on solo ventures, since an individual could face financial ruin if an entire cargo of commodities fell prey to pirates or went down with a ship that sank in a storm. Instead, like their counterparts in other postclassical societies, Abbasid entrepreneurs often pooled their resources in a variety of group investments designed to distribute individual risks.

As a result of improved transportation, expanded banking services, and refined techniques of business organization, long-distance trade surged in the early Islamic world. Muslim merchants dealt in silk and ceramics from China, spices and aromatics from India and southeast Asia, and jewelry and fine textiles from the Byzantine empire. Merchants also ventured beyond settled societies in China, India, and the Mediterranean basin to distant lands that previously had not engaged systematically in long-distance trade. They crossed the Sahara desert by camel caravan to trade salt, steel, copper, and glass for gold and slaves from the kingdoms of west Africa. They visited the coastal regions of east Africa, where they obtained slaves and exotic local commodities such as animal skins. They engaged in trade with Russia and Scandinavia by way of the Dnieper and Volga rivers and obtained commodities such as animal skins, furs, honey, amber, and slaves as well as bulk goods such as timber and livestock. The vigorous economy of the Abbasid empire thus helped to establish networks of communication and exchange throughout much of the eastern hemisphere.

**AL-ANDALUS**   The prosperity of Islamic Spain, known as al-Andalus, illustrates the far-reaching effects of long-distance trade during the Abbasid era. Most of the Iberian peninsula had fallen into the hands of Muslim Berber conquerors from north Africa during the early eighth century. As allies of the Umayyads, the governors of al-Andalus refused to recognize the Abbasid dynasty, and beginning in the tenth century they styled themselves caliphs in their own right rather than governors subject to Abbasid authority. Despite political and diplomatic tensions, al-Andalus participated actively in the commercial life of the larger Islamic world, which enabled merchants and manufacturers in al-Andalus to conduct thriving businesses in cities such as Córdoba, Toledo, and Seville.

## The Changing Status of Women

A patriarchal society had emerged in Arabia long before Muhammad's time, but Arab women enjoyed rights not accorded to women in many other lands. They could legally inherit property, divorce husbands on their own initiative, and engage in business ventures. Khadija, the first of Muhammad's four wives, managed a successful commercial business.

**THE QURAN AND WOMEN**   In some respects the Quran enhanced the security of women in Arabian society. It outlawed female infanticide, and it provided that dowries go directly to brides rather than to their husbands and male guardians. It portrayed women not as the property of their menfolk but as honorable individuals, equal to men before Allah, with their own rights and needs. Muhammad's own kindness and

*sakk* (sahk)

**al-Andalus** (al-ahn-duh-LUHS)

generosity toward his wives also served as an example that may have improved the lives of Muslim women.

For the most part, however, the Quran—and later the sharia as well—reinforced male dominance. The Quran and Islamic holy law recognized descent through the male line, and to guarantee proper inheritance, they placed a high premium on genealogical purity. To ensure the legitimacy of heirs, they subjected the social and sexual lives of women to the strict control of male guardians. The Quran and the sharia also permitted men to take up to four wives, whereas women could have only one husband. The Quran and the sharia thus provided a religious and legal foundation for a decisively patriarchal society.

VEILING OF WOMEN   When Islam expanded into the Byzantine and Sasanid empires, it encountered strong patriarchal traditions, and Muslims readily adopted long-standing customs such as the veiling of women. Social and family pressures had induced upper-class urban women to veil themselves in Mesopotamia as early as the thirteenth century B.C.E., and long before Muhammad the practice of veiling had spread to Persia and the eastern Mediterranean. When Muslim Arabs conquered these lands, they adopted the practice. A conspicuous symbol of male authority thus found a prominent place in the early Islamic community.

Although the Quran served as the preeminent source of authority in the Islamic world, over the centuries jurists and legal scholars interpreted the Quran in ways that progressively limited the rights of women. To a large extent the increased emphasis on male authority in Islamic law reflected the influence of the strongly hierarchical and patriarchal societies of Mesopotamia, Persia, and eastern Mediterranean lands as Islam developed from a local faith to a large-scale complex society.

# ISLAMIC VALUES AND CULTURAL EXCHANGES

Since the seventh century C.E., the Quran has served as the cornerstone of Islamic society. Arising from a rich tradition of bedouin poetry and song, the Quran established Arabic as a flexible and powerful medium of communication. When carrying their faith to new lands during the era of Islamic expansion, Muslim missionaries spread the message of Allah and provided instruction in the Quran's teachings, although they also permitted continued observance of pre-Islamic traditions. Muslim intellectuals drew freely from the long-established cultural traditions of Persia, India, and Greece, which they became acquainted with during the Umayyad and Abbasid eras.

## The Formation of an Islamic Cultural Tradition

Muslim theologians and jurists looked to the Quran and other sources of Islamic doctrine in their efforts to formulate moral guidelines appropriate for their society. The body of civil and criminal law embodied in the *sharia* provided a measure of cultural unity for the vastly different lands of the Islamic world. Islamic law did not by any means erase differences, but it established a common cultural foundation that facilitated dealings between peoples of various Islamic lands and that lent substance to the concept of the *dar al-Islam*.

PROMOTION OF ISLAMIC VALUES   On a more popular level, *ulama, qadis,* and missionaries helped to spread Islamic values throughout the *dar al-Islam. Ulama* and *qadis* held positions at all Islamic courts. By resolving disputes according to Islamic law and ordering public observance of Islamic social and moral standards, they helped to bring the values of the Quran and the sharia into the lives of peoples living far from the birthplace of Islam.

**SUFIS.** | Through song, dance, and ecstatic experiences, sometimes enhanced by wine, Persian Sufis expressed their devotion to Allah, as in this sixteenth-century painting.

Formal educational institutions also helped promote Islamic values. For example, many mosques maintained schools that provided an elementary education and religious instruction. By the tenth century, institutions of higher education known as *madrasas* had begun to appear, and by the twelfth century they had become established in the major cities of the Islamic world. Muslim rulers often supported the madrasas in the interests of recruiting literate and learned students for administrative positions.

SUFIS    Among the most effective Islamic missionaries were mystics known as Sufis. The term *Sufi* probably came from the patched woolen garments favored by the mystics. Sufis did not deny Islamic doctrine, but they also did not find formal religious teachings to be especially meaningful. Thus, instead of concerning themselves with fine points of doctrine, Sufis worked to deepen their spiritual awareness. Most Sufis led pious and ascetic lives. Some devoted themselves to helping the poor. Many sought a mystical, ecstatic union with Allah, relying on rousing sermons, passionate singing, or spirited dancing to bring them to a state of high emotion. Muslim theologians sometimes mistrusted Sufis, fearing that in their lack of concern for doctrine they would adopt erroneous beliefs. Nevertheless, after the ninth century Sufis became increasingly popular in Muslim societies because of their piety, devotion, and eagerness to minister to the needs of their fellow human beings.

SUFI MISSIONARIES    Sufis were especially effective as missionaries because they emphasized devotion to Allah above mastery of doctrine. They sometimes encouraged individuals to revere Allah in their own ways, even if their methods did not have a basis in the Quran. They tolerated the continued observance of pre-Islamic customs, for example, as well as the association of Allah with deities recognized and revered in other faiths. Because of their kindness, holiness, tolerance, and charismatic appeal, Sufis attracted numerous converts, particularly in lands such as Persia and India, where long-established religious faiths such as Zoroastrianism, Christianity, Buddhism, and Hinduism had enjoyed a mass following for centuries.

HAJJ    The symbol of Islamic cultural unity was the Ka'ba at Mecca, which from an early date attracted pilgrims from all parts of the Islamic world. Indeed, individuals from far-flung regions made their way to Mecca, visited the holy sites, and learned firsthand the traditions of Islam. Over the centuries these pilgrims helped to spread Islamic beliefs and values to all parts of the Islamic world, and alongside the work of *ulama, qadis,* and Sufi missionaries, their efforts helped to make the *dar al-Islam* not just a name but also a reality.

## Islam and the Cultural Traditions of Persia, India, and Greece

As the Islamic community expanded, Muslims of Arab ancestry interacted regularly with peoples from other cultural traditions, especially those of Persia, India, and Greece. In some cases, particularly in lands ruled by the Umayyad and Abbasid dynasties, large numbers of conquered peoples converted to Islam, and they brought elements of their inherited cultural traditions into Islamic society. In other cases, particularly in lands beyond

**madrasas** (MAH-drahs-ahs)
**Sufis** (SOO-fees)

the authority of Islamic rulers, Muslims became acquainted with the literary, artistic, philosophical, and scientific traditions of peoples who chose not to convert.

PERSIAN INFLUENCES ON ISLAM    Persian traditions quickly found a place in Islamic society, since the culturally rich land fell under Islamic rule at an early date. After the establishment of the Abbasid dynasty and the founding of its capital at Baghdad, Persian administrative techniques were crucial for the organization of the imperial structure through which rulers governed their vast empire. Meanwhile, Persian ideas of kingship—in which kings were wise, benevolent, but nonetheless absolute rulers—profoundly influenced Islamic political thought.

Persian influence was also noticeable in literary works from the Abbasid dynasty. Whereas Arabic served as the language of religion, theology, philosophy, and law, Persian was the principal language of literature, poetry, history, and political reflection. The marvelous collection of stories known as *The Arabian Nights* or *The Thousand and One Nights,* for example, presented popular tales of adventure and romance set in the Abbasid empire and the court of Harun al-Rashid.

INDIAN INFLUENCES ON ISLAM    Indian mathematics, science, and medicine also captured the attention of Arab and Persian Muslims who established Islamic states in northern India. Muslims readily adopted what they called "Hindi" numerals, which European peoples later called "Arabic" numerals, since they learned about them through Arab Muslims. Hindi numerals enabled Muslim scholars to develop an impressive tradition of advanced mathematics, concentrating on algebra (an Arabic word) as well as trigonometry and geometry. From a more practical point of view, Indian numerals vastly simplified bookkeeping for Muslim merchants.

Muslims also found much to appreciate in the scientific and medical thought they encountered in India. With the aid of their powerful and flexible mathematics, Indian scholars were able to carry out precise astronomical calculations, which helped inspire the development of Muslim astronomy. Similarly, Indian medicine appealed to Muslims because of its treatments for specific ailments and its use of antidotes for poisons.

GREEK INFLUENCES ON ISLAM    Muslims also admired the philosophical, scientific, and medical writings of classical Greece. They became especially interested in Plato and Aristotle, whose works they translated and interpreted in commentaries. For example, Ibn Rushd (1126–1198), *qadi* of Seville in the caliphate of Córdoba, followed Aristotle in seeking to articulate a purely rational understanding of the world. Ibn Rushd's work not only helped to shape Islamic philosophy but also found its way to the schools and universities of western Europe, where Christian scholars knew Ibn Rushd as Averroës. During the thirteenth century, his work profoundly influenced the development of scholasticism, the effort of medieval European philosophers to harmonize Christianity with Aristotelian thought. However, after the thirteenth century, Greek philosophy fell out of favor with Muslim philosophers and theologians, who turned instead to teachings from the Quran and Sufi mystics.

Quite apart from philosophy, Greek mathematics, science, and medicine also appealed strongly to Muslims. Greek mathematics did not make use of Indian numerals, but it offered a solid body of powerful reasoning, particularly when dealing with calculations in algebra and geometry. Greek mathematics supported the development of astronomical and geographical scholarship, and studies of anatomy and physiology served as foundations for medical thought. Muslim scholars quickly absorbed these Greek traditions, combined them with influences from India, and used them as points of departure for their own studies. The result was a brilliant flowering of mathematical, scientific, and medical scholarship that provided Muslim societies with powerful tools for understanding the natural world.

**Ibn Rushd** (IB-uhn RUSHED)

# SUMMARY

The prophet Muhammad did not intend to found a new religion. Instead, his intention was to express his faith in Allah and perfect the teachings of earlier Jewish and Christian prophets by announcing a revelation more comprehensive than those Allah had entrusted to his predecessors. His message soon attracted a circle of devout and committed disciples, and by the time of his death most of Arabia had accepted Islam. During the two centuries following the prophet's death, Arab conquerors spread Islam throughout southwest Asia and north Africa and introduced their faith to central Asia, India, the Mediterranean islands, and Iberia. This rapid expansion of Islam encouraged the development of an extensive trade and communications network: merchants, diplomats, and other travelers moved easily throughout the Islamic world exchanging goods and introducing agricultural crops to new lands. Rapid expansion also led to encounters between Islam and long-established religious and cultural traditions, Persian literature and political thought, and classical Greek philosophy and science. Muslim rulers built a society that made a place for those of different faiths, and Muslim thinkers readily adapted earlier traditions to their own needs. As a result of its expansion, its extensive trade and communications networks, and its engagement with other religious and cultural traditions, the *dar al-Islam* became one of the most prosperous and cosmopolitan societies of the postclassical world.

# STUDY TERMS

Abbasid dynasty (213)
Abu Bakr (211)
Allah (207)
caliph (211)
dar al-Islam (206)
Five Pillars of Islam (209)
*hadith* (207)
hajj (205)
*hijra* (208)

Islam (205)
jihad (209)
*jizya* (212)
Ka'ba (207)
madrasas (218)
Mecca (205)
Medina (205)
Muhammad (205)
Muslim (205)

*qadis* (213)
Quran (207)
*sakk* (216)
sharia (209)
Shia (212)
Sunni (212)
*ulama* (213)
Umayyad dynasty (212)
*umma* (208)

Richard C. Foltz. *Spirituality in the Land of the Noble: How Iran Shaped the World's Religions.* Oxford, 2004. Includes an accessible discussion of Persian influences on the Islamic faith.

Abu Hamid Muhammad al-Ghazzali. *The Alchemy of Happiness.* Trans. by Claude Field. Rev. by Elton L. Daniel. New York, 1991. Translation of one of the classic works of early Islamic religious and moral thought.

Mahmood Ibrahim. *Merchant Capital and Islam.* Austin, 1990. Examines the role of trade in Arabia during Muhammad's time and in early Islamic society.

Ira M. Lapidus. *A History of Islamic Societies.* Cambridge, 1988. Authoritative survey of Islamic history, concentrating on social and cultural issues.

M. Lombard. *The Golden Age of Islam.* Princeton, 2004. Concentrates on the social and economic history of the Abbasid period.

William H. McNeill and Marilyn R. Waldman, eds. *The Islamic World.* New York, 1973. An excellent collection of primary sources in translation.

F. E. Peters. *The Hajj: The Muslim Pilgrimage to Mecca and the Holy Places.* Princeton, 1994. Draws on scores of travelers' reports in studying the Muslim practice through the ages of making a pilgrimage to Mecca.

*Al Qur'an: A Contemporary Translation.* Trans. by Ahmed Ali. Princeton, 1984. A sensitive translation of the holy book of Islam.

Francis Robinson, ed. *The Cambridge Illustrated History of the Islamic World.* Cambridge, 1996. An excellent and lavishly illustrated introduction to Islam and the Muslim world.

Frances Wood. *The Silk Road: Two Thousand Years in the Heart of Asia.* Berkeley, 2002. A brilliantly illustrated volume discussing the history of the silk roads from antiquity to the twentieth century.

# The Resurgence of Empire in East Asia

## 12

Early in the seventh century C.E., the emperor of China issued an order forbidding his subjects to travel beyond Chinese borders into central Asia. In 629, however, a young Buddhist monk slipped past imperial watchtowers under cover of darkness and made his way west. His name was Xuanzang, and his destination was India, homeland of Buddhism. As a young man, Xuanzang had followed his older brother into a monastery, where he became devoted to Buddhism. While studying the Sanskrit language, Xuanzang noticed that Chinese writings on Buddhism contained many teachings that were confusing or even contradictory to those of Indian Buddhist texts. He decided to travel to India, visit the holy sites of Buddhism, and study with the most knowledgeable Buddhist teachers and sages to learn about his faith from the purest sources.

Xuanzang could not have imagined the difficulties he would face. Immediately after his departure from China, his guide abandoned him in the Gobi desert. After losing his water bag and collapsing in the heat, Xuanzang made his way to the oasis town of Turpan on the silk roads. The Buddhist ruler of Turpan provided the devout pilgrim with travel supplies and rich gifts to support his mission. Among the presents were twenty-four letters of introduction to rulers of lands on the way to India (each one attached to a bolt of silk), thirty horses, twenty-five laborers, and five hundred bolts of silk, along with gold, silver, and silk clothes for Xuanzang to use as travel funds. After departing from Turpan, Xuanzang crossed three of the world's highest mountain ranges—the Tian Shan, Hindu Kush, and Pamir ranges—and lost one-third of his party to exposure and starvation in the Tian Shan.

Yet Xuanzang persisted and arrived in India in 630. He lived there for more than twelve years, devoting himself to the study of languages and Buddhist doctrine, especially at Nalanda, the center of advanced Buddhist education in India. He also amassed a huge collection of relics and images as well as some 657 books, all of which he transported back to China to advance the understanding of Buddhism in his native land.

By the time of his return in 645, Xuanzang had logged more than 16,000 kilometers (10,000 miles) on the road. News of the holy monk's efforts had reached the imperial court, and even

《 *Buddhist temple in mountain detail.* The Nelson-Atkins Museum of Art, Kansas City, Missouri. Purchase: William Rockhill Nelson Trust, 47-71. Photograph by John Lamberton.

**Xuanzang** (SHWEN-ZAHNG)

**Buddhism** (BOO-diz'm)

**Sanskrit** (SAHN-skriht)

**Tian Shan** (tyahn shahn)

# CHRONOLOGY

though Xuanzang had violated the ban on travel, he received a hero's welcome and an audience with the emperor. Until his death in 664, Xuanzang translated Buddhist treatises into Chinese and promoted his faith. His efforts helped to popularize Buddhism and bring about nearly universal adoption of the faith throughout China.

Xuanzang undertook his journey at a propitious time. For more than 350 years after the fall of the Han dynasty, war, invasion, conquest, and foreign rule disrupted Chinese society. Toward the end of the sixth century, however, centralized imperial rule returned to China. The Sui and Tang dynasties restored order and presided over an era of rapid economic growth in China, especially in the areas of agricultural yields and technological innovations. As a result, China stood alongside the Byzantine and Abbasid empires as a political and economic anchor of the postclassical world.

For China the postclassical era was an age of intense interaction with other peoples. Chinese merchants participated in trade networks that linked most regions of the eastern hemisphere. Buddhism spread beyond its homeland of India and attracted a large popular following in China. A resurgent China also made its influence felt throughout east Asia, especially in Korea, Vietnam, and Japan. Although these lands retained their distinctiveness, each drew deep inspiration from China and participated in a larger east Asian society centered on China.

# THE RESTORATION OF CENTRALIZED IMPERIAL RULE IN CHINA

For several centuries following the Han dynasty, none of the remaining regional kingdoms was able to assert lasting authority over all of China. In the late sixth century, however, Yang Jian, an ambitious ruler in northern China, embarked on a series of military campaigns that brought all of China once again under centralized imperial rule. Yang Jian's Sui dynasty survived less than thirty years, but the tradition of centralized rule outlived his house. The Tang dynasty replaced the Sui, and the Song succeeded the Tang. The Tang and Song dynasties organized Chinese society so efficiently that China became a center of exceptional agricultural and industrial production, creating an economy so powerful that it affected much of the eastern hemisphere.

## The Sui Dynasty

ESTABLISHMENT OF THE SUI DYNASTY   Like Qin Shihuangdi some eight centuries earlier, Yang Jian imposed tight political discipline on his own state and then extended his rule to the rest of China. Yang Jian began his rise to power when a Turkish ruler appointed him duke of Sui in northern China. In 580 Yang Jian's patron died, and one year later he claimed both the throne and the Mandate of Heaven for himself. During the next decade Yang Jian sent military expeditions into central Asia and southern China. By 589 the house of Sui ruled all of China.

**Yang Jian** (yahng jyahn)

Like the rulers of the Qin dynasty, the emperors of the Sui dynasty (589–618 C.E.) built a strong, centralized government, but only at great human and financial cost. Indeed, the Sui emperors ordered construction projects, repaired defensive walls, and conducted military campaigns, but did so by levying high taxes and demanding compulsory labor services from their subjects.

THE GRAND CANAL    The most elaborate project undertaken during the Sui dynasty was the construction of the Grand Canal, which was one of the world's largest waterworks projects before modern times. The second emperor, Sui Yangdi (reigned 604–618 C.E.), wanted the canal to facilitate trade between northern and southern China, particularly to make the abundant supplies of rice and other food crops from the Yangzi River valley available to residents of northern regions. Since Chinese rivers generally flow from west to east, only an artificial waterway could support such a large volume of bulky trade goods trade between north and south.

The Grand Canal was a series of artificial waterways that ultimately reached from Hangzhou in the south to the imperial capital of Chang'an in the west to a terminus near modern Beijing in the north. Sui Yangdi used canals dug as early as the Zhou dynasty, but he linked them into a network that served much of China. When completed, the Grand Canal extended almost 2,000 kilometers (1,240 miles) and reportedly was forty paces wide, with roads running parallel to it on either side.

Though expensive to construct, Sui Yangdi's investment in the Grand Canal paid dividends for more than a thousand years. It integrated the economies of northern and southern China, thereby establishing an economic foundation for political and cultural unity. Until the arrival of railroads in the twentieth century, the Grand Canal served as the principal conduit for internal trade. Indeed, the canal continues to function even today.

Sui Yangdi's construction projects served China well for a long time, but their dependence on high taxes and forced labor generated hostility toward his rule. The Grand Canal alone required the services of conscripted laborers by the millions. In the late 610s, discontented subjects began to revolt against Sui rule. In 618 a disgruntled minister assassinated the emperor and brought the dynasty to an end.

## The Tang Dynasty

Soon after Sui Yangdi's death, a rebel leader seized Chang'an and proclaimed himself emperor of a new dynasty that he named Tang after his hereditary title. The dynasty survived for almost three hundred years (618–907 C.E.), and Tang rulers organized China into a powerful, productive, and prosperous society.

TANG TAIZONG    Much of the Tang success was due to the energy, ability, and policies of the dynasty's second emperor, Tang Taizong (reigned 627–649 C.E.). Taizong was both ambitious and ruthless: in making his way to the imperial throne, he murdered two of his brothers and pushed his father aside. Once on the throne, however, he displayed a high sense of duty and strove conscientiously to provide an effective, stable government. He built a splendid capital at Chang'an, and he saw himself as a Confucian ruler who heeded the interests of his subjects. Contemporaries reported that banditry ended during his reign, that the price of rice remained low, and that taxes levied on peasants amounted to only one-fortieth of the annual harvest—a 2.5 percent tax rate. These reports suggest that China enjoyed an era of unusual stability and prosperity during the reign of Tang Taizong.

Three policies in particular help to explain the success of the early Tang dynasty: maintenance of a well-articulated transportation and communications network, distribution of land according to the principles of the equal-field system, and reliance on a bureaucracy

**Sui Yangdi** (sway yahng-dee)

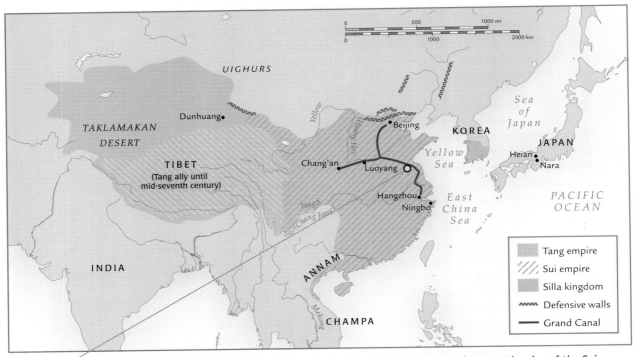

**The Grand Canal integrated the economies of northern and southern China.**

**MAP 12.1** | The Sui and Tang dynasties, 589–907 C.E. Compare the size of the Sui and Tang empires. *Why was the Tang dynasty able to extend its authority over such vast distances?*

based on merit. All three policies originated in the Sui dynasty, but Tang rulers applied them more systematically and effectively than their predecessors.

**TRANSPORTATION AND COMMUNICATIONS** Apart from the Grand Canal, which served as the principal route for long-distance transportation within China, Tang rulers maintained an extensive network of roads. Along the main routes, Tang officials maintained inns, postal stations, and stables. Using couriers traveling by horse, the Tang court could communicate with the most distant cities in the empire in about eight days. Even human runners provided speedy services: relay teams of some 9,600 runners supplied the Tang court at Chang'an with fresh seafood from Ningbo, more than 1,000 kilometers (620 miles) away!

**THE EQUAL-FIELD SYSTEM** The equal-field system governed the allocation of agricultural land. Its purpose was to ensure an equitable distribution of land and to avoid the concentration of landed property that had caused social problems during the Han dynasty. The system allotted land to individuals and their families according to the land's fertility and the recipients' needs. About one-fifth of the land became the hereditary possession of the recipients, and the rest remained available for redistribution when the original recipients' needs and circumstances changed.

For about a century, administrators were able to apply the principles of the equal-field system relatively consistently. By the early eighth century, however, a rapidly rising population brought pressure on the land available for distribution. Meanwhile, influential families found ways to retain land scheduled for redistribution. Furthermore, large parcels of land fell out of the system altogether when Buddhist monasteries acquired them. Nevertheless, during the first half of the Tang dynasty, the system provided a foundation for stability and prosperity in the Chinese countryside.

**BUREAUCRACY OF MERIT** The Tang dynasty also relied heavily on a bureaucracy based on merit. Following the example of the Han dynasty, Sui and Tang rulers recruited government officials from the ranks of candidates who had progressed through

**GRAND CANAL.** | Barges make their way through a portion of the Grand Canal near the city of Wuxi in southern China.

the Confucian educational system based on the classic works of Chinese literature and philosophy. As a result, most officeholders won their posts because of intellectual ability. Members of this talented class were generally loyal to the dynasty, and they worked to preserve and strengthen the state. In fact, the Confucian educational system and the related civil service served Chinese governments so well that with modifications and an occasional interruption, they survived until the collapse of the Qing dynasty in the early twentieth century.

**MILITARY EXPANSION**    Soon after its foundation, the powerful and dynamic Tang state began to flex its military muscles. In the north, Tang forces brought Manchuria under imperial authority and forced the Silla kingdom in Korea to acknowledge the Tang emperor as overlord. To the south, Tang armies conquered the northern part of Vietnam. To the west, they extended Tang authority as far as the Aral Sea and brought a portion of the high plateau of Tibet under Tang control. Territorially, the Tang empire ranks among the largest in Chinese history.

**TANG FOREIGN RELATIONS**    In an effort to fashion a stable diplomatic order, the Tang emperors revived the Han dynasty's practice of the tribute system. According to Chinese political theory, China was the Middle Kingdom and had the responsibility of bringing order to subordinate lands through a system of tributary relationships. Neighboring lands and peoples would recognize Chinese emperors as their overlords, and envoys from those states would regularly deliver gifts to the court of the Middle Kingdom and perform the kowtow—a ritual prostration during which subordinates knelt before the emperor and touched their foreheads to the ground. In return, tributary states received confirmation of their authority as well as lavish gifts. Because Chinese authorities often had little real influence in these supposedly subordinate lands, there was always something of a fictional quality to the system. Nevertheless, it was extremely important because it institutionalized relations between China and neighboring lands, fostering trade and cultural exchanges as well as diplomatic contacts.

**TANG DECLINE**    Under able rulers such as Taizong, the Tang dynasty flourished. During the mid–eighth century, however, the careless leadership of an emperor more interested in music and his favorite concubine brought the dynasty to a crisis. In 755 one of the dynasty's foremost military commanders, An Lushan, mounted a rebellion and captured the capital at Chang'an and the secondary capital at Luoyang. His revolt was short-lived: by 763 Tang forces had suppressed An Lushan's army and recovered their capitals. But the rebellion left the dynasty gravely weakened, because Tang commanders had to ask a nomadic Turkish people, the Uighurs, to help them win back their capitals. In return, the Uighurs demanded the right to sack Chang'an and Luoyang after the expulsion of the rebels.

The Tang imperial house never again regained control of affairs. The equal-field system deteriorated, and tax receipts dwindled. Imperial armies were unable to resist invasions of Turkish peoples in the late eighth century. During the ninth century a series of rebellions devastated the Chinese countryside. In an effort to control the rebellions, the Tang emperors granted progressively greater power and authority to regional military commanders, who gradually became the effective rulers of China. In 907 the last Tang emperor abdicated his throne, and the dynasty came to an end.

## The Song Dynasty

PSI map
The Song dynasty
www.mhhe.com/
bentleybrief2e

Following the Tang collapse, warlords ruled China until the Song dynasty reimposed centralized imperial rule in the late tenth century. Though it survived for more than three centuries, the Song dynasty (960–1279 C.E.) never built a very powerful state. Song rulers mistrusted military leaders, and they placed much more emphasis on civil administration, industry, education, and the arts than on military affairs.

SONG TAIZU   The first Song emperor, Song Taizu (reigned 960–976 C.E.), inaugurated this policy. Song Taizu began his career as a junior military officer for a powerful warlord in northern China. He had a reputation for honesty and effectiveness, and in 960 his troops proclaimed him emperor. During the next several years, he and his army subjected the warlords to their authority and consolidated Song control throughout China. He then set about organizing a centralized administration that placed military forces under tight supervision.

Song rulers vastly expanded the bureaucracy by creating more opportunities for individuals to seek a Confucian education and take civil service examinations. They accepted many more candidates into the bureaucracy than their Sui and Tang predecessors, and they provided generous salaries for those who qualified for government appointments. They even placed civil bureaucrats in charge of military forces.

SONG WEAKNESSES   The Song approach to administration resulted in a more centralized imperial government than earlier Chinese dynasties had enjoyed, but it caused two big problems that eventually caused the dynasty to fall. The first problem was financial: as the number of bureaucrats and the size of their rewards grew, the imperial treasury came under tremendous pressure. That pressure, in turn, aggravated the peasantry, who were expected to shoulder increased taxes.

The second problem was military. Scholar bureaucrats generally had little talent for military affairs, yet they led Song armies in the field and made military decisions. It was no coincidence that nomadic peoples flourished along China's northern border throughout the Song dynasty. In the early twelfth century, the nomadic Jurchen overran northern China, captured the Song capital at Kaifeng, and proclaimed establishment of the Jin empire. Thereafter the Song dynasty moved its capital to the prosperous port city of Hangzhou and survived only in southern China, so that the latter part of the dynasty is commonly known as the

THINKING ABOUT
*Traditions*

**TRADITIONS IN THE RESURGENT EAST ASIAN EMPIRES.** During the postclassical period, traders and travelers from a wide variety of Eurasian locations came to China, bringing foreign beliefs and values with them. Discuss some of the ways the Chinese transformed these foreign influences into ideas and practices that fit into long-established traditions.

**Uighurs** (WEE-goors)

**Song Taizu** (sawng tahy-zoo)

MAP 12.2 | The Song dynasty, 960–1279 C.E. After the establishment of the Jin empire, the Song dynasty moved its capital from Kaifeng to Hangzhou. **What advantages did Hangzhou offer to the Song rulers?**

The new capital of the Song dynasty.

Southern Song. This truncated Southern Song shared a border with the Jin empire about midway between the Yellow River and the Yangzi River until 1279, when Mongol forces ended the dynasty altogether.

# THE ECONOMIC DEVELOPMENT OF TANG AND SONG CHINA

Although the Song dynasty did not develop a strong military capacity, it benefited from a remarkable series of agricultural, technological, industrial, and commercial developments. This economic development originated in the Tang dynasty, but its results became most clear during the Song, which presided over a land of enormous prosperity. The economic surge of Tang and Song times had implications that went well beyond China, since it stimulated trade and production throughout much of the eastern hemisphere for more than half a millennium, from about 600 to 1300 C.E.

## *Agricultural Development*

**FAST-RIPENING RICE** The foundation of economic development in Tang and Song China was a surge in agricultural production. When Sui and Tang armies ventured into Vietnam, they encountered new strains of fast-ripening rice that enabled cultivators to harvest two crops per year. Transferred to the fertile fields of southern China, fast-ripening rice quickly resulted in an expanded supply of food.

**Jurchen** (JUHR-chehn)

**CHINESE PEASANT LIFE.** | A wall painting in a Buddhist cave depicts a peasant plowing his field in the rain with the aid of an ox and a heavy plow. Other peasants have found shelter from the rain and consume a mid-day meal brought to them by their wives. *How would peasant life have differed from the lives of scholar-bureaucrats?*

NEW AGRICULTURAL TECHNIQUES   Chinese cultivators also increased their productivity by adopting improved agricultural techniques. They made increased use of heavy iron plows, and they harnessed oxen (in the north) and water buffaloes (in the south) to help prepare land for cultivation. They enriched the soil with manure and composted organic matter. They also organized extensive irrigation systems. Artificial irrigation made it possible to extend cultivation to new lands, including terraced mountainsides—a development that vastly expanded China's agricultural potential.

POPULATION GROWTH   Increased agricultural production resulted in rapid population growth. After the fall of the Han dynasty, the population of China reached a low point of about 45 million in 600 C.E. By 1000 C.E. it had increased to 60 million. By 1127, when the Jurchen conquered the northern half of the Song state, the Chinese population had passed the 100 million mark, and by 1200 it stood at about 115 million.

URBANIZATION   Increased food supplies encouraged the growth of cities. During the Tang dynasty the imperial capital of Chang'an was the world's most populous city with as many as two million residents. During the Song dynasty, China was the most urbanized land in the world. In the late thirteenth century, Hangzhou, capital of the Southern Song dynasty, had more than one million residents. They supported hundreds of restaurants, taverns, teahouses, brothels, music halls, theaters, clubhouses, gardens, markets, craft shops, and specialty stores dealing in silk, gems, porcelain, lacquerware, and other goods.

Another result of increased food production was the emergence of a commercialized agricultural economy. Because fast-ripening rice yielded bountiful harvests, many cultivators could purchase inexpensive rice and raise vegetables and fruits for sale on the commercial market. Cultivators specialized in crops that grew well in their own regions, and they often exported their harvests to distant regions. By the twelfth century, for example, the wealthy southern province of Fujian imported rice and devoted its land to the production of lychees, oranges, and sugarcane, which fetched high prices in northern markets.

**PATRIARCHAL SOCIAL STRUCTURES**    Alongside increasing wealth and agricultural productivity, Tang and especially Song China experienced a tightening of patriarchal social structures. During the Song dynasty, for example, the veneration of family ancestors became much more elaborate than before. Indeed, descendants diligently sought the graves of their earliest traceable forefathers and then arranged elaborate graveside rituals in their honor. Whole extended families often traveled great distances to attend annual rituals venerating deceased ancestors—a practice that strengthened the sense of family identity and cohesiveness.

**FOOT BINDING**    Strengthened patriarchal authority also helps to explain the popularity of foot binding, which spread among privileged classes during the Song era. Foot binding involved the tight wrapping of young girls' feet with strips of cloth, which prevented natural growth and resulted in tiny, malformed, curved feet. Women with bound feet could not walk easily or naturally. Usually they needed canes to walk by themselves, and sometimes they depended on servants to carry them around in litters. Foot binding never became universal in China—it was impractical for peasants or lower-class working women in the cities—but wealthy families often bound the feet of their daughters to enhance their attractiveness, display their high social standing, and gain increased control over the girls' behavior. Like the practice of veiling women in the Islamic world, foot binding placed women of privileged classes under tight supervision of their male guardians, who then managed the women's affairs in the interests of the larger family.

Foot binding
www.mhhe.com/
bentleybrief2e

## *Technological and Industrial Development*

**PORCELAIN**    Abundant supplies of food enabled many people to pursue technological and industrial interests. During the Tang and Song dynasties, Chinese crafts workers generated a remarkable range of technological innovations. During Tang times they discovered techniques for producing high-quality porcelain, which was lighter, thinner, and adaptable to more uses than earlier pottery. Porcelain technology gradually diffused to other societies, yet demand for Chinese porcelain remained high, and the Chinese exported vast quantities of porcelain during the Tang and Song dynasties. Indeed, Chinese porcelain graced the tables of wealthy and refined households in southeast Asia, India, Persia, and the port cities of east Africa. Tang and Song products gained such a reputation that fine porcelain has come to be known generally as *chinaware.*

**METALLURGY**    Tang and Song craftsmen also improved metallurgical technologies, which resulted in a surge of iron and steel production. Chinese craftsmen discovered that they could use coke instead of coal in their furnaces and produce stronger and more useful grades of metal. Between the early ninth and the early twelfth centuries, iron production increased almost tenfold, according to official records. Most of the increased supply of iron and steel went into weaponry and agricultural tools: during the early Song dynasty, imperial armaments manufacturers produced 16.5 million iron arrowheads per year. As in the case of porcelain technology, metallurgical techniques soon diffused to lands beyond China. Indeed, Song military difficulties stemmed partly from the fact that nomadic peoples quickly learned Chinese techniques and fashioned their own iron weapons for use in campaigns against them.

**GUNPOWDER**    Tang and Song craftsmen also invented entirely new products, tools, and techniques, most notably gunpowder, printing, and naval technologies. During the Tang dynasty, Daoist alchemists seeking elixirs to prolong life soon learned that it was unwise to mix charcoal, saltpeter, sulphur, and arsenic because of the volatility of the resulting compound. Military officials, however, recognized opportunity in the explosive mixture. By the mid–tenth century they were using gunpowder in bamboo "fire lances," a kind of flamethrower, and by the eleventh century they had fashioned primitive bombs.

The earliest gunpowder weapons had limited military effectiveness. Over time, however, refinements enhanced their capabilities. Knowledge of gunpowder chemistry quickly

**GUNPOWDER.** | During the Han Dynasty, Chinese alchemists discovered that a combination of saltpeter, charcoal, and sulfur exploded when lit with a flame. By the 8th century C.E., Chinese strategists began to use gunpowder for military uses.

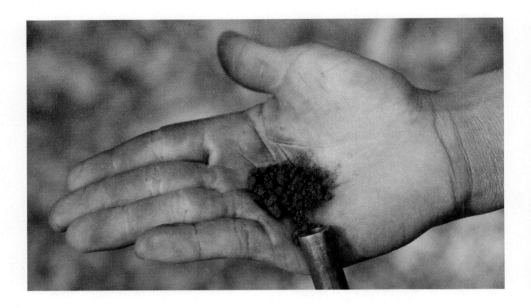

diffused through Eurasia, and by the late thirteenth century peoples of southwest Asia and Europe were experimenting with metal-barreled cannons.

**PRINTING**   The precise origins of printing are obscure. It is clear, however, that it became common during the Tang era. The earliest printers employed block-printing techniques: they carved a reverse image of an entire page into a wooden block, inked the block, and then pressed a sheet of paper on top. By the mid–eleventh century, printers had also begun to experiment with reusable, movable type: instead of carving images into blocks, they fashioned dies in the shape of ideographs, arranged them in a frame, inked them, and pressed the frame over paper sheets. Printing made it possible to produce texts quickly, cheaply, and in huge quantities. By the late ninth century, printed copies of Buddhist texts, Confucian works, calendars, agricultural treatises, and popular works were abundant, particularly in southwestern China (modern Sichuan province).

**NAVAL TECHNOLOGY**   Chinese inventiveness extended also to naval technology. Before Tang times, Chinese mariners did not venture very far from land, relying instead on foreign ships for long-distance maritime trade. During the Tang dynasty, however, Chinese consumers developed a taste for the spices and exotic products of southeast Asian islands, and Chinese mariners increasingly visited those lands in their own ships. By the time of the Song dynasty, Chinese seafarers sailed ships fastened with iron nails, waterproofed with oils, furnished with watertight bulkheads, driven by canvas and bamboo sails, steered by rudders, and navigated with the aid of the "south-pointing needle"—the magnetic compass. Chinese ships mostly plied the waters between Japan and the Malay peninsula, but some of them called at ports in India, Ceylon, Persia, and east Africa. These long-distance travels helped to diffuse elements of Chinese naval technology, particularly the compass, which soon became the common property of mariners throughout the Indian Ocean basin.

## *The Emergence of a Market Economy*

Increased agricultural production, improved transportation systems, population growth, urbanization, and industrial production combined to stimulate the Chinese economy. China's various regions increasingly specialized in the cultivation of particular food crops or the production of particular manufactured goods. To be sure, the government played an important role in the Chinese economy by regulating the distribution of staple foods and the production of militarily sensitive enterprises such as the iron industry. Nevertheless, millions of cultivators produced fruits and vegetables for sale on the open market, and manufacturers of silk, porcelain, and other goods supplied both domestic and foreign markets. The Chinese economy became more tightly integrated than ever before, and foreign demand for Chinese products fueled rapid economic expansion.

**FINANCIAL INSTRUMENTS**   In fact, trade grew so rapidly during Tang and Song times that China experienced a shortage of the copper coins that served as money for most transactions. To alleviate the shortage, letters of credit came into common use during the early Tang dynasty. Later developments included the use of promissory notes, checks, and even paper money. Indeed, wealthy merchants pioneered the use of printed paper money in the late ninth century. In return for cash deposits from their clients, they issued printed notes that the clients could redeem for merchandise. In a society short of cash, these notes greatly facilitated commercial transactions. Yet they also caused disorder, and sometimes even riots, in the event that merchants were not able to honor their notes.

In the eleventh century, in an effort to forestall such disorder, the Chinese government stepped in and assumed the sole right to issue paper money. The first government-issued paper money appeared in 1024 in Sichuan province, and by the end of the eleventh century it existed throughout imperial China. In spite of continuing problems with paper currency—including counterfeit notes and lapses of public confidence in the government's ability to honor its own notes—printed paper money provided a powerful stimulus to the Chinese economy under the Song.

**A COSMOPOLITAN SOCIETY**   Trade and urbanization transformed Tang and Song China into a prosperous, cosmopolitan society. Trade came to China both by land and by sea. Muslim merchants from the Abbasid empire and central Asia—and even subjects of the Byzantine empire—helped to revive the silk roads network and flocked to large Chinese trading centers. Residents of large Chinese cities such as Chang'an and Luoyang became quite accustomed to merchants from foreign lands. Indeed, musicians and dancers from Persia became popular entertainers in the cities of the Tang dynasty. Meanwhile, Arab, Persian, Indian, and Malay mariners arriving by way of the Indian Ocean and South China Sea established sizable merchant communities in the bustling southern Chinese port cities of Guangzhou and Quanzhou.

**CHINA AND THE HEMISPHERIC ECONOMY**   Indeed, high productivity and trade brought the Tang and Song economy a dynamism that China's borders could not restrain. Chinese consumers developed a taste for exotic goods, which stimulated trade throughout much of the eastern hemisphere. Spices from the islands of southeast Asia made their way to China, along with products as diverse as kingfisher feathers and tortoise shell from Vietnam, pearls and incense from India, and horses and melons from central Asia. In exchange for such exotic items, Chinese sent abroad vast quantities of silk, porcelain, and lacquerware. In central Asia, southeast Asia, India, Persia, and the port cities of east Africa, wealthy merchants and rulers wore Chinese silk and set their tables with Chinese porcelain. China's economic surge during the Tang and Song dynasties thus promoted trade and economic growth throughout much of the eastern hemisphere.

# CULTURAL CHANGE IN TANG AND SONG CHINA

Interactions with peoples of other societies encouraged cultural change in postclassical China. The Confucian and Daoist traditions did not disappear, but they made way for a foreign religion—Mahayana Buddhism—and they developed along new lines that reflected the conditions of Tang and Song society.

---

**Guangzhou** (gwahng-joh)

**Quanzhou** (chwahn-joh)

## The Arab Merchant Suleiman on Business Practices in Tang China

*The Arab merchant Suleiman made several commercial ventures by ship to India and China during the early ninth century C.E. In 851 an Arab geographer wrote an account of Suleiman's travels, describing India and China for Muslim readers in southwest Asia. His report throws particularly interesting light on the economic conditions and business practices of Tang China.*

Young and old Chinese all wear silk clothes in both winter and summer, but silk of the best quality is reserved for the kings. . . . During the winter, the men wear two, three, four, five pairs of pants, and even more, according to their means. This practice has the goal of protecting the lower body from the high humidity of the land, which they fear. During the summer, they wear a single shirt of silk or some similar material. They do not wear turbans. . . .

In China, commercial transactions are carried out with the aid of copper coins. The Chinese royal treasury is identical to that of other kings, but only the king of China has a treasury that uses copper coins as a standard. These copper coins serve as the money of the land. The Chinese have gold, silver, fine pearls, fancy silk textiles, raw silk, and all this in large quantities, but they are considered commodities, and only copper coins serve as money.

Imports into China include ivory, incense, copper ingots, shells of sea turtles, and rhinoceros horn, with which the Chinese make ornaments. . . .

The Chinese conduct commercial transactions and business affairs with equity. When someone lends money to another person, he writes up a note documenting the loan. The borrower writes up another note on which he affixes an imprint of his index finger and middle finger together. Then they put the two notes together, roll them up, and write a formula at the point where one touches the other [so that part of the written

formula appears on each note]. Next, they separate the notes and entrust to the lender the one on which the borrower recognizes his debt. If the borrower denies his debt later on, they say to him, "Present the note that the lender gave to you." If the borrower maintains that he has no such note from the lender, and denies that he ever agreed to the note with his fingerprints on it, and if the lender's note has disappeared, they say to him, "Declare in writing that you have not contracted this debt, but if later the lender brings forth proof that you have contracted this debt that you deny, you will receive twenty blows of the cane on the back and you will be ordered to pay a penalty of twenty million copper coins." This sum is equal to about 2,000 dinars [gold coins used in the Abbasid empire]. Twenty blows of the cane brings on death. Thus no one in China dares to make such a declaration for fear of losing at the same time both life and fortune. We have seen no one who has agreed when invited to make such a declaration. The Chinese are thus equitable to each other. No one in China is treated unjustly.

■ In what ways might Chinese policies have encouraged business and trade during the Tang dynasty?

SOURCE: Gabriel Ferrand, trans. *Voyage du marchand arabe Sulayman en Inde et en Chine.* Paris, 1922, pp. 45, 53–54, 60–61. (Translated into English by Jerry H. Bentley.)

## *The Establishment of Buddhism*

**FOREIGN RELIGIONS IN CHINA** Buddhist merchants traveling the ancient silk roads visited China as early as the second century B.C.E. During the Han dynasty their faith attracted little interest: Confucianism, Daoism, and cults that honored family ancestors were the most popular cultural alternatives. During the unsettled centuries following the fall of the Han, however, several foreign religions—including Nestorian Christianity, Manichaeism, Zoroastrianism, and Islam—established communities in China. Yet these religions of salvation mostly served the needs of foreign merchants trading in China and converts from nomadic societies and did not win a large popular following.

**Confucianism** (kuhn-FYEW-shuhn-iz'm)

**Daoism** (dow-iz'm)

**Manichaeism** (mahn-ih-kee-iz'm)

**DUNHUANG**  Mahayana Buddhism was different in that it gradually found a popular following in Tang and Song China. Buddhism came to China over the silk roads via the oasis cities of central Asia, and by the fourth century C.E., a sizable Buddhist community had emerged at Dunhuang in western China (modern Gansu province). Between about 600 and 1000 C.E., Buddhists built hundreds of cave temples in the vicinity of Dunhuang and decorated them with murals depicting events in the lives of the Buddha and the boddhisattvas. They also assembled libraries of religious literature and operated scriptoria to produce Buddhist texts. Missions supported by establishments such as those at Dunhuang helped Buddhism to establish a foothold in China.

**BUDDHISM IN CHINA**  Buddhism attracted Chinese interest partly because of its high standards of morality, its intellectual sophistication, and its promise of salvation. Yet practical concerns also help to account for its appeal. Buddhist monastic communities in China accumulated sizable estates donated by wealthy converts, and they commonly stored a portion of their harvests for distribution among local residents during hard times. As a result, Buddhist monasteries became important elements in the local economies of Chinese communities.

**BUDDHISM AND DAOISM**  In some ways Buddhism posed a challenge to Chinese cultural and social traditions. Buddhist theologians typically placed great emphasis on written texts and used them to explore elaborate investigations into metaphysical themes such as the nature of the soul. Among Chinese intellectuals, however, only the Confucians placed equal emphasis on written texts, and they devoted their energies mostly to practical rather than metaphysical issues. Meanwhile, Daoists had limited interest in written texts of any kind. Buddhist morality also called for individuals to observe an ascetic ideal by following a celibate, monastic lifestyle. In contrast, Chinese morality centered on the family unit and strongly encouraged procreation so that generations of offspring would be available to venerate family ancestors. Some Chinese held that Buddhist monasteries were economically harmful, because they paid no taxes, whereas others scorned Buddhism because of its foreign origins.

Because of these differences and concerns, Buddhist missionaries sought to tailor their message to Chinese audiences. They explained Buddhist concepts in vocabulary borrowed from Chinese cultural traditions, particularly Daoism. They translated the Indian term *dharma* (the basic Buddhist doctrine) as *dao* ("the way" in the Daoist sense of the term), and they translated the Indian term *nirvana* (personal salvation that comes after an individual soul escapes from the cycle of incarnation) as *wuwei* (the Daoist ethic of noncompetition). While encouraging the establishment of monasteries and the observance of celibacy, they also recognized the validity of family life and offered Buddhism as a religion that would benefit the extended Chinese family: one son in the monastery, they taught, would bring salvation for ten generations of his kin.

**CHAN BUDDHISM**  The result was a syncretic faith, a Buddhism with Chinese characteristics. One of the more popular schools of Buddhism in China, for example, was the Chan (also known by its Japanese name, Zen). Chan Buddhists had little interest in written texts but, instead, emphasized sudden flashes of insight in their search for spiritual enlightenment. In that respect they resembled Daoists as much as they did Buddhists.

During the Tang and Song dynasties, this syncretic Buddhism became an immensely popular and influential faith in China. Monasteries appeared in all the major cities, and stupas dotted the Chinese landscape. The monk Xuanzang (602–664) was only one of many devout pilgrims who traveled to India to visit holy sites and learn about Buddhism

**COSMOPOLITAN SOCIETY.** | Foreign music and dance were very popular in the large cities of Tang China. This ceramic model depicts a troupe of musicians from southwest Asia performing on a platform mounted on a camel. Many such models survive from Tang times.

Boddhisattva Guide of Souls
www.mhhe.com/bentleybrief2e

Mount Wudang
www.mhhe.com/bentleybrief2e

**nirvana** (nuhr-VAH-nuh)

*wuwei* (woo-WAY)

**Chan Buddhism** (CHAHN BOO-diz'm)

in its homeland. Like Xuanzang, many of those pilgrims returned with copies of treatises that deepened the understanding of Buddhism in China. In the process, they played significant roles in establishing Buddhism as a popular faith in China.

**HOSTILITY TO BUDDHISM**  In spite of its popularity, Buddhism met determined resistance from Daoists and Confucians. Daoists resented the popular following of Buddhism, which resulted in diminished resources available for their own tradition. Confucians despised Buddhists' exaltation of celibacy, and they denounced the faith as an alien superstition.

**PERSECUTION**  During the late Tang dynasty, Daoist and Confucian critics of Buddhism found allies in the imperial court. Beginning in the 840s the Tang emperors ordered the closure of monasteries and the expulsion of Buddhists as well as Zoroastrians, Nestorian Christians, and Manichaeans. Yet Tang rulers did not implement the policy in a thorough way, and foreign faiths were not eradicated. Buddhism in particular enjoyed continued support that enabled it not only to survive but also to influence the development of Confucianism during the Song dynasty.

## Neo-Confucianism

The Song emperors did not persecute Buddhists, but they actively supported native Chinese cultural traditions in hopes of limiting the influence of foreign religions. They contributed particularly generously to the Confucian tradition by sponsoring the studies of Confucian scholars and subsidizing the printing and dissemination of Confucian writings.

**CONFUCIANS AND BUDDHISM**  Yet the Confucian tradition of the Song dynasty differed from that of earlier times. The earliest Confucians had concentrated resolutely on practical issues of politics and morality, since they were mainly concerned with establishing social order. Confucians of the Song dynasty studied the classic works of their tradition, but they also were inspired by many aspects of Buddhist thought. Indeed, Buddhism both offered a tradition of logical thought and argumentation and dealt with issues not systematically explored by Confucian thinkers, such as the nature of the soul. Because Confucian thought during the Song dynasty reflected the influence of Buddhism as well as original Confucian values, it has come to be known as neo-Confucianism.

**neo-Confucianism** (nee-oh-kuhn-FYEW-shuhn-iz'm)

**NEO-CONFUCIAN INFLUENCE** Neo-Confucianism ranks as an important cultural development for two reasons. First, it illustrates the deep influence of Buddhism in Chinese society. Even though the neo-Confucians rejected Buddhism as a faith, their writings adapted Buddhist themes and reasoning to Confucian interests and values. Second, neo-Confucianism influenced east Asian thought over a very long term. In China, neo-Confucianism enjoyed the status of an officially recognized creed from the Song dynasty until the early twentieth century, and in lands that fell within China's cultural orbit—particularly Korea, Vietnam, and Japan—neo-Confucianism shaped philosophical, political, and moral thought for half a millennium and more.

# CHINESE INFLUENCE IN EAST ASIA

**THINKING ABOUT** *Encounters*

**ENCOUNTERS IN THE RESURGENT EAST ASIAN EMPIRES.** The postclassical period in China was a time of intense cultural interaction with societies throughout Asia and beyond. In what ways did this interaction influence the long-term development of other east Asian societies in Korea, Vietnam, and Japan?

Like societies in Byzantium and the *dar al-Islam,* Chinese society influenced the development of neighboring lands during postclassical times. Chinese armies periodically invaded Korea and Vietnam, and Chinese merchants established commercial relations with Japan as well as with Korea and Vietnam. Chinese techniques of government and administration helped shape public life in all three lands, as did Chinese values and cultural traditions. By no means did these lands become absorbed into China: all maintained distinctive identities. Yet they also drew deep inspiration from Chinese examples and built societies that reflected their participation in a larger east Asian society revolving around China.

## Korea and Vietnam

During the Tang dynasty, Chinese imperial armies followed in the footsteps of the Qin and Han dynasties by mounting large-scale campaigns of expansion in both Korea and Vietnam. Although the two lands responded differently to Chinese imperial expansion, both borrowed Chinese political and cultural traditions and used them in their own societies.

**THE SILLA DYNASTY** In the seventh century, Tang armies conquered much of Korea before the native Silla dynasty rallied. Both Tang and Silla authorities preferred to avoid a long and costly conflict, so they agreed to a political compromise: Chinese forces withdrew from Korea, and the Silla king recognized the Tang emperor as his overlord.

Thus Korea entered into a tributary relationship with China. Envoys of the Silla kings regularly delivered gifts to Chinese emperors and performed the kowtow, but those concessions brought considerable benefits to the Koreans. In return for their recognition of Chinese supremacy, they received gifts more valuable than the tribute they delivered to China. Moreover, the tributary relationship opened the doors for Korean merchants to trade in China.

**CHINESE INFLUENCE IN KOREA** Meanwhile, the tributary relationship facilitated the spread of Chinese political and cultural influences to Korea. Korean rulers began to model their court along Chinese lines, and the Silla kings even built a new capital at Kumsong modeled on the Tang capital at Chang'an. Korean scholars went to China to study Chinese thought and literature and took copies of Chinese writings back to Korea. Their efforts helped to build elite Korean interest in the Confucian tradition, and Chinese schools of Buddhism attracted widespread popular interest.

China and Korea differed in many respects. Most notably, perhaps, aristocrats and royal houses dominated Korean society much more than in China. Although the Korean monarchy sponsored Chinese schools and a Confucian examination system, Korea never

Sokkuram Grotto
www.mhhe.com/
bentleybrief2e

**VIETNAMESE DANCER.**
This Tang dynasty pottery figure is testament to the fact that commercial and tributary relationships introduced southeast Asian performers to China. *Why might sophisticated urban communities in China have appreciated this kind of entertainment?*

Todaiji
www.mhhe.com/
bentleybrief2e

Shinto temple
www.mhhe.com/
bentleybrief2e

established a bureaucracy based on merit, and political initiative remained firmly in the hands of the ruling classes. Nevertheless, extensive dealings with its powerful neighbor ensured that Korea reflected the influence of Chinese political and cultural traditions.

CHINA AND VIETNAM    Chinese relations with Vietnam were far more tense than their relations with Korea. When Tang armies ventured into the land that Chinese called Nam Viet, they encountered spirited resistance on the part of the Viet people, who had settled in the region around the Red River. Tang forces soon won control of Viet towns and cities, and they launched efforts to absorb the Viets into Chinese society. The Viets readily adopted Chinese agricultural methods and irrigation systems as well as Chinese schools and administrative techniques. Like their Korean counterparts, Viet elites studied Confucian texts and took examinations based on a Chinese-style education, and Viet traders marketed their wares in China. Vietnamese authorities even entered into tributary relationships with the Chinese court. Yet the Viets resented Chinese efforts to dominate them, and they mounted a series of revolts against Tang authorities. As the Tang dynasty fell during the early tenth century, the Viets won their independence and successfully resisted later Chinese efforts at imperial expansion to the south.

Like Korea, Vietnam differed from China in many ways. Although Buddhism won a large popular following, many Vietnamese retained their indigenous religions in preference to Chinese cultural traditions. Women played a much more prominent role in Vietnamese society and economy than did their Chinese counterparts. Southeast Asian women had dominated local and regional markets for centuries, and they participated actively in business ventures closed to women in the more rigidly patriarchal society of China. Nevertheless, Chinese traditions found a place in the southern land. Indeed, like Korea, Vietnam absorbed political and cultural influence from China and reflected the development of a larger east Asian society centered on China.

# Early Japan

Chinese armies never invaded Japan, but Chinese traditions deeply influenced Japanese political and cultural development. The earliest inhabitants of Japan were nomadic peoples from northeast Asia. They migrated to Japan, perhaps across land bridges that formed during an ice age, about two hundred thousand years ago. Their language, material culture, and religion derived from their parent society in northeast Asia. Later migrants, who arrived in several waves from the Korean peninsula, introduced cultivation of rice, bronze and iron metallurgy, and horses into Japan. As the population of the Japanese islands grew and built a settled agricultural society, small states dominated by aristocratic clans emerged. By the middle of the first millennium C.E., several dozen states ruled small regions.

NARA JAPAN    The establishment of the powerful Sui and Tang dynasties in China had repercussions in Japan, where they suggested the value of centralized imperial government. One of the aristocratic clans in Japan insisted on its precedence over the others, although in fact it had never wielded effective authority outside its own territory in central Japan. Nevertheless, inspired by the Tang example, this clan claimed imperial authority and introduced a series of reforms designed to centralize Japanese politics. The imperial house established a court modeled on that of the Tang, instituted a Chinese-style bureaucracy, implemented an equal-field system, provided official support for Confucianism and Buddhism, and in the year 710 moved to a new capital city at Nara (near modern Kyoto) that was a replica of the Tang capital at Chang'an. Never was Chinese influence more prominent in Japan than during the Nara period (710–794 C.E.).

Yet Japan did not lose its distinctive characteristics. While adopting Confucian and Buddhist traditions from China, for example, the Japanese continued to observe the rites of Shinto, their indigenous religion, which revolved around the veneration of ancestors and a host of nature spirits and deities.

**HEIAN JAPAN**   The experiences of the Heian, Kamakura, and Muromachi periods clearly illustrate the distinctiveness of Japanese society. Under the Heian (794–1185 C.E.), local rulers on the island of Honshu mostly recognized the emperor as Japan's supreme political authority. Unlike their Chinese counterparts, however, Japanese emperors rarely ruled but, rather, served as ceremonial figureheads and symbols of authority. Effective power lay in the hands of the Fujiwara family, an aristocratic clan that controlled affairs from behind the throne through its influence over the imperial house and manipulation of its members. Indeed, since the Heian period the Japanese political order has almost continuously featured a split between a publicly recognized imperial authority and a separate agent of effective rule. This pattern helps to account for the remarkable longevity of the Japanese imperial house: because emperors have not ruled, they have not been subject to deposition during times of turmoil.

The cultural development of Heian Japan also reflected both the influence of Chinese traditions and the elaboration of peculiarly Japanese ways. Most literature imitated Chinese models and indeed was written in the Chinese language. Boys and young men who received a formal education in Heian Japan learned Chinese, read the classic works of China, and wrote in the foreign tongue. Officials at court conducted business and kept records in Chinese, and literary figures wrote histories and treatises in the style popular in China. Even Japanese writing reflected Chinese influence, since scholars borrowed many Chinese characters and used them to represent Japanese words. They also adapted some Chinese characters into a Japanese syllabic script, in which symbols represent whole syllables rather than a single sound, as in an alphabetic script.

**DECLINE OF HEIAN JAPAN**   In the late eleventh century, changes in the countryside brought an end to the Heian court. The equal-field system gradually fell into disuse, and aristocratic clans accumulated most of the islands' lands into vast estates. Two clans in particular—the Taira and the Minamoto—overshadowed the others. During the mid–twelfth century the two engaged in outright war, and in 1185 the Minamoto emerged victorious. Like the Fujiwara family, the Minamoto did not seek to abolish imperial authority in Japan but, rather, claimed to rule the land in the name of the emperor. They installed the clan leader as *shogun*—a military governor who ruled in place of the emperor—and established the seat of their government at Kamakura, near modern Tokyo, while the imperial court remained at Kyoto. For most of the next four centuries, one branch or another of the Minamoto clan dominated political life in Japan.

**POLITICAL DECENTRALIZATION**   In the Kamakura (1185–1333 C.E.) and Muromachi (1336–1573 C.E.) periods, Japanese society grew ever more distinctive. Indeed, Japan developed a decentralized political order in which provincial lords wielded effective power and authority in local regions where they controlled land and economic affairs. As these lords and their clans vied for power and authority in the countryside, they found little use for the Chinese-style bureaucracy that Nara and Heian rulers had instituted in Japan and still less use for the elaborate protocol and refined conduct that prevailed at the courts. In place of etiquette and courtesy, they valued military talent and discipline. The mounted warrior, the *samurai,* thus came to play the most distinctive role in Japanese political and military affairs.

**Shinto** (SHIHN-toh)

**Heian** (HAY-ahn)

**shogun** (SHOH-gun)

**samurai** (SAM-uhr-eye)

Thus, although it had taken its original inspiration from the Tang empire in China, the Japanese political order developed along lines different from those of the Middle Kingdom. Yet Japan clearly had a place in the larger east Asian society centered on China. Japan borrowed from China, among other things, Confucian values, Buddhist religion, a system of writing, and the ideal of centralized imperial rule. Though somewhat suppressed during later periods, these elements of Chinese society not only survived in Japan but also decisively influenced Japanese development over the long term.

# SUMMARY

The revival of centralized imperial rule in China had profound implications for all of east Asia and indeed for most of the eastern hemisphere. When the Sui and Tang dynasties imposed their authority throughout China, they established a powerful state that guided political affairs throughout east Asia. Tang armies extended Chinese influence to Korea, Vietnam, and central Asia. They did not invade Japan, but the impressive political organization of China prompted the islands' rulers to imitate Tang examples. Moreover, the Sui and Tang dynasties laid a strong political foundation for rapid economic development. Chinese society prospered throughout the postclassical era, partly because of technological and industrial innovation. Tang and Song prosperity touched all of China's neighbors, since it encouraged surging commerce in east Asia. Chinese silk, porcelain, and lacquerware were prized commodities among trading peoples from southeast Asia to east Africa. Chinese inventions such as paper, printing, gunpowder, and the magnetic compass found a place in societies throughout the eastern hemisphere as they diffused across the silk roads and sea-lanes. The postclassical era was an age of religious as well as commercial and technological exchanges: Nestorian Christians, Zoroastrians, Manichaeans, and Muslims all maintained communities in Tang China, and Buddhism became the most popular religious faith in all of east Asia. During the postclassical era, Chinese social organization and economic dynamism helped to sustain interactions between the peoples of the eastern hemisphere on an unprecedented scale.

# STUDY TERMS

Chan Buddhism (235)
equal-field system (226)
foot binding (231)
Grand Canal (225)
gunpowder (231)
Heian Japan (239)
Kamakura Japan (239)
Mahayana Buddhism (233)
Muromachi Japan (239)

Nam Viet (238)
Nara period (238)
neo-Confucianism (236)
nirvana (235)
paper money (233)
porcelain (231)
Shinto (239)
Silla dynasty (237)

Song dynasty (228)
Song Taizu (228)
Sui dynasty (224)
Sui Yangdi (225)
Tang dynasty (225)
tribute system (227)
*wuwei* (235)
Yang Jian (224)

Kenneth Ch'en. *Buddhism in China: A Historical Survey*. Princeton, 1964. A clear and detailed account by an eminent scholar.

Hugh R. Clark. *Community, Trade, and Networks: Southern Fujian Province from the Third to the Thirteenth Century*. Cambridge, 1991. Excellent scholarly study exploring the transformation of a region by trade and market forces.

Patricia Buckley Ebrey. *Chinese Civilization: A Sourcebook*. 2nd ed. New York, 1993. A splendid collection of documents in translation.

Mark Elvin. *The Pattern of the Chinese Past*. Stanford, 1973. A brilliant analysis of Chinese history, concentrating particularly on economic, social, and technological themes.

Jacques Gernet. *Daily Life in China on the Eve of the Mongol Invasion, 1250–1276*. Trans. by H. M. Wright. New York, 1962. Rich portrait of Southern Song China, emphasizing social history.

Peter D. Hershock. *Chan Buddhism*. Honolulu, 2005. An accessible introduction to Chan Buddhism focusing on far renowned masters.

Edward H. Schafer. *The Golden Peaches of Samarkand: A Study of T'ang Exotics*. Berkeley, 1963. Deals with relations between China and central Asian lands during the Tang dynasty.

H. Paul Varley. *Japanese Culture*. 4th ed. Honolulu, 2000. An authoritative analysis of Japanese cultural development from early times to the present.

Sally Hovey Wriggins. *Xuanzang: A Buddhist Pilgrim on the Silk Road*. Boulder, 1996. A fascinating and well-illustrated account of Xuanzang's journey to India and his influence on the development of Buddhism in China.

# India and the Indian Ocean Basin

## 13

Buzurg ibn Shahriyar was a tenth-century shipmaster from Siraf, a prosperous and bustling port city on the Persian Gulf coast. He probably sailed frequently to Arabia and India, and he may have ventured also to Malaya, the islands of southeast Asia, China, and east Africa. Like all sailors, he heard stories about the distant lands that mariners had visited, the different customs they observed, and the adventures that befell them during their travels. About 953 C.E. he compiled 136 such stories in his *Book of the Wonders of India*.

Buzurg's collection included a generous proportion of tall tales. He told of mermaids and sea dragons, of creatures born from human fathers and fish mothers, of serpents that ate cattle and elephants, of birds so large that they crushed houses, and of a talking lizard. Yet alongside the tall tales, many of Buzurg's stories accurately reflected the conditions of his time. One recounted the story of a king from northern India who converted to Islam and requested translations of Islamic law. Others reported on Hindu customs, shipwrecks, encounters with pirates, and slave trading.

Several of Buzurg's stories tempted readers with visions of vast wealth attainable through maritime trade. For example, Buzurg mentioned a Jewish merchant who left Persia penniless and returned from India and China with a shipload of priceless merchandise. Despite their embellishments, his stories faithfully reflected the trade networks that linked the lands surrounding the Indian Ocean in the tenth century. Although Buzurg clearly thought of India as a distinct land with its own customs, he also recognized a larger world of trade and communication that extended from east Africa to southeast Asia and beyond to China.

Just as China served as the principal inspiration of a larger east Asian society in the postclassical era, India influenced the development of a larger cultural zone in south and southeast Asia. Yet China and India played different roles in their respective spheres of influence. In east Asia, China was clearly the dominant power. In south and southeast Asia, however, there emerged no centralized imperial authority like the Tang dynasty in China. Indeed, although several states organized large regional kingdoms, no single state was able to extend its authority to all parts of the Indian subcontinent, much less to the mainland and islands of southeast Asia.

Though politically disunited, during the postclassical era India remained a coherent and distinct society as a result of powerful social and cultural traditions—especially the caste system and the Hindu religion. Beginning in the seventh century, Islam also began to attract a popular following in India, and after the eleventh century, Islam deeply influenced Indian society alongside the caste system and Hinduism.

❮ *Kabir, the blind guru, weaves cloth while discussing religious matters with disciples.*

# CHRONOLOGY

| | |
|---|---|
| 1st to 6th century | Kingdom of Funan |
| 606–648 | Reign of Harsha |
| 670–1025 | Kingdom of Srivijaya |
| 711 | Conquest of Sind by Umayyad forces |
| 850–1267 | Chola kingdom |
| 889–1431 | Kingdom of Angkor |
| 1001–1027 | Raids on India by Mahmud of Ghazni |
| 11th to 12th century | Life of Ramanuja |
| 12th century | Beginning of the bhakti movement |
| 1206–1526 | Sultanate of Delhi |
| 1336–1565 | Kingdom of Vijayanagar |

Beyond the subcontinent Indian traditions helped to shape a larger cultural zone extending to the mainland and islands of southeast Asia. Throughout most of the region, ruling classes adopted Indian forms of political organization and Indian techniques of statecraft. Indian merchants took their Hindu and Buddhist faiths to southeast Asia, where they attracted sustained interest. Somewhat later, Indian merchants also helped introduce Islam to southeast Asia.

While Indian traditions influenced the political and cultural development of southeast Asia, the entire Indian Ocean basin began to move toward economic integration during the postclassical era, as Buzurg ibn Shahriyar's stories suggest. Indeed, innovations in maritime technology, the development of a well-articulated network of sea-lanes, and the building of port cities enabled peoples living around the Indian Ocean to trade and communicate more actively than ever before. As a result, peoples from east Africa to southeast Asia and China increasingly participated in the larger economic, commercial, and cultural life of the Indian Ocean basin.

# ISLAMIC AND HINDU KINGDOMS

Like the Han and Roman empires, the Gupta dynasty came under severe pressure from nomadic invaders. From the mid–fourth to the mid–fifth century C.E., Gupta rulers resisted the pressures and preserved order throughout much of the Indian subcontinent. Beginning in 451 C.E., however, White Huns from central Asia invaded India, and by the mid–sixth century the Gupta state had collapsed. Effective political authority quickly devolved to invaders and independent regional power brokers. From the end of the Gupta dynasty until the sixteenth century, when a Turkish people known as the Mughals extended their authority to most of the subcontinent, India remained a politically divided land.

## *The Quest for Centralized Imperial Rule*

 **States of postclassical India** www .mhhe.com/ bentleybrief2e

Northern and southern India followed different political trajectories after the fall of the Gupta empire. In the north, local states contested for power and territory, and politics were turbulent and frequently violent. Nomadic Turkish-speaking peoples from central Asia contributed to this unsettled state of affairs by forcing their way into India. They eventually found niches for themselves in the caste system and became completely absorbed into Indian society. However, until processes of social absorption worked themselves out, the arrival of nomadic peoples caused additional disruption in northern India.

HARSHA   Even after the collapse of the Gupta dynasty, the ideal of centralized imperial rule did not entirely disappear. During the first half of the seventh century, King Harsha (reigned 606–648 C.E.) temporarily restored unified rule in most of northern India and sought to revive imperial authority. Using a massive military force from his kingdom in the lower Ganges valley, by about 612 Harsha had subdued those who refused to recognize his authority.

COLLAPSE OF HARSHA'S KINGDOM   Yet even though Harsha was young, energetic, and an able ruler, he was unable to restore permanent centralized rule. Local rulers had established their authority too securely in India's regions for Harsha to overcome them. Ultimately, he fell victim to an assassin and left no heir to maintain his realm. His empire immediately disintegrated, and local rulers once again turned northern India into a battleground as they sought to enlarge their realms at the expense of their neighbors.

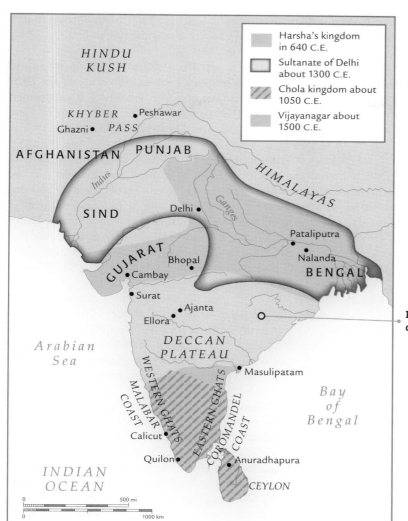

**MAP 13.1** | Major states of postclassical India, 600–1600 C.E. Several large rivers and river valleys offered opportunities for inhabitants of northern India. *How did peoples of southern India organize flourishing states and societies in the absence of major rivers?*

In the postclassical period, India was not dominated by one powerful state.

Map labels:
- Harsha's kingdom in 640 C.E.
- Sultanate of Delhi about 1300 C.E.
- Chola kingdom about 1050 C.E.
- Vijayanagar about 1500 C.E.

HINDU KUSH, KHYBER PASS, Peshawar, Ghazni, AFGHANISTAN, PUNJAB, HIMALAYAS, Indus, SIND, Delhi, Ganges, GUJARAT, Bhopal, Cambay, Pataliputra, Nalanda, BENGAL, Surat, Ajanta, Ellora, DECCAN PLATEAU, Arabian Sea, Masulipatam, WESTERN GHATS, MALABAR COAST, EASTERN GHATS, COROMANDEL COAST, Bay of Bengal, Calicut, Quilon, Anuradhapura, INDIAN OCEAN, CEYLON

0    500 mi
0    1000 km

# The Introduction of Islam to Northern India

**THE CONQUEST OF SIND**   Amid nomadic incursions and contests for power, northern India also experienced the arrival of Islam and the establishment of Islamic states. Islam reached India by several routes. One was military: Arab forces entered India as early as the mid–seventh century, although their first expeditions were exploratory ventures rather than campaigns of conquest. In 711, however, a well-organized expedition conquered Sind, the Indus River valley in northwestern India, and incorporated it as a province of the expanding Umayyad empire. At midcentury, along with most of the rest of the *dar al-Islam,* Sind passed into the hands of the Abbasid caliphs. Although political elites eventually took advantage of their distance from the centers of Islamic power to reassert their control over most of Sind, the region remained nominally under the jurisdiction of the caliphs until the collapse of the Abbasid dynasty in 1258.

**MERCHANTS AND ISLAM**   While conquerors brought Islam to Sind, Muslim merchants took their faith to coastal regions in both northern and southern India. Indeed, Muslims dominated trade and transportation networks between India and western lands from the seventh through the fifteenth century. Muslim merchants formed small communities in all the major cities of coastal India, where they played a prominent role in Indian business and commercial life. They frequently married local women, and in many cases they also found places for themselves in Indian society. Thus Islam entered India's port cities in a more gradual but no less effective way than was the case in Sind.

**TURKISH MIGRANTS AND ISLAM**    Islam also entered India by a third route: the migrations and invasions of Turkish-speaking peoples from central Asia. During the tenth century, several Turkish groups had become acquainted with Islam through their dealings with the Abbasid caliphate and had converted to the faith. Some of these Muslim Turks moved into Afghanistan, where they established an Islamic state.

**MAHMUD OF GHAZNI**    Mahmud of Ghazni, leader of the Turks in Afghanistan, soon turned his attention to the rich land to the south. Between 1001 and 1027 he mounted seventeen raiding expeditions into India. Taking advantage of infighting between local rulers, he annexed several states in northwestern India and the Punjab. For the most part, however, Mahmud had less interest in conquering India than in plundering the wealth stored in its many temples. Mahmud and his forces demolished hundreds of Hindu and Buddhist structures and frequently established mosques or Islamic shrines in their place. Not surprisingly, however, Mahmud's raids did not encourage Indians to turn to Islam.

**THE SULTANATE OF DELHI**    During the late twelfth century, Mahmud's successors mounted a more systematic campaign to conquer northern India and place it under Islamic rule. By the early thirteenth century, they had conquered most of the Hindu kingdoms in northern India and established an Islamic state known as the sultanate of Delhi. The sultans established their capital at Delhi, a strategic site controlling access from the Punjab to the Ganges valley, and they ruled northern India at least in name for more than three centuries, from 1206 to 1526.

During the fourteenth century the sultans of Delhi commanded an army of three hundred thousand, and their state ranked among the most powerful in the Islamic world. Yet for the most part, the authority of the sultans did not extend far beyond Delhi. They had no permanent bureaucracy or administrative apparatus. Even in their immediate domain, they imposed a thin veneer of Islamic political and military authority on a land populated mostly by Hindus, and they depended on the goodwill of Hindu kings to carry out their policies and advance their interests in local regions. They did not even enjoy comfortable control of their own court: of the thirty-five sultans of Delhi, nineteen were killed by assassins. Nevertheless, the sultans prominently sponsored Islam and helped to establish a secure place for their faith in the cultural landscape of India.

PSI img    Medieval fortress from the sultanate of Delhi, 14th C.
www.mhhe.com/bentleybrief2e

## *The Hindu Kingdoms of Southern India*

PSI img    Bronze statues from the Chola Dynasty
www.mhhe.com/bentleybrief2e

**THE CHOLA KINGDOM**    Although it too remained politically divided, the southern part of the Indian subcontinent largely escaped the invasions, chronic war, and turmoil that troubled the north. Most Hindu rulers in the south presided over small, loosely administered states and did not engage in prolonged or frequent conflicts. Two kingdoms, however, were able to expand enough to exercise at least nominal rule over much of southern India. The first was the Chola kingdom, situated in the deep south, which ruled the Coromandel coast for more than four centuries, from 850 to 1267 c.e. At its high point, during the eleventh century, Chola forces conquered Ceylon and parts of southeast Asia, and its navy dominated the waters from the South China Sea to the Arabian Sea.

Chola rulers did not build a tightly centralized state: they allowed considerable autonomy for local and village institutions as long as they maintained order and delivered tax revenues on time. By the twelfth century, however, revolts reduced the size and power of the Chola state, and it reverted to the status of one regional kingdom among many others in southern India.

**Mahmud of Ghazni** (mah-muhd of gahz-nee)

**Coromandel** (kawr-uh-MAN-dul)

THE KINGDOM OF VIJAYANAGAR    The second state that dominated much of southern India was the kingdom of Vijayanagar, based in the northern Deccan. The kingdom owed its origin to efforts by the sultans of Delhi to extend their authority to southern India. Officials in Delhi dispatched two brothers, Harihara and Bukka, to represent the sultan and implement court policies in the south. Although they had converted from their native Hinduism to Islam, Harihara and Bukka recognized an opportunity to establish themselves as independent rulers. In 1336 they renounced Islam and proclaimed the establishment of an independent empire of Vijayanagar (meaning "city of victory"). Indeed, the Hindu kingdom of Vijayanagar was the dominant state in southern India from the mid–fourteenth century until 1565, when it fell to Mughal conquerors from the north.

As in northern India, then, political division and conflict between states in southern India characterized its political history in postclassical times. India did not generate the sort of large-scale, centralized, imperial state that guided the fortunes of postclassical societies in the eastern Mediterranean, southwest Asia, or China. Nevertheless, on the basis of trade, common social structures, and inherited cultural traditions, a coherent and distinctive society flourished in postclassical India.

## THINKING ABOUT *Traditions*

**TRADITIONS IN INDIA AND THE INDIAN OCEAN BASIN.** Although Indian societies experienced much economic, social, and religious change during the postclassical period, they nevertheless remained culturally unified by particular social traditions. What were the most important of these traditions, and in what ways did they promote cultural unity?

# PRODUCTION AND TRADE IN THE INDIAN OCEAN BASIN

As in the Mediterranean, southwest Asia, and China, agricultural yields increased significantly in postclassical India, enabling large numbers of people to devote themselves to trade and manufacturing rather than the production of food. Trade forged links between the various regions of the subcontinent and fostered economic development in southern India. Trade also created links between India and distant lands, as merchants and manufacturers transformed the Indian Ocean basin into a vast zone of communication and exchange. Yet even though the increasing prominence of trade and industry brought change to Indian society, caste identities and loyalties also remained strong, and the caste system continued to serve as the most powerful organizing feature of Indian society.

**Vijayanagar** (vih-juh-yuh-NUH-guhr)

**ELEPHANT STABLES IN VIJAYANAGAR.** | The kings of Vijayanagar endowed their capital with splendid buildings and even provided these handsome domed stables for their elephants. *Why would the kings have invested so much in the construction of these stables?*

# Agriculture in the Monsoon World

**MONSOONS**  Because of the rhythms of the monsoons, irrigation was essential for the maintenance of a large, densely populated, agricultural society. During the spring and summer, warm, moisture-laden winds from the southwest bring most of India's rainfall. During the autumn and winter, cool and very dry winds blow from the northeast. To achieve their agricultural potential, Indian lands required a good watering by the southern monsoon, supplemented by irrigation during the dry months. Light rain during the spring and summer months or short supplies of water for irrigation commonly led to drought, reduced harvests, and widespread famine.

**IRRIGATION SYSTEMS**  In northern India, large rivers and plentiful surface water provided abundant opportunities to build irrigation systems. Indeed, irrigation had been a fixture of the countryside in northern India since Harappan times. For the most part, however, southern India is an arid land without rivers that can serve as sources for large-scale irrigation. Thus, as southern India became more densely populated, irrigation systems became crucial. Dams, reservoirs, canals, wells, and tunnels appeared in large numbers. Particularly impressive were monumental reservoirs lined with brick or stone that captured the rains of the spring and summer months and held them until the dry season, when canals carried them to thirsty fields. Projects of this size required enormous investments of human energy, both for their original construction and for continuing maintenance, but they led to significant increases in agricultural productivity.

**POPULATION GROWTH**  As a result of this increased productivity, India's population grew steadily throughout the postclassical era. In 600 C.E., shortly after the fall of the Gupta dynasty, the subcontinent's population stood at about 53 million. By 1000 it had grown 45 percent, to 79 million. During the following centuries the rate of growth slowed, but it took off again about 1500. By 1500, the population of the subcontinent had reached 105 million.

**URBANIZATION**  This demographic surge encouraged the concentration of people in cities. During the fourteenth century, the high point of the sultanate of Delhi, the capital city had a population of about four hundred thousand, which made it second only to Cairo among Muslim cities. Many other cities—particularly ports and trading centers such as Cambay, Surat, Calicut, Quilon, and Masulipatam—had populations well over one hundred thousand.

# Trade and the Economic Development of Southern India

Political fragmentation of the subcontinent did not prevent robust trade between the different states and regions of India. As the population grew, opportunities for specialized work became more numerous. Increased trade was a natural result of this process.

**INTERNAL TRADE**  Most regions of the Indian subcontinent were self-sufficient in staple foods such as rice, wheat, barley, and millet. The case was different, however, with metals, salt, and specialized crops that grew well only in certain regions. Iron came mostly from the Ganges River valley near Bengal, copper mostly from the Deccan Plateau, salt

**Surat** (soo-RAHT)

**Quilan** (kee-yawn)

**Masulipatam** (mahsu-lih-pah-tahm)

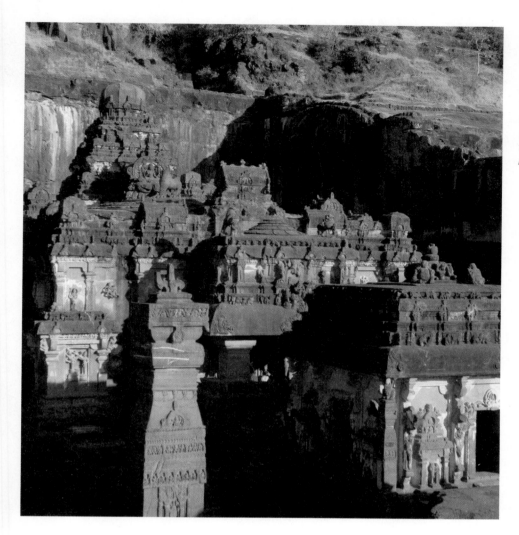

**TEMPLE AT ELLORA.**
During the eighth century c.e., workers carved a massive temple out of sheer rock at Ellora in central India. Temple communities like the one that grew up at Ellora controlled enormous resources in postclassical India. *Why did these temple communities control so many resources?*

mostly from coastal regions, and pepper from southern India. These and other commodities sometimes traveled long distances to consumers in remote parts of the subcontinent.

Southern India and Ceylon benefited especially handsomely from this trade. As invasions and conflicts disrupted northern India, southern regions experienced rapid economic development. The Chola kingdom provided relative stability in the south, and Chola expansion in southeast Asia opened markets for Indian merchants and producers.

**TEMPLES AND SOCIETY**   The Chola rulers allowed considerable autonomy to their subjects, and the towns and villages of southern India largely organized their own affairs. Public life revolved around Hindu temples, which organized agricultural activities, coordinated work on irrigation systems, and maintained reserves of surplus production for use in times of need. Temples often possessed large tracts of agricultural land, and they sometimes employed hundreds of people. To meet their financial obligations to employees, temple administrators collected a portion of the agricultural yield from lands subject to temple authority.

Temple at Mamallapuram
www.mhhe.com/
bentleybrief2e

Administrators were also responsible for keeping order in their communities and delivering tax receipts to the Cholas and other political authorities. In addition, temple authorities served as bankers, made loans, and invested in commercial and business ventures. They also frequently cooperated with the leaders of merchant guilds in seeking commercial opportunities to exploit. Temples thus grew prosperous and became crucial to the economic health of southern India.

## Cosmas Indicopleustes on Trade in Southern India

*Cosmas Indicopleustes was a Christian monk from Egypt who lived during the sixth century C.E. and traveled widely throughout north Africa and southwest Asia. On one of his trips, he ventured as far as India and Ceylon, which he described at some length in a work titled* The Christian Topography. *Cosmas's account clearly shows that sixth-century India and Ceylon played prominent roles in the larger economy of the Indian Ocean basin.*

Ceylon lies on the other side of the pepper country [southern India]. Around it are numerous small islands all having fresh water and coconut trees. They nearly all have deep water close up to their shores. . . . Ceylon is a great market for the people in those parts. The island also has a church of Persian Christians who have settled there, and a priest who is appointed from Persia, and a deacon and a complete ecclesiastical ritual. But the natives and their kings are heathens. . . .

Since the island of Ceylon is in a central position, it is much frequented by ships from all parts of India and from Persia and Ethiopia, and it likewise sends out many of its own. And from the remotest countries—I mean China and other trading places—it receives silk, aloes, cloves, sandalwood, and other products, and these again are passed on to markets on this side, such as Male [the western coast of southern India], where pepper grows, and to Calliana [a port city near modern Bombay], which exports copper and sesame logs and cloth for making dresses, for it also is a great place of business. And also to Sind [Gujarat], where musk and castor and spice are procured, and to Persia and the Homerite country [Anatolia], and to Adule [in Ethiopia]. And this island [Ceylon] receives imports from all these markets that we have mentioned and passes them on to the remoter ports, while at the same time exporting its own produce in both directions. . . .

The kings of various places in India keep elephants. . . . They may have six hundred each, or five hundred, some more, some fewer. Now the king of Ceylon gives a good price both for the elephants and for the horses that he has. The elephants he pays for by the cubit [a unit of measurement equivalent to about half a meter or twenty inches]. For the height is measured from the ground, and the price is reckoned at so many gold coins for each cubit—fifty [coins] it may be, or a hundred, or even more. Horses they bring to him from Persia, and he buys them, exempting the importers of them from paying custom duties. The kings of the Indian subcontinent tame their elephants, which are caught wild, and employ them in war.

■ Why did Ceylon become such an important location for Indian Ocean trade?

SOURCE: Cosmas Indicopleustes. *The Christian Topography of Cosmas, an Egyptian Monk.* Trans. by J. W. McCrindle. London: Hakluyt Society, 1897, pp. 364–72. (Translation slightly modified.)

## Cross-Cultural Trade in the Indian Ocean Basin

Indian prosperity sprang partly from the productivity of Indian society, but it depended also on the vast wealth that circulated in the commercial world of the Indian Ocean basin. Trade in the Indian Ocean was not new in postclassical times: Indian merchants had already ventured to southeast Asia during the classical era, and they dealt regularly with mariners from the Roman empire who traveled to India in search of pepper. During the postclassical era, however, larger ships and improved commercial organization supported a dramatic surge in the volume and value of trade in the Indian Ocean basin.

As larger, more stable ships came into use, mariners increasingly entrusted their crafts and cargoes to the reasonably predictable monsoons and sailed directly across the Arabian Sea and the Bay of Bengal. In the age of sail, however, it was impossible to make a round trip across the entire Indian Ocean without spending months at distant ports waiting for the winds to change, so merchants usually conducted their trade in stages.

EMPORIA   Because India stood in the middle of the Indian Ocean basin, it was a natural site for emporia and warehouses. Merchants coming from east Africa or Persia exchanged their cargoes at Cambay, Calicut, or Quilon for goods to take back west with the winter monsoon. Mariners from China or southeast Asia called at Indian ports and traded their cargoes for goods to ship east with the summer monsoon. Indeed, because of their central location, Indian ports became the principal clearinghouses of trade in the Indian Ocean basin, and they became remarkably cosmopolitan centers. Hindus, Buddhists, Muslims, Jews, and others who inhabited the Indian port cities did business with counterparts from all over the eastern hemisphere.

Particularly after the establishment of the Umayyad and Abbasid dynasties in southwest Asia and the Tang and Song dynasties in China, trade in the Indian Ocean surged. Generally, Arabs and Persians dominated the carrying trade between India and points west. During the Song dynasty, Chinese junks also ventured into the western Indian Ocean and called at ports as far away as east Africa. To the east, in the Bay of Bengal and the China seas, Malay and Chinese vessels were most prominent.

SPECIALIZED PRODUCTION    As the volume of trade in the Indian Ocean basin increased, lands around the ocean began to engage in specialized production of commodities for the commercial market. Indian artisans, for example, built thriving local industries around the production of high-quality cotton textiles. These industries influenced the structure of the Indian economy: they created a demand for specific agricultural products, provided a livelihood for thousands of artisans, and enabled consumers to import goods from elsewhere in the Indian Ocean basin.

Other lands concentrated on the production of different manufactured goods and agricultural commodities: China produced silk, porcelain, and lacquerware; southeast Asian lands provided fine spices; incense, horses, and dates came from southwest Asia; and east Africa contributed gold, ivory, and slaves. Thus trade encouraged specialized production

**Note India's central position in the Indian Ocean basin.**

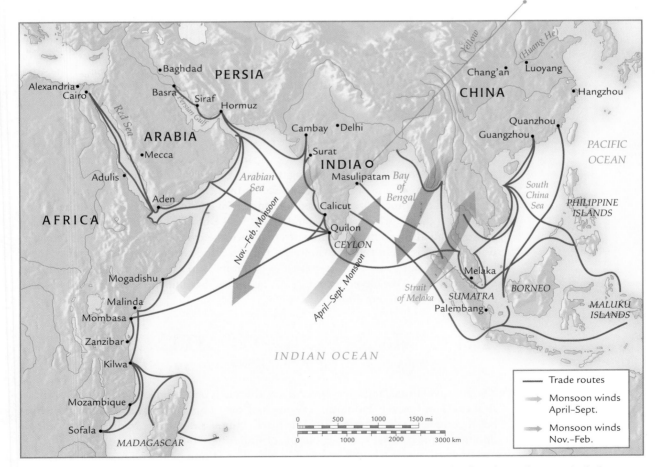

MAP 13.2 | The trading world of the Indian Ocean basin, 600–1600 C.E. Note the directions of seasonal winds in the Indian Ocean basin. *How would mariners take advantage of these winds to reach their destinations?*

and economic development in all lands participating in the trade networks of the Indian Ocean: cross-cultural trade in postclassical times influenced the structure of economies and societies throughout much of the eastern hemisphere.

## Caste and Society

The political, economic, and social changes of the postclassical era brought a series of challenges for India's caste system. Migrations, the growing prominence of Islam, economic development, and urbanization all placed pressures on the caste system as it had developed during the Vedic and classical eras. But the caste system has never been a rigid, unchanging structure. Rather, individuals and groups have continuously adjusted it and adapted it to new circumstances. Adjustments and adaptations of the postclassical era resulted in a caste system that was more complex than in earlier ages and that also extended its geographic reach deeper into southern India than ever before. In the absence of strong central governments, the caste system helped maintain order in local communities by providing guidance on individuals' roles in society and their relationships with others.

CASTE AND MIGRATION    The caste system closely reflected changes in Indian society. It adapted to the arrival of migrants, for example, and helped to integrate them into Indian society. As Turkish peoples or Muslim merchants pursued opportunities in India, they gained recognition as distinct groups under the umbrella of the caste system. They established codes of conduct both for the regulation of behavior within their own groups and for guidance in dealing with members of other castes. Within a few generations their descendants had become absorbed into Indian society.

CASTE AND SOCIAL CHANGE    The caste system also accommodated the social changes brought about by trade and economic development. Even before the postclassical era, individuals tended to identify most closely with their *jati* (subcastes), which were usually organized by occupation. In postclassical times, as merchants and manufacturers became increasingly important in the larger economy, they organized powerful workers' guilds to represent their interests. These guilds, however, were largely incorporated into the caste system as distinct *jati*. Thus merchants specializing in particular types of commerce, such as the silk, cotton, or spice trade, established themselves as subcastes, as did artisans working in particular industries, such as the iron, steel, or leather business.

EXPANSION OF THE CASTE SYSTEM    Besides becoming more complex, the caste system also extended its geographic reach. Caste distinctions first became prominent in northern India following the Aryan migrations. During the postclassical era, the caste system became securely established in southern India as well. Economic development aided this process by encouraging commercial relationships between southern merchants and their caste-conscious counterparts in the north. The emergence of merchant and craft guilds in southern regions strengthened the caste system, since guild members usually organized as a subcaste. Powerful temples also fostered caste distinctions, largely because of the influence of caste-conscious brahmins who supervised temple activities. As a result, by about the eleventh century C.E., caste had become the principal basis of social organization in southern India.

# THE MEETING OF HINDU AND ISLAMIC TRADITIONS

The Indian cultural landscape underwent a thorough transformation during the postclassical era. Jainism and Buddhism lost much of their popular following, although neither belief completely disappeared. In their place, Hindu and Islamic traditions increasingly dominated the cultural and religious life of India after 1000 C.E.

Hinduism and Islam differed profoundly. The Hindu pantheon made places for numerous gods and spirits, for example, whereas Islamic theology stood on the foundation of a firm and uncompromising monotheism. Yet both religions attracted large popular followings throughout the subcontinent, with Hinduism predominating in southern India and Islam in the north.

## The Development of Hinduism

Toward the end of the first millennium C.E., Buddhism flourished in east Asia, central Asia, and parts of southeast Asia but came under great pressure in India. Like Mahayana Buddhism, both Hinduism and Islam promised salvation to devout individuals, and they gradually attracted Buddhists to their own communities. Invasions of India by Turkish peoples also hastened the decline of Buddhism because the invaders looted and destroyed Buddhist stupas and shrines. In 1196 Muslim forces overran the Buddhist schools in the city of Nalanda, torched the libraries, and killed or exiled thousands of monks. Buddhism soon became a minor faith in the land of its birth.

**VISHNU AND SHIVA** Hinduism benefited from the decline of Buddhism. One reason for the increasing popularity of Hinduism was the remarkable growth of devotional cults, particularly those dedicated to Vishnu and Shiva, two of the most important deities in the Hindu pantheon. Vishnu was the preserver of the world, a god who observed the universe from the heavens and who occasionally entered the world in human form to resist evil or communicate his teachings. In contrast, Shiva was both a god of fertility and a destructive deity: he brought life but also took it away when its season had passed.

**DEVOTIONAL CULTS** Hindus embraced the new cults warmly because they promised salvation. Devotional cults became especially popular in southern India, where individuals or family groups went to great lengths to honor their chosen deities. Often cults originated when individuals identified Vishnu or Shiva with a local spirit or deity associated with a particular region or a prominent geographic feature. By venerating images of Vishnu or Shiva, offering them food and drink, and meditating on the deities and their qualities, Hindus hoped to achieve a mystic union with the gods that would bring grace and salvation.

**SHANKARA** The significance of Hinduism extended well beyond popular religion: it also influenced philosophy. Just as Buddhism, Christianity, and Islam influenced moral thought and philosophy in other lands, devotional Hinduism guided the efforts of the most prominent philosophers in postclassical India. Brahmin philosophers such as Ramanuja took the Upanishads as a point of departure for subtle reasoning and sophisticated metaphysics. Ramanuja, a devotee of Vishnu who was active during the eleventh and early twelfth centuries C.E., believed that genuine bliss came from salvation and identification of individuals with their gods. He followed the *Bhagavad Gita* in recommending intense devotion to Vishnu, and he taught that by placing themselves in the hands of Vishnu, devotees would win the god's grace and live forever in his presence. Thus, Ramanuja's

**SHIVA.** | Southern Indian artists often portrayed Shiva in bronze sculptures as a four-armed lord of dancers. In this figure from the Chola dynasty, Shiva crushes with his foot a dwarf demon symbolizing ignorance. One hand holds a bell to awaken his devotees, another bears the fire used by Shiva as creator and destroyer of the world, and a third gestures Shiva's benevolence toward his followers.

Vishnu dreaming the universe
www.mhhe.com/bentleybrief2e

**Buddhism** (BOO-diz'm)

**Vishnu** (VIHSH-noo)

**Shiva** (SHIH-vuh)

**Bhagavad Gita** (BUHG-uh-vuhd gee-tah)

philosophy pointed toward a Hindu theology of salvation. Indeed, his thought inspired the development of devotional cults throughout India, and it serves even today as a philosophical foundation for Hindu popular religion.

## Islam and Its Appeal

The Islamic faith did not attract much immediate interest among Indians when it arrived in the subcontinent. It won gradual acceptance in merchant communities where foreign Muslim traders took local spouses and found a place in Indian society. Elsewhere, however, circumstances did not favor its adoption, since it often arrived with conquering peoples. Muslim conquerors generally reserved important political and military positions for their Arab, Persian, and Turkish companions. Only rarely did they allow Indians—even those who had converted to Islam—to hold sensitive posts. Because of that policy, conquerors offered little incentive for Indians to convert to Islam.

CONVERSION TO ISLAM  Gradually, however, many Indians converted to Islam. By 1500 C.E. Indian Muslims numbered perhaps twenty-five million—about one-quarter of the subcontinent's population. Some Indians adopted Islam in hopes of improving their positions in society: Hindus of lower castes, for example, hoped to escape discrimination by converting to a faith that recognized the equality of all believers. In fact, Hindus rarely improved their social standing by conversion. Often members of an entire caste or subcaste adopted Islam en masse, and after conversion they continued to play the same social and economic roles that they had before.

SUFIS  In India as elsewhere, the most effective agents of conversion to Islam were Sufi mystics. Sufis encouraged a personal, emotional, devotional approach to Islam. They did not insist on fine points of doctrine, and they sometimes even permitted their followers to observe rituals or venerate spirits not recognized by the Islamic faith. Because of their piety and sincerity, however, Sufi missionaries attracted individuals searching for a faith that could provide comfort and meaning for their personal lives. Thus, like Hinduism, Indian Islam emphasized piety and devotion. Even though Hinduism and Islam were profoundly different religions, they encouraged the cultivation of similar spiritual values that transcended the social and cultural boundary lines of postclassical India.

THE BHAKTI MOVEMENT  In some ways the gap between Hinduism and Islam narrowed in postclassical India because both religions drew on long-established and long-observed cultural traditions. Sufis, for example, often attracted schools of followers in the manner of Indian gurus, spiritual leaders who taught Hindu values to disciples who congregated around them. Even more important was the development of the *bhakti* movement, a cult of love and devotion that ultimately sought to erase the distinction between Hinduism and Islam. The bhakti movement emerged in southern India during the twelfth century, and it originally encouraged a traditional piety and devotion to Hindu values. As the movement spread to the north, bhakti leaders increasingly encountered Muslims and became deeply attracted to certain Islamic values, especially monotheism and the notion of spiritual equality of all believers. Eventually, the bhakti movement rejected the exclusive features of both Hinduism and Islam, and some believers taught that Shiva, Vishnu, and Allah were all manifestations of a single, universal deity. The bhakti movement did not succeed in harmonizing Hinduism and Islam. Nevertheless, like the Sufis, bhakti teachers promoted values that helped build bridges between India's social and cultural communities.

**Sufis** (SOO-fees)
**bhakti** (BHUK-tee)

# THE INFLUENCE OF INDIAN SOCIETY IN SOUTHEAST ASIA

Just as China stood at the center of a larger east Asian society, India served as the principal source of political and cultural traditions widely observed throughout south and southeast Asia. For a millennium and more, southeast Asian peoples adapted Indian political structures and religions to local needs and interests. Although Indian armed forces rarely ventured into the region, southeast Asian lands reflected the influence of Indian society, as merchants introduced Hinduism, Buddhism, Sanskrit writings, and Indian forms of political organization. Beginning about the twelfth century, Islam also found solid footing in southeast Asia, as Muslim merchants, many of them Indians, established trading communities in the important port cities of the region. Over the next five hundred years, Islam attracted a sizable following and became a permanent feature in much of southeast Asia.

## The States of Southeast Asia

**INDIAN INFLUENCE IN SOUTHEAST ASIA**   Indian merchants visited the islands and mainland of southeast Asia from an early date, perhaps as early as 500 B.C.E. By the early centuries C.E., they had become familiar figures throughout southeast Asia, and their presence brought opportunities for the native ruling elites of the region. In exchange for spices and exotic products, Indian merchants brought textiles, beads, gold, silver, and manufactured metal goods. Southeast Asian rulers used the profits from this trade to consolidate their political control.

Meanwhile, southeast Asian ruling elites became acquainted with Indian political and cultural traditions. Without necessarily giving up their own traditions, they borrowed Indian forms of political organization and accepted Indian religious faiths. On the model of Indian states, for example, they adopted kingship as the principal form of political authority, and they surrounded themselves with courts featuring administrators and rituals similar to those found in India.

Ruling elites also sponsored the introduction of Hinduism or Buddhism—sometimes both—into their courts. They embraced Indian literature such as the *Ramayana* and the *Mahabharata,* which promoted Hindu values, as well as treatises that explained Buddhist views of the world. At the same time, however, they did not show much enthusiasm for the Indian caste system and continued to acknowledge the deities and nature spirits that southeast Asian peoples had venerated for centuries.

**FUNAN**   The first state known to have incorporated Indian influence into its own traditions was Funan, which dominated the lower reaches of the Mekong River (including parts of modern Cambodia and Vietnam) between the first and the sixth centuries C.E. Funan grew enormously wealthy because it dominated the Isthmus of Kra, the narrow portion of the Malay peninsula where merchants transported trade goods between China and India. (The short portage enabled them to avoid a long voyage around the Malay peninsula.) The rulers of Funan used the profits from this trade to construct an elaborate irrigation system that supported a highly productive agricultural economy in the Mekong delta.

As trade with India became an increasingly important part of Funan's economy, the ruling classes adopted Indian political, cultural, and religious traditions. They took the Sanskrit term *raja* ("king") for themselves and claimed divine sanction for their rule in the manner of Hindu rulers in India. They established positions for administrators and bureaucrats such as those found at Indian courts and conducted official business in

**Isthmus of Kra** (ihs-muhs of krah)

## THINKING ABOUT *Encounters*

**ENCOUNTERS IN INDIA AND THE INDIAN OCEAN BASIN.** During the post-classical period, Indian societies became critical players in the vast trading networks that crisscrossed the Indian Ocean basin. Why did these trading relationships encourage other societies, particularly in southeast Asia, to adopt Indian social, religious, and political structures? How did these adoptions shape the development of southeast Asian societies?

Sanskrit. They introduced Indian ceremonies and rituals and worshiped Vishnu, Shiva, and other Hindu deities. They continued to honor local deities, but they eagerly welcomed Hinduism, which offered additional recognition and divine legitimacy for their rule. At first, Indian cultural and religious traditions were most prominent and most often observed at ruling courts. Over the longer term, however, those traditions extended well beyond ruling elites and won a secure place in southeast Asian society.

SRIVIJAYA    During the sixth century C.E., a bitter power struggle weakened Funan internally, and by late century it had passed into oblivion. After the fall of Funan, political leadership in southeast Asia passed to the kingdom of Srivijaya (670–1025 C.E.) based on the island of Sumatra. The kings of Srivijaya built a powerful navy and controlled commerce in southeast Asian waters. They compelled port cities in southeast Asia to recognize their authority, and they financed their navy and bureaucracy from taxes levied on ships passing through the region. They maintained an all-sea trade route between China and India, eliminating the need for the portage of trade goods across the Isthmus of Kra. As the volume of trade with India increased in the postclassical era, the rulers of Srivijaya—like the rulers of Funan—borrowed heavily from Indian cultural traditions. Unlike their

raja (RAH-juh)

Srivijaya (sree-vih-JUH-yuh)

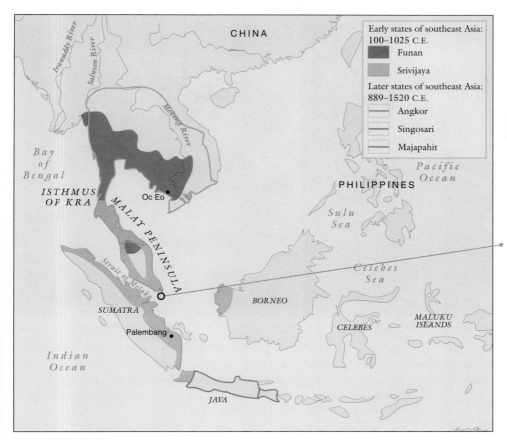

MAP 13.3 | Major states of southeast Asia between about 100 and 1520 C.E. Notice the strategic location of these southeast Asian states on the trade routes between China to the east and India to the west. *How might this have affected the development of states in southeast Asia?*

Most postclassical southeast Asian states grew powerful as a result of their position between China and India.

counterparts in Funan, however, the rulers of Srivijaya were most attracted to the teachings and practices associated with Buddhism. The Srivijaya kingdom prospered on the fruits of the Indian Ocean trade until the expansive Chola kingdom of southern India eclipsed it in the eleventh century. In the process, Srivijaya played an important role in facilitating cultural exchange in the Indian Ocean world.

With the decline of Srivijaya, the kingdoms of Angkor (889–1431 C.E.), Singosari (1222–1292 C.E.), and Majapahit (1293–1520 C.E.) dominated affairs in southeast Asia. Whereas Angkor had its base in Cambodia, Singosari and Majapahit were island states based on Java. Angkor made deep commitments to Buddhism; Majapahit was largely a Hindu state. Singosari represented a unique blend of Indian and indigenous traditions. Indeed, at the court of Singosari, religious authorities fashioned a cultural blend of Hindu, Buddhist, and indigenous values. Sculptures at the Singosari court depicted Hindu and Buddhist personalities, for example, but used them to honor local deities and natural spirits rather than Indian deities.

ANGKOR    The magnificent monuments of Angkor testify eloquently to the influence of Indian traditions in southeast Asia. Beginning in the ninth century, the kings of the Khmers began to build a capital city at Angkor Thom. With the aid of brahmin advisors from India, the kings designed the city as a microcosmic reflection of the Hindu world order. At the center, they built a temple representing the Himalayan Mount Meru, the sacred abode of Shiva, and surrounded it with numerous smaller temples representing other parts of the Hindu universe.

Angkor Wat
www.mhhe.com/
bentleybrief2e

**Angkor** (AHN-kohr)

**Singosari** (sihng-oh-sah-ree)

**Majapahit** (mah-jah-PAH-hit)

**BUDDHIST TEMPLE CARVING.** | Maritime trade flourished in southeast Asia during postclassical times. This ninth-century relief carving from the Buddhist temple at Borobodur in Java depicts a typical southeast Asian ship.

As the Khmers turned to Buddhism during the twelfth and thirteenth centuries, they added Buddhist temples to the complex, though without removing the earlier structures inspired by Hinduism. The entire complex formed a square with sides of about three kilometers (two miles), surrounded by a moat filled from the nearby Tonle Sap River. During the twelfth century the Khmer kings constructed a smaller but even more elaborate temple center at Angkor Wat, about one kilometer (just over half a mile) from Angkor Thom.

The Khmers abandoned Angkor in 1431 after Thai peoples invaded the capital and left much of it in ruins. Soon the jungle reclaimed both Angkor Thom and Angkor Wat, which remained largely forgotten until French missionaries and explorers rediscovered the sites in the mid–nineteenth century. Today the temple complexes of Angkor stand as vivid reminders of the influence of Indian political, cultural, and religious traditions in southeast Asia.

## The Arrival of Islam

Muslim merchants had ventured into southeast Asia by the eighth century, but only during the tenth century did they become prominent in the region. Some came from southern Arabia or Persia, but most were Indians from Gujarat or the port cities of southern India. Thus Indian influence helped to establish Islam as well as Hinduism and Buddhism in southeast Asia.

CONVERSION TO ISLAM   For several centuries Islam maintained a quiet presence in southeast Asia. Small communities of foreign merchants observed their faith in the port cities of the region but attracted little interest on the part of the native inhabitants. Gradually, however, ruling elites, traders, and others who had regular dealings with foreign Muslims became interested in the faith.

Like Hinduism and Buddhism, Islam did not enter southeast Asia as an exclusive faith. Ruling elites who converted to Islam often continued to honor Hindu, Buddhist, or native southeast Asian traditions. They adopted Islam less as an absolute creed than as a faith that facilitated their dealings with foreign Muslims and provided additional divine sanction for their rule. Rarely did they push their subjects to convert to Islam, although they allowed Sufi mystics to preach their faith before popular audiences. As in India, Sufis in southeast Asia appealed to a large public because of their reputation for sincerity and holiness. They allowed converts to retain inherited customs while adapting the message of Islam to local needs and interests.

MELAKA   During the fifteenth century the spread of Islam gained momentum in southeast Asia, largely because the powerful state of Melaka sponsored the faith throughout the region. Founded during the late fourteenth century by Paramesvara, a rebellious prince from Sumatra, Melaka took advantage of its strategic location in the Strait of Melaka, near modern Singapore, and soon became prominent in the trading world of southeast Asia. By the mid–fifteenth century, Melaka had built a substantial navy that patrolled the waters of southeast Asia and protected the region's sea-lanes. Melakan fleets compelled ships to call at the port, where ruling authorities levied taxes on the value of their cargoes. Thus, like southeast Asian states of earlier centuries, Melaka became a powerful state through the control of maritime trade.

In one respect, though, Melaka differed significantly from the earlier states. Although it began as a Hindu state, Melaka soon became predominantly Islamic. About the mid–fifteenth century the Melakan ruling class converted to Islam. It welcomed theologians, Sufis, and other Islamic authorities to Melaka and sponsored missionary campaigns to spread Islam throughout southeast Asia. By the end of the fifteenth century, mosques had begun to define the urban landscapes of Java, Sumatra, and the Malay peninsula, and Islam had made its first appearance in the spice-bearing islands of Maluku and in the southern islands of the Philippine archipelago.

Thus, within several centuries of its arrival, Islam was a prominent feature in the cultural landscape of southeast Asia. Along with Hinduism and Buddhism, Islam helped link southeast Asian lands to the larger cultural world of India and to the larger commercial world of the Indian Ocean basin.

**Melaka** (may-LAHK-kah)

## SUMMARY

With respect to political organization, India differed from postclassical societies in China, southwest Asia, and the eastern Mediterranean basin: it did not experience a return of centralized imperial rule such as that provided by the Tang and Song dynasties, the Umayyad and Abbasid dynasties, and the Byzantine empire. In other respects, however, India's development was similar to that of other postclassical societies. Increased agricultural production fueled population growth and urbanization, while trade encouraged specialized industrial production and rapid economic growth. The vigorous and voluminous commerce of the Indian Ocean basin influenced the structure of economies and societies from east Asia to east Africa. It brought prosperity especially to India, which not only contributed cotton, pepper, sugar, iron, steel, and other products to the larger hemispheric economy but also served as a major clearinghouse of trade. Like contemporary societies, postclassical India experienced cultural change, and Indian traditions deeply influenced the cultural development of other lands. Hinduism and Islam emerged as the two most popular religious faiths within the subcontinent, and Indian merchants helped to establish Hinduism, Buddhism, and Islam in southeast Asian lands. Throughout the postclassical era, India participated fully in the larger hemispheric zone of cross-cultural communication and exchange.

# STUDY TERMS

Angkor (257)
Angkor Thom (257)
Angkor Wat (258)
bhakti movement (254)
Buddhism (253)
caste system (252)
Chola kingdom (246)
Funan (255)

Gupta dynasty (244)
irrigation systems (248)
*jati* (252)
King Harsha (244)
Mahmud of Ghazni (246)
Majapahit (257)
Melaka (259)
Ramanuja (253)

Shiva (253)
Singosari (257)
Srivijaya (256)
Sufis (254)
Sultanate of Delhi (246)
Vijayanagar Kingdom (247)
Vishnu (253)

# FOR FURTHER READING

Aziz Ahmad. *Studies in Islamic Culture in the Indian Environment.* Oxford, 1964. A scholarly analysis of the arrival of Islam and its effects in India.

Buzurg ibn Shahriyar. *The Book of the Wonders of India: Mainland, Sea and Islands.* Trans. by G. S. P. Freeman-Grenville. London, 1981. Stories and tall tales of a tenth-century mariner who sailed frequently between Persia and India.

K. N. Chaudhuri. *Asia before Europe: Economy and Civilisation of the Indian Ocean from the Rise of Islam to 1750.* Cambridge, 1990. Controversial and penetrating analysis of economic, social, and cultural structures shaping societies of the Indian Ocean basin.

Ainslie T. Embree and Stephen Hay, eds. *Sources of Indian Tradition.* 2 vols. 2nd ed. New York, 1988. An important collection of primary sources in English translation.

Kenneth R. Hall. *Maritime Trade and State Development in Early Southeast Asia.* Honolulu, 1985. Examines the link between long-distance trade and state building in southeast Asia.

Charles Higham. *The Civilization of Angkor.* London, 2001. Draws usefully on recent archaeological research in placing Angkor in historical context.

S. M. Ikram. *Muslim Civilization in India.* Ed. by A. T. Embree. New York, 1964. Important survey of Islam and its impact in India.

Patricia Risso. *Merchants and Faith: Muslim Commerce and Culture in the Indian Ocean.* Boulder, 1995. Surveys the activities of Muslim merchants in the Indian Ocean basin from the seventh to the nineteenth century.

Burton Stein. *Vijayanagara.* Cambridge, 1989. A study of the southern Hindu kingdom concentrating on political and economic history.

Ramila Thapar. *Early India: From the Origins to A.D. 1300.* Berkeley, 2003. A fresh view by one of the leading scholars of early Indian history.

# Bringing It All Together

## Part III  The Postclassical Era, 500 to 1000 C.E.

After the collapse of classical societies in Persia, China, India, and the Mediterranean, societies in much of the eastern hemisphere were faced with the monumental tasks of restoring internal order as well as rebuilding networks of contact and exchange that had fallen into disuse. Although the ways societies accomplished these tasks varied, it is nevertheless clear that large portions of Eurasia and North Africa once again came under stable rule between 500 and 1000 C.E. As a consequence, during the postclassical era much of the eastern hemisphere both reintegrated and enhanced the trade networks that had once linked so many of the classical societies.

Religion played an important role in the maintenance of internal order in most postclassical societies, including the Byzantine Empire, the Islamic world, and India. Byzantine emperors claimed divine status within the Christian Orthodox church, dramatically enhancing their authority among their subjects. In the Islamic world, the new Muslim faith provided a common language, doctrine, culture, and legal system that served to unite diverse conquered peoples in a common community of believers. In India, the caste system central to Hinduism lent cultural unity to the subcontinent even though it was not ruled by a single power. Because the caste system determined the social role of both groups and individuals, it was a critical factor in maintaining a stable society.

Once they had restored internal order, the postclassical societies reestablished and expanded the trade networks that had once linked the classical societies. This encouraged the exchange of goods, of course, but also encouraged the transfer of technologies and food items that allowed for improved agricultural practices and greater crop productivity—both of which led to population growth. As in the classical era, interaction triggered by trade was also accompanied by cultural interaction. The vast networks of roads and sea-lanes that linked postclassical societies became highways for the exchange of ideas and beliefs as well.

Of these myriad cultural interactions, the spread of religion—including Islam, Buddhism, Hinduism, and Christianity—was perhaps the most obvious and important. In fact, each of these religions spread far beyond their origins in the postclassical era. As a result of Indian Ocean trading networks, Indian merchants brought Hinduism to much of southeast Asia; Islamic traders from both India and Arabia later did the same with their faith. Meanwhile, Buddhists from India and central Asia brought their faith to China, where for a time it enjoyed immense popularity. Finally, Orthodox Christians in Byzantium introduced their faith to the peoples of eastern Europe, who adopted it as their own. As a result of these and other exchanges, the legacies of postclassical societies remain very much with us in the present day.

# An Age of Cross-Cultural Interaction, 1000 to 1500 C.E.

AZTECS AND TOLTECS (CH. 17)

PEOPLES OF NORTH
AMERICA (CH. 17)

MONGOL EMPIRES (CH. 14)

TURKISH EMPIRES (CH. 14)

HOLY ROMAN EMPIRE (CH. 16)

REGIONAL STATES OF EUROPE (CH. 16)
THE RENAISSANCE (CH. 18)

INCA EMPIRE (CH. 17)

PORTUGUESE SLAVE TRADE (CH. 18)

KINGDOMS & EMPIRES OF
SUB-SAHARAN AFRICA (CH. 15)

MING DYNASTY (CH. 18)

PACIFIC ISLAND SOCIETIES (CH. 17)

The half millennium from 1000 to 1500 C.E. differed markedly from earlier eras. During classical and postclassical times, large, regional societies situated in China, India, southwest Asia, and the Mediterranean basin dominated the eastern hemisphere. From 1000 to 1500 C.E., however, nomadic Turkish and Mongol peoples overran settled societies and established vast transregional empires from China to eastern Europe.

Nomadic peoples toppled several postclassical states, most notably the Song empire in China and the Abbasid realm in southwest Asia. By building empires that transcended the boundaries of postclassical states, however, nomadic Turks and Mongols laid a political foundation for sharply increased trade and communication between peoples of different societies and cultural regions.

Increased trade in the Indian Ocean basin also promoted more intense cross-cultural communications. Maritime trade built on the political stability, economic expansion, and demographic growth of the postclassical era. This trade indicated a movement toward economic integration as societies of the Indian Ocean basin concentrated increasingly on cultivating crops or producing goods for export while importing foods or goods that they could not produce very well themselves.

Demographic growth, economic expansion, and increased trade were not limited to the Indian Ocean basin, China, and southwest Asia in this period. Indeed, the intensification of trade across much of Eurasia also brought relatively isolated areas like sub-Saharan Africa and western Europe into sustained cross-cultural relationships with far distant places. These relationships brought increased prosperity to both regions, which in turn encouraged political centralization and the consolidation of state power.

The indigenous peoples of the Americas and Oceania also built larger and more centralized societies from 1000 to 1500 C.E., with centralized empires appearing in Meso-america and Andean South America and agricultural societies emerging in several regions of North America. Although Pacific islanders had limited resources with which to build empires, within their own agricultural and fishing societies they established tightly centralized kingdoms.

During the fourteenth and fifteenth centuries C.E., much of the eastern hemisphere experienced difficulties not only because of warfare arising from the conquests of nomadic peoples but also because of epidemic bubonic plague and global climatic changes that brought cooler temperatures. Together, these problems led to political, social, and economic turmoil throughout much of the eastern hemisphere.

Nevertheless, by the mid–fifteenth century, peoples from China to western Europe were recovering from those difficulties and rebuilding prosperous societies. In their own quest for prosperity, western European peoples unwittingly laid the foundations of a new era in world history. While searching for sea routes to Asian markets, European mariners happened on the continents of North and South America. Their voyages brought the world's various peoples for the first time into permanent and sustained communication, and their interactions triggered a series of consequences that profoundly influenced modern world history. Yet it is important to remember that the European voyages that gave rise to this interdependent and interconnected world occurred precisely because Europeans were seeking to become more involved in the vibrant trade networks that characterized much of the eastern hemisphere in the half-millennium after 1000 C.E.

# Nomadic Empires and Eurasian Integration

## 14

Guillaume Boucher was a goldsmith who lived during the early and middle decades of the thirteenth century. During the 1230s, he left his native Paris and went to Budapest, which was then a part of the kingdom of Hungary. There he was captured by Mongol warriors campaigning in Hungary. The Mongols noticed and appreciated Boucher's talents, and when they left Hungary in 1242, they took him and other skilled captives to their central Asian homeland.

For at least the next fifteen years, Boucher lived at the Mongol capital at Karakorum. Though technically a slave, he enjoyed some prestige. He supervised fifty assistants in a workshop that produced decorative objects of gold and silver for the Mongol court. His most ingenious creation was a spectacular silver fountain in the form of a tree. Four pipes, concealed by the tree's trunk, carried wines and other intoxicating drinks to the top of the tree and then dispensed them into silver bowls from which guests filled their cups. Apart from his famous fountain, Boucher also produced statues in gold and silver, built carriages, designed buildings, and even sewed ritual garments for Roman Catholic priests who conducted services for Christians living at Karakorum.

Boucher was by no means the only European living at the Mongol court. His wife was a woman of French ancestry whom Boucher had met and married in Hungary. The Flemish missionary William of Rubruck visited Karakorum in 1254, and during his sojourn there he encountered men and women from France, Russia, Greece, and England. Other European visitors to the Mongol court found Germans, Slavs, and Hungarians as well as Chinese, Koreans, Turks, Persians, and Armenians, among others. Many thirteenth-century roads led to Karakorum.

Nomadic peoples had made their influence felt throughout much of Eurasia as early as classical times. The Xiongnu confederation dominated central Asia and threatened the Han dynasty in China from the third to the first century B.C.E. During the second and third centuries C.E., the Huns and other nomadic peoples from central Asia launched migrations that helped bring down the western Roman empire, and later migrations of the White Huns destroyed the Gupta state in India. Turkish peoples ruled a large central Asian empire from the sixth through the ninth century, and the Uighur Turks even seized the capital cities of the Tang dynasty in the mid–seventh century.

Between the eleventh and fifteenth centuries, nomadic peoples became more prominent than ever before in Eurasian

❮ *Chabi, a Nestorian Christian and the favorite wife of Khubilai Khan, wearing the distinctive headgear reserved for Mongol women of the ruling class.*

**Karakorum** (kahr-uh-KOR-uhm)

# CHRONOLOGY

| | |
|---|---|
| 1055 | Tughril Beg named sultan |
| 1071 | Battle of Manzikert |
| 1206–1227 | Reign of Chinggis Khan |
| 1211–1234 | Mongol conquest of northern China |
| 1219–1221 | Mongol conquest of Persia |
| 1237–1241 | Mongol conquest of Russia |
| 1258 | Mongol capture of Baghdad |
| 1264–1279 | Mongol conquest of southern China |
| 1264–1294 | Reign of Khubilai Khan |
| 1279–1368 | Yuan dynasty |
| 1295 | Conversion of Ilkhan Ghazan to Islam |
| 1336–1405 | Life of Tamerlane |
| 1453 | Ottoman capture of Constantinople |

affairs. Turkish peoples migrated to Persia, Anatolia, and India, where they established new states. During the thirteenth and fourteenth centuries, the Mongols established themselves as the most powerful people of the central Asian steppes and then turned on settled societies in China, Persia, Russia, and eastern Europe. By the early fourteenth century, the Mongols had built the largest empire the world has ever seen, stretching from Korea and China in the east to Russia and Hungary in the west.

Most of the Mongol states collapsed during the late fourteenth and fifteenth centuries, but the decline of the Mongols did not signal the end of nomadic peoples' influence on Eurasian affairs. Although a native Chinese dynasty replaced the Mongol state in China, the Mongols continued to threaten its central Asian frontier. Moreover, from the fourteenth through the seventeenth century, Turkish peoples embarked on new campaigns of expansion that eventually brought most of India, much of central Asia, all of Anatolia, and a good portion of eastern Europe under their domination.

The military campaigns of nomadic peoples were sometimes exceedingly destructive. Nomadic warriors demolished cities, slaughtered urban populations, and ravaged surrounding agricultural lands. Yet those same forces also encouraged systematic peaceful interaction between peoples of different societies. Between the eleventh and fifteenth centuries, the imperial campaigns of Turkish and Mongol peoples forged closer links than ever before between Eurasian lands. By fostering cross-cultural communication and exchange on an unprecedented scale, the nomadic empires integrated the lives of peoples throughout much of the eastern hemisphere.

# TURKISH MIGRATIONS AND IMPERIAL EXPANSION

Turkish peoples never formed a single, homogeneous group but, rather, organized themselves into clans and tribes that often fought bitterly with one another. All Turkish peoples spoke related languages, and all were nomads or descendants of nomads. From modest beginnings they expanded their influence until they dominated not only the steppes of central Asia but also settled societies in Persia, Anatolia, and India.

## Nomadic Economy and Society

Nomadic societies in central Asia developed by adapting to the ecological conditions of arid lands. Central Asia does not receive enough rain to support large-scale agriculture. Oases permit cultivation of limited regions, but for the most part only grasses and shrubs grow on the central Asian steppe lands, and there are no large rivers or other sources of water to support large-scale irrigation systems. Yet grazing animals thrive on grasses and shrubs, and the peoples of central Asia took advantage of this by herding sheep, horses, cattle, goats, and camels.

NOMADIC PEOPLES AND THEIR ANIMALS Nomadic peoples drove their herds and flocks to lands with abundant grass and then moved them along as the animals thinned the vegetation. They carefully followed migratory cycles that took account of the seasons and local climatic

**NOMADIC LIFE.** | A painting from the late fourteenth century by the central Asian artist Mehmed Siyah Qalem suggests the physical hardships of nomadic life. In this scene from a nomadic camp, two men wash clothes (upper left), while another blows on a fire, and a companion tends to a saddle. Bows, arrows, and other weapons are readily available (top right).

conditions and lived mostly off the meat, milk, and hides of their animals. They used animal bones for tools and animal dung as fuel. They made shoes and clothes out of wool from their sheep and skins from their other animals. Their dwellings—large tents called *yurts*—were fashioned with felt made from the wool of their sheep. They even prepared an alcoholic drink from their animals by fermenting mare's milk into a potent concoction known as *kumiss*.

**NOMADIC AND SETTLED PEOPLES** The aridity of the climate and the nomadic lifestyle limited the development of human societies in central Asia. Intensive agriculture was impossible except in oases, and the need to regularly follow the herds made large-scale craft production impractical. As a result, nomads avidly sought opportunities to trade with settled peoples. Much of that commerce took place on a small scale as nomads sought agricultural products and manufactured goods to satisfy their immediate needs. Often, however, nomads also participated in long-distance trade networks. Because of their mobility and their familiarity with large regions of central Asia, nomadic peoples were ideally suited to organize and lead the caravans that crossed central Asia and linked settled societies from China to the Mediterranean basin. During the postclassical era and later, Turkish peoples were especially prominent on the caravan routes of central Asia.

**NOMADIC SOCIETY** Nomadic society generated two social classes: nobles and commoners. Charismatic leaders won recognition as nobles and thereby acquired the prestige needed to organize clans and tribes into alliances. Normally, nobles did little governing, since clans and tribes looked after their own affairs and resented interference. During times of war, however, nobles wielded absolute authority over the forces within their alliances.

**yurts** (yuhrts)

The nobility was a fluid class. Leaders passed noble status along to their heirs, but the heirs could lose their status if they did not continue to provide appropriate leadership for their clans and tribes. Over the course of a few generations, nobles could return to the status of commoners. Meanwhile, commoners could win recognition as nobles by outstanding conduct, particularly by courageous behavior during war. Then, if they were clever diplomats, they could arrange alliances between clans and tribes and gain enough support to displace established leaders.

NOMADIC RELIGION    The earliest religion of the Turkish peoples revolved around shamans—religious specialists who possessed supernatural powers, communicated with the gods and nature spirits, and invoked divine aid on behalf of their communities. Yet many Turkish peoples became attracted to the religious and cultural traditions they encountered when trading with peoples of settled societies, and by the sixth century C.E. many Turks had converted to Buddhism, Nestorian Christianity, or Manichaeism. Partly because of their newly adopted religious traditions and partly because of their prominence in Eurasian trade networks, Turkish peoples also developed a written script.

TURKISH CONVERSION TO ISLAM    Between the tenth and the fourteenth centuries, most Turkish clans on the steppes of central Asia converted to Islam. Their conversion had great significance. When Turkish peoples began to migrate into settled societies in large numbers, they helped spread Islam to new lands, particularly Anatolia and northern India. The boundaries of the Islamic world thus expanded along with the political and military influence of Turkish peoples.

MILITARY ORGANIZATION    This expansion took place when nomadic leaders organized vast confederations of peoples under the leadership of a *khan* ("ruler"). In fact, khans rarely ruled directly, instead ruling through the leaders of allied tribes. Yet when organized on a large scale, nomadic peoples wielded enormous military power due mostly to their outstanding cavalry forces. Nomadic warriors had superior equestrian skills. Their arrows flew with deadly accuracy even when launched from the backs of galloping horses. Moreover, units of warriors coordinated their movements to outmaneuver and overwhelm their opponents. Indeed, few armies were able to resist the mobility and discipline of well-organized nomadic warriors. With such military capabilities, several groups of Turkish nomads began in the tenth century C.E. to seize the wealth of settled societies and build imperial states in the regions surrounding central Asia.

## Turkish Empires in Persia, Anatolia, and India

SALJUQ TURKS AND THE ABBASID EMPIRE    Turkish peoples entered Persia, Anatolia, and India at different times and for different purposes. They approached Abbasid Persia much as Germanic peoples had earlier approached the Roman empire. From about the mid–eighth to the mid–tenth century, Turkish peoples lived mostly on the borders of the Abbasid realm. By the mid– to late tenth century, large numbers of Saljuq Turks served in Abbasid armies and lived in the Abbasid realm itself. By the mid–eleventh century the Saljuqs overshadowed the Abbasid caliphs so much that in 1055 the caliph recognized the Saljuq leader Tughril Beg as *sultan* ("chieftain"). Tughril first consolidated his hold on the Abbasid capital at Baghdad, then he and his successors extended Turkish rule to Syria, Palestine, and other parts of the realm. For the last two

---

**Nestorian** (neh-STOHR-eeuhn)

**Manichaeism** (MAN-ih-kee-ism)

**Abbasid** (ah-BAH-sih)

**Saljuqs** (sahl-JYOOKS)

**MAP 14.1** | Turkish empires and their neighbors, ca. 1210 C.E. After about 1000 C.E., nomadic Turkish peoples conquered and ruled settled agricultural societies in several regions of Eurasia and north Africa. *How were Turkish peoples able to venture so far from their central Asian homeland?*

**Homeland of Turkish peoples**

centuries of the Abbasid state, the caliphs served only as figureheads: actual governance lay in the hands of the Turkish sultans.

**SALJUQ TURKS AND THE BYZANTINE EMPIRE** Some Saljuq Turks began to turn their attention to the rich land of Anatolia, and in the early eleventh century they began migrating there in large numbers. In 1071 Saljuq forces inflicted a devastating defeat on the Byzantine army at Manzikert in eastern Anatolia and took the Byzantine emperor captive. Following that victory Saljuqs and other Turkish groups entered Anatolia almost at will. The peasants of Anatolia, who mostly resented their Byzantine overlords, tended to look on the Saljuqs as liberators rather than as conquerors.

The migrants thoroughly transformed Anatolia. Turkish groups displaced Byzantine authorities and set up their own political and social institutions. They levied taxes on the Byzantine church, restricted its activities, and sometimes confiscated church property. Meanwhile, they welcomed converts to Islam and made political, social, and economic opportunities available to them. By 1453, when Ottoman Turks captured the Byzantine capital at Constantinople, Byzantine and Christian Anatolia had become largely a Turkish and Islamic land.

**GHAZNAVID TURKS AND THE SULTANATE OF DELHI** While the Saljuqs spearheaded Turkish migrations in Abbasid Persia and Byzantine Anatolia, in the early eleventh century Mahmud of Ghazni led the Turkish Ghaznavids of Afghanistan in raids on lucrative sites in northern India. Although their original goal was plunder, they gradually became more interested in permanent rule. They asserted their authority first over the Punjab and then over Gujarat and Bengal. By the thirteenth century the Turkish sultanate of Delhi claimed authority over all of northern India. Several of the Delhi sultans conceived plans to conquer southern India, but none was able to realize those ambitions. Indeed, the sultans faced constant challenges from Hindu princes in neighboring lands, and they periodically had to defend their northern frontiers from new Turkish or Mongol invaders. They maintained an enormous army with a large elephant corps, but those forces only enabled them to hold on to territories they already had.

Turkish rule had great social and cultural implications in India, as it did in Anatolia. Mahmud of Ghazni was a zealous foe of Buddhism and Hinduism alike, and his forces stripped Buddhist and Hindu establishments of their wealth, destroyed their buildings, and often slaughtered their residents and attendants as well. As Mahmud of Ghazni's forces repressed Buddhism and Hinduism, they encouraged conversion to Islam and enabled their faith to establish a secure presence in northern India.

Though undertaken by different groups and for different reasons, the Turkish conquests of Persia, Anatolia, and India represented part of a larger expansive movement by nomadic peoples. In all three cases the formidable military prowess of Turkish peoples enabled them to dominate settled societies. By the thirteenth century, the influence of nomadic peoples was greater than ever before in Eurasian history. Yet the Turkish conquests represented only a prelude to an astonishing round of empire building launched by the Mongols during the thirteenth and fourteenth centuries.

# THE MONGOL EMPIRES

For most of history the nomadic Mongols lived on the high steppe lands of eastern central Asia. Like other nomadic peoples, they displayed deep loyalty to kin groups organized into families, clans, and tribes. They frequently allied with Turkish peoples who built empires on the steppes, but they rarely played a leading role in the organization of states before the thirteenth century. Strong loyalties to kinship groups made it difficult for the Mongols to organize a stable society on a large scale. During the early thirteenth century, however, Chinggis Khan (sometimes spelled "Genghis Khan") forged the various Mongol tribes into a powerful alliance that built the largest empire the world has ever seen. Although the vast Mongol realm soon dissolved into a series of smaller empires—most of which disappeared within a century—the Mongols' imperial venture brought the societies of Eurasia into closer contact than ever before.

## *Chinggis Khan and the Making of the Mongol Empire*

The unifier of the Mongols was Temüjin, born about 1167 into a noble family. His father was a prominent warrior who forged an alliance between several Mongol clans and seemed likely to become a powerful leader. When Temüjin was about ten years old, however, rivals poisoned his father and destroyed the alliance. Abandoned by his father's allies, Temüjin led a precarious existence for some years. He lived in poverty, since rivals seized the family's animals, and several times eluded enemies seeking to eliminate him. A rival once captured him and imprisoned him in a wooden cage, but Temüjin made a daring midnight escape and regained his freedom.

**CHINGGIS KHAN'S RISE TO POWER** During the late twelfth century, Temüjin made an alliance with a prominent Mongol clan leader. He also mastered the art of steppe diplomacy, which called for displays of personal courage in battle, combined with intense loyalty to allies, a willingness to betray others to improve one's position, and the ability to entice other tribes into cooperative relationships. Temüjin gradually strengthened his position, sometimes by forging useful alliances, often by conquering rival contenders for power, and occasionally by turning suddenly against a troublesome

**Chinggis Khan** (CHIHN-gihs Kahn)
**Temüjin** (TEM-oo-chin)

ally. He eventually brought all the Mongol tribes into a single confederation, and in 1206 an assembly of Mongol leaders recognized Temüjin's supremacy by proclaiming him Chinggis Khan ("universal ruler").

### MONGOL POLITICAL ORGANIZATION

Chinggis Khan's policies greatly strengthened the Mongol people. Earlier nomadic state builders had ruled largely through the leaders of allied tribes. But Chinggis Khan mistrusted the Mongols' tribal organization, so he broke up the tribes and forced men of fighting age to join new military units with no tribal affiliations. He chose high military and political officials not on the basis of kinship or tribal status but because of their talents or their loyalty to him. Although he spent most of his life on horseback, Chinggis Khan also established a capital at Karakorum—present-day Har Horin, located about 300 kilometers (186 miles) west of the modern Mongolian capital of Ulaanbaatar—where he built a luxurious palace. As command center of Chinggis Khan's empire, Karakorum symbolized a source of Mongol authority superior to the clan or tribe. Chinggis Khan's policies created a Mongol state that was not only much stronger than any earlier nomadic confederation but also less troubled by conflicts between clans and tribes.

The most important institution of the Mongol state was the army, which magnified the power of the small population. In the thirteenth century the Mongol population stood at about one million people—less than 1 percent of China's numbers. During Chinggis Khan's life, his army numbered only 100,000 to 125,000 Mongols, although allied peoples also contributed forces. How was it possible for so few people to conquer the better part of Eurasia?

### MONGOL ARMS

Like earlier nomadic armies, Mongol forces relied on outstanding equestrian skills. In addition, their bows were short enough for archers to use while riding, and their arrows could fell enemies at 200 meters (656 feet). Mongol horsemen were among the most mobile forces of the premodern world, sometimes traveling more than 100 kilometers (62 miles) per day to surprise an enemy. Furthermore, the Mongols understood the psychological dimensions of warfare and used them to their advantage. If enemies surrendered without resistance, the Mongols usually spared their lives, and they provided generous treatment for artisans, crafts workers, and those with military skills. In the event of resistance, however, the Mongols ruthlessly slaughtered whole populations, sparing only a few, whom they sometimes drove before their armies as human shields during future conflicts.

Once he had united the Mongols, Chinggis Khan turned his army and his attention to other parts of central Asia, particularly to nearby settled societies. He attacked the various Turkish peoples ruling in Tibet, northern China, Persia, and the central Asian steppes. Those conquests were important because they protected him against the possibility that other nomadic leaders might challenge his rule. But the Mongol campaigns in China and Persia had especially far-reaching consequences.

### MONGOL CONQUEST OF NORTHERN CHINA

Chinggis Khan himself extended Mongol rule to northern China, dominated since 1127 C.E. by the nomadic Jurchen people, while the Song dynasty continued to rule in southern China. In 1211 C.E. Mongol raiding parties invaded the Jurchen realm, and by 1215 the Mongols

**CHINGGIS KHAN.** | This painting by a Chinese artist depicts Chinggis Khan at about age sixty. Though most of his conquests were behind him, Chinggis Khan's focus and determination are readily apparent in this portrait.

The Palace of Great Khan
www.mhhe.com/bentleybrief2e

The Mongol empires
www.mhhe.com/bentleybrief2e

**Ulaanbaatar** (OOLAHN-bah-tahr)
**Jurchen** (JUHR-chehn)
**Song** (SOHNG)

**CHINGGIS KHAN AT WAR.** | A Persian manuscript illustration depicts Chinggis Khan and his cavalry in hot pursuit of retreating forces.

History of the Mongols
www.mhhe.com/
bentleybrief2e

had captured the capital near modern Beijing. This city, under the new name of Khanbaliq ("city of the khan"), also served as the Mongol capital in China. By 1220 the Mongols had largely established control over northern China.

**MONGOL CONQUEST OF PERSIA** Next, Chinggis Khan led another force to Afghanistan and Persia, ruled at that time by a successor to the Saljuqs known as the Khwarazm shah. The mission was one of revenge, for in 1218 the Khwarazm shah had spurned a diplomatic envoy sent by Chinggis Khan by murdering the whole group. In response, the following year Chinggis Khan took his army west, pursued the Khwarazm shah to an island in the Caspian Sea (where he died), shattered his army, and seized control of his realm.

To ensure that the shah's state would never constitute a challenge to his own empire, Chinggis Khan wreaked destruction on the conquered land. The Mongols ravaged one city after another, demolishing buildings and massacring hundreds of thousands of people. Some cities never recovered. The Mongols also destroyed the delicate *qanat* irrigation systems that sustained agriculture in the arid region, resulting in severely reduced agricultural production. For centuries after the Mongol conquest, Persian chroniclers cursed the invaders and the devastation they visited on the land.

By the time of his death in 1227, Chinggis Khan had laid the foundation of a vast and mighty empire. He had united the Mongols, established Mongol supremacy in central Asia, and extended Mongol control to northern China in the east and Persia in the west. But Chinggis Khan was a conqueror, not an administrator. He ruled the Mongols themselves through his control over the army, but he did not establish a central government for the lands that he conquered. Instead, he assigned Mongol overlords to supervise local administrators and to extract a generous tribute for the Mongols' own uses. Chinggis Khan's heirs continued his conquests, but they also undertook the task of designing a more permanent administration to guide the fortunes of the Mongol empire.

## *The Mongol Empires after Chinggis Khan*

Chinggis Khan and his sons
www.mhhe.com/
bentleybrief2e

Chinggis Khan's death touched off a struggle for power among his sons and grandsons. Eventually, his heirs divided Chinggis Khan's vast realm into four regional empires. The great khans ruled China, the wealthiest of Mongol lands. Descendants of Chaghatai, one of Chinggis Khan's sons, ruled the khanate of Chaghatai in central Asia. Persia fell under the authority of rulers known as the ilkhans, and the khans of the Golden Horde dominated Russia. The great khans were nominally superior to the others, but they were rarely able to enforce their claims to authority. In fact, for as long as the Mongol empires survived, ambition fueled constant tension and occasional conflict among the four khans.

**KHUBILAI KHAN** The consolidation of Mongol rule in China came during the reign of Khubilai (sometimes spelled Qubilai), one of Chinggis Khan's grandsons. Khubilai was perhaps the most talented of the great conqueror's descendants. He unleashed ruthless attacks against his enemies, but he also took an interest in cultural matters and worked to improve the welfare of his subjects. He actively promoted Buddhism, and he provided support also for Daoists, Muslims, and Christians in his realm. The famous Venetian traveler Marco Polo, who lived almost two decades at Khubilai's court, praised him for his generosity toward the poor and his efforts to build roads. From 1264 until his death in 1294, Khubilai Khan presided over the Mongol empire at its height.

**Khubilai** (KOO-bih-lie)
**Buddhism** (BOO-diz'm)

*The Venetian Marco Polo traveled extensively through central Asia and China in the late thirteenth century, when Mongol empires dominated Asia. His book of travel writings is an especially valuable source of information about the Mongol age. Among other things, he described the Mongol way of making war.*

Their arms are bows and arrows, sword and mace; but above all the bow, for they are capital archers, indeed the best that are known. . . .

When a Mongol prince goes forth to war, he takes with him, say, 100,000 men. Well, he appoints an officer to every ten men, one to every hundred, one to every thousand, and one to every ten thousand, so that his own orders have to be given to ten persons only, and each of these ten persons has to pass the orders only to another ten, and so on, no one having to give orders to more than ten. And every one in turn is responsible only to the officer immediately over him; and the discipline and order that comes of this method is marvellous, for they are a people very obedient to their chiefs. . . .

When they are going on a distant expedition they take no gear with them except two leather bottles for milk, a little earthenware pot to cook their meat in, and a little tent to shelter them from rain. And in case of great urgency they will ride ten days on end without lighting a fire or taking a meal. On such an occasion they will sustain themselves on the blood of their horses, opening a vein and letting the blood jet into their mouths, drinking till they have had enough, and then staunching it. . . .

When they come to an engagement with the enemy, they will gain the victory in this fashion. They never let themselves get into a regular medley, but keep perpetually riding round and shooting into the enemy. And as they do not count it any shame to run away in battle, they will sometimes pretend to do so, and in running away they turn in the saddle and shoot hard and strong at the foe, and in this way make great havoc. Their horses are trained so perfectly that they will double hither and thither, just like a dog, in a way that is quite astonishing. Thus they fight to as good purpose in running away as if they stood and faced the enemy because of the vast volleys of arrows that they shoot in this way, turning round upon their pursuers, who are fancying that they have won the battle. But when the Mongols see that they have killed and wounded a good many horses and men, they wheel round bodily and return to the charge in perfect order and with loud cries, and in a very short time the enemy are routed. In truth they are stout and valiant soldiers, and inured to war. And you perceive that it is just when the enemy sees them run, and imagines that he has gained the battle, that he has in reality lost it, for the Mongols wheel round in a moment when they judge the right time has come. And after this fashion they have won many a fight.

■ In what ways do the military practices described by Marco Polo reflect the influence of the steppe environment on the Mongols?

SOURCE: Marco Polo. *The Book of Ser Marco Polo,* 3rd ed. Trans. and ed. by Henry Yule and Henri Cordier. London: John Murray, 1921, pp. 260–63. (Translation slightly modified.)

**MONGOL CONQUEST OF SOUTHERN CHINA** Khubilai extended Mongol rule to all of China. From his base at Khanbaliq, he relentlessly attacked the Song dynasty in southern China. The Song capital at Hangzhou fell to Mongol forces in 1276, and within three years Khubilai had eliminated resistance throughout China. In 1279 he proclaimed himself emperor and established the Yuan dynasty, which ruled China until its collapse in 1368.

Beyond China, Khubilai had little success as a conqueror. During the 1270s and 1280s, he launched several unsuccessful invasions of Vietnam, Cambodia, and Burma as well as a failed naval expedition against Java involving 500 to 1,000 ships and twenty thousand troops. In 1274 and again in 1281, Khubilai also attempted seaborne invasions of Japan, but on both occasions typhoons thwarted his plans. The storm of 1281 was especially vicious:

**Khanbaliq** (Kahn-bah-LEEK)

**Yuan** (yoo-AHN)

**The Mongol capital under Chinggis Khan**

**MAP 14.2** | The Mongol empires, ca. 1300 C.E. The Mongol empires stretched from Manchuria and China to Russia and eastern Europe. *In what ways did Mongol empires and Mongol policies facilitate trade, travel, and communication throughout Eurasia?*

it destroyed about 4,500 Mongol vessels carrying more than one hundred thousand armed troops—the largest seaborne expedition before World War II.

**THE GOLDEN HORDE**   As Khubilai consolidated his hold on east Asia, his cousins and brothers tightened Mongol control on lands to the west. Mongols of the group known as the Golden Horde overran Russia between 1237 and 1241 and then mounted exploratory expeditions into Poland, Hungary, and eastern Germany in 1241 and 1242. Mongols of the Golden Horde prized the steppes north of the Black Sea as prime pastureland for their horses, and they used them to maintain a large army. They did not occupy Russia, which they regarded as an unattractive land of forests, but they extracted tribute from the Russian cities and agricultural provinces. The Golden Horde maintained its hegemony in Russia until the mid–fifteenth century, when the princes of Moscow built a powerful Russian state. By the mid–sixteenth century Russian conquerors had extended their control to the steppes, but Mongol khans descended from the Golden Horde continued to rule the Crimea until the late eighteenth century.

**THE ILKHANATE OF PERSIA**   While the Golden Horde established its authority in Russia, Khubilai's brother Hülegü toppled the Abbasid empire and established the Mongol ilkhanate in Persia. In 1258 he captured the Abbasid capital of Baghdad after a brief siege. His troops looted the city, executed the caliph, and massacred more than two hundred thousand residents. From Persia, Hülegü's army ventured into Syria, but Muslim forces from Egypt soon expelled them and placed a limit on Mongol expansion to the southwest.

When the Mongols crushed ruling regimes in large settled societies, they discovered that they needed to become governors as well as conquerors. The Mongols had no experience administering complex societies, where successful governance required talents

**Hülegü** (Hoo-LAY-goo)

**ilkhanate** (EEL-kahn-ate)

beyond the equestrian and military skills esteemed on the steppes. They had a difficult time adjusting to their role as administrators, and in fact most of their conquests fell out of their hands within a century.

MONGOL RULE IN PERSIA    The Mongols adopted different tactics in the different lands they ruled. In Persia they made important concessions to local interests. Although Mongols and their allies occupied the highest administrative positions, they basically allowed the Persians to run the ilkhanate as long as they delivered tax receipts and maintained order.

Over time, the Mongols even assimilated to Persian cultural traditions. The early Mongol rulers of Persia mostly observed their native shamanism, but they tolerated all religions—including Islam, Nestorian Christianity, Buddhism, and Judaism. Gradually, however, the Mongols gravitated toward Islam. In 1295 Ilkhan Ghazan publicly converted to Islam, and most of the Mongols in Persia followed his example. Ghazan's conversion sparked large-scale massacres of Christians and Jews, and it signaled the absorption of the Mongols into Muslim Persian society.

MONGOL RULE IN CHINA    In China, in contrast, the Mongol overlords stood aloof from their subjects, whom they scorned as mere cultivators. They outlawed intermarriage between Mongols and Chinese and forbade the Chinese to learn the Mongol language. Some of the victors went so far as to suggest that the Mongols exterminate the Chinese people and convert China itself into pastureland for their horses. In the end, the Mongols decided simply to extract as much revenue as possible from their Chinese subjects. Unlike their counterparts in Persia, the Mongols in China did not make much use of native administrative talent. Instead, they brought foreign administrators—including Arabs, Persians, and even Europeans—into China and placed them in charge.

The Mongols also resisted assimilation to Chinese cultural traditions. They ended the privileges enjoyed by the Confucian scholars, and they dismantled the Confucian educational and examination system, which had produced generations of civil servants for the Chinese bureaucracy. They did not persecute Confucians, but they allowed the Confucian

shamanism (SHAH-mah-niz'm)

tradition to wither in the absence of official support. Meanwhile, although the Mongols mostly continued to follow their native shamanist cults, they tolerated all cultural and religious traditions in China, including Confucianism, Daoism, Buddhism, and Christianity. Of Khubilai Khan's four wives, his favorite was Chabi, a Nestorian Christian.

## The Mongols and Eurasian Integration

In building their vast empire, the Mongols brought tremendous destruction to lands throughout much of the Eurasian landmass. Yet they also sponsored interaction among peoples of different societies and linked Eurasian lands more directly than ever before. Indeed, Mongol rulers positively encouraged travel and communication over long distances. Recognizing the value of regular communications for their vast empire, Chinggis Khan and his successors maintained a courier network that rapidly relayed news, information, and government orders. The network included relay stations with fresh horses and riders so that messages could travel almost nonstop throughout Mongol territories. The Mongols' encouragement of travel and communication facilitated trade, diplomatic travel, missionary efforts, and movements of peoples to new lands.

THE MONGOLS AND TRADE    As a nomadic people dependent on commerce with settled agricultural societies, the Mongols worked to secure trade routes and ensure the safety of merchants passing through their territories. The Mongol khans frequently fought among themselves, but they maintained reasonably good order within their realms and allowed merchants to travel unmolested through their empires. As a result, long-distance travel and trade became much less risky than in earlier times. Merchants increased their commercial investments, and the volume of long-distance trade across central Asia dwarfed that of earlier eras. Lands as distant as China and western Europe became directly linked for the first time because of the ability of individuals to travel across the entire Eurasian landmass.

DIPLOMATIC MISSIONS    Like trade, diplomatic communication was essential to the Mongols, and their protection of roads and travelers benefited ambassadors as well as merchants. Throughout the Mongol era the great khans in China, the ilkhans in Persia, and the other khans maintained close communications by means of diplomatic embassies. They also had diplomatic dealings with rulers in Korea, Vietnam, India, and western Europe, and in other lands as well. Some diplomatic travelers crossed the entire Eurasian landmass. Several European ambassadors traveled to Mongolia and China to deliver messages from authorities seeking to ally with the Mongols against Muslim states in southwest Asia. Diplomats also traveled west: Rabban Sauma, a Nestorian Christian monk born in Khanbaliq, visited Italy and France as a representative of the Persian ilkhan.

MISSIONARY EFFORTS    Like the silk roads in earlier times, Eurasian routes during the era of the Mongol empires served as highways for missionaries as well as merchants and diplomats. Sufi missionaries helped popularize Islam among Turkish peoples in central Asia, and Nestorian Christians found new opportunities to win converts when they went to China to serve as administrators for Mongol rulers. Roman Catholic Christians also mounted missionary campaigns in China. (See chapter 18 for further discussion of travel during the Mongol era.)

RESETTLEMENT    Another Mongol policy that encouraged Eurasian integration was the practice of resettling peoples in new lands. As a nomadic people, the Mongols had limited numbers of skilled artisans and educated individuals, but the more their empire expanded, the more they needed the services of specialized crafts workers and literate administrators. Mongol overlords recruited the talent they needed largely from the ranks

Daoism (DOW-iz'm)

of their allies and the peoples they conquered, and they often moved people far from their homelands to sites where they could best make use of their services. Among the most important of the Mongols' allies were the Uighur Turks, who lived mostly in oasis cities along the silk roads. The Uighurs were literate and often highly educated, and they provided not only many of the clerks, secretaries, and administrators who ran the Mongol empires but also units of soldiers who bolstered Mongol garrisons. Arab and Persian Muslims were also prominent among those who administered the Mongols' affairs far from their homelands.

Conquered peoples also supplied the Mongols with talent. When they overcame a city, Mongol forces surveyed the captured population, separated out those with specialized skills, and sent them where there was demand for their services. After the 1230s the Mongols often took censuses of lands they conquered, partly to levy taxes and conscript military forces and partly to locate talented individuals. The Parisian goldsmith Guillaume Boucher was only one among thousands of foreign-born individuals who became permanent residents of the Mongol capital at Karakorum because of their special talents. Like their protection of trade and diplomacy, the Mongols' policy of resettling allies and conquered peoples promoted Eurasian integration by increasing communication and exchange between peoples of different societies.

**THINKING ABOUT** *Encounters*

**ENCOUNTERS IN NOMADIC EMPIRES AND EURASIAN INTEGRATION.** In the thirteenth and fourteenth centuries, the Mongols conquered vast portions of the Eurasian landmass, creating the largest empire in history. Why, despite the extreme violence of Mongol conquest in many areas, did Mongol rule lead to greater cultural interaction among the peoples of Eurasia than ever before?

## Decline of the Mongols in Persia and China

**COLLAPSE OF THE ILKHANATE** Soon after the long and prosperous reign of Khubilai Khan, the Mongols encountered serious difficulties governing Persia and China. In Persia excessive spending strained the treasury, and overexploitation of the peasantry led to reduced revenues. When the ilkhan tried to resolve his financial difficulties by ordering the use of paper money in the 1290s, merchants refused to accept paper they regarded as worthless. Commerce ground to a halt until the ilkhan rescinded his order. Meanwhile, factional struggles plagued the Mongol leadership. When the last of the Mongol rulers died without an heir in 1335, the ilkhanate itself simply collapsed. Government in Persia devolved to local levels until late in the fourteenth century, when Turkish peoples reintroduced effective central government.

**DECLINE OF THE YUAN DYNASTY** Mongol decline in China was a more complicated affair. As in Persia, it had an economic dimension. The Mongols continued to use the paper money that the Chinese had introduced during the Tang and Song dynasties, but they did not maintain adequate reserves of the bullion that backed up paper notes. The general population soon lost confidence in paper money, and its value plummeted. As in Persia, too, factions and infighting hastened Mongol decline in China. Beginning in the 1320s power struggles, imperial assassinations, and civil war convulsed the Mongol regime in China.

**BUBONIC PLAGUE** Apart from financial difficulties and factional divisions, the Mongol rulers of China also faced an onslaught of epidemic disease. By facilitating trade and communications throughout Eurasia, the Mongols unwittingly expedited the spread of bubonic plague (discussed in chapter 18). During the 1330s plague erupted in southwestern China. From there it spread throughout China and central Asia, and by the late 1340s it had reached southwest Asia and Europe, where it became known as the Black Death. Bubonic plague sometimes killed half or more of an exposed population, particularly during the furious initial years of the epidemic, and it seriously disrupted economies

---

**Uighurs** (WEE-goors)

and societies throughout much of Eurasia. In China depopulation and labor shortages that followed on the heels of epidemic plague weakened the Mongol regime.

Because they treated their Chinese subjects as inferiors, the Mongols also faced a rebellious subject population in China. Beginning in the 1340s southern China became a hotbed of peasant rebellion and banditry, which the Mongols could not control. In 1368 rebel forces captured Khanbaliq, and the Mongols departed China en masse and returned to the steppes.

**SURVIVING MONGOL KHANATES**   Despite the collapse of the Mongol regimes in Persia and China, Mongol states did not completely disappear. The khanate of Chaghatai continued to prevail in central Asia, and Mongols posed a threat to the northwestern borders of China until the eighteenth century. Meanwhile, the khanate of the Golden Horde continued to dominate the Caucasus and the steppe lands north of the Black Sea and Caspian Sea until the mid–sixteenth century, when a resurgent Russian state brought the Golden Horde down. Like Mongols in China, however, Mongols in Russia continued to threaten until the eighteenth century, and Mongols who had settled in the Crimean peninsula retained their identity until Josef Stalin forcibly moved them to other parts of the Soviet Union in the mid–twentieth century.

# AFTER THE MONGOLS

By no means did the decline of the Mongols signal the end of nomadic peoples' influence in Eurasia. As Mongol strength waned, Turkish peoples resumed the expansive campaigns that the Mongols had interrupted. During the late fourteenth and early fifteenth centuries, the Turkish conqueror Tamerlane built a central Asian empire rivaling that of Chinggis Khan himself. Although Tamerlane's empire foundered soon after his death, it deeply influenced three surviving Turkish Muslim states—the Mughal empire in India, the Safavid empire in Persia, and the Ottoman empire based in Anatolia—and embraced much of southwest Asia, southeastern Europe, and north Africa.

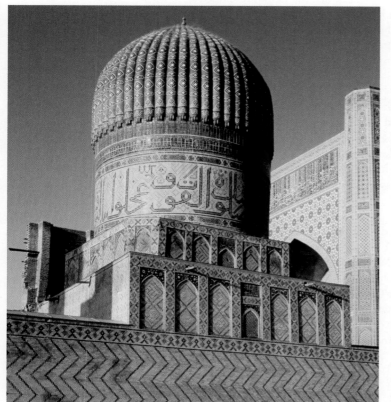

**TAMERLANE'S TOMB.** Spoils from Tamerlane's campaigns and raids enriched the conqueror's capital at Samarkand. They financed, among other buildings, the magnificent tomb where Tamerlane's remains still rest.

## *Tamerlane the Whirlwind*

**THE LAME CONQUEROR**   The rapid collapse of the Mongol states left gaping power vacuums in China and Persia. While the native Ming dynasty filled the vacuum in China, a self-made Turkish conqueror named Timur moved on Persia. Because he walked with a limp, contemporaries referred to him as Timur-i lang—"Timur the Lame," an appellation that made its way into English as Tamerlane.

Born about 1336 near Samarkand, Tamerlane took Chinggis Khan as his model. Like Chinggis Khan, Tamerlane came from a family of the minor nobility and had to make his own way to power. Also like Chinggis Khan, he was a charismatic leader and a courageous warrior, and he attracted a band of loyal followers. During the 1360s he eliminated rivals to power, either by persuading them to join him as allies or by defeating their armies on the battlefield, and he won recognition as leader of his own tribe. By 1370

**Timur-i lang** (tee-MOOR-yee LAHNG)

**MAP 14.3** | Tamerlane's empire, ca. 1405 C.E. Notice the similarity between Tamerlane's empire and the ilkhanate of Persia shown on Map 14.2. *To what extent do you think the cities and the administrative infrastructure of the region facilitated Tamerlane's efforts to control his empire?*

**Samarkand was the capital of Tamerlane's empire.**

he had extended his authority throughout the khanate of Chaghatai and had begun to build a magnificent imperial capital in Samarkand.

For the rest of his life, Tamerlane led his armies on campaigns of conquest. He turned first to the region between Persia and Afghanistan, and he took special care to establish his authority in the rich cities so that he could levy taxes on trade and agricultural production. Next he attacked the Golden Horde in the Caucasus region and Russia, and by the mid-1390s he had severely weakened it. During the last years of the century, he invaded India and subjected Delhi to a ferocious sack. Later Tamerlane campaigned along the Ganges, although he never attempted to incorporate India into his empire. He opened the new century with campaigns in southwest Asia and Anatolia. In 1404 he began preparations for an invasion of China, and he was leading his army east when he fell ill and died in 1405.

Like his model Chinggis Khan, Tamerlane was a conqueror, not a governor. He spent most of his adult life planning and fighting military campaigns. He did not create an imperial administration but, rather, ruled through tribal leaders who were his allies. He appointed overlords in the territories he conquered, but they relied on existing bureaucratic structures and simply received taxes and tributes on his behalf.

**TAMERLANE'S HEIRS** Given its loose organization, it is not surprising that Tamerlane's empire experienced stresses and strains after the conqueror's death. Tamerlane's sons and grandsons engaged in a long series of bitter conflicts that resulted in the contraction of his empire and its division into four main regions. For a century after Tamerlane's death, however, they maintained control over the region from Persia to Afghanistan. When the last vestiges of Tamerlane's imperial creation disappeared, in the early sixteenth century, the Mughal, Safavid, and Ottoman empires that replaced it all clearly reflected the Turkish Muslim legacy of the lame conqueror.

**Tamerlane the Conqueror**
www.mhhe.com/
bentleybrief2e

# The Foundation of the Ottoman Empire

Chapter 25 will discuss the Mughal Empire in India and the Safavid Empire in Persia, both of which emerged during the early sixteenth century as Tamerlane's empire finally dissolved. The early stages of Ottoman expansion predated Tamerlane, however, and the foundation of the Ottoman empire throws additional light on the influence of nomadic peoples during the period 1000 to 1500 C.E.

**OSMAN** After the Mongol conquest of Persia, large numbers of nomadic Turks migrated from central Asia to the ilkhanate and beyond to the territories in Anatolia that the Saljuq Turks had seized from the Byzantine empire. There they followed charismatic leaders who organized further campaigns of conquest. Among those leaders was Osman, who during the late thirteenth and early fourteenth centuries carved a small state for himself in northwestern Anatolia. In 1299 Osman declared independence from the Saljuq sultan and launched a campaign to build a state at the expense of the Byzantine empire. After every successful operation Osman attracted more and more followers, who came to be known as Osmanlis or Ottomans.

**OTTOMAN CONQUESTS** During the 1350s the Ottomans gained a considerable advantage over their Turkish rivals when they established a foothold across the Dardanelles at Gallipoli on the Balkan peninsula. The Ottomans quickly moved to expand the boundaries of their Balkan holdings. By the 1380s they had become by far the most powerful people in the Balkan peninsula, and by the end of the century they were poised to capture Constantinople and take over the Byzantine empire.

Tamerlane temporarily delayed Ottoman expansion in the Byzantine realm. In 1402 his forces crushed the Ottoman army, captured the sultan, and subjected the Ottoman state to the conqueror's authority. After Tamerlane's death, Ottoman leaders had to reestablish their rule in their own realm. Yet by the 1440s the Ottomans had recovered their balance and had begun again to expand in the Byzantine empire.

The siege of Constantinople
www.mhhe.com/
bentleybrief2e

**THE CAPTURE OF CONSTANTINOPLE** The campaign culminated in 1453 when Sultan Mehmed II, known as Mehmed the Conqueror, captured the Byzantine capital of Constantinople. After subjecting it to a sack, he made the city his own capital under the Turkish name of Istanbul. With Istanbul as a base, the Ottomans quickly absorbed the remainder of the Byzantine empire. By 1480 they controlled all of Greece and the Balkan region. They continued to expand throughout most of the sixteenth century as well, extending their rule to southwest Asia, southeastern Europe, Egypt, and north Africa. Once again, then, a nomadic people asserted control over a long-settled society and quickly built a vast empire.

**Osman** (os-MAHN)

## SUMMARY

During the half millennium from 1000 to 1500 C.E., nomadic peoples of central Asia played a larger role than ever before in world history. As early as the second millennium B.C.E., they had periodically threatened states from China to the eastern Mediterranean region, and from classical times on they had traded regularly and actively with peoples of settled societies. From 1000 to 1500 their relations with neighboring peoples changed, as they dominated affairs in most of Eurasia through their conquests and their construction of vast transregional empires. Turkish peoples built the most durable of the nomadic empires, but the spectacular conquests of the Mongols most clearly demonstrated the potential of nomadic peoples to project their formidable military power to settled agricultural societies. By establishing connections that spanned the Eurasian landmass, the nomadic empires laid the foundation for increasing communication, exchange, and interaction among peoples of different societies and thereby fostered the integration of the eastern hemisphere. The age of nomadic empires, from 1000 to 1500 C.E., foreshadowed the integrated world of modern times.

## STUDY TERMS

Abbasids (268)
Chinggis Khan (270)
Ghaznavids (269)
Hülegü (274)
Ilkhan Ghazan (275)
ilkhans (272)
Karakorum (271)
khan (268)
khanate of Chagatai (272)

Khanbaliq (272)
khans of the Golden Horde (272)
Khubilai Khan (272)
Khwarazm shah (272)
Mehmed the Conqueror (280)
Mongols (270)
Osman (280)
Rabban Sauma (276)

Saljuqs (268)
shamanism (268)
sultan (268)
sultanate of Delhi (269)
Tamerlane (278)
Turkish peoples (266)
Uighur Turks (277)
Yuan dynasty (273)

## FOR FURTHER READING

S. A. M. Adshead. *Central Asia in World History.* New York, 1993. A provocative essay on central Asia and its place in the larger world.

Thomas J. Barfield. *The Nomadic Alternative.* Englewood Cliffs, N.J., 1993. A sensitive study of nomadic societies in Africa and Eurasia by a leading anthropologist.

Charles J. Halperin. *Russia and the Golden Horde: The Mongol Impact on Medieval Russian History.* Bloomington, 1985. An insightful study of the Golden Horde and its influence on Russian society.

Halil Inalcik. *The Ottoman Empire: The Classical Age, 1300–1600.* Trans. by N. Itzkowitz and C. Imber. New York, 1973. The best short introduction to early Ottoman history.

Paul Kahn, ed. *The Secret History of the Mongols: The Origin of Chingis Khan.* Adapted from the translation of F. W. Cleaves. San Francisco, 1984. A translation of the Mongols' history of their own society, adapted for modern readers.

Adam T. Kessler. *Empires beyond the Great Wall: The Heritage of Genghis Khan.* Los Angeles, 1993. Well-illustrated survey of nomadic states in central Asia from the Xiongnu to the Mongols.

Beatrice Forbes Manz. *The Rise and Rule of Tamerlane.* Cambridge, 1989. Scholarly analysis of Tamerlane's career and his empire.

David Morgan. *Medieval Persia, 1040–1797.* London, 1988. A brief and insightful survey concentrating on the eras of Turkish and Mongol dominance in Persia.

———. *The Mongols.* Oxford, 1986. Lucid and witty study: the best short work on the Mongols.

Morris Rossabi. *Khubilai Khan: His Life and Times.* Berkeley, 1988. Excellent scholarly study of the greatest of the great khans.

# States and Societies of Sub-Saharan Africa

## 15

A remarkable oral tradition preserves the story of the lion prince Sundiata, thirteenth-century founder of the Mali empire in west Africa. Oral traditions include stories, histories, epics, and other accounts transmitted by professional singers and storytellers known in Africa as griots. Until scholars began to collect and publish African oral traditions in the middle of the twentieth century, the story of Sundiata was available only when a griot recited it.

According to the oral tradition, Sundiata's father ruled a small west African kingdom in the northeastern part of what is now Guinea. Despite his royal parentage, Sundiata had a difficult childhood, because a congenitally defective leg left him partially crippled. When the old king died, his enemies invaded the kingdom and killed the royal offspring, sparing Sundiata because they thought his physical condition would prevent him from posing a threat to their ambitions. But Sundiata overcame his injury, learned to use the bow and arrow, and strengthened himself by hunting in the forest. As Sundiata grew stronger, his enemies began to fear him, and they forced him to seek refuge in a neighboring kingdom. While in exile, Sundiata distinguished himself as a warrior and assembled a powerful cavalry force staffed by loyal followers and allies.

About 1235 Sundiata returned to his homeland and claimed the throne. His cavalry slashed through the countryside and defeated his enemies. Within a few years he had overcome resistance, established the Mali empire, and consolidated his rule throughout the valley of the Niger River. Although he respected traditional religious beliefs and magical powers, Sundiata was a Muslim, and he welcomed Muslim merchants from north Africa into his realm. He built a capital city at Niani, which soon became a thriving commercial center. For two centuries after Sundiata's death about 1260, the lion prince's legacy shaped the lives of west African peoples and linked west Africa with north Africa and the Mediterranean basin.

From the classical era forward, peoples from east Asia to the Mediterranean basin established extensive networks of trade and communication. African peoples living south of the Sahara desert participated in the larger economy of the eastern hemisphere, though not as fully as their counterparts in north Africa. Geographic conditions help to explain why trade and communication networks

❮ *The magnificent mosque at Jenne, constructed in the fourteenth century, served as a principal center of Islamic education and scholarship in the Mali empire.*

**Sundiata** (soon-JAH-tuh)

**Mali** (MAH-lee)

**griot** (GREE-oh)

## EFFECTS OF EARLY AFRICAN MIGRATIONS

Agriculture and Population Growth

African Political Organization

## AFRICAN SOCIETY AND CULTURAL DEVELOPMENT

Social Classes

African Religion

The Arrival of Christianity

## ISLAMIC KINGDOMS AND EMPIRES

Trans-Saharan Trade and Islamic States in West Africa

The Indian Ocean Trade and Islamic States in East Africa

# CHRONOLOGY

| | |
|---|---|
| 4th century C.E. | Introduction of bananas to Africa |
| 11th to 13th century | Kingdom of Ghana |
| 11th to 15th century | Swahili cities |
| 12th to 15th century | Kingdom of Great Zimbabwe |
| 12th to 16th century | Christian kingdom of Axum |
| 13th to 15th century | Mali empire |
| 1230–1255 | Reign of Sundiata |
| 14th to 17th century | Kingdom of Kongo |
| 1312–1337 | Reign of Mansa Musa |
| 1324–1325 | Mansa Musa's pilgrimage to Mecca |

did not embrace sub-Saharan Africa as readily as they did other regions: the Sahara desert poses a formidable challenge to overland travelers, the African coastlines offer few good natural harbors, and cataracts complicate travel up the continent's major rivers.

Nevertheless, like their Eurasian and north African counterparts, peoples of sub-Saharan Africa organized productive societies, built powerful states, and participated in large-scale networks of communication and exchange. Internal African processes drove much of this development. Between 1000 and 1500 C.E., in the wake of the Bantu and other migrations (discussed in chapter 2), population increases in sub-Saharan Africa led societies there to organize states, develop centers of economic specialization, and conduct interregional trade. Alongside these internal processes, relations with other peoples of the eastern hemisphere also profoundly influenced the development of African societies. From the early centuries C.E. to 1500 and later as well, trade with lands of the Mediterranean and the Indian Ocean basins encouraged African peoples to produce commodities desired by consumers throughout much of the eastern hemisphere. This trade promoted urban development, the organization of large states and empires, and the introduction of new food crops and new religious beliefs into sub-Saharan Africa.

# EFFECTS OF EARLY AFRICAN MIGRATIONS

By 1000 C.E. Bantu-speaking peoples had settled in most parts of Africa south of the equator, and Kushite, Sudanese, Mande, and other peoples had also established communities in lands far from their original homes. For the next several centuries, African peoples built societies on the foundation of small communities that the Bantu and other migrations had generated.

## Agriculture and Population Growth

The principal early result of the Bantu and other migrations was to spread agriculture and herding to almost all parts of Africa. As they established agricultural societies, cultivators and herders displaced or absorbed many of the hunting, gathering, and fishing peoples who previously inhabited sub-Saharan Africa. After about 500 B.C.E., most Bantu peoples possessed iron metallurgy, which enabled them to fashion iron tools that facilitated further clearing of lands and extension of agriculture. By the early centuries C.E., cultivation and herding had reached the southernmost parts of Africa. The expansion of agriculture, in turn, resulted in increased agricultural production, rising population, and pressure for continuing migration to new territories.

BANANAS    The introduction of bananas to Africa encouraged a fresh migratory surge. First domesticated in southeast Asia, bananas entered Africa by way of the Indian Ocean. Between about 300 and 500 C.E., Malay seafarers from the islands that make up modern Indonesia colonized the island of Madagascar and established banana cultivation there. From Madagascar, bananas easily made the jump to the east African mainland. By 500 C.E. several varieties of bananas had become well established in Africa.

Cultivation of bananas allowed the Bantu to expand into heavily forested regions where yams and millet did not grow well. Indeed, bananas increased the supply of available food, enriched the Bantu diet, and allowed sub-Saharan populations to expand more rapidly than before.

**POPULATION GROWTH**     The population history of sub-Saharan Africa clearly reflects the significance of iron metallurgy and bananas. In 400 B.C.E., before iron working had deeply influenced the continent's societies, the population of sub-Saharan Africa stood at about 3.5 million. By 800 C.E., after banana cultivation had spread throughout the continent, the sub-Saharan population had climbed to 17 million. And by 1000, when the Bantu migrations had introduced agriculture and iron metallurgy to most regions of sub-Saharan Africa, the population had passed 22 million.

The continuing Bantu migrations, the expansion of Bantu population, and the establishment of new Bantu communities contributed to changes in relationships between Bantu and foraging peoples such as the forest dwellers of central Africa (the people once referred to as pygmies). In the past, the Bantu had often relied on the foragers as guides as they expanded into unfamiliar forest environments. However, as Bantu populations surged, many foragers were displaced by growing numbers of agricultural settlements. As a result, some forest peoples joined the cultivators and effectively integrated into Bantu society, while others retreated deeper into the forest to sustain their small-scale societies.

## *African Political Organization*

By 1000 C.E., the Bantu had approached the limits of their expansion. Because agricultural peoples already occupied most of the continent, migrating into new territories and forming new settlements was much more difficult than before. Instead of migrating in search of new lands to cultivate, then, African peoples developed increasingly complex forms of government that enabled them to organize their existing societies more efficiently.

**KIN-BASED SOCIETIES**     Most early Bantu societies did not depend on an elaborate hierarchy of officials or a bureaucratic apparatus to administer their affairs. Instead, Bantu peoples governed themselves mostly through family and kinship groups. Usually, Bantu peoples settled in villages with populations averaging about one hundred people. Male heads of families constituted a village's ruling council, which decided public affairs for the entire group. The most prominent of the family heads presided over the village as a chief and represented the settlement when it dealt with neighboring peoples. A group of villages constituted a district, which became the principal focus of loyalties. Usually, there was no chief or larger government for the district. Instead, village chiefs negotiated on matters concerning two or more villages. Meanwhile, within individual villages, family and kinship groups disciplined their own members as necessary.

**CHIEFDOMS**     This type of organization lends itself particularly well to small-scale communities, but kin-based societies often grew to large proportions. After about 1000 C.E., kin-based societies faced difficult challenges as population growth strained resources. Conflicts between villages and districts became more frequent and more intense. Increased conflict encouraged Bantu communities to organize military forces for both offensive and defensive purposes, and military organization in turn encouraged the development of more formal structures of government.

Many districts fell under the leadership of powerful chiefs, who overrode kinship networks and imposed authority on their territories. Some of these chiefs conquered their neighbors and consolidated their lands into small kingdoms. These local kingdoms emerged in several regions of sub-Saharan Africa after about 1000 C.E. The kingdoms of Ife and Benin, for example, arose in the forested regions of west Africa. Both realms were city-states in which the court and urban residents controlled the surrounding countryside through family relationships and political alliances. Both Ife and Benin also produced magnificent sculptures that put human faces and figures to the early history of sub-Saharan Africa. Local kingdoms appeared also in southern Africa and central Africa.

**Ife** (EE-fehy)
**Benin** (beh-NEEN)

**IFE SCULPTURE.** | According-
ing to legend, this handsome
terra-cotta head represents an
ambitious warrior who usurped
power in the small state of Ife
(in modern Nigeria). Produced
shortly after 1000 C.E., it testifies
to the increasing tensions in sub-
Saharan politics after the turn of
the millennium.

**KINGDOM OF KONGO** One of the most active areas of political development was the basin of the Congo River (also known as the Zaire River). After about 1000 C.E. population pressures and military challenges encouraged kin-based societies in the Congo region to form small states embracing a few villages each. By 1200 conflict between these small states had resulted in the organization of larger, regional principalities that could better resist political and military pressures. One of the more prosperous of the Congolese states was the kingdom of Kongo, which participated actively in trade networks involving copper, raffia cloth, and nzimbu shells from the Atlantic Ocean. During the fourteenth century the kingdom of Kongo came to embrace much of the modern-day Republic of the Congo and Angola.

The central government of Kongo included the king and officials who oversaw military, judicial, and financial affairs (including a royal currency system based on cowry shells). Beneath the central government were six provinces administered by governors, each of whom supervised several districts administered by subordinate officials. Within the districts, villages ruled by chiefs provided local government. Though not the only kingdom in sub-Saharan Africa, Kongo was perhaps the most tightly centralized of the early Bantu kingdoms. The kingdom of Kongo provided effective organization from the fourteenth until the mid–seventeenth century, when Portuguese slave traders undermined the authority of the kings and the central government.

Kin-based societies did not disappear with the emergence of formal states. In fact, many survived well into the nineteenth century. Yet regional states and large kingdoms became increasingly prominent during the centuries after 1000 C.E. as Bantu and other African peoples responded to population pressures and military challenges facing their societies.

# AFRICAN SOCIETY AND CULTURAL DEVELOPMENT

By the eleventh century C.E., Africa was a land of enormous diversity. The peoples of sub-Saharan Africa spoke some eight hundred languages, and the continent supported a wide variety of societies and economies: mobile bands of hunting and gathering peoples, fishing peoples who lived alongside the continent's lakes and coasts, nomadic herders, subsistence farmers who migrated periodically to fresh lands, settled cultivators, and city-based societies that drew their livelihoods from mining, manufacturing, and trade. Although that diversity makes it difficult to speak of African society and cultural development in general terms, certain social forms and cultural patterns appeared widely throughout sub-Saharan Africa.

## Social Classes

In kingdoms, empires, and city-states, such as Kongo, Mali, and Kilwa, respectively, African peoples developed complex societies with clearly defined classes: ruling elites, military nobles, administrative officials, religious authorities, merchants, artisans, peasants, and slaves. These societies more or less resembled those found in other settled, agricultural lands of Eurasia organized by powerful states.

In the small states and kin-based societies of sub-Saharan Africa, however, social structures were different. Small states often generated an aristocratic or ruling elite, and they always recognized a class of religious authorities. Yet in general, kinship, sex and gender expectations, and age groupings were the principal considerations that determined social position in such societies.

**KINSHIP GROUPS** Extended families and clans served as the main foundation of social and economic organization in small-scale agricultural societies. The institution of privately owned property, found in most societies in north Africa and Eurasia, did not exist in sub-Saharan

Africa. Instead, communities claimed rights to land and used it in common. The villages of sub-Saharan Africa, where most of the population lived, generally consisted of several extended family groups. Male heads of families jointly governed the village and organized the work of their own groups. They allocated portions of the communal lands for their relatives to cultivate and were responsible for distributing harvests equitably among all members of their groups.

SEX AND GENDER RELATIONS   Sex and gender relations also influenced the roles and occupations of individuals in society. Workers with special skills were mostly men. Leather tanning, for example, was the work of men who carefully guarded knowledge of their techniques and passed them down to their heirs. Iron working, which was highly prestigious, was also the work of men. Blacksmiths often served as community leaders, and like leather tanners, they passed knowledge of their craft down to their heirs. Men usually undertook the heavy labor of clearing land and preparing it for cultivation, although both men and women participated in the planting and harvesting of crops. Women's roles also included tending to domestic chores and taking primary responsibility for child rearing.

WOMEN'S ROLES   As in other societies, men largely monopolized public authority. Yet women in sub-Saharan Africa generally had more opportunities open to them than did their counterparts in other lands. Women enjoyed high honor as the sources of life. On at least a few occasions, women made their ways to positions of power, and aristocratic women often influenced public affairs. Women merchants commonly traded at markets, and they participated actively in both local and long-distance trade in Africa. Sometimes women even engaged in combat and organized all-female military units.

The arrival of Islam did not change the status of women in sub-Saharan Africa as dramatically as it did in Arabia and southwest Asia. South of the Sahara, early converts to Islam came mostly from the ranks of the ruling elites and the merchant classes. Because it did not become a popular faith for several centuries after its introduction, Islam did not deeply influence the customs of most Africans. Even at royal courts where Islam attracted eager converts, Muslims of sub-Saharan Africa simply did not honor the same social codes as their counterparts elsewhere. For the most part, Muslim women in sub-Saharan Africa socialized freely with men outside their immediate families, and they continued to appear and work openly in society. Thus Islam did relatively little to curtail the opportunities available to women or to compromise their status in sub-Saharan Africa.

AGE GRADES   Apart from kinship and expectations based on sex and gender roles, African society also made a place for age groups that included all individuals within a given community born within a few years of one another. Members of age grades performed tasks appropriate for their levels of development, and they often bonded with one another to form tight circles of friends and political allies. Members of an age grade might provide labor for community projects, for example, or take joint responsibility for looking after village elders. They aided members who experienced adversities and helped one another at crucial junctures, such as marriage and the building of a new household. Thus age grades had the effect of establishing social ties that crossed the lines of family and kinship.

SLAVERY   One class of individuals stood apart from the other social groups: slaves. As in other lands, the institution of slavery had had a place in Africa since antiquity. Most slaves were captives of war. Others came from the ranks of debtors, suspected witches, and criminals. Within Africa most slaves probably worked as agricultural laborers, although many also worked as construction laborers, miners, or porters. Slaves were an important form of personal wealth in sub-Saharan Africa. In the absence of private property, sub-Saharans could not become wealthy through the accumulation of landholdings. Instead, the accumulation of slaves enabled individuals or families to display their wealth, to enhance their positions in society, and also to increase their agricultural production. For those reasons, slave trading and slaveholding were prominent features of sub-Saharan African society.

**SLAVE TRADING**   After about the ninth century C.E., the expansion of the trans-Saharan and Indian Ocean trade networks stimulated increased traffic in African slaves. In previous centuries, eastern Europeans had been the main source of slaves in the trading networks of Muslim merchants. Yet the demand for slaves became greater than eastern Europe could supply. As a result, Muslim merchants turned increasingly to sub-Saharan Africa as an alternative source for slaves.

In response to that demand, slave raiding became an increasingly prominent activity within Africa itself. Rulers of large-scale states and empires began to make war on smaller, weaker states and kin-based societies in search of captives. In some years, ten to twenty thousand Africans left their homes as slaves. Indeed, although smaller than the Atlantic slave trade of modern times, the Islamic slave trade was a sizable affair: between 750 and 1500 C.E. the number of African slaves transported to foreign lands may have exceeded ten million. The high demand led to the creation of networks within Africa that supplied slaves and served as a foundation for the Atlantic slave trade in later centuries. Although records of the Islamic slave trade are scarce, a lengthy uprising known as the *Zanj* revolt allows a glimpse of the harsh conditions under which many of these slaves toiled. The term *Zanj* referred to black slaves from the Swahili coast, many of whom worked on sugarcane plantations or cleared land for cultivation in southern Mesopotamia by the seventh century C.E. Slave revolts were not uncommon, and about 869 a rebel slave named Ali bin Muhammad organized about fifteen thousand Zanj slaves into a massive force that captured Basra, the most important city of southern Mesopotamia. The rebels then proceeded to establish a state in the region, which was only defeated by the Abbasid rulers fourteen years later.

## African Religion

Peoples of sub-Saharan Africa developed a wide range of languages, societies, and cultural traditions. Religious beliefs and practices in particular took many forms. The continent's peoples referred to their deities by different names, told different stories about them, and honored them with different rituals. Yet certain features were common to many religions of sub-Saharan Africa. In combination, these features offer considerable insight into the cultural and religious climate of sub-Saharan Africa in premodern times.

**CREATOR GOD**   Many African peoples had held monotheistic beliefs from the early days of Sudanic agriculture. Although those beliefs were not static over time, many peoples recognized a single divine force as the agent responsible for setting the world in motion and providing it with order. Some peoples believed that this god also sustained the world, intervening indirectly, through spirits, to influence the course of human affairs. Some considered this deity to be all-powerful, others regarded it as all-knowing, and many considered it both omnipotent and omniscient.

**LESSER GODS AND SPIRITS**   Apart from the superior creator god, Africans recognized many lesser gods and spirits often associated with the elements and with natural features. Unlike the creator god, these lesser deities participated actively in the workings of the world. They could confer or withhold benefits and bring favor or injury to humans. Similarly, most Africans believed that the souls of departed ancestors had the power to intervene in the lives of their descendants: the departed could bring good fortune to descendants who behaved properly and honored their ancestors, and they could also bring misfortune as punishment for evil behavior and neglect of their ancestors' memory. Much of the ritual of African religions focused on honoring deities, spirits, or ancestors' souls to win their favor or regain their goodwill. The rituals included prayers, animal sacrifices, and ceremonies marking important stages of life—such as birth, circumcision, marriage, and death.

**DIVINERS**   Like other peoples of the world, Africans recognized classes of religious specialists—individuals who had the power to mediate between humanity and supernatural beings. Often referred to as diviners, they were intelligent people, usually men though

**Zanj** (zahn-jee)

sometimes women, who understood clearly the networks of political, social, economic, and psychological relationships within their communities. When afflicted by illness, sterility, crop failure, or some other disaster, individuals or groups consulted diviners to learn the cause of their misfortune. Diviners then consulted oracles, identified the causes of the trouble, and prescribed medicine, rituals, or sacrifices designed to eliminate the problem and bring about a return to normality.

For the most part, African religion concerned itself not with matters of theology but, rather, with the more practical business of explaining, predicting, and controlling the experiences of individuals and groups in the world. Thus African religion strongly emphasized morality and proper behavior as essential to the maintenance of an orderly world. Failure to observe high moral standards would displease deities, spirits, and departed ancestors and ensure that misfortune befell the negligent parties. Because proper moral behavior was so important to their fortunes, family and kinship groups took responsibility for policing their members and disciplining those who fell short of expected standards.

## *The Arrival of Christianity*

**EARLY CHRISTIANITY IN NORTH AFRICA** Alongside religions that concentrated on the practical matter of maintaining an orderly world, Christianity reached Egypt and north Africa during the first century C.E., soon after the faith's appearance. Alexandria in Egypt became one of the most prominent centers of early Christian thought, and north Africa was the home of St. Augustine, an important leader of the fledgling church.

**CONGOLESE MASK.** | Entrancing and enthralling masks like this one from Congo were essential to the proper observance of religious rituals, which often involved communicating with natural or animal spirits. Masks transformed diviners and provided them with powers not accessible to normal humans. *What kinds of feelings might a mask like this have elicited from observers?*

**THE CHRISTIAN KINGDOM OF AXUM** About the middle of the fourth century C.E., Christianity established a foothold in the kingdom of Axum, located in the highlands of modern Ethiopia. The first Axumite converts were probably local merchants who traded with Mediterranean Christians calling at the port of Adulis on the Red Sea. As missionaries visited Ethiopia, the kings of Axum also converted to Christianity. Indeed, the kings of Axum were some of the first royal converts to Christianity, adopting the faith shortly after the Roman emperor Constantine himself. Missionaries later established monasteries, translated the Bible into the Ethiopian language, and worked to popularize Christianity throughout the kingdom.

The fortunes of Christianity in Ethiopia reflected the larger political experience of the region. In the late seventh century C.E., the ruling house of Axum fell into decline, and during the next several centuries the expansion of Islam left an isolated island of Christianity in the Ethiopian highlands. During the twelfth century, however, a new ruling dynasty undertook a centralizing campaign and enthusiastically promoted Christianity as a faith that could provide cultural unity for the land. From the twelfth through the sixteenth century, Christianity enjoyed particular favor in Ethiopia. During the twelfth century, the Ethiopian kings ordered the carving of eleven massive churches out of solid rock—a monumental work of construction that required enormous resources. During the thirteenth century, rulers of Ethiopia's Solomonic dynasty claimed descent from the Israelite kings David and Solomon in an effort to lend additional biblical luster to their authority. The fictional work *Kebra Negast (The Glory of Kings),* which undertook to trace that lineage, has recently become popular among Rastafarians and devotees of reggae music in Ethiopia, Jamaica, and other lands. Meanwhile, Christianity retained its privileged status in Ethiopia until it fell out of favor following the socialist revolution of 1974.

**Axum** (AHK-soom)

*Kebra Nagast* (kee-brah NAH-gahst)

**CHURCH OF ST. GEORGE.** Worshipers gather at the church of St. George at Lalibela, Ethiopia, a massive structure in the form of a cross. Workers excavated the surrounding earth and then carved the church itself out of a rock.

ETHIOPIAN CHRISTIANITY During the centuries after the Islamic conquests of Egypt, the Sudan, and northern Africa, Ethiopian Christians had little contact with Christians in other lands. As a result, although Ethiopian Christianity retained basic Christian theology and rituals, it increasingly reflected the interests of its African devotees. Ethiopian Christians believed that a large host of evil spirits populated the world, for example, and carried amulets or charms for protection against these menacing spirits. The twelfth-century carved-rock churches themselves harked back to pre-Christian values, since rock shrines had long been a prominent feature in Ethiopian religion. Not until the sixteenth century, when Portuguese mariners began to visit Ethiopia en route to India, did Ethiopians reestablish relations with Christians from other lands. By that time the Portuguese had introduced their Roman Catholic faith to the kingdom of Kongo, and Christianity began to win a place for itself elsewhere in sub-Saharan Africa.

# ISLAMIC KINGDOMS AND EMPIRES

After the eighth century C.E., Islam was also introduced to Africa. Islam arrived by two routes: it went to west Africa overland by trans-Saharan camel caravans, and it traveled to coastal east Africa over the sea-lanes of the Indian Ocean in the vessels of merchant mariners. After its introduction, Islam profoundly influenced the political, social, and economic development of sub-Saharan Africa as well as its cultural and religious development. At the same time, Africans in both west and east Africa adapted Islam to their own cultures, giving African Islam distinctly African characteristics.

# Trans-Saharan Trade and Islamic States in West Africa

The Sahara desert has never served as an absolute barrier to communication between human societies. Small numbers of nomadic peoples have lived in the desert itself since about 5000 B.C.E. These nomads migrated around the desert and had dealings with other peoples settled on its fringes. In addition, merchants occasionally organized commercial expeditions across the desert even in ancient and classical times.

CAMELS    Yet travel across the Sahara quickened substantially with the arrival of the camel. Camels came to north Africa from Arabia about the seventh century B.C.E. During the late centuries B.C.E., a special camel saddle, which took advantage of the animals' distinctive physical structure, also made its way to north Africa. Because a caravan took seventy to ninety days to cross the Sahara and because camels could travel long distances before needing water, they proved to be extremely useful beasts of burden in such an arid region. After about 300 C.E. camels became the preferred transport animals throughout the Sahara.

When Arab conquerors established their Islamic faith in north Africa during the seventh and eighth centuries, they also integrated the region into a rapidly expanding zone of commerce and communication. Soon afterward, Muslims in north Africa began to explore the potential of trade across the Sahara. By the late eighth century, Islamic merchants had trekked across the desert and established commercial relations with societies in sub-Saharan west Africa. There they found a series of long-established trading centers such as Gao, a terminus of caravan routes across the Sahara that offered access to the Niger River valley, which was a flourishing market for copper, ironware, cotton textiles, salt, grains, and carnelian beads.

THE KINGDOM OF GHANA    The principal state of west Africa at the time of the Muslims' arrival was the kingdom of Ghana (not related to the modern state of Ghana), situated between the Senegal and Niger rivers in a region straddling the border between the modern states of Mali and Mauritania. Ghana emerged as a kingdom at an uncertain but early date: according to legends preserved by Arab travelers, as many as twenty-two kings ruled in Ghana before Muhammad and his companions embarked on the *hijra*. Ghana probably developed as a state during the fourth or fifth century C.E. when agricultural peoples sought to protect their societies from the raids of camel-riding nomads who increasingly came out of the Sahara. When Muslims arrived in west Africa, the kingdom of Ghana was a regional state much like others that were emerging elsewhere in sub-Saharan Africa.

Kingdoms & empires of Africa
www.mhhe.com/bentleybrief2e

GOLD TRADE    As trade and traffic across the desert increased, Ghana underwent a dramatic transformation. It became the most important commercial site in west Africa because it was the center for trade in gold, which was in high demand throughout the eastern hemisphere. Muslim merchants flocked to camel caravans traveling across the Sahara to Ghana in search of gold for consumers in the Mediterranean basin and elsewhere in the Islamic world. Ghana itself did not produce gold, but the kings procured nuggets from lands to the south— probably from the region around the headwaters of the Niger, Gambia, and Senegal rivers, which enjoyed the world's largest supply of gold available at the time. By controlling and taxing trade in the precious metal, the kings both enriched and strengthened their realm. Apart from gold, merchants from Ghana provided ivory and slaves for traders from north Africa. In exchange, they received horses, cloth, small manufactured wares, and salt.

KOUMBI-SALEH    Integration into trans-Saharan trade networks brought enormous wealth and considerable power to Ghana. The kingdom's capital and principal trading site stood at Koumbi-Saleh, a small town today but a thriving commercial center with a population of some fifteen to twenty thousand people at its peak between the ninth and twelfth centuries. Al-Bakri, a Spanish Muslim traveler of the mid–eleventh century,

**Ghana** (GAH-nuh)

**MAP 15.1** | Kingdoms, empires, and city-states of sub-Saharan Africa, 800–1500 C.E. After the emergence of Islam, trans-Saharan overland routes linked sub-Saharan west Africa with the Mediterranean region, and maritime trade routes linked sub-Saharan east Africa to the Indian Ocean basin. *What role did trade play in the emergence of cities and states in sub-Saharan Africa?*

It took 70–90 days for a camel caravan to cross the Sahara Desert.

described Koumbi-Saleh as a flourishing site with buildings of stone and more than a dozen mosques. From taxes levied on trade passing through Ghana, the kings financed a large army—al-Bakri reported that they could field two hundred thousand warriors—that protected the sources of gold, maintained order in the kingdom, kept allied and tributary states in line, and defended Ghana against nomadic incursions from the Sahara.

**ISLAM IN WEST AFRICA**   By about the tenth century, the kings of Ghana had converted to Islam. Their conversion led to improved relations with Muslim merchants from north Africa as well as Muslim nomads from the desert who transported trade goods across the Sahara. It also brought them recognition and support from Muslim states in north Africa. The kings of Ghana made no attempt to impose Islam forcibly on their society, nor did they accept Islam exclusively even for their own purposes. Instead, they continued to observe traditional religious customs: al-Bakri mentioned, for example, that native religious specialists practiced magic and kept idols in the woods surrounding the royal palace at Koumbi-Saleh. Even in the absence of efforts to impose Islam on Ghana, however, the faith attracted converts, particularly among those engaged in trade with Muslim merchants from the north.

As the kingdom expanded to the north, it became vulnerable to attacks by nomadic peoples from the Sahara who sought to seize some of the kingdom's wealth. During the early thirteenth century, raids from the desert weakened the kingdom, and it soon collapsed. Political leadership in west Africa then fell to the powerful Mali empire, which emerged just as the kingdom of Ghana dissolved.

**SUNDIATA** The lion prince Sundiata (reigned 1230–1255) built the Mali empire during the first half of the thirteenth century. Through alliances with local rulers, a reputation for courage in battle, and a large army dominated by cavalry, Sundiata had consolidated his hold on the Mali empire by about 1235. The empire embraced Ghana as well as other, neighboring kingdoms in the regions surrounding the Senegal and Niger rivers.

**THE MALI EMPIRE AND TRADE** Mali benefited from trans-Saharan trade on an even larger scale than Ghana had. From the thirteenth until the late fifteenth century, Mali controlled and taxed almost all trade passing through west Africa. Enormous caravans with as many as twenty-five thousand camels linked Mali to north Africa. The capital city of Niani attracted merchants seeking gold, and market cities on the caravan routes such as Timbuktu, Gao, and Jenne grew crowded and wealthy. Like the earlier kings of Ghana, the rulers of Mali honored Islam and provided protection, lodging, and comforts for Muslim merchants from the north. Also like the Ghanaian kings, they did not force Islam on their realm. Rather, they encouraged its spread on a voluntary basis.

**MANSA MUSA** The significance of trade and Islam for west Africa became clearest during the reign of Sundiata's grand-nephew Mansa Musa, who ruled Mali from 1312 to 1337, during the high point of the empire. Mansa Musa observed Islamic tradition by making his pilgrimage to Mecca in 1324–1325. His party formed a huge caravan that included thousands of soldiers, attendants, subjects, and slaves as well as a hundred camels carrying satchels of gold. In fact, during his three-month visit to Cairo along the way, Mansa Musa distributed so much gold that the metal's value declined by as much as 25 percent on local markets.

**MANSA MUSA AND ISLAM** Mansa Musa drew great inspiration from his pilgrimage to Mecca, and on returning to Mali he took his religion even more seriously than before. He built mosques, and he sent promising students to study with distinguished Islamic scholars in north Africa. He also established religious schools and brought in Arabian and north African teachers, including four descendants of Muhammad, to make Islam better known in Mali.

Within a century of Mansa Musa's reign, Mali was in serious decline: factions crippled the central government, provinces seceded from the empire, and military pressures came both from neighboring kingdoms and from desert nomads. By the late fifteenth century, the Songhay empire had completely overcome Mali. Yet Mansa Musa and other Mali rulers had established a tradition of centralized government that the Songhay realm would continue, and they had ensured that Islam would have a prominent place in west African society over the long term.

**WEST AFRICAN SCULPTURE.** This terra-cotta sculpture from the thirteenth or fourteenth century depicts a helmeted and armored warrior astride a horse with elaborate harness and head protection. *What can this sculpture tell us about the values of the society that produced it?*

Mansa Musa, king of Mali
www.mhhe.com/
bentleybrief2e

Great Mosque at Timbuktu
www.mhhe.com/
bentleybrief2e

# The Indian Ocean Trade and Islamic States in East Africa

While trans-Saharan caravan traffic linked west Africa to the larger trading world of the eastern hemisphere, merchant mariners sailing the sea-lanes of the Indian Ocean performed a similar service for Swahili societies in coastal east Africa. *Swahili* is an Arabic term meaning "coasters," referring to those who engaged in trade along the east African coast. Swahili society developed as a result of Bantu migrations to east Africa in the early centuries C.E. These migrants introduced agriculture, cattle herding, and iron metallurgy to the region, and here, as elsewhere in sub-Saharan Africa, they founded complex societies governed by small, local states. As their population increased, Bantu peoples founded settlements on the coasts and

**Timbuktu** (tim-buhk-TOO)

**Gao** (gou)

**Jenne** (jehn-neh)

**Mansa Musa** (MAHN-suh MOO-suh)

offshore islands as well as the interior regions of east Africa. These coast dwellers supplemented their agricultural production with ocean fishing and maritime trade.

**THE SWAHILI**   The Swahili dominated the east African coast from Mogadishu in the north to Kilwa, the Comoro Islands, and Sofala in the south. They spoke a Bantu language, also known as Swahili, supplemented with words and ideas borrowed from Arabic. Swahili peoples developed different dialects, but they communicated readily among themselves because individuals frequently visited other Swahili communities in their ocean-going craft. Indeed, all along the east African coast, Swahili society underwent similar patterns of development with respect to language, religion, architecture, and technology.

In the tenth century, Swahili society attracted increasing attention from Islamic merchants. From the interior regions of east Africa, the Swahili obtained gold, slaves, ivory, and exotic local products, which they traded for pottery, glass, and textiles that Muslim merchants brought from Persia, India, and China.

**THE SWAHILI CITY-STATES**   By the eleventh and twelfth centuries, trade had brought important changes to coastal east Africa, just as it had done in west Africa. By controlling and taxing trade within their jurisdictions, local chiefs grew wealthy, strengthened their own authority, and increased the influence of their communities. Gradually, trade concentrated at several coastal and island port cities that enjoyed especially convenient locations: Mogadishu, Lamu, Malindi, Mombasa, Zanzibar, Kilwa, Mozambique, and Sofala. Each of these sites developed into a powerful city-state governed by a king who supervised trade and organized public life in the region.

The cities themselves underwent an impressive transformation. Whereas most buildings were traditionally made of wood and dried mud, by about the twelfth century Swahili peoples began to construct large coral buildings, and by the fifteenth century the main Swahili towns boasted handsome stone mosques and public buildings. Meanwhile, urban Swahili elites dressed in silk and fine cotton clothes, and they set their tables with porcelain imported from China.

**KILWA**   Travelers' reports and recent archaeological discoveries have thrown especially clear light on the development of Kilwa, one of the busiest city-states on the east African coast. With a population of about twelve thousand, Kilwa was a thriving city with many stone buildings and mosques. Residents imported cotton and silk textiles as well as perfumes and pearls from India, and archaeologists have unearthed a staggering amount of Chinese porcelain. Merchants of Kilwa imported these products in exchange for gold, slaves, and ivory obtained from interior regions. By the late fifteenth century, Kilwa exported about a ton of gold per year.

**Swahili** (swah-HEE-lee)

**ZIMBABWE** The influence of long-distance trade also had important effects on the interior regions of east Africa. Indeed, trade and the wealth that it brought underwrote the establishment of large and powerful kingdoms in east and central Africa. The best known of these kingdoms was Zimbabwe. The term *zimbabwe* simply refers to the dwelling of a chief. About the early thirteenth century, interior peoples built a magnificent stone complex known as Great Zimbabwe near Nyanda in the modern state of Zimbabwe. Within stone walls 5 meters (16 feet) thick and 10 meters (32 feet) tall, Great Zimbabwe was a city of stone towers, palaces, and public buildings that served as the capital of a large kingdom. At the time of its greatest extent in the late fifteenth century, up to eighteen thousand people may have lived in the vicinity of Great Zimbabwe, and the kingdom stretched from the outskirts of the Swahili city of Sofala deep into the interior of south-central Africa.

Kings residing at Great Zimbabwe controlled and taxed the trade between the interior and coastal regions. They organized the flow of gold, ivory, slaves, and local products from sources of supply to the coast. Their control over these products enabled them to forge alliances with local leaders and to profit handsomely from commercial transactions. Just as the trans-Saharan trade encouraged the building of states and empires in west Africa, the Indian Ocean trade generated wealth that financed the organization of city-states on the coast and large kingdoms in the interior regions of east and central Africa.

**ISLAM IN EAST AFRICA** In east Africa, as in west Africa, trade brought cultural as well as political changes. Like their counterparts in west Africa, the ruling elites and the wealthy merchants of east Africa converted to the Islamic faith. They did not necessarily give up their religious and cultural traditions but, rather, continued to observe them for purposes of providing cultural leadership in their societies. By adopting Islam, however, they laid a cultural foundation for close cooperation with Muslim merchants. Moreover, Islam served as a fresh source of legitimacy for their rule, since they gained recognition from Islamic states in southwest Asia, and their conversion opened the door to political alliances with Muslim rulers in other lands. Even though the conversion of elite classes did not bring about the immediate spread of Islam throughout their societies, it enabled Islam to establish a presence in east Africa under the sponsorship of influential patrons. The faith eventually attracted interest in larger circles and became one of the principal cultural and religious traditions of east Africa.

Kilwa (KILH-wah)

Zimbabwe (zihm-BAHB-way)

Distant view of Great Zimbabwe
www.mhhe.com/bentleybrief2e

**GREAT ZIMBABWE.** Built between the 11th and 15th centuries C.E. in what is now modern Zimbabwe, this stone city complex covered 1,800 acres.

# Ibn Battuta on Muslim Society at Mogadishu

*During the fourteenth century the Moroccan jurist Ibn Battuta traveled throughout much of the eastern hemisphere. Twice he visited sub-Saharan Africa: in 1331, when he traveled along the Swahili coast, and in 1351–1352, when he visited the Mali empire. His account of his visit to the Swahili city of Mogadishu offers insight into the mercantile and social customs of the city as well as the hospitality accorded to distinguished visitors.*

[Mogadishu] is a town of enormous size. Its inhabitants are merchants possessed of vast resources: they own large numbers of camels, of which they slaughter hundreds every day [for food], and also have quantities of sheep. In this place are manufactured the woven fabrics called after it, which are unequalled and exported from it to Egypt and elsewhere. It is the custom of the people of this town that, when a vessel reaches the anchorage, the sumbuqs, which are small boats, come out to it. In each sumbuq there are a number of young men of the town, each one of whom brings a covered platter containing food and presents it to one of the merchants on the ship saying "This is my guest," and each of the others does the same. The merchant, on disembarking, goes only to the house of his host among the young men, except those of them who have made frequent journeys to the town and have gained some acquaintance with its inhabitants; these lodge where they please. When he takes up residence with his host, the latter sells his goods for him and buys for him; and if anyone buys anything from him at too low a price or sells to him in the absence of his host, that sale is held invalid by them. This practice is a profitable one for them.

When the young men came on board the vessel in which I was, one of them came up to me. My companions said to him "This man is not a merchant, but a doctor of the law," whereupon he called out to his friends and said to them "This is the guest of the qadi." There was among them one of the qadi's men, who informed him of this, and he came down to the beach with a number of students and sent one of them to me. I then disembarked with my companions and saluted him and his party. He said to me "In the name of God, let us go to salute the Shaikh." "And who is the Shaikh?" I said, and he answered, "The Sultan," for it is their custom to call the sultan "the Shaikh." . . .

When I arrived with the qadi . . . at the sultan's residence, one of the serving-boys came out and saluted the qadi, who said to him "Take word to the intendant's office and inform the Shaikh that this man has come from the land of al-Hijaz [Arabia]." So he took the message, then returned bringing a plate on which were some leaves of betel and areca nuts, the same to the qadi, and what was left on the plate to my companions and the qadi's students. He brought also a jug of rose-water of Damascus, which he poured over me and over the qadi [i.e., over our hands], and said "Our master commands that he be lodged in the students' house," this being a building equipped for the entertainment of students of religion. . . .

We stayed there three days, food being brought to us three times a day, following their custom. On the fourth day, which was a Friday, the qadi and students and one of the Shaikh's viziers came to me, bringing a set of robes; these [official] robes of theirs consist of a silk wrapper which one ties round his waist in place of drawers (for they have no acquaintance with these), a tunic of Egyptian linen with an embroidered border, a furred mantle of Jerusalem stuff, and an Egyptian turban with an embroidered edge. They also brought robes for my companions suitable to their position. We went to the congregational mosque and made our prayers behind the maqsura [private box for the sultan]. When the Shaikh came out of the door of the maqsura I saluted him along with the qadi; he said a word of greeting, spoke in their tongue with the qadi, and then said in Arabic "You are heartily welcome, and you have honored our land and given us pleasure."

■ From Ibn Battuta's report, how could you characterize the role of hospitality on the Swahili coast?

SOURCE: H. A. R. Gibb, trans. *The Travels of Ibn Battuta, A.D. 1325–1354,* 4 vols. Cambridge: Hakluyt Society, 1958–94, 2:374–77.

# SUMMARY

States and societies of sub-Saharan Africa differed considerably from those in other parts of the eastern hemisphere. The foundations of most sub-Saharan societies were the agricultural economy and iron-working skills that Bantu and other peoples spread throughout most of the African continent. As these peoples migrated to new regions and established new communities, they usually based their societies on kin groups rather than the state structures that predominated elsewhere in the eastern hemisphere. When different societies came into conflict with one another, however, they increasingly established formal political authorities to guide their affairs. African peoples organized states of various sizes, some very small and others quite large. When they entered into commercial relationships with Muslim peoples in southwest Asia and north Africa, they also built formidable imperial states in west Africa and bustling city-states in coastal east Africa. These states had far-reaching implications for sub-Saharan societies because they depended on a regular and reliable flow of trade goods—particularly gold, ivory, and slaves—and they encouraged African peoples to organize themselves politically and economically to satisfy the demands of foreign Muslim merchants. Trade also had cultural implications because it facilitated the introduction of Islam, which together with native African traditions profoundly influenced the development of sub-Saharan societies. After the eighth century, ruling elites in both west Africa and coastal east Africa mostly accepted Islam and strengthened its position in their societies by building mosques, consulting Muslim advisors, and supporting Islamic schools. By 1500 C.E. African traditions and Islamic influences had combined to fashion a series of powerful, productive, and distinctive societies in sub-Saharan Africa.

## STUDY TERMS

age grades (287)
Axum (289)
bananas (284)
Bantu peoples (284)
Benin (285)
camels (291)
Ghana (291)

Great Zimbabwe (295)
Ife (285)
Islamic slave trade (288)
*Kebra Negast* (289)
Kilwa (294)
kin-based societies (285)
kingdom of Kongo (286)

Koumbi-Saleh (291)
Mansa Musa (293)
Sundiata (283)
Swahili (293)
trans-Saharan trade (291)
*Zanj* revolt (288)

## FOR FURTHER READING

Ibn Battuta. *Ibn Battuta in Black Africa*. Ed. and trans. by Said Hamdun and Noel King. Princeton, 1998. Translations of travel accounts of visits to coastal east Africa and the empire of Mali by a famous fourteenth-century Moroccan traveler.

Paul Bohannan and Philip D. Curtin. *Africa and Africans*. 3rd ed. Prospect Heights, Ill., 1988. Exploration of themes in African history, society, and culture by an anthropologist and a historian.

Christopher Ehret. *The Civilizations of Africa: A History to 1800*. Charlottesville, Va., 2002. An important contribution that views Africa in the context of world history.

J. F. P. Hopkins and N. Levtzion, eds. *Corpus of Early Arabic Sources for West African History*. Princeton, 2000. Translations of numerous important accounts by Muslim merchants and geographers who reported on conditions in west Africa before modern times.

Ali A. Mazrui. *The Africans: A Triple Heritage*. Boston, 1986. Emphasizes the legacies of indigenous, Islamic, and western influences on African history.

John S. Mbiti. *African Religions and Philosophy*. 2nd ed. London, 1990. A thorough and systematic study of traditional African religions in their cultural context.

Roderick James McIntosh. *The Peoples of the Middle Niger: The Island of Gold*. Oxford, 1998. Fascinating volume emphasizing the environmental context of west African history.

John Middleton. *The World of the Swahili: An African Mercantile Civilization*. New Haven, 1992. Rich scholarly analysis that places modern Swahili society and culture in its historical context.

D. T. Niane, ed. *Sundiata: An Epic of Old Mali*. Trans. by G. D. Pickett. London, 2006. Translation of the story of Sundiata, founder of the Mali empire, as preserved in African oral tradition.

Jan Vansina. *Paths in the Rainforests: Toward a History of Political Tradition in Equatorial Africa*. Madison, 1990. A brilliant synthesis of early African history by one of the world's foremost historians of Africa.

# Christian Western Europe during the Middle Ages

n 1260 C.E. two brothers, Niccolò and Maffeo Polo, traveled from their native Venice to Constantinople. The Polo brothers were jewel merchants, and while in Constantinople, they decided to pursue opportunities farther east. They went first to trading cities on the Black Sea and the Volga River and then spent three years in the great central Asian trading city of Bokhara. While in Bokhara, they received an invitation to join a diplomatic embassy going to the court of Khubilai Khan. They readily agreed and traveled by caravan to the Mongol court, where the great khan received them and inquired about their land, rulers, and religion.

Khubilai was especially interested in learning more about Roman Catholic Christianity. Thus he asked the Polo brothers to return to Europe and request the pope to send learned theologians who could serve as authoritative sources of information on Christian doctrine. They accepted the mission and returned to Italy in 1269 as envoys of the great khan.

The Polo brothers were not able to satisfy the great khan's desire for expertise in Christian doctrine. The pope designated two missionaries to accompany the Polos, and the party set out in 1271, together with Niccolò's seventeen-year-old son, Marco Polo. Soon, however, the missionaries became alarmed at fighting along the route, and they decided to abandon the embassy and return to Europe. Only the Polos completed the journey, arriving at the Mongol court of Shangdu in 1274. Although they presented Khubilai with presents and letters from the pope rather than the requested missionaries, the great khan received them warmly. In fact, they remained in China in the service of the great khan for the next seventeen years. Their mission gave rise to Marco Polo's celebrated account of his travels, and it signaled the reintegration of Europe into the political and economic affairs of the larger eastern hemisphere.

**PSI img** Khubilai Khan with the Polo brothers
www.mhhe.com/
bentleybrief2e

During the early middle ages—from about 500 to 1000 C.E.—western Europe was a violent and disorderly land. The collapse of the western Roman empire and invasions by migratory peoples wrecked European society and the economy. The Germanic Carolingian empire—ruled most famously by Charlemagne—provided order in much of Europe only for a short time before a new series of invasions brought it down in 843 C.E. As a result of the turmoil and disarray that plagued Europe during the half millennium from 500 to 1000 C.E., western Europeans played little role in the development of a hemispheric economy during the era dominated by the Tang, Song, Abbasid, and Byzantine empires.

《 *A street scene of fabric and furniture merchants.*

**Khubilai Khan** (KOO-bih-lie Kahn)

# CHRONOLOGY

| | |
|---|---|
| 476 | Fall of the western Roman empire |
| 480–547 | Life of St. Benedict of Nursia |
| 481–511 | Reign of Clovis |
| 482–543 | Life of St. Scholastica |
| 590–604 | Reign of Pope Gregory I |
| 751–843 | Carolingian kingdom |
| 768–814 | Reign of Charlemagne |
| 800 | Coronation of Charlemagne as emperor |
| 843 | Dissolution of the Carolingian empire |
| 936–973 | Reign of King Otto I of Saxony |
| 962 | Coronation of Otto I as Holy Roman Emperor |
| 1066 | Norman invasion of England |
| 1096–1099 | First crusade |
| 1170–1221 | Life of St. Dominic |
| 1182–1226 | Life of St. Francis |
| 1187 | Recapture of Jerusalem by Saladin |
| 1202–1204 | Fourth Crusade |
| 1225–1274 | Life of St. Thomas Aquinas |
| 1271–1295 | Marco Polo's trip to China |

However, Europeans did begin to lay the foundations of a more dynamic society in the early middle ages. For example, regional states began to provide a stable political order. New tools and technologies led to increased agricultural production and economic growth. In addition, the western Christian church brought cultural and religious unity to most of Europe. Based on such political, economic, and cultural foundations, Europeans were able to build a vibrant and powerful society from about 1000 to 1300 C.E.—the period known in Europe as the "high middle ages."

Although the idea of empire continued to fascinate European leaders, no one managed to bring all of Europe under their control during the high middle ages. Instead, local rulers organized powerful regional states. Increased agricultural production fueled rapid population growth. Economic expansion led to increased long-distance trade, enriched cities, and helped to create new towns.

Political organization, demographic increase, and economic growth pushed Europeans once again into the larger world. European merchants began to participate directly in the commercial economy of the eastern hemisphere, sometimes traveling as far as China in search of luxury goods. Ambitious military and political leaders expanded the boundaries of Christendom by seizing Muslim-held territories in Spain and the Mediterranean islands. European forces even mounted a series of military crusades that sought to recapture Palestine and the city of Jerusalem from Muslim control. Those efforts clearly demonstrated that Europeans were beginning to play a much larger role in the world than they had for the previous half millennium.

# THE QUEST FOR ORDER AND THE ESTABLISHMENT OF REGIONAL STATES

Long after its disappearance in the late fifth century C.E. the Roman empire inspired European leaders, who dreamed of a centralized political structure embracing all of Christian Europe. Yet it was not until the late eighth and ninth centuries that a Germanic group, the Franks, temporarily reestablished imperial authority in western Europe. Even then, imperial authority was short-lived and collapsed by the late ninth century. In the late tenth century, a new attempt was made by German princes who formed the Holy Roman Empire, which they viewed as a Christian revival of the earlier Roman empire. In fact, however, the Roman empire returned only in name. All attempts to extend its influence beyond Germany met stiff resistance from the popes and from the princes of other European lands. Medieval Europe became a political mosaic of independent and competing regional states. Independent monarchies emerged in France and England, and other authorities ruled the various regions of Italy and Spain. These states frequently clashed with one another, and they all faced perennial challenges from within. Yet they organized their own territories efficiently, and they laid the foundations for the emergence of powerful national states in a later era.

# The Franks and the Temporary Revival of Empire

Just a few decades after the Germanic general Odovacer deposed the last of the western Roman emperors in 476 C.E., the invaders organized a series of Germanic kingdoms as successor states in place of the Roman Empire. However, from the fifth through the eighth centuries, continuing invasions and conflicts among the invaders themselves left western Europe in a shambles. A major problem was that none of the Germanic peoples possessed the resources—much less the political and social organization—to dominate all the others and establish their hegemony throughout western Europe. Yet by the ninth century, one of these groups—the Franks—not only became the most powerful of the Germanic peoples, but also built an impressive imperial state that temporarily organized about half of the territories formerly embraced by the western Roman empire.

**CHARLEMAGNE.** | A bronze statue depicts Charlemagne riding a horse and carrying an orb symbolizing his imperial authority.

**CHARLEMAGNE**  The Franks had won their dominance over other Germanic peoples as a result of strong military leadership as well as the support of the popes in Rome, who appreciated the Franks' conversion to Roman Christianity in the late fifth century. The Frankish realm reached its high point under the rule of the Carolingian family line during the reign of Charlemagne ("Charles the Great"), who ruled from 768 to 814. Charlemagne possessed enormous energy, and the building of the Carolingian empire was in large measure his personal accomplishment. Although barely literate, Charlemagne was extremely intelligent. He spoke Latin, understood some Greek, and regularly conversed with theologians and other learned men. He also maintained diplomatic relations with the Byzantine empire and the Abbasid caliphate. When Charlemagne inherited the Frankish throne, his realm included most of modern France as well as the lands that now form Belgium, the Netherlands, and southwestern Germany. By the time of his death in 814, Charlemagne had extended his authority to northeast Spain, Bavaria, northern Germany, and Italy as far south as Rome.

**CHARLEMAGNE'S ADMINISTRATION**  Charlemagne established a court and capital at Aachen (in modern Germany), but he spent most of his reign traveling throughout his realm to maintain his authority. In his absence, Charlemagne relied on aristocratic deputies, known as counts, who held political, military, and judicial authority in local jurisdictions. However, because the counts often had their own political ambitions that were not the same as those of the central government, Charlemagne instituted a new group of imperial officials known as *missi dominici* ("envoys of the lord ruler"), who traveled annually to review the accounts of all local authorities.

**CHARLEMAGNE AS EMPEROR**  Charlemagne worked extremely hard to keep his territories together. Although he had built the Frankish kingdom into an empire, he hesitated to call himself emperor because he knew the title would constitute a direct challenge to the Byzantine emperors who had inherited the eastern Roman empire. In 800, however, Charlemagne did accept the title when Pope Leo III publicly recognized his accomplishments by proclaiming him emperor during religious services on Christmas Day.

**DISSOLUTION OF THE CAROLINGIAN EMPIRE**  Yet Charlemagne's empire did not last long after his death. Indeed, both internal disunity and external invasions brought the Carolingian empire to an early end. By 843 Charlemagne's

**Odoacer** (AHD-oh-ah-cer)

**Charlemagne** (SHAHR-leh-mane)

**Carolingian** (kah-roe-LIN-gee-uhn)

**Aachen** (AH-kehn)

MAP 16.1 | The Carolingian empire, 814 C.E. Notice the location of Charlemagne's capital at Aachen and also the extent of his empire. *What geographical challenges did he face in his efforts to hold his empire together?*

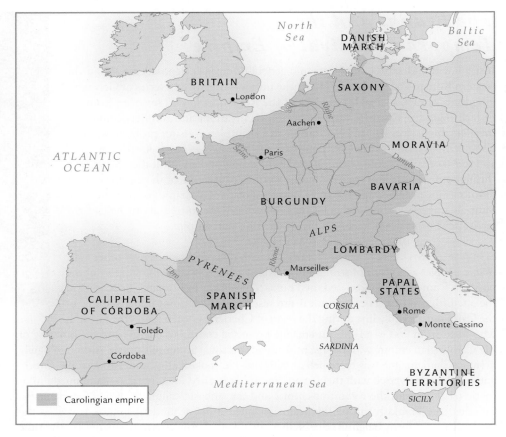

three grandsons—who fought bitterly between themselves for the title of emperor—decided that they would solve the problem by dividing the empire into three kingdoms. Even had the empire remained unified, however, it was already apparent that local counts in the empire's vast realms were increasingly ignoring the central imperial government in favor of their own interests. Moreover, Muslim invaders from the south, Hungarian Magyar invaders from the east, and Viking invaders from the north all contributed to massive instability in the region and helped to ensure the ultimate dissolution of the empire.

# The Holy Roman Empire

OTTO I    As the Carolingian empire faded during the ninth century, local authorities took responsibility for providing order in their own regions. Gradually, some of them extended their influence beyond their own jurisdictions and built larger states. Otto of Saxony was particularly aggressive. By the mid–tenth century, he had established himself as king in northern Germany, and twice he ventured into Italy to quell political disturbances, protect the church, and seek opportunities in the south. In appreciation for his aid to the church, Pope John XII proclaimed Otto emperor in 962 C.E. Thus was born the Holy Roman Empire.

The imperial title had considerable cachet, and on several occasions energetic emperors almost transformed the Holy Roman Empire into a hegemonic state that might have reintroduced imperial unity to Europe. Conflict with the papacy, however, prevented the emperors from building a strong and dynamic state. Although the popes crowned the medieval emperors, their relations were usually tense, since both popes and emperors made large claims to authority in Christian Europe. Relations became especially strained when emperors sought to influence the selection of church officials, which the popes regarded as their own prerogative, or when emperors sought to extend their authority into

**MAP 16.2** | The regional states of medieval Europe, 1000–1300 C.E. Note the large number of states and the different kinds of states that claimed sovereignty in medieval Europe. *How would this variety of states have contributed to instability in Europe?*

The Holy Roman Emperors claimed more territory than they could effectively rule.

Italy, where the popes had long provided political leadership. Thus when the popes felt threatened by the pretensions of the Holy Roman Empire, they entered into alliances with other European authorities to check the power of the emperors. Because of that, the Holy Roman Empire remained an empire principally in name. Voltaire, the eighteenth-century French writer, once quipped that the Holy Roman Empire was "neither holy, nor Roman, nor an empire." Instead, it was a regional state that ruled Germany and occasionally sought to wield influence in eastern Europe and Italy.

## *Regional Monarchies in France and England*

In the absence of an effective imperial power, regional states emerged throughout medieval Europe. In France and England, princes established regional monarchies on the basis of relationships between lords and their retainers.

CAPETIAN FRANCE    The French monarchy grew slowly from humble beginnings. When the last of the Carolingians died, in 987 C.E., the lords of France elected a minor noble named Hugh Capet to serve as king. Capet held only a small territory around

**Capet** (KAHP-it)

Paris, and some of his retainers were far more powerful than he. Over the next three centuries, however, his descendants, known as the Capetian kings, gradually added to their resources, expanded their political influence, and established the right to administer justice throughout the realm. By the early fourteenth century, the Capetian kings had gradually centralized power and authority in France.

Statutes of William the Conqueror
www.mhhe.com/ bentleybrief2e

**THE NORMANS**    The English monarchy developed quite differently. Its founders were Normans—descendants of Vikings who carved out a state on the peninsula of Normandy in France during the ninth century. Though nominally subject to Carolingian and later to Capetian rulers, the dukes of Normandy in fact pursued their own interests with little regard for their lords. Within Normandy the dukes built a tightly centralized state in which all authority stemmed from the dukes themselves. The dukes also retained title to all land in Normandy and strictly limited the right of their retainers to grant land to others. In 1066 Duke William of Normandy invaded England, then ruled by descendants of the Angles, the Saxons, and other Germanic peoples. Following a speedy military victory, the duke, now known as William the Conqueror, introduced Norman principles of government and land tenure to England and quickly established a tightly centralized realm.

Both the Capetians and the Normans faced internal challenges from retainers seeking to pursue independent policies or enlarge their powers. Both dynasties also faced external challenges: indeed, they often battled each other, since the Normans periodically sought to expand their possessions in France. On the basis of relationships between lords and retainers, however, both the Capetians and the Normans managed to organize regional monarchies that maintained order and provided reasonably good government.

## Regional States in Italy and Iberia

**ITALIAN STATES**    Regional states emerged also in other lands of medieval Europe, though not on such a large scale as the monarchies of France and England. In Italy, for example, a series of ecclesiastical states, city-states, and principalities competed for power and position. By about the twelfth century, a series of prosperous city-states—including Florence, Bologna, Genoa, Milan, and Venice—dominated not only their own urban districts but also the surrounding hinterlands. Meanwhile, in southern Italy, Norman adventurers invaded territories still claimed by the Byzantine empire and various Muslim states. With papal approval and support, they overcame Byzantine and Muslim authorities, brought southern Italy into the orbit of Roman Catholic Christianity, and laid the foundations for the emergence of the powerful kingdom of Naples.

The Alhambra in Granada
www.mhhe.com/ bentleybrief2e

**CHRISTIAN AND MUSLIM STATES IN IBERIA**    As in Italy, a series of regional states competed for power on the Iberian peninsula. From the eighth to the eleventh century, Muslim conquerors ruled most of the peninsula except for a few small states in northern Spain. Beginning in the mid–eleventh century, though, Christian adventurers from these states began to attack Muslim territories and enlarge their own domains. By the late thirteenth century, the Christian kingdoms of Castile, Aragon, and Portugal controlled most of the Iberian peninsula, leaving only the small kingdom of Granada in Muslim hands.

With its Holy Roman Empire, regional monarchies, ecclesiastical principalities, city-states, and new states founded on conquest, medieval Europe might seem to present a stark contrast to a centralized, reunified land such as China. Moreover, European rulers constantly campaigned to enlarge their holdings at the expense of their neighbors and thus endlessly complicated medieval European politics. Yet the regional states of the middle ages effectively tended to public affairs in limited regions. In doing so, they fashioned alternatives to a centralized empire as a form of political organization.

# ECONOMIC GROWTH AND
# SOCIAL DEVELOPMENT

As regional states provided increasingly effective political organization, regional lords and their vassals took charge of political and military affairs in a system historians have commonly referred to as feudalism. The relative order and stability provided by feudalism eventually encouraged dramatic economic growth and social development in medieval Europe. This economic revival closely resembled the processes that in an earlier era had strengthened China, India, and the Islamic world. Thus, even in the absence of centralized imperial authority, the increased agricultural production, urbanization, manufacturing, and trade spurred by feudalism transformed Europe and drew it once again into commercial relationships with distant lands.

## *Organizing a Decentralized Society*

When the short-lived Carolingian empire dissolved, European nobles had little choice but to take responsibility for maintaining order in their own territories. Although most nobles owed nominal allegiance to a higher authority, in reality they acted with growing independence: they collected rents and fees, administered local affairs, mobilized armed forces, and decided legal disputes.

**LORDS AND RETAINERS**   To organize their territories the local nobles built military and political relationships with other prominent individuals in their territories. In doing so, they mobilized small private armies by attracting armed retainers into their service with grants of land or money. These grants enabled retainers to devote their energies to the service of their lords rather than the tasks of cultivating food for their families. Retainers became responsible for the organization of local public works projects, the resolution of disputes, and the administration of justice. In exchange, retainers owed loyalty, obedience, and military service to their lords. As a result of these mutual obligations, lords and retainers merged into a hereditary noble class that lived off the surplus agricultural production it extracted from cultivators.

This decentralized political order developed into a complicated network of relationships between lords and retainers. Indeed, a lord with several retainers might himself be a retainer to a higher lord, who in turn might be one of several retainers to an even greater lord in a web of relationships extending from local communities to a king. Although this decentralized political order had the potential to lead to chaos if retainers decided to pursue their own interests, in several places—including England, Germany, and France—high-ranking lords built powerful states on such foundations.

## *Serfs, Manors, and the Growth of the Agricultural Economy*

**SERFS**   The development of a decentralized political order accompanied fundamental changes in European society. Among the most important of these changes was the creation, during the mid-seventh century, of a new category of peasants called serfs. Serfs were not slaves subject to sale, but neither were they fully free. Instead, landlords allocated serfs a certain portion of land to farm, and in exchange required both labor services as well as a portion of the serfs' harvest. Male serfs typically worked three days a week in the fields of their lords and provided additional labor services during planting and harvesting seasons, while women churned butter, made cheese, brewed beer, spun thread, wove cloth, or sewed clothes for the lords and their families. Because landlords provided them with land to cultivate and sometimes with tools and animals as well, serfs had little opportunity to move to different lands. Indeed, they were able to do so only with the permission of their lord. They even had to pay a fee for the right to marry a serf who worked for a different lord.

**MANORS** During the early middle ages, the institution of serfdom encouraged the development of the manor as the principal form of agricultural organization in western Europe. A manor was a large estate consisting of fields, meadows, forests, domestic animals, and serfs bound to the land. The lord of the manor was a prominent political or military figure who provided government, administration, and justice for the manor. In the absence of thriving cities, manors became largely self-sufficient communities. Lords of the manors maintained mills, bakeries, breweries, and wineries, and serfs produced most of the iron tools, leather goods, domestic utensils, and textiles that the manorial community needed. During the high middle ages, craft skills developed on manors would help fuel an impressive round of economic development in western Europe.

**NEW CROPS AND TOOLS** Peasant cultivators on manors also cleared forests, drained swamps, and increased the amount of land devoted to agriculture during the middle ages. As they did so, they also experimented with new agricultural techniques and implements. By the high middle ages European cultivators were experimenting with new crops and with different cycles of crop rotation to ensure the most abundant harvests without compromising the fertility of the soil. They increased cultivation especially of beans, which not only provided dietary protein but also enriched the land because of their property of fixing nitrogen in the soils where they grow. In addition, European peoples expanded their use of watermills and heavy plows, and introduced new tools like the horseshoe and horse collar—both of which increased the efficiency of agricultural labor. By the thirteenth century, observation and experimentation with new crops and new techniques had vastly increased understanding of agricultural affairs. News of these discoveries circulated widely throughout Europe in books and treatises on household economics and agricultural methods, which in turn led to increased agricultural productivity.

**POPULATION GROWTH** Expansion of land under cultivation, improved methods of cultivation, and the use of new tools combined to increase both the quantity and the quality of food supplies. During the centuries from 1000 to 1300, European diets expanded from an almost complete reliance on grains to include meat, dairy products, fish, vegetables, and legumes such as beans and peas. This increase in agricultural productivity supported rapid population growth. In 600 C.E., as the Franks were beginning to

*Some useful insights into the lives and experiences of common people come from a decree known as the "Capitulary de Villis" issued by the emperor Charlemagne in 807 C.E. as a guide for stewards of Carolingian estates. The decree envisions a community with sophisticated agricultural and craft skills. Probably few estates observed all provisions of Charlemagne's decree, but the capitulary nonetheless communicates clearly how lords hoped to control their manors and profit from their production.*

Each steward shall make an annual statement of all our income: an account of our lands cultivated by the oxen which our ploughmen drive and of our lands which the tenants of farms ought to plough; an account of the pigs, of the rents, of the obligations and fines; of the game taken in our forests without our permission; . . . of the mills, of the forest, of the fields, of the bridges, and ships; of the free men and the hundreds who are under obligations to our treasury; of markets, vineyards, and those who owe wine to us; of the hay, firewood, torches, planks, and other kinds of lumber; of the waste lands; of the fruits of the trees, of the nut trees, larger and smaller; of the grafted trees of all kinds; of the gardens; of the turnips; of the fish ponds; of the hides, skins, and horns; of the honey, wax; of the fat, tallow and soap; of the mulberry wine, cooked wine, mead, vinegar, beer, wine new and old; of the new grain and the old; of the hens and eggs; of the geese; the number of fishermen, [metal] smiths, sword-makers, and shoemakers; . . . of the forges and mines, that is iron and other mines; of the lead mines; . . . of the colts and fillies; they shall make all these known to us, set forth separately and in order, at Christmas, in order that we may know what and how much of each thing we have. . . .

[Stewards] must provide the greatest care, that whatever is prepared or made with the hands, that is, lard, smoked meat, salt meat, partially salted meat, wine, vinegar, mulberry wine, cooked wine . . . mustard, cheese, butter, malt, beer, mead, honey, wax, flour, all should be prepared and made with the greatest cleanliness. . . .

[Stewards should ensure] that in each of our estates, the chambers [living quarters] shall be provided with counterpanes, cushions, pillows, bed clothes, coverings for the tables and benches; vessels of brass, lead, iron and wood; andirons, chains, pot-hooks, adzes, axes, augers, cutlasses and all other kinds of tools, so that it shall never be necessary to go elsewhere for them, or to borrow them. And the weapons, which are carried against the enemy, shall be well cared for, so as to keep them in good condition; and when they are brought back they shall be placed in the chamber.

For our women's work they are to give at the proper time, as has been ordered, the materials, that is the linen, wool, woad, vermillion, madder, wool-combs, teasels, soap, grease, vessels and the other objects which are necessary.

Of the food products other than meat, two-thirds shall be sent each year for our own use, that is of the vegetables, fish, cheese, honey, mustard, vinegar, millet, panic [a grain similar to millet], dried and green herbs, radishes, and in addition of the wax, soap and other small products; and they shall tell us how much is left by a statement, as we have said above; and they shall not neglect this as in the past; because from those two-thirds, we wish to know how much remains.

Each steward shall have in his district good workmen, namely, blacksmiths, goldsmiths, silversmiths, shoemakers, [wood] turners, carpenters, sword-makers, fishermen, foilers [fine metalworkers], soap-makers, men who know how to make beer, cider, berry, and all other kinds of beverages, bakers to make pastry for our table, net-makers who know how to make nets for hunting, fishing and fowling, and the others who are too numerous to be designated.

■ On the basis of the "Capitulary de Villis," how would you characterize the conditions of material life in the Carolingian countryside?

SOURCE: *Translations and Reprints from the Original Sources of European History*, vol. 2. Philadelphia: University of Pennsylvania Press, 1900. (Translation slightly modified.)

---

gain dominance in western Europe, the European population stood at about twenty-six million. By 1000, when regional states had ended invasions and restored order, it had edged up to thirty-six million. By 1300, only three hundred years later, the population had reached seventy-nine million. Such rapid demographic growth in turn helped stimulate a vigorous revival of towns and trade in medieval Europe.

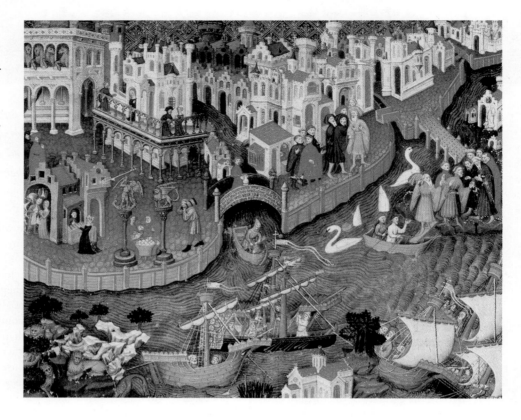

**VENICE.** | This city, the home of Marco Polo and a legion of merchants, drew enormous prosperity from trade. Street vendors, shopkeepers, and merchant ships figure prominently in this illustration from a fourteenth-century manuscript. *What advantages did proximity to the water lend to Venetian merchants?*

# The Revival of Towns and Trade

**URBANIZATION** With the abundant supplies of food produced on manors during the middle ages, by 1000 C.E. European society was able to support large numbers of urban residents. Attracted by urban opportunities, people from the countryside flocked to established cities and founded new towns at strategically located sites. Cities founded during Roman times, such as Paris, London, and Toledo, became thriving centers of government and business, and new urban centers—such as Venice in northern Italy—also emerged. Northern Italy and Flanders (the northwestern part of modern Belgium) experienced especially strong urbanization. Thus, for the first time since the fall of the western Roman empire, cities began to play a major role in European economic and social development.

**TEXTILE PRODUCTION** The growth of towns and cities brought about increasing specialization of labor, which in turn resulted in the dramatic expansion of manufacturing and trade. Manufacturing concentrated especially on the production of wool textiles. In fact, trade in wool products helped to fuel economic development, commercial exchange, and urbanization throughout Europe.

**MEDITERRANEAN TRADE** The revival of urban society was most pronounced in Italy, which was geographically well situated to participate in the trade networks of the Mediterranean basin. During the tenth century, for example, the cities of Amalfi and Venice served as ports for merchants engaged in trade with Byzantine and Muslim partners in the eastern Mediterranean. Italian merchants exchanged salt, olive oil, wine, wool fabrics, leather products, and glass for luxury goods such as gems, spices, silk, and other goods from India, southeast Asia, and China that Muslim merchants brought to eastern Mediterranean markets.

As trade expanded, Italian merchants established sizable communities in the major ports and commercial centers of the Mediterranean and the Black Sea, and by the mid–

thirteenth century some were even beginning to venture as far as central Asia, India, and China in search of commercial opportunities.

**THE HANSEATIC LEAGUE**   Although medieval trade was most active in the Mediterranean basin, a lively commerce grew up also in the northern seas. The Baltic Sea and the North Sea were sites of a particularly well-developed trade network known as the Hanseatic League, or more simply as the Hansa—an association of trading cities stretching from Novgorod to London and embracing all the significant commercial centers of northern Europe. The Rhine, the Danube, and other major European rivers linked the Hansa trade network with that of the Mediterranean.

**IMPROVED BUSINESS TECHNIQUES**   As in postclassical China and the Islamic world, a rapidly increasing volume of trade encouraged the development of credit, banking, and new forms of business organization in Europe. Bankers issued letters of credit to merchants traveling to distant markets, which could then be exchanged for merchandise or cash in the local currency.

Meanwhile, merchants devised new ways of spreading and pooling the risks of commercial investments. They entered into partnerships with other merchants, and they limited the liability of partners to the extent of their individual investments. These arrangements encouraged the formation of commercial partnerships, thus further stimulating the European economy.

## Social Change

**THE THREE ESTATES**   Medieval social commentators frequently held that European society embraced three estates or classes: "those who pray, those who fight, and those who work." Those who prayed were clergy of the Roman Catholic Church. From lowly parish priests to bishops, cardinals, and popes, the clergy constituted a spiritual estate owing its loyalty to the church rather than to secular rulers. The fighters came from the ranks of nobles. They inherited their positions in society and received an education that concentrated on equestrian skills and military arts. Finally, there were those who worked—the vast majority of the population—who mostly cultivated land as peasants.

The formula dividing society neatly into three classes captures some important truths about medieval Europe. It clearly reflects a society marked by political, social, and economic inequality: although they did not necessarily lead lives of luxury, those who prayed and those who fought enjoyed rights and honors denied to those who worked.

**CHIVALRY**   Yet, though expressing some truths, the formula overlooks processes that brought considerable change to medieval European society. Within the ranks of the nobles, for example, an emphasis on chivalry and courtly behavior gradually introduced expectations of high ethical standards and refined manners that encouraged warriors to become cultivated leaders of society. Chivalry was an informal but widely recognized code of ethics and behavior considered appropriate for nobles. Church officials originally promoted the chivalric code in an effort to curb fighting within Christendom. By the twelfth century the ritual by which a young man became initiated into the nobility as a knight commonly called for the candidate to place his sword on a church altar and pledge his service to God. Thus, the noble who observed the chivalric code would devote himself to the causes of order, piety, and the Christian faith. Over the long term, then, the code of chivalry helped to soften the manners of the nobility.

**INDEPENDENT CITIES**   Social change also touched those who worked. By the twelfth century the ranks of workers included not only peasants but also increasing numbers of merchants, artisans, crafts workers, and professionals who filled the growing

**Hanseatic** (han-see-AT-ik)

**FISH MARKET.** This painting from 1568 depicts a woman fishmonger working alongside her husband.

towns of medieval Europe. Because of their military power, lords could dominate these growing towns and tax their wealth. As towns grew larger, however, urban populations were increasingly able to resist the demands of nobles and guide their own affairs. By the late eleventh century, inhabitants of prosperous towns were demanding that local lords grant them charters of incorporation that exempted them from political regulation and allowed them to manage their own affairs. Sometimes groups of cities organized leagues to advance their commercial interests, as in the case of the Hansa, or to protect themselves against the encroachments of political authorities.

GUILDS   The cities of medieval Europe were by no means egalitarian societies. Yet medieval towns and cities also reflected the interests and contributions of the working classes. Merchants and workers in all the arts, crafts, and trades organized guilds that regulated the production and sale of goods within their jurisdictions. By the thirteenth century the guilds had come to control much of the urban economy of medieval Europe. For example, guilds oversaw the teaching of the various trades, established standards of quality for manufactured goods, determined the prices at which members had to sell their products, and regulated the entry of new workers into their groups.

Guilds had social as well as economic significance in that they provided a focus for friendship and mutual support in addition to work. Guild members regularly socialized with one another, and prosperous guilds often built large halls where members held meetings, banquets, and sometimes boisterous drinking parties. Guilds often came to the aid of members and their families by providing financial and moral support for those who fell ill. They also arranged funeral services for their deceased and provided support for survivors. Thus guilds constituted a kind of social infrastructure that made it possible for medieval cities to function.

URBAN WOMEN   Medieval towns and cities offered fresh opportunities for women as well as for men. Although few routes to public authority were open to women, in the larger towns and cities women worked alongside men as butchers, brewers, bakers, fishmongers, innkeepers, merchants, and occasionally physicians and pharmacists. Women dominated some occupations, particularly those involving textiles and decorative arts, such as sewing, spinning, weaving, and the making of hats, wigs, and fur garments.

In addition, most guilds admitted women into their ranks, and some guilds had exclusively female memberships. Indeed, the increasing prominence of women in European society illustrates the significance of towns and cities as agents of social change in medieval Europe.

# EUROPEAN CHRISTIANITY DURING THE MIDDLE AGES

One of the most important developments of the early middle ages was the conversion of western Europe to Roman Christianity. The Franks, the popes, and the monasteries played important roles in bringing about this conversion. The adoption of Roman Christianity ensured that medieval Europe would inherit crucial cultural elements from classical Roman society, including the Latin language and the institutional Roman church. In addition, Roman Catholic Christianity guided European thought on religious, moral, and ethical matters. Representatives of the Roman church administered the rituals associated with birth, marriage, and death. Most of the art, literature, and music of the middle ages drew inspiration from Christian doctrines and stories. Just as mosques and minarets defined the skylines of Muslim cities, the spires of churches and cathedrals dominated the landscape of medieval Europe, testifying visually to the importance of religion and the pervasive presence of the Roman Catholic church.

Western Christianity also changed in several ways during the late middle ages. As the Roman Catholic church developed an identity distinct from the Eastern Orthodox church, western theologians became reacquainted with the works of Aristotle—mostly unknown to European scholars of the early middle ages—and they produced an impressive synthesis of Aristotelian philosophy and Christian values. Meanwhile, lay classes elaborated a rich tradition of popular religion that represented an effort to express Christianity in meaningful terms.

## *The Politics of Conversion*

**THE FRANKS AND THE CHURCH**    Although Christianity was the principal source of religious, moral, and cultural authority in the Mediterranean basin by the time the Roman empire collapsed, western Europeans did not demonstrate a deep commitment to Christianity until the Franks converted to the religion in the late fifth century. By the time of Charlemagne, the Carolingian Franks viewed themselves as protectors of the papacy, and offered the popes both political and military support. Charlemagne also worked to spread Christianity in northern lands through both peaceful and military means. Between 772 and 804, for example, he waged a bitter campaign against the Saxons, a pagan people inhabiting northern Germany. When he finally claimed victory, Charlemagne insisted, not only that the Saxons acknowledge him as their political lord, but that they replace their pagan traditions with Christianity. Through campaigns such as this, as well as through diplomacy and the work of missionaries, by the year 1000 C.E. Christianity had won the allegiance of most people throughout western Europe and the Nordic lands.

## *The Papacy*

In addition to the support it received from the Franks, the Roman church increased its authority in Europe through strong papal leadership. When the western Roman empire collapsed, the papacy survived and claimed spiritual authority over all the lands formerly embraced by the empire. Initially, the popes cooperated closely with the Byzantine emperors, who as leaders of the eastern Roman empire seemed to be the natural heirs to Roman authority. Beginning in the late sixth century, however, the popes began increasingly to distinguish the western Christian church based in Rome from the eastern Christian church based in Constantinople. By 1054 C.E., the two churches differed so violently on so many issues that the pope and the patriarch of the eastern church excommunicated each other. After the eleventh century the two branches of Christianity formed distinct identities as the Roman Catholic and Eastern Orthodox churches.

POPE GREGORY I   The individual most important in providing the Roman church with its sense of identity and direction was Pope Gregory I (590–604 C.E.), also known as Gregory the Great. Most important, Gregory strengthened the pope's control over church doctrine by reasserting papal primacy—the claim that the bishop of Rome was the ultimate authority in the Christian church. Gregory also enhanced the influence of the Roman church in the lives of individuals by emphasizing the sacrament of penance, which required individuals to confess their sins to their priests and then to atone for their sins by penitential acts prescribed by the priests. In addition, Gregory further strengthened the Roman church by extending its appeal and winning new converts in western Europe through the efforts of missionaries, most of whom were monks. Indeed, Pope Gregory himself was a monk, and he relied heavily on the energies of his fellow monks in seeking converts throughout Europe.

## *Monasticism*

Christian monasticism had its origin in the second century C.E. in Egypt, where devout Christians had formed communes to devote themselves to the pursuit of holiness. When Christianity became legal during the fourth century, the monastic lifestyle became an increasingly popular alternative throughout the Roman empire.

ST. BENEDICT AND THE *RULE*   During the early days of monasticism, each community developed its own rules, procedures, and priorities. Some communities demanded that their inhabitants follow extremely austere lifestyles that sapped the energy of the monks, whereas others did not establish any clear expectations of their recruits. In response to those haphazard conditions, St. Benedict of Nursia (480–547 C.E.) strengthened the early monastic movement by providing it with discipline and a sense of purpose. In 529 St. Benedict prepared a set of regulations known as Benedict's *Rule* for the monastic community that he had founded at Monte Cassino, near Rome. The *Rule* required monks to take vows to lead communal, celibate lives under the absolute direction of the abbot who supervised the monastery: poverty, chastity, and obedience became the prime virtues for Benedictine monks.

ST. SCHOLASTICA   Through the influence of St. Benedict's sister, the nun St. Scholastica (482–543), an adaptation of the *Rule* soon provided guidance for the religious life of women living in convents. Within a century most European monasteries and convents observed the Benedictine *Rule*. Even today most Roman Catholic monasteries observe rules that reflect the influence of the Benedictine tradition.

Strengthened by the discipline that the Benedictine *Rule* introduced, monasteries became a dominant feature in the social and cultural life of western Europe throughout the middle ages. Monasteries helped to provide order in the countryside, for example, and to expand agricultural production. Monasteries accumulated large landholdings—as well as authority over serfs working their lands—from the bequests of wealthy individuals, and on those lands they mobilized both monks and serfs to clear forests, drain swamps, and prepare lands for cultivation. Indeed, monasteries organized much of the labor that brought about the expansion of agricultural production in early medieval Europe.

MONASTICISM AND SOCIETY   Like Buddhist monasteries in Asian lands and charitable religious foundations in Muslim lands, European monasteries provided a variety of social services. They served as inns, places of refuge, orphanages, hospitals,

**St. Scholastica** (skuh-LAS-tih-kah)

and schools. Some monasteries maintained libraries and scriptoria, where monks copied works of classical literature and philosophy as well as the scriptures and other Christian writings. Almost all works of Latin literature that have come down to the present survive because of copies made by medieval monks. Finally, monasteries served as a source of literate, educated, and talented individuals whose secretarial and administrative services were crucial for the organization of effective government in early medieval Europe.

Because of the various roles they played in the larger society, monasteries were particularly effective agents in the spread of Christianity. While they organized life in the countryside and provided social services, monks also zealously preached Christianity and tended to the spiritual needs of rural populations. Monks patiently and persistently served the needs of rural populations, and over the decades and centuries they helped to instill Christian values in countless generations of European peasants.

## *Schools, Universities, and Scholastic Theology*

**MONASTERY LIFE.** Monasteries were the principal centers of literacy in western Europe during the early middle ages. In this manuscript illustration, one monk copies a manuscript, another makes geometric calculations, and a third cuts parchment, while two work on the building and one more rings the bells that call monks and members of the surrounding community to religious services.

Founding of the University of Heidelberg
www.mhhe.com/bentleybrief2e

**CATHEDRAL SCHOOLS**   By the high middle ages, Europe's increasing wealth and social complexity created a strong demand for educated individuals who could deal with complicated political, legal, and theological issues. In response to such demand, by the eleventh century bishops and archbishops in France and northern Italy organized schools in their cathedrals and invited well-known scholars to serve as master teachers.

By the twelfth century the cathedral schools had established formal curricula. Instruction concentrated on the liberal arts, especially literature and philosophy. Students read the Bible and the writings of the church fathers, as well as classical Latin literature and the few works of Plato and Aristotle that were available in Latin translation. Some cathedral schools also offered advanced instruction in law, medicine, and theology.

**UNIVERSITIES**   About the mid–twelfth century, students and teachers organized academic guilds and persuaded political authorities to grant charters guaranteeing their rights. Student guilds demanded rigorous, high-quality instruction from their teachers, while faculty sought to vest teachers with the right to bestow academic degrees and to control the curriculum in their own institutions. These guilds had the effect of transforming cathedral schools into universities. By the late thirteenth century, universities had appeared in cities throughout Europe.

**SCHOLASTICISM: ST. THOMAS AQUINAS**   The evolution of the university coincided with the rediscovery of the works of Aristotle, which European scholars learned about through increased contacts with Byzantine as well as Muslim philosophers. During the thirteenth century, Latin translations of Aristotle's works spread throughout Europe, and they profoundly influenced almost all branches of thought. The most notable result was the emergence of scholastic theology, which sought to synthesize the beliefs and values of Christianity with the logical rigor of Greek philosophy. The most famous of the scholastic theologians was St. Thomas Aquinas (1225–1274), who spent most of his career teaching at the University of Paris. While holding fervently to his Christian convictions, St. Thomas believed that Aristotle had understood and explained the workings of the world better than any other thinker. St. Thomas saw no contradiction between Aristotle and Christian revelation. In his view, Aristotle explained the world according to human reason, while Christianity explained it as part of a divine plan. Thus, scholastic theology represented the synthesis of reason and faith. Like the neo-Confucianism of Zhu Xi or

St. Thomas Aquinas (uh-KWAHY-nuhs)

**NÔTRE DAME CATHE-DRAL.** | Architects and laborers sometimes worked more than a century to construct the massive gothic cathedrals of medieval Europe. Built during the twelfth and thirteenth centuries, the magnificent cathedral of Notre Dame in Paris honors the Virgin Mary. *What kinds of feelings might such massive structures have evoked in worshipers?*

the Islamic philosophy of Ibn Rushd, scholastic theology reinterpreted inherited beliefs in light of the most advanced knowledge of the time.

## Popular Religion

St. Thomas and the other scholastic theologians addressed a sophisticated, intellectual elite rather than the common people of medieval Europe. The popular masses neither knew nor cared much about Aristotle. For their purposes, Christianity was important primarily as a set of beliefs, ceremonies, and rituals that gave meaning to individual lives and that bound them together into coherent communities.

SACRAMENTS    Popular piety generally entailed observance of the sacraments and devotion to the saints recognized by the Roman Catholic church. Sacraments are holy rituals that bring spiritual blessings on the observants. The church recognized seven sacraments, including baptism, matrimony, penance, and the Eucharist. By far the most popular was the Eucharist, during which priests offered a ritual meal commemorating Jesus' last meal with his disciples before his trial and execution by Roman authorities. Because the sacrament kept individuals in good standing with the church, conscientious believers observed it weekly, and the especially devout on a daily basis. Popular beliefs held that the sacrament would protect individuals from sudden death and advance their worldly interests.

DEVOTION TO SAINTS    Popular religion also took the form of devotion to the saints. According to church teachings, saints were human beings who had led such exemplary lives that God held them in special esteem. As a result, they enjoyed special influence with heavenly authorities and were able to intervene on behalf of individuals living in the world. Medieval Europeans frequently invoked the aid of saints, who had reputations for helping living people as well as souls of the dead. Tradition held that certain saints could cure diseases, relieve toothaches, and guide sailors through storms to a port.

THE VIRGIN MARY    During the high middle ages, the most popular saint was always the Virgin Mary, mother of Jesus, who personified the Christian ideal of womanhood, love, and sympathy, and who reportedly lavished aid on her devotees. During the twelfth and thirteenth centuries, Europeans dedicated hundreds of churches and cathedrals to the Virgin, among them the splendid cathedral of Notre Dame ("Our Lady") of Paris.

**SAINTS' RELICS**    Medieval Europeans went to great lengths to express their adoration of the Virgin and other saints through veneration of their relics and physical remains, widely believed to retain the powers associated with the holy individuals themselves. Churches assembled vast collections of relics, such as clothes, locks of hair, teeth, and bones of famous saints. Especially esteemed were relics associated with Jesus or the Virgin, such as the crown of thorns that Jesus reportedly wore during his crucifixion or drops of the Virgin's milk miraculously preserved in a vial.

**PILGRIMAGE**    Some collections of relics became famous well beyond their own regions. Like Muslims making the hajj, pilgrims trekked long distances to honor the saints the relics represented. The making of pilgrimages became so common during the high middle ages that a travel industry emerged to serve the needs of pilgrims. Inns dotted the routes leading to popular churches and shrines, and guides shepherded groups of pilgrims to religious sites and explained their significance. There were even guidebooks that pointed out the major attractions along pilgrims' routes and warned them of difficult terrain and unscrupulous scoundrels who took advantage of visitors.

> **THINKING ABOUT** *Traditions*
>
> **TRADITIONS IN WESTERN EUROPE DURING THE MIDDLE AGES.** When a strong and sustained imperial authority failed to emerge in Europe in the centuries after the fall of the Roman empire, a wide variety of regional, self-sufficient states emerged to organize local affairs. In the early middle ages, most of these states did not have the wealth or capability to engage in long-distance trade or communication with the rest of the eastern hemisphere. In what ways did the relative isolation of European states in this period affect the development of cultural, political, and social traditions?

# THE MEDIEVAL EXPANSION OF EUROPE

During the high middle ages, the relationship between western European peoples and their neighbors underwent dramatic change. Powerful states, economic expansion, and demographic growth all strengthened European society, while church officials encouraged the colonization of pagan and Muslim lands as a way to extend the influence of Roman Catholic Christianity. Beginning about the mid–eleventh century, Europeans embarked on expansive ventures on several fronts: Atlantic, Baltic, and Mediterranean. All those ventures signaled clearly that Europeans were beginning to play a much larger role in the affairs of the eastern hemisphere than they had during the early middle ages.

 **Relic of John the Baptist** www.mhhe.com/ bentleybrief2e

## *Atlantic and Baltic Colonization*

**VINLAND**    During the ninth and tenth centuries, seafaring peoples from the Nordic Scandinavian lands began to venture far from Europe to the islands of the North Atlantic Ocean. They occupied Iceland beginning in the late ninth century, and by the end of the tenth century they had discovered Greenland and established a small colony there. About 1000 C.E. Leif Ericsson left the colony at Greenland and took an exploratory party south and west, arriving eventually at modern Newfoundland in Canada. Because of the wild grapes growing in the region, Leif called it Vinland. During the years following Leif's voyage, Greenlanders made several efforts to establish permanent colonies in Vinland. Ultimately, however, their efforts failed because they did not have the resources to sustain a settlement over the stormy seas of the North Atlantic Ocean. Nonetheless, the establishment of even a short-lived colony indicated a growing capacity of Europeans to venture into the larger world.

**CHRISTIANITY IN SCANDINAVIA**    While Scandinavians explored the North Atlantic, the Roman Catholic church drew Scandinavia itself into the community of Christian Europe. The kings of Denmark and Norway converted to Christianity in the

**Leif Ericsson** (leef ER-ik-suhn)

tenth century. Conversion of their subjects came gradually and with considerable resistance, but royal support for the Roman Catholic church ensured that Christianity would have a place in Danish and Norwegian societies. Between the twelfth and fourteenth centuries, Sweden and Finland followed their neighbors into the Christian faith.

**CRUSADING ORDERS AND BALTIC EXPANSION**  In the Baltic lands of Prussia, Livonia, and Lithuania, Christian authority arrived in the wake of military conquest. During the era of crusades, zealous Christians formed a series of military-religious orders. The most prominent were the Templars, Hospitallers, and Teutonic Knights, who pledged to devote their lives to the struggle against Muslims and pagans. The Teutonic Knights were most active in the Baltic region, where they waged military campaigns against the pagan Slavic peoples during the twelfth and thirteenth centuries. Aided by German missionaries, the Knights founded churches and monasteries in the territories they subdued. By the late thirteenth century, the Roman Catholic church had established its presence throughout the Baltic region, which progressively became absorbed into the larger society of Christian Europe.

## The Reconquest of Sicily and Spain

The boundaries of Christian Europe also expanded in the Mediterranean basin. There Europeans came into conflict with Muslims, whose ancestors had conquered the major Mediterranean islands and most of the Iberian peninsula between the eighth and tenth centuries. As their society became stronger, Europeans undertook to reconquer those territories and reintegrate them into Christian society.

**THE RECONQUEST OF SICILY**  Most important of the islands was Sicily, which Muslims had conquered in the ninth century. During the eleventh century, Norman warriors returned Sicily to Christian hands after almost twenty years of conflict. Islam did not disappear immediately, but as Muslims either left Sicily or converted to Christianity, Islam gradually disappeared from the island.

**THE RECONQUISTA OF SPAIN**  The reconquest of Spain—known as the *reconquista*—took a much longer time than the recapture of Sicily. Following the Muslim invasion and conquest of the early eighth century, the caliphate of Córdoba ruled almost all of the Iberian peninsula. A small Christian state survived in Catalonia in the far northeast, and the kingdom of León resisted Muslim advances in the far northwest. The process of *reconquista* began in the 1060s from these Christian toeholds. By 1150 Christian forces had recaptured Lisbon and established their authority over half of the peninsula. Their successes lured reinforcements from France and England, and in the first half of the thirteenth century a new round of campaigns brought most of Iberia into Christian hands. Only the kingdom of Granada in the far south of the peninsula remained Muslim. It survived as an outpost of Islam until 1492, when Christian forces mounted a campaign that conquered Granada and completed the *reconquista*.

The political, economic, and demographic strength of Christian Europe helps to explain the reconquests of Sicily and Spain as military ventures. Especially in the case of Spain, however, it is clear that religious concerns also helped to drive the *reconquista*. The popes and other leading clergy of the Roman Catholic church regarded Islam as an affront to Christianity, and they enthusiastically encouraged campaigns against the Muslims. When reconquered territories fell into Christian hands, church officials immediately established bishoprics and asserted Christian authority. They also organized campaigns to convert local populations. As a result of those efforts, the Roman Catholic church began to displace Islam in conquered Spain.

*reconquista* (ray-kohn-KEES-tah)

**MAP 16.3** | Medieval expansion of Europe, 1000–1250 C.E. Observe the paths taken by the European crusaders and invaders. ***What does the distance of these paths tell you about the military and organizational capabilities of Europeans in the high middle ages?***

The fourth crusade was diverted to Constantinople, where crusaders sacked the city.

# The Crusades

The term *crusade* refers to a holy war. It derives from the Latin word *crux,* meaning "cross," the device on which Roman authorities had executed Jesus. When a pope declared a crusade, warriors would "take up the cross" as a symbol of their faith, sew strips of cloth in the form of a cross on the backs of their garments, and venture forth to fight on behalf of Christianity. The most famous of these crusades were the enormous expeditions that Roman Catholic Christians mounted in an effort to recapture Palestine and the holy city of Jerusalem from Muslim authorities.

Summons to the crusade
www.mhhe.com/
bentleybrief2e

**URBAN II** Pope Urban II launched these crusades in 1095. The response to Urban's appeal was immediate and enthusiastic. A zealous preacher named Peter the Hermit traveled throughout France, Germany, and the Low Countries whipping up support among popular audiences. Within a year of Pope Urban's call, the Hermit had organized a ragtag army of poor knights and enthusiastic peasants—including women—and set out for Palestine without training, discipline, weapons, supplies, or plans. Not surprisingly, the campaign was a disaster: many members of Peter's band died, and few made it back to Europe. Yet the campaign indicated the high level of interest that the crusading idea generated among the European public.

**THE THIRD CRUSADE.** This painting commemorates the fall of Ptolemais (St. Jean d'Acre) to the Christian forces of King Richard I (the Lionheart) of England and King Philip II of France in 1191.

The crusades www.mhhe.com/bentleybrief2e

**PSI map** The crusades www.mhhe.com/bentleybrief2e

## THINKING ABOUT *Encounters*

**ENCOUNTERS IN WESTERN EUROPE DURING THE MIDDLE AGES.** By the high middle ages, increasing wealth and productivity in Europe encouraged many Europeans to rebuild lines of communication with the rest of the eastern hemisphere through trade, diplomacy, religious crusades, and exploration. In what specific ways did these encounters with a wider world change European trading patterns, tastes, technologies, and ideas?

**THE FIRST CRUSADE** Shortly after Peter's ill-fated venture, French and Norman nobles organized a more respectable military expedition to the holy land. In late 1096 the crusading armies began the long trek to Palestine. In 1097 and 1098 they captured Edessa, Antioch, and other strategic sites. In 1099 Jerusalem itself fell to the crusaders, who then proceeded to extend their conquests and carve conquered territories into Christian states.

Although the crusaders did not realize it, hindsight shows that their quick victories came largely because of division and disarray in the ranks of their Muslim foes. The crusaders' successes, however, encouraged Turks, Egyptians, and other Muslims to settle their differences, at least temporarily, in the interests of expelling European Christians from the eastern Mediterranean. By the mid–twelfth century the crusader communities had come under tremendous pressure. The crusader state of Edessa fell to Turks in 1144, and the Muslim leader Salah al-Din, known to Europeans as Saladin, recaptured Jerusalem in 1187. Crusaders maintained several of their enclaves for another century and even embarked on several more military expeditions, but Saladin's victories sealed the fate of Christian forces in the eastern Mediterranean.

Europeans did not immediately concede Palestine to the Muslims. By the mid–thirteenth century they had launched five major crusades, but none of the later ventures succeeded in reestablishing a Christian presence in Palestine. The fourth crusade (1202–1204) went badly astray. Venetian authorities contracted with military leaders to supply enough ships to transport some thirty thousand crusaders to Palestine. When crusaders could not come up with sufficient funds, Venetians directed them instead to conquer the Italian port city of Zara—a commercial rival of Venice—and then to attack Constantinople, the most important commercial center in the eastern Mediterranean. In fact, the fourth crusade never made it to Palestine. The ignoble venture ended after the crusaders conquered Constantinople, subjected the city to a ruthless sack, and installed a Roman Catholic regime that survived until 1261. The

Byzantine empire never fully recovered from this blow, and lumbered along in serious decline until Ottoman Turks toppled it in 1453. Yet even though the later crusades failed in their principal objective, they inspired European dreams of conquest in the eastern Mediterranean until the late sixteenth century.

**CONSEQUENCES OF THE CRUSADES**   As holy wars intended to reestablish Roman Catholic Christianity in the eastern Mediterranean basin, the crusades were wars of military and political expansion. Yet in the long run, the crusades were much more important for their social, economic, commercial, and cultural consequences. Even as European armies built crusader states in Palestine and Syria, European scholars and missionaries dealt with Muslim philosophers and theologians, and European merchants traded eagerly with their Muslim counterparts. The result was a large-scale exchange of ideas, technologies, and trade goods that profoundly influenced European development. Through their sojourns in Palestine and their regular dealings with Muslims throughout the Mediterranean basin, European Christians became acquainted with the works of Aristotle, Islamic science and astronomy, "Arabic" numerals (which Muslims had borrowed from India), and techniques of paper production (which Muslims had learned from China). They also learned to appreciate new food and agricultural products such as spices, granulated sugar, coffee, and dates as well as trade goods such as silk products, cotton textiles, carpets, and tapestries.

In the early days of the crusades, Europeans had little to exchange for those products other than rough wool textiles, furs, and timber. During the crusading era, however, Italian merchants seeking to meet the rising demand for luxury goods developed new products and marketed them in commercial centers and port cities. Thus Niccolò, Maffeo, and Marco Polo traded in gems and jewelry, and other merchants marketed fine woolen textiles or glassware. By the thirteenth century, large numbers of Italian merchants had begun to travel well beyond Egypt, Palestine, and Syria to avoid Muslim intermediaries and to deal directly with the producers of silks and spices in India, China, and southeast Asia. Thus, although the crusades largely failed as military ventures, they helped encourage the reintegration of western Europe into the larger economy of the eastern hemisphere.

# SUMMARY

Like societies in China, India, southwest Asia, and the eastern Mediterranean, western European society experienced massive change from 500 to 1300 C.E. Unlike those societies, however, rulers of medieval Europe were unable to reinstate an imperial form of government for long, and for centuries they did not participate actively in the larger trading world of the eastern hemisphere. Yet western Europeans found ways to maintain relative order and stability by decentralizing political responsibilities and relying on local authorities and regional states for political organization. The development of self-sufficient manors allowed western Europeans to expand agricultural production, which in turn spurred population growth as well as trade. In addition, western Christianity preserved elements of classical Roman society and established a foundation for cultural unity in western Europe. It was on these solid foundations that western Europe underwent thorough political and economic reorganization in the later middle ages. Regional states maintained good order and fostered rapid economic growth. Agricultural improvements brought increased food supplies, which encouraged urbanization, manufacturing, and trade. By the thirteenth century, European peoples traded actively throughout the Mediterranean, Baltic, and North Sea regions, and a few merchants even ventured as far away as China in search of commercial opportunities. The Roman Catholic church prospered, and advanced educational institutions reinforced the influence of Christianity throughout Europe. Christianity even played a role in European political and military expansion, since church officials encouraged crusaders to conquer pagan and Muslim peoples in Baltic and Mediterranean lands. Thus even in the absence of a strong imperial power, by 1300 western European peoples had strengthened their own society and began in various ways to interact regularly with their counterparts in other regions of the eastern hemisphere.

# STUDY TERMS

Capetian kings (303)
Carolingian empire (301)
cathedral schools (313)
Charlemagne (301)
chivalry (309)
crusades (317)
Eastern Orthodox Church (311)
Eucharist (314)
feudalism (305)
Franks (301)

guilds (310)
Hanseatic League (309)
Holy Roman Empire (302)
manors (306)
Normans (304)
Otto of Saxony (302)
Pope Gregory I (312)
Pope Urban II (317)
relics (315)

*reconquista* (316)
Roman Catholic Church (311)
sacraments (314)
scholasticism (313)
serfs (305)
St. Benedict of Nursia (312)
St. Scholastica (312)
St. Thomas Aquinas (313)
William the Conqueror (304)

# FOR FURTHER READING

Robert Bartlett. *The Making of Europe: Conquest, Colonization, and Cultural Change, 950–1350.* Princeton, 1993. A well-documented examination of European expansion from a cultural point of view.

Rosalind Brooke and Christopher Brooke. *Popular Religion in the Middle Ages: Western Europe, 1000–1300.* London, 1984. Well-illustrated essays on the faith of the masses.

Peter Brown. *The Rise of Western Christendom: Triumph and Diversity, A.D. 200–1000.* 2nd ed. Oxford, 2003. A landmark analysis of early Christian history that incorporates the findings of recent scholarship.

Georges Duby. *Rural Economy and Country Life in the Medieval West.* Trans. by C. Postan. Columbia, S.C., 1968. Authoritative and well-documented study of the medieval agrarian world by a distinguished scholar.

Patrick J. Geary, ed. *Readings in Medieval History.* Lewiston, N.Y., 1989. Offers substantial English translations of primary sources.

David Herlihy. *Opera Muliebra: Women and Work in Medieval Europe.* New York, 1990. Examines women's roles both in their own households and in the larger society of medieval Europe.

Richard Hodges and David Whitehouse. *Mohammed, Charlemagne, and the Origins of Europe: Archaeology and the Pirenne Thesis.* Ithaca, 1983. Draws on archaeological discoveries in placing the early medieval European economy in hemispheric context.

Hans Eberhard Mayer. *The Crusades,* 2nd ed. Oxford, 1988. Perhaps the best short history of the crusades.

Michael McCormick. *Origins of the European Economy: Communications and Commerce, A.D. 300–900.* Cambridge, Mass., 2001. A thorough and comprehensive analysis that emphasizes the participation of early medieval Europe in a larger Mediterranean economy.

J. R. S. Phillips. *The Medieval Expansion of Europe.* Oxford, 1988. Excellent survey of European ventures in the larger world during the high and late middle ages.

Susan Reynolds. *Kingdoms and Communities in Western Europe, 900–1300.* Oxford, 1984. An imaginative study focusing on the political and social values that undergirded western European society.

———. *Fiefs and Vassals: The Medieval Evidence Reinterpreted.* Oxford, 1994. A powerful scholarly critique of the concept of feudalism.

# Worlds Apart: The Americas and Oceania

I n November 1519 a small Spanish army entered Tenochtitlan, capital city of the Aztec empire. Although they had heard many reports about the wealth of the Aztec empire, nothing prepared them for what they saw. Years after the conquest of the Aztec empire, Bernal Díaz del Castillo, a soldier in the Spanish army, described Tenochtitlan at its high point. The city itself sat in the water of Lake Texcoco, connected to the surrounding land by three broad causeways, and, as in Venice, canals allowed canoes to navigate to all parts of the city. The imperial palace included many large rooms and apartments, and its armory was well stocked with swords, lances, knives, bows, arrows, slings, armor, and shields.

To Bernal Díaz the two most impressive sights were the markets and the temples of Tenochtitlan. The markets astonished him because of their size, the variety of goods they offered, and the order that prevailed there. In the principal market at Tlatelolco, a district of Tenochtitlan, Bernal Díaz found gold and silver jewelry, gems, feathers, embroidery, slaves, cotton, cacao, animal skins, maize, beans, vegetables, fruits, poultry, meat, fish, salt, paper, and tools. It would take more than two days, he said, to walk around the market and investigate all the goods offered for sale. His well-traveled companions-in-arms compared the markets favorably to those of Rome and Constantinople.

 **The city of Tenochtitlan** www.mhhe.com/ bentleybrief2e

The temples also struck Bernal Díaz, though in a different way. Aztec temples were the principal sites of rituals involving human sacrifice. Bernal Díaz described interior rooms of the temple so encrusted with blood that their walls and floors had turned black. Some of the interior rooms held the dismembered limbs of sacrificial victims, and others were resting places for thousands of human skulls and bones.

The contrast between Tenochtitlan's markets and temples challenged Bernal Díaz and his fellow soldiers. In the markets they witnessed peaceful exchange of the kind that took place all over the world. In the temples, however, they saw signs of human sacrifice on a scale

**Aztec human sacrifice** www.mhhe.com/ bentleybrief2e

rarely matched, if ever, anywhere else in the world. Yet, by the cultural standards of the Aztec empire, both the commercial activity of the marketplaces and the human sacrifice of the temples had a place in the maintenance of the world: trade enabled a complex society to function, and

❮ *A Mexica manuscript known as the Codex Borgia depicts Quetzalcóatl (left) as the lord of life and Tezcatlipoca (right) as the god of death.*

**Tenochtitlan** (teh-noch-tee-TLAHN)

**Texcoco** (TEHS-co-co)

**Tlatelolco** (tl-tay-LOL-ko)

# CHRONOLOGY

sacrificial rituals pleased the gods and persuaded them to keep the world going.

Although the peoples of Africa, Asia, and Europe interacted regularly before modern times, before 1492 the indigenous peoples of the Americas had only fleeting and random dealings with their contemporaries across the oceans. Yet between 1000 and 1500 C.E. the peoples of North and South America, like their counterparts in the eastern hemisphere, organized large empires with distinctive cultural and religious traditions, and they created elaborate trade networks touching most regions of the Americas.

The indigenous peoples of Australia and the Pacific islands had irregular and sporadic dealings with peoples outside Oceania. Within Oceania itself, Pacific islanders did maintain links between various island groups by sailing over the open ocean. Yet to a greater extent than their counterparts in the eastern hemisphere, the indigenous peoples of Australia and the Pacific islands built self-sufficient societies that tended to their own needs. Even though they had extremely limited amounts of land and other natural resources to work with, by the thirteenth century C.E. they had established well-organized agricultural societies and chiefly states throughout the Pacific islands.

## 17

# STATES AND EMPIRES IN MESOAMERICA AND NORTH AMERICA

Mesoamerica entered an era of war and conquest in the eighth century C.E. Great stores of wealth had accumulated in Teotihuacan, the largest early city in Mesoamerica. When Teotihuacan declined, it became a target for less-prosperous but well-organized forces from the countryside and northern Mexico. Attacks on Teotihuacan opened a long era of militarization and empire building in Mesoamerica that lasted until Spanish forces conquered the region in the sixteenth century. Most prominent of the peoples contesting for power in Mesoamerica were the Mexica, the architects of the Aztec empire.

## The Toltecs and the Mexica

During the ninth and early tenth centuries, after the collapse of Teotihuacan, several regional states dominated portions of the high central valley of Mexico, the area surrounding Mexico City. Although these successor states and their societies shared the religious and cultural traditions of Teotihuacan, they fought relentlessly among themselves. Their capital cities all stood on well-defended hill sites, and warriors figured prominently in their works of art.

**Teotihuacan** (teh-o-tee-WAH-kahn)
**Mexica** (MEHK-si-kah))

**TOLTECS** With the emergence of the Toltecs and later the Mexica, much of central Mexico again came under unified rule. The Toltecs began to migrate into the area from the arid land of northwestern Mexico about the eighth century. They settled mostly at Tula, about 50 kilometers (31 miles) northwest of modern Mexico City. There, the Toltecs tapped the waters of the nearby River Tula to irrigate crops of maize, beans, peppers, tomatoes, chiles, and cotton. At its high point, from about 950 to 1150 C.E., Tula supported a population that might have reached sixty thousand people, and another sixty thousand lived in the surrounding region.

The Toltecs also built a compact regional empire with their large and powerful army, and they transformed their capital into a wealthy city with the tribute they exacted from subject peoples. Indeed, the city of Tula became an important center of weaving, pottery, and obsidian work, and residents imported large quantities of jade, turquoise, animal skins, exotic bird feathers, and other luxury goods from elsewhere in Mesoamerica. The Toltecs maintained close relations with societies on the Gulf coast as well as with the Maya of Yucatan. Indeed, Tula shared numerous architectural designs and art motifs with the Maya city of Chichén Itzá some 1,500 kilometers (932 miles) to the east.

Beginning about 1125 C.E. the Toltec empire faced serious difficulties as conflicts between the different ethnic groups living at Tula led to civil strife. By the mid–twelfth century large numbers of migrants—mostly nomadic peoples from northwestern Mexico—had entered Tula and settled in the surrounding area. By 1175 the combination of civil conflict and nomadic incursion had destroyed the Toltec state.

**THE MEXICA** Among the migrants drawn to central Mexico from northwestern regions was a people who called themselves the Mexica, often referred to as Aztecs because they dominated the alliance that built the Aztec empire in the fifteenth century. (The term *Aztec* derives from *Aztlán,* "the place of the seven legendary caves," which the Mexica remembered as the home of their ancestors.) The Mexica arrived in central Mexico about the middle of the thirteenth century. They had a reputation for making trouble by kidnapping women from nearby communities and seizing land already cultivated by others. On several occasions their neighbors became tired of their disorderly behavior and forced them to move. For a century they migrated around central Mexico, fighting with other peoples and sometimes surviving only by eating fly eggs and snakes.

**TENOCHTITLAN** About 1345 the Mexica settled on an island in a marshy region of Lake Texcoco and founded the city that would become their capital—Tenochtitlan, on top of which Spanish conquerors later built Mexico City. The site offered several advantages. The lake harbored plentiful supplies of fish, frogs, and waterfowl, and it also enabled the Mexica to develop the *chinampa* system of agriculture. The Mexica dredged the fertile muck from the lake's bottom and built it up into small plots of land known as *chinampas.* During the dry season, cultivators tapped water from canals leading from the lake to their plots, and in the temperate climate they grew crops year-round. *Chinampas* were so productive that cultivators were sometimes able to harvest seven crops per year. The lake also served as a natural defense: waters protected Tenochtitlan on all sides, and Mexica warriors patrolled the three causeways that eventually linked their capital to the surrounding mainland.

**THE AZTEC EMPIRE** By the early fifteenth century, the Mexica were powerful enough to overcome their immediate neighbors and demand tribute from their new subjects. During the middle decades of the century, the Mexica launched ambitious campaigns of imperial expansion. Under the rule of "the Obsidian Serpent" Itzcóatl (1428–1440) and Motecuzoma I (1440–1469), also known as Moctezuma or Montezuma, they

Toltec and Aztec empires
www.mhhe.com/
bentleybrief2e

Yucatan (yoo-kuh-TAN)

Itzcóatl (tsee-ko-atl)

Motecuzoma (mo-tec-oo-ZO-ma)

**The Aztec built their capital in the middle of Lake Texcoco, which made for easier defense.**

**MAP 17.1** | The Toltec and Aztec empires, 950–1520 C.E. The Aztec empire stretched from the Gulf of Mexico to the Pacific Ocean. *How were Aztec rulers able to control these diverse territories?*

first advanced against Oaxaca in southwestern Mexico. After conquering the city and slaying many of its inhabitants, they populated Oaxaca with colonists, and the city became a bulwark for the emerging Mexica empire.

The Mexica next turned their attention to the Gulf coast. Finally, they conquered the cities of the high plateaus between Tenochtitlan and the Gulf coast. About the mid–fifteenth century the Mexica joined forces with two neighboring cities, Texcoco and Tlacopan (modern Tacuba), to create a triple alliance that guided the Aztec empire. Dominated by the Mexica and Tenochtitlan, the allies imposed their rule on about twelve million people and most of Mesoamerica, excluding only the arid northern and western regions and a few small, independent states.

**TRIBUTE AND TRADE**  The main objective of the triple alliance was to exact tribute from subject peoples. From nearby peoples the Mexica and their allies received food crops and manufactured items. Tribute obligations were sometimes very oppressive for subject peoples. The annual tribute owed by the state of Tochtepec on the Gulf coast, for example, included 9,600 cloaks, 1,600 women's garments, 200 loads of cacao (the source of cocoa and chocolate), and 16,000 rubber balls. Ruling elites entrusted some of these tribute items to officially recognized merchants, who took them to distant lands and exchanged them for local products including luxury items such as translucent jade, tortoise shells, jaguar skins, parrot feathers, and seashells. The tropical lowlands also supplied vanilla beans and cacao, from which Mexica elites prepared tasty beverages.

Unlike imperial states in the eastern hemisphere, the Aztec empire had no elaborate bureaucracy or administration. The Mexica and their allies simply conquered their subjects and assessed tribute, leaving local governance and the collection of tribute in the hands of the conquered peoples themselves. The allies did not even maintain military garrisons throughout their empire. Nor did they keep a permanent, standing army. Nevertheless, the Mexica in particular had a reputation for military prowess, and fear of reprisal kept most subject peoples in line.

At the high point of the Aztec empire in the early sixteenth century, tribute from some 489 subject territories flowed into Tenochtitlan, which was an enormously wealthy city.

**Oaxaca** (wah-hah-kah)

**Tlacopan** (Tee-laaa-co-pawn)

The Mexica capital had a population of about two hundred thousand people, and three hundred thousand more lived in nearby towns and suburban areas. The principal market had separate sections for merchants dealing in gold, silver, slaves, cloth, shoes, animal skins, turkeys, dogs, wild game, maize, beans, peppers, cacao, and fruits.

## Mexica Society

More information survives about the Mexica and their subjects than about any other people of the pre-Columbian Americas. A few Mexica books survived the Spanish conquest of the Aztec empire, and they offer direct testimony about the Mexica way of life. Moreover, a great deal of information survives from interviews conducted by Spanish missionaries with priests, elders, and other leaders of the Mexica during the mid–sixteenth century. In combination, these sources shed considerable light on Mexica society.

SOCIAL STRUCTURE    Mexica society was rigidly hierarchical, with public honors and rewards going mostly to the military elite. The Mexica looked on all males as potential warriors, but for the most part the military elite came from the Mexica aristocracy. Men of noble birth received the most intense training in military affairs, and they enjoyed the best opportunities to display their talents on the battlefield.

MEXICA TRIBUTE LIST.
A Spanish copy of a Mexica list records tribute owed by six northwestern towns to the ruler Motecuzoma II. Every two years the towns delivered, among other items, women's skirts and blouses, men's shirts, warriors' armor and shields, an eagle, and various quantities of maize, beans, and other foods.

WARRIORS    The Mexica showered wealth and honors on the military elite. Accomplished warriors received extensive land grants as well as tribute from commoners for their support. The most successful warriors formed a council whose members selected the ruler, discussed public issues, and filled government positions. They ate the best foods, and they consumed most of the luxury items that came into Mexica society by way of trade or tribute. Even dress reflected social status in Mexica society. Sumptuary laws required commoners to wear coarse, burlaplike garments made of henequen but permitted aristocrats to drape themselves in cotton. Successful warriors also enjoyed the right to don brightly colored capes and adorn themselves with lip plugs and eagle feathers.

MEXICA WOMEN    Women played almost no public role in a society so dominated by military values, but they wielded influence within their families and enjoyed honor as mothers of warriors. Mexica women did not inherit property or hold official positions, and the law subjected them to the strict authority of their fathers and husbands. However, women were prominent in the marketplaces, as well as in crafts involving embroidery and needlework.

With the exception of a few who dedicated themselves to the service of a temple, all Mexica women married. Mexica values taught that their principal function was to bear children, and society recognized the bearing of children as equal to a warrior's capture of enemies in battle. Indeed, women who died in childbirth won the same fame as warriors who died valiantly on the battlefield.

PRIESTS    Alongside the military aristocracy, a priestly class also ranked among the Mexica elite. Priests received a special education in calendrical and ritual lore, and they presided over religious ceremonies that the Mexica viewed as crucial to the continuation of the world. Priests read omens and explained the forces that drove the world, thereby wielding considerable influence as advisors to Mexica rulers. On a few occasions, priests even became supreme rulers of the Aztec empire: the ill-fated Motecuzoma II (reigned 1502–1520), ruler of the Aztec empire when Spanish invaders appeared in 1519, was a priest of the most popular Mexica cult.

**CULTIVATORS AND SLAVES**  The bulk of the Mexica population consisted of commoners who lived in hamlets cultivating lands allocated to their families by community groups known as *calpulli*. Originally, *calpulli* members claimed descent from common ancestors, but over time ancestry became less important than the fact that groups of families lived together in communities, organized their own affairs, and allocated community property to individual families. In addition to cultivating plots assigned by their *calpulli*, Mexica commoners also worked on the lands of aristocrats or warriors and contributed labor services to public works projects. Cultivators delivered periodic tribute payments to state agents, who distributed a portion of what they collected to the elite classes and stored the remainder in state granaries and warehouses. In addition to these cultivators of common birth, Mexica society included a large number of slaves, who usually worked as domestic servants. Most slaves were not foreigners, but Mexica who entered slavery because of financial distress or criminal behavior.

**ARTISANS AND MERCHANTS**  Skilled artisans, particularly those who worked with gold, silver, and other items destined for consumption by the elite, enjoyed considerable prestige in Mexica society. Merchants specializing in long-distance trade occupied an important but somewhat more tenuous position in Mexica society. Indeed, although these merchants supplied important luxuries to the elite as well as political and military intelligence about the lands they visited, they often fell under suspicion as greedy profiteers.

## *Mexica Religion*

When they migrated to central Mexico, the Mexica already spoke the Nahuatl language, which had been the prevalent tongue in the region since the time of the Toltecs. The Mexica soon adopted other cultural and religious traditions, some of which dated from the time of the Olmecs, shared by all the peoples of Mesoamerica. Most Mesoamerican peoples played a ball game in formal courts, for example, and maintained a complicated calendar based on a solar year of 365 days and a ritual year of 260 days. The Mexica enthusiastically adopted the ball game, and they also kept a sophisticated calendar.

**MEXICA GODS**  The Mexica also absorbed the religious beliefs common to Mesoamerica. Two of their principal gods—Tezcatlipoca, "the Smoking Mirror," and Quetzalcoatl, "the Feathered Serpent"—had figured in Mesoamerican pantheons at least since the time of Teotihuacan. Tezcatlipoca was a powerful figure, the giver and taker of life and the patron deity of warriors, whereas Quetzalcoatl supported arts, crafts, and agriculture. Like their predecessors, the Mexica believed that their gods had set the world in motion through acts of individual sacrifice. By letting their blood flow, the gods had given the earth the moisture it needed to bear maize and other crops. To win the favor of the gods and ensure the continuation of the world, the Mexica also engaged in sacrificial bloodletting. Mexica priests regularly performed acts of self-sacrifice, piercing their earlobes or penises with cactus spines in honor of the primeval acts of their gods.

**RITUAL BLOODLETTING**  Mexica priests also presided over the sacrificial killing of human victims. From at least the time of the Olmecs, Mesoamerican peoples had regarded the ritual sacrifice of human beings as essential to the world's survival. The Mexica, however, placed much more emphasis on human sacrifice than their predecessors had. To a large extent the Mexica enthusiasm for human sacrifice followed from their devotion to the god Huitzilopochtli as the patron deity of Mexica warriors. Military successes in the fourteenth century, when the Mexica subjected neighboring peoples to their

*calpulli* (kal-po-lee)

**Nahuatl** (na-watl)

**Tezcatlipoca** (tehs-cah-tlee-poh-cah)

**Quetzalcoatl** (keh-tzahl-koh-AHTL)

rule, increasingly persuaded them of Huitzilopochtli's favor. As Mexica military successes
mounted, the priests of Huitzilopochtli's cult demanded sacrificial victims to keep the
war god appeased.

Some of the victims were Mexica criminals, and others came as tribute from neighboring peoples or from the ranks of warriors captured on the battlefield. In all cases the Mexica
viewed human sacrifice not as a gruesome form of entertainment but, rather, as a ritual
essential to the world's survival. They believed that the blood of sacrificial victims sustained
the sun and secured a continuing supply of moisture for the earth, thus ensuring that human communities would be able to cultivate their crops and perpetuate their societies.

## Peoples and Societies of the North

Beyond Mexico the peoples of North America developed a rich variety of political, social,
and cultural traditions. Many North American peoples depended on hunting, fishing, and
foraging. In the arctic and subarctic regions, for example, diets included whale, seal, and
walrus supplemented by land mammals such as moose and caribou. Peoples in coastal regions consumed fish, and in interior regions they hunted large animals such as bison and
deer. Throughout the continent nuts, berries, roots, and grasses supplemented the meat
provided by hunters and fishers. Like their counterparts elsewhere, hunting, fishing, and
foraging peoples of North America built societies on a relatively small scale, since food
resources in the wild would not support dense populations.

PUEBLO AND NAVAJO SOCIETIES   In several regions of North Amer-
ica, agricultural economies enabled peoples to maintain settled societies with large populations. In what is now the American southwest, for example, Pueblo and Navajo peoples
tapped river waters to irrigate crops of maize, which constituted as much as 80 percent of

Huitzilopochtli (we-tsee-loh-POCK-tlee)
Pueblo (PWEB-loh)
Navajo (NAH-vah-ho)

**TRADITIONS IN THE AMERICAS AND OCEANIA.** In contrast to societies in Eurasia, which were linked across vast areas through complex networks of seaborne and overland trade, societies in the Americas and in Oceania were unable to maintain similar connections across areas of comparable size. In what ways can geographical obstacles in both the Americas and Oceania help to explain the difficulties of maintaining comparable long-distance connections? How might the presence of these obstacles have shaped the development of cultural, social, and political traditions?

PSI
img
Cahokia
www.mhhe.com/
bentleybrief2e

their diets. Although the hot and dry environment periodically brought drought and famine, by about 700 C.E. the Pueblo and the Navajo had begun to construct permanent stone and adobe buildings. Archaeologists have discovered about 125 sites where agricultural peoples built such communities.

**IROQUOIS PEOPLES**  Large-scale agricultural societies also emerged in the woodlands east of the Mississippi River. Woodlands peoples began to cultivate maize and beans during the early centuries C.E., and after about 800 these cultivated foods made up the bulk of their diets. By 1000 the Owasco people had established a distinct society in what is now upstate New York, and by about 1400 the five Iroquois nations (Mohawk, Oneida, Onondaga, Cayuga, and Seneca) had emerged from Owasco society. Women were in charge of Iroquois villages and longhouses, in which several related families lived together, and supervised cultivation of fields surrounding their settlements. Men took responsibility for affairs beyond the village—hunting, fishing, and war.

**MOUND-BUILDING PEOPLES**  The most impressive structures of the woodlands were the enormous earthen mounds that dotted the countryside throughout the eastern half of North America. Woodlands peoples used these mounds as stages for ceremonies and rituals, as platforms for dwellings, and occasionally as burial sites. Although modern development has destroyed most of these mounds, several surviving examples demonstrate that they sometimes reached gigantic proportions.

**CAHOKIA**  The largest surviving structure is a mound at Cahokia near East St. Louis, Illinois. More than 30 meters (100 feet) high, 300 meters (1,000 feet) long, and 200 meters (650 feet) wide, it was the third-largest structure in the western hemisphere before the arrival of Europeans. Only the temple of the sun in Teotihuacan and the tem-

Iroquois (EER-uh-kwah)
Cahokia (kuh-HOH-kee-uh)

**THE GREAT SERPENT MOUND.** | Originally constructed about 1000 C.E., this mound sits atop a ridge in modern Ohio. The serpent's coiled tail is visible at the left, while its open mouth holds an egg on the right. *Why would the builders of this mound have adopted an aerial perspective?*

ple of Quetzalcóatl in Cholula were larger. When the Cahokia society was at its height, from approximately 900 to 1250 C.E., more than one hundred smaller mounds stood within a few kilometers of the highest and most massive mound. Scholars have estimated that during the twelfth century, fifteen thousand to thirty-eight thousand people lived in the vicinity of the Cahokia mounds.

TRADE   Because peoples north of Mexico had no writing, information about their societies comes almost exclusively from archaeological discoveries. Burial sites reveal that mound-building peoples recognized social classes, since they bestowed grave goods of differing quality and quantities on their departed kin. Archaeologists have shown, too, that trade linked widely separated regions and peoples of North America. An elaborate network of rivers—notably the Mississippi, Missouri, Ohio, and Tennessee rivers—facilitated travel and trade by canoe in the eastern half of North America. Throughout the eastern woodlands, archaeologists have turned up stones with sharp cutting edges from the Rocky Mountains, copper from the Great Lakes region, seashells from Florida, minerals from the upper reaches of the Mississippi River, and mica from the southern Appalachian mountains. Indeed, the community at Cahokia probably owed its size and prominence to its location at the hub of North American trade networks. Situated near the confluence of the Mississippi, Missouri, and Ohio rivers, Cahokia was most likely the center of trade and communication networks linking the eastern woodlands of North America with the lower Mississippi valley and lands bordering the Gulf of Mexico.

# STATES AND EMPIRES IN SOUTH AMERICA

Like the peoples north of Mexico, South American peoples had no tradition of writing before the arrival of Spanish invaders in the early sixteenth century. As a result, the experiences of early South American societies have been reconstructed largely on the basis of archaeological evidence and information recorded by Spanish conquerors. As in Mesoamerica, cities and secular government in South America began to overshadow ceremonial centers and priestly regimes during the centuries from 1000 to 1500 C.E. Toward the end of the period, like the Mexica in Mesoamerica, the Incas built a powerful state, extended their authority over a vast region, and established the largest empire South America had ever seen.

## The Coming of the Incas

After the disappearance of the Chavín and Moche societies, a series of autonomous regional states organized public affairs in Andean South America. The states frequently clashed, but rarely did one of them gain a long-term advantage over the others. For the most part they controlled areas either in the mountainous highlands or in the valleys and coastal plains.

CHUCUITO   In the highlands, people depended on the cultivation of potatoes and the herding of llamas and alpacas—camel-like beasts that were the only large domesticated animals anywhere in the Americas before the sixteenth century. After the twelfth century the kingdom of Chucuito dominated the highland region on the border between modern Peru and Bolivia. There, inhabitants built elaborately terraced fields where cultivators harvested potatoes of many different colors, sizes, and tastes.

CHIMU   Inhabitants of the coastal lowlands depended not on potatoes but on maize and sweet potatoes, which were grown with the aid of irrigation networks that tapped the rivers and streams flowing from the Andes mountains. Some lowland societies, such as

Chucuito (CHEW-keeto)

The Inca capital of Cuzco was situated high in the Andes mountains.

Andean South America
www.mhhe.com/
bentleybrief2e

Keeper of the quipu
www.mhhe.com/
bentleybrief2e

the kingdom of Chimu, grew large and powerful in the half millennium before the emergence of the Incas in the mid–fifteenth century. Indeed, Chimu's capital city, Chanchan, had a population that exceeded fifty thousand and may have approached one hundred thousand.

For several centuries, regional states such as Chucuito and Chimu maintained order in Andean South America. Yet within a period of about thirty years, they and other regional states fell under the domination of the dynamic and expansive society of the Incas. The word *Inca* originally was the title of the rulers of a small kingdom in the valley of Cuzco, but in modern usage the term refers more broadly to those who spoke the Incas' Quechua language, or even to all subjects of the Inca empire.

THE INCA EMPIRE   After a long period of migration in the highlands, the Incas settled in the highland region around Lake Titicaca about the mid–thirteenth century. At first they lived as one among many peoples inhabiting the region. About 1438, however, the Inca ruler Pachacuti (reigned 1438–1471) launched a series of military campaigns that vastly expanded the Incas' authority. Pachacuti first extended Inca control over the southern and northern highlands and then turned his forces on the coastal kingdom of Chimu. Though well defended, Chimu had to submit to the Incas when Pachacuti gained control of the waters that supplied Chimu's irrigation system.

By the late fifteenth century, the Incas had built a huge empire stretching more than 4,000 kilometers (2,500 miles) from modern Quito to Santiago. It embraced almost all of modern Peru, most of Ecuador, much of Bolivia, and parts of Chile and Argentina. Only the tropical rain forests of the Amazon and other river valleys set a limit to Inca expansion to the east, and the Pacific Ocean defined its western boundary. With a population of about 11.5 million, the Inca empire easily ranked as the largest state ever built in South America.

The Incas ruled as a military and administrative elite. They led armies composed mostly of conquered peoples, and they staffed the bureaucracy that managed the empire's political affairs. But the Incas themselves were not numerous enough to overwhelm their subjects. Thus, they sought to encourage obedience among subject peoples by taking hostages from their ruling classes and forcing them to live at the Inca capital. Also, when conquered peoples became restive or uncooperative, the Incas sent loyal subjects to colonize the area and to establish military garrisons. When conquered peoples rebelled, Inca armies resettled them in distant parts of the empire.

QUIPU AND INCA ADMINISTRATION   Administration of the Inca empire rested with a large class of bureaucrats. In the absence of writing, bureaucrats relied on a mnemonic aid known as *quipu* to keep track of their responsibilities. Quipu consisted of an array of small cords of various colors and lengths, all suspended from one large, thick

**Chanchan** (CHAHN-chahn)

**Quechua** (keh-CHUA)

**Pachacuti** (pah-cha-KOO-tee)

**quipu** (KEE-poo)

**INCA CITY.** | Machu Picchu, an Inca settlement built beginning in 1430, was 8,000 feet above sea level. *What kinds of technology would the Inca have needed to construct a stone city at such a high altitude?*

cord. Experts tied a series of knots in the small cords, which sometimes numbered a hundred or more, to help them remember certain kinds of information. Most quipu recorded statistical information having to do with population, state property, taxes, and labor services that communities owed to the central government. Occasionally, though, quipu also helped experts to remember historical information having to do with the establishment of the Inca empire, the Inca rulers, and their deeds. Although much more unwieldy and less flexible than writing, quipu enabled Inca bureaucrats to keep track of information well enough to run an orderly empire.

CUZCO    The Inca capital at Cuzco served as the administrative, religious, and ceremonial center of the empire. At its high point in the late fifteenth century, Cuzco's population may have reached three hundred thousand. Most prominent of the residents were the Inca rulers and high nobility, the high priests of the various religious cults, and the hostages of conquered peoples who lived with their families under the watchful eyes of Inca guardians. Cuzco had many handsome buildings of red stone, and the most important temples and palaces sported gold facings.

INCA ROADS    A magnificent and extensive road system enabled the central government at Cuzco to communicate with all parts of the far-flung Inca empire and to dispatch large military forces rapidly to distant trouble spots. Two roads linked the Inca realm from north to south—one through the mountains, the other along the coast. Scholars have estimated the combined length of these roads at 16,000 kilometers (9,944 miles). A corps of official runners carried messages along the roads so that news and information could travel between Cuzco and the most distant parts of the empire within a few days. When the Inca rulers desired a meal of fresh fish, they dispatched runners from Cuzco to the coast more than 320 kilometers (200 miles) away and had their catch within two days. Like roads in empires in other parts of the world, the Incas' roads favored their efforts at centralization.

## Inca Society and Religion

TRADE    Despite these splendid roads, Inca society did not generate large classes of merchants and skilled artisans. On the local level the Incas and their subjects bartered agricultural produce and handcrafted goods among themselves. Long-distance trade, however, fell under the supervision of the central government. Administrators organized

**INCA GOD-KING.** | This painting depicts Pachacuti (r. 1438–1471), the ruler responsible for expanding Inca territory into an empire.

exchanges of agricultural products, textiles, pottery, jewelry, and craft goods, but the Inca state did not permit individuals to become independent merchants. In the absence of a market economy, then, there was no opportunity for a large class of professional, skilled artisans to emerge.

**RULING ELITES** The main classes in Inca society were the rulers, aristocrats, priests, and peasant cultivators of common birth. The Incas considered their chief ruler a deity descended from the sun. In theory, this god-king owned everything in the Inca realm, which he governed as an absolute and infallible ruler. Inca rulers retained their prestige even after death. Their descendants mummified the royal remains and regarded departed kings as intermediaries with the gods. Succeeding rulers often deliberated state policy in the presence of royal mummies so as to benefit from their counsel. Indeed, on the occasion of certain festivals, rulers brought out the mummified remains of their ancestors, dressed them in fine clothes, and presented them with offerings of food and drink to maintain cordial relations with former rulers.

**ARISTOCRATS AND PRIESTS** Like the ruling elites, Inca aristocrats and priests led privileged lives. Aristocrats consumed fine foods and dressed in embroidered clothes provided by common subjects. Aristocrats also had the right to wear large ear spools that distended their lobes so much that Spanish conquerors referred to them as "big ears." Priests often came from royal and aristocratic families. They led celibate and ascetic lives, but they deeply influenced Inca society because of their education and their responsibility for overseeing religious rituals. The major temples supported hundreds of priests, along with attendants and virgin women devoted to divine service who prepared ceremonial meals and wove fine ritual garments for the priestly staff.

**PEASANTS** The cultivators were mostly peasants of common birth who lived in communities known as *ayllu,* similar to the Mexica's *calpulli,* which were the basic units of rural society. Ranging in size from small villages to larger towns, each *ayllu* consisted of several families who lived together, sharing land, tools, animals, crops, and work. Instead of paying taxes or tribute, peasants also worked on state lands administered by aristocrats. Much of the production from these state lands went to support the ruling, aristocratic, and priestly classes. The rest went into state storehouses for public relief in times of famine and for the support of widows, orphans, and others unable to cultivate land for themselves. Apart from agricultural work, peasants also owed compulsory labor services to the Inca state. Men provided the heavy labor required for the construction, maintenance, and repair of roads, buildings, and irrigation systems. Women delivered tribute in the form of textiles, pottery, and jewelry. With the aid of quipu, Inca bureaucrats kept track of the labor service and tribute owed by local communities.

**INCA GODS: INTI AND VIRACOCHA** Members of the Inca ruling class venerated the sun as a god and as their major deity, whom they called Inti. They also recognized the moon, the stars, the planets, the rain, and other natural forces as divine. Some Incas, including the energetic ruler Pachacuti, also showed special favor to the god Viracocha, creator of the world, humankind, and all else in the universe. The cult of the

**Inti** (ihn-tee)

**Viracocha** (veer-rah-coh-chah)

sun, however, outshone all the others. In Cuzco alone some four thousand priests, attendants, and virgin devotees served Inti, whose temple attracted pilgrims from all parts of the Inca empire. Priests of all cults honored their deities with sacrifices, which in Inca society usually took the form of agricultural produce or animals such as llamas and guinea pigs rather than humans.

MORAL THOUGHT   Alongside sacrifices and ritual ceremonies, Inca religion had a strong moral dimension. The Incas taught a concept of sin as a violation of the established social or natural order, and they believed in a life beyond death during which individuals would receive rewards or punishments based on the quality of their earthly lives. Sin, they believed, would bring divine disaster both for individuals and for their larger communities. The Incas also observed rituals of confession and penance by which priests absolved individuals of their sins and returned them to the good graces of the gods.

# THE SOCIETIES OF OCEANIA

Inhabitants of Oceania did not interact with peoples of different societies as frequently or systematically as did their counterparts in the eastern hemisphere, but they built and maintained flourishing societies. The aboriginal peoples of Australia ventured over vast stretches of their continent and created networks of trade and exchange between hunting and gathering societies. Meanwhile, throughout the Pacific Ocean, islanders built complex agricultural societies. By the time European mariners sailed into the Pacific Ocean in the sixteenth century, the larger island groups had sizable populations, hierarchical social orders, and hereditary chiefly rulers. In the central and western Pacific, mariners sailed regularly between island groups and established elaborate trade networks. Islanders living toward the eastern and western edges of the Pacific Ocean also had occasional dealings with American and Asian peoples, sometimes with significant consequences for the Pacific island societies.

## The Nomadic Foragers of Australia

Although the aboriginal peoples of Australia learned how to expertly exploit the resources of the continent, they did not turn to agriculture as did their neighbors to the north in New Guinea. The inhabitants of New Guinea began to herd swine and cultivate root crops about 5000 B.C.E., and the inhabitants of islands in the Torres Strait (which separates Australia from New Guinea) took up gardening soon thereafter. In contrast, the aboriginal peoples of northern Australia maintained nomadic, foraging societies until European peoples migrated to Australia in large numbers during the nineteenth and twentieth centuries.

Aborigine of the Naomi tribe
www.mhhe.com/bentleybrief2e

TRADE   As a result of their mobile and nomadic way of life, aboriginal Australians frequently interacted with peoples of neighboring societies. Even though as nomads they did not accumulate large quantities of material goods, groups regularly exchanged surplus food and small items when they met. Eventually, this sort of small-scale exchange enabled trade goods to spread throughout most of Australia. Pearly oyster shells were among the most popular trade items. Archaeologists have turned up many of these shells fashioned into jewelry more than 1,600 kilometers (1,000 miles) from the waters where the oysters bred. Peoples on the north coast also engaged in a limited amount of trade with mariners from New Guinea and the islands of southeast Asia. Australian spears and pearly shells went north in exchange for items such as iron axes, which were much coveted by aboriginal peoples who had no tradition of metallurgy.

CULTURAL AND RELIGIOUS TRADITIONS   In spite of seasonal migrations, frequent encounters with peoples from other aboriginal societies, and trade, the cultural traditions of Australian peoples did not diffuse much beyond the regions inhabited by individual societies. Aboriginal peoples paid close attention to the prominent geographic features of the lands around them. Often they conducted religious observances designed to ensure continuing supplies of animals, plant life, and water. Given the intense concern of aboriginal peoples with their immediate environments, their cultural and religious traditions focused on local matters and did not appeal to peoples from other regions.

## The Development of Pacific Island Societies

By the early centuries C.E., human migrants had established agricultural societies in almost all the island groups of the Pacific Ocean. About the middle of the first millennium C.E., they ventured to the large islands of New Zealand—the last large, habitable region of the earth to receive members of the human species. After 1000 C.E. Polynesians inhabiting the larger Pacific islands grew especially numerous, and their surging population prompted remarkable social and political development.

**TRADE BETWEEN ISLAND GROUPS** In the central and western regions of the Pacific, where several clusters of islands are relatively close to one another, mariners linked island societies. Regional trade networks facilitated exchanges of useful goods such as axes and pottery, exotic items such as shells and decorative ornaments, and sometimes even foodstuffs. Regional trade within individual island groups served social and political as well as economic functions, since it helped ruling elites establish and maintain harmonious relations with one another. In some cases, trade crossed longer distances and linked different island groups. Inhabitants of the Tonga, Samoa, and Fiji islands traded mats and canoes, for example, and also intermarried, thus creating political and social relationships.

New Zealand was the last large habitable area to be settled by humans.

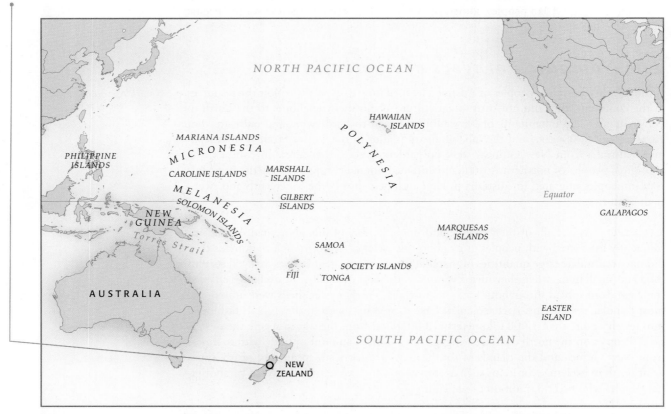

**MAP 17.3** | The societies of Oceania. Islands are much more numerous and much closer together in the western Pacific than in the eastern Pacific. *In what ways did proximity to or distance from other islands influence the development of Pacific island societies?*

LONG-DISTANCE VOYAGING  Elsewhere in Polynesia, vast stretches of deep blue water made it much more complicated to travel between different island groups and societies. As a result, regular trade networks did not emerge in the eastern Pacific Ocean. Nevertheless, mariners undertook lengthy voyages on an intermittent basis, sometimes with momentous results. After the original settlement of Easter Island about 300 C.E., for example, Polynesian mariners probably ventured to the western coast of South America, where they learned about the cultivation of sweet potatoes. Between about 400 and 700 C.E., mariners spread sweet potatoes throughout Polynesia and beyond. The new crop quickly became a prominent source of food in all the islands it reached. Thus long-distance voyages were responsible for the dissemination of sweet potatoes to remote islands situated thousands of kilometers from the nearest inhabited lands.

Another case of long-distance voyaging prompted social changes in the Hawaiian Islands. For centuries after the voyages that brought the original settlers to the islands in the early centuries C.E., there was little travel or communication between Hawai`i and other Polynesian societies. During the twelfth and thirteenth centuries, however, a series of two-way voyages linked Hawai`i with Tahiti and the Marquesas Islands. Memories of those voyages survive in oral traditions that relate the introduction into Hawai`i of new chiefly and priestly lines from Tahiti. Evidence for the voyages comes also from Hawaiian adoption of fishhook styles from Tahiti and words from the Tahitian language.

POPULATION GROWTH  While undertaking regular or intermittent voyages over long distances, islanders throughout the Pacific Ocean also built productive agricultural and fishing societies. They cultivated taro, yams, sweet potatoes, bananas, breadfruit, and coconuts, and they kept domesticated pigs and dogs. They also fed on abundant supplies of fish. After about the fourteenth century, as their population increased, the inhabitants of Hawai`i built ingenious fishponds that allowed small fry to swim from the ocean through narrow gates into rock-enclosed spaces but prevented larger fish from escaping. Fishponds thus enabled Hawaiians to harvest large quantities of mature fish with relative ease. The establishment of agricultural and fishing societies led to rapid population growth in all the larger Pacific island groups. In Hawai`i, the most heavily populated of the Polynesian island groups, the human population may have exceeded five hundred thousand when European mariners arrived in the late eighteenth century.

Dense populations sometimes led to environmental degradation and social strife on small islands with limited resources. Easter Island in particular was the site of dramatic problems arising from overpopulation. Polynesian migrants originally settled Easter Island in the early centuries C.E., and during the era from about 1100 to 1500, their descendants numbered about ten thousand. This population placed tremendous pressure on the island's resources. By 1500, islanders fought one another ferociously for those resources, engaging in brutal massacres of their enemies and the desecration of their bodies. As their society disintegrated, they sometimes resorted to cannibalism for lack of sufficient food.

NAN MADOL   In other lands, dense populations promoted social organization on a scale never before seen in Oceania. On Pohnpei in the Caroline Islands, for example, the Sandeleur dynasty built a powerful state and organized construction of a massive stone palace and administrative center at Nan Madol. Built mostly during the period from 1200 to 1600, the complex included ninety-three artificial islets protected by seawalls and breakwaters on three sides.

DEVELOPMENT OF SOCIAL CLASSES   Indeed, beginning about the thirteenth century, expanding populations prompted residents of many Pacific islands to develop increasingly complex social and political structures. Especially on the larger islands, workers became more specialized: some concentrated on cultivating certain crops while others devoted their efforts to fishing or crafts production. Distinct classes emerged as well. The islands of Tonga, Tahiti, and Hawai`i had especially stratified societies with sharp distinctions between various classes of high chiefs, lesser chiefs, and commoners. Hawaiian society also recognized distinct classes of priests and skilled artisans as well as common classes.

THE FORMATION OF CHIEFLY STATES   In addition to distinct social classes, island societies generated strong political leadership. Ruling chiefs generally oversaw public affairs in portions of an island, in an entire island, or occasionally in several islands situated

## THINKING ABOUT *Encounters*

**ENCOUNTERS IN THE AMERICAS AND OCEANIA.** Within limited regions, societies in the Americas and Oceania established trade networks, tributary relations, or imperial authority over neighboring peoples. In addition, some societies supported networks of long-distance trade. What are some examples in which long-distance trade altered or shaped societies in either the Americas or Oceania?

*A group of Polynesian oral traditions preserves memories of numerous two-way voyages between Tahiti and Hawai`i in the twelfth and thirteenth centuries. One of them has to do with Mo`ikeha, a high chief who left Tahiti because of domestic difficulties and migrated to Hawai`i, where he founded a new chiefly line. The legend recounts several voyages between Tahiti and Hawai`i. The following excerpts deal with Mo`ikeha's establishment as a chief in Hawai`i and the later arrival of his Tahitian son La`amaikahiki, who is credited with the introduction of Tahitian religious and cultural traditions to Hawai`i.*

It was dark by the time they arrived [at the Hawaiian island of Kaua`i], so they did not land, instead, mooring their canoe offshore. Early the next morning the people saw this double-hulled canoe floating offshore with the kapu sticks of a chief aboard. The canoe was brought ashore and the travelers got off. Meanwhile the locals were gathering in a crowd to go surf-riding. . . . Among them were the two daughters of the ali`i nui [chief] of Kaua`i, Ho`oipoikamalanai and Hinauu.

Mo`ikeha and his companions saw the crowd and followed along to take part in the morning exercise. Mo`ikeha was a handsome man with dark reddish hair and a tall, commanding figure.

When Ho`oipoikamalanai and her sister saw Mo`ikeha, they immediately fell in love with him, and they decided to take him for their husband. Mo`ikeha in the meantime was also struck with the beauty and grace of the two sisters, and he, too, fell in love with them and decided to take one of them to be his wife. After enjoying the surf for a time, Ho`oipoikamalanai and her sister returned home and told their father about the new arrival and said: "We wish to take that young chief as a husband for one of us." The father approved.

Orders were issued that Mo`ikeha be brought to the house of the two ali`i women. Mo`ikeha and his company were sent for and brought in the presence of the king [the ali`i nui of Kaua`i]. The love of these young people being mutual, Ho`oipoikamalanai and Hinauu took Mo`ikeha to be their husband. Mo`ikeha became ali`i nui of Kaua`i after the death of his father-in-law. . . .

Mo`ikeha worked to make his two wives and five children happy, giving his undivided attention to the bringing up of his boys. He thought no more of Lu`ukia [his lover in Tahiti], but after a while, he began to feel a yearning desire to see his son La`amaikahiki, his child by his first wife Kapo. So he called

his five sons together and said to them: "I'm thinking of sending one of you boys to bring your elder brother to Hawai`i.". . .

[After Mo`ikeha's son Kila sailed to Tahiti and found his elder half-brother] La`amaikahiki immediately prepared to accompany his brother to Hawai`i, as Mo`ikeha wished. La`amaikahiki took his priests and his god Lonoika`ouali`i, and set sail for Hawai`i with the men who had come with Kila. When they were approaching Kaua`i, La`amaikahiki began beating his drum. Mo`ikeha heard his drum and ordered everything, the land as well as the house, to be made ready for the reception of the chief La`amaikahiki. Upon the arrival of La`amaikahiki and Kila, the high priest of Kaua`i, Poloahilani, took La`amaikahiki and his god Lonoika`ouali`i ("Lono at the Chiefly Supremacy") to the heiau [temple]. It is said that La`amaikahiki was the first person to bring a god (akua) to Hawai`i. . . .

[After returning to Tahiti, then sailing again to Hawai`i, La`amaikahiki] set sail again, going up the Kona coast [of Hawai`i Island]. . . . It was on this visit that La`amaikahiki introduced hula dancing, accompanied by the drum, to Hawai`i. . . .

La`amaikahiki stayed a long time on Kaua`i teaching the people the art of dancing. From Kaua`i La`amaikahiki visited all the other islands of this group and thus the drum dance (hula ka`eke) spread to the other islands.

■ How would you characterize the political, social, and cultural significance of two-way voyaging between Tahiti and Hawai`i?

SOURCE: Teuira Henry and others. *Voyaging Chiefs of Havai`i.* Ed. by Dennis Kawaharada. Honolulu: Kalamaku Press, 1995, pp. 138–39, 144–46.

close to one another. In Tonga and Hawai`i, high chiefs frequently launched campaigns to bring additional islands under their control and create large centralized states. Rarely, however, were these militant chiefs able to overcome geographic and logistic difficulties and realize their expansionist ambitions before the nineteenth century.

Nevertheless, high chiefs guided the affairs of complex societies throughout Polynesia. They allocated lands to families, mobilized labor for construction projects, and organized men into military forces. They commanded enormous respect within their societies. In Hawai`i, for example, the classes of high chiefs known as *ali`i nui* intermarried, ate the best fish and other foods that were *kapu* ("taboo") to commoners, and had the right to wear magnificent cloaks adorned with thousands of bright red and yellow bird feathers. Indeed, a *kapu* forbade commoners to approach or even cast a shadow on the *ali`i nui*.

POLYNESIAN RELIGION   High chiefs worked closely with priests, who served as intermediaries between human communities and the gods. Gods of war and agriculture were common throughout the Pacific islands, but individual islands and island groups recognized deities particular to their own regions and interests. The most distinctive architecture of early Pacific societies was the ceremonial precinct and temple structure known as *marae* (or *heiau* in Hawaiian). *Marae* often had several terraced floors, with a rock or coral wall designating the boundaries of the sacred space. In Tonga and Samoa, temples made of timber and thatched roofs served as places of worship, sacrifice, and communication between priests and the gods, whereas in eastern Polynesia religious ceremonies took place on platforms in open-air courtyards.

Pacific island societies did not enjoy access to the range of technologies developed by continental peoples until after the sixteenth century. Yet Pacific islanders cleverly exploited their environments, established productive agricultural economies, built elaborate, well-organized societies, and reached out when possible to engage in trade with their neighbors. Their achievements testify anew to the human impulses toward densely populated communities and interaction with other societies.

# SUMMARY

The original inhabitants of the Americas and Oceania lived in societies that were considerably smaller than those of the eastern hemisphere. Unlike their counterparts in the eastern hemisphere, they did not possess metallurgical technologies or transportation technologies based on wheeled vehicles and domesticated animals. Nevertheless, long before they entered into sustained interaction with European and other peoples, they built complex societies and developed sophisticated cultural and religious traditions. Indigenous peoples established foraging, fishing, and agricultural societies throughout the Americas, and they fashioned tools from wood, stone, and bone that enabled them to produce enough food to support sizable communities. In Mesoamerica and Andean South America, they also built imperial states that organized public affairs on a large scale.

The original inhabitants of Australia and the Pacific islands built societies on a smaller scale than did the peoples of the Americas, but they too devised effective means of exploiting the natural environment and organizing flourishing communities. Australia was a continent of foraging nomadic peoples, whereas the Pacific islands supported densely populated agricultural societies. Although they had limited communication with peoples of the Americas or the eastern hemisphere, the peoples of Oceania traded and interacted regularly with their neighbors, and inhabitants of the Pacific islands sometimes undertook lengthy voyages to trade with distant island groups.

aboriginal peoples (335)
*ali'i nui* (340)
*ayllu* (334)
Aztec (325)
Cahokia (330)
*calpulli* (328)
Chimu (331)
*chinampa* system (325)
Cuzco (333)
Huitzilopochtli (328)

Inca (332)
Inti (334)
Iroquois (330)
*kapu* (340)
*marae* (340)
Mexica (324)
Nahuatl (328)
Nan Madol (338)
Navajo (329)
Pachacuti (332)

Polynesians (336)
Pueblo (329)
Quechua (332)
Quetzalcoatl (328)
quipu (332)
Tenochtitlan (323)
Teotihuacan (324)
Tezcatlipoca (328)
Toltecs (324)
Viracocha (334)

## FOR FURTHER READING

Peter Bellwood. *The Polynesians: Prehistory of an Island People.* Rev. ed. London, 1987. Well-illustrated popular account emphasizing the origins and early development of Polynesian societies.

Geoffrey Blainey. *Triumph of the Nomads: A History of Aboriginal Australia.* Melbourne, 1975. A sympathetic account of Australia before European arrival, well informed by archaeological discoveries.

Inga Clendinnen. *Aztecs: An Interpretation.* Cambridge, 1991. A brilliant re-creation of the Mexica world, concentrating on cultural and social themes.

George A. Collier, Renato I. Rosaldo, and John D. Wirth, eds. *The Inca and Aztec States, 1400–1800: Anthropology and History.* New York, 1982. Seventeen well-focused essays represent approaches that scholars have taken to the Inca and Aztec empires.

Ben Finney. *Voyage of Rediscovery: A Cultural Odyssey through Polynesia.* Berkeley, 1994. Fascinating account of efforts to understand ancient Polynesian techniques of seafaring and to chart the courses of Polynesian migrations.

Patrick V. Kirch. *On the Road of the Winds: An Archaeological History of the Pacific Islands before European Contact.* Berkeley, 2000. A valuable synthesis of recent scholarship by the foremost contemporary archaeologist of the Pacific islands.

Miguel León-Portilla. *The Aztec Image of Self and Society: An Introduction to Nahua Culture.* Salt Lake City, 1992. An excellent guide to Mexica social and cultural history by the foremost student of the Mexica.

Charles C. Mann. *1491: New Revelations of the Americas before Columbus.* New York, 2006. Summarizes a great deal of archaeological research on the pre-Columbian Americas.

Lynda Norene Shaffer. *Native Americans before 1492: The Mound-building Centers of the Eastern Woodlands.* Armonk, N.Y., 1992. Places the societies of mound-building peoples in larger historical context.

Muriel Porter Weaver. *The Aztecs, Maya, and Their Predecessors: Archaeology of Mesoamerica.* 3rd ed. New York, 1993. An up-to-date survey based on historical and archaeological research.

# Reaching Out: Cross-Cultural Interactions

# 18

One of the great world travelers of all time was the Moroccan legal scholar Ibn Battuta. Born in 1304 at Tangier, Ibn Battuta followed family tradition and studied Islamic law. In 1325 he left Morocco to make a pilgrimage to Mecca. He traveled by caravan across north Africa and through Egypt, Palestine, and Syria, arriving at Mecca in 1326. After completing his hajj, Ibn Battuta spent a year visiting Mesopotamia and Persia, then traveled by ship through the Red Sea and down the east African coast as far south as Kilwa. By 1330 he had returned to Mecca, but then soon set off for India when he learned that the sultan of Delhi offered handsome rewards to foreign legal scholars. In 1333 he arrived in Delhi after following a long and circuitous land route that took him through Egypt, Syria, Anatolia, Constantinople, the Black Sea, and the great trading cities of central Asia, Bokhara and Samarkand.

**Ibn Battuta in China**
www.mhhe.com/
bentleybrief2e

For the next eight years, Ibn Battuta remained in India, serving mostly as a *qadi* (judge) in the government of the sultan of Delhi. In 1341 Ibn Battuta began his travels again, this time making his way around southern India, Ceylon, and the Maldive Islands before continuing to China about 1345. He visited the bustling southern Chinese port cities of Quanzhou and Guangzhou, where he found large communities of Muslim merchants, before returning to Morocco in 1349 by way of southern India, the Persian Gulf, Syria, Egypt, and Mecca.

Still, Ibn Battuta's travels were not complete. In 1350 he made a short trip to the kingdom of Granada in southern Spain, and in 1353 he joined a camel caravan across the Sahara desert to visit the Mali empire, returning to Morocco in 1355. During his travels Ibn Battuta visited the equivalent of forty-four modern countries and logged more than 117,000 kilometers (73,000 miles). His account of his adventures stands with Marco Polo's book among the classic works of travel literature.

Between 1000 and 1500 C.E., the peoples of the eastern hemisphere traveled, traded, communicated, and interacted more regularly and intensively than ever before. The large empires of the Mongols and other nomadic peoples provided a political foundation for that cross-cultural interaction. When they conquered and pacified vast regions, nomadic peoples provided safe roads for merchants, diplomats, missionaries, and other travelers. Quite apart from the nomadic empires, improvements in maritime technology led to increased traffic in the sea-lanes of the Indian Ocean and the South China Sea. As a result, long-distance travel became much more common than in earlier eras.

❮ *A giraffe from east Africa sent as a present to China in 1414 and painted by a Chinese artist at the Ming zoo.*

**Ibn Battuta** (ih-bun BAH-too-tah)

Merchants and travelers exchanged more than trade goods. They diffused technologies and spread religious faiths. They also exchanged diseases that caused deadly epidemics. During the middle decades of the fourteenth century, bubonic plague traveled the trade routes and spread through most of Eurasia. During its initial, furious onslaught, bubonic plague caused death and destruction on a huge scale and interrupted long-distance trade networks.

By the early fifteenth century, however, societies had begun to recover from the plague. Chinese and western European peoples in particular had restabilized their societies and begun to renew cross-cultural contacts. In Europe, this effort had profound consequences for modern world history. As they sought entry to the markets of Asia, European mariners sailed to the western hemisphere and the Pacific Ocean. Their voyages brought the peoples of the eastern hemisphere, the western hemisphere, and Oceania into permanent and sustained interaction with one another. Thus between 1000 and 1500, cross-cultural interactions pointed toward global interdependence, a principal characteristic of modern world history.

# LONG-DISTANCE TRADE AND TRAVEL

Travelers embarked on long-distance journeys for a variety of reasons. Three of the more important motives for long-distance travel between 1000 and 1500 C.E. were trade, diplomacy, and missionary activity. The cross-cultural interactions that resulted helped spread technological innovations throughout the eastern hemisphere.

## *Patterns of Long-Distance Trade*

Merchants engaged in long-distance trade relied on two principal networks of trade routes. Luxury goods of high value relative to their weight, such as silk textiles and precious stones, often traveled overland on the silk roads. Bulkier commodities, such as steel, stone, and building materials, traveled the sea-lanes of the Indian Ocean, because it would have been unprofitable to transport them overland. The silk roads linked all of the Eurasian landmass, and trans-Saharan caravan routes drew west Africa into the larger economy of the eastern hemisphere. The sea-lanes of the Indian Ocean served ports in southeast Asia, India, Arabia, and east Africa while also offering access via the South China Sea to ports in China, Japan, Korea, and the islands of southeast Asia. Thus, in combination, land and sea routes touched almost every corner of the eastern hemisphere.

TRADING CITIES    As the volume of trade increased, the major trading cities and ports grew rapidly, attracting buyers, sellers, brokers, and bankers from parts near and far. When a trading or port city enjoyed a strategic location, maintained good order, and resisted the temptation to levy excessive customs fees, it had the potential to become a major emporium. A case in point is Melaka (in modern Malaysia). Founded in the 1390s, within a few decades Melaka became the principal clearinghouse of trade in the eastern Indian Ocean. The city's authorities policed the strategic Strait of Melaka and maintained

**Melaka** (may-LAH-kah)

a safe market that welcomed all merchants and levied reasonable fees on goods exchanged there. By the end of the fifteenth century, Melaka had a population of some fifty thousand people, and, according to one report, more than eighty languages could be heard in the city's streets.

Although the early period of Mongol conquest in the first half of the thirteenth century caused economic decline, especially in China and southwest Asia, eventually Mongol rule proved to be a boon for overland trade. Under Mongol rule, merchants traveling the silk roads faced less risk of banditry or political turbulence than in previous times. Meanwhile, strong economies in China, India, and western Europe fueled demand for foreign commodities.

**MARCO POLO** The best-known long-distance traveler of Mongol times was the Venetian Marco Polo (1253–1324), who, with his father and his uncle, traveled and traded throughout Mongol lands in the late thirteenth century. When Marco Polo returned to Europe in 1295, stories of his adventures were compiled by a third party and circulated widely throughout Europe. In spite of occasional exaggerations and tall tales, Marco's stories about the textiles, spices, gems, and other goods he observed during his travels deeply influenced European readers eager to participate in the lucrative trade networks of Eurasia. Indeed, in the wake of the Polos came hundreds of others, whose travels helped to increase European participation in the larger economy of the eastern hemisphere.

## *Political and Diplomatic Travel*

Marco Polo came from a family of merchants, and merchants were among the most avid readers of his stories. Yet his experiences also throw light on long-distance travel undertaken for political and diplomatic purposes. Khubilai Khan and the other Mongol rulers of China did not entirely trust their Chinese subjects and regularly appointed foreigners to administrative posts. Indeed, while in China Marco reported that Khubilai appointed him governor of the large trading city of Yangzhou, and that he represented Khubilai Khan's interests on diplomatic missions.

Khubilai Khan with the Polos
www.mhhe.com/ bentleybrief2e

**MONGOL-CHRISTIAN DIPLOMACY** The emergence of elaborate trading networks and the establishment of vast imperial states created great demand for political and diplomatic representation during the centuries after 1000 C.E. The thirteenth century was a time of especially active diplomacy involving distant parties. During the 1240s and 1250s, for example, Pope Innocent IV dispatched a series of envoys who invited the Mongol khans to convert to Christianity and join Europeans in an alliance against the Muslims in control of Jerusalem. The khans declined the invitation, proposing in reply that the pope and European Christians submit to Mongol rule or face destruction.

**RABBAN SAUMA** Although the early round of Mongol-European diplomacy offered little promise of cooperation, the Mongols later initiated another effort. In 1287 the Mongol ilkhan of Persia planned to invade the Muslim-held lands of southwest Asia and capture Jerusalem. In hopes of attracting support for the project, he dispatched Rabban Sauma, a Nestorian Christian priest of Turkish ancestry, as an envoy to the pope and European political leaders. Although his efforts did not succeed in garnering European support for Mongol plans, such diplomatic activity illustrates the complexity of political affairs in the eastern hemisphere and the need for diplomatic consultation over long distances.

The expansion of Islamic influence in the eastern hemisphere encouraged a different kind of politically motivated travel. Legal scholars and judges played a crucial role in Islamic societies, since the *sharia* prescribed religious observances and social relationships based on the Quran. Conversions to Islam and the establishment of Islamic states in India, southeast Asia, and sub-Saharan Africa created a demand for Muslims educated in Islamic law. After about the eleventh century, educated Muslims from southwest Asia and north Africa regularly traveled to recently converted lands to help instill Islamic values.

**MAP 18.1** | Travels of Marco Polo and Ibn Battuta. Compare the routes taken by Marco Polo and Ibn Battuta during their travels. *How did the two men choose where to travel? What conditions made it possible for them to travel so far from their homes?*

Between them, Ibn Battuta and Marco Polo traveled across much of the Eurasian landmass as well as parts of Africa and southeast Asia.

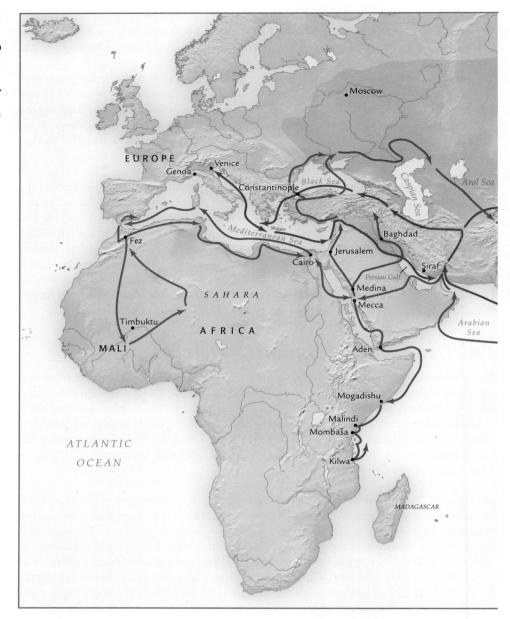

**IBN BATTUTA** Best known of the Muslim travelers was Ibn Battuta (1304–1369). Islamic rulers governed most of the lands Ibn Battuta visited, but very few Muslims educated in the law were available in those lands. With his legal credentials Ibn Battuta had little difficulty finding government positions. As *qadi* and advisor to the sultan of Delhi, he supervised the affairs of a wealthy mosque and heard cases at law, which he strictly enforced according to Islamic standards of justice. On one occasion Ibn Battuta sentenced a man to receive eighty lashes because he had drunk wine eight years earlier. Ibn Battuta also served as *qadi* in both east and west Africa, where he consulted with Muslim rulers and offered advice about government, women's dress, and proper relationships between the sexes. Like many other legal scholars whose stories went unrecorded, Ibn Battuta provided guidance in the ways of Islam in societies recently converted to the faith.

*qadi* (KAH-dee)

Mongol empires
Marco Polo's travels
Ibn Battuta's travels

# Missionary Campaigns

**SUFI MISSIONARIES**   Islamic values spread not only through the efforts of legal scholars but also through the missionary activities of Sufi mystics. As in the early days of Islam, Sufis in the period from 1000 to 1500 ventured to recently conquered or converted lands and sought to win a popular following for the faith in India, southeast Asia, and sub-Saharan Africa. Sufis did not insist on a strict, doctrinally correct understanding of Islam but, rather, emphasized piety and devotion to Allah. They even tolerated continuing reverence of traditional deities. By taking a flexible approach to their missions, the Sufis spread Islamic values without facing the resistance that unyielding and doctrinaire campaigns might have provoked.

**Sufis** (SOO-fees)

**CHRISTIAN MISSIONARIES** Meanwhile, Roman Catholic missionaries also traveled long distances in the interests of spreading Christianity. Missionaries accompanied the crusaders and other forces to all the lands where Europeans extended their influence after the year 1000. In lands where European conquerors maintained a long-term presence—such as the Baltic lands, the Balkan region, Sicily, and Spain—missionaries attracted converts in large numbers, and Roman Catholic Christianity became securely established.

The most ambitious missions sought to convert Mongols and Chinese to Roman Catholic Christianity. Yet even though Roman Catholic authorities in Europe dispatched many priests and missionaries to China during the early fourteenth century, they ultimately won few converts. In part, east Asia was just too distant for the resources available to the Roman Catholic church. Moreover, Christianity seemed to have little appeal to east Asian peoples, who already possessed sophisticated religious and cultural traditions.

## Long-Distance Travel and Cross-Cultural Exchanges

**CULTURAL EXCHANGES** Long-distance travel of all kinds, whether for commercial, political, diplomatic, or missionary purposes, encouraged cultural exchanges between peoples of different societies. Songs, stories, religious ideas, philosophical views, and scientific knowledge all passed readily among travelers who ventured into the larger world during the era from 1000 to 1500 C.E. The troubadours of western Europe, for example, drew on the poetry, music, and love songs of Muslim performers when developing the literature of courtly love. Similarly, European scientists avidly consulted their Muslim and Jewish counterparts in Sicily and Spain to learn about their understanding of the natural world.

Large numbers of travelers also facilitated agricultural and technological diffusion during the period from 1000 to 1500. The magnetic compass, for example, invented in China during the Tang or Song dynasty, spread throughout the Indian Ocean basin during the eleventh century, and by the mid–twelfth century European mariners used compasses in the Mediterranean and the Atlantic Ocean. The compass was a boon to maritime trade,

**THE SIEGE OF BAGHDAD.** | Mongol troops under the leadership of Hulagu Khan storm and capture Baghdad in 1258 after besieging the city. *How did the Mongols make use of catapults during the siege?*

## Ibn Battuta on Customs in the Mali Empire

*Long-distance travelers often encountered unfamiliar customs in foreign societies. The Moroccan traveler Ibn Battuta approved heartily when staying with hosts who honored the values of his own Muslim society, but he had little tolerance for those who did not. Here he describes what he witnessed at the sultan's court in the Mali empire.*

The blacks are the most humble of men before their king and the most extreme in their self-abasement before him. They swear by his name, saying "Mansa Sulaimanki" [the law of Mansa Sulaiman, the Mali sultan]. When he calls one of them while he is in session . . . the man invited takes off his clothes and wears patched clothes, takes off his turban, puts on a dirty cap, and goes in raising his clothes and trousers up his legs halfway to his knees. He advances with humility looking like a beggar. He hits the ground with his elbows, he hits it hard. He stands bowed, like one . . . in prayer, listening to what the king says. When one of them speaks to the sultan and he gives him an answer, he removes his clothes from his back and throws dust on his head and back, as a person does when bathing with water. I used to wonder how they do not blind their eyes. . . .

Sometimes one of them would stand before him and recall what he had done in his [the sultan's] service, saying, "I did such and such on such a day," and, "I killed so and so on such a day." Those who know this confirm that he is telling the truth. Their confirmation is by pulling the strings of their bows and letting them go, as one does when one is shooting. If the sultan says to him that he has spoken the truth or thanks him, he takes off his clothes and dusts. This is good manners among them. . . .

Amongst their good qualities is the small amount of injustice amongst them, for of all people they are the furthest from it. . . .

Another of the good habits amongst them is the way they meticulously observe the times of the prayers and attendance at them, so also it is with regard to their congregational services and their beating of their children to instill these things in them.

When it is Friday, if a man does not come early to the mosque he will not find a place to pray because of the numbers of the crowd. It is their custom for every man to send his boy [i.e., servant] with his prayer mat. He spreads it for him in a place commensurate with his position and keeps the place until he comes to the mosque. . . .

Among their good qualities is their putting on of good white clothes on Friday. If a man among them has nothing except a tattered shirt, he washes and cleans it and attends the Friday prayer in it. Another of their good qualities is their concern for learning the sublime Quran by heart. . . .

Among the bad things which they do—their serving women, slave women and little daughters appear before people naked, exposing their private parts. I used to see many of them in this state in [the fasting month of] Ramadan, for it was the custom of the *farariyya* [commanders] to break the fast in the sultan's house. Everyone of them has his food carried in to him by twenty or more of his slave girls and they are naked, every one. Also among their bad customs is the way women will go into the presence of the sultan naked, without any covering; and the nakedness of the sultan's daughters—on the night of the twenty-seventh of Ramadan, I saw about a hundred slave girls coming out of his palace with food, with them were two of his daughters, they had full breasts and no clothes on. Another of their bad customs is their putting of dust and ashes on their heads as a sign of respect. . . . And another is that many of them eat animals not ritually slaughtered, and dogs and donkeys.

■ **Discuss the various ways in which Islamic influences and established local customs came together in the Mali empire.**

SOURCE: Said Hamdun and Noel King, eds. *Ibn Battuta in Black Africa.* Princeton: Markus Wiener, 1998, pp. 49–50, 58–59.

because it allowed mariners to sail over long stretches of deep water with confidence in their ability to find their destinations and return home safely.

SPREAD OF CROPS   Long-distance journeys enabled Muslim travelers to introduce new food and commercial crops—such as citrus fruits and Asian rice—to sub-Saharan Africa, which enriched west African diets after the eleventh century. Muslims also introduced cotton to west Africa, and by 1500 it was the principal textile produced in sub-Saharan Africa.

SUGARCANE    Muslims were also instrumental in the continuing diffusion of sugarcane. Muslim merchants and other travelers had begun large-scale cultivation of sugarcane in southwest Asia and north Africa during the Abbasid caliphate. After the twelfth century, Muslims facilitated the westward spread of sugarcane by acquainting European crusaders with crystallized sugar refined from cane. Up to that time Europeans had little access to refined sugar, and they relied on honey and fruits as sweeteners. They immediately appreciated the convenience of refined sugar. Italian entrepreneurs began to organize sugarcane plantations on Mediterranean islands such as Sicily, Cyprus, Crete, and Rhodes, and investors began to seek suitable locations throughout the Mediterranean basin. The cultivation of sugarcane had deep social and economic implications. Like their Muslim predecessors, European sugar producers often staffed their plantations with slave laborers, and the growth of plantations fueled an increasing demand for Muslim war captives and black Africans who could supply labor services.

GUNPOWDER TECHNOLOGIES    Although Muslim merchants and travelers were especially prominent agents of diffusion, Mongols also contributed to the process, notably by helping to spread gunpowder technologies west from China. Mongol invaders learned about gunpowder from Chinese military engineers in the early thirteenth century and soon incorporated gunpowder-based weapons into their arsenal. During the 1250s, as they campaigned in Persia and southwest Asia, the Mongols used catapults and trebuchets to lob gunpowder bombs into cities under siege. Muslim armies soon developed similar weapons in response.

By the mid–thirteenth century gunpowder had reached Europe. By the early fourteenth century, armies from China to Europe possessed primitive cannons. Although not especially accurate, the weapons were powerful enough to blow holes in the defensive walls of cities under siege. Thus, with the assistance of Mongol warriors, gunpowder technology rapidly spread from its homeland in China across the entire Eurasian landmass and changed forever the nature of war.

Agricultural and technological diffusions of the era 1000 to 1500 were by no means unique processes in world history. For millennia, agricultural crops and technological skills had spread widely whenever peoples of different societies interacted with one another. Because of the particularly intense interactions of the period from 1000 to 1500, however, agricultural and technological diffusion profoundly influenced the lives of peoples throughout the eastern hemisphere on an unprecedented scale.

# CRISIS AND RECOVERY

As Eurasian peoples traveled over long distances, they exchanged trade goods, agricultural crops, and technological expertise, and they also unwittingly spread disease pathogens. When diseases broke out among previously unexposed populations, they often caused widespread epidemics that severely disrupted whole societies. During the fourteenth century, bubonic plague erupted in epidemics that ravaged societies throughout most of Asia, Europe, and north Africa. Epidemic plague struck intermittently until the seventeenth century, but by the fifteenth century Chinese and western European societies in particular had begun to recover from its effects.

## Bubonic Plague

THE LITTLE ICE AGE    About 1300 C.E. a process of global climatic change caused temperatures to decline significantly throughout the world. For more than five hundred years, the earth experienced a "little ice age," when temperatures were much cooler than before. Markedly cooler temperatures meant shorter growing seasons, which caused agricultural production to decline in many lands. That, in turn, led to famine and sometimes even starvation. In some northerly lands, such as Greenland, agriculture ceased to be a practical possibility.

## ORIGINS OF EPIDEMIC BUBONIC PLAGUE

Just after the onset of the little ice age, peoples in much of the eastern hemisphere suddenly encountered a new challenge in the form of devastating epidemic disease. Bubonic plague spread from the Yunnan region of southwestern China, where it probably had been endemic for centuries. The plague bacillus infects rodents such as rats, squirrels, and prairie dogs, and fleas transmit the pathogen from one rodent to another. If rodent populations decline, fleas seek other hosts and sometimes spread the disease to human victims. In the early fourteenth century, Mongol military campaigns helped spread plague from Yunnan to China's interior, and by the 1350s it had spread to widely scattered regions of China. In some afflicted areas contemporaries reported that plague carried away two-thirds of the population.

**SPREAD OF PLAGUE** During the 1340s Mongols, merchants, and other travelers helped spread the disease along trade routes west of China. By 1346 it had reached the Black Sea ports of Caffa and Tana. In 1347 Italian merchants fled plague-infected Black Sea ports and unwittingly spread the disease throughout the Mediterranean basin. By 1348, following the trade routes, plague had sparked epidemics in most of western Europe.

Wherever it appeared, bubonic plague—which Europeans referred to as the "Black Death"—struck with frightful effects. Victims developed inflamed lymph nodes, particularly in the neck, armpit, and groin areas, and most died within a few days after the onset of symptoms. Internal hemorrhaging often discolored the inflammations to a black or purple hue. These swellings were called buboes, which gave rise to the term *bubonic plague*. Bubonic plague typically killed 60 to 70 percent of its human victims. In some small villages and towns, disease wiped out the entire population. Plague also returned to claim new victims. In Europe plague erupted intermittently from the 1340s until the late 1600s.

Some parts of the eastern hemisphere did not suffer directly from plague epidemics. The long, cold winters of Scandinavia, for example, discouraged the proliferation of plague-bearing rodents and fleas. For reasons unknown, India also seems to have avoided the worst effects of the plague. In fact, Indian population grew from 91 million in the year 1300 to 97 million a century later. Epidemics also largely bypassed sub-Saharan Africa.

**THE BUBONIC PLAGUE IN EUROPE.** A painting of 1503 graphically communicates the horror felt by medieval Europeans when bubonic plague struck their communities. Here death takes away a victim, while others die beside the road.

The bubonic plague
www.mhhe.com/
bentleybrief2e

**POPULATION DECLINE** In lands hard hit by plague, however, it took a century and more to begin recovery from the demographic consequences of the disease. In 1300 China's population, already reduced by conflicts with the Mongols, stood at eighty-five million. In 1400, after about seventy years of epidemic plague, China's population amounted to only seventy-five million. A century later demographic recovery was under way, and China's population rebounded to one hundred million. European society also reeled from the effects of bubonic plague. From seventy-nine million in 1300, European population dropped by almost 25 percent to sixty million in 1400. As in China, demographic recovery in Europe was under way in 1500, when European population climbed to eighty-one million. Islamic societies in southwest Asia, Egypt, and north Africa also suffered devastating population losses, and demographic recovery took much longer there than in China and Europe. In Egypt, human population probably did not reach pre-plague levels until the nineteenth century.

**SOCIAL AND ECONOMIC EFFECTS** Because of its heavy demographic toll, bubonic plague disrupted societies and economies throughout Eurasia and north Africa. Such high death rates caused huge labor shortages, which in turn generated social unrest. In western Europe, for example, urban workers demanded higher wages, and many left their homes in search of better conditions. Political authorities responded by freezing wages and forbidding workers to leave their homes. Peasants in the countryside also sought to improve their circumstances by moving to regions where landlords offered better terms. Landlords responded to this challenge by restricting the freedom of peasants to move. As a result of sharply conflicting interests, disgruntled workers and peasants mounted a series of rebellions that rocked both the towns and the countryside of western Europe and were extinguished only after considerable social disruption and loss of life.

By the seventeenth century the plague had lost much of its ferocity. Epidemics occurred more sporadically, and they did not seriously diminish human populations. Since the 1940s antibiotic drugs have brought the disease largely under control among human populations, although it survives in rodent communities throughout much of the world.

## *Recovery in China: The Ming Dynasty*

By the mid–fourteenth century the Mongol's Yuan dynasty was experiencing very difficult times. Financial mismanagement led to serious economic difficulties, and political conflicts led to factional fighting among the Mongols themselves. In 1368, with bubonic plague raging, the Yuan dynasty collapsed, and the Mongols departed China en masse, leaving China in a state of both demographic and political turmoil. However, an increasing birthrate soon helped to replenish human numbers, and political recovery accompanied the demographic rebound.

HONGWU     When the Yuan dynasty fell, the governance of China returned to Chinese hands. The new emperor came from a family so poor that he spent much of his youth as a beggar. Because of his size and strength, he came to the notice of military commanders, and he made his way through the ranks to lead the rebellious forces that toppled the Yuan dynasty. In 1368 he became Emperor Hongwu, and he proclaimed the establishment of the Ming ("brilliant") dynasty, which lasted until 1644.

MING CENTRALIZATION     Hongwu immediately set about eliminating all traces of Mongol rule and establishing a government on the model of traditional Chinese dynasties. Although Hongwu had little interest in scholarly matters, he reestablished the Confucian educational and civil service systems to ensure a supply of talented officials and bureaucrats. At the same time, he moved to centralize his authority. In 1380, when he suspected his chief minister of involvement in a treasonous plot, Hongwu executed the minister and his allies and then abolished the minister's position altogether. From that time forward the Ming emperors ruled directly, without the aid of chief ministers.

MANDARINS AND EUNUCHS     The Ming emperors insisted on absolute obedience to the policies and initiatives of the central government. They relied heavily on the mandarins, a special class of officials sent out as emissaries of the central government to ensure local compliance with imperial policy. The Ming emperors also relied more heavily on eunuchs than had any of their predecessors. Eunuchs had long been considered reliable because they could not generate families and build power bases that might challenge ruling houses. Yet Ming emperors intent on centralization placed even more importance on the service of eunuchs, because they expected that servants whose fortunes depended exclusively on the emperors' favor would work especially diligently to advance the emperors' interests.

The tightly centralized administration instituted by the early Ming emperors lasted more than five hundred years. Although the dynasty fell in 1644 to Manchu invaders, who founded the Qing dynasty, the Manchus retained the administrative framework of

**Yuan** (yoo-AHN)

**Hongwu** (hawng-woo)

**eunuchs** (YOO-nihks)

the Ming state, which largely survived until the collapse of the Qing dynasty in 1911.

**ECONOMIC RECOVERY**    While building a centralized administration, the Ming emperors also worked toward economic recovery. The new rulers conscripted laborers to rebuild irrigation systems that had fallen into disrepair, and agricultural production surged as a result. At the same time, they promoted the manufacture of porcelain, lacquerware, and fine silk and cotton textiles. They did not actively promote trade with other lands, but private Chinese merchants conducted a thriving business marketing Chinese products in ports and trading cities from Japan to the islands of southeast Asia. Meanwhile, domestic trade surged within China, reflecting increasing productivity and prosperity.

**CULTURAL REVIVAL**    Alongside political and economic recovery, the Ming dynasty sponsored a kind of cultural revival in China. Emperor Hongwu tried to eradicate all signs of the recent nomadic occupation by discouraging the use of Mongol names and the wearing of Mongol dress. Ming emperors actively promoted Chinese cultural traditions, particularly the Confucian and neo-Confucian schools. Hongwu's successor, Yongle, even organized the preparation of a vast encyclopedia that compiled all significant works of Chinese history, philosophy, and literature. This *Yongle Encyclopedia* ran to almost twenty-three thousand manuscript rolls, each equivalent to a medium-size book, and was a clear signal of Ming interest in supporting native Chinese cultural traditions.

**MING JAR.** | Ming artisans won worldwide fame for their blue-and-white porcelain, which inspired the founders of the Delft porcelain factory in the Netherlands. This covered jar dates from the early fifteenth century.

## Recovery in Western Europe: State Building

Ming dynasty tea shop
www.mhhe.com/
bentleybrief2e

Demographic recovery strengthened states in western Europe as it did in China. In Europe, however, political authority rested with a series of regional states rather than a centralized empire. By the late fifteenth century, states in Italy, Spain, France, and England had devised techniques of government that vastly enhanced their power.

During the later middle ages (1300–1500), internal problems as well as bubonic plague complicated European political affairs. The Holy Roman Empire survived in name, but effective authority lay with the German princes and the Italian city-states rather than the emperor. In Spain descendants of Muslim conquerors held the kingdom of Granada in the southern portion of the Iberian peninsula. Meanwhile, the kings of France and England sparred constantly over lands claimed by both.

**TAXES AND ARMIES**    By the late fifteenth century, however, regional states in western Europe had greatly strengthened their societies. The state-building efforts of the later middle ages involved two especially important elements. The first was the development of fresh sources of finance, usually through new taxes levied directly on citizens and subjects. The second was the maintenance of large standing armies, often composed of mercenary forces and equipped with gunpowder weapons, supported by state funds.

**ITALIAN STATES**    The state-building process began in Italy, where profits from industrial production and trade enriched the major cities. Beginning in the thirteenth century, the principal Italian states—the city-states of Milan, Venice, and Florence, the papal state based in Rome, and the kingdom of Naples—began to finance their needs for military forces and larger bureaucracies by levying direct taxes and issuing long-term bonds that they repaid from treasury receipts. With fresh sources of finance, the principal

**Qing** (ching)

**Yongle** (YAWNG-leh)

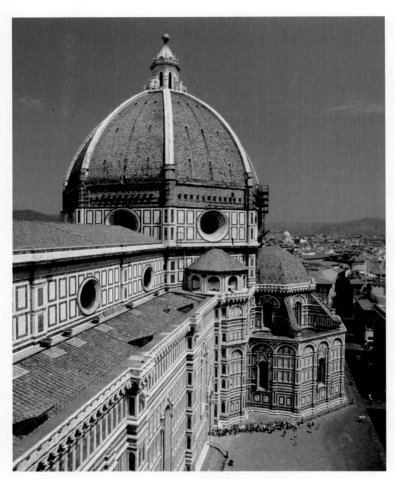

**THE CATHEDRAL OF FLORENCE.** | Brunelleschi's magnificent dome on the cathedral of Florence dominates the city's skyline even today. *Why was such a dome considered revolutionary during the Renaissance?*

Fernando and Isabel receive Boabdil
www.mhhe.com/bentleybrief2e

Italian states strengthened their authority within their boundaries as well as in their surrounding areas.

**FRANCE AND ENGLAND** During the fourteenth and fifteenth centuries, Italian administrative methods made their way beyond the Alps. Partly because of the enormous expenses they incurred during wars against each other, the kings of France and England began to levy direct taxes and assemble powerful armies. Rulers in both lands asserted the authority of the central government over the nobility. In France, King Louis XI (reigned 1461–1483) accomplished this by maintaining a permanent army of about fifteen thousand well-armed troops. Because the expense of maintaining such forces was beyond the means of the nobility, Louis and his successors enjoyed a decisive edge over ambitious subordinates seeking to challenge royal authority.

**SPAIN** The process of state building was most dramatic in Spain, where the marriage in 1469 of Fernando of Aragon and Isabel of Castile united the two wealthiest Iberian realms. Receipts from the sales tax, the primary source of royal income, supported a powerful standing army. Under Fernando and Isabel, popularly known as the Catholic Kings, Christian forces completed the *reconquista* by conquering the kingdom of Granada and absorbing it into their state. The Catholic Kings also projected their authority beyond Iberia. When a French army threatened the kingdom of Naples in 1494, they seized southern Italy, and by 1559 Spanish forces had established their hegemony throughout most of the Italian peninsula.

Competition between European states intensified as they tightened their authority in their territories. This competition led to frequent small-scale wars between European states, and it encouraged the rapid development of military and naval technology. As states sought technological advantages over their neighbors, they encouraged the refinement and improvement of weapons, ships, and sails. When one state acquired powerful weapons—such as ships equipped with cannons—neighboring states sought to outdo their rivals with more advanced devices. Thus technological innovations vastly strengthened European armies just as they began to venture again into the larger world.

## *Recovery in Western Europe: The Renaissance*

Demographic recovery and state-building efforts in western Europe coincided with a remarkable cultural flowering known as the Renaissance. The French word *renaissance* means "rebirth," and it refers here to a period of artistic and intellectual creativity from the fourteenth to the sixteenth century in western Europe. Painters, sculptors, and architects of the Renaissance era drew inspiration from classical Greek and Roman artists rather

---

**Fernando of Aragon** (fer-NAWN-doh of ah-ruh-GAWN)

**Isabel of Castile** (IHZ-uh-bel of ka-steel)

*reconquista* (ray-kohn-KEES-tah)

**Renaissance** (ren-uh-SAHNS)

than from their medieval predecessors. In their efforts to revive classical aesthetic standards, they transformed European art. Meanwhile, Renaissance scholars known as humanists looked to classical rather than medieval literary models, and they sought to update medieval moral thought and adapt it to the needs of a bustling urban society.

**ITALIAN RENAISSANCE ART** Just as they pioneered new techniques of statecraft, the Italian city-states also pioneered Renaissance innovations in art and architecture. In search of realistic depictions, Italian artists studied the human form and represented the emotions of their subjects. Italian painters such as Leonardo da Vinci (1452–1519) relied on the technique of linear perspective to represent the three dimensions of real life on two-dimensional surfaces. Sculptors such as Donatello (1386–1466) and Michelangelo Buonarotti (1475–1564) sought to depict their subjects in natural poses that reflected the actual workings of human muscles rather than the awkward and rigid postures of earlier sculptures.

The Vitruvian Man
www.mhhe.com/
bentleybrief2e

**RENAISSANCE ARCHITECTURE** Renaissance architects designed buildings in the simple, elegant style preferred by their classical Greek and Roman predecessors. Their most impressive achievement was the construction of domed buildings. Roman architects had built domes, but their technology and engineering did not survive the collapse of the Roman empire. In the early fifteenth century, however, the Florentine architect Filippo Brunelleschi (1377–1446) reinvented equipment and designs for a large dome. During the 1420s and 1430s, he oversaw the construction of a magnificent dome on the cathedral of Florence, which residents took as a symbol of the city's wealth and leadership in artistic and cultural affairs.

**THE HUMANISTS** Like Renaissance artists and architects, scholars and literary figures known as humanists drew inspiration from classical models. The term *humanist* referred to scholars interested in the humanities—literature, history, and moral philosophy. Renaissance humanists were also deeply committed to Christianity. Several humanists worked diligently to prepare accurate texts and translations of the New Testament and other important Christian writings. Most notable of them was Desiderius Erasmus of Rotterdam (1466–1536), who in 1516 published the first edition of the Greek New Testament along with a revised Latin translation and copious annotations.

Humanists scorned the dense and often convoluted writing style of the scholastic theologians. Instead, they preferred the elegant and polished language of classical Greek and Roman authors and the early church fathers, whose works they considered more engaging and more persuasive than those of medieval philosophers and theologians. Thus humanists such as the Florentine Francesco Petrarca, known in English as Petrarch (1304–1374), traveled throughout Europe searching for manuscripts of classical works. In the monastic libraries of Italy, Switzerland, and southern France, they found hundreds of Latin writings that medieval scholars had overlooked. During the fifteenth century, Italian humanists became acquainted with Byzantine scholars and enlarged the body of classical Greek as well as Latin works available to scholars.

**HUMANIST MORAL THOUGHT** Classical Greek and Latin values encouraged the humanists to reconsider medieval ethical teachings. Medieval moral philosophers had taught that the most honorable calling was that of monks and nuns who withdrew from the world and dedicated their lives to prayer and contemplation, but the humanists drew inspiration from classical authors such as Cicero, who demonstrated that it was possible to lead a morally virtuous life while participating actively in the affairs of the world.

**Leonardo da Vinci** (lee-uh-NAHR-doh duh VIHN-chee)

**Michelangelo Buonarotti** (mik-uhl-AN-juh-loh baw-nahr-RAW-tee)

**Desiderius Erasmus** (des-i-DEER-ee-uhs ih-raz-muhs)

**Francesco Petrarca** (frahn-CHES-kaw PEE-trahrk-a)

Renaissance humanists argued that it was perfectly honorable for Christians to enter into marriage, business relationships, and public affairs. Humanist moral thought thus represented an effort to reconcile Christian values and ethics with the increasingly urban and commercial society of Renaissance Europe.

**RENAISSANCE EUROPE AND THE LARGER WORLD**  Quite apart from the conscious effort to draw inspiration from classical antiquity, Renaissance art and thought also reflected increasing European participation in the affairs of the eastern hemisphere. As merchants linked Europe to the larger hemispheric economy, European peoples experienced increased prosperity, which enabled them to invest resources in artistic production and support for scholarship. Renaissance painters filled their canvases with images of silk garments, lacquered wood, spice jars, and foreign peoples that had recently come to European attention. Princes and wealthy patrons commissioned hundreds of these paintings, which brought a cosmopolitan look to their palaces, residences, and places of business.

# EXPLORATION AND COLONIZATION

As peoples of the eastern hemisphere recovered from demographic collapse and restored order to their societies, they also sought to revive the networks of long-distance trade and communication that epidemic plague had disrupted. Most active in that effort were China and western Europe—the two societies that recovered most rapidly from the disasters of the fourteenth century. During the early Ming dynasty, Chinese ports accommodated foreign traders, and mariners mounted a series of enormous naval expeditions that visited almost all parts of the Indian Ocean basin. Meanwhile, by the end of the fifteenth century, Europeans not only had established sea-lanes to India but also had made several return voyages to the American continents, thus inaugurating a process that brought all the world's peoples into permanent and sustained interaction.

## The Chinese Reconnaissance of the Indian Ocean Basin

Having ousted the Mongols, the early Ming emperors were not eager to have large numbers of foreigners residing in China. Yet the emperors permitted foreign merchants to trade in the closely supervised ports of Quanzhou and Guangzhou, where they obtained Chinese silk, porcelain, and manufactured goods in exchange for pearls, gems, spices, and cotton fabrics. The early Ming emperors also refurbished the large Chinese navy built during the Song dynasty, and they allowed Chinese merchants to participate in overseas trading ventures in Japan and southeast Asia.

**ZHENG HE'S EXPEDITIONS**  Moreover, for almost thirty years, the Ming government sponsored a series of seven unprecedented naval expeditions designed to establish a Chinese presence in the Indian Ocean basin. Emperor Yongle organized the expeditions for two main purposes: to impose imperial control over foreign trade with China and to impress foreign peoples with the power and might of the Ming dynasty. Indeed, he might well have hoped to extend the tributary system, by which Chinese dynasties traditionally recognized foreign peoples, to lands in the Indian Ocean basin.

The expeditions took place between 1405 and 1433. Leading them was the eunuch admiral Zheng He, a Muslim from Yunnan in southwestern China who became a trusted advisor of Yongle. Zheng He embarked on each voyage with an awesome fleet of vessels

**Zheng He** (jung ha)

complemented by armed forces large enough to overcome resistance at any port where the expedition called. On the first voyage, for example, Zheng He's fleet consisted of 317 ships accompanied by almost twenty-eight thousand armed troops. Many of these vessels were mammoth, nine-masted ships with four decks capable of accommodating five hundred or more passengers. Measuring up to 124 meters (408 feet) long and 51 meters (166 feet) wide, these ships were by far the largest marine craft the world had ever seen.

On the first three voyages, Zheng He took his fleet to southeast Asia, India, and Ceylon. The fourth expedition went to the Persian Gulf and Arabia, and later expeditions ventured down the east African coast, calling at ports as far south as Malindi in modern Kenya. Throughout his travels, Zheng He liberally dispensed gifts of Chinese silk, porcelain, and other goods. In return he received rich and unusual presents, including African zebras and giraffes.

CHINESE NAVAL POWER    Zheng He generally sought to attain his goals through diplomacy, and for the most part he had little need to engage in hostilities. But a contemporary reported that Zheng He did not shrink from violence when he considered it necessary to impress foreign peoples with China's military might. He ruthlessly suppressed pirates who had long plagued Chinese and southeast Asian waters. He also intervened in a civil disturbance to establish his authority in Ceylon, and he made displays of military force when local officials threatened his fleet in Arabia and east Africa. The seven expeditions established a Chinese presence and reputation in the Indian Ocean basin. Returning from his fourth voyage, Zheng He brought envoys from thirty states who traveled to China and paid their respects at the Ming court.

END OF THE VOYAGES    Yet suddenly, in the mid-1430s, the Ming emperors decided to end the expeditions. Confucian ministers, who mistrusted Zheng He and the eunuchs who supported the voyages, argued that resources committed to the expensive expeditions should go to better uses. Moreover, during the 1420s and 1430s the Mongols mounted a new military threat from the northwest, and land forces urgently needed financial support.

Thus in 1433, after Zheng He's seventh voyage, the expeditions ended. Chinese merchants continued to trade in Japan and southeast Asia, but imperial officials destroyed most of the nautical charts that Zheng He had carefully prepared. The decommissioned ships sat in harbors until they rotted away, and Chinese craftsmen forgot the technology of building such large vessels. Yet Zheng He's voyages demonstrated clearly that China could exercise military, political, and economic influence throughout the Indian Ocean basin.

## European Exploration in the Atlantic and Indian Oceans

As Chinese fleets reconnoitered the Indian Ocean, European mariners were preparing to enter both the Atlantic and the Indian Ocean basins. Unlike Zheng He and his companions, however, Europeans ventured onto the seas not for diplomatic reasons but to expand the boundaries of Roman Catholic Christianity and to profit from commercial opportunities.

PORTUGUESE EXPLORATION    The experience of Portugal illustrates that mixture of motives. During the fifteenth century Prince Henrique of Portugal, often called Prince Henry the Navigator, embarked on an ambitious campaign to spread Christianity and increase Portuguese influence on the seas. In 1415 he watched as Portuguese forces seized the Moroccan city of Ceuta, which guarded the Strait of Gibraltar from the south. He regarded his victory both as a blow against Islam and as a strategic move enabling Christian vessels to move freely between the Mediterranean and the Atlantic.

King Afonso V to his sea captains
www.mhhe.com/ bentleybrief2e

Ceuta (SYOO-tuh)

**MAP 18.2** | Chinese and European voyages of exploration, 1405–1498. Although they followed different routes, all the voyagers represented on this map were seeking destinations in the Indian Ocean basin. *Why did Chinese and Iberian mariners want to establish a presence in the Indian Ocean during the fifteenth century?*

Columbus believed he had found a shorter route to the Indian Ocean basin when he landed on San Salvador.

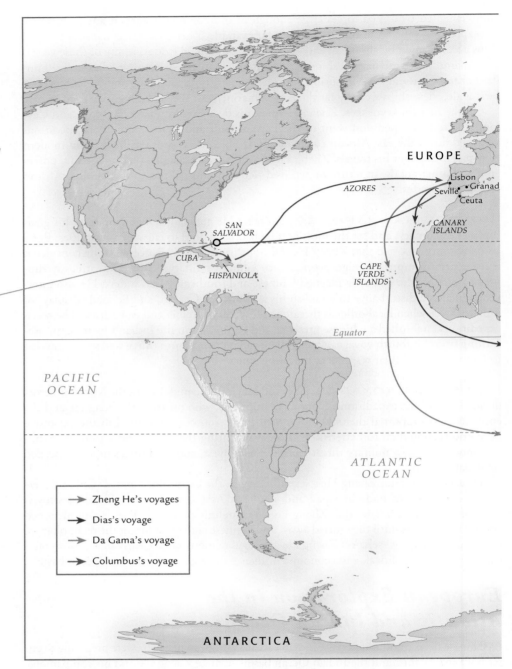

COLONIZATION OF THE ATLANTIC ISLANDS    Following the capture of Ceuta, Henrique encouraged Portuguese mariners to venture into the Atlantic. During their voyages they discovered the Madeiras and Azores Islands, all uninhabited, which they soon colonized. Later discoveries included the Cape Verde Islands, Fernando Po, São Tomé, and Principe off the west African coast. Because these Atlantic islands enjoyed fertile soils and a Mediterranean climate, Portuguese entrepreneurs soon began to cultivate sugarcane there, often in collaboration with Italian investors. Italians had financed sugar plantations in the Mediterranean islands since the twelfth century, and their commercial networks provided a ready means to distribute sugar to Europeans, who were rapidly developing a taste for sweets.

SLAVE TRADE   During the middle decades of the fifteenth century, a series of Portuguese fleets also explored the west African coast. Originally, the Portuguese traded guns, textiles, and other manufactured items for African gold and slaves. Soon, Portuguese traders changed the nature of the African slave trade by dramatically increasing its volume and by sending slaves to new destinations. In the mid–fifteenth century the Portuguese dispatched thousands of slaves annually to recently founded plantations in the Atlantic islands, where the slaves worked as laborers. The use of African slaves to perform heavy labor on commercial plantations soon became common practice, and it fueled the development of a huge, Atlantic-wide trade that, by the end of the nineteenth century, delivered as many as twelve million enslaved Africans to destinations in North America, South America, and the Caribbean region.

# THINKING ABOUT
## *Encounters*

**ENCOUNTERS IN CROSS-CULTURAL INTERACTIONS.** The period from 1000 to 1500 C.E. witnessed enormous and unprecedented cross-cultural trade and travel across Eurasia and Africa and, for the first time, between Eurasia and the Americas. Using specific examples, discuss the ways in which these numerous encounters encouraged technological, intellectual, and material changes in far-distant societies.

**INDIAN OCEAN TRADE** While some Portuguese mariners traded profitably in west Africa, others sought to eliminate the role of Muslim and Italian intermediaries in the Asian silk and spice trades by finding a sea-lane from Europe around Africa and into the Indian Ocean. By 1488 Bartolomeu Dias had sailed around the Cape of Good Hope and entered the Indian Ocean. In 1497 Vasco da Gama departed Portugal with the intention of sailing to India. After rounding the Cape of Good Hope, he cruised up the east African coast and found a Muslim pilot who showed him how to take advantage of the seasonal monsoon winds to sail across the Arabian Sea to India. In 1498 he arrived at Calicut, and by 1499 he had returned to Lisbon with a hugely profitable cargo of pepper and spices.

For most of the following century, Portuguese merchants and mariners dominated trade between Europe and Asia. Indeed, they attempted to control all shipping in the Indian Ocean by overpowering the vessels of Arabs, Persians, Indians, and southeast Asians. They did not have enough ships to oversee all trade in the region, but the entry of Portuguese mariners into the Indian Ocean signaled the beginning of European imperialism in Asia.

**CHRISTOPHER COLUMBUS** While Portuguese seafarers sought a sea route around Africa to India, the Genoese mariner Cristoforo Colombo, known in English as Christopher Columbus, conceived the idea of sailing west to reach Asian markets. Because geographers in the eastern hemisphere knew nothing of the Americas, Columbus's notion made a certain amount of sense, although many doubted that his plan could lead to profitable trade because of the long distances involved. After the king of Portugal declined to sponsor an expedition to test Columbus's plan, Fernando and Isabel of Spain agreed to underwrite a voyage. In 1492 Columbus set sail. Later that year his fleet of three ships reached land at San Salvador (Watling Island) in the Bahamas.

**Bartolomeu Dias** (bahr-tol-oh-mew DEE-uhs)

**Vasco da Gama** (VAS-koh duh GAM-uh)

**Cristoforo Colombo** (crihs-toh-for-oh kuh-LUHM-boh)

**SIXTEENTH-CENTURY EUROPEAN MAP OF THE WORLD.** | Although Christopher Columbus believed that he had sailed into Asian waters, later mariners soon realized that the Americas were continents unknown to geographers of the eastern hemisphere. This map, prepared in 1532 by the German cartographer Sebastian Münster, shows that by the early sixteenth century European geographers had acquired a rough but accurate understanding of South America but had reconnoitered only the Atlantic coastline of North America.

Columbus returned to Spain without the gold, silk, and spices that he had expected to find, but he persistently held that he had reached islands near the Asian mainland and the markets of China and Japan. Yet although Columbus himself never acknowledged that his expeditions had not reached Asia, by the end of the fifteenth century other mariners who came to explore the Caribbean and the American continents realized that the western hemisphere constituted a world apart from Europe, Asia, and Africa.

# SUMMARY

In the five centuries between 1000 and 1500 C.E., peoples in the eastern hemisphere interacted with more frequency than ever before. In part this was because of the stability created by the large empires of the Mongols and other nomadic peoples. Although conquest by these empires brought initial destruction to many societies, the pacification of large areas that occurred after conquest allowed safe travel for traders, diplomats, and missionaries. The relative safety of long-distance travel encouraged peoples of the eastern hemisphere to exchange technologies, ideas, crops, and religious faiths with one another with ever-increasing frequency. Yet just as we saw at the end of the classical period, one of the unintended consequences of increased cross-cultural interaction was the spread of epidemic disease to distant regions. Indeed, in the fourteenth century bubonic plague tore through much of Eurasia, leaving death and destruction in its wake and severely weakening cross-cultural ties. However, by the early fifteenth century societies had begun to recover from the plague, and China and Europe in particular began to renew cross-cultural contacts. Although both Chinese and European efforts at renewing these contacts had momentous consequences, the ocean voyages of Europeans in this period fundamentally shaped modern world history when they accidentally made contact with peoples from the western hemisphere. For the first time in human history, cross-cultural interactions began to connect peoples from both hemispheres, with enormous significance for the entire globe.

# STUDY TERMS

Bartolomeu Dias (360)
bubonic plague (344)
Christopher Columbus (360)
Desiderius Erasmus (355)
eunuchs (352)
Filippo Brunelleschi (355)
gunpowder (350)
Hongwu (352)
Ibn Battuta (343)

Isabel of Castile and Fernando
    of Aragon (354)
Khubilai Khan (345)
Leonardo da Vinci (355)
mandarins (352)
Marco Polo (345)
Melaka (344)
Michelangelo Buonarotti (355)
Ming dynasty (352)

Petrarch (355)
Prince Henry the Navigator (357)
reconquista (354)
Renaissance (354)
Sufis (347)
sugarcane (350)
Vasco da Gama (360)
Yongle (353)
Zheng He (356)

# FOR FURTHER READING

Janet L. Abu-Lughod. *Before European Hegemony: The World System, A.D. 1250–1350.* New York, 1989. An important study of long-distance trade networks during the Mongol era.

Jerry H. Bentley. *Old World Encounters: Cross-Cultural Contacts and Exchanges in Pre-modern Times.* New York, 1993. Studies cultural and religious exchanges in the eastern hemisphere before 1500 C.E.

Jerry Brotton. *The Renaissance Bazaar: From the Silk Road to Michelangelo.* Oxford, 2002. A provocative and well-illustrated study arguing that encounters in the larger world deeply influenced Renaissance cultural development in Europe.

K. N. Chaudhuri. *Asia before Europe: Economy and Civilisation of the Indian Ocean from the Rise of Islam to 1750.* Cambridge, 1990. Controversial and penetrating analysis of economic, social, and cultural structures shaping societies of the Indian Ocean basin.

Ross E. Dunn. *The Adventures of Ibn Battuta: A Muslim Traveler of the 14th Century.* Berkeley, 1986. Fascinating reconstruction of Ibn Battuta's travels and experiences.

Robert S. Gottfried. *The Black Death: Natural and Human Disaster in Medieval Europe.* New York, 1983. The best general study of bubonic plague and its effects in Europe.

John Larner. *Marco Polo and the Discovery of the World.* New Haven, 1999. Excellent study of Marco Polo and his significance, based on a thorough review of both textual evidence and recent scholarship.

Louise L. Levathes. *When China Ruled the Seas: The Treasure Fleet of the Dragon Throne, 1405–1433.* New York, 1994. Excellent popular account of Zheng He's voyages.

William D. Phillips Jr. and Carla Rahn Phillips. *The Worlds of Christopher Columbus.* New York, 1992. The best general work on Christopher Columbus.

Frances Wood. *The Silk Road: Two Thousand Years in the Heart of Asia.* Berkeley, 2002. A brilliantly illustrated volume discussing the history of the silk roads from antiquity to the twentieth century.

# Bringing It All Together

## Part IV | An Age of Cross-Cultural Interaction, 1000 to 1500 C.E.

Although the postclassical societies of the eastern hemisphere had restored order and stability to the region by 1000 C.E., invasions and conquest by nomadic peoples caused most postclassical societies to collapse between the eleventh and the fourteenth centuries. These nomadic invaders included the Mongols, who conquered so much of Eurasia in the thirteenth and fourteenth centuries that they built the largest empire the world has ever seen.

Mongol conquest initially resulted in monumental human and physical destruction. However, once conquest was complete, Mongol overlords facilitated accelerated communication within their vast imperial domains. Thus, from China to eastern Europe, traders, diplomats, missionaries, travelers, and pilgrims moved overland with greater ease than ever before, and encouraged ever-stronger networks of communication and exchange.

The Indian Ocean basin also grew far more integrated in the centuries between 1000 and 1500 C.E. Indeed, by 1500 the Indian Ocean served as a highway linking peoples from China to east Africa. As with the overland routes of the Mongol empire, this Indian Ocean highway encouraged the diffusion of scientific and intellectual knowledge, technologies like gunpowder and the compass, and food crops such as cotton and sugarcane—all of which profoundly influenced the development of societies throughout the eastern hemisphere.

Yet as at the end of the classical period, increased overland and seaborne interaction in the eastern hemisphere also led to the diffusion of disease pathogens. In the fourteenth century, the bubonic plague spread rapidly from China across most of Eurasia, leaving millions dead in its wake. Such massive fatalities severely disrupted networks of communication and trade. However, by the end of the fifteenth century these networks had recovered once again. Indeed, they recovered so well that western Europeans—who had long been on the margins of Eurasian trade networks—sought eagerly to find alternate routes to the lucrative markets of east and southeast Asia. In one attempt to reach these markets by sailing west rather than east, Europeans instead stumbled on the Americas.

As European mariners ventured across the Atlantic and into the Americas, they unwittingly inaugurated a new era in world history, because they initiated a long-term process that brought all regions and peoples of the earth into permanent and sustained interaction for the first time in human history. Indeed, the formation and reconfiguration of global networks of power, communication, and exchange that followed from the initial contact between the two hemispheres rank among the most prominent themes of modern world history.

| | |
|---|---|
| **A** | short *a* sound, as in *asp, fat, parrot* |
| **AH** | *a* sound, as in *car, father* |
| **AHW** | diphthong *au* in Romance languages, similar to vowel sound in *ouch* |
| **AHY** | diphthong *ai* in Romance languages, similar to vowel sound in *die* |
| **AW** | diphthong *a* sound, as in *awful, paw, law* |
| **AY** | long *a* sound, as in *ape, date, play* |
| **EE** | long *e* sound, as in *even, meet, money* |
| **EH** | short *e* sound, as in *ten, elf, berry, how, bow* |
| **EHY** | diphthong *ei* in Romance languages, similar to "ay" in *day* |
| **EW** | diphthong *iu* in Romance languages, similar (but shorter than) *you* |
| **EYE** | long *i* sound, as in *ice, high, bite* |
| **IH** | short *i* sound, as in *fit, his, mirror* |
| **KH** | hard *k* sound |
| **OH** | long *o* sound, as in *open, go, tone* |
| **OHI** | diphthong *oi* in Romance languages, similar to "oy" in *toy* |
| **OO** | long *o* sound, as in *ooze, tool, crew* |
| **'R** | tapped *r* like *dd* or *tt* in *latter* and *butter* |
| **RR** | trilled *r* (repeated taps) |
| **UH** | short *u* sound, as in *up, cut, color* |
| **WA** | diphthong *ua* in Romance languages, similar to the "wa" in *want* and *waffle* |
| **WE** | diphthong *ui* in Romance languages, similar to the word *we* |
| **Y** | like *ll* in *million* or *ny* in *canyon* |
| **YA** | diphthong *ia* in Romance languages, similar to "ya" in *yacht* |
| **YE** | diphthong *ie* in Romance languages, similar to "ye" in *yet* |
| **YO** | diphthong *io* in Romance languages, similar to "yo" in the suffix *yoke* |

*Note on emphasis:* Syllables in capital letters receive the stress. If there is no syllable in capitals, then all syllables get equal stress.

**Aachen** (AH-kehn) A city in western Germany; formerly Charlemagne's northern capital.

**Abbasid** (ah-BAH-sihd) Cosmopolitan Arabic dynasty (750–1258) that replaced the Umayyads; founded by Abu al-Abbas and reaching its peak under Harun al-Rashid.

**Abolitionism** Antislavery movement.

**Absolutism** Political philosophy that stressed the divine right theory of kingship: the French king Louis XIV was the classic example.

**Abu Bakr** (ah-BOO BAHK-uhr) First caliph after the death of Muhammad.

**Achaemenid empire** (ah-KEE-muh-nid) First great Persian empire (558–330 B.C.E.), which began under Cyrus and reached its peak under Darius.

**Aegean** (ih-JEE-uhn) Bronze Age civilization that flourished near the Aegean Sea.

**Aeschylus** (ES-kuh-luhs) Greek tragedian, author of the *Oresteia*.

**Age of Access** Label for contemporary times regarding the ability of communication technologies to change the social, economic, and political solution of the past.

**Age grades** Bantu concept in which individuals of roughly the same age carried out communal tasks appropriate for that age.

**Agricultural transition** The gradual transition from a dependence on hunting and gathering for subsistence to a dependence on cultivation and animal husbandry. First evidence of transition is from around 12,000 B.C.E.

**Aguinaldo, Emilio** (AH-gee-NAHL-daw, ee-MEE-lyaw) Filipino independence leader who fought for independence from Spain and then the United States.

**Ahimsa** (uh-HIM-suh) A Buddhist, Hindu, and Jainist doctrine that all life is sacred and that violence should be avoided at all costs.

**Ahmosis** (AH-moh-sis) Egyptian pharaoh (c. 1500 B.C.E.), founder of the New Kingdom.

**Ahura Mazda** (uh-HOORE-uh MAHZ-duh) Main god of Zoroastrianism who represented truth and goodness and was perceived to be in an eternal struggle with the malign spirit Angra Mainyu.

**AIDS** Acquired immune deficiency syndrome.

**Akhenaton** (ahk-eh-NAH-ton) Early ruler of Egypt who created a tradition of sun worship.

**Al-Andalus** (al-ahn-dah-LOOS) Islamic Spain.

**Alboquerque, Afonso d'** (AL-buh-kur-kee, al-FAWN-soo d') Portuguese nobleman who established the Portuguese colonial empire in the Indian Ocean.

**Aliæi nui** Hawaiian class of high chiefs.

**Allah** (AH-lah) God of the monotheistic religion of Islam.

**Al Qaeda** A radical Sunni Muslim organization dedicated to the elimination of a Western presence in Arab countries and militantly opposed to Western foreign policy.

**Amon-Re** (AH-mohn RAY) Egyptian god, combination of the sun god Re and the air god Amon.

**Ancestor worship** Belief that dead ancestors can influence one's fortunes in this life. People who practice ancestor worship characteristically practice rituals and ceremonies to the memory or remains of their ancestors.

**Ancien régime** (ahn-syan rey-ZHEEM) The political and social system that existed in France before the French Revolution.

**Angkor** (AHN-kohr) Southeast Asian Khmer kingdom (889–1432) that was centered around the temple cities of Angkor Thom and Angkor Wat.

**Anschluss** (AHN-shloss) 1938 annexation of Austria into Greater Germany by the Nazi regime.

**Antigonus** (an-TIG-uh-nuhs) A general of Alexander the Great and king of Macedonia.

**Anti-Semitism** Term coined in late nineteenth century that was associated with a prejudice against Jews and the political, social, and economic actions taken against them.

**Antonianism** African syncretic religion, founded by Doña Beatriz, that taught that Jesus Christ was a black African man and that heaven was for Africans.

**Apartheid** (ah-PAHR-teyed) South African system of "separateness" that was implemented in 1948 and that maintained the black majority in a position of political, social, and economic subordination.

**Appeasement** British and French policy in the 1930s that tried to maintain peace in Europe in the face of German aggression by making concessions.

**Arianism** Early Christian heresy that centered around teaching of Arius (250–336 C.E.) and contained the belief that Jesus was a mortal human being and not coeternal with God; Arianism was the focus of Council of Nicaea.

**Aristotle** (AHR-ih-stot-uhl) One of the greatest ancient Athenian philosophers and pupil of Plato.

**Artha** Hindu concept for the pursuit of economic well-being and honest prosperity.

**Arthashastra** (UHRR-th-sha-strrah) Ancient Indian political treatise from the time of Chandragupta Maurya; its authorship was traditionally ascribed to Kautalya, and it stressed that war was inevitable.

**Aryans** (AYR-ee-uhns) Indo-European tribes who settled in India after 1500 B.C.E.; their union with indigenous Dravidians formed the basis of Hinduism.

**Asante** (uh-SAN-tee) Empire that emerged in 1670 in what is now modern Ghana.

**Asceticism** (uh-SET-uh-siz-uhm) Doctrine that through the renunciation of worldly pleasure one can achieve a high spiritual or intellectual state.

**Association of Southeast Asian Nations** (ASEAN) Regional alliance established in 1967 by Thailand, Malaysia, Singapore, Indonesia, and the Philippines; the alliance was designed to promote economic progress and political stability; it later became a free-trade zone.

**Assyrians** (uh-SEER-ee-uhns) Southwest Asian people who built an empire that reached its height during the eighth and seventh centuries B.C.E.; it was known for a powerful army and a well-structured state.

**Astrolabe** (as-truh-leyb) Navigational instrument for determining latitude.

**Atahualpa** (ah-tah-WAHL-pah) The last sovereign emperor of the Inca empire, executed by the Spanish.

**Aten** Monotheistic god of Egyptian pharaoh Akhenaten (r. 1353–1335 B.C.E.) and arguably the world's first example of monotheism.

**Audiencias** (AW-dee-uhns-cee-ahs) Spanish courts in Latin America.

**Australopithecus** (ah-strah-loh-PIHTH-uh-kuhs) "Southern ape," oldest known ancestor of humans; it lived from around four million down to around one million years ago, and it could walk on hind legs, freeing up hands for use of simple tools.

**Austronesians** People who, by as early as 2000 B.C.E., began to explore and settle islands of the Pacific Ocean basin.

**Avesta** Book that contains the holy writings of Zoroastrianism.

**Axum** (AHK-soom) Capital of ancient Ethiopian kingdom.

**Azores** (uh-ZAWRZ) Volcanic islands in the Northern Atlantic belonging to Portugal.

**Aztec empire** Central American empire constructed by the Mexica and expanded greatly during the fifteenth century during the reigns of Itzcoatl and Motecuzoma I.

**Babur** (BAH-ber) Founder of the Mughal dynasty in India.

**Bakufu** (bah-kuh-fuh) Military government under the Japanese shoguns.

**Balfour Declaration** British declaration from 1917 that supported the creation of a Jewish homeland in Palestine.

**Bantu** (BAHN-too) African peoples who originally lived in the area of present-day Nigeria; around 2000 B.C.E. they began a centuries-long migration that took them to most of sub-Saharan Africa; the Bantu were very influential, especially linguistically.

**Bechuanaland** (bech-oo-AH-nuh-land) Protectorate established in 1885 by the British in southern Africa.

**Bedouins** (BEHD-oh-ihnz) Nomadic Arabic tribespeople.

**Belisarius** (bel-uh-SAIR-ee-uhs) Byzantine general who fought against the Persians and recovered Roman territories in northern Africa.

**Benefice** Grant from a lord to a vassal, usually consisting of land, which supported the vassal and signified the relationship between the two.

**Benin** (beh-NEEN) Large precolonial African state in what is now modern Nigeria.

**Berdiaev, Nikolai** (ber-dee-ev, nih-koh-LYE) Late nineteenth- and early twentieth-century Russian philosopher.

**Berlin Conference** Meeting organized by German chancellor Otto von Bismarck in 1884–1885 that provided the justification for European colonization of Africa.

**Berlin Wall** Wall that separated West Berlin from East Germany.

**Bhagavad Gita** (BUHG-uh-vuhd GEE-tah) Sacred "song of god" composed in 200 B.C.E. and incorporated into the *Mahabharata,* a Sanskrit epic.

**Bhakti** (BHUK-tee) Indian movement that attempted to transcend the differences between Hinduism and Islam.

**Biodiversity** Diversity among and within plant and animal species in an environment.

**Black Hand** Pre–World War I secret Serbian society; one of its members, Gavrilo Princip, assassinated Austrian archduke Francis Ferdinand and provided the spark for the outbreak of the Great War.

**Blitzkrieg** German style of rapid attack through the use of armor and air power that was used in Poland, Norway, Denmark, Belgium, the Netherlands, and France in 1939–1940.

**Boddhisatvas** (BOH-dih-SAT-vuhs) Buddhist concept regarding individuals who had reached enlightenment but who stayed in this world to help people.

**Bolshevik** (BOHL-shih-vehk) Russian communist party headed by Lenin.

**Bourgeoisie** Middle class in modern industrial society.

**Boyars** (BOY-ahrs) Russian nobles.

**Brahmins** (BRAH-minz) Hindu caste of priests.

**Brezhnev Doctrine** Policy developed by Leonid Brezhnev (1906–1982) that claimed for the Soviet Union the right to invade any socialist country faced with internal or external enemies; the doctrine was best expressed in the Soviet invasion of Czechoslovakia.

**Bubonic plague** Epidemic that swept Eurasia, causing devastating population loss and economic disruption. It was known as the Black Death in Europe after around 1350 C.E.

**Buddha** (BOO-duh) The "enlightened one," the term applied to Siddhartha Gautama after his discoveries that would form the foundation of Buddhism.

**Buddhism** (BOO-diz'm) Religion, based on Four Noble Truths, associated with Siddhartha Gautama (563–483 B.C.E.), or the Buddha; its adherents desired to eliminate all distracting passion and reach nirvana.

**Buenos Aires** (BWE-naws AHY-res) Capital and largest city in Argentina.

**Bunraku** (boon-RAH-koo) A form of traditional Japanese puppet theater.

**Bush Doctrine of Deterrence** U.S. policy after 9/11 that preemptively attacks any supposed terrorist threat.

**Bushido** (BOH-shee-DOH) The "way of the warrior," the code of conduct of the Japanese samurai that was based on loyalty and honor.

**Byzantine** (BIHZ-uhn-teen) Long-lasting empire centered at Constantinople; it grew out of the end of the Roman empire and carried the legacy of Roman greatness and was the only classical society to survive into the early modern age; it reached its early peak during the reign of Justinian (483–565).

**Caesaropapism** Concept relating to the mixing of political and religious authority, as with the Roman emperors, that was central to the church versus state controversy in medieval Europe.

**Cahokia** (kuh-HOH-kee-uh) Large structure in modern Illinois that was constructed by the mound-building peoples; it was the third largest structure in the Americas before the arrival of the Europeans.

**Caliph** (KAH-leef) "deputy," Islamic leader after the death of Muhammad.

**Calpulli** (kal-po-lee) An organizational unit and geographical area of the Aztec capital Tenochtitlan.

**Cambyses** (kam-BIE-sees) Son of the Persian leader Cyrus the Great.

**Candomblé** (kan-duhm-BLEH) African-oriented religion practiced mainly in Brazil.

**Capet** (KAHP-ay) Surname of the founder of the French dynasty by the same name.

**Capetian** (cah-PEE-shuhn) Early French dynasty that started with Hugh Capet.

**Capitalism** An economic system with origins in early modern Europe in which private parties make their goods and services available on a free market.

**Capitulation** Highly unfavorable trading agreements that the Ottoman Turks signed with the Europeans in the nineteenth century that symbolized the decline of the Ottomans.

**Caporetto** (kap-uh-RET-oh) 1917 Battle of World War I in which the Italians were defeated by a combined Austro-German force.

**Carolingian** (kar-uh-LIHN-jee-uhn) Germanic dynasty that was named after its most famous member, Charlemagne.

**Carthage** (KAHR-thihj) Northern African kingdom, main rival to early Roman expansion, that was defeated by Rome in the Punic Wars.

**Caste** A social class system with distinctions that are transferred through generations or through occupation. Restrictions are placed on marriage, occupation, handling of food, and other matters, according to caste. Caste usually refers to the social system of India.

**Çatal Hüyük** (chat-l-hoo-yook) Important Neolithic settlement in Anatolia (7250–6150 B.C.E.).

**Cathars** Medieval heretics, also known as the Albigensians, who considered the material world evil; their followers renounced wealth and marriage and promoted an ascetic existence.

**Catholic Reformation** Sixteenth-century Catholic attempt to cure internal ills and confront Protestantism; it was inspired by the reforms of the Council of Trent and the actions of the Jesuits.

**Caucasus** (KAW-kuh-suhs) Mountain range between the Black and Caspian seas.

**Caudillos** (kahw-DEE-yohs) Latin American term for nineteenth-century local military leaders.

**Central Powers** World War I term for the alliance of Germany, Austria-Hungary, and the Ottoman empire.

**Ceuta** (SYOO-tuh) An autonomous Spanish city situated on the north African side of the Straits of Gibraltar.

**Chagatai** (chah-guh-TAHY) One of the sons of Chinggis Khan.

**Chalcedon** (kal-SED-n) An ancient city in northwest Asia Minor on the Bosphorus, opposite Byzantium.

**Chaldiran** (chahld-ih-rahn) Site of a battle between the Safavids and Ottomans in 1514, where the Safavids were badly defeated.

**Chamorro** (chuh-MAWR-oh) Indigenous peoples of the Mariana Islands.

**Chan Buddhism** (CHAHN BOO-diz'm) Most popular branch of Buddhism in China, with an emphasis on intuition and sudden flashes of insight instead of textual study.

**Chan Chan** (chahn chahn) Capital of the pre-Incan, South American Chimu society that supported a large population of fifty thousand.

**Chang'an** (chahng-ahn) Ancient capital in China during the Han, Sui, and Tang dynasties.

**Charlemagne** (SHAHR-leh-mane) King of the Franks and the Holy Roman Emperor.

**Charvaka** (CHAHR-vah-kuh) Indian philosophy based on philosophical skepticism.

**Chauvinism** (SHOH-vuh-niz-uhm) Prejudiced belief in the superiority of one's own kind, particularly with respect to nation or biological sex.

**Chavín cult** Mysterious but very popular South American religion (1000–300 B.C.E.).

**Chimu** Pre-Incan South American society that fell to the Incas in the fifteenth century.

**Chinampas** Style of agriculture used by Mexica (Aztecs) in which fertile muck from lake bottoms was dredged and built up into small plots.

**Chinggis Khan** (CHIHN-gihs kahn) Conqueror of much of Eurasia in the thirteenth century, from China in the east to the Abbasid empire in the west.

**Chivalry** European medieval concept, a code of conduct for the knights based on loyalty and honor.

**Chola** Southern Indian Hindu kingdom (850–1267), a tightly centralized state that dominated sea trade.

**Christianity** Religious doctrine that emerged in southeast Asia in the first century C.E. and then spread through Europe, north Africa, parts of Asia, and eventually to the Americas. Central to the religion is the belief that Jesus was the son of God and sacrificed himself on behalf of humankind.

**Chucuito** (choo-CWE-toh) Pre-Incan South American society that rose in the twelfth century and fell to the Incas in the fifteenth century.

**Cicero** (SIHS-ser-oh) Roman senator and bitter enemy of Marc Antony.

**City-state** Urban areas that controlled surrounding agricultural regions and that were often loosely connected in a broader political structure with other city-states.

**Clemenceau, Georges** (klem-uhn-SOH, jawrj) French statesman who played a key role in negotiating the Treaty of Versailles.

**Coen, Jan Pieterszoon** (KOH-uhn, yahn PEE-tuhr-sohn) Governor-general of the Dutch East Indies in the sixteenth century.

**Cohong** Specially licensed Chinese firms that were under strict government regulation.

**Cold War** Strategic struggle that developed after World War II between the U.S. and USSR.

**Collectivization** Process beginning in the late 1920s by which Stalin forced the Russian peasants off their own land and onto huge collective farms run by the state; millions died in the process.

**Colombo, Cristoforo** (kuh-LUHM-boh, crihs-toh-for-oh) Italian navigator who discovered the Caribbean islands for Europeans while trying to find a western route to China.

**Columbian Exchange** The trans-Atlantic exchange of plants, animals, and diseases that followed European contact with the Americas at the end of the fifteenth century.

**COMECON** The Council for Mutual Economic Assistance, which offered increased trade within the Soviet Union and eastern Europe; it was the Soviet alternative to the United States's Marshall Plan.

**Communalism** A term, usually associated with India, that placed an emphasis on religious rather than national identity.

**Communism** Philosophy and movement that began in middle of the nineteenth century with the work of Karl Marx; it has the same general goals as socialism, but it includes the belief that violent revolution is necessary to destroy the bourgeois world and institute a new world run by and for the proletariat.

**Confucianism** (kuhn-FEW-shuhn-iz'm) Philosophy, based on the teachings of the Chinese philosopher Kong Fuzi (551–479 B.C.E.), or Confucius, that emphasizes order, the role of the gentleman, obligation to society, and reciprocity.

**Congress of Vienna** Gathering of European diplomats in Vienna, Austria, from October 1814 to June 1815. The representatives of the "great powers" that defeated Napoleon—Britain, Austria, Prussia, and Russia—dominated the proceedings, which aimed to restore the prerevolutionary political and social order.

**Conquistadores** (kohn-kees-tah-DOH-rays) Spanish adventurers like Cortés and Pizarro who conquered Central and South America in the sixteenth century.

**Conservatism** A political philosophy that emphasizes gradual change, continuity of traditions, and established authority. Although the word has taken on many shades of meaning, nineteenth-century conservatives generally opposed democracy and supported traditional institutions such as the church, monarchy, and nobility.

**Constantine** (KAHN-stuhn-teen) Emperor of Rome who made Christianity the official religion of the Roman empire in 324.

**Constitutionalism** Movement in England in the seventeenth century that placed power in Parliament's hands as part of a constitutional monarchy and that increasingly limited the power of the monarch; the movement was highlighted by the English Civil War and the Glorious Revolution.

**Containment** U.S. policy to block further expansion of Soviet power.

**Coromandel** (kawr-uh-MAN-dul) Southeastern coast of India.

**Corporation** A concept that reached mature form in 1860s in England and France; it entailed private business owned by thousands of individual and institutional investors who financed the business through the purchase of stocks.

**Corpus iuris civilis** (KOR-poos EW-rees sih-VEE-lees) *Body of the Civil Law,* the Byzantine emperor Justinian's attempt to codify all Roman law.

**Cortés, Hernán** (kawr-TEZ, er-NAHN) Spanish conquistador who defeated the Aztecs and conquered Mexico.

**Cossacks** (KAW-sacks) Russian "free men" recruited by Ivan III to settle conquered land in return for their freedom; the strategy eventually played a key role in Russian expansion eastward.

**Criollos** (kree-OH-lohs) The term for Spaniards born in the Americas during the Spanish colonial period.

**Croesus** (CREE-suhs) The last king of Lydia who died in 546 B.C.E.

**Cro-Magnon** (CROH MAHG-nohn) *Homo sapiens sapiens,* who appeared forty thousand years ago during the Paleolithic age and were the first human beings of the modern type.

**Cross staff** Device that sailors used to determine latitude by measuring the angle of the sun or pole star above the horizon.

**Ctesiphon** (TES-uh-phon) Ancient city of central Iraq on the Tigris River southeast of Baghdad.

**Cuneiform** Written language of the Sumerians, probably the first written script in the world.

**Cuzco** (KOOS-koh) A town in the Andes in southern Peru; former capital of the Inca empire.

**Cyrus** (SIGH-ruhs) King of Persia and founder of the Persian empire.

**Dahomey Oyo** (dah-HO-meh OH-yoh) Precolonial West African empire in what is now modern Nigeria.

**Daimyo** (DEYEM-yoh) Powerful territorial lords in early modern Japan.

**Dao** Key element in Chinese philosophy that means the "way of nature" or the "way of the cosmos."

**Daodejing** (DOW-DAY-JIHNG) Book that is the fundamental work of Daoism.

**Daoism** (dow-ism) Chinese philosophical system advocating a simple, honest life and following the natural patterns of the universe.

**Dar al-Islam** The "house of Islam," a term for the Islamic world.

**Declaration of Independence** Drafted by Thomas Jefferson in 1776; the document expressed the ideas of John Locke and the Enlightenment, represented the idealism of the American rebels, and influenced other revolutions.

**Declaration of the Rights of Man and Citizen** Document from the French Revolution (1789) that was influenced by the American Declaration of Independence and in turn influenced other revolutionary movements.

**Decolonization** Process by which former colonies achieved their independence, as with the newly emerging African nations in the 1950s and 1960s.

**Degas, Edgar** (day-GAH, ED-gahr) Nineteenth- and early twentieth-century French impressionist painter.

**Deism** (DEE-iz'm) An Enlightenment view that accepted the existence of a god but denied the supernatural aspects of Christianity; in deism, the universe was an orderly realm maintained by rational and natural laws.

**Demographic transition** Adjustments in the rate of births and deaths that usually accompany industrialization. The demographic transition is often triggered by improvements in health and nutrition, which result in lower death rates. Birthrates remain high initially, but after a period of rapid population growth, birthrates fall in response to the lower death rates. Eventually, in highly industrialized societies, birthrates and death rates stabilize at low levels.

**Descamisados** "Shirtless ones," Argentine poor who supported Juan and Eva Perón.

**De-Stalinization** The policy of ending Stalin's reign of terror after his death in 1953.

**Détente** A reduction in cold war tension between the United States and the Soviet Union from 1969 to 1973.

**Devshirme** Ottoman requirement that the Christians in the Balkans provide young boys to be slaves of the sultan.

**Dharma** (DHUHR-muh) Hindu concept of obedience to religious and moral laws and order.

**Dhimmi** (DIHM-mee) Islamic concept of a protected people that was symbolic of Islamic toleration during the Mughal and Ottoman empires.

**Dhow** Indian, Persian, and Arab ships, one hundred to four hundred tons, that sailed and traded throughout the Indian Ocean basin.

**Dias, Bartolomeu** (dee-as, bahr-tol-uh-MEY-oh) The first European explorer (Portu-guese) to sail around the southern tip of Africa.

**Diaz, Porfirio** (DEE-ahs, pawr-FEER-eeo) Mexican politician who became president of Mexico from 1876 to 1880 and from 1884 to 1911.

**Diaspora** (dahy-AS-per-uh) The dispersion of peoples outside their homeland.

**Diocletian** (dah-yuh-KLEE-shuhn) Roman emperor who divided the empire into two parts, east and west, in 286 C.E.

**Dionysus** Greek god of wine, also known as Bacchus; Greek plays were performed in his honor.

**Domestic Containment** Concern that Communist spies had infiltrated the United States.

**Domino Theory** Theory that if one country becomes Communist, neighboring countries will also "collapse" to communism the way dominoes fall.

**Dravidian** (drah-VIHD-een) A member of one of the aboriginal groups of India.

**Dreadnoughts** A class of British battleships whose heavy armaments made all other battleships obsolete overnight.

**Duma** Russian parliament, established after the Revolution of 1905.

**Dutch learning** European knowledge that reached Tokugawa Japan.

**East India Company** British joint-stock company that grew to be a state within a state in India; it possessed its own armed forces.

**Eastern Orthodox Christianity** An eastern branch of Christianity that evolved after the division of the Roman Empire and the subsequent development of the Byzantine Empire in the east and the medieval European society in the west. The Eastern Orthodox Church acknowledged what became known as the Byzantine rite and recognized the primacy of the patriarch of Constantinople.

**Eight-legged essay** Eight-part essays that an aspiring Chinese civil servant had to compose, mainly based on a knowledge of Confucius and the Zhou classics.

**Einsatzgruppen** (ain-zats-groopen) Paramilitary group run by the German SS in World War II, whose main task was to annihilate Jews, Gypsies, and Slavs as the German army moved east, invading the Soviet Union.

**Encomienda** (ehn-koh-MYEN-dah) System that gave the Spanish settlers (*encomenderos*) the right to compel the indigenous peoples of the Americas to work in the mines or fields.

**Engenho** (ehn-GEN-yo) Portuguese term for a sugar mill and its facilities.

**Enlightenment** Eighteenth-century philosophical movement that began in France; its emphasis was on the preeminence of reason rather than faith or tradition; it spread concepts from the Scientific Revolution.

**Epicureans** (ehp-ih-KYOOR-eeuhns) Hellenistic philosophers who taught that pleasure—as in quiet satisfaction—was the greatest good.

**Equal-field system** Chinese system during the Han dynasty in which the goal was to ensure an equitable distribution of land.

**Equiano, Olaudah** (ay-kwee-AHN-oh, oh-LAU-duh) An ex-slave who became deeply involved in the fight against slavery and the slave trade.

**Erasmus, Desiderius** (ih-raz-muhs, des-i-DEER-ee-uhs) Dutch humanist and leading Renaissance scholar in northern Europe.

**Essenes** Jewish sect that looked for the arrival of a savior; they were similar in some of their core beliefs to the early Christians.

**Etruscans** (ih-TRUHS-kuhns) Northern Italian society that initially dominated the Romans; the Etruscans helped convey Greek concepts to the expanding Romans.

**Eunuch** (YOO-nuhk) A castrated man.

**European Community (EC)** Organization of European states established in 1957; it was originally called the European Economic Community and was renamed the EC in 1967; it promoted economic growth and integration as the basis for a politically united Europe.

**European Union** Established by the Maastricht Treaty in 1993, a supranational organization for even greater European economic and political integration.

**Fascism** Political ideology and mass movement that was prominent in many parts of Europe between 1919 and 1945; it sought to regenerate the social, political, and cultural life of societies, especially in contrast to liberal democracy and socialism; fascism began with Mussolini in Italy, and it reached its peak with Hitler in Germany.

**Fatehpur Sikri** (fah-teh-poor SIH-kree) City built by the Mughal emperor Akbar to serve as the Mughal capital.

**Feminist Movement** The movement of women in postwar industrialized nations to gain political and economic equality.

**Fernando of Aragon** (fer-NAWN-doh of ah-ruh-GAWN) Husband of Isabella of Castille, who jointly funded Cristoforo Colombo's expedition to search for a western trade route to China.

**Ferreira, Christovao** (feh-RAY-rah, chris-STOH-voh) Portuguese Jesuit who renounced his faith in Japan in 1632.

**Fief** (FEEF) A grant of land from a lord to a vassal.

**Five Pillars** The foundation of Islam; (1) profession of faith, (2) prayer, (3) fasting during Ramadan, (4) alms, and (5) pilgrimage, or hajj.

**Five-year plans** First implemented by Stalin in the Soviet Union in 1928; five-year plans were a staple of communist regimes in which every aspect of production was determined in advance for a five-year period; five-year plans were the opposite of the free market concept.

**Four Noble Truths** The foundation of Buddhist thought: (1) life is pain, (2) pain is caused by desire, (3) elimination of desire will bring an end to pain, (4) living a life based on the Noble Eightfold Path will eliminate desire.

**Free trade** Economic doctrine, first argued by Adam Smith in the late eighteenth century, of unrestricted trade between nations without protective tariffs or duties. Smith and his followers argue that, through free trade and competition, the forces of supply and demand will ensure that the best product is available at the best price. Free trade has gained wide acceptance since World War II.

**Freud, Sigmund** (froid, SIG-muhnd) Nineteenth- and early twentieth-century Austrian neurologist who developed psychoanalysis.

**Front de Libération Nationale (FLN)** The Algerian organization that fought a bloody guerilla war for freedom against France.

**Fulani** (foo-LAH-nee) Sub-Saharan African people who, beginning in the seventeenth century, began a series of wars designed to impose their own strict interpretation of Islam.

**Gandhi, Mohandas Karamchand** (GAHN-dee, moh-huhn-DAHS kuhr-uhm-CHUND) Political and spiritual leader of the Indian Independence movement, assassinated by a Hindu extremist in 1948.

**Gao** (gou) City that served as capital of the Mali Empire in Africa.

**Garibaldi, Giuseppe** (gar-uh-BAWL-dee, juh-SEP-eh) Nineteenth-century Italian nationalist who led the Italian unification movement.

**Gathas** (GATH-uhs) Zoroastrian works believed to be compositions by Zarathustra.

**GATT** General Agreement on Tariffs and Trade, promoted unrestricted free trade.

**Gauchos** (GAHW-chohs) Argentine cowboys, highly romantic figures.

**Gaugamela** (GAW-guh-mee-luh) Site, in modern Iraq, of Alexander the Great's final victory over Darius III in 331 B.C.E.

**Gaunahani** (gwah-nah-nee) The name indigenous peoples called the island Columbus called San Salvador in the Caribbean.

**Geechee** (GEE-chee) See Gullah.

**General Agreement on Tariffs and Trade (GATT)** Free trade agreement first signed in 1947; by 1994 it had grown to 123 members and formed the World Trade Organization (WTO).

**Ghana** (GAH-nuh) Eighth- through eleventh-century empire in West Africa that grew wealthy from the trans-Saharan trade.

**Ghazi** (GAH-zee) Islamic religious warrior.

**Ghaznavids** Turkish tribe under Mahmud of Ghazni who moved into northern India in the eleventh century and began a period of greater Islamic influence in India.

**Gilgamesh** Legendary king of the Mesopotamian city-state of Uruk (ca. 3000 B.C.E.), subject of the *Epic of Gilgamesh,* world's oldest complete epic literary masterpiece.

**Glasnost** (GLAHS-nohst) Russian term meaning "openness" introduced by Mikhail Gorbachev in 1985 to describe the process of opening Soviet society to dissidents and public criticism.

**Global warming** The emission of greenhouse gases, which prevents solar heat from escaping the earth's atmosphere and leads to the gradual heating of the earth's environment.

**Globalization** The breaking down of traditional boundaries in the face of increasingly global financial and cultural trends.

**Golden Horde** Mongol tribe that controlled Russia from the thirteenth to the fifteenth centuries.

**Gorbachev, Mikhail** Leader of the USSR in the 1980s, responsible for the opening up of the USSR in social and economic policy.

**Gouges, Olympe de** (gouj, oh-LIMP de) French playwright and journalist who advocated that women and men should share equal rights during the French Revolution.

**Great Game** Nineteenth-century competition between Great Britain and Russia for the control of central Asia.

**Great Leap Forward** The vision by Mao that planned how China could overtake the industrial production of more developed nations.

**Great Proletarian Cultural Revolution** Attempt by Mao to mobilize the Chinese and reignite revolutionary spirit.

**Great Zimbabwe** Large sub-Saharan African kingdom in the fifteenth century.

**Greater East Asia Co-Prosperity Sphere** Japanese plan for consolidating Asia under their control during World War II.

**Greenpeace** An environmental organization founded in 1970 and dedicated to the preservation of earth's natural resources.

**Guadalupe Hidalgo** (gwahd-i-LOOP hee-DAHL-goh) Peace treaty that ended the Mexican-American War in 1848.

**Guangxu** (wang-soo) Tenth Qing emperor who initiated the Hundred Days' Reform in 1898, but was removed from power by the Empress Dowager Cixi.

**Guarani** (gwahr-uh-NEE) Ethnic group of indigenous people from modern Paraguay and Bolivia, as well as their language.

**Guild** Organizations whose membership is based on occupation. They often regulate the production and sale of goods and serve as mutual aid societies for their members. They were particularly powerful in medieval European cities.

**Gullah** (GUHL-uh) Also known as Geechee, the Gullah are African Americans who live in the low country of South Carolina and Georgia. They have preserved much of their syncretic African culture from the days of slavery, including the creole Gullah language.

**Guomindang** (GWOH-mihn-dahng) Chinese nationalist party founded by Sun Yat-sen (1866–1925) and later led by Jiang Jieshi; it has been centered in Taiwan since the end of the Chinese civil war.

**Gupta** (GOOP-tah) Indian dynasty (320–550 C.E.) that briefly reunited India after the collapse of the earlier Mauryan dynasty.

**HAART** The active antiretroviral therapy that treats AIDS.

**Hacienda** (ah-SYEN-dah) Large Latin American estates.

**Hagia Sophia** (HAH-yah soh-FEE-uh) Greek orthodox temple constructed by the Byzantine emperor Justinian and later converted into a mosque.

**Hajj** (HAHJ) Pilgrimage to Mecca.

**Hammurabi's Code** (hahm-uh-RAH-beez cohd) Sophisticated law code associated with the Babylonian king Hammurabi (r. 1792–1750 B.C.E.).

**Han Feizi** (hahn fay-zi) Chinese philosopher who developed the doctrine of Legalism.

**Han Wudi** (hahn woo-dee) Seventh emperor of the Han dynasty who developed a strong, centralized, Confucian state.

**Hanseatic** (han-see-AT-ik) A commercial and defensive confederation of free cities in northern Germany and surrounding areas in the thirteenth and fourteenth centuries.

**Harappan** (huh-RUHP-puhn) Early brilliant Indian society centered around Harappa and Mohenjo-Daro.

**Harijans** (har-i-jahns) Literally meaning the "children of God," very low-status Indian people who are outside the caste system.

**Hatshepsut** (hat-SHEP-soot) Queen of Egypt (1505 B.C.E.) who shared her throne with her nephew Tuthmosis III.

**Hebrews** Semitic-speaking nomadic tribe influential for monotheistic belief in Yahweh.

**Heian** (HAY-ahn) Japanese period (794–1185), a brilliant cultural era notable for the world's first novel, Murasaki Shikibu's *The Tale of Genji.*

**Heisenberg, Werner** (HAHY-zuyn-burg, VER-nuhr) Twentieth century German theoretical physicist responsible for the development of uncertainty theory.

**Hellenic Era** First phase in Greek history (ca. 2000–328 B.C.E.), which was highlighted by the Golden Age of Athens in the fifth century B.C.E.

**Hellenistic Era** Second phase in Greek history (328–146 B.C.E.), from the conquest of Greece by Philip of Macedon until Greece's fall to the Romans; this era was a more cosmopolitan age facilitated by the conquests of Alexander the Great.

**Herzl, Theodore** (HER-tsuhll, TEY-aw-dohr) Hungarian Jewish journalist and author of the book *Judenstaat,* he is considered by many to be the father of modern Zionism.

**Hidalgo, Miguel de** (hee-DHAHL-goh, mee-GEL de) Priest and leader of the Mexican War of Independence in 1810–1821.

**Hieratic** (hahy-uh-RAT-tik) A cursive form of Egyptian hieroglyphics.

**Hieroglyphics** (heye-ruh-GLIPH-iks) Ancient Egyptian written language.

**Hijra** (HIHJ-ruh) The migration of Muhammed and his followers to the city of Medina in 622 C.E.

**Hinayana** (HEE-nah-yah-nuh) Branch of Buddhism known as the "lesser vehicle," also known as Theravada Buddhism; its beliefs include a strict, individual path to enlightenment, and it is popular in south and southeast Asia.

**Hinduism** Main religion of India, a combination of Dravidian and Aryan concepts; Hinduism's goal is to reach spiritual purity and union with the great world spirit; its important concepts include dharma, karma, and samsara.

**Ho Chi Minh** Leader of Vietnam during revolution.

**Holocaust** German attempt in World War II to exterminate the Jews of Europe.

**Holy Roman Empire** A confederation of states mostly in central and western Europe. It began in 962 C.E. with the crowning of Otto I by the pope.

**Home front** Term made popular in World War I and World War II for the civilian "front" that was symbolic of the greater demands of total war.

**Hominid** (HAW-mih-nihd) A creature belonging to the family Hominidae, which includes human and humanlike species.

**Homo erectus** (HOH-moh ee-REHK-tuhs) "Upright-walking human," which existed from 1.5 million to two hundred thousand years ago; *Homo erectus* used cleavers and hand axes and learned how to control fire.

**Homo sapiens** (HOH-moh SAY-pyans) "Consciously thinking human," which first appeared around two hundred fifty thousand years ago and used sophisticated tools.

**Homo sapiens sapiens** (HOH-moh SAY-pyans SAY-pyans) First human being of the modern type, which appeared roughly one hundred thousand years ago; Cro-Magnon falls into this category.

**Hong Xiuquan** (hoong shee-OH-chew-an) The leader of the nineteenth-century Taiping Rebellion.

**Hongwu** (hawng-woo) The first Ming emperor, who overthrew the Yuan dynasty in 1368.

**Huitzilopochtli** (we-tsee-loh-POCK-tlee) Sun god and patron deity of the Aztecs.

**Hulegu** (Hoo-LAY-goo) Grandson of Chinggis Khan and leader of the Ilkhan khanate, who was responsible for the destruction of Baghdad.

**Humanism** Cultural movement during the Renaissance that drew inspiration from the humanities, that is, literature, history, philosophy, and the arts. In contrast to medieval theologians, humanists argued that one could live a moral life and still be actively engaged in the affairs of the world.

**Hundred Days of Reform** Chinese reforms of 1898 led by Kang Youwei and Liang Qichao in their desire to turn China into a modern industrial power.

**Hunting/gathering culture** Any culture whose primary means of subsistence is through hunting and gathering from the environment. Humans survived this way for millions of years before the agricultural transition, and some hunting/gathering cultures persisted into the twenty-first century C.E.

**Hyksos** (HICK-sohs) Invaders who seized the Nile delta and helped bring an end to the Egyptian Middle Kingdom.

**Ibn Battuta** (ih-bun BAH-too-tah) A famous fourteenth-century traveler and historian of Africa and Asia.

**Ibn Rushd** (IB-uhn RUSHED) A twelfth-century Muslim philosopher, born in Cordoba in modern Spain, whose philosophy influenced European thought.

**Iconoclasts** (eye-KAHN-oh-klasts) Supporters of the movement, begun by the Byzantine Emperor Leo III (r. 717–741), to destroy religious icons because their veneration was considered sinful.

**Ife** (EE-fehy) Eighth- to tenth-century kingdom in what is now modern Nigeria.

**Ilkhanate** (EEL-kahn-ate) Mongol state that ruled Persia after abolition of the Abbasid empire in the thirteenth century.

**IMF** International Monetary Fund.

**Imperialism** Term associated with the expansion of European powers and their conquest and colonization of African and Asian societies, mainly from the sixteenth through the nineteenth centuries.

**Inca empire** Powerful South American empire that would reach its peak in the fifteenth century during the reigns of Pachacuti Inca and Topa Inca.

**Indentured labor** Labor source in the Americas; wealthy planters would pay the European poor to sell a portion of their working lives, usually seven years, in exchange for passage.

**Indo-Europeans** Series of tribes from southern Russia who, over a period of millennia, embarked on a series of migrations from India through western Europe; their greatest legacy was the broad distribution of Indo-European languages throughout Eurasia.

**Indra** Early Indian god associated with the Aryans; Indra was the king of the gods and was associated with warfare and thunderbolts.

**Indus** (IN-duhs) A river with its source in Tibet that flows southwest through India to the Bay of Bengal.

**Intelligentsia** Refers to an educated and literate class in Russia that often advocated social and political reform. In the late nineteenth century the Russian intelligentsia became frustrated when reform efforts failed, and many turned to anarchism and violence. Some members of the intelligentsia supported the Bolshevik rise to power in the revolution of 1917.

**Inti** (ihn-tee) The Inca sun god.

**Investiture** (ihn-VEHST-tih-tyoor) The granting of church offices by a lay leader; one aspect of the medieval European church versus state controversy.

**Iran-Contra Scandal** Political scandal over arms for hostages in Iran and funding for Nicaraguan contras.

**Iranian Revolution** Islamist revolution to throw out the U.S.-backed shah in 1979.

**Iron Curtain** Dividing line between the two blocs of Europe, with one supported by the USSR and the other by the U.S.

**Iroquois** (EER-uh-kwah) Eastern American Indian confederation made up of the Mohawk, Oneida, Onondaga, Cayuga, and Seneca tribes.

**Isabel of Castile** (IHZ-uh-bel of ka-steel) Queen of Castile and Leon and wife of Fernando II of Aragon, who together funded Cristoforo Colombo's expedition to discover a westerly route to China.

**Islam** Monotheistic religion of the prophet Muhammad (570–632); influenced by Judaism and Christianity, Muhammad was considered the final prophet because the earlier religions had not seen the entire picture; the Quran is the holy book of Islam.

**Islamism** The reassertion of Islamic values in Muslim politics.

**Israel** A Jewish state created after World War II.

**Istanbul** (iss-TAHN-bull) Capital city of the Ottoman Empire, built on the site of the capital city of the Byzantine Empire, Constantinople.

**Isthmus of Kra** (ihs-muhs of krah) A narrow isthmus linking the Malay peninsula to the Asian mainland.

**Itzcoatl** (tsee-ko-atl) The name of the fourth emperor of the Aztecs who ruled from 1427 to 1440.

**Jainism** (JEYEN-iz'm) Indian religion associated with the teacher Vardhamana Mahavira (ca. 540–468 B.C.E.) in which every physical object possessed a soul; Jains believe in complete nonviolence to all living beings.

**Jati** Indian word for a Hindu subcaste.

**Jenne** (jehn-neh) City in what is now modern Mali, famous for its role in the trans-Saharan trade and for its mud-brick mosque.

**Jiaozhou** (jyou-joh) A city in the Shandong province of China.

**Jieshi, Jiang** (jeh-she, jyahng) Also known as Chiang Kai-shek, Jiang became leader of the Kuomintang party after the death of Sun Yat-sen in 1925. After the communist victory in 1949, Jiang and the Kuomintang retreated to the island of Taiwan.

**Jihad** Arabic word meaning "struggle." In Islam this word is understood to be one's duty to struggle on behalf of the faith. Although this struggle might be a personal and spiritual effort, it has frequently been a call for holy war against perceived enemies. In recent years, radical Islamists such as al-Qaeda have called for a *jihad* against the United States and other "nonbelievers."

**Jizya** (JIHZ-yuh) Tax in Islamic empires that was imposed on non-Muslims.

**Joint-stock companies** Early forerunner of the modern corporation; individuals who invested in a trading or exploring venture could make huge profits while limiting their risk.

**Judaism** The monotheistic religion of the Jewish people that traces its origins to Abraham (ca. 2000 B.C.E.).

**Judenstaat** (juh-dehn-STAHT) 1896 book written by Theodore Herzl advocating the creation of a Jewish state.

**Junzi** (juhn-zee) Confucian idea of the ideal human, who lives according to virtue.

**Jurchen** (JUHR-chehn) A people who inhabited Manchuria until the seventeenth century.

**Ka'ba** (KAH-bah) Main shrine in Mecca, goal of Muslims embarking on the hajj.

**Kabuki** (kah-BOO-kee) Japanese theater in which actors were free to improvise and embellish the words.

**Kama** Hindu concept of the enjoyment of physical and sexual pleasure.

**Kamikaze** (KAH-mih-kah-zee) A Japanese term meaning "divine wind" that is related to the storms that destroyed Mongol invasion fleets; the term is symbolic of Japanese isolation and was later taken by suicide pilots in World War II.

**Kangxi** (kahng shee) The third emperor of the Qing dynasty, famous for his learning and work ethic.

**Kanun** (KUH-noon) Laws issued by the Ottoman Süleyman the Magnificent, also known as Süleyman Kanuni, "the Lawgiver."

**Kapu** Hawaiian concept of something being taboo.

**Karakorum** (kahr-uh-KOR-uhm) Capital of the Mongol empire in the thirteenth century.

**Karma** (KAHR-mah) Hindu concept that the sum of good and bad in a person's life will determine his or her status in the next life.

**Kautalya** (KAHT-ahl-yah) A minister of Chandragupta, founder of the Mauryan dynasty in India.

**Kebra Nagast** (kee-brah NAH-gahst) A book written in the priestly Ethiopian language Ge'ez, that traces the Solomonic origins of the Ethiopian emperors.

**Kemal, Mustafa** (kuh-MAHL, MOOS-fah) Turkish statesman and World War I hero who abolished the caliphate and established Turkey as a modern secular state.

**Khanbaliq** (Kahn-bah-LEEK) Name of the capital of the Yuan dynasty in China.

**Khartoum** (khar-TOOM) The capital of Sudan, located at the confluence of the Blue Nile and the White Nile.

**Khoikhoi** (KOI-koi) An ethnic group in southern Africa.

**Khubilai Khan** (KOO-bih-lie kahn) Prominent Mongol ruler in the thirteenth century and founder of the Yuan dynasty.

**Kilwa** (KILH-wah) A thriving Swahili city-state in east Africa between the twelfth and sixteenth centuries.

**Kin-based society** A society that governs itself primarily through family and clan relationships; many existed in sub-Saharan Africa throughout history.

**Kongo** Central African state that began trading with the Portuguese around 1500; although their kings, such as King Afonso I (r. 1506–1543), converted to Christianity, they nevertheless suffered from the slave trade.

**Korean Conflict** The Korean War between North and South Korea.

**Koumbi-Saleh** Important trading city along the trans-Saharan trade route from the eleventh to the thirteenth centuries.

**Kowtow** (kou-tou) A former Chinese custom of bowing the forehead to touch the ground as an act of submission.

**Kshatriayas** (SHUHT-ree-uhs) Hindu caste of warriors and aristocrats.

**Kulaks** Land-owning Russian peasants who benefited under Lenin's New Economic Policy and suffered under Stalin's forced collectivization.

**Kush** (kuhsh) An ancient African state of the Nile River Valley, also known as Nubia.

**Lamaist Buddhism** (LAH-muh-ihst BOO-diz'm) Branch of Buddhism that was similar to shamanism in its acceptance of magic and supernatural powers.

**Lapita** (Lah-PEE-tah) The pottery style of an ancient Pacific Ocean culture.

**La Reforma** Political reform movement of Mexican president Benito Juárez (1806–1872) that called for limiting the power of the military and the Catholic church in Mexican society.

**Latifundia** (lah-tee-FOON-dya) Huge state-run and slave-worked farms in ancient Rome.

**League of Nations** Forerunner of the United Nations, the dream of American president Woodrow Wilson, although its potential was severely limited by the refusal of the United States to join.

**Lebensraum** (LAY-behnz-rahwm) German term meaning "living space"; the term is associated with Hitler and his goal of carving out territory in the east for an expanding Germany.

**Legalism** Chinese philosophy from the Zhou dynasty that called for harsh suppression of the common people.

**Legazpi, Miguel Lopez de** (le-GAHS-pee, mee-GEHL LOH-pess de) Spanish conquistador who established one of the first European settlements in the East Indies.

**Leif Ericson** (leef ER-ik-suhn) A Norse explorer who probably landed in North America in the eleventh century.

**Lenin, Vladimir Ilyich** (LEHN-in, VLAD-uh-meer IL-yich) Founder of the Bolshevik party, leader of the Russian Revolution, and first leader of the Soviet Union from 1917 to 1924.

**Leonardo da Vinci** (lee-uh-NAHR-doh duh VIHN-chee) Italian artist and scientist of the Italian Renaissance.

**Levée en Masse** (leh-VAY ahn MAS) A term signifying universal conscription during the radical phase of the French revolution.

**Lex talionis** (lehks tah-LYO-nihs) "Law of retaliation," laws in which offenders suffered punishments similar to their crimes; the most famous example is Hammurabi's Laws.

**Li** (LEE) Confucian concept, a sense of propriety.

**Liaodong peninsula** (lyou-dawng) A peninsula in northeastern China that extends into the Yellow Sea.

**Liberalism** A political philosophy inspired by John Locke and the ideals of the Enlightenment that advocated individual liberty, constitutional government, and free trade. Nineteenth-century liberals favored representative government but not necessarily democracy.

**Liberation theology** The beliefs of Christian thinkers and social activists who emphasize Jesus' role in helping those who were oppressed, a view that gained wide support in Latin America in the late twentieth century. Liberation theologians question the historic role of the church in supporting traditional regimes.

**Lil'iuokalani** (lee-lee-oo-oh-kah-LAH-nee) The last monarch of Hawaii before it was annexed by the United States.

**Linear A** Minoan written script.

**Linear B** Early Mycenaean written script, adapted from the Minoan Linear A.

**Little Tigers** Asian countries that followed the Japanese model for economic development.

**Louis** (LOO-ee) French name for many of the Capetian kings.

**Luddites** Early-nineteenth-century artisans who were opposed to new machinery and industrialization.

**Macedon** (MAS-ih-don) The ancient kingdom of Alexander the Great in the southeastern Balkans.

**Machismo** (mah-CHEEZ-moh) Latin American social ethic that honored male strength, courage, aggressiveness, assertiveness, and cunning.

**Madeiras** (muh-DEER-uhs) A group of islands in the Atlantic Ocean to the west of Morocco.

**Madrasas** (MAH-drahs-ahs) Islamic institutions of higher education that originated in the tenth century.

**Magellan, Ferdinand** (muh-JEHL-uhn, FUR-dih-nand) Portuguese navigator who commanded an expedition that was the first to circumnavigate the world.

**Magyars** (MAH-jahrs) Hungarian invaders who raided towns in Germany, Italy, and France in the ninth and tenth centuries.

**Mahabharata** (mah-hah-BAH-rah-tah) Massive ancient Indian epic that was developed orally for centuries; it tells of an epic civil war between two family branches.

**Mahayana** (mah-huh-YAH-nah) The "greater vehicle," a more metaphysical and popular northern branch of Buddhism.

**Mahmud of Ghazni** (mah-muhd of gahz-nee) Founder of the Ghaznavid empire in what is now Afghanistan.

**Mahmud II** (mah-MOOD) The thirtieth sultan of the Ottoman Empire, famous for instituting extensive military and legal reforms.

**Majapahit** (mah-jah-PAH-hit) An Indianized kingdom of eastern Java, powerful from the late thirteenth to the end of the fourteenth century.

**Mali** (MAH-lee) West African kingdom founded in the thirteenth century by Sundiata; it reached its peak during the reign of Mansa Musa.

**Malindi** (mah-LIN-dee) East African town on the Indian Ocean.

**Malintzin** (mal-een-tzen) Also known as La Malinche, Malintzin was an indigenous woman who acted as interpreter and guide for Hernán Cortés during his conquest of Mexico.

**Manchus** Manchurians who conquered China, putting an end to the Ming dynasty and founding the Qing dynasty (1644–1911).

**Mandate of Heaven** Chinese belief that the emperors ruled through the mandate, or approval, of heaven contingent on their ability to look after the welfare of the population.

**Mandate system** System that developed in the wake of World War I when the former colonies ended up as mandates under European control, a thinly veiled attempt at continuing imperialism.

**Manichaeism** (man-ih-KEE-iz'm) Religion founded by the prophet Mani in the third century C.E., a syncretic version of Zoroastrian, Christian, and Buddhist elements.

**Manifest destiny** The idea, popular in the United States in the mid-nineteenth century, that the North American continent was intended by God to be settled by white Americans. This notion helped justify the Mexican war of 1846–1848 and the Indian wars of the 1870s and 1880s.

**Manor** Large estates of the nobles during the European middle ages, home for the majority of the peasants.

**Mansa Musa** (MAHN-suh MOO-suh ) Emperor of the Kingdom of Mali in Africa who made a famous pilgrimage to Mecca.

**Mao Zedong** (mow zuh-doong) Revolutionary leader of the Chinese Communist Party, who came to power in 1949 and ruled until 1976.

**Maori** (MAY-oh-ree) Indigenous peoples of New Zealand.

**Marae** Polynesian temple structure.

**Marathon** Battlefield scene of the Athenian victory over the Persians in 490 B.C.E.

**Maroons** Runaway African slaves.

**Marshall Plan** U.S. plan, officially called the European Recovery Program, that offered financial and other economic aid to all European states that had suffered from World War II, including Soviet bloc states.

**Masulipatam** (mahsu-lih-pah-tahm) Ancient port town in east-central India.

**Mau Mau revolution** Revolution in Kenya, forcing out the British.

**Maurya, Chandragupta** (MORE-yuh, chuhn-drah-GOOP-tah) Founder of the Indian Mauryan empire.

**Mauryan empire** Indian dynasty (321–185 B.C.E.) founded by Chandragupta Maurya and reaching its peak under Ashoka.

**May Fourth Movement** Chinese movement that began 4 May 1919 with a desire to eliminate imperialist influences and promote national unity.

**Maya** (MY-uh) Brilliant Central American society (300–1100) known for math, astronomy, and a sophisticated written language.

**Mazzini, Giuseppe** (maht-TSEE-nee, joo-ZEP-pe) Italian nationalist whose writings spurred the movement for a unified Italy in the nineteenth century.

**McDonaldization** The term for cultural homogenization created by globalization.

**Medes** (meeds) Indo-European branch that settled in northern Persia and eventually fell to another branch, the Persians, in the sixth century.

**Meiji Restoration** (MAY-jee) Restoration of imperial rule under Emperor Meiji in 1868 by a coalition led by Fukuzawa Yukichi and Ito Hirobumi; the restoration enacted western reforms to strengthen Japan.

**Melaka** (may-LAHK-ah) Southeast Asian kingdom that was predominantly Islamic.

**Mencius** (MEN-shi-us) Chinese philosopher who refined the ideas of Confucius and spread them across China.

**Menes** (mee-neez) The Egyptian pharoah who unified Egypt in 3100 B.C.E.

**Mesoamerica** (mez-oh-uh-MER-i-kuh) The region comprising Mexico and Central America.

**Mesopotamia** Term meaning "between the rivers," in this case the Tigris and Euphrates; Sumer and Akkad are two of the earliest societies.

**Mestizo** (mehs-TEE-soh) Latin American term for children of Spanish and native parentage.

**Metallurgy** The process of extracting metal from ores, or purifying metals, and of creating objects from metals.

**Métis** (may-TEE) Canadian term for individuals of mixed European and indigenous ancestry.

**Mexica** (meh-SHEE-kah) An indigenous people of the Valley of Mexico who became the rulers of the Aztec empire.

**Michelangelo Buonarotti** (mik-uhl-AN-juh-loh baw-nahr-RAW-tee) Famous Italian Renaissance painter, sculptor, and architect.

**Millet** An autonomous, self-governing community in the Ottoman empire.

**Mindanao** (min-duh-NAH-oh) Second largest island in the Philippines.

**Ming** Chinese dynasty (1368–1644) founded by Hongwu and known for its cultural brilliance.

**Minoan** (mih-NOH-uhn) Society located on the island of Crete (ca. 2000–1100 B.C.E.) that influenced the early Mycenaeans.

**Missi dominici** (MEE-see doh-mee-NEE-chee) "Envoys of the lord ruler," the noble and church emissaries sent out by Charlemagne.

**Mission civilisatrice** (mee-see-on sih-vihl-ihs-a-trihs) Belief by French colonial rulers in the duty to bring Western civilization to colonized subjects.

**Mithradates** (mihth-rah-DAY-teez) Ancient king of Pontus who expanded his kingdom by defeating the Romans.

**Mithraism** (MIHTH-rah-iz'm) Mystery religion based on worship of the sun god Mithras; it became popular among the Romans because of its promise of salvation.

**Mochica** (moh-CHEE-kah) Pre-Incan South American society (300–700) known for their brilliant ceramics.

**Moksha** Hindu concept of the salvation of the soul.

**Monotheism** (mah-noh-THEE-iz'm) Belief in only one god, a rare concept in the ancient world.

**Monroe Doctrine** American doctrine issued in 1823 during the presidency of James Monroe that warned Europeans to keep their hands off Latin America, and that expressed growing American strength and also growing American imperialistic views regarding Latin America.

**Motecuzoma** (mo-tec-oo-ZO-ma) Aztec emperor who ruled when Hernán Cortés conquered Mexico.

**Mozambique** (moh-zam-BEEK) A country on the southeast coast of Africa that became independent from Portugal in 1975.

**Mughals** (MOO-guhls) Islamic dynasty that ruled India from the sixteenth through the eighteenth centuries; the construction of the Taj Mahal is representative of their splendor; with the exception of the enlightened reign of Akbar, the increasing conflict between Hindus and Muslims was another of their legacies.

**Muhammad** (muh-HAHM-mahd) Prophet of Islam (570–632).

**Muhammed Ali Jinnah** (moo-HAM-id ah-lee JIN-uh) Indian statesman and founder of the state of Pakistan.

**Mumtaz Mahal** (moom tahz muh-HAHL) Beloved wife of the Mughal emperor Shah Jahan, whose death inspired him to build the Taj Mahal.

**Muslim** A follower of Islam.

**Mutsuhito** (MOO-tsoo-HEE-taw) Emperor of Japan who encouraged the modernization of Japan after the Meiji Restoration.

**Mycenaean** (meye-suh-NEE-uhn) Early Greek society on the Peloponese (1600–1100 B.C.E.) that was influenced by the Minoans; the Mycenaeans' conflict with Troy is immortalized in Homer's *Odyssey.*

**Nahuatl** (na-watl) Ancient language of the Valley of Mexico, and language of the Aztec empire.

**Napoleon Bonaparte** (nuh-POH-lee-uhn BOH-nuh-pahrt) French general who became emperor of the French from 1804 until his defeat by enemy European powers in 1815.

**Nara era** Japanese period (710–794), centered around city of Nara, that was the highest point of Chinese influence.

**Nasser, Gamal Abdel** Leader of Egypt and founder of pan-Arab nationalism.

**National Policy** Nineteenth-century Canadian policy designed to attract migrants, protect industries through tariffs, and build national transportation systems.

**NATO** The North Atlantic Treaty Organization, which was established by the United States in 1949 as a regional military alliance against Soviet expansionism.

**Navajo** (NAH-vah-ho) Native American group that settled in what is now Arizona, New Mexico, and Utah.

**Ndebele** (uhn-duh-BEE-lee) A people of South Africa that split from King Shaka of the Zulu in the 1820s.

**Ndongo** (n'DAWN-goh) Angolan kingdom that reached its peak during the reign of Queen Nzinga (r. 1623–1663).

**Neandertal** (nee-ANN-duhr-tawl) Early humans (100,000 to 35,000 years ago) who were prevalent during the Paleolithic period.

**Nebuchadnezzar** (neb-uh-kud-NEZ-er) Chaldean king of Babylon.

**Negritude** (NEH-grih-tood) "Blackness," a term coined by early African nationalists as a means of celebrating the heritage of black peoples around the world.

**Neo-Confucianism** (nee-oh-kuhn-FYEW-shuhn-iz'm) Philosophy that attempted to merge certain basic elements of Confucian and Buddhist thought; most important of the early Neo-Confucianists was the Chinese thinker Zhu Xi (1130–1200).

**Neolithic** (nee-uh-LITH-ik) New Stone Age (10,000–4000 B.C.E.), which was marked by the discovery and mastery of agriculture.

**Nestorian** (neh-STOHR-eeuhn) Early branch of Christianity, named after the fifth-century Greek theologian Nestorius, that emphasized the human nature of Jesus Christ.

**New Economic Policy (NEP)** Plan implemented by Lenin that called for minor free market reforms.

**Nian** (neen) An armed uprising that occurred in China in 1851 contemporaneously with the Taiping rebellion.

**Nicaea** (nahy-SEE-uh) The first ecumenical council in 325 C.E. that produced the wording of the Nicene Creed and condemned heresy.

**Nirvana** (ner-VAHN-nah) Hindu belief in the state of having transcended the cycle of reincarnation and ending the human cycle of desire and suffering.

**Nkrumah, Kwame** The leader of Ghana who gained freedom from Britain for Ghana.

**Noble Eightfold Path** Final truth of the Buddhist Four Noble Truths that called for leading a life of balance and constant contemplation.

**Nonalignment** Countries not associated with the two powers in the cold war, the USSR and the U.S.

**North American Free Trade Agreement (NAFTA)** Regional alliance established in 1993 between the United States, Canada, and Mexico; it formed the world's second largest free-trade zone.

**Northern Alliance** A multiethnic coalition in Afghanistan opposed to the Taliban.

**Nostrum** (NAHS-truhm) Latin word for "our."

**Nubia** (NOO-bee-uh) Area south of Egypt; the kingdom of Kush in Nubia invaded and dominated Egypt from 750 to 664 B.C.E.

**Nurhaci** (NOOR-hacheh) Founding father of the Manchu state.

**Nzinga Mbemba** (IN-zinga MEHM-bah) Also called King Afonso I, he was ruler of the kingdom of Kongo in the first half of the sixteenth century.

**Oaxaca** (wah-hah-kah) A city in southeastern Mexico.

**Oceania** Term referring to the Pacific Ocean basin and its lands.

**Odovacer** (AHD-oh-vah-cer) Germanic general and first non-Roman ruler after 476.

**Olmecs** Early Central American society (1200–100 B.C.E.) that centered around sites at San Lorenzo, La Venta, and Tres Zapotes and that influenced later Maya.

**Omdurman** (om-door-MAHN) 1898 battle in the Sudan in which a British and Egyptian force defeated the Sudanese.

**Operation Iraqi Freedom** The Iraq War.

**Oprichnina** (oh-PREEK-nee-nah) A Russian term meaning the "land apart," Muscovite territory that the Russian Tsar Ivan IV (r. 1533–1584) demanded to control; the tsar created a new class of nobles called the *oprichniki* for this territory.

**Oracle bones** Chinese Shang dynasty (1766–1122 B.C.E.) means of foretelling the future.

**Organization of African Unity (OAU)** An organization started in 1963 by thirty-two newly independent African states and designed to prevent conflict that would lead to intervention by former colonial powers.

**Organization of Petroleum Exporting Countries (OPEC)** An organization begun in 1960 by oil-producing states originally for purely economic reasons but that later had more political influence.

**Osama bin Laden** Founder of Al Qaeda and terrorist wanted for 9/11 attack on the U.S.

**Osiris** Ancient Egyptian god that represented the forces of nature.

**Osman** (oz-MAHN) Founder of the dynasty that ruled the Ottoman Empire from 1289–1923.

**Otto von Bismarck** (oht-toh fuhn BIZ-mahrk) German statesman under whose leadership Germany was united.

**Ottoman empire** Powerful Turkish empire that lasted from the conquest of Constantinople (Istanbul) in 1453 until 1918 and reached its peak during the reign of Süleyman the Magnificent (r. 1520–1566).

**Pachacuti** (pah-cha-KOO-tee) Ruler of Inca society from 1438 to 1471, whose military campaigns greatly extended Inca control.

**Paleolithic** (pey-lee-oh-LITH-ik) Old Stone Age, a long period of human development before the development of agriculture.

**Palestinian Liberation Organization (PLO)** Ruling party of the Palestinian territories occupied by Israel.

**Paris Peace Accords** Agreement reached in 1973 that marked the end of the United States's role in the Vietnam War.

**Parsis** (pahr-SEES) Indian Zoroastrians.

**Parthians** Persian dynasty (247 B.C.E.–224 C.E.) that reached its peak under Mithradates I.

**Pasargadae** (pah-SAR-gah-dee) Capital city of ancient Persia.

**Pasion** (pahs-ee-on) Fourth-century B.C.E. Athenian slave who eventually became a wealthy Athenian citizen.

**Pataliputra** (pah-tal-ih-puh-trah) Capital city of the Indian Mauryan and Gupta empires.

**Pater familias** (PAH-tehrr fah-MEE-lyas) Roman term for the "father of the family," a theoretical implication that gave the male head of the family almost unlimited authority.

**Patriarch** (PAY-tree-ahrk) Leader of the Greek Orthodox church, which in 1054 officially split with the Pope and the Roman Catholic church.

**Patriarchy** A system of social organization in which males dominate the family and in which the public institutions and descent and succession are traced through the male line.

**Patricians** Roman aristocrats and wealthy classes.

**Pax Americana** "American Peace," a term that compares American domination in the years after World War II with the power of Rome at its peak.

**Pax Romana** (Pahks roh-MAH-nah) "Roman Peace," a term that relates to the period of political stability, cultural brilliance, and economic prosperity beginning with unification under Augustus and lasting through the first two centuries C.E.

**Peloponnesian** (pell-uh-puh-NEE-suhn) A large peninsula in southern Greece.

**Peloponnesus** (pell-uh-puh-NEE-suhs) See Peloponnesian.

**Peninsulares** (peh-neen-soo-LAH-rehs) Latin American officials from Spain or Portugal.

**Perestroika** (PAYR-eh-stroy-kuh) Economic policy adopted by the USSR to increase labor efficiency.

**Pericles** (PEH-rih-kleez) Athenian orator and statesman whose leadership contributed to the political and cultural supremacy of Athens.

**Persepolis** (per-SEP-uh-lis) Ancient capital of the Persian empire.

**Petrarca, Francesco** (pe-TRAHRK-a, frahn-CHES-kaw) Fourteenth-century Italian poet famous for his love poems.

**Pharaohs** (FARE-ohs) Egyptian kings considered to be gods on earth.

**Philosophes** (fil-uh-sofs) Enlightenment intellectuals who sought to apply the methods of science to the improvement of society.

**Phoenicians** (fi-NEE-shins) Inhabitants of ancient Phoenicia, a narrow coastal plain north of Palestine between the Mediterranean Sea and the Lebanon Mountains.

**Piri Reis** (pir-ree reys) An Ottoman Turkish admiral and cartographer famous for his maps and charts.

**Plebeians** (plih-BEE-uhns) Roman common people.

**Polis** (POH-lihs) Greek term for the city-state.

**Popol Vuh** (poh-pohl VOO) Mayan creation epic.

**Potosi** (paw-taw-SEE) City in what is now Bolivia, where Spanish conquerors discovered one of the richest silver veins in the world in 1545.

**Prehistory** The period before the invention of writing.

**Procopius** (proh-KOH-pee-uhs) Roman member of the Constantinian dynasty.

**Proletariat** Urban working class in a modern industrial society.

**Protestant Reformation** Sixteenth-century European movement during which Luther, Calvin, Zwingli, and others broke away from the Catholic church.

**Ptolemaic** (tawl-oh-MAY-ihk) Term used to signify both the Egyptian kingdom founded by Alexander the Great's general Ptolemy and the thought of the philosopher Ptolemy of Alexandria (second century C.E.), who used mathematical formulas in an attempt to prove Aristotle's geocentric theory of the universe.

**Pueblo** (PWEB-loh) Native American groups native to what is now the southwestern United States, called such because they lived in communal adobe homes called pueblos.

**Putting-out system** Method of getting around guild control by delivering unfinished guild materials to rural households for completion.

**Qadi** (KAH-dee) An Islamic judge.

**Qanat** (kah-NAHT) Persian underground canal.

**Qi** (chee) Chinese concept of the basic material that makes up the body and the universe.

**Qianlong** (chyahn-lawng) The fifth Qing emperor of China who ruled at the end of the eighteenth century and was famous for his erudition.

**Qin** (chihn) Chinese dynasty (221–207 B.C.E.) that was founded by Qin Shihuangdi and was marked by the first unification of China and the early construction of defensive walls.

**Qin Shihuangdi** (chin she-huang-dee) Founder of the Qin dynasty.

**Qing** (chihng) Chinese dynasty (1644–1911) that reached its peak during the reigns of Kangxi and Qianlong.

**Qizilbash** (gih-ZIHL-bahsh) Term meaning "red heads," Turkish tribes that were important allies of Shah Ismail in the formation of the Safavid empire.

**Quanzhou** (chwahn-joh) Chinese city-port established during the Tang dynasty.

**Quecha** (keh-CHUA) South American ethnic group of Peru who were once the ruling people of the Inca Empire.

**Quetzalcoatl** (keh-tzahl-koh-AHT'l) Aztec god, the "feathered serpent," who was borrowed originally from the Toltecs; Quetzalcoatl was believed to have been defeated by another god and exiled, and he promised to return.

**Quiché** (keesh-AY) Mayan ethnic group of south-central Guatemala.

**Quinto** (KEEN-toh) The one-fifth of Mexican and Peruvian silver production that was reserved for the Spanish monarchy.

**Quipu** (KEE-poo) Incan mnemonic aid comprised of different colored strings and knots that served to record events in the absence of a written text.

**Quran** (koorr-AHN) Islamic holy book that is believed to contain the divine revelations of Allah as presented to Muhammad.

**Raja** (RAH-juh) A prince or king in India.

**Ramayana** (rah-MAHY-yuh-nah) Ancient Indian masterpiece about the hero Rama that symbolized the victory of *dharma* (order) over *adharma* (chaos).

**Rape of Nanjing** Japanese conquest and destruction of the Chinese city of Nanjing in the 1930s.

**Realpolitik** (ray-AHL-poh-lih-teek) The Prussian Otto von Bismarck's "politics of reality," the belief that only the willingness to use force would actually bring about change.

**Reconquista** (ray-kohn-KEES-tah) Crusade, ending in 1492, to drive the Islamic forces out of Spain.

**Reconstruction** System implemented in the American South (1867–1877) that was designed to bring the Confederate states back into the union and also extend civil rights to freed slaves.

**Remus** (REE-muhs) Along with his brother Romulus, one of the twin founders of Rome.

**Renaissance** (ren-uh-SAHNS) A period of European history between the fourteenth and mid-seventeenth century in which culture and the arts experienced a rebirth.

**Repartimiento** (ray-pahrr-tee-MYEN-toh) Spanish labor system in Latin America, supposed to replace the *encomienda* system, in which native communities were compelled to provide laborers for the farms or mines and the Spanish employers were expected to pay fair wages.

**Rhodes, Cecil** (rhohdz, see-sihl) British financier and statesman in Southern Africa who made his fortune in gold and diamonds.

**Ricci, Matteo** (REET-chee, maht-TAY-oh) Italian Jesuit priest famous for his service in China during the sixteenth century.

**Richelieu** (RISH-uh-loo) French statesman and principal minister to king Louis XIII of France.

**Richet, Charles** (ri-SHEY, shawrl) French physiologist in the late nineteenth and early twentieth centuries.

**Romanov** (ROH-muh-nawf) The Russian imperial dynasty that ruled from 1613 to 1917.

**Romulus** (ROM-yuh-luhs) Along with his brother Remus, one of the twin founders of Rome.

**Rosas, Juan Manuel de** (roh-sahs, HWAHN mahn-WEL de) A conservative Argentine politician who ruled the country from 1829 to 1852.

**Rubaiyat** (ROO-beye-aht) "Quatrains," famous poetry of Omar Khayyam that was later translated and transformed by Edward Fitzgerald.

**Saddam Hussein** President of Iraq before the U.S. operation in 2003.

**Safavid** (SAH-fah-vihd) Later Persian empire (1501–1722) that was founded by Shah Ismail and that became a center for Shiism; the empire reached its peak under Shah Abbas the Great and was centered around the capital of Isfahan.

**Saint-Domingue** (san doe-MANG) French colony in the Caribbean in what is now the republic of Haiti.

**Sakk** Letters of credit that were common in the medieval Islamic banking world.

**Saljuqs** (sahl-JYOOKS) Turkish tribe that gained control over the Abbasid empire and fought with the Byzantine empire.

**Samsara** (suhm-SAH-ruh) Hindu term for the concept of transmigration, that is, the soul passing into a new incarnation.

**Samurai** (SAM-uhr-eye) A Japanese warrior who lived by the code of *bushido*.

**Sandinistas** A socialist Nicaraguan political party in the 1960s and 1970s looking to overthrow the government.

**Sanskrit** (SAHN-skriht) An ancient classical language of India.

**Santeria** (sahn-tuh-REE-uh) A syncretic Afro-Caribbean religion.

**Sao Jorge de Mina** (Sou hor-hay day meena) The first Portuguese trading post built on the Gulf of Guinea, which later became an important site for the Atlantic slave trade.

**São Tomé** (SOU tuh-MEY) Island in the Atlantic west of Africa's Kongo kingdom, used by the Portuguese beginning in the fifteenth century to produce sugar.

**Saramaka** (sar-ah-mah-kah) A group of Maroons (runaway slaves) who established themselves in the interior of Suriname.

**Sasanids** (suh-SAH-nids) Later powerful Persian dynasty (224–651) that would reach its peak under Shapur I and later fall to Arabic expansion.

**Sati** (suh-TEE) Also known as *suttee,* Indian practice of a widow throwing herself on the funeral pyre of her husband.

**Satraps** (SAY-traps) Persian administrators, usually members of the royal family, who governed a satrapy.

**Satyagraha** (suh-TYA-gruh-hah) "Truth and firmness," a term associated with Gandhi's policy of passive resistance.

**Schlieffen** (SHLEE-fn) Early twentieth century German plan for fighting a continental European war on two fronts.

**Scholar-bureaucrats** Describes the administrative apparatus of China created by the Ming dynasty (1368–1644) and continued by the Qing dynasty (1644–1911). Under this system, Confucian scholars, chosen through a highly competitive series of examinations, ran the country. This system meant that China was a meritocracy, but a very conservative one.

**Scholasticism** Medieval attempt of thinkers like St. Thomas Aquinas to merge the beliefs of Christianity with the logical rigor of Greek philosophy.

**Scientific racism** Nineteenth-century attempt to justify racism by scientific means; an example would be Gobineau's *Essay on the Inequality of the Human Races.*

**Sebiumeker** (sehb-ih-meh-kur) Ancient Nubian creator god.

**Seleucid** (sih-LOO-sid) A successor state of Alexander the Great that comprised modern Syria, Iraq, and Iran in the Hellenistic era.

**Self-determinism** Belief popular in World War I and after that every people should have the right to determine their own political destiny; the belief was often cited but ignored by the Great Powers.

**Self-strengthening movement** Chinese attempt (1860–1895) to blend Chinese cultural traditions with European industrial technology.

**Semitic** (suh-MIHT-ihk) A term that relates to the Semites, ancient nomadic herders who spoke Semitic languages; examples of Semites were the Akkadians, Hebrews, Aramaics, and Phoenicians, who often interacted with the more settled societies of Mesopotamia and Egypt.

**Sengoku** (sehn-goh-koo) Also called the "Warring States" period, a time in Japan of social upheaval and military conflict between the fifteenth and seventeenth centuries.

**Sepoys** Indian troops who served the British.

**Seppuku** A Japanese term for ritual suicide committed by the samurai when he had been dishonored.

**Serfs** Peasants who, while not chattel slaves, were tied to the land and who owed obligation to the lords on whose land they worked.

**Shah Ismail** (shah IZ-may-el) Founder of the Safavid dynasty that ruled Persia in the sixteenth and seventeenth centuries.

**Shah Jahan** (shah jah-han) Mughal emperor of India, famous for building the Taj Mahal in memory of his beloved wife.

**Shamanism** (SHAH-mah-niz'm) Belief in shamans or religious specialists who possessed supernatural powers and who communicated with the gods and the spirits of nature.

**Shanfei** (shahn-fahy) Twentieth-century communist revolutionary in China.

**Sharia** (shah-RREE-ah) The Islamic holy law, drawn up by theologians from the Quran, and accounts of Muhammad's life.

**Shaykh Salim Christi** (sheyk sah-LEEM KRIS-tee) Sufi saint whose correct prophecy to Akbar prompted the Mughal emperor to move his capital to Fatehpur Sikri.

**Shia** (SHEE-ah) Islamic minority in opposition to the Sunni majority; their belief is that leadership should reside in the line descended from Ali.

**Shintoism** (SHIHN-toh-iz'm) Indigenous Japanese religion that emphasizes purity, clan loyalty, and the divinity of the emperor.

**Shiva** (SHIH-vuh) Hindu god associated with both fertility and destruction.

**Shogun** (SHOH-gun) Japanese military leader who ruled in place of the emperor.

**Shudras** (SHOO-druhs) Hindu caste of landless peasants and serfs.

**Siddhartha Gautama** (sih-DHAR-thuh GAHW-tah-mah) Indian *kshatriya* who achieved enlightenment and became known as the Buddha, the founder of Buddhism.

**Sikhs** (SIHKS) Indian syncretic faith that contains elements of Hinduism and Islam.

**Silk roads** Ancient trade routes that extended from the Roman empire in the west to China in the east.

**Sinan Pasha** (sih-NAHN pah-cha) Ottoman military commander who was appointed governor of Egypt in 1569.

**Singosari** (sihng-oh-sah-ree) Thirteenth-century kingdom in east Java.

**Sioux** (soo) Native North American tribe that ranged from Lake Michigan to the Rocky Mountains.

**Social Darwinism** Nineteenth-century philosophy, championed by thinkers such as Herbert Spencer, that attempted to apply Darwinian "survival of the fittest" to the social and political realm; adherents saw the the elimination of weaker nations as part of a natural process and used the philosophy to justify war.

**Socialism** Political and economic theory of social organization based on the collective ownership of the means of production; its origins were in the early nineteenth century, and it differs from communism by a desire for slow or moderate change compared to the communist call for revolution.

**Socrates** (SAHK-rah-teez) Ancient Athenian philosopher and teacher of Plato.

**Solidarity** Polish trade union and nationalist movement in the 1980s that was headed by Lech Walesa.

**Song** (SOHNG) Chinese dynasty (960–1279) that was marked by an increasingly urbanized and cosmopolitan society.

**Song Taizu** (sawng tahy-zoo) Founder of the tenth-century Song dynasty in China.

**Songhay** (song-AHY) Fifteenth- through sixteenth-century empire in west Africa specializing in the gold trade.

**Soviets** Russian elected councils that originated as strike committees during the 1905 St. Petersburg disorders; they represented a form of local self-government that went on to become the primary unit of government in the Union of Soviet Socialist Republics. The term was also used during the cold war to designate the Soviet Union.

**Spanish Inquisition** Institution organized in 1478 by Fernando and Isabel of Spain to detect Protestant heresy and the secret practice of Judaism or Islam.

**Spartacus** (SPAHR-tah-cus) A Roman slave who became the leader of an uprising meant to overthrow the Roman Republic.

**Spheres of influence** A region dominated by an outside power. Generally refers to the intrusion of western imperial powers into China in the late nineteenth century. China, although technically a sovereign state, was divided into "spheres," each one occupied by a European state that had license to conduct business without any interference.

**Sputnik** The first manmade satellite to orbit Earth, made by the USSR.

**Srivijaya** (sree-vih-JUH-yuh) Southeast Asian kingdom (670–1025), based on the island of Sumatra, that used a powerful navy to dominate trade.

**Stateless societies** Term relating to societies such as those of sub-Saharan Africa after the Bantu migrations that featured decentralized rule through family and kinship groups instead of strongly centralized hierarchies.

**Stoicism** A Hellenistic philosophy that emphasized strict adherence to duty and personal self-discipline. It became very popular among the Roman upper classes.

**Stoics** (STOH-ihks) Hellenistic philosophers who encouraged their followers to lead active, virtuous lives and to aid others.

**Strabo** (STRAH-boh) Greek geographer (first century C.E.).

**Strategic Arms Limitations Talk (SALT)** Agreement in 1972 between the United States and the Soviet Union.

**St. Scholastica** (skuh-LAS-tih-kah) The twin sister of St. Benedict of Nursia, the compiler of *The Rule of St. Benedict,* which provided a guide to monastic living based on poverty, obedience, and service. St. Scholastica (480–547 C.E.) is believed to have spread the *Rule* among communities of nuns.

**St. Thomas Aquinas** (uh-KWAHY-nuhs) Thirteenth-century Italian theologian best remembered for his attempt to reconcile faith and reason in Christian theology.

**Stupas** (STOO-pahs) Buddhist shrines.

**Sudetenland** (soo-DEYT-n-land) The name used to describe the western regions of Czechoslovakia inhabited mostly by ethnic Germans.

**Suez Crisis** When Britain, France, and Israel attacked Egypt in 1956 to regain the Suez Canal.

**Sufis** (SOO-fees) Islamic mystics who placed more emphasis on emotion and devotion than on strict adherence to rules.

**Sui** (SWAY) Chinese dynasty (589–618) that constructed Grand Canal, reunified China, and allowed for the splendor of the Tang dynasty that followed.

**Sui Yangdi** (sway-yahng-dee) Second emperor of the Sui dynasty, famous for completing the Grand Canal and reconstructing the Great Wall in the early seventh century.

**Süleyman** (SOO-lehy-mahn) Ottoman Turkish ruler Süleyman the Magnificent (r. 1520–1566), who was the most powerful and wealthy ruler of the sixteenth century.

**Sumerians** (soo-MEHR-ee-uhns) Earliest Mesopotamian society.

**Sundiata** (soon-JAH-tuh) Founder of the Mali empire (r. 1230–1255), also the inspiration for the *Sundiata,* an African literary and mythological work.

**Sunni** (SOON-nee) "Traditionalists," the most popular branch of Islam; Sunnis believe in the legitimacy of the early caliphs, compared to the Shiite belief that only a descendent of Ali can lead.

**Sunni Ali** (soon-ee ah-lee) First great king of the Songhay empire in West Africa.

**Surat** (soo-RAHT) Port city on India's northwest coast with an important historical role in trade.

**Suriname** (SOOR-uh-nahm) Former Dutch colony in northeastern South America that achieved independence in 1975.

**Suu Kyi, Aung San** (SOO KEE, AWNG SAHN) Opposition leader (1945–) in Myanmar; she was elected leader in 1990 but she was not allowed to come to power; she was a Nobel Peace Prize recipient in 1991.

**Swahili** (swah-HEE-lee) East African city-state society that dominated the coast from Mogadishu to Kilwa and was active in trade.

**Taino** (tah-EE-noh) A Caribbean tribe who were the first indigenous peoples from the Americas to come into contact with Christopher Columbus.

**Taiping rebellion** (TEYE-pihng) Rebellion (1850–1864) in Qing China led by Hong Xiuquan, during which twenty to thirty million were killed; the rebellion was symbolic of the decline of China during the nineteenth century.

**Taliban** A fundamentalist Islamic militia in Afghanistan.

**Tang Taizong** (TAHNG TEYE-zohng) Chinese emperor (r. 627–649) who founded the Tang dynasty (618–907).

**Tanzimat** (TAHNZ-ee-MAT) A period of reform in the Ottoman Empire between 1845 and 1876.

**Temüjin** (TEM-oo-chin) Mongol conqueror (ca. 1167–1227) who later took the name Chinggis Khan, "universal ruler."

**Tenochtitlan** (teh-noch-tee-TLAHN) Capital of the Aztec empire, later Mexico City.

**Teotihuacan** (tay-oh-tee-wa-KAHN) Central American society (200 B.C.E.–750 C.E.); its Pyramid of the Sun was the largest structure in Mesoamerica.

**Terrorism** The use of violence against civilians in order to gain political or religious goals.

**Teutonic Knights** Crusading European order that was active in the Baltic region.

**Texcoco** (TEHS-co-co) A major city-state in the Valley of Mexico during the Aztec period, and a member of the Aztec Triple Alliance.

**Tezcatlipoca** (tehs-cah-tlee-poh-cah) A central deity in the Aztec religion.

**Theodosius** (thee-uh-DOH-see-uhs) The last emperor of a united Roman Empire. He became a Christian in 391 C.E.

**Theravada** (thehr-ah-VAH-dah) One of two schools of Buddhism emphasizing personal salvation through one's own efforts.

**Third Rome** Concept that a new power would rise up to carry the legacy of Roman greatness after the decline of the Second Rome, Constantinople; Moscow was referred to as the Third Rome during the fifteenth century.

**Three Principles of the People** Philosophy of Chinese Guomindang leader Sun Yat-sen (1866–1925) that emphasized nationalism, democracy, and people's livelihood.

**Tian** (TEE-ehn) Chinese term for heaven.

**Tian Shan** (tyahn shahn) A mountain range located in central Asia.

**Tikal** (tee-KAHL) Maya political center from the fourth through the ninth centuries.

**Timbuktu** (tim-buhk-TOO) A city in what is now central Mali, famous for its historical role in the gold trade.

**Timur-i lang** (tee-MOOR-yee LAHNG) "Timur the Lame," known in English as Tamerlane (ca. 1336–1405), who conquered an empire ranging from the Black Sea to Samarkand.

**Tlacopan** (tee-laaa-co-pawn) A major city-state in the Valley of Mexico during the Aztec period, and a member of the Aztec Triple Alliance.

**Tlatelolco** (tl-tay-LOL-ko) Once a separate island city in Lake Texcoco, it was later incorporated into the Aztec capital of Tenochtitlan.

**Tokugawa** (TOH-koo-GAH-wah) Last shogunate in Japanese history (1600–1867); it was founded by Tokugawa Ieyasu who was notable for unifying Japan.

**Toltecs** Central American society (950–1150) that was centered around the city of Tula.

**Topkapi** (TOHP-kah-pih) A palace in Istanbul that was the main residence of the Ottoman sultans from 1465 to 1853.

**Trail of Tears** Forced relocation of the Cherokee from the eastern woodlands to Oklahoma (1837–1838); it was symbolic of U.S. expansion and destruction of indigenous Indian societies.

**Treaty of Sevres** (SEV-ruh) The peace treaty (1920) between the Ottoman Empire and the Allies after World War I.

**Tres Zapotes** (TRACE-zah-POE-tace) Ancient Olmec city in what is now Veracruz state in Mexico.

**Triangular trade** Trade between Europe, Africa, and the Americas that featured finished products from Europe, slaves from Africa, and American products bound for Europe.

**Triple Alliance** Pre–World War I alliance of Germany, Austria-Hungary, and Italy.

**Triple Entente** (ahn-TAHNT) Pre–World War I alliance of England, France, and Russia.

**Truman Doctrine** U.S. policy instituted in 1947 by President Harry Truman in which the United States would follow an interventionist foreign policy to contain communism.

**Tsar** (ZAHR) Old Russian term for king that is derived from the term *caesar.*

**Tsuyoshi, Inukai** (ts-yo-she, ee-NO-kigh) Prime Minister of Japan from December 1931 to May 1932.

**Tungan** (tuhn-gahn) A term used to describe a Muslim people of Chinese origin.

**Tuthmosis** (tuh-MOE-sis) Egyptian pharaoh from the eighteenth dynasty.

**Twelver Shiism** (SHEE'i'zm) Branch of Islam that stressed that there were twelve perfect religious leaders after Muhammad and that the twelfth went into hiding and would return someday; Shah Ismail spread this variety through the Safavid empire.

**Tyre** (tah-yer) A port in what is now southern Lebanon, formerly an important Phoenician city for trade in silk.

**Uighurs** (WEE-goors) Turkish tribe.

**Ukiyo** Japanese word for the "floating worlds," a Buddhist term for the insignificance of the world that came to represent the urban centers in Tokugawa Japan.

**Ulaanbaatar** (OO-lahn-bah-tahr) Mongolian city.

**Ulama** (oo-lah-MAH) Islamic officials, scholars who shaped public policy in accordance with the Quran and the *sharia.*

**Umayyad** (oo-MEYE-ahd) Arabic dynasty (661–750), with its capital at Damascus, that was marked by a tremendous period of expansion to Spain in the west and India in the east.

**Umma** (UM-mah) Islamic term for the "community of the faithful."

**United Nations (UN)** Successor to the League of Nations, an association of sovereign nations that attempts to find solutions to global problems.

**Universal Declaration of Human Rights** United Nations bill of rights protecting all human beings.

**Upanishads** (oo-pan-NIH-shuhds) Indian reflections and dialogues (800–400 B.C.E.) that reflected basic Hindu concepts.

**Urdu** (OOR-doo) A language that is predominant in Pakistan.

**Uruk** (OO-rook) Ancient Mesopotamian city from the fourth millennium B.C.E. that was allegedly the home of the fabled Gilgamesh.

**Vaishyas** (VEYESH-yuhs) Hindu caste of cultivators, artisans, and merchants.

**Vaqueros** (bah-KEH-rohs) Latin American cowboys, similar to the Argentine gaucho.

**Vardhamana** (vahr-duh-MAH-duh) Indian sage who developed the central tenets of Jainism.

**Vargas, Getúlio Dornelles** (VAHR-guhs, zhi-TOO-lyoo door-NE-lis) Twentieth century Brazilian statesman who ruled Brazil as a virtual dictator.

**Varna** (VUHR-nuh) Hindu word for caste.

**Varuna** (vuh-ROO-nuh) Early Aryan god who watched over the behavior of mortals and preserved the cosmic order.

**Vasco da Gama** (VAS-koh duh GAM-uh) Portuguese explorer who was the first to sail directly from Europe to India in 1498.

**Vedas** (VAY-duhs) "Wisdom," early collections of prayers and hymns that provide information about the Indo-European Aryans who migrated into India around 1500 B.C.E.; *Rig Veda* is most important collection.

**Velvet revolution** A term that describes the nonviolent transfer of power in Czechoslovakia during the collapse of Soviet rule.

**Venta, La** (BEHN-tah, lah) Early Olmec center (800–400 B.C.E.).

**Venus figurines** Small Paleolithic statues of women with exaggerated sexual features.

**Vernacular** (ver-NA-kyoo-lar) The language of the people; Martin Luther translated the Bible from the Latin of the Catholic church into the vernacular German.

**Versailles** (vehr-SEYE) Palace of French King Louis XIV.

**Vichy** (vee-SHEE) A city in France that served as the capital of unoccupied France during World War II.

**Viet Minh** North Vietnamese nationalist communists under Ho Chi Minh.

**Vijayanagar** (vih-juh-yuh-NUH-guhr) Southern Indian kingdom (1336–1565) that later fell to the Mughals.

**Villa, Francisco** (VEE-uh, frahn-SEES-kow) General in the Mexican Revolution, also known as "Pancho Villa."

**Viracocha** (veer-rah-coh-chah) A deity in the Inca religion believed to have been responsible for the creation of civilization.

**Virgin of Guadalupe** (gwah-dah-LOO-pay) Iconic image of the Virgin Mary who appeared to a peasant in Mexico in 1531, after which a shrine was built to commemorate the vision. It is an enduring symbol of Mexican national identity.

**Vishnu** (VIHSH-noo) Hindu god, preserver of the world, who was often incarnated as Krishna.

**Volksgeist** (FOHLKS-geyest) "People's spirit," a term that was coined by the German philosopher Herder; a nation's volksgeist would not come to maturity unless people studied their own unique culture and traditions.

**Volta do mar** (VOHL-tah doh MAHR) "Return through the sea," a fifteenth-century Portuguese sea route that took advantage of the prevailing winds and currents.

**Voltaire** (vohl-TAIR) French writer who embodied the spirit of the eighteenth-century Enlightenment.

**Von Herder, Johann Gottfried** (fuhn HER-duhr, YOH-hahn GAWT-freet) Eighteenth-century German philosopher who advocated the power of intuition over reason.

**Von Metternich, Klemens** (fuhn MET-er-nik, kleh-mens) German-Austrian politician who was critical in the negotiations of the Congress of Vienna after the end of the Napoleonic wars.

**Voudou** (voo-doo) A polytheistic West African religion that traveled with African slaves and was adapted to conditions in the Caribbean, particularly on the island of Haiti.

**Wahhabi** (wuh-HAH-bee) Orthodox Sunni Muslim sect from Saudi Arabia that rejects any changes in Islam after the third century of its existence.

**Waldensians** Twelfth-century religious reformers who criticized the Roman Catholic church and who proposed that the laity had the right to preach and administer sacraments; they were declared heretics.

**Walesa, Lech** (WAH-lehn-sah, LEHK) Leader of the Polish Solidarity movement.

**Wanli** (wahn-LEE) Chinese Ming emperor (r. 1572–1620) whose refusal to meet with officials hurried the decline of Ming dynasty.

**War Communism** The Russian policy of nationalizing industry and seizing private land during the civil war.

**Warsaw Pact** Warsaw Treaty Organization, a military alliance formed by Soviet bloc nations in 1955 in response to rearmament of West Germany and its inclusion in NATO.

**Westphalia** (west-FEY-lee-uh) Peace treaties that ended the Thirty Years' War.

**Wind wheels** Prevailing wind patterns in the Atlantic and Pacific Oceans north and south of the equator; their discovery made sailing much safer and quicker.

**Witte, Sergei** (VIHT-tee, SAYR-gay) Late-nineteenth-century Russian minister of finance who pushed for industrialization.

**World Health Organization (WHO)** United Nation organization designed to deal with global health issues.

**World Trade Organization (WTO)** An organization that was established in 1995 with more than 120 nations and whose goal is to loosen barriers to free trade.

**Wuwei** (woo-WAY) Daoist concept of a disengagement from the affairs of the world.

**Xavier, Francis** (ZEY-vee-er, fran-sis) Jesuit missionary who introduced Christianity to Japan.

**Xenophobia** (zen-uh-FOH-bee-uh) A fear of foreigners or strangers.

**Xhosa** (KOH-suh) An agriculturalist people in southeast South Africa who speak a Bantu language.

**Xia** (shyah) Early Chinese dynasty (2200–1766 B.C.E.) that is known mainly from legend.

**Xi'an** (shee-ahn) One of the oldest cities in Chinese history, and one of the capitals of the Zhou, Qin, Han, Sui, and Tang dynasties.

**Xianyang** (SHYAHN-YAHNG) Capital city of Qin empire.

**Xiao** (SHAYOH) Confucian concept of respect for one's parents and ancestors.

**Xinjiang** (shin-jyahng) Western Chinese province.

**Xiongnu** (SHE-OONG-noo) A nomadic people of Central Asia who frequently invaded Han dynasty China.

**Xuantong** (soo-ahn-tohng) Also known as Puyi, the twelfth and final Qing emperor to rule China.

**Xuanzang** (SHWEN-ZAHNG) Seventh-century Chinese monk who made a famous trip to India to collect Buddhist texts.

**Xunzi** (SHOON-dzuh) Chinese philosopher who lived during the Warring States period, who believed human nature was essentially bad.

**Yahweh** (YAH-way) God of the monotheistic religion of Judaism that influenced later Christianity and Islam.

**Yangshao** (YAHNG-shaw) Early Chinese society (2500–2200 B.C.E.).

**Yangzi** (YAHNG-zuh) River in central China.

**Yemelian Pugachev** (yehm-eel-ian puh-gah-chehf) Leader of a major Cossack rebellion during the reign of Catherine II in eighteenth-century Russia.

**Yongle** (YAWNG-leh) Chinese Ming emperor (r. 1403–1424) who pushed for foreign exploration and promoted cultural achievements such as the *Yongle Encyclopedia.*

**Young Turks** Nineteenth-century Turkish reformers who pushed for changes within the Ottoman empire, such as universal suffrage and freedom of religion.

**Yu** (yoo) Legendary founder of the Xia dynasty (ca. 2200 B.C.E.).

**Yuan** (yoo-AHN) Chinese dynasty (1279–1368) that was founded by the Mongol ruler Khubilai Khan.

**Yucatan** (yoo-kah-TAN) Peninsula in Central America, home of the Maya.

**Yurts** (yuhrts) Tents used by nomadic Turkish and Mongol tribes.

**Zacatecas** (sah-kah-TEH-kahs) The capital of the Mexican state of Zacatecas.

**Zahir al-Din Muhammad** (zah-here ahl-dihn muh-HAHM-mud) Also known as Babur, founder of the Mughal dynasty in India.

**Zaibatsu** (zeye-BAHT-soo) Japanese term for "wealthy cliques," which are similar to American trusts and cartels but usually organized around one family.

**Zambos** (SAHM-bohs) Latin American term for individuals born of indigenous and African parents.

**Zamudio, Adela** (sah-MOO-dyo, ah-DEH-lah) Nineteenth-century Bolivian poet, author of "To Be Born a Man."

**Zanj** (zahn-jee) Slave revolt led by Ali bin Muhammed in 869 C.E. The rebels successfully captured Basra in Mesopotamia and established a state in the region until they were defeated by the Abbasid Empire fourteen years later.

**Zapata, Emiliano** (zuh-PAH-tuh, eh-mee-LYAH-no) Revolutionary who was a leading figure in the Mexican Revolution of 1910.

**Zarathustra** (zar-uh-THOO-struh) Persian prophet (ca. 628–551 B.C.E.) who founded Zoroastrianism.

**Zemstvos** (ZEHMST-voh) District assemblies elected by Russians in the nineteenth century.

**Zen Buddhism** Japanese version of Chinese Chan Buddhism, with an emphasis on intuition and sudden flashes of insight instead of textual study.

**Zhang Qian** (jung-chen) Imperial envoy during the Han dynasty in the second century B.C.E., who was the first to bring reliable information about central Asia back to the Emperor.

**Zheng He** (jung ha) Chinese eunuch mariner who commanded the famous Seven Voyages from 1405 to 1433.

**Zhou** (JOH) Chinese dynasty (1122–256 B.C.E.) that was the foundation of Chinese thought formed during this period: Confucianism, Daoism, Zhou Classics.

**Zhu Xi** (ZHOO-SHEE) Neo-Confucian Chinese philosopher (1130–1200).

**Zhuangzi** (joo-wong-dz) Fourth-century B.C.E. Chinese philosopher who developed the Hundred Schools of Thought tradition.

**Ziggurats** (ZIG-uh-rahts) Mesopotamian temples.

**Zimbabwe** (zihm-BAHB-way) Former colony of Southern Rhodesia that gained independence in 1980.

**Zoroastrianism** (zohr-oh-ASS-tree-ahn-iz'm) Persian religion based on the teaching of the sixth-century B.C.E. prophet Zarathustra; its emphasis on the duality of good and evil and on the role of individuals in determining their own fate would influence later religions.

# CREDITS

*Egyptian Literature,* Three Volumes: Vol. 1. Berkeley: University of California Press, 1973. Copyright © 1973–1980 Regents of the University of California. Pp. 25–27. **Chapter 3** James Legge, trans. *The Chinese Classics,* 5 vols. London: Henry Frowde, 1893, 4:171–72. **Chapter 4** From POPOL VUH by Dennis Tedlock. Copyright © 1985, 1996 by Dennis Tedlock. Pp. 163–65, 167. Reprinted with the permission of Simon & Schuster, Inc., from POPOL VUH: *The Definitive Edition of the Mayan Book of the Dawn of Life* by Dennis Tedlock. Copyright © 1985, 1996, by Dennis Tedlock. All rights reserved. **Chapter 5** D.J. Irani, *The Divine Songs of Zarathustra,* George Allen & Unwin, 1924. **Chapter 6** James Legge, trans. *The Chinese Classics,* 7 vols. Oxford: Clarendon Press, 1893, 1:145, 146, 152, 254, 258–59, 266. **Chapter 7** "The Teachings of the Buddha," Thomas Sanders, et al, *Encounters in World History: Sources and Themes from the Global Past,* Vol I, McGraw-Hill, 2006, pp. 113–114. **Chapter 8** F.J. Church, trans. *The Trial and Death of Socrates,* 2nd ed. London: Macmillan, 1886, pp. 76–78. **Chapter 9** Wilhelm von Hartel, ed. S. *Thasci Caecili Cypriani opera onmia in Corpus scriptorum ecclesiasticorum latinorum.* Vienna: 1868, vol. 3, pp. 305–6. (Translation by Jerry H. Bentley.) **Chapter 10** From THE ALEXIAD OF ANNA COMNENEA translated by E.R.A. Sewter (Penguin Classics, 1969). Copyright © E.R.A. Sewter, 1969. **Chapter 11** *Al-Qur'an: A Contemporary Translation.* Trans. By Ahmed Ali. Princeton: Princeton University Press, 1984, pp. 11, 358, 359, 540, 559. **Chapter 12** Gabriel Ferrand, trans. *Voyage du marchand arage Sulayman en Inde et en Chine.* Paris, 1922, pp. 45, 53-54, 60 – 61 (Translated into English by Jerry H. Bentley). **Chapter 13** *Cosmas Indicopleustes. The Christian Topography of Cosmas, an Egyptian Monk.* Trans. By J.W. McCrindle. London: Hakluyt Society, 1897, pp. 364–72. **Chapter 14** Marco Polo. *The Book of Ser Marco Polo,* 3rd ed. Trans. and ed. by Henry Yule and Henri Cordier. London: John Murray, 1921, pp. 260–63. **Chapter 15** H.A.R. Gibb, trans. *The Travels of Ibn Battuta,* A.D. 1325–1354. 4 vols., Cambridge: Hakluyt Society, 1958–1994, vol. 2, pp. 374–77. **Chapter 16** *Translations and Reprints from the Original Sources of European History,* vol. 2. Philadelphia: University of Pennsylvania Press, 1900. **Chapter 17** Teuira Henry and others, Dennis Kawaharada, ed., *Voyaging Chiefs of Havai'i.* Copyright 1995. pp. 138–39, 144–46. Kalamaku Press. **Chapter 18** From Said Hamdun and Noel King, *Ibn Battuta in Black Africa.*

266, 267–68, 270. *See also* kinship groups

Clark, William (1770–1838), 537

classes. *See* social classes

classical societies: characteristics of, 85, 183, 187; silk roads and, 85, 166, 168–69, 177, 195; trade and, 85, 166, 168–69, 183; Persian empires, 87–101, 89 (*map*), 95 (*map*). *See also specific classical societies*

Clemenceau, Georges (1841–1929), 596

Cleopatra, Mark (c. 31 B.C.E.), 157

climatic change, 29, 50, 263, 350. *See also* global warming

clocks, mechanical, 451, 462

coal, 515, 516, 517, 518, 518 (*illus.*), 520 (*map*)

Code of Hammurabi, 12, 12 (*illus.*), 13, 19

Codex Borgia, 322 (*illus.*), 323

Coen, Jan Pieterszoon (seventeenth century), 379

coffee, 444, 478–79, 479 (*illus.*)

coins. *See* money and coins

coke (coal), 518

cold war (1947–1991), 665 (*map*); capitalism, communism and, 581, 657–58, 668, 681; U.S., Soviet Union and, 638, 652–54, 657–66, 663 (*source document*), 665 (*map*), 668–69, 677–79; origins of, 652–53; decolonization and, 658–59, 666–77, 682, 685, 686; in Europe, 659–61; societies during, 661–62; cultural traditions in, 669, 686; dissent to dissolution in, 677–81; encounters in, 679; end of, 679–81

collectivization of agriculture, 612, 669–70

Colombia, 573

colonies and colonization: Greek, 144–45, 144 (*map*), 147–48; Atlantic and Baltic, 315–16; exploration and, 356–61, 358–59 (*map*), 365; of Atlantic islands, 358, 368–69; European, 378–80, 628, 629 (*illus.*), 634; in Americas, 416–26, 418 (*map*), 503–4, 517, 547; relations with indigenous peoples, 417, 418–19, 421, 422–23; in Pacific Islands, 426–29, 571–72, 572 (*map*); in south Africa, 436–37, 568–70; anticolonial movements, 489, 574; American revolution, 492, 493–96, 494 (*map*); Africa and, 555, 568–70, 627–30, 674–75; cultural traditions and, 566; agriculture and, 575; conflict and, 576; WWI and, 584, 585–86, 591, 593; mandate system and, 597–99. *See also* decolonization; imperialism; *specific countries*

Columbian exchange, 381–83, 383 (*illus.*), 385, 400, 451, 478

Columbus, Christopher (1451–1506), 358–59 (*map*), 360–61, 370, 371 (*map*), 372, 373 (*source document*), 374, 412

COMECON. *See* Council for Mutual Economic Assistance

"comfort women," 652

commercial exchanges, 365, 376, 380–81

Committee of Public Safety (France), 497

commoners, 16, 16 (*illus.*), 267–68, 328, 460. *See also* peasants

communication, 363; in Persian empires, 91; in China, 110–11, 226; technologies, 558–60; globalization and, 686, 691–92, 703. *See also* railroads; roads; silk roads; trade

communism: Marx and Engels on, 526–27; capitalism and, 581, 584, 611, 657–58, 668, 670, 681; in Russia, 610–12; in China, 619, 624–26, 638–39, 669–71; "containment" of, 653, 661–62, 664; end of, 679–80, 686

compass, 215, 232, 348–49, 370

complex society: agriculture in, 3, 5–8; characteristics of, 3, 5–6, 20, 24, 83; cultural traditions and, 3, 14–18, 24, 35–41; defined, 3; trade and, 3, 6, 14–16, 24; encounters in, 23

concentration camps, 569, 650–51, 650 (*illus.*), 651 (*map*)

concrete aqueducts, 159

confession, 335

Confucianism: in China, 103–6, 108, 113–14, 118, 177, 235, 352, 452, 456, 457, 458, 460–61, 462–63, 700; neo-Confucianism, 236–37, 461–62, 466–67, 468; Mongols on, 275–76

Confucius (551–479 B.C.E.), 62, 104–6, 105, 105 (*illus.*), 107 (*source document*), 457

Congo, Belgian, 568, 568 (*illus.*), 627, 676

Congo, Democratic Republic of the, 286, 435, 568, 676

Congo Free State (modern-day Democratic Republic of the Congo), 568

Congo-Ocean railway, 629

Congress of Vienna (1814–1815), 509–10, 511, 512

*conquistadores* (conquerors), 414

conscription: of commoners, 16; in China, 111, 225, 353; of Tainos, 413; during WWI, 590, 628; of "comfort women," 652

conservatism, 472, 483, 484–85, 486, 504–5

Constantine, Roman emperor (reigned 313–337 C.E.), 178, 178 (*illus.*), 180, 188, 196–97

Constantinople (Istanbul), 179 (*map*), 189 (*map*), 311; founding of, 178, 188; Ottoman Turks in, 188, 200, 269, 280, 319; riots in, 190; Islamic sieges of, 191; trade and, 194–95; housing in, 195; attractions in, 196; conquering of, 199, 200, 473; crusades and, 199, 318–19; Polo, N. and Maffeo, in, 299

constitutional states, 394–96

constitutions: Roman republican, 154, 155, 156; U.S. (1787), 495; Mexican (1857), 542; Mexican (1917), 544

consumer culture, 691–92

"containment," of communism, 653, 661–62, 664

Continental Congress (1774), 494, 495 (*illus.*)

Contras, 677

Convention (French), 497–500

Convention on the Rights and Duties of States, 633

Cook, Capt. James (1728–1779), 80, 374–75 (*map*), 376, 376 (*illus.*), 426–27, 428, 571

Copernican universe, 404, 405 (*source document*)

Copernicus, Nicolaus (1473–1543), 404, 405

copper metallurgy, 14

Coptic ("Egyptian") script, 39

Córdoba (Spain), 216, 216 (*illus.*), 316

Coromandel coast (India), 245 (*map*), 246

corporations, 521, 687

*Corpus iuris civilis* (Justinian), 191

Cortés, Hernán (1485–1547), 410 (*illus.*), 411, 414, 415 (*illus.*)

Cosmas Indicopleustes on Trade in Southern India, 250 (*source document*)

cosmopolitan society, 233, 235

Costa Rica, 504

cotton, 71, 126, 251, 294, 349, 444, 517–18, 528

cotton gin, 521

Council for Mutual Economic Assistance (COMECON), 653–54

Council of Chalcedon (451), 181

Council of Nicaea (325), 181, 196–97

Council of Trent (1545–1563), 390

courier service, 91, 276

creation stores, Harappan, 50

creator god, African, 288

creoles, 421, 446, 503, 504, 506, 512

Crete (Greece), 141, 142 (*map*)

Crimea, 274, 278, 473

Crimean War (1853–1856), 529, 531

*criollos* (creoles), 421, 503

Croesus, king of Lydia (c. 560–546 B.C.E.), 87

Crompton, Samuel (1753–1827), 517

crop rotation, 214, 306

cross-staffs, 370, 370 (*illus.*)

crusades, 199, 300, 316, 317–20, 317 (*map*), 318 (*illus.*), 348, 370

Crystal Palace exhibition (1851), 522 (*illus.*)

Ctesiphon (Parthian empire), 94, 95 (*map*)

Cuba, 413, 632 (*map*); abolition of slavery by, 447, 506; Spanish-Cuban-American War, 573; Bay of Pigs, 664

Cuban missile crisis, 664, 666

cubism, 607 (*illus.*)

cult of motherhood, 616

"cult of reason," 497

cultivators, in Mexica society, 328

cults: of Osiris, 40, 40 (*illus.*), 41, 153; in Greece, 152; in Rome and Roman empire, 160–61, 162; Hindu, 171, 253–54; of sun, 334–35

cultural exchanges: Greece and, 144; Hellenistic empires and, 148; trade and, 166, 343–44, 348–50; along silk roads, 170–73; encounters and, 177, 360; Byzantium and, 203; Islam and, 217–19; Tang dynasty and, 227, 348; Srivijaya kingdom and, 257; travel and, 343–44, 348–50, 361; Muslims and, 349–50

cultural nationalism, 508

Cultural Revolution (China, 1966–1976), 670–71, 671 (*illus.*)

cultural traditions, 365; complex society and, 3, 14–18, 24, 35–41; in Mesopotamia, 6, 14–18, 24; in Egypt and Nubia, 28, 35–41; in Harappan society, 49–50; in east Asia, 56, 228; in south Asia, 56; of China, 59–60, 104, 109, 174, 176–77, 233–37, 353, 453, 458, 461–63; in Americas, 76, 330, 417, 419, 420–21, 548, 553; in Oceania, 76, 330, 335–36, 419; in Teotihuacan, 76, 324; of classical societies, 85, 177; of Persian empires, 93; in India, 121–22, 125, 135, 243–44, 247, 561; of Rome and Roman empire, 140, 152, 174; in Hellenistic empire, 147–48; in Greece, 149–53; in Byzantine empire, 196; in Islamic empires, 211, 217–19, 471–72, 479, 481–82, 484–85; in Japan, 238–40, 468; in nomadic empires and Eurasian integration, 270; in Africa, 286–90, 295, 437, 630; Europe and, 311, 315, 378, 390, 407; crusades and, 319, 348; of Aztec empire, 323; in Mesoamerica, 328; of North America, 329; in Atlantic world, 437; of African Americans, 445–47; in revolutions, 503; in industrial society, 529; in U.S., 549–50, 691–92; in Canada, 550–51; migrations and, 551, 703; of Latin America, 551–52, 692; imperialism and, 557–58; colonization and, 566; globalization and, 581, 690–92; in WWI, 585; after WWI, 604–7; in nationalism and political identities, 625; in WWII, 644; in cold war, 669, 686

cuneiform writing, 17–18, 20

currency. *See* money and coins

currents, winds and, 370

Custer, George Armstrong (1839–1876), 538

Cuzco (Peru), 332 (*map*), 333, 335, 414–15

Cybele (goddess), 160, 161

Cyprian, Saint, bishop of Carthage (third century), 175 (*source document*)

Cyril, Saint, 201

Cyrillic alphabet, 201–2

Cyrus the Achaemenid, king of Persia (reigned 558–530 B.C.E.), 87, 88–89, 92, 145

Czech Republic, 680, 681 (*map*)

Czechoslovakia, 678, 680

# Taking Sides Content

**Taking Sides: Clashing Views in World History: Volume 1-the Ancient World to the Pre-Modern Era 4/e, 0078050073**

# ISSUE 5

# Did Christianity Liberate Women?

**YES: Karen L. King,** from "Women in Ancient Christianity: The New Discoveries," A Report from *FRONTLINE* (April 6, 1998)

**NO: Lisa Bellan-Boyer,** from "Conspicuous in Their Absence: Women in Early Christianity," *Cross Currents* (Spring 2003)

## ISSUE SUMMARY

**YES:** Professor of New Testament Studies and the History of Ancient Christianity Karen L. King presents evidence from biblical and other recently discovered ancient texts to illuminate women's active participation in early Christianity—as disciples, apostles, prophets, preachers, and teachers.

**NO:** Art historian Lisa Bellan-Boyer uses mimetic theory to explain why women's richly diverse roles were severely circumscribed in the name of unity and in order to make the new religion of Christianity acceptable in the Greco-Roman world.

**H**ave women been excluded from leadership roles in the Christian Church from the beginning? The ordination of women as ministers and priests during the twentieth century sometimes gave the impression that new ground was being broken by women who sought to lead congregations. Some charged that these women were carrying the movement for women's liberation in civil society inappropriately into churches and defying a two thousand year tradition that had properly excluded them. Radical, however, means "from the roots" and a return to ancient sources may link modern claims with ancient practices.

It is deeply challenging to our modern notions of progress to think that, even by present standards, women may have been more "liberated" two thousand years ago than they are today. Our greatest challenge might come from trying to imagine how early Christian women regarded their own status in what was frequently called the Jesus Movement. Did they feel liberated from the more patriarchal world of first century Palestinian Judaism and Hellenistic paganism? And, regardless of how they felt, does our assessment of their status merit claiming that Christianity liberated them?

Before the Christian Church became institutionalized and before a theology was clearly defined, early converts acted out of intense personal conviction and met informally to share their faith. Most churches were based in people's homes and some state that it was this private dimension that made women's leadership

1

possible. Gender conventions of the time declared the public sphere male and confined the woman's sphere of influence to the home. An outcast sect because its followers refused to worship the Emperor, Christianity remained an underground religion until the early fourth century when Constantine, the Roman Emperor, forbade government persecution and, eventually, made Christianity the state religion.

Missionaries converted many Greeks to Christianity, resulting in more Gentile or non-Jewish Christians than Jewish Christians by the third century. The Greek-speaking world, where many of the women in these selections lived, was the first to accept Christianity in large numbers. If Christian women in both Jewish and Gentile environments during the early centuries enjoyed equality with men, what happened to create the climate of misogyny or hatred of women during later centuries?

In the sixth century a Christian Church Council actually debated whether or not women had souls. The question seemed to be whether women were made in the image and likeness of God, as men were, or merely in the image and not in the likeness. Women are still barred from the Roman Catholic priesthood, primarily using a theological argument introduced by Thomas Aquinas in the thirteenth century. He stated that women are inferior by nature and incapable of assuming leadership positions. If only males can "image" God to their congregations, women must be barred from the priesthood.

How did this happen? The Yes-side emphasizes the evidence we have for the truly radical character of the early Jesus movement. The No-side chronicles the process by which Christianity became mainstream and details the sacrifices that were made to reach this state. According to mimetic theory, as uncovered by Rene Girard, we begin by imitating and envying those we admire. As the process unfolds, we sacrifice what gets in the way and unconsciously become what we originally opposed. According to the No-side, this mimetic process can help us understand how Christianity, which began as anti-establishment, could become, within a few centuries, the state religion of the Roman Empire.

Karen L. King, who teaches in the Divinity School at Harvard University, is widely regarded as a leading authority on women in ancient Christianity. Using both the scrolls included in the Bible and newly-discovered texts from the same period, she reconstructs the enthusiastic and welcome participation of women in every aspect of the early Christian Church. Once Christianity moved from house churches to public meeting places and became the state religion of the Roman Empire, however, women's roles were restricted in a bid for legitimacy and in conformity with prevailing gender conventions.

Art historian Lisa Bellan-Boyer describes how the full and equal participation of early Christian women has been eclipsed by forcing them into a pre-existing honor/shame system, based in Greco-Roman goddess attributes and social expectations For example, the many Marys in the gospels were sorted into one good Mary (the mother of Jesus) and one bad Mary (Mary Magdelene). The latter, a disciple, apostle, and missionary, has been merged and then identified with the repentent prostitute. According to Bellan-Boyer, we become what we profess to hate; and Christianity abandoned its radical beginnings in order to fit into an existing set of gender conventions. Women, Bellan-Boyer claims, were the sacrifice that got the early church to a state the victorious called "unity."

# YES

Karen L. King

# Women in Ancient Christianity: The New Discoveries

**I**n the last twenty years, the history of women in ancient Christianity has been almost completely revised. As women historians entered the field in record numbers, they brought with them new questions, developed new methods, and sought for evidence of women's presence in neglected texts and exciting new findings. For example, only a few names of women were widely known: Mary, the mother of Jesus; Mary Magdalene, his disciple and the first witness to the resurrection; Mary and Martha, the sisters who offered him hospitality in Bethany. Now we are learning more of the many women who contributed to the formation of Christianity in its earliest years.

Perhaps most surprising, however, is that the stories of women we thought we knew well are changing in dramatic ways. Chief among these is Mary Magdalene, a woman infamous in Western Christianity as an adulteress and repentant whore. Discoveries of new texts from the dry sands of Egypt, along with sharpened critical insight, have now proven that this portrait of Mary is entirely inaccurate. She was indeed an influential figure, but as a prominent disciple and leader of one wing of the early Christian movement that promoted women's leadership.

◦◦❀◦◦

Certainly, the New Testament Gospels, written toward the last quarter of the first century CE [Christian Era], acknowledge that women were among Jesus' earliest followers. From the beginning, Jewish women disciples, including Mary Magdalene, Joanna, and Susanna, had accompanied Jesus during his ministry and supported him out of their private means (Luke 8:1–3). He spoke to women both in public and private, and indeed he learned from them. According to one story, an unnamed Gentile woman taught Jesus that the ministry of God is not limited to particular groups and persons, but belongs to all who have faith (Mark 7:24–30; Matthew 15:21–28). A Jewish woman honored him with the extraordinary hospitality of washing his feet with perfume. Jesus was a frequent visitor at the home of Mary and Martha, and was in the habit of teaching and eating meals with women as well as men. When Jesus was arrested, women remained firm, even when his male disciples are said to have fled, and they accompanied him to the foot of the cross. It was women who were reported as the first witnesses to the resurrection, chief among them again Mary Magdalene. Although the details of these gospel stories may be questioned, in general they reflect the prominent historical roles women played in Jesus' ministry as disciples.

## Women in the First Century of Christianity

After the death of Jesus, women continued to play prominent roles in the early movement. Some scholars have even suggested that the majority of Christians in the first century may have been women.

The letters of Paul—dated to the middle of the first century CE—and his casual greetings to acquaintances offer fascinating and solid information about many Jewish and Gentile women who were prominent in the movement. His letters provide vivid clues about the kind of activities in which women engaged more generally. He greets Prisca, Junia, Julia, and Nereus' sister, who worked and traveled as missionaries in pairs with their husbands or brothers (Romans 16:3, 7, 15). He tells us that Prisca and her husband risked their lives to save his. He praises Junia as a prominent apostle, who had been imprisoned for her labor. Mary and Persis are commended for their hard work (Romans 16:6, 12). Euodia and Syntyche are called his fellow-workers in the gospel (Philippians 4:2–3). Here is clear evidence of women apostles active in the earliest work of spreading the Christian message.

Paul's letters also offer some important glimpses into the inner workings of ancient Christian churches. These groups did not own church buildings but met in homes, no doubt due in part to the fact that Christianity was not legal in the Roman world of its day and in part because of the enormous expense to such fledgling societies. Such homes were a domain in which women played key roles. It is not surprising then to see women taking leadership roles in house churches. Paul tells of women who were the leaders of such house churches (Apphia in Philemon 2; Prisca in I Corinthians 16:19). This practice is confirmed by other texts that also mention women who headed churches in their homes, such as Lydia of Thyatira (Acts 16:15) and Nympha of Laodicea (Colossians 4:15). Women held offices and played significant roles in group worship. Paul, for example, greets a deacon named Phoebe (Romans 16:1) and assumes that women are praying and prophesying during worship (I Corinthians 11). As prophets, women's roles would have included not only ecstatic public speech, but preaching, teaching, leading prayer, and perhaps even performing the eucharist meal. (A later first century work, called the Didache, assumes that this duty fell regularly to Christian prophets.)

## Mary Magdalene: A Truer Portrait

Later texts support these early portraits of women, both in exemplifying their prominence and confirming their leadership roles (Acts 17:4, 12). Certainly the most prominent among these in the ancient church was Mary Magdalene. A series of spectacular 19th and 20th century discoveries of Christian texts in Egypt dating to the second and third century have yielded a treasury of new information. It was already known from the New Testament gospels that Mary was a Jewish woman who followed Jesus of Nazareth. Apparently of independent means, she accompanied Jesus during his ministry and supported him out of her own resources (Mark 15:40–41; Matthew 27:55–56; Luke 8:1–3; John 19:25).

Although other information about her is more fantastic, she is repeatedly portrayed as a visionary and leader of the early movement.( Mark 16:1–9; Matthew 28:1–10; Luke 24:1–10; John 20:1, 11–18; Gospel of Peter). In the Gospel of John, the risen Jesus gives her special teaching and commissions her as an apostle to the apostles to bring them the good news. She obeys and is thus the first to announce the resurrection and to play the role of an apostle, although the term is not specifically used of her. Later tradition, however, will herald her as "the apostle to the apostles." The strength of this literary tradition makes it possible to suggest that historically Mary was a prophetic visionary and leader within one sector of the early Christian movement after the death of Jesus.

The newly discovered Egyptian writings elaborate this portrait of Mary as a favored disciple. Her role as "apostle to the apostles" is frequently explored, especially in considering her faith in contrast to that of the male disciples who refuse to believe her testimony. She is most often portrayed in texts that claim to record dialogues of Jesus with his disciples, both before and after the resurrection. In the Dialogue of the Savior, for example, Mary is named along with Judas (Thomas) and Matthew in the course of an extended dialogue with Jesus. During the discussion, Mary addresses several questions to the Savior as a representative of the disciples as a group. She thus appears as a prominent member of the disciple group and is the only woman named. Moreover, in response to a particularly insightful question, the Lord says of her, "You make clear the abundance of the revealer!" (140.17–19). At another point, after Mary has spoken, the narrator states, "She uttered this as a woman who had understood completely"(139.11–13). These affirmations make it clear that Mary is to be counted among the disciples who fully comprehended the Lord's teaching (142.11–13).

In another text, the Sophia of Jesus Christ, Mary also plays a clear role among those whom Jesus teaches. She is one of the seven women and twelve men gathered to hear the Savior after the resurrection, but before his ascension. Of these only five are named and speak, including Mary. At the end of his discourse, he tells them, "I have given you authority over all things as children of light," and they go forth in joy to preach the gospel. Here again Mary is included among those special disciples to whom Jesus entrusted his most elevated teaching, and she takes a role in the preaching of the gospel.

In the Gospel of Philip, Mary Magdalene is mentioned as one of three Marys "who always walked with the Lord" and as his companion (59.6–11). The work also says that Lord loved her more than all the disciples, and used to kiss her often (63.34–36). The importance of this portrayal is that yet again the work affirms the special relationship of Mary Magdalene to Jesus based on her spiritual perfection.

In the Pistis Sophia, Mary again is preeminent among the disciples, especially in the first three of the four books. She asks more questions than all the rest of the disciples together, and the Savior acknowledges that: "Your heart is directed to the Kingdom of Heaven more than all your brothers" (26:17–20).

Indeed, Mary steps in when the other disciples are despairing in order to intercede for them to the Savior (218:10–219:2). Her complete spiritual comprehension is repeatedly stressed.

She is, however, most prominent in the early second century Gospel of Mary, which is ascribed pseudonymously to her. More than any other early Christian text, the Gospel of Mary presents an unflinchingly favorable portrait of Mary Magdalene as a woman leader among the disciples. The Lord himself says she is blessed for not wavering when he appears to her in a vision. When all the other disciples are weeping and frightened, she alone remains steadfast in her faith because she has grasped and appropriated the salvation offered in Jesus' teachings. Mary models the ideal disciple: she steps into the role of the Savior at his departure, comforts, and instructs the other disciples. Peter asks her to tell any words of the Savior which she might know but that the other disciples have not heard. His request acknowledges that Mary was preeminent among women in Jesus' esteem, and the question itself suggests that Jesus gave her private instruction. Mary agrees and gives an account of "secret" teaching she received from the Lord in a vision. The vision is given in the form of a dialogue between the Lord and Mary; it is an extensive account that takes up seven out of the eighteen pages of the work. At the conclusion of the work, Levi confirms that indeed the Saviour loved her more than the rest of the disciples (18.14–15). While her teachings do not go unchallenged, in the end the Gospel of Mary affirms both the truth of her teachings and her authority to teach the male disciples. She is portrayed as a prophetic visionary and as a leader among the disciples.

## Other Christian Women

Other women appear in later literature as well. One of the most famous woman apostles was Thecla, a virgin-martyr converted by Paul. She cut her hair, donned men's clothing, and took up the duties of a missionary apostle. Threatened with rape, prostitution, and twice put in the ring as a martyr, she persevered in her faith and her chastity. Her lively and somewhat fabulous story is recorded in the second century Acts of Thecla. From very early, an order of women who were widows served formal roles of ministry in some churches (I Timothy 5:9–10). The most numerous clear cases of women's leadership, however, are offered by prophets: Mary Magdalene, the Corinthian women, Philip's daughters, Ammia of Philadelphia, Philumene, the visionary martyr Perpetua, Maximilla, Priscilla (Prisca), and Quintilla. There were many others whose names are lost to us. The African church father Tertullian, for example, describes an unnamed woman prophet in his congregation who not only had ecstatic visions during church services, but who also served as a counselor and healer (On the Soul 9.4). A remarkable collection of oracles from another unnamed woman prophet was discovered in Egypt in 1945. She speaks in the first person as the feminine voice of God: Thunder, Perfect Mind. The prophets Prisca and Quintilla inspired a Christian movement in second century Asia Minor (called the New Prophecy or Montanism) that spread around the Mediterranean and lasted for at least four centuries. Their oracles were collected and published, including the account of a vision in which Christ appeared to the prophet in the form of a woman and "put wisdom" in her (Epiphanius, *Panarion* 49.1). Montanist Christians ordained women as presbyters and bishops, and women held the title of prophet. The third century African bishop Cyprian also tells of an ecstatic woman prophet from Asia Minor who celebrated the eucharist and performed baptisms (*Epistle* 74.10). In the early second century, the Roman governor Pliny tells of two slave women he tortured who were deacons (*Letter to Trajan* 10.96). Other women were ordained as priests in fifth century Italy and Sicily (Gelasius, *Epistle* 14.26).

Women were also prominent as martyrs and suffered violently from torture and painful execution by wild animals and paid gladiators. In fact, the earliest writing definitely by a woman is the prison diary of Perpetua, a relatively wealthy matron and nursing mother who was put to death in Carthage at the beginning of the third century on the charge of being a Christian. In it, she records her testimony before the local Roman ruler and her defiance of her father's pleas that she recant. She tells of the support and fellowship among the confessors in prison, including other women. But above all, she records her prophetic visions. Through them, she was not merely reconciled passively to her fate, but claimed the power to define the meaning of her own death. In a situation where Romans sought to use their violence against her body as a witness to their power and justice, and where the Christian editor of her story sought to turn her death into a witness to the truth of Christianity, her own writing lets us see the human being caught up in these political struggles. She actively relinquishes her female roles as mother, daughter, and sister in favor of defining her identity solely in spiritual terms. However horrifying or heroic her behavior may seem, her brief diary offers an intimate look at one early Christian woman's spiritual journey.

## Early Christian Women's Theology

Study of works by and about women is making it possible to begin to reconstruct some of the theological views of early Christian women. Although they are a diverse group, certain reoccurring elements appear to be common to women's theology-making. By placing the teaching of the Gospel of Mary side-by-side with the theology of the Corinthian women prophets, the Montanist women's oracles, Thunder Perfect Mind, and Perpetua's prison diary, it is possible to discern shared views about teaching and practice that may exemplify some of the contents of women's theology:

- Jesus was understood primarily as a teacher and mediator of wisdom rather than as ruler and judge.
- Theological reflection centered on the experience of the person of the risen Christ more than the crucified savior. Interestingly enough, this is true even in the case of the martyr Perpetua. One might expect her to identify with the suffering Christ, but it is the risen Christ she encounters in her vision.
- Direct access to God is possible for all through receiving the Spirit.
- In Christian community, the unity, power, and perfection of the Spirit are present now, not just in some future time.
- Those who are more spiritually advanced give what they have freely to all without claim to a fixed, hierarchical ordering of power.

- An ethics of freedom and spiritual development is emphasized over an ethics of order and control.
- A woman's identity and spirituality could be developed apart from her roles as wife and mother (or slave), whether she actually withdrew from those roles or not. Gender is itself contested as a "natural" category in the face of the power of God's Spirit at work in the community and the world. This meant that potentially women (and men) could exercise leadership on the basis of spiritual achievement apart from gender status and without conformity to established social gender roles.
- Overcoming social injustice and human suffering are seen to be integral to spiritual life.

Women were also actively engaged in reinterpreting the texts of their tradition. For example, another new text, the Hypostasis of the Archons, contains a retelling of the Genesis story ascribed to Eve's daughter Norea, in which her mother Eve appears as the instructor of Adam and his healer.

The new texts also contain an unexpected wealth of Christian imagination of the divine as feminine. The long version of the Apocryphon of John, for example, concludes with a hymn about the descent of divine Wisdom, a feminine figure here called the Pronoia of God. She enters into the lower world and the body in order to awaken the innermost spiritual being of the soul to the truth of its power and freedom, to awaken the spiritual power it needs to escape the counterfeit powers that enslave the soul in ignorance, poverty, and the drunken sleep of spiritual deadness, and to overcome illegitimate political and sexual domination. The oracle collection Thunder Perfect Mind also adds crucial evidence to women's prophetic theology-making. This prophet speaks powerfully to women, emphasizing the presence of women in her audience and insisting upon their identity with the feminine voice of the Divine. Her speech lets the hearers transverse the distance between political exploitation and empowerment, between the experience of degradation and the knowledge of infinite self-worth, between despair and peace. It overcomes the fragmentation of the self by naming it, cherishing it, insisting upon the multiplicity of self-hood and experience.

These elements may not be unique to women's religious thought or always result in women's leadership, but as a constellation they point toward one type of theologizing that was meaningful to some early Christian women, that had a place for women's legitimate exercise of leadership, and to whose construction women contributed. If we look to these elements, we are able to discern important contributions of women to early Christian theology and praxis. These elements also provide an important location for discussing some aspects of early Christian women's spiritual lives: their exercise of leadership, their ideals, their attraction to Christianity, and what gave meaning to their self-identity as Christians.

# Undermining Women's Prominence

Women's prominence did not, however, go unchallenged. Every variety of ancient Christianity that advocated the legitimacy of women's leadership was eventually declared heretical, and evidence of women's early leadership roles was erased or suppressed.

This erasure has taken many forms. Collections of prophetic oracles were destroyed. Texts were changed. For example, at least one woman's place in history was obscured by turning her into a man! In Romans 16:7, the apostle Paul sends greetings to a woman named Junia. He says of her and her male partner Andronicus that they are "my kin and my fellow prisoners, prominent among the apostles and they were in Christ before me." Concluding that women could not be apostles, textual editors and translators transformed Junia into Junias, a man.

Or women's stories could be rewritten and alternative traditions could be invented. In the case of Mary Magdalene, starting in the fourth century, Christian theologians in the Latin West associated Mary Magdalene with the unnamed sinner who anointed Jesus' feet in Luke 7:36–50. The confusion began by conflating the account in John 12:1–8, in which Mary (of Bethany) anoints Jesus, with the anointing by the unnamed woman sinner in the accounts of Luke. Once this initial, erroneous identification was secured, Mary Magdalene could be associated with every unnamed sinful woman in the gospels, including the adulteress in John 8:1–11 and the Syro-phoenician woman with her five and more "husbands" in John 4:7–30. Mary the apostle, prophet, and teacher had become Mary the repentant whore. This fiction was invented at least in part to undermine her influence and with it the appeal to her apostolic authority to support women in roles of leadership.

Until recently the texts that survived have shown only the side that won. The new texts are therefore crucial in constructing a fuller and more accurate portrait. The Gospel of Mary, for example, argued that leadership should be based on spiritual maturity, regardless of whether one is male or female. This Gospel lets us hear an alternative voice to the one dominant in canonized works like I Timothy, which tried to silence women and insist that their salvation lies in bearing children. We can now hear the other side of the controversy over women's leadership and see what arguments were given in favor of it.

It needs to be emphasized that the formal elimination of women from official roles of institutional leadership did not eliminate women's actual presence and importance to the Christian tradition, although it certainly seriously damaged their capacity to contribute fully. What is remarkable is how much evidence has survived systematic attempts to erase women from history, and with them the warrants and models for women's leadership. The evidence presented here is but the tip of an iceberg.

**Lisa Bellan-Boyer**  **NO**

# Conspicuous in Their Absence: Women in Early Christianity

**I**n recent decades, a great deal of work has been done to reconstruct our understanding of the ancient world and the early church, particularly in regard to the women who participated in early Christian communities. Enriched by interdisciplinary collaboration with cultural and social anthropologists, the findings of archeologists and the interpretations of art historians, we can visualize a fuller, more colorful picture of women's lives in the late Classical period than we have had available to us heretofore.

There was a much greater diversity of ministries available to early church-women than we have been led to think by the historiography of the past. It is now clear that the "open commensality" of Jesus was absolutely scandalous; the nearly infinite implications of women and men actually eating together are hard for modern people to grasp. Contemporary and interdisciplinary biblical scholarship has helped widen our knowledge of what open commensality meant in that social context. Psychology has brought some insight into the shadowy corners in the divided minds of the men of the early church, immersed in a deeply honor/shame-based culture and desiring social acceptability for the sake of church growth. Mimetic theory, as it has germinated following the work of Rene Girard, can provide some further tools to analyze and interweave the historical fragments in order to discern wider systemic patterns at work.

Other than the well-known statement of Caiaphas, in the Gospel of John's passion narrative, that "It is better for one man to die for the people than that the whole nation should perish" (John 11:50), there is no more concise formulation of the scapegoat mechanism in action than the sentence that is placed in the mouth of Simon Peter in the last part of the Gospel of Thomas: "Make Mary (Magdalene) leave us, for women are not worthy of life."

A close friend of mine, with a long record of church-based social activism, recently reminded me that: "The Orthodox are the Orthodox not because they are fight, but because they won." My understanding of what Girard has brought to our ability to see into our cultural shadows makes it imperative that we look at history and myth, as written by those who won, with deep suspicion and an ever-present concern for what has been silenced and covered. This is the process of normalizing a view; relentlessly pursued by what Walter Wink calls "the domination system." I ask you to suspend what you think you may know about some cherished church traditions.

My approach uses both art history and mimetic theory, learned from the community of scholars working with tools uncovered by Rene Girard, to compose a picture of what happened during the long mystification and traditionalizing process. Art history can play an important part in helping clarify what affect the early church battles over dogma had on people and culture in the long centuries that followed. Simplistically depicted as a struggle of true-believing Orthodoxy over a bewildering assortment of heresies unhelpfully labeled "gnosticism," the history of the early church, as it is most commonly written, bears the perduring stain of mimetic rivalry.

I contend that women were the sacrifice that got the early church to a state that the victorious called "unity." This can be read in the surviving texts, both in and between the lines, and also in the visual tradition. Who is and is not present or absent in the icons, frescoes, woodcuts, and canvasses? What do these compositions say about their subjects as cultural objects? Given all the knowledge now available about the lives of women in the early church, who is conspicuous by their absence?

Contemporary scholars of the early Christian communities, such as Margaret MacDonald and Luise Schottroff, have offered practical and convincing circumstantial evidence for the robust presence and activity of women from all livelihoods and class levels in fostering the new religion. Women were often very successful as evangelists precisely because they could permeate barriers between the "inside" realm of women and the "outside" realm of men, either by the power-behind-authority of matriarchs in noble households (a la the present-day examples of Barbara and Laura Bush) or through the intermediary functions of craftswomen and tradeswomen who staffed the workshops associated with wealthy houses. Schottroff, in particular, has emphasized the stark necessity that women had to work alongside their husbands in trades and agriculture, and that there was no such thing as a stay-at-home farm wife or fish wife. Raw economics precluded such a luxury.

Women's tending of home and children was so much of an expectation that no special mention or commendation of it was thought of; and by the time of the Roman occupation of Palestine and the displacement of the peasantry off the land, the outside labor of women for supplementary income meant the difference between living or starving to death. So there were many peasant women working in the fields as hired laborers and shepherds, in workshops of all sorts, and as fisherwomen.

Women lived their lives in the tension between social standards that required women to stay indoors and hidden away as the coveted symbols of honor and shame-based cultural systems; and economic forces driving them out and into the fields and the streets of the city. Women in the Dustbowl era had to do sharecropping and migrant picking to secure their families' survival. In the Ellis Island immigration period, it was sweatshops and piece work at home in their tenement kitchen—all the while cooking meals, raising children, and caring for the sick and elderly. It was no different from the state of economic desperation so common to the majority of the women living in first- and second-century Palestine. Incorporating this understanding changes the way we exegete passages such as the Parable of the Lost Coin or the way we picture life on the shore of the Galilean Sea. This is fundamental to expanding our understanding of women in the time of Jesus.

Women could function as fluid intermediaries in part, because they "didn't count." As a consequence, they could escape notice, or "fly under the radar" in conducting house churches, catechizing converts in pagan households, seeing to the needs of prisoners, and acting as "look-outs." Margaret MacDonald's insightful mining of Greco-Roman records provides a vivid description of how valuable these ministries must have been in fostering the early church. The orders of widows provided the believing community with a safety net that was even commended by Christianity's pagan critics: well-off widows took in poor widows, who looked after orphans, thus forming viable and sustaining "family."

The patronage of wealthy widows accounts for much travel under sponsorship for both female and male evangelists, as for other types of emissaries, and it is well known that travel was extremely important in nurturing the early church. The Deacon, Phoebe, is one example of a traveling woman, and the Ethiopian eunuch traveling as the emissary of Candace are some examples from canonical texts. Mary Magdalene, the "Apostle to the Apostles" and John the Evangelist are said, in Eastern Church tradition, to have traveled together as partner-evangelists.

This may have been a model of partnership ministry that was not uncommon in the early church, and might well account for Paul's reference to "sister-wives" in First Corinthians. It would have been a very effective model in that time and place, as well as many others: the men more able, in terms of social acceptability, to speak in public places and proselytize on the streets, and the women able to go places denied to the men: in the confines of private, family space, and in the workshops and warehouses of those who supplied the material needs of large households.

Roman critics slandered early Christians by spreading rumors having to do with this cult of wicked, home-wrecking women under the spell of evil men: they will insinuate themselves inside your honorable household and subvert it, with their sexual immorality, hysteria, witchcraft, incest, and cannibalism. Later, orthodox churchmen concerned with fostering church growth and assimilation used these very same languages of contagion and scandal about fellow Christians in putting down the groups of heretics and "Gnostics" in which women played significant roles, controlling and subduing the "house churches" in the process. The perennial reappearance of these coded attributes of sin and scandal should sound a bell for those with an ear for the mimetic processes at work, as they lead up to acts of sacrificial violence.

In both the first and second centuries, the radical hospitality and table culture of the house churches, following the example of Jesus, was an invitation to scandal: Uncovered women, eating and talking with men-teaching men! They could be nothing else but prostitutes and courtesans. Celibate women—in particular-were thought of as sexual deviants and outlaws, because of their defiance of the enforced convention. They rebelled against the state, which imposed strict marriage and childbearing requirements on women, backed up by severe punishments written into the Roman law codes. The very existence of Christian women who had deliberately chosen a life of celibacy posed an embarrassment to the honor of the law-abiding, paternalistic Roman household. It is instructive to recall a twentieth-century example of similar marriage and childbearing requirements for women: Nazi Germany.

"Holy in body and spirit," they challenged the cultural structures of the honor/shame system, which MacDonald has succinctly described with the sentence: "Men defend honor, women embody shame." Sadly, it is not hard to find this system hard at work in our own historical period, fuelling millions of episodes of domestic violence, perhaps most dramatically illustrated by the prevalence of "honor killings" in the Middle East.

The Pastoral Epistles, especially 1st and 2nd Timothy and Titus, reveal the ambivalent position of celibate women in the church community. Paul and his followers endorsed celibacy, but this led to many dilemmas of practical theology: believing women married to pagan husbands, the legally mandated remarriage of young widows (under sixty), Christian women who defied their paterfamilias by refusing arranged marriages to pagans, etc. As the ideal of celibacy placed into practice began to impact public opinion about Christians, churchmen revealed what Luise Schottroff calls a "divided mind" toward women who embraced celibacy as a way to an independent, spiritually free way of life. This "divided mind" is evident in the second-century text: The Acts of Paul and Thecla, sometimes known as just The Acts of Paul. Hmm. . . .

Thecla becomes a follower of Paul after hearing him preaching outside her window, where she is transfixed by his words. Leaving family and fiance, she becomes active in a house church and lives under the protection of the wealthy widow, Tryphaena. She travels and evangelizes, eventually becoming a spiritual teacher in her own right, independent of Paul. As a result of this boldly public ministry, several attempts are made to kill her. Celibate Thecla is accused of sorcery and adultery. In an echo of Peter's denial, Paul stands weakly by as Thecla is stripped in public. Accused of being shameless, she is ritually shamed. As she is traveling with Paul in Antioch, a Syrian named Alexander sexually assaults her, but she escapes and causes him to be ridiculed. For this mortal blow to his honor, she is sent to the beasts in the arena.

Why has Thecla disappeared? Saint Thecla was removed from the Vatican's list of official Saints in the 1960s, when St. Christopher and many others were also removed. There is a continuing tradition about her in the Eastern Churches, though it is but a glimmer.

Looking at Church hagiographies about early Christian female martyrs shows that conflicted, ambivalent thinking about their sister Christians continued in the minds and hearts of the Christian men who set down their stories.

The medieval repression of the Beguines is only one later example of how this ambivalence carried on. In the hagiographies, female saints who resisted the patronal systems of Mediterranean household law by clinging to celibacy and dying as martyrs are generally depicted in the most passive, meek, and mild terms—like sacrificial lambs. Their roll call is a long one: St. Ursula and the 11,000 Virgins, St. Barbara, St. Catherine, St. Agatha, St. Lucia, et al.

Women of the early church who were known to not be purely virginal were even more problematic to the honorable status of the men in the community. Female slaves were expected to be sexually available to their owners, and former slaves came with this in their (often immediate) past. How did the church's valuation of celibacy work for them? How easy for them to declare themselves a "born-again virgin by choice" in the wording of today's faith-based sexual abstinence for teens movement? That female slaves were active participants in church communities, and even bore some leadership authority is attested to by the correspondence of Pliny the Younger to the Emperor Trajan, circa 112 G.E., in which he reports on the torture of two female slaves (ancilla) who are called deacons (ministra). Pliny states that these two deacons had been turned in by an informant. MacDonald posits the likelihood that they either annoyed the pagan patriarch of the household they belonged to and were simply dumped on Pliny, or sacrificed in order to deflect suspicion from a Christian master or mistress.

All the major objections against "Gnostic" groups mimicked pagan criticisms of early Christians, and included all the major headings from the list of archaic accusations familiar to mimetic theorists. As orthodox doctrine developed in the Byzantine era, it distinguished itself from the horde of heretics by claiming that their theology was more incarnational, thereby affirming the true humanity of Christ. While the centuries wore on, however, Greco-Roman goddess attributes and social conventions migrated onto churchwomen to reflect social systems of honor/shame, "good girl/bad girl" dualities. This was calcified into the culture of the Roman Church by Pope Gregory (for whom the chant form is named) in the sixth century, in a famous series of sermons that merely made official what had been a popular trend for some time.

This was to conflate all the women who supported and participated in the life and ministry of Jesus into as few women as possible, making the many Marys into one honorable Mary and one Mary who bore the mark of shame. Mary, the Mother of Jesus, like her son, become less and less Jewish and more and more divinized. She became increasingly separated from all other women, "blessed among women" so as to become ostracized from them, or they from her. One can never be as good as the Blessed Virgin Mary, no matter how unassailable one's bodily purity may be or how selfless a mother. You could be "as good" as Mary Magdalene, though.

Mary Magdalene's reputation as a prostitute, however undeserved, clings to her today, despite having been officially rescinded by the Vatican in 1969 and thoroughly deconstructed by New Testament scholars and historians of church art such as Jane Schaberg and Susan Haskins. The stain of a reputation is a hard thing to lose even now—clearly impossible for the women who embodied the shame and honor of their house church communities. By the Medieval period, Magdalene Houses all over Western Europe provided the public with a steady supply of designated penitents who enacted the community's shame, functioning as female versions of the Spanish colonial orders of Penitente. Interestingly, while the Beguinage where independent communities of women lived and worked were violently suppressed, the Magdalene Houses for public penitents were officially fostered and supported.[1]

The casting of Mary Magdalene as a prostitute happened concurrently with the development of the Cult of the Virgin Mary, and this is no coincidence at all. Gradually, pagan goddess attributes sorted themselves out between the "good" girl and the "bad" girl with astonishing continuity: portraits of Mary, the Mother of Jesus, were decorated with starry crowns and crescent moons, attributes of the ever-virgin Athena/Diana. Pomegranates and vineyards, attributes of Demeter and Persephone and the Syrian Mother Goddess, become associated with Mary Magdalene. Many of the clues to this syncretic divination process have their roots and ruins at Ephesus, the great temple city dedicated to the Mother Goddess centuries before the Greek conquest. A city that was, of course, a center of Paul's ministry. It is said, in the Eastern Church's tradition, to be a place where Mary, the Mother of Jesus spent time in her later years. It is also the place where Mary Magdalene is said to have been buried.

White doves were an attribute of the Syrian Mother Goddess, and of Venus to the Romans. So familiar to Christians as the symbol of the Holy Spirit: in the classical period, white doves were strongly associated with this then-ancient Temple at Ephesus. Demolished in the Byzantine era, the great columns of the Temple to the Mother Goddess at Ephesus were transported to Constantinople by Justinian to become the great columns in the Cathedral of Hagia Sophia, or Holy Wisdom. They are still there today.

Between the time when Christianity became a state-sponsored religion and the period of the schism between the Eastern and Roman Churches, the Cult of the Virgin gradually crystallized into its own form of inherently anti-incarnational "Gnostic" heresies, and the process of "becoming what you profess to hate," a basic principle of mimetic theory, had come full circle. The "law of anti-idolatry" spoken of so eloquently by Sandor Goodhart calls us to unpack this history, to look at what kinds of sacrifices women and their friends have had to make in order for the domination system to ensure that the repetitive duality of who can wear the white dress and who must wear the red dress will be preserved.

Theologies of Mary's immaculate conception and emphases on "pure vessel" and "ever virgin" language about her isolates and denatures her in a way not far distant from the kind of Goddess who is spawned from the forehead of her Father. Because this "blessed among women" is said in legends to have visited Mount Athos in Greece, for centuries the Orthodox monasteries there have dedicated themselves to barring female humans and domestic animals from the place of pilgrimage, calling this an honor to Mary. Of course, the monks have no way of preventing Holy Sophia from sending female flora and fauna there, anyway. And a question, for me, hangs in the air: Wouldn't this way of being "honored" make a real flesh-and-blood Mary feel lonely? When she had her important news to tell, the Mary of the text sought out the company of other women—her cousin, Elizabeth, and the circle of women that were certainly a big part of her cousin's village life.

"Pure vessel" theology has been the subject of long dispute between the Eastern and Roman Churches, and then the Roman Church and the Protestant

Reformers and secular Enlightenment. These rivalries reached a climax in the middle of the nineteenth century with the declaration of the Doctrine of the Immaculate Conception and were closely tied to the declaration of the Doctrine of Papal Infallibility. These are intimately related to the idea of Mary as a cosmic "Beatrix Mundi," of which John Paul II is so fond. What does it mean for a Church hierarchy that refuses to even consider the ordination of women, to call Mary "The Queen of Priests" in the ordination liturgy?

It is critically important to pay attention to language about the Church, who genders it, and how it is done. Hearing Cardinals talk about how the Church is working to uphold Her honor is quite instructive in this era of sexual scandal.

The "true-believing" (as the term "orthodox" is commonly translated) leadership of the Church became what they professed to hate. This can be detected in the phenomenon of "reversing the text." This is something the early Church "fathers" accused opposing groups of doing on a regular basis—turning a text inside out and standing it on its head so that it means the opposite of what it says, solely for the evil purpose of spreading chaos and confusion.

As concerns the place of women in the faith community, two texts come immediately to mind as nominations for orthodoxy's "text reversal." First is Matthew 23:9, where Jesus says: "Call no man on earth your father, for you have one Father who is in Heaven." Structuring that title as a necessary resume requirement for Churchly office has proven to be a reversal of this instruction from Jesus, turning away from his radical re-visioning of what it could mean to be family to one another, and back toward the old paternalistic domination system of the pagan world.

The second text is the frequently ignored (excluded from the common lectionary) passage in Luke 11:27, a scene which also appears in the Gospel of Thomas 79:1–2. When Jesus is on the street, a woman calls out to him: "Blessed is the womb that bore you and the breasts that nursed you!" He answers: "Blessed rather are those who hear the word of God and obey it!" Beyond virginity, honor/shame based patriarchal systems value women primarily for their fertility, especially for being "fruitful" in bearing strong sons. I read this text as a rebuke of the woman for her admiration (envy'?) of Mary as a particularly blessed mother. Jesus tells her that is not what it's about: in the realm of God, biology is not destiny.

The missing pieces of history surrounding the family life of this woman of first-century Palestine (and all the other women of her era); and the structures of the sacred that have been erected to fill those pieces in still have power to provoke the honor/shame reflex today. Lest you doubt this, I remind you of Mayor Giuliani's rage at the Brooklyn Museum over the Chris Ofili painting/collage of the Madonna, adorned with pictures clipped from pornographic magazines and elephant dung.

The overarching cultural motifs clarified by mimetic theory are evident in this history. It is a history in which real women lived out their lives in social systems where their roles were largely circumscribed, as symbols of family honor and social acceptability. Their passion and commitment still shine through, if we will not neglect to keep their lamps faithfully filled. In their time, the women of the early church were sacrificial victims to a rivalry over honor and "true belief." Let them now be inspired and inspiring "Sheroes for Christ"—models of resistance and reform.

## Note

1. On Sunday, January 19, 2003, ABC "World News Tonight" aired a segment on the Magdalene Houses of Ireland. Terry Moran, the anchor introduces the segment by relating how this has become yet another variety of scandal in the Roman Catholic Church, and with a few phrases about the history of the Magdalene House system. The news writers for the network provided him with this sentence: "These workhouses in Ireland were named after Mary Magdalene, who is identified as a repentant prostitute in the Gospel of Saint Luke."(?!) The broadcast went on to talk about the recent coverage of this story on BBC-TV, and shows clips from a BBC docudrama about the Magdalene Houses, titled: "Sinners." Operated as profit-making convent laundries, they were actually prisons, dumping places for "wayward" girls and unwed mothers, some of whom spent their entire lives in these dismal places. Told that they must remain there to "wash away their sins," the girls and women were called by numbers, not names. Hilary Brown, the correspondent reporting from County Cork, interviewed two of the surviving witnesses to the cruelties of the Magdalene Houses, Sadie Williams and Mary Norris, who have campaigned for a memorial to the women who died in the Magdalene House system, known as the "Irish Gulag." The last Magdalene House was closed seven years ago, in 1996. There was at least one in every city in Ireland.

# POSTSCRIPT

## Did Christianity Liberate Women?

The Bible provides ample evidence of women's active roles during the early years of what would later be called Christianity. For a look at this early period, see *First Converts: Rich Pagan Women and the Rhetoric of Mission in Early Judaism and Christianity* (Stanford University Press, 2001). Eusebius (263–339 C.E.), a Greek Christian and intimate friend of Emperor Constantine, mentions women by name and identity in his account of the first 300 years, *The History of the Church* (Dorset Press, 1984). Fifth-century historians often omitted names and changed narratives in the process depersonalizing and shaming the women, according to Anne Jensen in *God's Self-Confident Daughters: Early Christianity and the Liberation of Women* (Knox, 1996).

During the first centuries of Christianity, different schools of what would later become theology existed side by side. One of these was Gnosticism, a mystical worldview that predominated in Greece and Rome. Remarkable for its androgynous view of God as father and mother, Gnosticism was the first heresy condemned by the Christian Church because some of its views clashed with what had become orthodoxy. Four Gnostic Gospels, part of what scholars call the Nag Hammadi library, found in Egypt in the 1940s, are available in Marvin W. Meyer's translation in *The Secret Teachings of Jesus* (Vintage Books, 1986). Elaine Pagels, an authority in this field, has written a useful guide to Gnosticism in *The Gnostic Gospels* (Vintage Books, 1989). Her more recent *Beyond Belief: The Secret Gospel of Thomas* (Random House, 2004) contrasts the canonical gospel of John, in which salvation comes only through belief in Jesus, with the Gnostic Gospel of Thomas, in which each person is encouraged to know God directly, through the divinely-given capacity, granted to all who are created in the image of God. See also the PBS/Frontline website recommended for this issue on the On the Internet page for Part I.

Karen Jo Torjesen's *When Women Were Priests* (Harper-San Francisco, 1995) highlights women as deacons, priests, prophets, and bishops and documents their exclusion from many of these roles as the Christian Church joined the establishment and worship moved from private to public space. During the Patristic Age, holy women paid a high price for their piety, energy, and talent. Gilian Close captures this time in *'This Female Man of God': Women and Spiritual Power in the Patristic Age, AD 350–450* (Routledge, 1995). Any woman holy enough to be an exemplar of the faith must be spiritually male. Finally, former Boston College theologian Mary Daly in *The Church and the Second Sex* (Beacon Press, 1985) follows up on Simone de Beauvoir's feminist classic *The Second Sex* by documenting sexism in Christian Church history and the "otherness" of women.

# ISSUE 9

# Could the Crusades Be Considered a Christian Holy War?

**YES: Arthur Jones**, from "Memories of Crusades Live on in Today's War," *National Catholic Reporter* (October 26, 2001)

**NO: Jonathan Phillips**, from "Who Were the First Crusaders?" *History Today* (March 1997)

### ISSUE SUMMARY

**YES:** Editor-at-large Arthur Jones presents a case for calling the Crusades a Christian holy war and finds resonances of that long-ago conflict in today's Muslim-Christian conflicts.

**NO:** Lecturer in medieval history Jonathan Phillips finds motivations for the Crusades in religious fervor, the desire for wealth, and a family history of pilgrimage, not in holy war.

**A**rthur Jones begins his essay with President Bush's inadvertent use of the word "crusade" on September 16, 2001 ("This crusade, this war on terrorism, is going to take a long time)—a word he claims echoed into Muslim memories of centuries of Christian incursions. Point-of-view is pivotal. Christians might view the Crusades as a noble effort to reclaim the central sites of their faith, or as an unfortunate but long-forgotten chapter in world history. Muslims, by contrast, may have fresh memories of "the holy religious war of the Christians" and their own "war against the cross" that began in the eleventh century and continues today.

Christianity began as a persecuted sect in the Roman Empire that took seriously its founder's injunction to "turn the other cheek" and repay evil with good. Early Christians would have no part of war. But by the fourth century, Constantine, the Holy Roman Emperor, had won battles with the cross on his shield and made Christianity the official faith of the Empire. Even against this background, however, papally sanctioned violence was something new, Jones suggests.

Muhammad's revelation from God ignited a fervor on the Arabian Peninsula that swept across north Africa and into Christian Europe, beginning in the seventh century. By 750 it had spread throughout the Byzantine Empire. At least in part, Jones argues, the Crusades can be viewed as a Christian counteroffensive, designed to take back their conquered territories and reclaim the Holy Land, the site of Jesus's ministry, death, and burial.

Muslims regard both Jews and Christians as People of the Book, praise their prophets—Abraham, Moses, and Jesus—and permit them to worship freely. The higher head tax Jews and Christians had to pay in Muslim-controlled lands was another disincentive to convert them. So, in the Fertile Crescent, Muslims and Christians had lived together for centuries before the First Crusade—in mutual toleration, if not friendship. One key to the ferocity of the First Crusade is its point of origin. Most Frankish knights would have had no contact with Islam. However, their epic poem *The Song of Roland* changed the "enemy" that defeated Charlemagne's rearguard in the Pyrenees from the Basques, who were the actual victors, into the "treacherous" Muslims of Spain.

Jonathan Phillips situates the Crusades within the social, intellectual, religious, economic, and psychological realities of late eleventh-century Europe, which he calls "one of the most guilt-ridden societies in history." People, he argues, would have had many reasons for joining a crusade—the promise of salvation, the lure of wealth, and family traditions of pilgrimage. And, Pope Urban II's original goal was a very specific one—to assist the Byzantine emperor Alexius in his struggle against the Seljuk Turks of Asia Minor. These motivations, Phillips contends, are sufficient to account for the 60,000 who joined the first Crusade. It is not necessary to posit a holy war as motivation.

Fulcher of Chartres, the priest-chaplain of the First Crusade, described "a new path to heaven" and said confidently that those who undertook this "holy war" would experience "forgiveness of sins." Those who quest for God—in the eleventh century of the twenty-first—believe they will be blessed. During the Seventh Crusade, led by St. Louis, King of France, Yves le Breton reported encountering an old woman who wandered the streets with a dish of fire in her right hand and a bowl of water in her left hand. With the fire, she explained, she would burn up Paradise, until there was nothing left of it, And with the water, she would put out the fires of Hell, until nothing remained of them. "Because," she said, "I want no one to do good in order to receive the reward of Paradise, or from fear of Hell; but solely out of love of God."

## Memories of Crusades Live on in Today's War

**C**rusade!

On Sept. 16, the word shot around the Islamic world. And shocked it. President George W. Bush thought he'd used the term innocently enough. On that Sunday, walking from his helicopter to the White House, he said of U.S. retaliation to the Sept. 11 attacks, "this crusade, this war on terrorism, is going to take a long time."

As the Muslim uproar swelled, Bush quickly apologized. But damage had been done. The BBC, for example, in its Persian and Uzbeck broadcast news services, had translated Bush's remark in the way the Islamic world understands it, as "the war of those signed with the cross," and "the holy, religious war of the Christians." (In Islam's many national languages, from Arabic to Farsi to Urdu, the Muslims call their defense against the crusaders, "the war against the cross.")

Only a minority of Muslims actually believe America had declared a "holy war" against them, cautions Paul E. Chevedden of the University of California, Los Angeles. And Georgetown University's Zahid H. Bukhari, speaking of both Muslims and Westerners, said, "Certain lobbies, certain people, do use the word [crusade] to project what is happening because they have their own agendas to present. They like the terminology and can be more effective because of it."

To Muslims, whose memory of historic grievances may be sharper than that of most Christians, the concept of a "holy war" has implications lost in history's mists. To some millions of Muslims within the Islamic world, crusade still means centuries of bloody Western Christian incursions fought over the Holy Land. Those memories are like ghosts dancing to the U.S. drums of war.

NCR talked to historians of religion and those engaged in Muslim-Christian dialogue and, as the globe's sole superpower searches for one man among the rocks and caves of Islamic Afghanistan, learned lessons for today from the history of the medieval crusades. From today's perspective, there are some surprises, some odd similarities and parallels.

Christians did indeed at one time have their "holy wars," accompanied by language that could have come from bin Laden himself.

The historical record tells us that Fulcher of Chartres (1058–1130), priest-chaplain on the First Crusade, wrote in his eyewitness account that this Crusade was a *novum salutis genus*, "a new path to Heaven." Those Christians who followed this "holy war" path would, wrote Fulcher, experience "full and complete satisfaction" and "forgiveness of sins."

## A World Bursting Apart

To Chevedden, however, who is an associate at UCLA's Gustav E. von Grunebaum Center for Near Eastern Studies, the Crusades have to be understood as part of tremendous geo-political, socio-economic and religious shifts underway at the time. "The Mediterranean world of the 11th century was changing in a remarkable manner; it was witnessing the birth of a new world. The Crusades were the product of the sudden and all-transforming change that produced Western European civilization. An old world burst apart, and a new one took its place."

Bukhari, director and principal co-investigator for Georgetown's Muslims in the American Public Square project, and Fr. James Fredericks of Loyola Marymount theology department, see similar shifts underway today. Bukhari explained that during a period of great transformation "the Crusades were a clash of religions. In the transformations of modern times, we have a clash of civilizations. To some extent there is the same connotation, the whole West as a symbol of Christianity, the entire Muslim world as the symbol of Islam."

But what must be taken into account, he said, is the evolution underway. One aspect of that, he said, is "the evolving debate within Islam about living according to Islamic beliefs, to divine guidance. The notion of how to do that has been evolving since World War II, which triggered the end of colonialism. Among Muslim countries and the Muslim world (which includes those Muslims who live as minorities in non-Muslim countries), there is a debate over issues of democracy, civil rights, human rights, the role of women and living with people of other faiths."

And that debate, he said, "will be violent in some places, look absurd in others, be serious in others, but evolve ultimately, hopefully, in a positive direction."

Bukhari, a Pakistani who has lived in the West for 17 years, said that when "looked at in the time period of 30 to 40 years, things are going very much in a positive direction. Especially with those Muslims living in Western societies. But we are talking only about 30 to 40 years. What evolution will the next 30 to 40 years bring?"

Fredericks, a priest of the San Francisco archdiocese whose field is comparative religion, comments, "We Americans are so concerned with the violent [Islamic] fringe, we miss what's going on at a deeper level."

To Fredericks, the geo-politic transformations Islam is signaling are enormous. This is a huge, huge topic. First, Christianity and Islam—you cannot say it about Judaism—are religions that have been at the foundations of empires. Further, Christianity and Islam are the bases of entire cultural outlooks.

Christian nations today are, by and large, secular societies, in which Protestantism was able to adjust more quickly than Roman Catholicism. "Christianity has made its peace—an uneasy truce—with secular culture. Christianity," he continued, "has grudgingly yielded its place at the center of culture. It isn't that anymore."

The peace isn't total, and opposition to the peace does not just come from Christian reactionaries, traditionalists and conservatives. "We see opposition," he said, "not just from the new religious right, though in the culture wars they get all the publicity, but in the theology of liberation. The theology of liberation also says that religious voices, religious values, need to be very public realities at the center of culture.

"The other thing—and it's such a complicated picture," he said, "there is something in the very character of Christianity that resists privatization. Christianity wants to be a very public religion. So when Christianity becomes a private religion, it is in a rather anomalous situation."

The same statement, he said, can be made about Islam. "Islam wants to be a very public force, a very public reality." Islam wants of its very character to be the basis of society. It always has.

"From the beginnings of Islam," said Fredericks, "submitting to Islam meant renouncing one culture that was sinful and violent and discriminatory and based on petty racial and ethnic rivalries, and recognizing there is this universal humanity, universal morality. A powerful conversion takes place from an immoral society to a moral society." In fact, he said, submission—submission to Allah—is what Islam means.

For Islam to accept a privatized place within secular society "is very, very difficult. We in the West tend to presume that this is an inevitable process. I think that's naive."

Fredericks argues that because Christians "slowly and begrudgingly, and with a great deal of violence" more or less worked out a modus vivendi with the secular nation, Muslims will not necessarily follow suit.

"Why should we presume that that's normative?" he asked.

## "Alternative Modernities"

Speaking to Bukhari's point about Islam in the recent post-colonial period, Fredericks talked of "alternative modernities," of Islamic states developing in unique and non-Western ways.

He uses Indonesia, the largest of all Islamic nations, as an example. "If one allows, and it is controversial to do so, that Indonesia's Sukarno [1949–1967] and Suharto [1967–1998] regimes were aftermaths connected to Dutch colonialism, then what we're hearing from Indonesia's Muslims today is, 'We want to be a nation. We don't want to go back to the Middle Ages. And—the West doesn't get this—we want to be a modern nation. We just don't want to be modern the way you're modern. We think that's sick.' "

Think of such a development, says Fredericks, in terms "of 'religious nationalism' as an alternative to Western secularism. Islam saying our religious nationalism is a way of being a modern, national state: Economically competitive, a state able to provide basic social services to its population. We want to be a success. But secularism—with all the immorality that comes with it—isn't going to cut it for us. We're not that kind of people. We want to be an Islamic state."

What the world may be witnessing, contends Fredericks, is not just a violent fringe but manifestations of religious nationalism that from Egypt to

Iran to Indonesia "may have more in common with the theology of liberation than we've recognized. Both are a critique of Western secular, capitalist, consumerist, materialist, globalist secularism. And that's something we ought to pay attention to and be respectful of." Like Islam, liberation theology seeks to put Christian values, such as a preferential option for the poor, at the center of culture.

Scott Bartchy, director of the Center for the Study of Religion at UCLA, said Americans need to understand that at the deepest level they have been moving away from cultural values built around honor—shame—still the dominant framework for values around much of the world. In contrast, the United States "has an achievement-guilt culture focused almost entirely on the individual," he said.

"Certainly we have very little sense of honor," he said. "Most Americans will say honor is nice, but give me the check instead. And if we had any shame, we wouldn't have had the last 20 years of U.S. politics."

Bartchy said that in Germany in the 1970s, Chancellor Willi Brandt resigned as a matter of honor when an East German mole penetrated West Germany's security services. In Japan, "CEOs or government officers caught in whatever, resign." By contrast, he said, "in America if you get caught out, you back and fill. You don't resign, you just tough it out."

The 80 percent of the world living with honor-shame values have strict gender divisions and roles, systems that generate enormous competition among the males, and a sense of bonding within the family. "Islam," he said, "has created a sense of what anthropologists call 'fictive' and I choose to call 'surrogate' kinship: It goes beyond the family to create a sense of brotherhood. It's no accident that the extremist group in Egypt is the 'Brotherhood.'"

In many ways, said Bartchy, "Islam, for all the way it looks, is still kind of a thin overlay of ancient tribal cultures." For example, nothing in the Quran or the Islamic tradition supports honor killing of women, yet in some countries women are killed if they have been raped, he said. "If the father isn't strong enough, the brothers are supposed to go out there and kill that woman. And if they can kill her in public it's even better, because that at least eliminates the shame from the family."

The only groups in the United States that live up to these strong honor-shame codes, Bartchy said, are inner-city gangs and the Mafia. They cannot allow themselves or their family to be "dissed, or shamed." Every time they step over the threshold, they are in competition with the world outside. "From the time you're 3 years old until you die, you do and say those things that will bring honor back to your family."

Which, in part, said Bartchy, explains Osama bin Laden's popularity in Afghanistan. "Whatever else he was doing," he said, "Osama was accumulating an enormous amount of honor. Spending his own wealth initially on the widows and orphans of the mujahideen—an enormous contrast to what the royal elites back home in Saudi Arabia were doing."

In bin Laden's eyes, said Bartchy, these Saudis were not sharing, and Islam requires it. As bin Laden and those sympathetic to him looked at the United States, "they saw the ever-increasing gap between the elite—the enormously rich—and the Americans at the bottom. Then Osama and his allies looked at the Saudi leadership doing the same and reasoned: 'How did Saudis learn that those values are OK? Because they looked to the West.'" (Bartchy left unanswered the next question: "How did the West learn that those values are OK?")

"Basically," he said, "what Muslims in the Near East want is the same things we want. Even the most conservative bring their kids to the United States to be educated. What they can't understand is how we say we're so strong for democracy and participation and yet we continue to prop up regimes in their part of the world they regard as terribly oppressive and corrupt."

At home what bothers Bartchy is the tone of the American popular response, even among his students. They believe, he said, "the only way to look at us is as the victims. We can do anything we damn well please overseas, and that should never have any effect on what comes down."

## What the Peeves Really Are

Bush used the word crusade and apologized. He warned against racism and bigotry, and visited with Muslims at Islamic centers. Sound moves?

If Bush wants support, to prove he's not against Islam "the first place you start is at home," said Yvonne Haddad, professor of the history of Islam and Christian-Muslim relations at Georgetown University. "And his rhetoric—in the speech to Congress, listening to it as an American, I was impressed. Listening with the other ear, as Muslims overseas would hear it, it was awful: he talked about 'us' and 'them,' you're either with us or against us. He showed no reflection on what the issues, the peeves, really are."

And some of those peeves can be seen as related to the Crusades. Israel occupies the same geographic area the Crusades were about, she said. "Therefore anybody who supports Israel's policies is perceived as continuing the Crusades."

And a thousand years after the first one, the Crusades remain a source of contention.

## Pressures That Led to an Empire-wide Movement

The Nine Crusades, which took place in the 11th, 12th and 13th centuries, were a counteroffensive by Christians against Muslims occupying the Holy Land.

Was the Islamic threat real? "You betcha," said Professor Paul E. Chevedden. "Islamic conquest had taken from Christendom its choicest province—Syria, Egypt, North Africa and Iberia [Spain and Portugal]."

Islam pushed its way north into Italy until it captured Monte Cassino, St. Benedict's monastery, then moved into eastern Switzerland. On the Great St. Bernard Pass, Muslims even captured the abbot of Cluny, France.

The Crusades, in response, were applications of Roman Catholicism's "just war" tradition, said Chevedden of UCLA's Gustav E. von Grunebaum Center for Near Eastern Studies. Islam had the Holy Land, and the pope wanted it back.

A grave pitfall for today, insists Chevedden, would be to view the Crusades in isolation from the world-transforming events in the Mediterranean and in western Asia at the turn of the second millennium. Those events included pressures from expanding populations, rapidly developing urbanism, intellectual and technological inquiries and advances, plus rising commerce pushing into new areas.

The clash between Christendom and Islam was a 1,000-year struggle, the most protracted conflict in human history. What should not be overlooked, Chevedden said, is that, for the most part, Islam, rather than Christianity, was in the ascendancy.

Scott Bartchy, director of UCLA's Center for the Study of Religion, though well aware of what Islam gave to the West during those 1,000 years, looks at the early heritage of both Christianity and Islam from the perspective of violence/non-violence.

During the first 250 to 300 years of Christianity, it was initially persecuted, then scapegoated through four more tense periods, as it became an empire-wide movement. "Never," emphasized Bartchy, "never once during this period is anybody killed in the name of Jesus. The Christians are not a guerrilla band, they are not social bandits. They stay in the urban environment, gain a reputation not only for helping their own widows and orphans, but others' as well. Not only burying their own dead but—a major deal at that time—other people's as well. They never become violent."

Bartchy called it "remarkable" that Jesus' nonviolence had taken "such a hold" across those early centuries. It was Emperor Constantine's adopting Christianity as the Roman Empire's religion in the fourth century that "wrecked things. He never got it," said Bartchy. "He puts the Chi-Rho symbol on Roman shields, and for the first time Christians start killing people in the name of Jesus."

Bartchy contrasts that Jesus with Islam's Muhammad who, in the early seventh century, "goes into Medina and in effect becomes the civil authority. Functionally he's an innovator, a Jesus of Nazareth and a Constantine, all rolled into one."

Bartchy said Muhammad "never ever renounces violence, and for all the fine things in the Islamic tradition, there's never been any serious commitment to nonviolence. In a war, if you follow the prophet, you shouldn't hurt women or children. Or trees. Quite charming that. And the violence should be defensive."

Bartchy said that after the Crusades the Near Eastern Islamic world felt itself transgressed upon, "and there's a certain victim mentality." Culturally, he said, Muslims saved much from the Greek philosophers that the West later appropriated. Technologically Islam held its own, even into the 16th and 17th centuries. "But then the West got the technological edge in military stuff and began pushing," said Bartchy, "and the Muslims again get into the mentality of being victims."

Consequently, Bartchy summarized, today "some of the more extreme people have given themselves permission to do almost anything in the name of defense. And that's what we see."

The Crusades were religious, political and economic. The First Millennium had just ended, the 11th century was the setting of an enormous spiritual revival. For centuries, with the Holy Land under benign Islamic rule, pilgrims traveled together to Jerusalem under arms to protect themselves from robbers. Confessors in that era regularly gave pilgrimages as a penance, so ensuring the safety of pilgrims was one element of the Crusades.

Other elements included merchants in Italian cities wanting Eastern trading outlets and the ambitions of chivalrous knights—high-born youths looking for action and conquest.

There also was a shift within Islam precipitating the Crusades. The more restrictive Turkish Muslims had taken over the Holy Land, and the pope, disenchanted with the warring European nobles' inability to form a coalition to battle Islam, brought his own unifying authority to bear.

The scene was set, and all the elements combined in the urge to free the Holy Land from Islam. Thus nine Crusades, each generally less successful than the one before it.

## Crusaders Went from Victory to Disaster

In box scores, there were nine Crusades between 1095 and 1272. The outcome was Crusaders 2, Muslims 5, plus two negotiated ties. And the Muslims remained in control.

The Crusades (1095–1272) got their name from the crosses Pope Urban II distributed in 1095 after he called on the factious European kings and princes to band together and recover the Holy Sepulcher from the Muslim Seljuk Turks.

They agreed. It would be the first of nine crusades.

Even as the potential First Crusaders were looking into strategy and logistics, peasants in France heard the papal call. Less worried than their leaders about tactics and supplies, several thousand started marching. They resupplied themselves by sacking Belgrade. German peasants set out and financed themselves by attacking Jews.

At Constantinople, what was left of these ragtag bands joined forces, sailed to Jerusalem, dispersed the Turks and declared a victory.

The European nobility finally set off, led by Raymond IV of Toulouse and Bishop Ademar. The First Crusade (1096–99) took Nicea, Antioch and consolidated Western control over what they now called the Latin Kingdom of Jerusalem, with Godfrey of Bouillon as ruler.

The Muslims retaliated. The Second Crusade (1147–49) failed to recapture cities taken by the Turks; the Third Crusade (1189–91) failed to retake Jerusalem, which was back in Muslim hands. But Saladin decreed Christians could have access to the Holy Sepulcher.

The Fourth Crusade (1220–04) got bogged down in the more profitable venture of fighting Venice, sacking Constantinople, crushing the Byzantine Empire and establishing the Latin Empire of Constantinople.

Quite disastrous was the 1202 Children's Crusade, led by two young peasants. Stephen in France and Nicolas in Germany led several thousand children out of their homelands and into starvation and disease, and into the arms of adults who sold them into slavery and other fates worse than death.

The second longest crusade, the Fifth Crusade (1218–21) was an unsuccessful war against Egypt, and the Sixth Crusade (1228–29), which eschewed military arms, was led by Holy Roman Emperor Frederick II who negotiated a degree of Christian control over the holy sites.

France's Louis IX led the next two crusades, the Seventh (1248–50) and Eighth (1270), with no noticeable gains. Louis died in North Africa, and the Eighth Crusade was called off. The English launched the Ninth Crusade (1271–72) under Prince Edward. It changed nothing, though the prince later became King Edward I.

Jonathan Phillips  **NO**

# Who Were the First Crusaders?

**W**ho were the people who answered Urban II's call to crusade between 1096 and 1099? Jonathan Phillips investigates their origins and motives.

The canons of the council summarised the offer made by Urban II as he launched the First Crusade:

> Whoever, for devotion alone, not to gain honour or money, goes to Jerusalem to liberate the Church of God can substitute this journey for all penance.

In other words, if people fought God's enemies on earth and completed a pilgrimage to the Holy Land, their actions would receive a spiritual reward of remarkable magnitude. Urban blended the familiar ideas of pilgrimage and penance with the more radical notion of papally-sanctioned violence to produce what a contemporary writer described as "a new means of attaining salvation." He followed the speech at Clermont with an extensive preaching tour through France and by the dispatch of letters and legations elsewhere in Europe.

The response to his appeal was remarkable, and in total almost 60,000 people set out for the Holy Land. The population of Europe at the end of the eleventh century is estimated to have been around 20 million, so clearly the vast majority of people chose to remain in the West. If, however, one adds contact through ties of family and friendship then it is clear that the crusade touched the lives of millions.

Fulcher of Chartres, a participant in the crusade, wrote that people "of any and every occupation" took the cross. He also commented "whoever heard of such a mixture of languages in one army, since there were French, Flemings, Frisians, Gauls, Allobroges [Savoyards], Lotharingians, Allemani [South Germans and Swiss], Bavarians, Normans, English, Scots, Aquitainians, Italians, Danes, Apulians, Iberians, Bretons, Greeks and Armenians." Representatives of the last two groups probably joined the expedition en route, but the remainder had been attracted by Urban's initial call to arms. The crusade therefore appealed to people from almost every level of society right across Christian Europe. The purpose here is to give some insight into who the First Crusaders were, to explain why they took the cross, and to understand the importance of identifying those who took part in the expedition.

The reasons for such a wide-ranging response are complex. Our distance from events and the nature of the surviving evidence mean that we can never

From *History Today*, vol. 47, no. 3, March 1997. Copyright © 1997 by History Today, Ltd. Reprinted by permission.

achieve a perfect insight into a crusader's mind. We should not necessarily look for a single motive in determining an individual's desire to take the cross, although certain themes emerge more clearly than others. An understanding of the actions of each crusader must be grounded in the cultural, political and economic context of the time.

Spiritual concerns were a prominent factor governing people's lives in the late eleventh century. It was an intensely religious age; pilgrimage and monastic life flourished, and donations to ecclesiastical institutions were increasingly commonplace. Christian Europe was also one of the most guilt-ridden societies in history. Sin was ubiquitous in everyday life and the images of fire and torture so frequently depicted on churches reinforced the fear of eternal damnation. The need for all people—whether rich or poor, nobles or labourers—to atone for their actions helps to explain the level of enthusiasm for the First Crusade and also the crusaders' determination to fulfil their vows by completing the journey to Jerusalem.

The pope's original conception of the crusade was for a compact contingent of knights to assist Emperor Alexius of Byzantium in his struggle against the Seljuk Turks of Asia Minor before marching on to the Holy Land. His appeal was directed, therefore, towards the knightly classes of his native France, a region of weak central authority and endemic lawlessness which was often initiated by the knights themselves. The crusade may have been one way to channel this violence elsewhere as well as giving the knights an opportunity of salvation. The knights responded in large numbers and formed the backbone of the Christian army.

As we have seen, however, Urban's offer was so attractive that almost all elements of society were represented on the crusade. The most notable exception to this was the absence of any kings. Urban regarded the crusade as a papally-directed enterprise and had not explicitly invited the secular monarchs to become involved. In any case, Philip I of France was excommunicated on account of an adulterous relationship with the Countess of Anjou; Henry IV of Germany was the papacy's principal opponent in a bitter struggle concerning the supremacy of lay versus sacral power (known as the Investiture Contest), and William Rufus was too entangled in the government of England to be particularly interested. It was not until the crusade of Sigurd of Norway (1107–10), that a king participated in a campaign in the Holy Land, although it should be noted that the rulers of Spain had long been involved in the Reconquista, their own struggle against the Muslims.

While the non-participation of kings may be regarded as part of Urban's design, the pope had not anticipated that his call would appeal to monks. He wrote "we do not want those who have abandoned the world and vowed themselves to spiritual warfare either to bear arms or to go on this journey; we go so far as to forbid them to do so." Other churchmen such as priests and clerks, were permitted to join as long as they secured the permission of their bishop, and in any case, some religious officials were needed to administer to the crusaders' spiritual needs during the course of the expedition. Urban's message also struck a deep chord with the wider populace, including women, children, the old, the infirm and the poor. Clearly these groups would hinder the progress of an army because they had to be fed and protected. The pope tried to limit their involvement by requiring people to consult their parish priests before taking their vows, but this measure failed and the crusade set out accompanied by many noncombatants. In the course of the crusade the majority of this anonymous mass perished through starvation or disease, deserted, or were enslaved.

It is among the members of the noble and knightly classes that we can begin to pinpoint the individuals who took the cross. In part this is because, as men of standing, their deeds feature in the narrative accounts of the crusade. Some, such as the southern Italian knight, Hugh the Beserk, are mentioned on only one occasion for an act of particular bravery: in this case because Hugh had single-handedly defended a tower for an entire day against Turkish attacks during the siege of Antioch. For the leaders of the major contingents, however, there is a much fuller picture, particularly when their force happens to have included a chronicler. The anonymous author of the Gesta Francorum, for example, was a member of Bohemond of Taranto's army, and Raymond of Aguilers was the chaplain to Raymond of Saint-Gilles, the Count of Toulouse. The latter writer noted "It seems too tiresome to write of each journey . . . so we have taken care to write of the Count of Saint-Gilles without bothering with the others." In the case of Hugh of Vermandois, younger brother of Philip I of France, there is much less information because, as far as we are aware, no member of his contingent wrote an account of the crusade.

While narrative works provide the majority of our material they are not the only source of information for the crusade. In recent years the use of charters has enhanced our understanding of the motivation, financing and family networks of the crusaders. It is the nature of eleventh-century charters which holds the key to this. Charters from later periods tend to convey only a bare minimum of information, such as names, places, dates, and the exact subject of the transaction. Some charters from the time of the First Crusade, however, provide more of a clue to the hopes and fears of individual crusaders, as well as basic factual information.

Crusading was extremely expensive. To equip oneself with chainmail, horses and supplies would cost a great deal—some estimates suggest over four years' annual income. However, the recent experience of the Norman Conquest, for example, would have given people some idea of the resources needed to fight a large-scale and lengthy military expedition. In order to finance the crusade it was often necessary to mortgage or sell lands and rights to the church. The records of these transactions give further indication as to who took part and how they raised money for the journey. Incidentally, the issue of cost is another reason why the old cliche of crusaders being freebooting younger sons is deeply suspect, simply because such men would have been unable to afford to set out in the first instance.

In fact, largely through the use of charters, all sorts of combinations of family members can be found on the crusade. For example, Hugh of Merysur-Seine mortgaged lands at Rosnay to the abbey of Molesme in order to pay for both his own and his brother's journey. Jonathan Riley-Smith has traced the remarkable involvement of the Montlhery clan. One member, Miles of

Bray, was accompanied on the First Crusade by his son, Guy, his brother-in-law, Walter of St. Valery, and two of Walter's sons; his nephew, Baldwin (later Baldwin II of Jerusalem), and two other nephews—Humberge of Le Puiset and Everard III of Le Puiset—were amongst members of the network to take the cross in 1095–96.

Some crusader families had an existing tradition of pilgrimage to the Holy Land which may have formed a further reason for their taking the cross. For example, both the great-grandfather and the grandfather of the First Crusader, Adhemar III of Limoges, had been to Jerusalem in the course of the eleventh century. The influence of pilgrimage is a theme more thoroughly explored in the work of Marcus Bull.

Although the religious motivation of the First Crusaders should be emphasised, it would be naive to argue that other interests were absent. When a noble embarked upon the crusade it was inevitable that he would be accompanied by his household retainers. He would have to provide support for his knights, squires and servants. All were an integral part of a medieval army and, because of this, ties of allegiance and loyalty should be advanced as a further reason for taking the cross, even though such a commitment was, in theory, a strictly voluntary exercise. The desire for land was a further motive, but it did not apply to all the crusaders. Many charters contain clauses detailing financial arrangements that would come into force only if the crusader died during the expedition. Such measures suggest that the participants were well aware of the dangers of the crusade, but hoped to return home once the vow was completed. Two brothers, Bernard and Odo, entered into an agreement with the abbey of Cluny:

> For the remission of our sins, setting out with all the others on the journey to Jerusalem, we have made over for 100 solidi . . . a manor known as Busart. We are making this on the condition that if, on the pilgrimage that we are undertaking, we may die, the manor may remain in perpetuity under the control of . . . the monastery of Cluny. But if we may return . . . we may keep it in our lifetime, but after our death it may not come into the possession of our heirs . . . but will pass to Cluny.

The fact that the Crusader States were seriously undermanned throughout their existence also indicates that relatively few crusaders chose to remain in the Levant and become settlers. Some men, however, were explicit in their intention never to return to the West and clearly planned to carve out new territories for themselves in the East. Raymond of Saint-Gilles was rumoured to be one such person. The French knight Achard of Montmerle might also have been planning to stay in the Holy Land. The charter detailing his agreement with the abbey of Cluny includes the clause "if I die, or if I choose to remain in those lands [the Levant] . . ." shows at least an awareness of the possibility of settling in the East, a course of action which would presumably necessitate the taking of land.

The need to repay debts incurred in paying for the expedition, coupled with poor economic conditions—a series of droughts and bad harvests had marked the early 1090s—suggests that the desire for money may have been a priority for the crusaders. Perhaps the search for salvation and the wish for financial gain seem too mutually exclusive in our eyes. One has only to think of TV evangelism to shudder at the potential for abuse in this connection, yet it is not improbable or contradictory that pious men took the cross also hoping to improve their financial and material prospects. There must also have been crusaders for whom the wish to accumulate wealth predominated. The sources indicate that such people must have been gravely disappointed. There is remarkably little evidence of people returning from the crusade with new-found riches. One rare example is reported by Abbot Suger of Saint Denis. He wrote that Count Guy of Rochefort "returned from the expedition to Jerusalem renowned and rich," an ironic reversal of Urban II's injunction against crusaders seeking honour or money.

People certainly brought back relics from the Holy Land. Lord Riou of Loheac, for example, acquired a fragment of the True Cross and bequeathed it to his local church when he died in 1101. But the experience of the First Crusade does not suggest that it was the route to easy profit. None-the-less, the narrative sources contain frequent reports of the crusaders seeking booty. After the siege of Ma'arrat an Nu'man (December 1098) Muslim graves were dug up and the bodies slit open to check if any treasure had been swallowed. Acts of a similarly brutal nature were repeated elsewhere. The most likely explanation for this behaviour is that substantial sums of money were required to keep the expedition going.

The duration and rigour of the campaign exhausted the resources of the vast majority. Crusaders endured terrible suffering during the march across Asia Minor and at the siege of Antioch (October 1097–June 1098). Food prices became grossly inflated and losses of horses and equipment were enormous. It is an important distinction, therefore, that acts of greed were usually initiated in response to the need to survive, rather than the long-term motivation to accumulate treasure. For those interested solely in money, the cost of warfare and the duration of the expedition meant that the depredation of land closer to home had to be a safer option than going on crusade. If some had set out hoping to acquire untold riches it seems that the hardships of the expedition soon deterred them because throughout the course of the crusade a stream of deserters left the main army unable to endure the experience.

News of the expedition to Jerusalem spread rapidly across Northern and Central Europe and also down through Italy and to Sicily. The pope accepted the reality of the situation and began to dispatch letters of instruction and encouragement to these areas. The only region where he actively discouraged recruitment was the Iberian peninsula because he did not want people distracted from the "reconquista," although we know that some Spanish crusaders ignored him and travelled to Jerusalem. When the forces of the First Crusade began to assemble in 1096 the racial mix of the armies is an impressive testimony to the power of Urban's appeal. Another indication of the range of participants involved is provided by Raymond of Aguilers. He relates that in the Provencal contingent alone no less than seven different currencies were in circulation. He mentioned the use of coins from Lucca, Chartres, Le Mans, Melgueil, Le Puy, Valence and Poitou. Currency from the first five places have been discovered in a single collection at Antioch and tentatively associated with the siege that took place there.

Because almost every region of Latin Christendom was represented on the First Crusade difficulties emerged in communication and leadership. Problems also arose on account of hostility between regional contingents of the army. An episode related by Ralph of Caen—a visitor to the Levant soon after the First Crusade—serves to illustrate the tensions that sometimes broke out in the course of the campaign. As morale sagged during the siege of Antioch, gangs of northern and southern French grouped up on linguistic lines to forage for supplies. They assaulted or freed their captives according to the language they spoke, while those responding in tongues other than Occitan or a northern French dialect were spared as neutrals.

In the course of the crusade and afterwards, the Franks (as they were known collectively) established a series of states in the Levant. During the early years of settlement the polyglot nature of the crusader army was, to some extent, distilled. In some states the origins of the dominant Latin Christian element reflected the ancestry of the particular leader who had based himself there. Bohemond of Taranto's principality of Antioch had a strong contingent of Normans from Southern Italy. Similarly, because it was Raymond of Saint-Gilles who had set up the county of Tripoli, the area had a Provencal influence. The kingdom of Jerusalem, in consequence of its spiritual importance, attracted sellers from a wider number of regions and represented, therefore, a more diverse grouping.

The creation of the Frankish states, each with its own character and links to the West, as well as the over-arching bond of Latin Christianity, meant that strong ties existed between the settlers and their co-religionists in Europe. As the Muslim jihad gathered momentum in the course of the twelfth century, the Franks in the East needed military and financial help. It is interesting to note that traditions of crusading and ties of kinship between those in the Holy Land and the West were two ideas that the settlers emphasised in their attempts to secure support.

Pope Eugenius III drew attention to the concept of crusading ancestry in Quantum Praedecessores his appeal for the Second Crusade (1145–49). He wrote:

> It will be seen as a great token of nobility and uprightness if those things acquired by the efforts of the fathers are vigorously defended by you, their good sons. But if, God forbid, it comes to pass differently, then the bravery of the fathers will have proved to be diminished in the sons. We impress upon you . . . to defend in this way the Eastern Church, which was freed from their [the Muslims'] tyranny, as we have said before by the spilling of your fathers' blood.

In effect this amounted to an appeal to those families with traditions of crusading. The counts of Flanders were a group particularly receptive to such a message. They also had close family ties with the settlers. When Count Thierry took the cross in 1146 he was perpetuating a well-established line of involvement with the Holy Land. His grandfather, Robert I, had mounted a large-scale pilgrimage to Jerusalem in 1087–90. His uncle, Count Robert II, was one of the leading figures on the First Crusade. His cousin, Count Charles the Good, had visited Jerusalem around 1107, and was probably offered the throne of the kingdom of Jerusalem in 1123–24. In 1134 Thierry gained close links with the house of Jerusalem through his marriage to Sibylla of Anjou, a daughter of King Fulk. Thierry had also journeyed to the Holy Land in 1139 and seems to have planned another trip in 1142 only to turn back at an early stage.

An awareness of the identity of the First Crusaders reveals the impact of Pope Urban's call on the people of Europe in 1095–96. But answering the question "Who were the First Crusaders?" can tell us more. We are able to use the answer to start following traditions of crusading and the creation of family ties between the Levant and the West and from this information we have a better understanding of the nature of Latin settlement in the East and the subsequent history of the crusades.

# POSTSCRIPT

## Could the Crusades Be Considered a Christian Holy War?

**W**ith the emergence of Islamic revivalism in the modern world, the historical relationships between the West and the Muslim world have taken center stage. Are the Crusades at the root of this contemporary conflict? The Islamic world has always viewed the Crusades as an invasion of its territory by a foreign power; the West has not shared this perspective. This issue asks: To what extent can the Crusades be viewed as a Christian Holy War? As the West responds to radical Islamic-inspired terrorism today with shock and outrage, is it not possible that a millennium ago, Middle Eastern Muslims responded in the same manner to the European crusaders?

Both struggles spring, at least in part, from religious motivation present. Christian crusaders believed they were fighting a just war in the service of God; securing indulgences for services rendered; and the ultimate prize, gaining the right to eternal salvation. With a slight change in language, we hear the same promises in Islamic revivalism—fighting the infidels in the name of Allah; participating in a fierce struggle between the forces of good and evil; and ultimately acquiring a special place in heaven as martyrs of the faith. Failure to hear these resonances might prevent us from learning a lesson from history.

For sources on the Crusades from a Muslim viewpoint, see: Amin Maalouf, *The Crusades Through Arab Eyes* (Schocken Books, 1985); Francesco Gabrieli, ed., *Arab Historians of the Crusades* (University of California Press, 1984); and Carol Hillenbrand, *The Crusades: Islamic Perspectives* (Routledge, 2000). Karen Armstrong's *Holy War: The Crusades and their Impact on Today's World* (Anchor Books, 2001) is a Western source that speaks of the Crusades in an objective and critical manner, especially their links with contemporary conflicts among Muslims, Christians, and Jews in the Middle East.

As far as general sources on the Crusades are concerned, start with Steven Runciman's three-volume work *A History of the Crusades*, 4th ed. (Cambridge University Press, 1954). Jonathan Riley-Smith's *The First Crusaders, 1095–1131* (Cambridge University Press, 1997) represents current scholarship. Smith states that the Crusades "drew on the tradition of Pilgrimage to Jerusalem . . . and pious violence" as motivating forces. He also points out that many of the Crusaders from the times he researched came from the same families and clans, and concludes that the sustenance they received from these ties helped make the Crusades possible. A readable, popular account of the Crusades, which features many interesting illustrations and useful maps, is W. B. Bartlett, *God Wills It: An Illustrated History of the Crusades* (Oxford University Press, 1999). Another general source is Thomas F. Madden, *A Concise History of the Crusades* (Roman & Littlefield, 1999).